KU-619-594

THE EXPLORATION OF NORTH AMERICA 1630-1776

The Exploration of North America 1630-1776

W.P. Cumming
S.E. Hillier
D.B. Quinn
G. Williams

Paul Elek London

351,848 | 973·1

© Paul Elek Ltd 1974

Published in Great Britain by
ELEK BOOKS LIMITED
54-58 Caledonian Road London N1
No part of this book may be reproduced without
the permission of the publishers

ISBN 0 236 31055 0
Produced by Paul Elek Ltd.
Designed by Harold Bartram

Filmset in England by Photocomp Limited, Birmingham

I.G.D.A., Officine Grafiche, Novara 1974
Printed in Italy

Title page: Sketch of an Iroquois Indian from the *Codex Canadensis*, c. 1700.
Thomas Gilcrease Institute, Tulsa.

CONTENTS

PREFACE

The subject of this volume is the exploration of North America between about 1630 and the American Revolution a century and a half later. Generally, the same editorial conventions have been followed as in the previous volume which took the story of exploration up to 1630, *The Discovery of North America*. The textual selections and (with a very few exceptions) the accompanying illustrations and maps date from the actual period of discovery indicated above. The exact wording of the original narratives has been followed, with omissions indicated by points of suspension, and editorial interpolations shown in square brackets.

Professor D. B. Quinn has written the Introduction and Epilogue; Dr G. Williams, Chapters 1, 6 and 7; Dr S. E. Hillier, Chapter 2; and Professor W. P. Cumming, Chapters 3, 4 and 5; all the authors are also responsible for the captions to the illustrations and maps appearing in their chapters.

The authors and publishers wish to thank Mrs Elizabeth Cumming for her contributions to the book, especially in the preparation and writing of the chapter on Louisiana and the Southwest; Dr Brian Harley of the Department of Geography, University of Exeter, for advice and help from the beginning of the project; Dr Terence Armstrong of the Scott Polar Research Institute, Cambridge; Dr Helen Wallis, Superintendent of the Map Room, British Museum; Dr W. W. Ristow, Chief, Division of Geography and Maps, Library of Congress; together with the many archivists and librarians in the institutions listed in the Acknowledgements without whose help and cooperation a volume of this nature would be impossible. Finally, the authors wish to thank Miss Moira Johnston of Paul Elek Ltd for her patient guidance of their work, and for ensuring that the volume as it emerged reflected an even balance between the written word and the pictorial record.

Acknowledgement of author and title for all extracts quoted from published works is given in the text. However, the authors and publishers would like to acknowledge permission in particular for the following: the extract from *Early narratives of the northwest, 1634-1699* edited by Louise Phelps Kellogg, from Barnes & Noble Books, division of Harper & Row Publishers, Inc; the extract from *The discoveries of John Lederer* edited by W. P. Cumming, from University of Virginia Press; the extract from John Lawson, *A new voyage to Carolina*, from University of North Carolina Press; the extract from *William Byrd's histories of the Dividing Line* by permission of the Division of Archives and History, North Carolina Department of Cultural Resources; the extracts from *James Isham's observations on Hudson's Bay 1743 . . .*, and *Andrew Graham's observations on Hudson's Bay 1767-91*, published by permission of the Hudson's Bay Record Society; the extract from *The British search for the Northwest passage in the eighteenth century* edited by G. Williams, from the Longman Group Ltd; the extract from *Bering's successors 1745-80* edited by Masterton and Brower, from the University of Washington Press; the extract from *Anza's California expeditions* edited by H. E. Bolton, from the University of California Press; the extract from The journals of *Captain James Cook on his voyages of discovery* edited by J. C. Beaglehole, from the Hakluyt Society; and the extract from *The Kelsey Papers* edited by A. G. Doughty and C. Martin, reproduced by permission of Information Canada.

INTRODUCTION: IMPETUS AND IMAGINATION IN AMERICAN EXPLORATION

The earlier background of exploration

In the sixteenth century, Europeans became aware rather suddenly that the world had opened up around them, that they were no longer confined to a relatively small Christian world and a somewhat hazy Muslim and pagan sphere around it. Bartolomeu Dias, Vasco da Gama and Christopher Columbus had opened the seas to disclose strange, rich lands beyond the older limits of knowledge. But this was not the mere uncovering of a geographical picture, the disclosing of unrealized economic advantages to be gained; it was a revelation to the imagination also. A heightened awareness of the familiar, a sharper appreciation of the unfamiliar, a spirit of intellectual inquiry developed around the new discoveries though perhaps not originating solely in them. Then, too, older passions were released: the lust for conquest; the desire to master those non-Christian peoples who were enemies of European Christian faith and to convert them if possible; the greed for wealth which in the presence of infidels could be unrestrained by any church-bound scruples.

Portuguese and Spaniards, guided by Italians, hotly pursued by French, English and Dutch, spilled out in small or large parties over the newly accessible sea and land surfaces of the earth. This overspill, hungry for gold and spices, slaves and

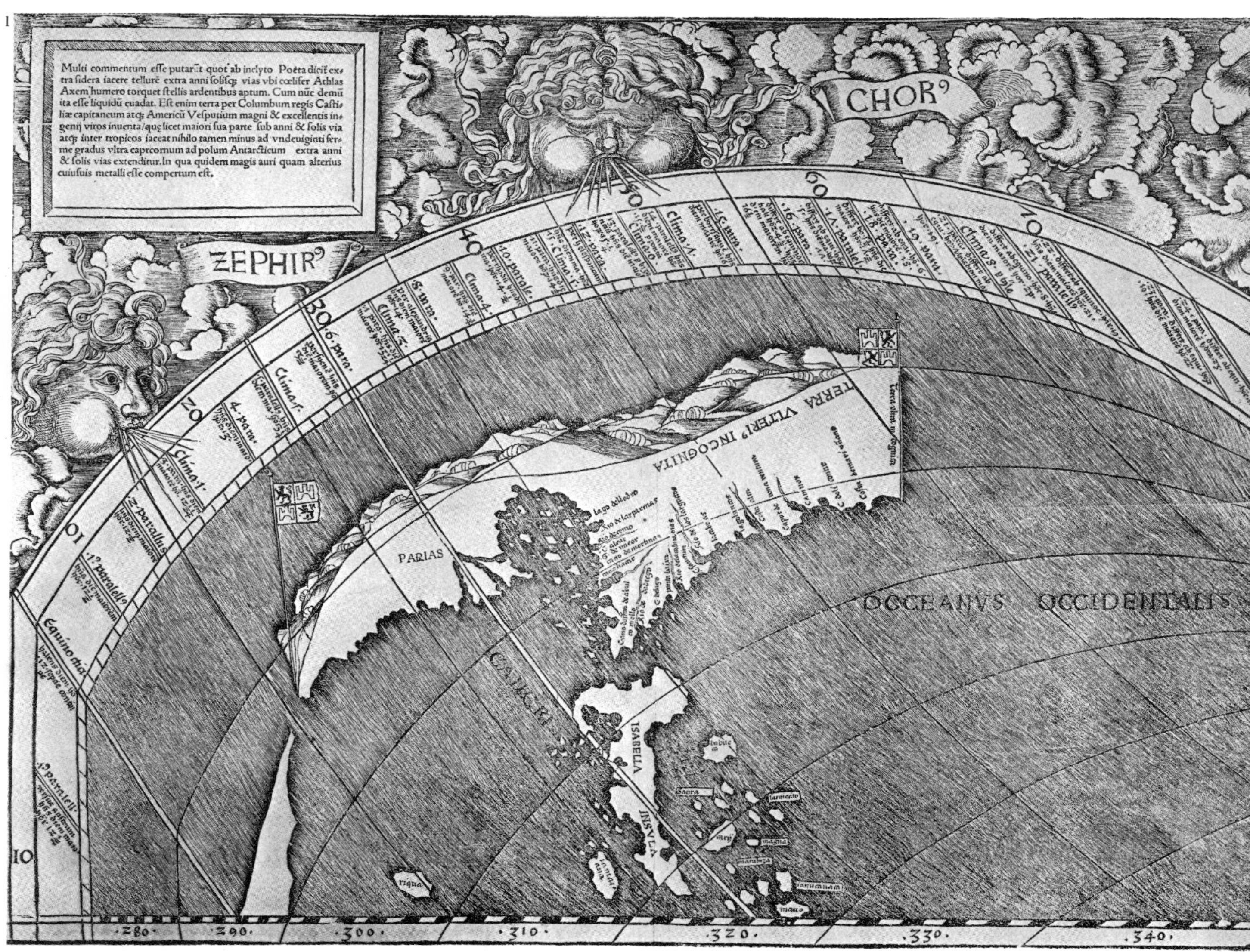

1 Detail from the world map of Martin Waldseemüller of St Die, 1507. *Wolfegg Castle, Austria.*
The brilliant guess which put the two American continents on the world and was proved to be right in the course of a few years. The name America (in honor of 'Americus', Amerigo Vespucci) was first attached to South America but by extension was within a few years applied to North America as well.

converts, created great trading empires in the east and greater landed empires in the west. But the men who went searching new oceans, probing novel shores and penetrating unfamiliar interior routes were also excited intellectually by what was new and strange in what they saw. They were able to use improved technical aids to exploration—better ships and navigating instruments, and also techniques of charting shorelines and compiling local maps which made it possible to gain a general picture of large new areas. Moreover, something of the depth and color of the new lands could be conveyed by the sketches, however simple, made by the traveller himself. Words were more powerful than pen and pencil when circulated in print. The stark journals of the explorers, with their sudden revelations of novel vegetation or people, or of dramatic events, tragic more often than comic, could convey something of the sharp clarity of the first sight of the strange, something of the sensation of the new, bring home to those who could read, from those who could write, that reality was sometimes more terrifying than fantasy or tradition.

America revealed itself slowly; men did not immediately tie up Columbus' islands with the mainlands in middle latitudes west of Europe, which he, Vespucci, Ojeda and so many others discovered during the first two decades after 1492. Nor were they easily linked with the islands and mainlands which John Cabot and the Corte Reals found in latitudes rather nearer to those of France and England until there appeared Martin Waldseemüller's map of 1507, an imaginative jump which showed the discoveries to be two new continents. But gradually America emerged in the minds of those who were aware of the new discoveries, and conscious of their implications. The discoveries in the East, the spices and jewels of Asia, were never so strange, so stirring as those of the western American world.

In the next stages a handful of Spaniards opened, to an astonished Europe, the Mexican treasure chest and condemned perhaps twenty million Amerindians to decay and penury. The struggles of Spain to make an empire out of a scattered chain of pioneer posts, the strivings of Spanish laymen to conquer the American pagans, and of priest and friar to assimilate some at least, many if possible, to the Christian fold as compensation in the next world for their robbery in this, made a tale which soaked slowly but certainly into European consciousness and would never leave it. Spanish missions crept out from Mexico into western North America and, round the gulf of Mexico, towards the southeastern fringes of the continent. The coasts as far north as Chesapeake Bay fairly soon became known to the Spaniards while the interior of the south and central parts of what are now the United States were penetrated by careful, quixotic and ultimately unsuccessful expeditions. After 1540 Spain turned rapidly away from the Pacific coast north of Mexico, and also from the southeast apart from the Florida peninsula. For the rest, North America beyond Mexico, except in New Mexico and later in Texas, had apparently nothing to confer on Spaniards; no gold, few attractive agricultural novelties, no millions of willing, laboring serfs, only native Amerindian people who preferred their own way of living to that of the European intruders. This left the coasts of eastern North America mainly to northern Europeans. Portuguese, Spanish Basques, French and English descended on the great fisheries of Newfoundland and the Maritimes but lived there in the summer only. There were no cod to be had through the cold North American winters. Otherwise it was Frenchmen who explored the eastern shores, worked their way into the St Lawrence, laid the firm outlines of New France on the map but never had the resources or the will to fill them in by settlements. Englishmen, too, followed up only half-heartedly the explorations of John and Sebastian Cabot, though they did have a share in defining the shores of eastern North America in detail.

2

2 Indians taking sea-birds, from François du Creux, *Historia Canadensis*, 1664. The islands of Newfoundland, especially Funk Island, and those in the Gulf of St Lawrence, in particular Bird Rock, provided plentiful bird-life for food for the Indians and the European fishermen who came to take advantage of the abundant quantities of fish. In this picture, Indians are killing the birds with clubs and removing them in a birchbark canoe; food was dried for keeping. The birds are not very clearly differentiated but are probably gannets, *Morus bassanus* (Linnaeus). See plate 57 for a note on Du Creux.

Exploration and the tempo of settlement

Colonies took a long time to adhere. Spain's planting of St Augustine in Florida in 1565 was the end product of a number of fruitless attempts and it never proved an effective nucleus for expansion northwards along the coast. France's first colonial enterprises on the St Lawrence under Cartier and Roberval failed utterly. Those of England much later on Roanoke Island failed also though they left a legacy to the early seventeenth century in the belief of the survival of a colony lost in 1587. Then France and England began again. English efforts between 1600 and 1606 were puny until the Virginia Company was able at last to plant Jamestown in 1607. So were those of France in comparable years until Quebec took root as a small but firmly established trading station after 1608. But the area in between, along the coast—Norumbega, southern New France, New England, whatever it might be called—was slow to be exploited. At length, in 1620, the Pilgrims showed that a determined, small company of people willing to work for subsistence only could survive in a land

and climate not too drastically unlike England itself. And so New England attracted other, more vigorous, more wealthy settlers who established a New England indeed in Massachusetts and in its adjoining territories after 1630. Farther south, through all its tribulations, Virginia was supported by a company until it could at last flourish as a tobacco garden and a royal colony. A little to the north Maryland followed on similar if not identical lines. The Dutch entered the Hudson and established themselves in its valley as traders. By 1635 a European fringe, lightly peopled, penetrating only a little way inland, except for French Quebec, had been created.

3

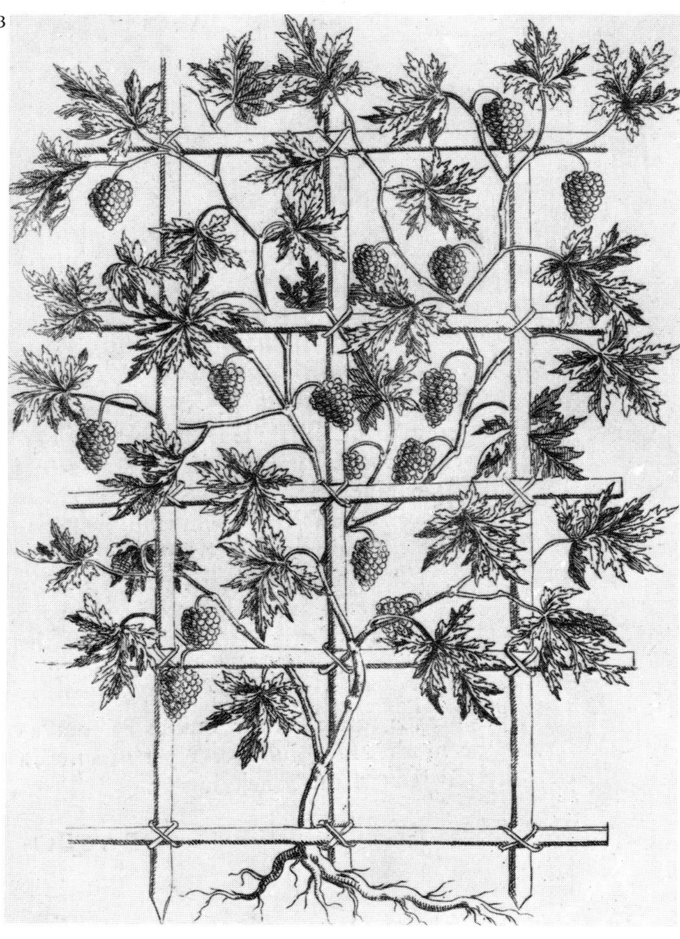

3 Summer grape: *Vitis aestwalis*, from Iac. Cornuti, *Canadensium plantarum*, 1635.
This is the first known illustration of the sweet, black summer grape, with fruit up to two centimeters in diameter, found in the more southerly parts of Canada. A vigorous, high-climbing and conspicuous grape, it was used experimentally for wine-making, and it is an ancestor of the Concord and other cultivated grapes.
Dr Cornuti prepared his book in Paris for publication using dried specimens sent from Quebec.

4

5

4 The falls of Montmorency, below Quebec, by an unknown artist; dated August 1765. *British Museum, London.*
One of a series of five early views. The falls are 160 feet high.

5 The Great Falls at Niagara, by an unknown artist; dated July 1765. *British Museum, London.*
The drawing was done from the east bank and shows the western, or Great Fall, now known as the Horseshoe Fall, 800 feet across and 140 feet high.

The one hundred and forty years between this date and the American Revolution slowly saw this situation transformed. North America was brought fully into European and world politics, building communities of her own which gradually asserted their individual qualities and made up a new society.

In the seventeenth century exploration outwards from the initial English settlements was on a microscale. The early settlers had first to find a place in which they wished to live, which they could clear and cultivate, could exploit in family units and with which they could soon identify as an element in a township community. This exploration was rarely dramatic. It seldom revealed great expanses of territory or unsuspected riches, but it enabled the coastal belt of settlement to widen, mile by mile, and made it possible for Europeans translated to North America gradually to know the land intimately, as they or their parents had known the districts in Europe from which they had sprung.

This gradual realization of the quality of the local environment was an especially marked feature of the early settlement of Massachusetts. The townships were laid out and occupied rapidly in the vicinity of Boston, Charles Town and Salem. They spread inland fast, but in general systematically, until they began to saturate the soil and lose the capacity to exploit agricultural land, woodland and rivers profitably. This tight, moderately intensive settlement, and its proliferation, together with the continued growth of urban nuclei within it, had much to do with the rapid emergence of the distinct community identity of the Commonwealth. Massachusetts continued to throw out pioneers beyond its limits, to the north into the later New Hampshire and Maine, westward into the farther extension of the Commonwealth, into Rhode Island and the rivers of Connecticut. Sometimes the pioneers were solitary trappers or fur traders or farmers, but more often they formed part of a group of settlers who laid out new townships, especially along the rivers.

In Virginia, though the initial land grants had envisaged some concentration of population, if only for defence, the unit came to be the individual holding rather than the township. Many were small, especially in the first years of the tobacco boom, but a number were relatively large from an early stage, and so a colonial aristocracy of landowners emerged. As the century wore on the average size of plantations became larger. The typical unit emerged as the great household, comprising owners, servants, tenants and negro slaves. The estates had to be large in order to be viable; tobacco farming demanded the breaking in of new land while old plots of ground were allowed to recover; and the demands of such households for corn, vegetables and livestock also led to exploitation of land on a fairly large-scale basis. Scattered, rather than intensive, settlement developed though small urban nuclei proved necessary to hold the colony's activities together. But a plantation economy provided incentives to expand in a rather different way from that of the more intensive farming settlements of New England. In order to prosper, or to break away from a plantation which has exhausted its profitable soil, it is necessary to acquire large new tracts of land. Virginia men, and those of Maryland too, were explorers on a wider scale than most New Englanders. They learned to occupy and use lands in the Piedmont as well as on the coastal plain. In the middle of the century they had reached modern North Carolina, though in the coastlands they exploited the fine natural timber resources rather than tobacco. They were influential in opening up South Carolina where plantation agriculture was varied by cotton and rice. Yet in the seventeenth century they were not explorers on any grand scale.

6

6 Immature redwing blackbird (not jay), and an ear of corn, from Edward Bland, *Discovery of New Britaine*, frontispiece, 1651.
Bland was an English merchant who arrived in Virginia in 1634. This illustration is drawn with considerable accuracy but attempts to discover the artist and whether the drawing was done in North America or England have so far been unsuccessful. Whoever the artist, he obviously sketched from life.

7

7 A beaver dam, from François du Creux, *Historia Canadensis*, 1664. Basing his account on the *Jesuit Relations* of 1633-4 and 1636, and Sagard's *Histoire du Canada*, 1632, Du Creux wrote: 'When beavers find a stream that suits them, but that is not quite deep enough, they dam it themselves in order to confine the water, an essential matter with them, and they show such skill and industry that one is forced to recognize the presence of higher intelligence. They cut down large trees by gnawing them with their teeth, convey the fallen logs to the channel of the stream, where they lay them crosswise one on the other so neatly that better workmanship could scarcely be expected from a skilled architect. When finished the dam is six feet wide . . . structures of this kind have been found which are more than two hundred paces long. . . .'

The mountains did not offer, at first, any notable economic attractions. It was only in the early eighteenth century that the settlers learned to know the passes on the Appalachian chain and had the impetus to work their way into the Roanoke River valley and towards the Ohio, though pioneers had penetrated far inland well before the end of the colonial period.

Seventeenth-century attitudes and achievements

The temper of the seventeenth century was different from that of the sixteenth. Europeans looked at North America with clearer eyes, with more calculating minds, with a more realistic appreciation of what was and what was not possible in the way of settlement, exploitation and exploration. The sense of excitement which characterized so many of the sixteenth-century narratives has not disappeared but it is restrained, channelled into practical ends. There are few drawings surviving from this period; it seemed that men preferred the semi-abstraction of maps and charts. There are only a few great chronicles, such as those composed to record and enshrine in words the original Spanish conquests. Histories and travel narratives tend to be local rather than general. Samuel Champlain and John Smith are almost the last in this century to think in terms of general histories. Piecemeal, the propaganda tracts, the journals, the records of missionaries, the recorders of internal colonial change build up a realistic view, but for the most part a narrow and partial one. Unless the contemporary reader took a good deal of trouble to study a wide range of materials, printed and manuscript, unless he was interested in the emergence of new patterns of life in field and town, the intricacies of local politics, the problems of religious belief or organization, the economic efforts (not frequently chronicled in detail) made to ensure the security, wealth and expansion of the new communities, he did not learn very much from individual sources. But now he could come in comparative safety to examine these characteristic European activities in North America for himself. He might even stay on to see something of the lands not yet fully explored, and so become an instrument of discovery, part of a cyclical process of advance, consolidation and renewed expansion, which was the dynamic element behind all exploration.

8

9

8 Milkweed: *Asclepias syriaca*, from Iac. Cornuti, *Canadensium plantarum* 1635.
It was hoped that down from the seed pods and fiber from the leaves of the milkweed would provide substitutes for silk; but nothing came from experiments in spinning and weaving. Its milky juice was also regarded by the American Indians as having curative properties and was recommended for use by Europeans.

9 Portrait of Tiscohan, chief of the Delaware of Pennsylvania, 1735; oil-painting by Gustavus Hesselius. *Historical Society of Pennsylvania, Philadelphia.*
The serious portraits of Tiscohan and his fellow-chief Lapowinsa form the finest pair of Indian portraits of the colonial period. In 1737 both men took part in the farce of the 'walking' purchase in which three white athletes walked sixty miles to the Pocono Mountains to take in such lands between the Delaware and Lehigh Rivers as might be walked in a day and a half by a white man.

The seventeenth century, more particularly in Canada, was the century of an ideal, one which proved to be largely illusory, that the soul of the Indian inhabitants was worth saving, could be saved, and if saved would entitle the Indian to set up as a white man, someone who farmed in the European way, traded as Europeans traded, resided in permanent European-style towns and became in time indistinguishable except perhaps in skin color from Frenchmen or even Englishmen. The missionary priests of French Canada, both Recollets and Jesuits, who pushed ahead into western and northwestern America, often abreast of the *voyageurs*, were driven forward by their zeal for hunting souls which was greater than that of the beaver hunters themselves. They hunted men, new Indian tribes whose indigenous beliefs were still untouched by Christian concepts of this world and the next, men who, it was thought, could be brought rapidly, completely, to salvation in Christ and his Church. Nevertheless, hard experience taught the missionaries that to communicate was difficult, that to have any appreciable effect on Indian ways of life or thought might in the end be impossible. At the same time they established some stable influence over many of the tribes. Their patience in learning to understand the way the Indian thought and what he believed was phenomenal. They braved harsh winters and squalid living conditions, and accompanied their Indian hosts on expeditions for hunting and war. One result of all this, particularly in the missionaries' reports related for the edification and charity of a French audience, is a feeling, unusual in European exploration literature, of close contact with the aboriginal population.

In the end, after a great deal of missionary effort, only a few handfuls of Indians were genuinely converted to Christian beliefs and practices and only very few of the tribes which were in contact with the missionaries obeyed the rules and regulations brought from Europe both for the services of the Church and for the social practices of the people. The missionaries were received on the whole sceptically but kindly, though sometimes indeed with cruel rejection. As they were, for much of the seventeenth and early eighteenth centuries, great explorers, the history of their journeyings west of the Appalachians, and in particular west and northwest of the Great Lakes, is largely the history of the earliest exploration of those regions by white men. Towards the end of the seventeenth century some began to enter into economic relationships with the fur traders, which blunted their exploring missionary zeal, so that by the early eighteenth century many of the mission posts were also frontier trading posts. Nevertheless the missionary influence on our knowledge of North America is almost impossible to overrate. The work of the Jesuits contrasts sharply with the efforts of the English and the Dutch, who did little missionary work on the frontiers. The Indians who were surrounded by the progress of white

10 A Nipissing Indian man, 1717;
11 An Indian in a grey costume, *c.* 1704. *Bibliothèque Nationale, Paris.*
The man on the left was a member of the Algonquin tribe, known to the French as 'Les Sorciers', who lived in the region of Lake Nipissing. It is not known by whom this drawing was made. The figure on the right is earlier, perhaps about 1704, but it is not known to what tribe he belonged.

10

11

settlement in New England and Virginia were indeed influenced and Christianized by English protestant missionaries, but they tended to remain enclaves of poor and underprivileged dependants in a white society.

On the whole, the European communities established in North America had no large ideas of subduing and enslaving the native inhabitants. They were determined to have such lands as they needed or could use and they were prepared to clear apparently vacant land or to purchase it from its Indian owners. After all, there appeared to be indefinite areas into which the mobile, or relatively mobile, tribes could be dispersed and so to shift them from their traditional hunting grounds did not seem like cruel dispossession. Nevertheless, as the growing areas of white settlement pushed the Indians into proximity and friction with other tribes farther west, a hostile Indian frontier was the almost inevitable result.

Neither the English nor the Dutch, nor for that matter the French traders, showed any great desire to interfere with Indian life beyond the frontier except to sell goods in return for skins and furs. The seventeenth century was very much the century of the beaver. He was the magnet which drew French and English, Dutch and colonial Americans west and northwest into the depths of North America. Apart from the records of the Hudson's Bay Company, which appear comparatively late in the seventeenth and early eighteenth centuries, there are few chronicles of the European hunt for his fur. The *voyageurs*, trail blazers in much exploration, left little record of their gypsy way of life. They were followed by more organized bodies of trappers and then traders. How many thousands of square miles the search for beaver, and other furs and skins, opened up has never been, can never be, fully estimated.

The French, English and other traders, even though they did not intend to destroy Indian society, gradually altered it through the distribution of European artefacts. Cloth was introduced to make the blanket a substitute in many cases for the skin mantle. The European-manufactured bead became the main ornament in native designs from quite early in the seventeenth century and spread far ahead of the traders and explorers. Metal tools and weapons altered the capacity of the Indians to control their environment and also to engage in military struggles with their neighbors. The tribes most closely in contact with the French and best organized to utilize European objects, the Iroquois, were able quite early to assimilate the gun into their armory, with devastating effects on their enemies, with whom they fought for beaver territories. Then, too, the introduction of liquor, mainly rum, had insidious and sometimes drastic effects on Indian society. But the greatest transformation came from the horse, traded

12

12 A buffalo. One of the early prints published of this formidable beast; from Louis Hennepin, *Nouvelle découverte d'un très grand pays*, 1697. The Recollet Father Hennepin was one of the best known explorers, through his accounts, sometimes fanciful, of his adventures in interior North America. The author's description, from the English edition of 1698, is graphic: 'Those Bulls have a very fine Coat, more like Wooll than Hair, and their Cows have it longer than the Males; their Horns are almost black, and much thicker, though somewhat shorter than those of *Europe*: Their Head is of a prodigious Bigness, as well as their Neck very thick, but at the same time exceeding short: They have a kind of Bump between the two Shoulders: Their Legs are big and short, cover'd with long Wooll; and they have between the two Horns an ugly Bush of Hair, which falls upon their Eyes, and makes them look horrid.'

from Mexico. Because they could, for the first time, subdue the buffalo with it, the life of the Plains Indians was gradually transformed in the seventeenth and eighteenth centuries. And as white men ultimately penetrated the plains the horse, together with European weapons, was to make the Indian a formidable foe. Although the assimilation of European customs tended on balance to weaken Indian society, there were compensations: more effective means of fighting and of transport, two factors which in the end made the conquest of the west much more a matter of serious warfare than was the occupation of the east.

An age of reason and consolidation

The spirit of the eighteenth century was confident and rationalist. There was sufficient knowledge of the world available to encourage those concerned with exploration—government officials, trading companies, individual adventurers—to make it a rational, reasonable, almost inevitable activity for the extension and completion of existing information. It was also being done for political, strategic and, above all, economic purposes but, in this period for the first time, governments spent money on mounting expeditions whose functions were recognizably scientific; enterprises, for example, to establish precisely the length of a degree of latitude, to observe a transit of Venus, to follow and check ocean currents and magnetic variation, to experiment with various horological devices for obtaining accurate longitudes, to locate (or eliminate) the great southern continent, or to reach out, for example, in the person of James Cook to complete one chapter in the long search for the Northwest Passage.

Because governments were becoming seriously involved, exploration tended to be based at least partly in London, Paris, Madrid or St Petersburg. Such concern meant that expeditions

14 Sketches of vessels seen in New England ports, 1739-49. *Marblehead Historical Society, Mass.*
Bowen's untrained but vivid sketches bring to life the shipping which carried explorers to and from America in the course of trade and naval activity. For the period of his youth these appear to be unique. ('Journals of Ashley Bowen (1728-1813)', P. C. F. Smith (Ed.), *Colonial Society of Massachusetts Collections*, XLIV-XLV, 1973.)

15 'Nouvelle decouverte de plusieres nations dans la Nouuelle France en l'annee 1673 et 1674', by Louis Jolliet. *John Carter Brown Library, Brown University, Providence.*
For long this manuscript map was thought to be the original map drawn by the explorer Jolliet from memory for Governor Frontenac in 1674 after he had lost all his papers of the 1673 expedition he undertook with Marquette down the Mississippi. Closer investigation of the map has shown that neither the handwriting nor the form of the signature 'Joliet' are the explorer's, and that the map is one of several copies of the lost original made in Quebec at about this time (see plates 46, 47 and 78). From the point of view of draughtsmanship and geographical concept the map is a poor production away from the areas actually traversed by Jolliet: the Mississippi is shown rising in three imaginary lakes, Lake Erie is triangular in form, and a more or less straight line serves for the east coast of North America. Even if these defects stem from the unknown copyist, it is unlikely that he made deliberate changes either in Jolliet's nomenclature or in the text of the dedicatory letter to Frontenac inscribed in the cartouche of the map. The latter is an important document in its own right, stressing the fertility of much of the country through which the Mississippi (called here the Buade by Jolliet in honor of Frontenac, whose family name it was) flowed, and also the ease with which Jolliet imagined the Missouri would take him to California and the Pacific.

13

13 Early seventeenth-century ship. Engraving by Joseph Furstenbach, from his *Architectura navalis*, 1624.
This type of vessel, apparently Dutch, represents broadly the developed ship of the first quarter of the seventeenth century, which was engaged in the transatlantic trade and which was capable of penetrating into Arctic waters. She has a well-developed sail-plan and flush main deck. She can be armed, as is shown in the engraving, for either offensive or defensive purposes, but is pre-eminently a cargo and passenger carrier.

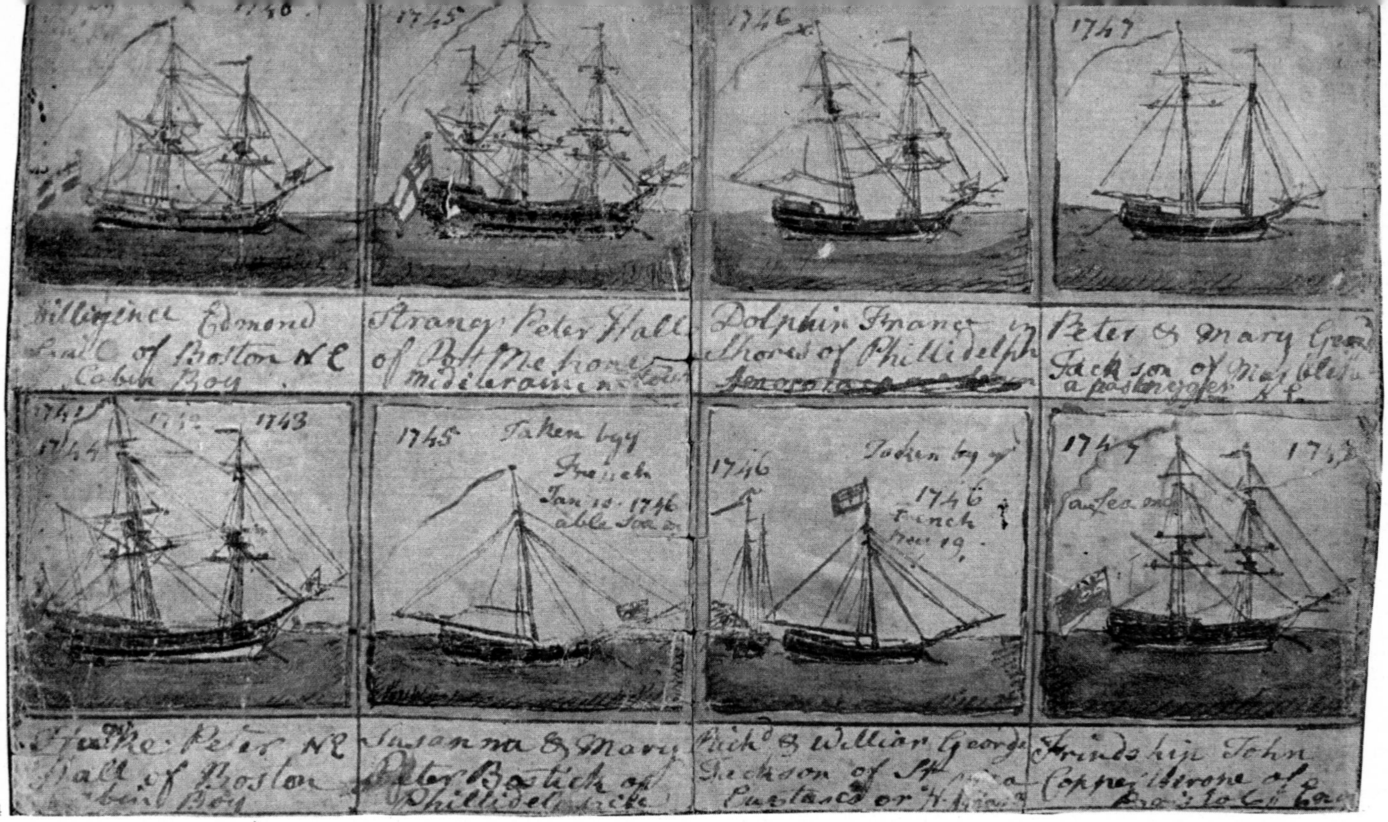
1745
1746
1747
Taken by y French

14

15

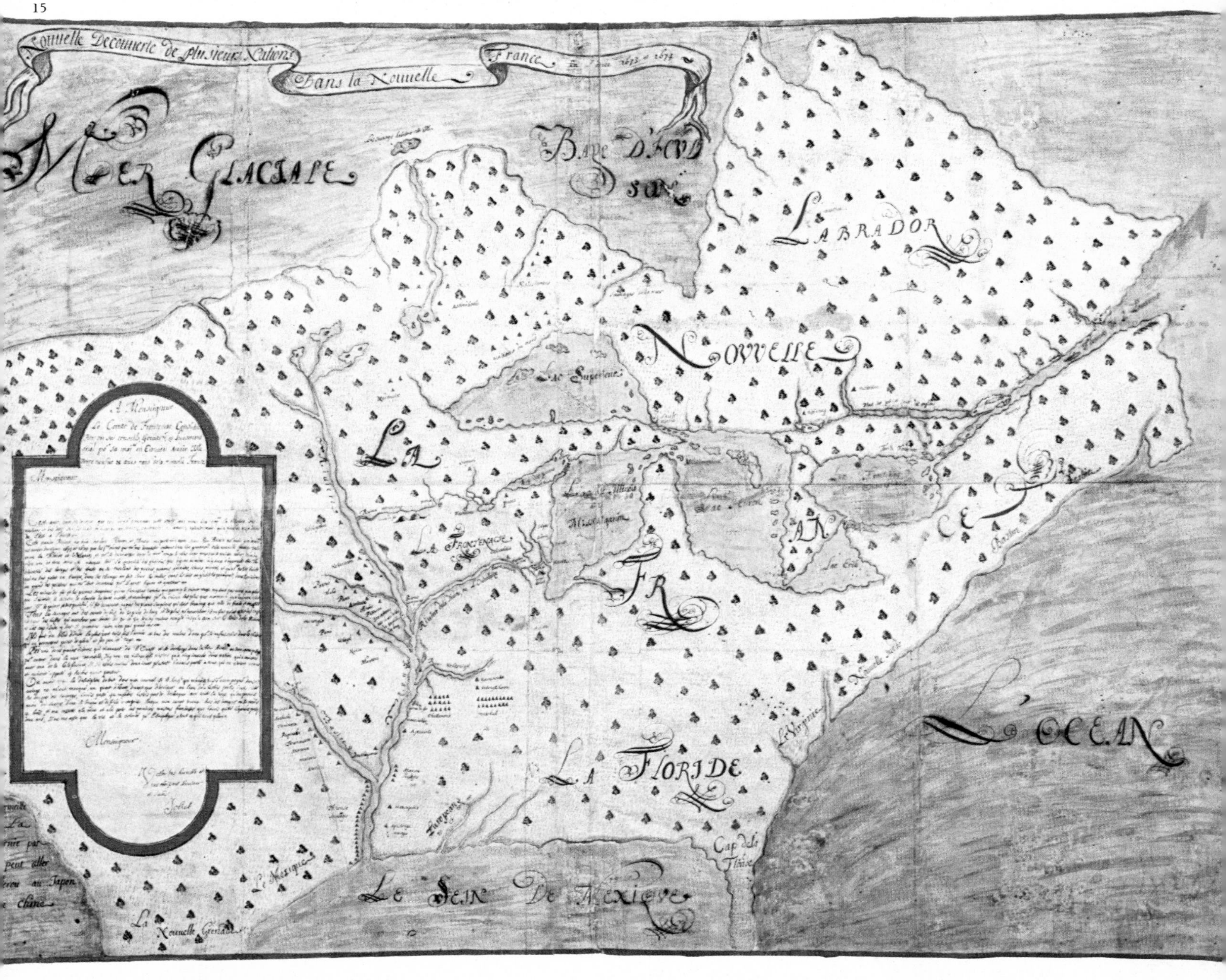
Nouvelle Decouverte de plusieurs Nations
Dans la Nouvelle
France
Mer Glaciale
Baye d'Hudson
Labrador
Nouvelle France
Lac Superieur
La Frontenacie
La Floride
L'Ocean
Le Sein de Mexique
Le Mexique
Cap de Floride

16

17

18

16 Portrait of Jean Talon, intendant of New France 1665-8 and 1670-2. *L'Hôtel-Dieu, Quebec.*
The portrait was painted by Frère Luc, possibly in 1670 on his voyage across the Atlantic with Talon. See plate 33 for a note on the painter.

17 Father Jean de Brébeuf, SJ. Artist unknown. *La Vielle Maison des Jésuites, Sillery, Quebec.*

18 The Jesuit martyrs, by Abbé Hugues Pommier, 1665. *L'Hôtel-Dieu, Quebec.*
Separate incidents during the period of the Iroquois hostilities of the 1640s are here gathered into a composite picture. An engraving of the same scene published the previous year in Du Creux has numbered captions in Latin which show that the following incidents were depicted: *foreground, from left to right*: the murder with an axe of Father Isaac Jogues in October 1646, and two of his French companions; the death at the stake of Father Gabriel Lalemant and Father Jean de Brébeuf in March 1649. *Background, from left to right*: the killing of Father Noël Chabanel by an apostate, who threw the corpse into a stream; Father Anne de Nouë who was frozen to death, February 1646; the death of Joseph Onahare, a young Algonquin Christian, who was tortured for three days by the Iroquois in 1650 for refusing to renounce his faith; Father Charles Garnier, shot in December 1649 among the Tobacco Hurons; in white vestments Father Antoine Daniel, shot at the end of his Mass in July 1648.

were usually larger, or better briefed and equipped than ever before, and had the advice of scientific bodies in the European capitals to guide them. At the same time, daring searches in western North America could still be mounted by companies and by individuals or small syndicates with favorable results. There was a growing obligation on explorers to make more effective maps and to bring back information on fauna, flora and minerals, together with details of native life and customs (often illustrated). Thus what was exceptional in the seventeenth century became usual in the eighteenth. There is, perhaps, less excitement to be obtained from records of eighteenth-century exploration in North America than in the previous century, but they are much fuller, more precise and more encyclopedic.

Water transport in American exploration

In the discovery of North America in the sixteenth and early seventeenth centuries the ship had been all-important but, in many cases, it was no longer directly involved in exploration once a string of colonies had been established along the eastern seaboard. Ships could indeed sail a thousand miles inland to Montreal and they continued to supply and service the forward bases of French expansionism; ships could and did penetrate some way up the Hudson and Delaware Rivers and so help to launch exploring parties farther inland; ships could probe the shoreline of Chesapeake Bay and its formidable tributaries but they were stopped at the Fall Line. Farther to the southwest they could not pierce inland beyond the coastal harbors and so did not contribute appreciably to the early exploration of the Mississippi Basin. Ships played a major part farther back in the exploring process; they carried European emigrants to the coastal colonies from which the later explorers were drawn. They carried on commerce between the colonies and Europe and they brought from Europe instructions for undertaking expeditions, and sometimes, too, the equipment required. They were the vital link between the two continents, sustaining the European inspiration to continue the process of understanding and exploiting North America by exploring it.

It was essential for the continuing settlement and exploration that ships should become more effective carriers. Adaptation for commercial purposes of designs worked out for fighting galleons, especially in England and France, produced faster and more seaworthy vessels. The adoption of Dutch types of cargo-carrying hulls, roomy and relatively cheap, was a

19

20

351,848 | 973.1

19 Satirical print showing Captain Woodes Rogers and his men being received by the Indian men (and maidens) of Lower California in January 1710, from Drake, *New universal collection of voyages*, 1770.
Rogers, as he tells in *A crossing voyage round the world*, 1712, with the *Duke* and *Dutchess*, had just taken one of the Manila galleons off the Lower California coast when he put into Puerto Seguro where 'we spent our Time refitting, wooding, and watering'. 'The Natives,' he says, 'grew very familiar with us, and came frequently aboard to view our ships'. The women, however, did not play the part indicated for them in the print: 'All of them that we saw were old, and miserably wrinkled. We suppose they were afraid to let any of their young ones come near us, but needed not; for besides the good Order we kept among our Men in that respect, if we may judge by what we saw, they could not be very tempting.' Such casual contacts were all that Englishmen had with the west coast until late in the eighteenth century.

20 'English whalers on the ice' by P. Brooking. Oil painting. *National Maritime Museum, Greenwich.*
This early eighteenth-century scene indicates the large-scale of the whaling industry in sub-Arctic and Arctic waters off North America at that period. Whaling accustomed masters and men alike to the harsh northern conditions and enabled them to provide expert personnel for exploring expeditions in northern waters then and later.

Leabharlann Chontae Longfoirt/Longphuirt

parallel development of equal importance in western Europe. In detail, ship design slowly becomes more sophisticated, rounder sterns give place to flat ones; hulls become straighter; there is some gradual modification of decking and accommodation at bow and stern. Mast and sail plans are not greatly altered in essentials, though fashions change in matters of detail as time goes on; the fixed spritsail topsail on the bowsprit and a single mizzen with a square topsail slowly become general. Gradually the transatlantic sailing ships grow larger and become more effective vehicles for carrying men and goods. Those built in Holland or France or England are soon joined by those built in Massachusetts, since timber could be most profitably exported in a fully manufactured form.

The growing navy of merchant vessels brought North America nearer to Europe, brought many Europeans into contact with American products and awakened a desire in an appreciable number to emigrate there. The transatlantic trade also created in a significant number of those who stayed at home a continuing interest in the novelties which North America offered, however familiar it was becoming in certain respects. This minority, anxious to inform itself, established a growing market for books, pamphlets and maps. In the seventeenth century the *Jesuit Relations* had an audience in France which could and did follow, year by year for more than a generation, every exploring step of the missionary fathers in the American north and west. And indeed, up until the middle of the eighteenth century, most of the French travel books on North America—and there were many of exceptional importance—continued to be written by clerics with some missionary-exploring experience or else by men who had close contacts inside the missionary Orders. The audience in England and the Netherlands was more miscellaneous in its demands. Economic information, material useful for merchants or intending emigrants, was in much call, but this too had many links with exploration, since prospectuses, for example, were often aimed at opening up recently discovered territories with some real or supposed potential for settlement. Map-makers in the Netherlands, dominant until late in the seventeenth century, found a continuous and growing demand for what cartographic information on North America they could display, including the course of exploration which the map-compilers attempted, however erratically, to satisfy. French and English map-compilers also responded to the rising demand and proved increasingly effective in producing representations, often well up-to-date, of the progress of exploration. The political rivalries of England and France, as they developed during the eighteenth century, helped to expand the audience for information on North America, not least on those frontier areas where exploration and political competition were taking place in uneasy double harness. Much of this growing consciousness of North America could not have taken root without effective shipping links. The ship was ultimately the vehicle which made continued exploration possible and which enabled the growing demand in Europe, both for discovery and for information about what had been discovered, to be satisfied.

There were, of course, several exceptional areas where ships could still be of some value in primary or secondary exploration. The opening of Hudson Bay by the Hudson's Bay Company was effected entirely by ship, and those involved in the northern fur trade were necessarily closely

21

21 View of La Lorette in Canada, inhabited by Catholic Indians Aug 1765. Anonymous drawing *British Museum, London.*
One of a series of drawings made in 1765 in the seigniory of Deschambault, one of the oldest feudal estates in French Canada. Houses of this period have survived into the present century.

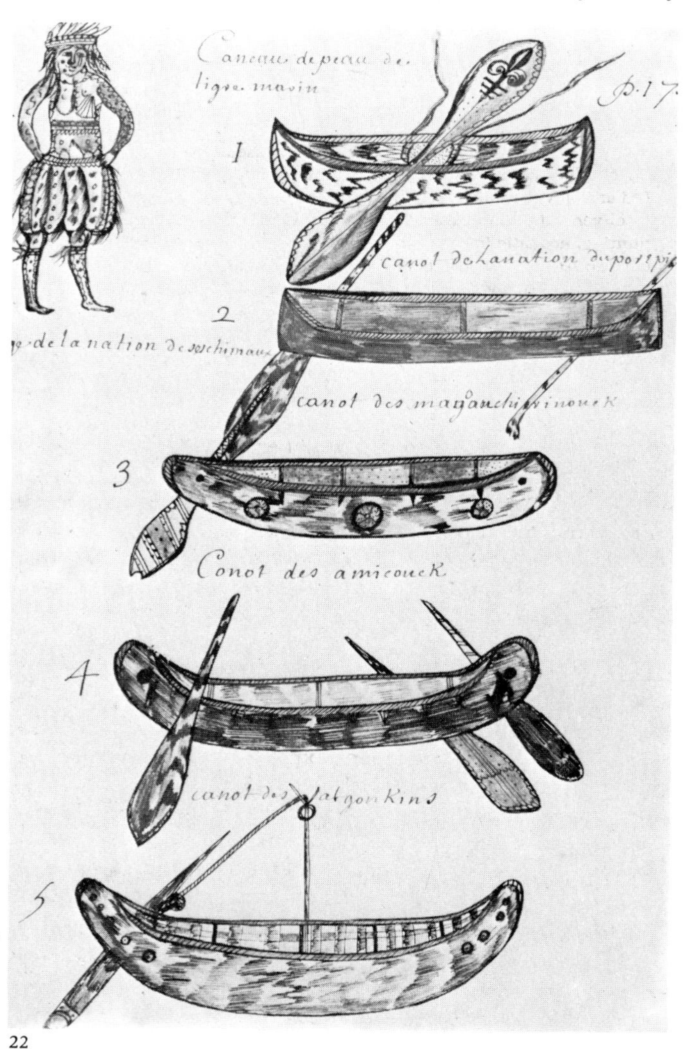

22

22 Indian canoes from the *Codex Canadensis*, c. 1700. *Thomas Gilcrease Institute, Tulsa.*
The five canoes (and the figure at the side) are all from Algonkian tribes of eastern Canada. No. 1 is a sealskin canoe. The Micmac Indians were known as Porcupines by the Malecite (no. 2); the 'Magoauchiwinouck' are probably a band rather than a tribe (3), as also may have been the 'Amicouck', unless they are Micmac in another form (4). The canoes and paddles show many interesting variations in design and decoration: no. 5 is fitted with a mast on which a sail can be hoisted. See plate 36 for a description of the *Codex Canadensis*.

linked with the maintenance and expansion of that trade. Though the search for the Northwest Passage by sea languished in the seventeenth century, the revival of interest in the next led to the re-employment of ships for discovery purposes, though no very striking achievements were to be recorded in these maritime efforts. The Greenland whale fishery, which enabled the English and Dutch to gain an intimate knowledge of the shores of Davis and Baffin Straits, was not primarily concerned with discovery but it constantly presented new aspects of these Arctic and sub-Arctic zones to the ships and crews involved.

24

24 Mariner's magnetic compass; Italian, 1719. *National Maritime Museum, Greenwich.*
This boxed compass with fly (the star-like painted wind rose) 'has undergone very little change since its first invention' (E. G. R. Taylor and M. W. Richey, *The geometrical seaman*, 1962, p. 21, tell us), yet it remained the basic instrument of navigation on water. Smaller, more portable versions of it were carried on land. The scale of 32 points of $11^\circ\frac{1}{4}$ lasted from the fourteenth to the twentieth centuries. (Diameter: 4.8 ins.)

23

23 A birchbark canoe from the Penobscot River. *The Peabody Museum of Salem.*
This is the earliest surviving example of this craft from the Maine-New Brunswick area, and has been in the Peabody Museum of Salem since 1826. 'Canoe-building was one of the most extensive and important skills among the Indians of Maine and of the Maritime Provinces where it furnished an easy, convenient mode of travel, and without which the economic life of the hunting, nomadic Indians would have been greatly restricted. . . . The importance of the birch canoe to the economic life of Indians during the exploration period, and to white men in the early colonial and fur-trading times, is forcibly brought to our minds by the many historical accounts mentioning its use as an aid in travelling and as a means for shipping supplies to and from remote posts.' (Hadlock and Dodge, *A canoe from the Penobscot River*, 1948, pp. 3-4.)

The other significant area was the west coast. So far as we are aware, only infrequent visits to California and the coasts to the north were made after 1603 and then only by privateers calling, like Drake earlier, for water or for respite from their journeying: Woodes Rogers's men found Lower California pleasant in 1709 but they did not penetrate along the shores of what we now reckon to be North America. It was the Russians, coming from Siberia, who first revived the exploration of the western extremities of North America. Bering and the rest put Alaska, however tentatively, on the map and began a course of Russian penetration into the fur trade there which was ultimately to be significant. Spain too, attracted by Russian activity and English interest in that activity, at last began to concern herself with the western shore, to send expeditions, to chart the islands off what is now British Columbia and to plan the establishment of military and naval posts. It was not until after James Cook's third voyage—when the Revolution was under way—that charts of any accuracy linked the Russian with the Spanish discoveries and set in motion the effective exploration of these areas, paralleling the efforts being made on land by the fur trading interests which culminated in Mackenzie's transcontinental journey; by the end of the century most of the main outlines of this region had been sketched out.

An active part in detailed exploration was played by smaller European-type vessels. Shallops and other small sailing craft enabled the lesser harbors to be brought into use, so as to exploit more intensively the eastern colonies, to penetrate the eastern rivers, sometimes in craft built or assembled above the Fall Line, and to exploit the Great Lakes from the time of Frontenac on or explore the Mississippi. But until well into the eighteenth century such vessels took only a rather limited part in the exploration process.

The main instruments of exploration of interior North America by water were canoes, mainly birchbark canoes, though the dugout canoe was also employed from time to time especially in the more southerly parts of North America. Skilfully constructed by the Indians of Canada from locally grown materials, the birchbark canoe was a very good means of transport. It could be made up to some twenty feet in length (with a beam of up to three feet) and, under French influence, by the late seventeenth century came to be built rather longer and wider, and was normally fitted with a sail. Capable of holding up to twenty-five men, it could also carry several thousand pounds of cargo. It was maneuverable in varied water conditions: having a slight draft it could be used in shallower rivers and lakes; being easily guided it could pass through fairly rapidly flowing waters. The smaller canoes could be portaged by one man in a hurry. Larger craft, together with their ladings, could be carried by their crews over less extended portages. Though fragile, canoes could be repaired or even rebuilt from local materials if their occupants had the necessary skill. (The canoe was significant in requiring in most cases the cooperation of whites and Indians.) It enabled the Great Lakes system to become a high road into the west and northwest, and also opened up the way into the Missouri, Mississippi and Ohio water systems. The paper birch which formed the essential skin of the canoe did not grow to sufficient size much below latitude 43°N. For exploration to the south, then, canoes, or their essential parts, had to be brought down from Canada or inferior substitutes found. The dugout canoe, especially when made with the axe and other European tools rather than fire and stone and shell scrapers, was not an ineffective exploring tool. Where yellow poplar large enough could be the raw material, it was serviceable, reasonably durable, and could accommodate twenty-five to thirty persons, but it was not as fast as the birchbark or nearly so maneuverable. Both birchbark and dugout canoes could, with some skill and the necessary materials, be sailed, the latter probably more safely than the former. But with the opening of the Mississippi river system European-type boats and sailing vessels of various types were eventually constructed for trading and, to some extent, exploring.

The explorer on land

The explorer usually had to use his feet. The frontiersman learned to walk steadily for long periods without undue fatigue. How far he was able to make use of means of navigation on land would naturally depend on how thoroughly he was equipped and for what purposes. Large exploring parties

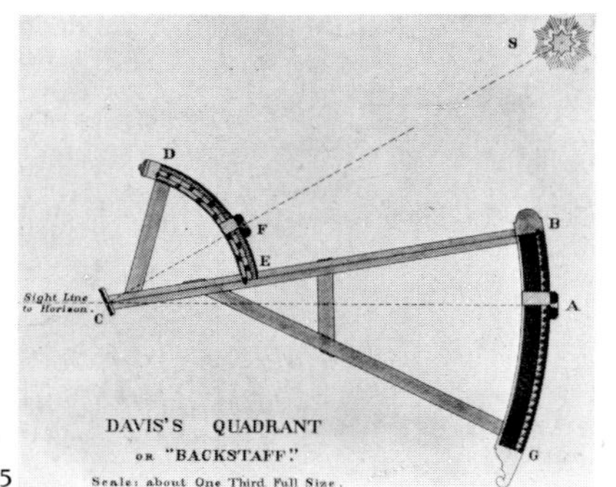

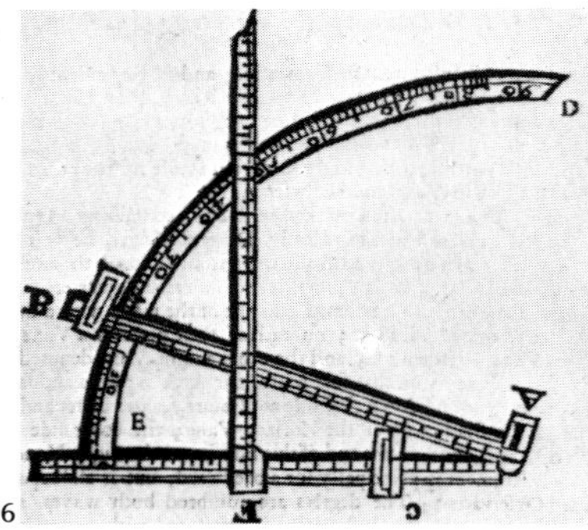

25 Davis quadrant. Diagram from *The Science Museum, London.*

26 Removing quadrant, from *The use of the removing quadrant.*
John Davis invented an ingenious variation of the cross-staff in about 1594 which enabled observers of star or sun to link their celestial observation with the establishment of the horizon so as to give a reasonably accurate angular reading. The observer turns his back on the sun and observes the altitude from the angle of the shadow cast. He sights the horizon from A and sets the first scale (B-G) from the horizon: the sun casts either a shadow or (in some cases) a bright spot on C when the second scale (D-E) is set correctly, thus recording angular height on this scale. This quadrant in many slightly varying forms was very popular, became known as the 'English quadrant' and remained in use until well into the eighteenth century. One variation was the 'Removing quadrant' as illustrated.

might well carry with them some instruments beside the basic magnetic compass for survey purposes (but plane table and theodolite would be part of the equipment of fairly specialized exploring groups only). A timepiece too came to be virtually indispensable, as those available became more reliable. Astrolabes, like Champlain's, probably continued in use. A large expedition by water might well include instruments for taking accurate latitude sights, such as a Davis staff or one of the more sophisticated quadrants. But means of determining time and distance and direction of travel, over land especially, were rather primitive and probably no more accurate than skilled direct observation of natural phenomena with the naked eye. Almanacs and the smaller sets of tables may well have been used. The explorer did, in most cases, carry some means of writing and material on which to write. He would try to make and keep some kind of journal, recording roughly distances, direction and 'occurrences', if his expedition was one on which he might have to report in detail. But he might, too, be wholly unused to keeping a written record, being either illiterate or indifferent to all except the end-objectives and the material returns of his expedition. Even if he were illiterate he might, on his return, be able to give an effective oral account of what he had seen, with reasonably accurate indications of where he had been; such verbal descriptions were often a matter of experience, memory and training rather than of education, and might be made the basis of narratives written by those to whom they were reported.

The explorer needed both tools and weapons and it is often difficult to draw any hard distinction between them. Firearms, however clumsy they might be, could be as essential for securing food as for defense against (or attacks on) enemies; pistols, if easier to carry, were less effective and had a much shorter range than the piece. Firearms, then, were normal, for a non-clerical traveller, essential. Axes were indispensable to clear a way through vegetation, live or dead, to cut firewood, to repair canoes, to dismember animals, as well as, if need be, to use as weapons against other humans. Knives were in much the same category, but even more intimate and at hand as a tool or a weapon. Many explorers wore European clothes, but most used, at the end if not the beginning of their travels, Indian-type garments, cloaks and mantles of fur or skin chiefly, more probably skins or furred garments cut on European lines, breeches, jackets, coats, and of course, gloves and furred hats. Choice and circumstances dictated whether they continued to wear stout European-designed shoes or boots or took to the softer native leggings and Moccasins; since often the explorer was obliged to adopt Indian footwear when his own had given way. Much depended on the season and the climate. Blankets, tents, other impedimenta of this sort might be taken, might be essential, if an expedition consisted of more than two or three people.

It was the Indian who killed by far the greater number of animals involved in the fur trade; he and his people prepared the skins so that they would reach Europe in condition good enough to be finished and tailored. He manned the canoes which brought most traders and explorers out from the trading posts, though sometimes the tribes insisted, themselves, on bringing the pelts to the posts. In the exploring process, the Indian was normally essential to the European trapper, explorer and missionary; he supplied the canoes and the skill to repair them; he propelled the canoes, if the European had insufficient skill or strength, or else the paddling and steering was shared. He knew the portages far beyond the limits of the explorer's knowledge: when he was in strange territory he was often still the guide, picking up animal trails, indications of changes of soil, rock and vegetation, co-operating in determining direction, giving advice about weather prospects and the means of mitigating the effects of bad weather. If the expedition had to hunt for food or skins the Indian was often able to take the initiative. Missionaries tended to depend on their native guides and canoes much more absolutely than other civilian explorers. Some learned how to imitate native ways, though Indians supplied essential foodstuffs, especially dried meats. Indian villages could give

27 Edmond Halley's isogonic chart, showing lines of equal magnetic variation, published in London in 1702. *National Maritime Museum, Greenwich.*
The mapping of the land and charting of the seacoasts went on hand in hand with the first maps of the regularities observed over the oceans themselves. Two charts, one of the world and the other of the Atlantic Ocean, in 1701 and 1702 incorporated the information on the variation of the compass Halley had gathered over many years, principally through his own Atlantic voyages. Angus Armitage says, 'He embodied all the magnetical material in two charts, constructed on a principle now familiar in physical geography but of which these are believed to have been the earliest printed examples. Curves were drawn through sets of places all having the same variation of the compass, so that the charts were inscribed with what . . . we call "Isogonics".' (*Edmond Halley*, London, pp. 146-8, 1966.)

28 Map of Louisiana, from N. de Fer, *Nouvelle France*, 1718.
The map shows the Mississippi Valley and the land to the west of it, as the boundaries of Louisiana were being sketched out but before New Orleans had been founded in 1718. It illustrates the routes of La Salle. The western part of the new province is inaccurately rendered. The lay-out of the Rio Grande and New Mexico are conventionalized, as are the illustrations of fauna and Indian activities on the map. The outline of the Mississippi is, however, firm and its major features reasonably well shown. Nevertheless, this map is really little more than a sketch with meager precise knowledge backing its features.

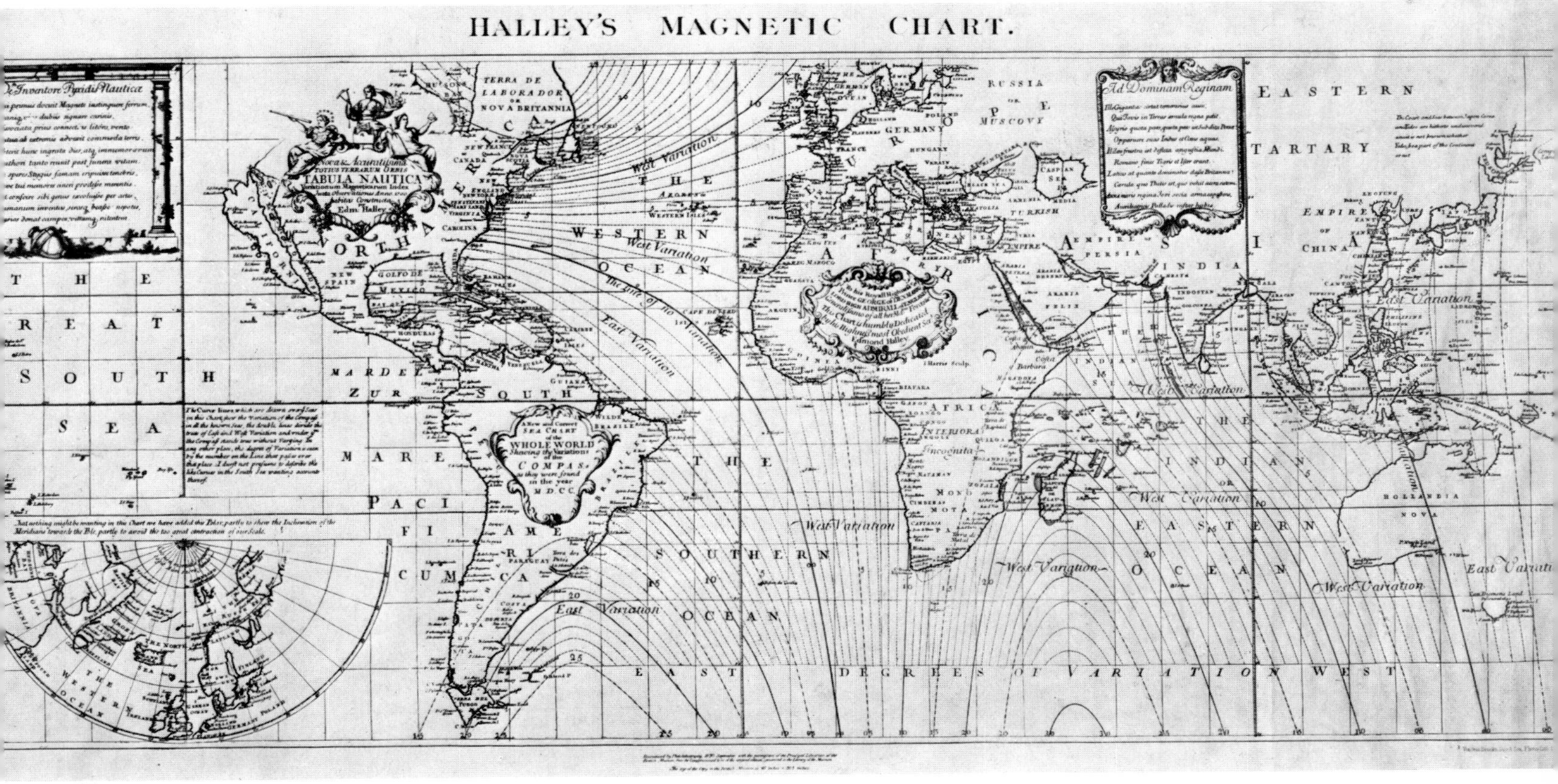
HALLEY'S MAGNETIC CHART.
TERRA DE LABORADOR OR NOVA BRITANNIA
RUSSIA
MUSCOVY
GERMANY
EASTERN
TARTARY
Ad Dominam Reginam
WESTERN
OCEAN
West Variation
East Variation
The Line of no Variation
EMPIRE OF CHINA
PERSIA
INDIA
MAR DEL ZUR
SOUTH
SEA
MARE
PACI
FI
CUM
SOUTHERN
OCEAN
INDIAN
EASTERN
OCEAN
A New and Correct SEA CHART of the WHOLE WORLD Shewing the Variations of the COMPASS as they were found in the year MDCC
AFRICA INTERIORA Incognita
EAST DEGREES OF VARIATION WEST

27

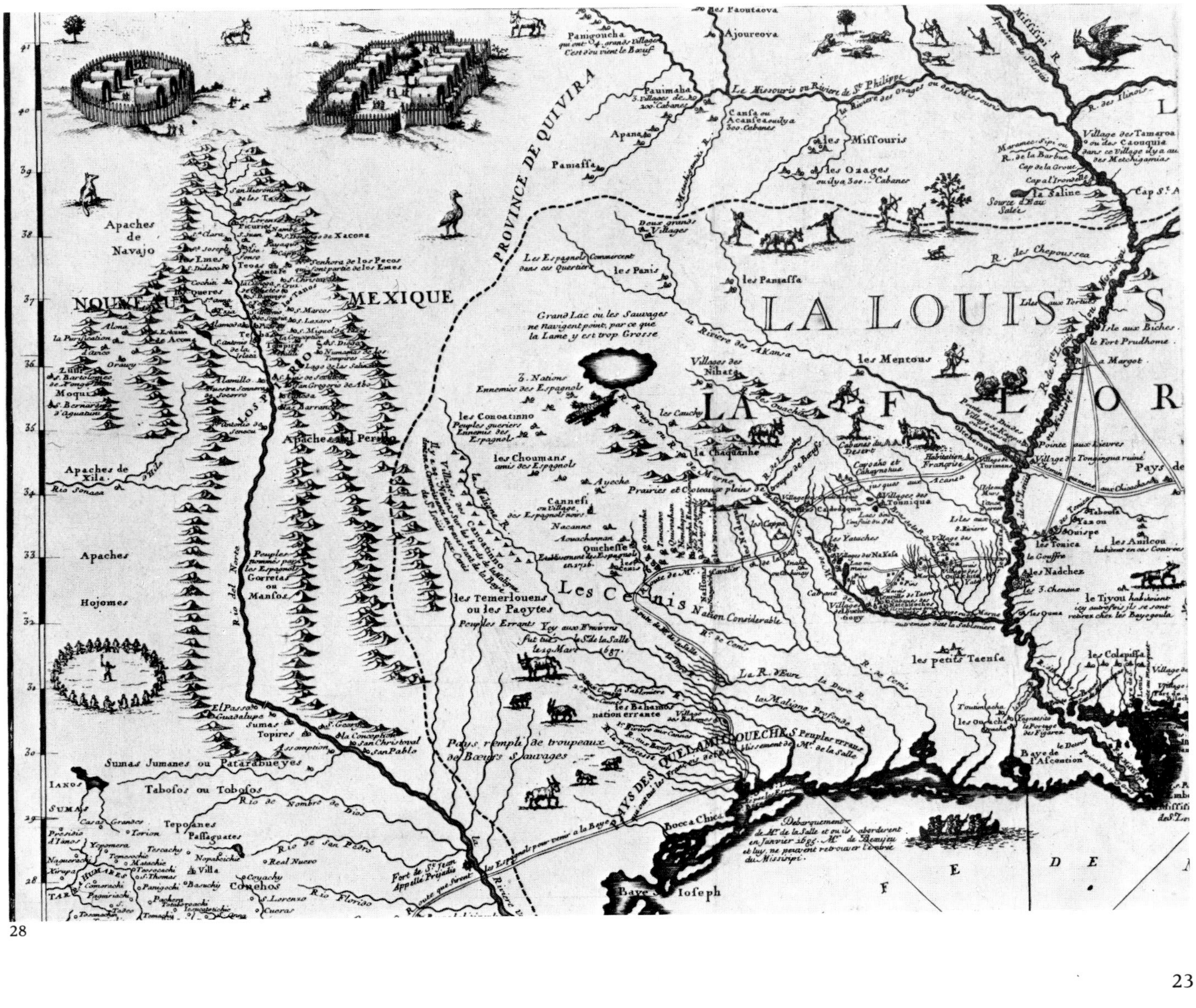
PROVINCE DE QUIVIRA
NOUVEAU MEXIQUE
LA LOUIS
LA FLOR
Apaches de Navajo
Apaches de Xila
Apaches
Hojomes
Les Cenis
les Missouris
les Ozages
les Panis
les Pantaffa
les Mentous
Grand Lac ou les Sauvages ne Navigent point, par ce que la Lame y est trop Grosse
Rio del Norte
Sumas Jumanes ou Patarabueyes
Tabosos ou Tobosos
Pays rempli de troupeaux de Bœufs sauvages
les Temerlouens ou les Paqytes
Peuples Errants
la Riviere des Akansa
Baye de l'Ascention
Baye Ioseph
Bocca Chica

28

29 A French explorer shares a meal with his Indian hosts. This fine drawing came from a late seventeenth-century manuscript, sold at Sotheby's on 17 February 1936 and since lost sight of. Apparently written by N. Foederis, with drawings by a Mons. Destrez, it was entitled *Dialogue ou entretient d'un Français avec un sauvage*. It compares well in its realism and its animation with the famous sixteenth-century drawings by John White. It is not known in what part of Canada it was drawn.

30 Wampum ceremony and pipe ceremony, from Père Lafitau, *Moeurs des sauvages Ameriquains*, II, p. 314, 1724.
Lafitau summed up in his book, and his illustrations to it, what was known by the eighteenth century about the Indian peoples encountered by Europeans (especially the French). Here he is illustrating two major ceremonial events in Indian life, seen especially amongst the Algonkian in Canada: the presentation of the wampum belt as a gift of great price to a chief with whom an alliance has been made; and the tobacco ceremony, when elaborately decorated pipes were smoked as a sign of friendship and might be exchanged for that purpose. The illustrations often provide good detail on the specific objects involved in the ceremonies, but lazily take the general setting and appearance of the Indians from stereotypes going back to De Bry at the end of the sixteenth century.

food and shelter and very often the Indian guides were essential as translators and mediators. Indians sometimes knew how to make maps on bark or in sand and could then aid very much the process of recording by sketches or observation so that mapping in outline of new areas could be done well. They could also greatly impede the process of discovery by their hostility, their calculated deception of exploring parties, and sometimes, unexpectedly, by their ignorance.

Enlightenment by map

Explorers carried maps and made them or, at the least, contributed to their creation. How much use the early maps of the interior of North America were is very doubtful. Champlain's maps had, by incorporating oral information from Indian informants, pointed to his successors the way westwards. The details of the eastern shoreline were only slowly conveyed on to the printed maps, though one suspects that they were earlier known on manuscript versions which have largely been lost. But most of the attempts to supplement the coastal outlines with information on the interior for long contained much fantasy and guesswork, nourished on a few miscellaneous and misleading data. Latitude determination offered a check on the course and direction of the major rivers, but longitude could not effectively be determined accurately by the explorer, certainly on overland journeys. The result was that, though successive explorers gradually built up something of a cartographic picture of the interior as they covered it in some degree systematically, the relation of parts to the whole often remained confused. Only if there were a major lake or river or other prominent natural feature could some distinctness in the character of a particular area be conveyed convincingly on a map. The tracts of low-land, which increased in extent as men travelled westward, and the multiplicity of lakes of no very pronouncedly individual character brought confusion, which meant that many of the more general maps compiled in London or Paris were of little or no use to the explorer in the field.

The explorer was handicapped in making original contributions to cartography. He might sketch prominent features in his journal; or he could draw in an impressionistic way the broader outlines of the places to which he had been (allowing considerable opportunities for error); or afterwards he might attempt to construct from his journal alone, or amplified by sketches, a map of his whole journey. More usually the task of putting discoveries on paper was done in the capital cities by cartographical compilers who could get outlines wrong as often, or more often, than they got them right.

Survey was very slow. If long distances in new territory were traversed it was not normally practicable. Systematic surveying tended to be deferred, unless there was an overriding need, until an area was at least moderately well known

30

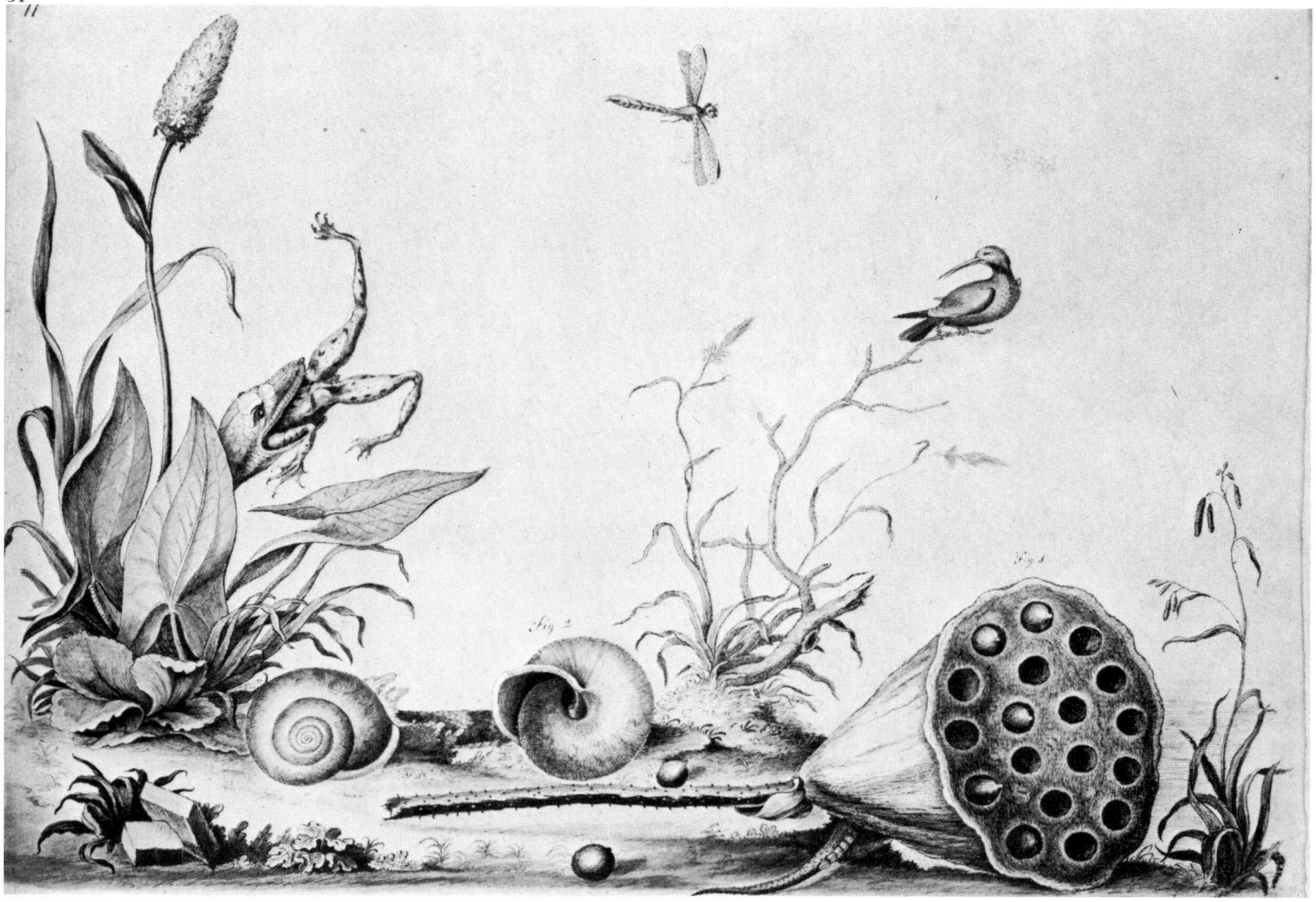

31 William Bartram. Snails and various plants, *c.* 1776. *Natural History Museum, London, Fothergill Album.*
A scarlet snake swallowing a frog; snails ('a large land snail of a straw colour'd shell & pale inside'—Bartram); American lotus. Other plants: blackroot ('the Floridians roast or boil the root of this plant'—Bartram to Dr Fothergill); arrow arum; water lettuce. Bartram's drawings are among the most accurate and attractive records of North American flora and fauna. William was a naturalist who explored widely in the southern colonies with John, his father, and later alone.

32 Des Barres. Vignette of falls on Sandwich Bay, Labrador, from the *Atlantic Neptune*, *c.* 1773.
Of all the late eighteenth-century cartographers, Joseph des Barres especially illustrated his charts with many views and vignettes which gave glimpses of coastal and river scenery. This typical view of falls near the Labrador coast gives some idea of how unattractive access to the interior could seem.

and until, often, some legal quarrel over boundaries or the acquisition of territory rendered correct delineation imperative and offical. But such surveys contained an element of exploration: they revealed the details of the partly known in areas not fully settled or exploited where communications tended to be confined to a few settled tracks or trails. William Byrd's *History of the Dividing Line*, for example, shows that even in 1728 the land between Virginia and North Carolina offered opportunity for many minor discoveries. The same might be said of the maps of the Mason-Dixon line and of the first attempts to put the whole area of one or more colony effectively on paper, such as the Jefferson and Fry map of Virginia of 1755. Again, James Cook, by accurately charting the coasts of Newfoundland, southern Labrador and the St Lawrence estuary between 1758 and 1765, revealed many spatial relationships which had not been precisely known. Even for the mainland coasts of the Maritimes and the Thirteen Colonies, the charting of Des Barres and others after 1763 pinned down many details of coastal topography which had remained obscure, and brought to light certain areas as truly as if they had for the first time been discovered.

Discovery and exploration are seen through the work of the cartographers as not a single process but one of first sight, of repetition, of selective recording and exploitation, of later revision and amplification of topographic detail which brings much new to light: a process which does not end in 1775 or even in the 1970s. But in the process, from the 1630s to the 1770s, much of the great continent emerged.

Fig1 The Great Lakes and the Mississippi Valley

33

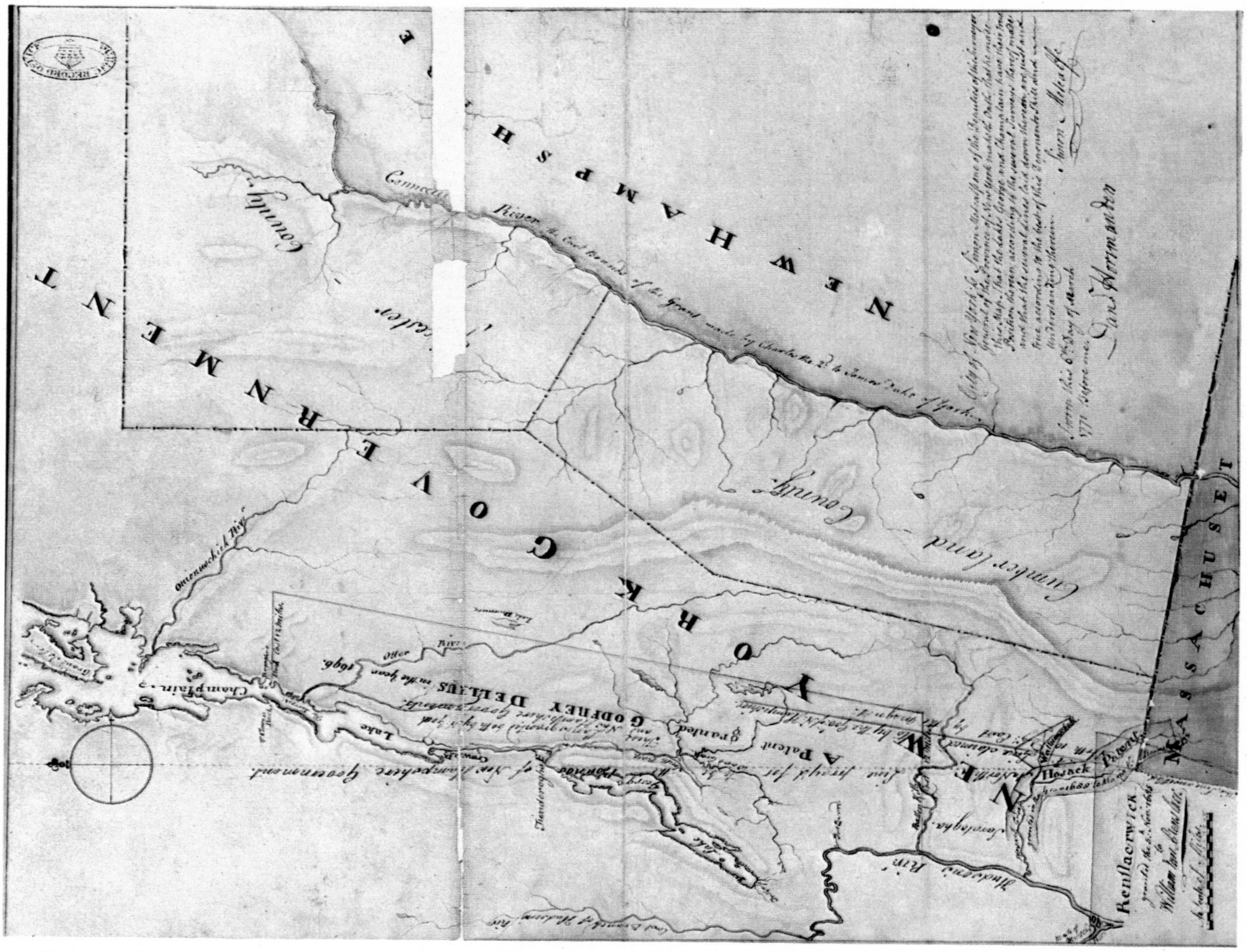

References

NEW YORK GOVERNMENT

NEW HAMPSHIRE

MASSACHUSET

Cumberland County

County

A Patent granted GODFREY DELLIUS in the year 1696.

Lake Champlain

Rensslaerwick granted the 5th Nov. 1685 to William Van Rensselaer

City of New York ss Simon Metcalfe one of the Deputies of the Surveyor General of the Province of New York maketh Oath that he made this Map. That the Lakes George and Champlain have their true Position thereon according to the several Surveys thereof made and that the several Lines laid down thereon are just and true according to the best of this Deponents Skill and Understanding therein.

Simon Metcalfe

Sworn this 6th Day of March 1771 Before me.

Danl Horsmanden

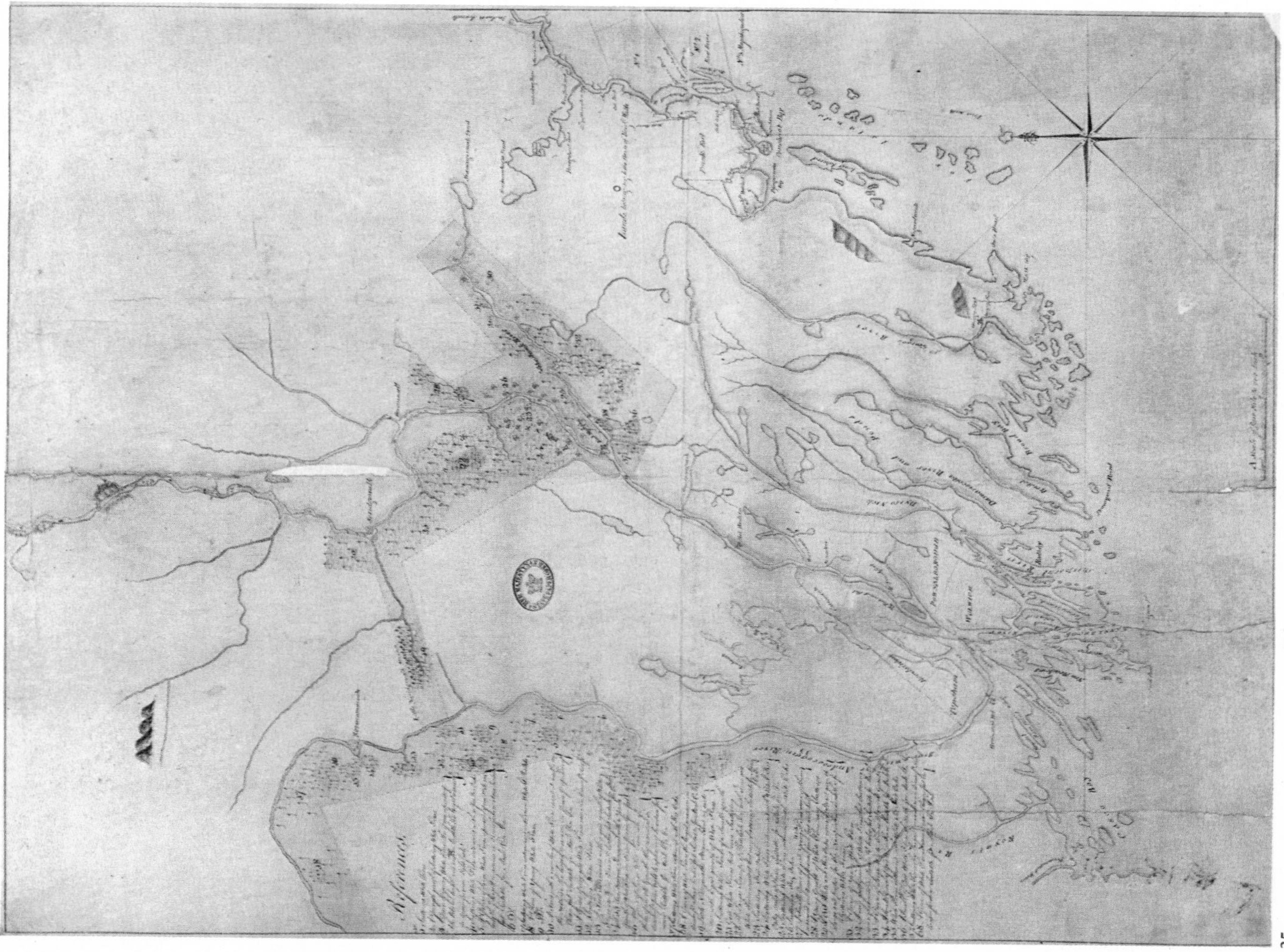

1 NEW FRANCE AFTER CHAMPLAIN: THE EXPLORATION OF THE GREAT LAKES AND THE MISSISSIPPI

1 The Great Lakes

In the course of a long and heroic career Samuel de Champlain (*c.* 1570-1635) did more than secure Acadia and the St Lawrence valley for the French. With his insistence on the commercial and mineral potentialities of northeast America, on the need to push ever farther west in quest of a short route to China, and with his linking of exploration to the profitable fur trade, he pointed the way to the spectacular expansion of New France in the later seventeenth century. Champlain's writings and maps (see plate 37) sketched the extent of his achievement: the exploration of modern Nova Scotia and New Brunswick, the discovery of the route from the St Lawrence through Lake Champlain to the Hudson, the opening up of the rugged terrain north of the St Lawrence by way of the Saguenay and St Maurice Rivers, and above all the realization that farther west lay a series of mighty lakes, veritable inland seas. It was the task of his successors to discover the character and relationship of these immense stretches of water, and these successors included not only men forged in Champlain's own image, empire-builders, fur traders, official agents of company or government, but also the black-robed Jesuits who returned to Quebec with Champlain in 1633 (after the brief interlude of English occupation) to take control of all missionary activity in New France. A unique amalgam of commercial enterprise, spiritual zeal and imperial ambition was within fifty years to reveal the full dimensions of the Great Lakes, and far away to the south trace the course of the imposing Mississippi River to its outlet on the sub-tropical shores of the Gulf of Mexico.

Although one of the fullest accounts of early French activity was written by a lay brother in the Recollet order (see selection 1) we follow the process of exploration for the most part through the eyes of the Jesuits; for the most valuable and comprehensive reports from New France to be published in the seventeenth century were the famed *Jesuit relations.* Each year the Jesuit fathers wrote at their mission posts detailed accounts of their activities which were edited by the superior at Quebec into a coherent narrative, sent to France, and there published as a regular series for forty years by the Parisian publishing house of Sébastien Cramoisy. At first the missionaries found it depressingly difficult to gain any insight into Indian life and customs. The societies encountered by the Jesuits on the coastal fringes of Asia, however alien and

33 'La France apportant la foi aux Indiens de la Nouvelle France', *c.* 1671, attributed to Frère Luc (baptized Claude François). *Ursuline Convent, Quebec.*
Frère Luc, a well-known Parisian painter of the period, was a member of the Recollet order and arrived in Quebec in 1670. This painting is described by J. Russell Harper in his *Painting in Canada*, 1966: 'France, symbolized by the Queen Mother, Anne of Austria, shows a painting of New France's spiritual patrons to an Indian kneeling on the shores of the broad St. Lawrence, with mission stations in the distance.'

34 Map showing the boundaries between New York and New Hampshire and the land grants in New York along Lake George and Lake Champlain and to the south of Lake Champlain, 1771. *Public Record Office, London, Class MPG 365.*
This map serves to illustrate a secondary phase of exploration, the process leading up to the acquisition of land. Speculators, especially in the eighteenth century, followed closely on the heels of explorers and traders. Although maps such as this were drawn up to show the division of land and the ownership of grants, often as a means of settling disputes, the land was not necessarily immediately occupied. Several years might pass before the settled frontier caught up with the speculators who were regarded with great suspicion by the colonists. In particular, successive governors of New York were condemned for granting huge acreages to speculators who had no intention of clearing, settling and utilizing the land. Further results of such expansion were disputes between the colonies and often two neighboring colonies would claim the same stretch of land. Maps such as this one were drawn up to further the claim of one party or another.

35 Map showing one of the New Hampshire timber areas set aside for the use of the Royal Navy, 1772. *Public Record Office, London, CO700, Maine No. 20.*
One of the chief reasons for the early exploration of America was the search for raw materials to provide, for the home government, alternative sources of supply. In particular it was hoped that the forests of the New World would replace those of the Baltic as a source of timber for the building of naval ships. To further this aim, the government allocated large areas of forest, to the annoyance of the settlers who constantly attempted to thwart official policy by removing the special marks put on each tree. New England provided most of the timber and this particular official map delineates an area of white pines in New Hampshire. An attempt was also made to distinguish between the quality and types of trees in a particular area.

36 Sketches from the *Codex Canadensis. Thomas Gilcrease Institute, Tulsa.*
This manuscript book of sketches can be dated with a fair degree of certainty to *c.* 1700, but the artist is less easy to establish. Once thought to be the work of Charles Bécart de Granville, a draughtsman and cartographer who lived in Quebec 1675-1703, the book's text has recently been shown to have been written by Louis Nicolas, and he may also have drawn the sketches. Nicolas was a Jesuit missionary in New France from 1667 to 1675, when he was defrocked. Whoever the artist, and whatever his technical limitations, the sketches have a vigor and spontaneity which stand in sharp contrast to many of the more formalized illustrations in the published works of this period. p. 8 A Sioux chieftain, a very early depiction.

36

MER DV NORT GLACIALLE
NOVVELLE FRANCE
Terres de la Brador
Groen lan dia
C. Wornam
C. Elizabeth
C. Harles
Le Golphe St Laurens
La grande baye
Terre neuue
Le grand banc
Banquereaux
Isle de sable
Nouuelle France
Mer douce
Grand lac
Virginia
Faicte l'an 1632 par le sieur de Champlain

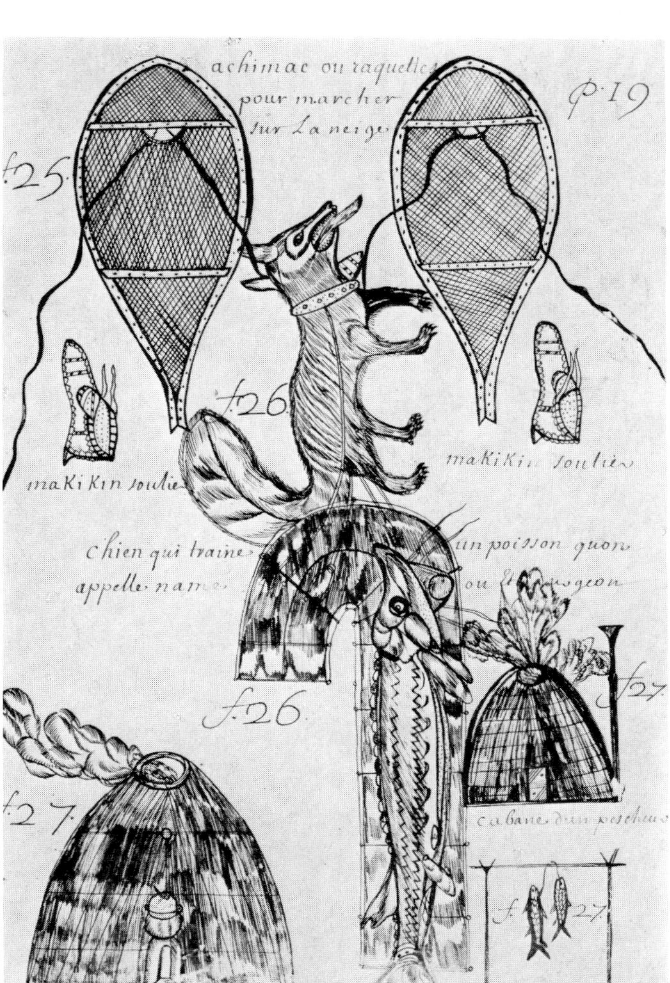

38

39

40

exotic they might be, at least had identifiable form and shape; but in the wilderness of North America the Jesuits found peoples without recognizable governmental structures, formal religions or written languages. The essential prelude to any attempt at understanding and conversion was the learning of the Indians' language. As Father Le Jeune wrote in 1638: 'First, we make expeditions to go and attack the enemy on their own ground, with their own weapons—that is to say, by a knowledge of the Montagnais, Algonkian, and Huron languages.'[1] This was no easy achievement. The multiplicity of Indian tongues, the lack of any formal, written grammar, the reluctance of the Indians to teach the eager missionaries their language, all conspired against Jesuit hopes. But despite the linguistic barrier (which some of the Fathers never overcame) the Jesuits, living day by day among the Indians in their bark lodges, produced a remarkable series of observations (see selection 2). They were not written with the calm impartiality of a modern anthropologist. The same writer might show within the space of a few paragraphs respect for the harmony of Indian family life, gratitude for Indian hospitality, and admiration for Indian fortitude, and then turn with disgust to the physical habits of the Indians, their sexual morality,

37 'Carte de la nouvelle France', by Samuel de Champlain, in *Voyages*, 1632. Champlain's last and finest map is of interest not only because of the comprehensive summary it provides of French knowledge of Acadia and the St Lawrence valley at this time, but above all because of its representation of the Great Lakes. For the first time all of them except Michigan appear, though most in distorted form: Ontario ('Lac St Louis') and Huron ('Mer douce') of both of which Champlain had personal knowledge; an unnamed Erie, looking more like a river than a lake, north of 'La nation neutre'; and finally distant Superior ('Grand Lac'), whose situation had probably been reported to Champlain by Etienne Brûlé.

38-40 Sketches from the *Codex Canadensis*, *c.* 1700. *Thomas Gilcrease Institute, Tulsa.* p. 19 Indian snowshoes, dog-sleigh etc; p. 6 An Ottawa Indian; p. 16 Indian warriors in their canoes.

and the horrific tortures they inflicted on prisoners. But for all their preconceptions and instinctive attitudes the Jesuits, by observing the Indians at close quarters over a long period of time, produced an incomparable picture of the tribes of the northeast at the moment of their calamitous contact with Europeans and their superior material culture, deadly diseases and aggressive religion. The Jesuit writings brought the Indian to life; he is far removed from the crude stereotype which often appears in the accounts of those explorers, traders and soldiers whose encounters with the Indians tended to be brief and sometimes bloody.

Human beings and their souls were the missionaries' first concern; but as they moved away from the little French settlements along the St Lawrence they were bound to acquire a knowledge of the land itself—its rivers and forests, swamps and portages, mosquito-ridden summers and icebound winters. The *Relations* are a treasure-house of information about the travels and explorations, not only of the Jesuits but also of their secular compatriots—traders and adventurers who were often unable or unwilling to express in written form their discoveries of the land and its people. It is usually in the Fathers' accounts that we catch glimpses of the rough *coureurs de bois*, the true pioneers of discovery, pushing far ahead of French officialdom in their never-ending quest for furs. By the early seventeenth century the French were tapping the continental fur trade as they received furs from Indian middlemen well to the west of their own areas of settlement. Furs were shipped to France in increasing volume, both for the domestic market and for re-export to the colder climes of the Baltic and Russia (for long, prime winter beaver was known as *castor de moscovie*). In the *Relations* too we appreciate the importance as well as the limitations of the Indian as a pathfinder. The mysterious land beyond the river or over the ridge was often familiar territory to the Indian; but his range of travel and therefore of knowledge was usually (though not invariably) limited, and even when he had come far his lack of the Europeans' surveying skills made it difficult for him to convey accurate information on routes and distances. Of more value to the white man was to observe and imitate the Indian's techniques of travel, and the birchbark canoe in summer and snowshoe in winter soon became the indispensable means by which Europeans moved across the roadless terrain of North America.

The death of Champlain in 1635 removed some of the impetus from French expansion, although one of his associates, Jean Nicollet, made at his instigation an important if ill-defined journey of exploration at about this time (see selection 3). For commercial reasons the Hurons were anxious to enlist French assistance in making peace between them and the 'Winnebagos' Indians who lived, they said, on the shores of a vast inland sea beyond Lake Huron. Accompanied by Huron guides Nicollet reached Green Bay on the western shores of Lake Michigan, and probably the Fox River. He was the first European to see Lake Michigan, the great sea of which the Hurons had spoken, to meet the Winnebagos or Menominee Indians, and to hear of the mighty Sioux nation farther west still. On the Fox he would have been only a short distance from the Wisconsin River, a tributary of the (as yet unknown) Mississippi. Indeed, Nicollet brought back with him vague references to a great river down which the sea lay a mere three days' sailing distance away and 'that from this sea there would be an outlet towards Japan and China'—or so his Jesuit narrator believed.[2] This optimistic note reflected the conviction of most Frenchmen that the Pacific lay not far distant; they would have been aghast if they had known that even when they reached the remote waters of Lake Superior they would still be only one-third of the way across the North American continent.

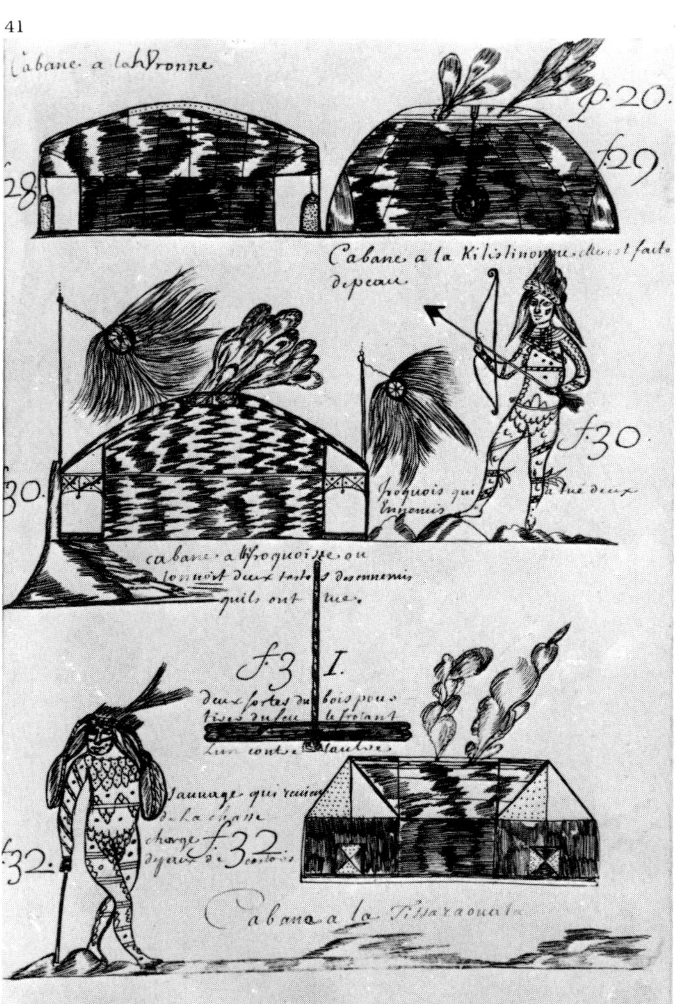

41 Indian cabins from the *Codex Canadensis*, c. 1700. *Thomas Gilcrease Institute, Tulsa.*
Note the scalps hanging outside the Iroquois lodge. In the bottom left-hand corner an Indian is shown carrying beaver skins on his shoulders.

Although speculation about the ocean to the west was never far removed from the French writings of this period, the immediate preoccupation of fur traders and missionaries alike was to explore and exploit the area of the Great Lakes. While the Company of New France, founded by Richelieu in 1627, sought to secure a regular trade route to the fur regions of the west by way of the Ottawa River and Lake Nipissing, the Jesuits pushed into Huronia, the land of Champlain's Indian allies, lying inland from Georgian Bay on the eastern shore of Lake Huron. Here the Hurons played an essential role as middlemen in the fur trade; the Indians to the west and north brought to the Huron villages vast quantities of furs, and received in return provisions and European trading goods. And here too the Jesuits saw opportunities for more profitable missionary work than among the nomadic and primitive Montagnais north of the Gulf of St Lawrence.

Using Huronia as a base, the missionaries followed the Indian trade routes into unfamiliar territory. By the early 1640s the Jesuits had reached in one direction the vital strategic point of Sault Ste Marie between Lakes Huron and Superior, where Indian tribes came from all directions to trade for the whitefish caught by the local Chippewa (see selection 4); and in another the northern shores of Lake Erie. Back on the St Lawrence they founded Montreal in 1642 (see plate 42) at the important site where the Ottawa River joined the St Lawrence and offered a route westward which, although difficult, was safer than the more southerly way through Lake Ontario which lay along the edge of the Iroquois country, land of the traditional rivals of the Hurons. Father Ragueneau explained the problem in the *Relation* of 1647-8:

'By that Lake Saint Louys [Ontario] we could go straight to Quebec in a few days, and with less trouble, having only three or four falls—or, rather, more rapid currents—to pass all the way to Mont-Real, which is distant only about sixty leagues from the outlet of Lake Saint Louys. But fear of the enemies who dwell along the shores of this Lake compels our Hurons, and us with them, to make a long detour to reach another branch of the River Saint Lawrence,—namely, that which flows to the North of Mont-Real, and which we call the River des Prairies [the Ottawa]. This lengthens our journey by almost one-half, and, moreover, compels us to pass more than sixty falls.'[3]

By the end of the decade Indian informants had given the Jesuits a rough idea of the size and relationship of all the Great Lakes, including Lake Superior (see selection 5), and of a new, formidable Indian nation farther west, the Sioux. It was at this moment that the work of proselytizing, trading and exploring was interrupted as the long-threatened Iroquois war broke over Huronia. Between 1648 and 1650 repeated attacks by the Iroquois—no longer just the Mohawks, for by now French observers were referring to the Iroquois confederacy, the Five Nations—wiped out most of the Huron villages, already ravaged by smallpox, measles and other European-borne diseases. They scattered and massacred the inhabitants, gave several Jesuits a fiery martyrdom, and wrecked the structure of the fur trade. With the French thrust back on the defensive, scarcely safe even at Quebec from the

42

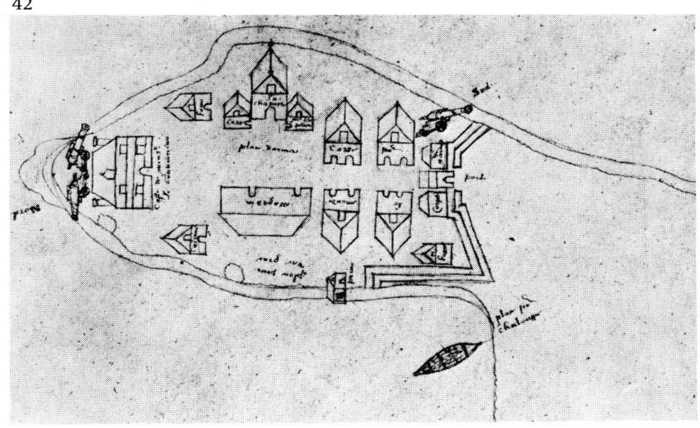

42 Montreal. A view of the first settlement of 1642, drawn by Jehan Bourdon, surveyor-general. *McGill University Library, Montreal.*
This is just a rough sketch but the church, dwelling-places, storehouses and cannon of the modest settlement can all be discerned.

rampaging Iroquois, with the rivers and the forests of the west now a death-trap for Frenchmen and their Indian allies, survival became the chief preoccupation of the two or three thousand threatened inhabitants of New France.

In 1653 the Iroquois over-extended themselves with simultaneous attacks towards Sault Ste Marie and the region south of Lake Michigan, and during the subsequent uneasy pause in the raiding some of the traders began to return west. Indians filtering in to the St Lawrence settlements from the west reported that in the aftermath of the Iroquois terror thousands of displaced Indians had been driven west of Lake Michigan into (modern) Wisconsin to the edge of Sioux territory, where they were eager to renew the fur trade. With the old Huron-dominated organization shattered, the French had little alternative but to move west and bring back the furs themselves, a radical departure from previous practice. Among the dozens of *coureurs de bois* who ventured westward in the mid 50s with licences from the French authorities were a remarkable pair, Médart Chouart (better known by his assumed title, Sieur des Groseilliers) and his brother-in-law Pierre Esprit Radisson. Together and separately the two men made a number of journeys to the west from 1654 onwards, but to decide the track or even the date of their wanderings from the perplexing ambiguities of Radisson's later narrative is a baffling business (see selection 6). They may have ranged as far as Hudson Bay and the Cree regions to the north, and

43

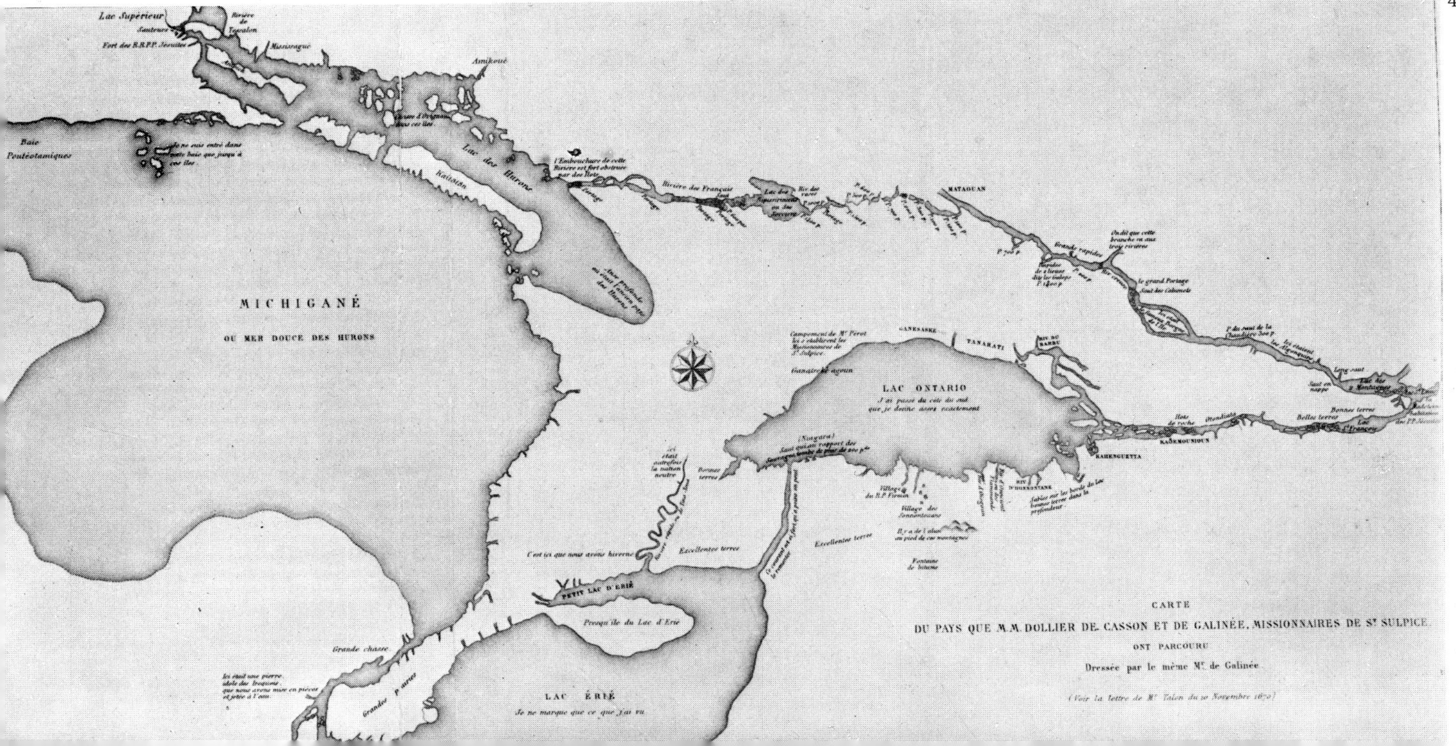

43 Map of the Upper Lakes, by Bréhant de Galinée, 1670. Reduction in Faillon, *Histoire de la Colonie Française en Canada*, III, 1685.
Galinée's rudimentary map-making skill was one reason why he accompanied the Sulpician expedition of 1669-70 which made a pioneering journey to the Upper Lakes, and whose members became the first known Europeans to winter on Lake Erie. For all its inaccuracies and omissions, the map (the original of which is lost) represents a conscientious attempt to draw from actual observation the Upper Lakes, until this time laid down on the maps mainly from report. Galinée wrote afterwards, probably to the intendant, Jean Talon: 'Everybody desired me to make the map of our journey, which I have done accurately enough; however, I recognise rather serious faults in it still, which I will correct when I have time. . . .
I have marked in it nothing but what I saw. Thus you will find only one side of each lake, since their width is so great that one cannot see the other' (Coyne, 1903, p. 75). Galinée drew the south shore of Lake Ontario, the north shore of Lake Erie, the east and north shores of Lake Huron, and the portage route from Sault Ste Marie to Montreal by way of Lake Nipissing and the Ottawa River. The north shore of Lake Ontario and some of the other details in regions not traversed by Galinée were presumably added by another hand.

44

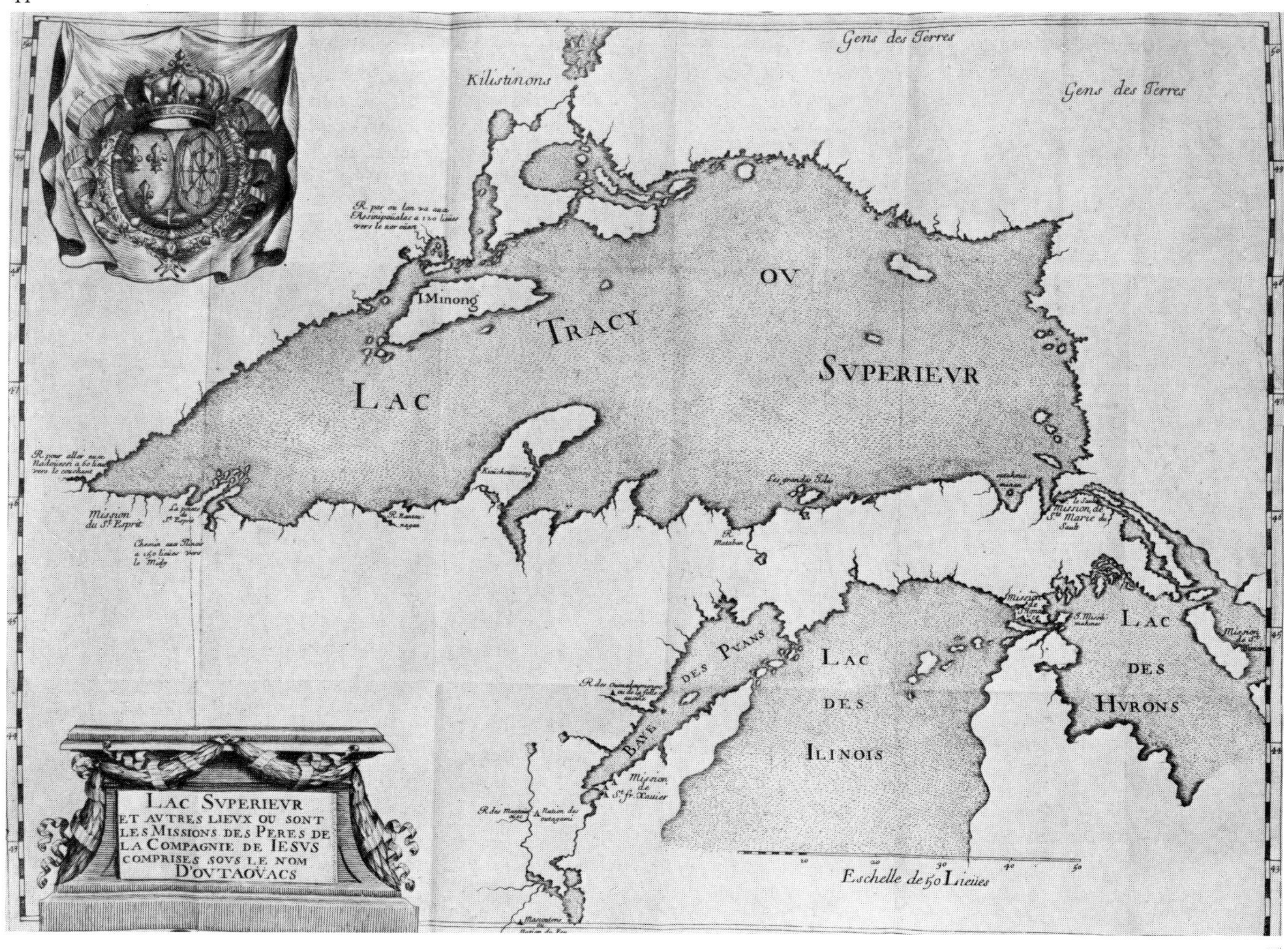

44 The Jesuit map of the Great Lakes, 1672. 'Lac Superieur et autres lieux ou sont les Missions des Peres de la Compagnie de Iesus . . .' from *Relation de ce qui s'est passé de plus remarquable en la Nouvelle France 1670 et 1671*, 1672. In terms of accurate observation and careful draughtsmanship, this map is one of the most impressive produced of any area of New France in the seventeenth century. Its delineation of Lake Superior and the northern parts of Lakes Michigan and Huron was not to be surpassed until the detailed surveys of the nineteenth century, and for the first time the western parts of the Great Lakes appear in a form not far removed from that shown on a modern map. It was the first map, for example, to distinguish between Lake Michigan and Green Bay ('Baye des Puans').

In the *Relation* of 1670-1 Father Claude Dablon wrote that a map had been drawn by two Fathers, 'of considerable intelligence, much given to research, and very exact, who determined to set down nothing that they had not seen with their own eyes.' (Thwaites, *Jesuit Relations*, vol 54, p. 255). The Jesuits involved were probably Dablon himself, and Father Claude Allouez. Dablon later continued (*ibid.*, vol 55, p. 95): 'By glancing, as one can, at a Map of the lakes, and of the territories on which are settled most of the tribes of these regions, one will gain more light upon all these Missions than by long descriptions that might be given of them.'

the Upper Mississippi and the Sioux to the southwest, but if so they failed to leave any convincing directions for their contemporaries, still less for posterity.[4] That they were major figures in the commercial expansion of New France there can be no dispute, but their real importance lies not so much in the shadowy explorations they may or may not have accomplished, as in the new impetus their observations among the Indians of the interior gave to the northern fur trade (see Chapter 6). Radisson's narrative, despite its jumbled, sometimes incomprehensible syntax, gives an authentic and unique account of life as a *coureur de bois* among the Huron and Mohawk Indians in the yet unspoiled forests and lakes of the northeast. It tells of life and death among the Indians, of the tortures inflicted and endured—of these Radisson had hideous, first-hand experience—and of the hardships of a wilderness existence. At times game was plentiful—bears, deer, buffalo, moose, and fish so numerous that 'scarcely we are able to draw out our net'; but at others Radisson and his half-starved companions were forced to live on tree-bark, beaver skins, and 'black and clammie' *tripe de roches*. The existence of a trader and explorer among the Indians was hard and precarious even by rough contemporary standards, and was summed up by Radisson in a memorable passage:

'It is a strange thing when victaulls are wanting, worke whole nights & dayes, lye downe on the bare ground, & not allwayes that hap[py], the breech in the water, the feare in ye buttocks, to have the belly empty, the wearinesse in the bones, and drowsinesse of ye body by the bad weather that you are to suffer, having nothing to keepe you from such calamity.'[5]

Some Jesuits, notably Father Simon Le Moyne in 1654, courageously took advantage of the lull in the fierce raiding to visit the Iroquois, and they brought back the first accounts of the Iroquois' homeland, stretching away south of Lake Ontario into the northern and central areas of modern New York State.[6] But in 1658 the Iroquois returned to the offensive, and New France seemed once more on the verge of collapse. Its fragile and vulnerable structure was saved only by a decision at the highest level in France, where the young king, Louis XIV, took control out of the hands of the moribund Company of New France, and in 1663 made Quebec a royal colony again. That this was more than just a change in legal status was shown when the experienced Carignan-Salières regiment of French soldiers was sent across the Atlantic, and by 1667 had defeated the Iroquois. With that hovering threat subdued, settlement and trade were renewed with a fresh confidence under the aegis of the forceful intendant of New France, Jean Talon. The *Jesuit relations* again fill with geographical detail, accompanied by much speculation about the alluring prospects of routes across the remaining unknown areas of land to the ocean (see selection 7). Into this context fitted easily enough renewed discussions about the great river first mentioned by Nicollet thirty years earlier; but whether it flowed south to the Gulf of Mexico, and was perhaps the 'Rio del Espíritu Santo' of the Spanish explorers of the sixteenth century, or was deflected west by mountain ranges to the Pacific, or even east to the Atlantic seaboard, was uncertain (see selection 8).

As the *coureurs de bois* moved along the western trails once more, so the Jesuits, and now also the Sulpicians from Montreal and the Recollets, undertook a series of explorations which defined the outline of the Great Lakes in the form shown on the Galinée map of 1670 and the Jesuit map of 1672 (plates 43 & 44). A Sulpician expedition led by a former cavalry officer, François Dollier de Casson, and by Bréhant de Galinée, and accompanied for part of the way by the young La Salle, became the first Europeans known to have entered the Niagara River from Lake Ontario, the first to winter on Lake Erie (in 1669-70), and the first to make adequate surveys along the shores of both lakes (see selection 9). Explorers, including Jean Peré and the Jolliet brothers (see below), prospected new portage routes which linked Lake Superior, Georgian Bay and Lake Ontario. These efforts were supplemented by the unflagging efforts of the Jesuits in collecting and collating information, typified by the detailed description Father Dablon gave in the *Relation* of 1669-70 of the greatest and most distant of the lakes, Superior. It was in this report that the celebrated passage about the lake's outline first appeared:

'This Lake has almost the form of a bent Bow, more than a hundred and eighty leagues long; the South side serves as its string, and the arrow seems to be a great Tongue of land projecting more than eighty leagues into the width of the Lake, starting from this same South side, at about its middle. . . .'[7]

The Jesuits themselves remained active in the field. They renewed their efforts to establish missions among the Iroquois south of Lake Ontario and, perhaps most important of all, in the west Father Allouez followed Nicollet's old route to Green Bay, and established a mission among the Siouan-speaking Menominee Indians of Wisconsin. It was along this path that the Mississippi was to be discovered, and in the *Relation* of 1669-70 Allouez hinted at this as he wrote of the Mascoutens along the upper Fox: 'These people are settled in a very attractive place, where beautiful Plains and Fields meet the eye as far as one can see. Their River leads by a six days' Voyage to the great River named Messi-Sipi.'[8]

2 The Mississippi

Behind the natural inclinations of the fur traders to find better routes, and of the religious to seek out fresh mission fields, lay a more resolute expansionist attitude in Quebec, not always in tune with Colbert's determination in Paris to set the colony on a firmer basis. Talon's arrival in Canada in 1670 to serve a second term as intendant marked official determination to mount a coherent program of westward exploration to find furs, minerals (copper had been reported in the Lake Superior region), new Indian allies, and perhaps even the route to China. Within two months of his arrival Talon was able to report to the King: 'I have dispatched persons of resolution, who promise to penetrate further than has ever been done; the one to the West and to the North West of Canada, and the others to the Southwest and South. Those adventurers are to keep journals in all instances . . . in all cases they are to take possession, display the King's arms and draw up *procès verbaux* to serve as titles.'[9]

Although the advocates of western expansion always had to compete with those who preferred to consolidate the centers of settlement in the St Lawrence valley, the summer of 1671 saw further evidence of the new spirit of expansionism with an impressive wilderness ceremony at the Jesuit mission post at Sault Ste Marie. There Talon's representative, Daumont de Saint-Lusson, met delegates from fourteen Indian nations to inform them that the King of France was taking possession 'of the territories lying between the east and the west, from Montreal as far as the South Sea, covering the utmost extent and range possible'. This solemn declaration was supported by the blessing of Father Allouez, who also delivered a panegyric on the power, majesty and wealth of the Indians' new protector, 'that great captain, our Great King', Louis XIV.[10] Talon's emissaries into the interior were soon followed by the fur traders, who established important bases near the Jesuit missions at the Sault and at Michilimackinac. The *coureurs de bois* now tended to accompany the Indians on their trapping expeditions and to trade furs from them on the spot. In their deceptively slender birchbark canoes the Frenchmen packed an amazing variety of trade goods, among which guns and ammunition, knives and hatchets, household utensils, cloth and brandy were in most demand. A wild, disturbing influence when they returned to the quiet St Lawrence settlements, the *coureurs de bois* came nearer to living on easy terms with the Indians of the forests than any other group of Europeans. Quick to pick up the customs as well as the wilderness skills of the Indians, usually with a squaw or two in attendance, they scandalized the missionaries at their stations, and alarmed the royal officials for reasons both economic and moral. That perceptive, if sometimes over-imaginative, observer of the Canadian scene, Lom d'Arce (better known as Baron Lahontan) wrote of them:

'You would be amaz'd if you saw how lewd these Pedlers are when they return; how they Feast and Game, and how prodigal they are, not only in their Cloaths, but upon Women. Some of 'em as are married, have the wisdom to retire to their own Houses; but the Batchelors act just as our East-Indian-Men, and Pirates are wont to do; for they Lavish, Eat, Drink, and Play all away as long as the Goods hold out; and when these are gone, they e'en sell their Embroidery, their Lace, and their Cloaths. This done, they are forc'd to go upon a new Voyage for Subsistance.'[11]

More serious as far as Colbert and his planners in Paris were concerned was that the attraction of the fur trade was drawing away to the west the pick of New France's young, energetic men. But at Quebec Talon was impressed by the potentialities opened up by the ceremony at Sault Ste Marie. In his report to the King of the event, which on paper at least brought most of the North American continent under French jurisdiction, Talon pointed out that another three hundred leagues would probably bring Frenchmen to the borders of countries on the Pacific coast.[12] The attempt by La Salle to cut across country from the Ontario/Erie area to find a southern river leading to the ocean had ended in obscure failure—if indeed it had ever begun—so the decision was taken to approach by way of Green Bay that great river flowing southward which Frenchmen had heard about since the days of Nicollet, but whose course and outlet were a complete mystery.

The task of finding the river, now often mentioned under its Indian name of Mesippi (or some variant spelling), was entrusted to the fur trader and explorer, Louis Jolliet, des-

45

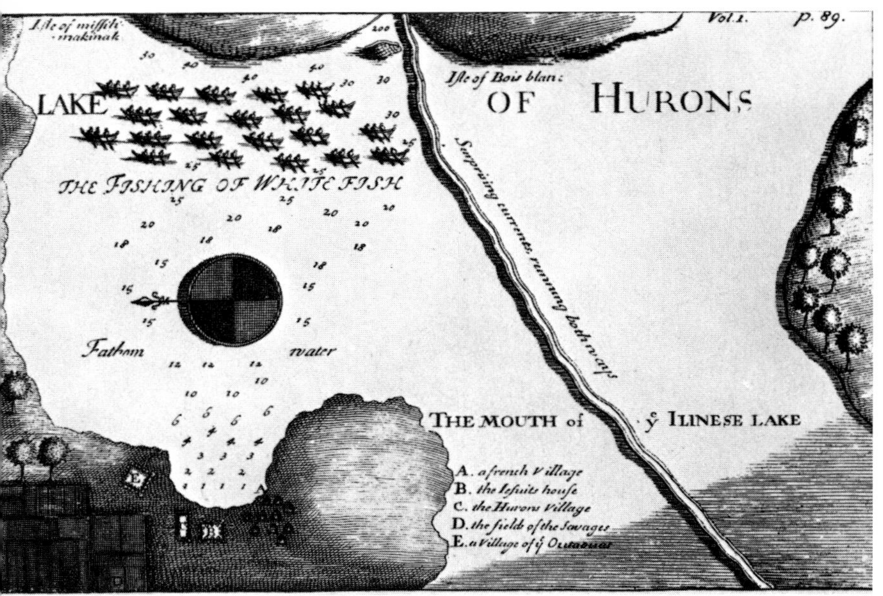

45 Map of the Straits of Mackinac, from Lahontan, *New voyages*, 1703. The map shows (B) 'the Iesuits house' at the St Ignace mission from which Marquette and Jolliet began their epic journey.

cribed by his companion on the expedition, the Jesuit Jacques Marquette, as 'a young man, born in this country, who possesses all the qualifications that could be desired for such an undertaking. He has experience and knows the languages . . . possesses Tact and prudence . . . has the courage to dread nothing where everything is to be feared.'[13] Marquette himself had been described in rather similar terms as having 'a good knowledge of Algonkian, is of sound health and strong body, of excellent character and tried virtue; and, because of his wonderfully gentle ways, most acceptable to the natives.'[14] With Talon's blessing and the grant of a *congé* or trading licence, though without any direct financial support, Jolliet and Marquette left the Jesuit mission post on the north shore of the Strait of Mackinac in May 1673 (see selection 10). Accompanied by five *voyageurs*, they followed the Fox River in their two canoes from Green Bay through wild-rice country to the marshy stretches of the Fox-Wisconsin portage. The Menominee Indians of Green Bay had tried to deter the Frenchmen with fearful tales—'horrible monsters which devoured men and canoes together; that there was even a demon, who was heard from a great distance, who barred the way, and swallowed all who ventured to approach him'[15]—but the explorers disregarded their warning and by mid-June had reached the wide, sluggish waters of the Upper Mississippi without mishap and 'with a Joy', wrote Marquette, 'that I cannot express'. It was a very different sight from the rock-strewn, foaming streams of the north, and for the most part the epic journey proved quietly uneventful. The land on either side was fertile; birds, fish and game were plentiful; but of Indians there was little sign. Not until the party had paddled two hundred miles downstream did it find Indians, and then only poor, relatively unsophisticated Illinois villagers.

Farther downstream the sedateness of the journey was unexpectedly broken by the thundering entry into the placid Mississippi of a large river coming from the west, the 'Pekitanoui' or 'Muddy' River. Jolliet and Marquette had sighted the Missouri in full flood, an exciting discovery since Indian reports insisted that it led westward to another river which flowed into the western ocean. As Jolliet optimistically reported on his return, 'I saw a village which is only five days' journey from a tribe which trade with the natives of California'.[16] Farther south, beyond the great ox-bow bend of the Mississippi, another considerable river came in, this time from the east. This was the 'Ouabouskigan' or 'Ohio', object of La Salle's vain search two years earlier. Then the explorers met Indians—perhaps Tuscaroras but more probably Cherokees—whose language reminded Marquette of Iroquoian, and who carried guns and powder which they had obtained from 'Europeans on the eastern side'. Jolliet and Marquette followed the Mississippi probably as far as its juncture with the Arkansas River, still close on four hundred miles from the delta, where fear of capture by Spaniards to the south persuaded them to turn back. Although their assessment that they were only a few days from the sea was over-sanguine, they had gone far enough south to realize that the river must flow into the Gulf of Mexico. In one sense the great discovery was an anti-climax: the explorers had found no gold, precious stones or furs, no wealthy Indian nations, no route to the Pacific. Apart from resolving one of the major geographical queries of the time, the most useful practical result of the expedition was the discovery on the return journey of a short cut through to Lake Michigan along the Illinois and Des Plaines Rivers to the Chicago portage. Marquette informed his superior, Dablon, that this route, with only moderate improvements, would take a sailing vessel from the Great Lakes to the Gulf of Mexico; moreover, the Illinois Valley justified all the stories Marquette had heard about its fertility. He had 'seen nothing like this river', he wrote, 'for the fertility of the land, its prairies, woods, wild cattle, stag, deer, wildcats, bustards, swans, ducks, parrots, and even beaver.'

Talon had returned to France before the expedition set out, and although in his report to Colbert the governor of New France, the Comte de Frontenac, made much of the water route now known to exist from the Great Lakes towards the Gulf of Mexico, broken by only one portage, and also stressed the importance of the river flowing into the Mississippi from the west, his letter showed no great sense of urgency to complete and exploit the discovery.[17] Indeed, in 1676 he was warned by the King in language which reflected Colbert's insistence on the desirability of a 'compact' colony, that 'Concerning these discoveries, you must on no account encourage them unless there be a great need and some obvious advantage . . . it is far more worthwhile to occupy a smaller area and have it well populated than to spread out and have several feeble colonies which could easily be destroyed by all manner of accidents.'[18] The final step on the Mississippi had to wait another nine years after the Jolliet-Marquette expedition, when it was taken by that far-seeing, ambitious and perhaps paranoiac explorer, René-Robert Cavelier de la Salle. La Salle's determination to reach the mouth

46 The 'Marquette map' of 1673-4. *Archives de la Compagnie de Jésus, Saint-Jérôme, Quebec.*
This manuscript map is the only known extant document by a member of the Jolliet-Marquette expedition which descended the Mississippi in 1673. It was probably drawn by Father Marquette in the winter of 1673-4 during his stay at the mission post on Green Bay after the expedition's return. The outline of that part of the Great Lakes area shown follows that of the Jesuit map of 1672 (plate 44). For the rest, the map represents the route followed by Jolliet and Marquette and, with the aid of a compass and astrolabe, the Jesuit had taken observations which resulted in a surprisingly well-proportioned map. Its sketchiness is deceptive; Marquette's refusal to indulge in fanciful cartography and his austere insistence on representing only those features he had actually seen resulted in a map much more accurate and realistic than those of later cartographers (though Marquette's latitudes are generally one degree too far south). The Wisconsin and Illinois Rivers are easily identifiable, and farther south we see the earliest appearance on map of the mouths of the Missouri ('PEKITTAN8i') and Ohio ('8AB8SKIG8' or 'Ouaboukigou'). The name for the Ohio the French later wrote as 'Ouabache' and the English as 'Wabash', and it was well into the eighteenth century before the confusion between the modern Ohio and Wabash Rivers was cleared.

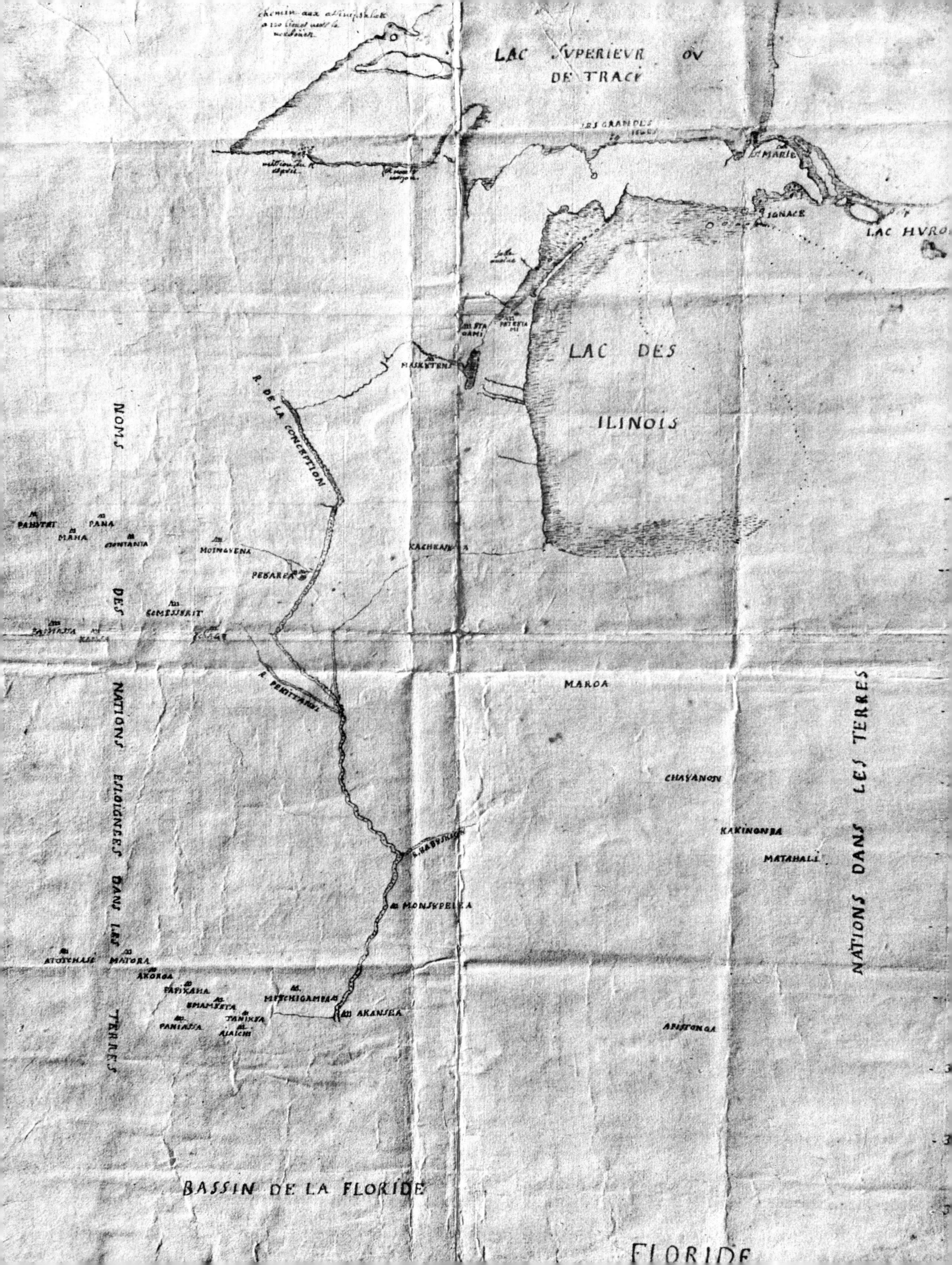
LAC SVPERIEVR OV DE TRACY
LES GRANDES ISLES
STE MARIE
SIGNACE
LAC HVRON
LAC DES ILINOIS
MASKOVTENS
R. DE LA CONCEPTION
NOMS DES NATIONS ELOIGNEES DANS LES TERRES
PANA
MAHA
MOINGVENA
PEBAREA
KACHKASKA
R. PEKITTANOVI
MAROA
CHAVANON
KAKINONBA
MATAHALI
NATIONS DANS LES TERRES
MONSOVPELEA
ATOTCHASI
MATORA
AKOROA
MITCHIGAMEA
AKANSEA
TANIKOA
PANIASSA
APISTONGA
BASSIN DE LA FLORIDE
FLORIDE

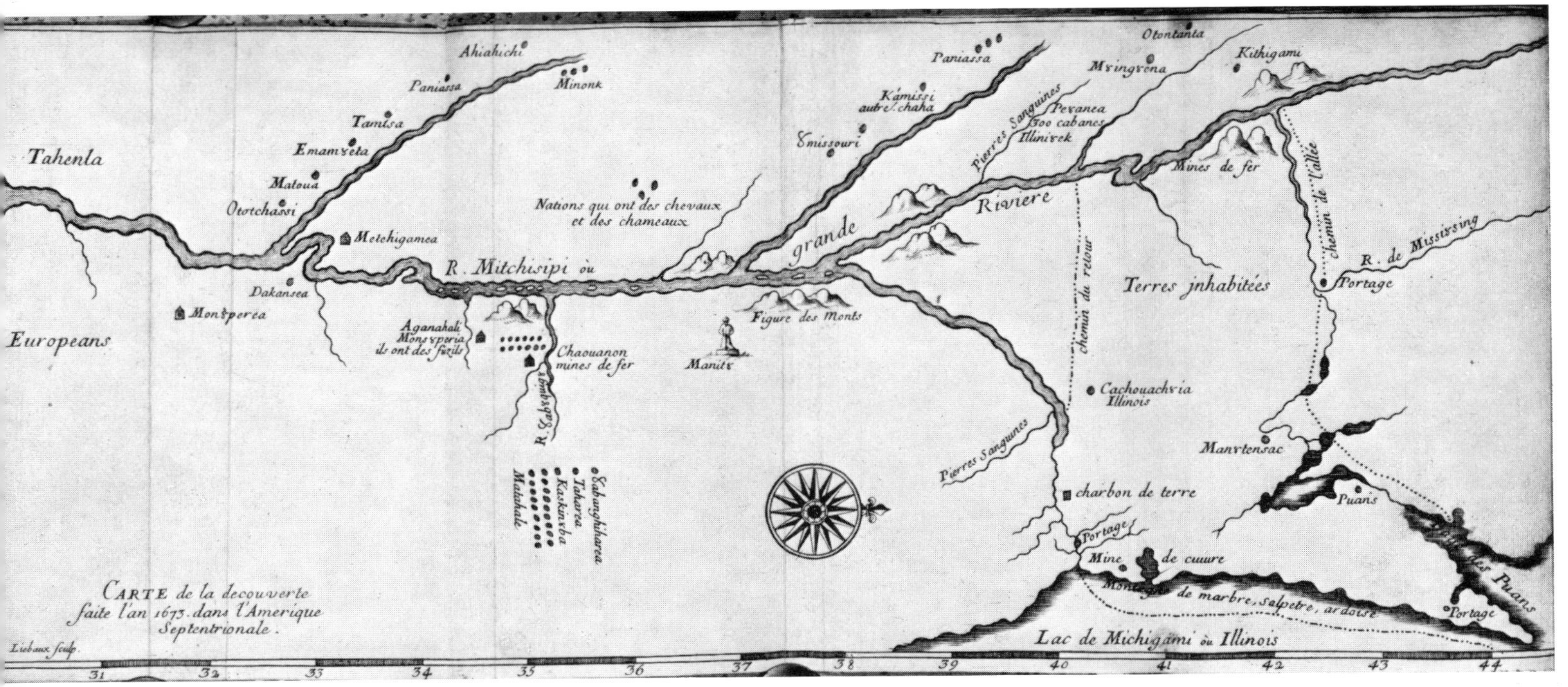

47

48

47 'Carte de la decouverte faite l'an 1673 dans l'Amerique Septentrionale', by Thevenot in his *Recueil de voyages de Mr Thevenot*, 1681.
This is apparently yet another map based upon Jolliet's lost map of 1674. It is the first published map to mark the Jolliet/Marquette discoveries of 1673, and also the earliest to attach the name Michigan (Michigami) to one of the Great Lakes. The original manuscript version of this map may have been drawn by Father Dablon, a speculation strengthened by the curious placing of a statue under which is written 'Manit 8' in a region between the Ohio and Illinois Rivers which had not yet been crossed by a Frenchman. The manuscript draft bears the legend 'Manit 8 Statue ou les Sauuages vont faire leurs adoration'; and this would appear to be a reference to the great painted rock idol tumbled into the river by Dablon and Allouez on their journey along the Fox River in 1670.

48 Oil painting, reputed to be a self-portrait of Louis Hennepin. *Minnesota Historical Society*. A note on the back of the canvas in the handwriting of the period reads 'Louis Hennepin 1694'.

49 The building of the *Griffon*, the first sailing vessel on the Great Lakes, 1679, from Louis Hennepin, *Voyage ou nouvelle découverte*, 1704.
To help his trading operations on the Lakes, La Salle in 1679 ordered the construction of a sailing vessel above Niagara. Hennepin at one time described the *Griffon* as a vessel of 45 tons, at another as being of 60 tons; if the proportions of vessel and men in this engraving are correct, she appears to be about 60 foot in length. She was certainly large enough to overawe the local Indians, to whom she appeared, wrote Hennepin, like 'a travelling fort'. The *Griffon*'s career was short-lived, for within a few months of her launching she sank with all hands in a storm on Lake Michigan in September 1679.

of the Mississippi (see Chapter 5) was part of his grandiose project for a vast commercial empire across the heartland of the North American continent. It was to stretch from the St Lawrence to the Gulf of Mexico, served by inland sailing vessels and protected by strategically-sited forts. Once secured, and with the English and Spaniards hemmed in along the coastal regions to the east and south, the way would be clear for the next great thrust—westward to the Pacific. La Salle's ideas were always larger than his resources, and his journey down the Mississippi in 1682 was made only after prodigious hardships and misadventures in the preceding years.

It was during the preparations for this expedition that La Salle was joined in 1678 by the Recollet Father Louis Hennepin, whose narratives of his adventures in the wilderness were to become the most widely-read books of French exploration in North America, and a fruitful source of controversy for later scholars attempting to discern the historical and geographical reality behind the web of exaggeration and self-glorification which Hennepin spun in so tantalizing a fashion in his writings.[19] Hennepin was unwittingly to provide a link between La Salle and another French explorer and projector operating farther north, Daniel Greysolon Dulhut (usually Anglicized to Duluth). Dulhut had left Sault Ste Marie in the spring of 1679 on a mission of pacification among the warlike Sioux and their neighbors the Chippewas, Assiniboines and Crees who lived west and north of Lake Superior, and were threatening to take their furs to the English posts on Hudson Bay. By July he had reached Lake Mille Lacs to the southwest of Lake Superior where he erected French arms 'in the great village of the Nadouecioux [Sioux] called Izatys' at the farthest point west any Frenchman had reached. In the winter of 1679-80 Dulhut continued his work of reconcilation among the Indians from his camp at the western end of Lake Superior, on the site of the modern city of Duluth, and during his stay sent three of his men to explore farther west. Where precisely they went is not known, but when they returned in the summer of 1680 they brought back salt and reports that a Sioux war party 'Had told them that it was only twenty days' journey from where they were to the discovery of the great lake whose water is not good to drink.'[20] Whether this was a reference to Lake Winnipeg or (improbably) the far distant Great Salt Lake is scarcely material; Dulhut was convinced that the Indians had been talking about the western ocean. His plans to explore in that direction were disrupted when he heard that the Sioux, despite his peace-making activities, had captured three Frenchmen. When Dulhut found and released the prisoners they proved to be Hennepin and two companions sent by La Salle to prepare the way for his attempt on the Mississippi. Their freedom was achieved at the cost of Dulhut's own hopes of pushing farther west, for he now turned back towards the settled areas where he soon became embroiled in the internal politics of the fur trade.

La Salle meanwhile was dissipating his energies in an endless series of arduous journeys between Quebec, the Great Lakes and the Upper Mississippi in an attempt to coordinate his scattered resources. He built posts at the southeast corner of Lake Michigan (Fort St Joseph) and on the Illinois River (Fort St Louis and Fort Crèvecoeur); but one result of this activity was that La Salle was not in a position to mount his much-postponed major expedition until the winter of 1681-2. Plans to sail down the Mississippi in a prototype of the armed vessels which La Salle hoped to see plying on the Great Lakes and the Mississippi under the French flag had long been abandoned, and the party of twenty-three Frenchmen with eighteen Indians and their families made the journey in less imposing fashion by canoe. For the second time Europeans

49

50

50 'Carte de la Nouvelle France et de la Louisiane Nouvellement decouverte', by Louis Hennepin, Paris, 1683.
Although it is difficult to disentangle fact from fiction in Hennepin's writings it is generally accepted that his assertions of 1683 that he and two companions explored along the Upper Mississippi, and discovered the Falls of St Anthony (marked on the map as 'Sault de St. Antoine de Padoü') are correct. Beyond the range of his own personal knowledge it is interesting that Hennepin pointed the Mississippi (his 'R. Colbert') straight to the south, the dotted line of its course reaching the Gulf of Mexico at about the right location—in contrast to the fanciful speculations of other cartographers of the 1680s and 1690s that it flowed into the western extremity of the Gulf. Hennepin's naming of the Mississippi Valley 'La Louisiane' was the first published mention of the name, although it has been contended that the term originated with La Salle. Nowhere does the map substantiate Hennepin's later claim that he had anticipated La Salle by two years by following the Mississippi down to the Gulf during his travels in 1680. If true, he would have had to have travelled more than 3000 miles in a month. Away to the west, California is shown, rather unusually for this period, as a peninsula, bordering on the Strait of Anian.

saw the turbulent mouth of the Missouri, 'a great river, which comes from the west', and the Ohio, flowing in 'from the east and is more than 500 leagues in length'.[21] Like Jolliet and Marquette nine years before, the party was impressed by the fertility of the region and its abundant animal life; and as they passed the farthest point south of the earlier expedition they encountered more Indian tribes—Taensa, Natchez and Choctaw. Among them were sun-worshippers living in cabins of mud and cane, who greeted the Frenchmen with music, drums and formal ceremonial, and on one occasion traded pearls with them. Although La Salle was confident that he was the first European to paddle these waters he was in fact following the track of some of De Soto's men almost a century and a half earlier as they made their last desperate bid for the sea and escape after the death of their leader. Early in 1682 the sea was sighted, and La Salle made as impressive a ceremony of the occasion as his straightened circumstances would allow. He raised a cross and the arms of France, and against a background of hymns and a fusillade of musket-fire declared that he 'took possession of that river, of all rivers that enter it and of all the country watered by them.'[22] (See selection 11.)

The vision which had beckoned La Salle to the mouth of the Mississippi was a glittering one, but it had no more substance than a dream. The French empire in North America was an outline, a plan rather than an achievement. When Colbert died in 1683 and was succeeded by men of lesser caliber the population of New France was still a mere ten thousand, stretched thin between agriculture, trading, exploring and soldiering, and less in total than the population of any one of several English colonies. Although the French had reached most of the inland vantage points the rapidity of their advance could not conceal the weaknesses of their position. Unhampered by the mountain ranges which confined the English to the Atlantic seaboard, Frenchmen had ranged across vast areas of the continent—westward beyond the Great Lakes, north to the sub-Arctic wastes of Hudson Bay, south to the Mississippi and the warm waters of the Gulf—but they had not occupied the regions they had explored. The economic necessities of the fur trade required the preservation rather than the conquest of the wilderness, and although the commercial and political impact of French activities was more far-reaching than the thin thread of the explorers' tracks on the map would suggest, on the ground the only visible sign of the Europeans' presence was a scattering of military forts, mission stations and fur trade posts. As yet the French empire in North America was a skeleton, lacking the flesh and blood of population, wealth and power.

51

51 Father Hennepin leaves Michilimackinac, 1681, from Louis Hennepin, *Voyage ou nouvelle découverte*, 1704. Hennepin is shown here, as in other illustrations from his books, in the friar's garb of the Recollet order. The birchbark canoes have greatly exaggerated bows and sterns.

52

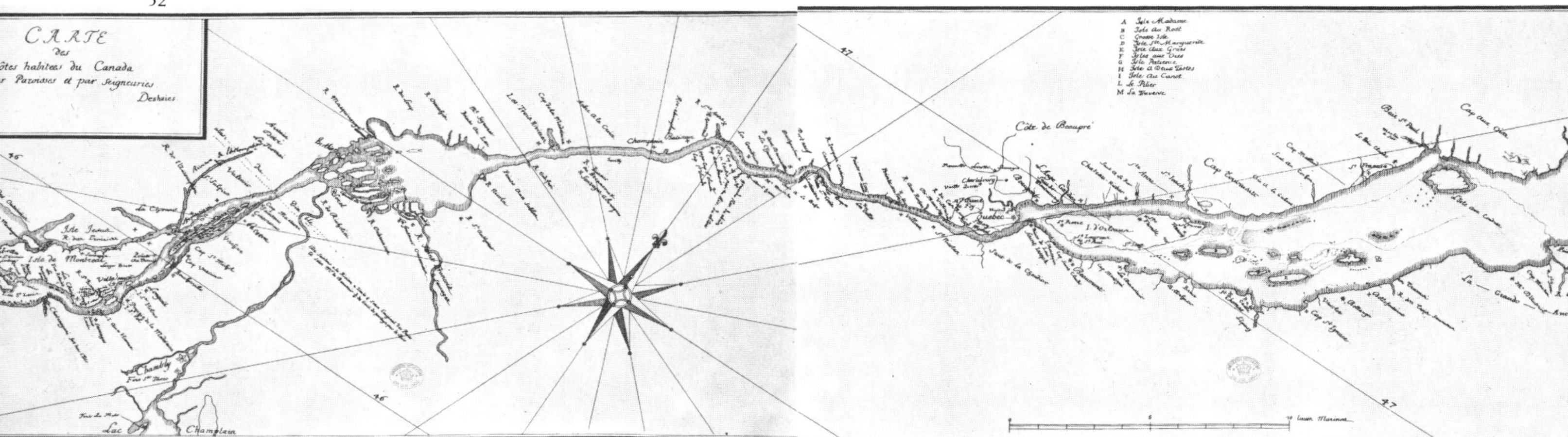

52 Jean Deshayes. 'Carte des Côtes habitees du Canada . . .', 1686, from A. L. Pinart, *Recueil de cartes, plans et vues relatifs aux Etats-Unis et au Canada . . .*, 1893.
The map illustrates the thickening of settlement along the St Lawrence in the twenty years after Quebec became a royal colony in 1663. Under the vigorous emigration policy pursued by the intendant Talon the population of New France doubled to about 7,500 inhabitants by 1673, and many of the gaps in the cultivated areas along the banks of the St Lawrence were filled in by the granting of new fiefs, and by an insistence that the old ones must be cleared. By the date of this map in 1686 the population had risen to about 10,000.

53 J. B. L. Franquelin. 'Carte de l'Amerique septentrionale . . .' [1688]. *Service Historique de la Marine, Paris, SHM66 (8-9-10-11)*.
Jean-Baptiste Louis Franquelin never travelled farther west than Montreal but he exercised an important influence for twenty years on many well-known cartographers. Two erroneous features on this map—both to be copied later—are the great westerly sweep of the lower Mississippi which brought its mouth on to the west coast of the Gulf of Mexico, and the delineation of the Missouri far to the west. This follows more closely the line of the Platte than the Missouri, and it may be that Franquelin was trying to reconcile Indian reports of another great river somewhere west of the Mississippi by merging it with the Missouri. The first error stems from the deliberate distortion of the course of the Lower Mississippi by La Salle and his supporters who, in order to promote the Louisiana settlement scheme of the mid 80s (see Chapter 5), claimed that the Mississippi entered the Gulf of Mexico some 400 or 500 miles west of its true outlet (see also plates 221 and 231).

In two respects the map was ahead of its time. It succeeds in distinguishing between the Ohio and the Wabash. Away to the northeast the Albanel overland route of 1671-2 from Tadoussac to James Bay is shown (see Chapter 6), and Lake Mistassini at last appears on a map, though under the name of 'Lac Timagaming'.

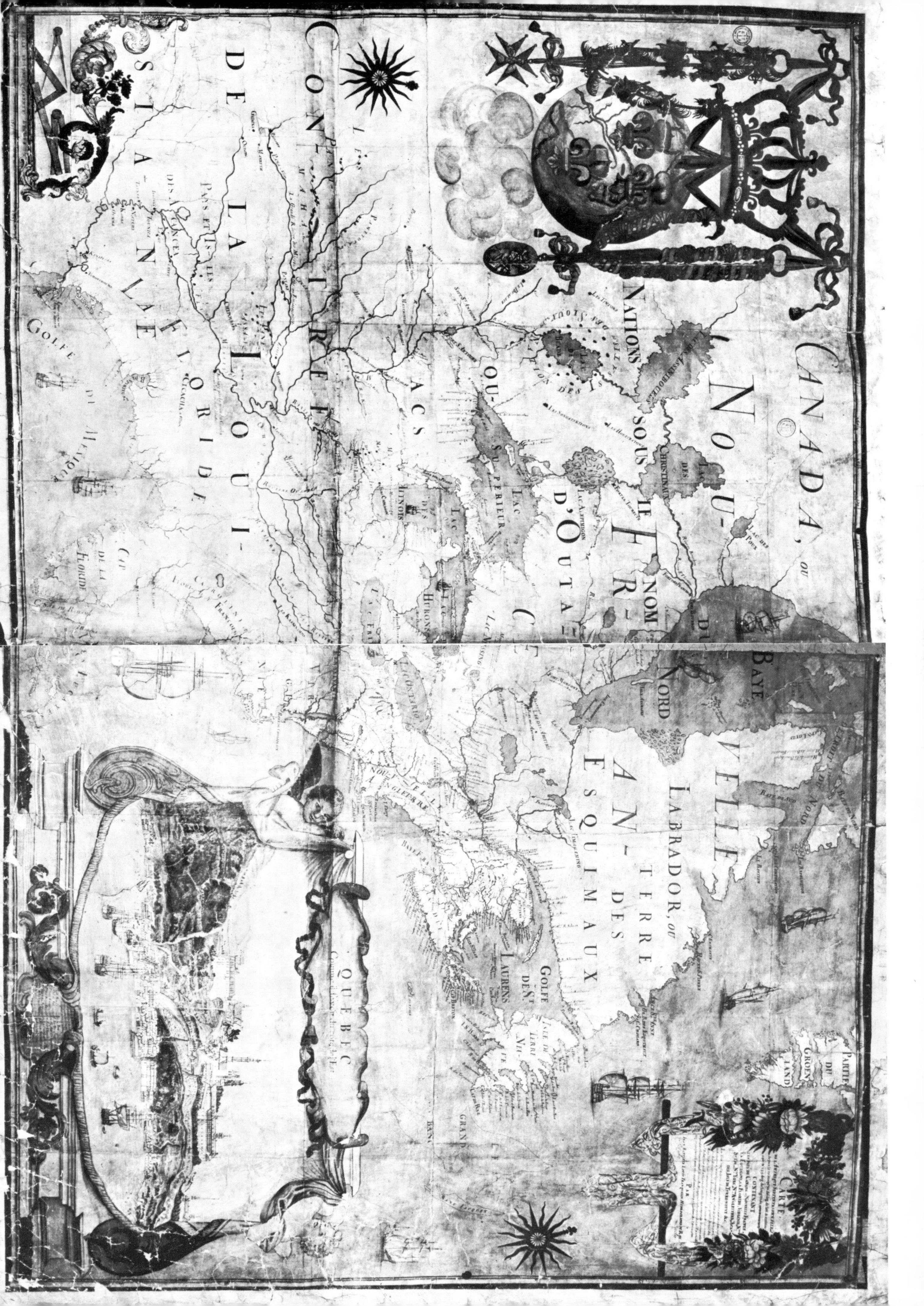

CANADA, ou

NOUVELLE FRANCE

NATIONS SOUS LE NOM D'OUTAOUACS

LES CONTRÉES DE LA LOUISIANE

LA FLORIDE

BAYE DU NORD

LABRADOR, ou TERRE DES ESQUIMAUX

PARTIE DU GROENLAND

LAC DES CHRISTINAUX

LAC SUPERIEUR

LAC DES ILINOIS

LAC DES HURONS

LAC ONTARIO

LAC ERIE

GOLFE DE ST LAURENS

ISLE DE TERRE NEUVE

GRAND BANC

CAP DE LA FLORIDE

GOLFE DU MEXIQUE

NOUVELLE ANGLETERRE

QUEBEC

Comme il se voit du coté de l'Est

CARTE DE L'AMERIQUE SEPTENTRIONALE ... CONTENANT LE PAIS DE CANADA OU NOUVELLE FRANCE, LA LOUISIANE, LA FLORIDE, VIRGINIE, N^LLE SUEDE, N^LLE YORK, N^LLE ANGLETERRE, ACADIE, ISLE DE TERRENEUVE &c.

PAR JEAN BAPTISTE LOUIS FRANQUELIN HYDROGRAPHE DU ROY

1
The country of the Hurons

From Gabriel Sagard, *Le Grand Voyage du Pays des Hurons*, Paris, 1632

Father Gabriel Sagard was a lay brother in the mendicant order, the Recollets, pioneers of Roman Catholic missionary enterprise in Canada. The first Recollets arrived in Quebec in 1615, but they soon left Champlain's settlement for mission work among the nearby Montagnais and in the Huron villages some hundreds of miles to the west. Sagard arrived in Quebec in 1623, and remained in Canada until the English seizure of Quebec in 1629. Here he describes the Huron country, lying between Georgian Bay and Lake Simcoe.

Now to speak generally about the country of the Hurons, its situation, the manners of its inhabitants, and their principal ceremonies and activities, let us say first that it is situated in forty-four and a half degrees of latitude and extends westward two hundred and thirty leagues in length with a breadth of ten. It is a well-cleared country, pretty and pleasant, and crossed by streams which empty into the great lake. There is no ugly surface of great rocks and barren mountains such as one sees in many places in Canadian and Algonquin territory. The country is full of fine hills, open fields, very beautiful broad meadows bearing much excellent hay, which is of no use except to set fire to as an amusement when it is dry; and in many places there is much uncultivated wheat, which has an ear like rye and grains like oats. I was deceived by it, supposing when first I saw it that these were fields that had been sown with good grain. I was also mistaken in the wild peas which in some places are as thick as if they had been sown and cultivated; and, as a demonstration of the richness of the soil, where a savage of Toënchen had planted a few peas brought from the trading-place, they produced pease twice as big as usual, which astonished me, for I had seen none so big either in France or in Canada.

There are fine forests, consisting of great oaks, beeches, maples, cedars, spruces, yews, and other kinds of trees, far finer beyond comparison than in the other provinces of Canada that we have seen. Moreover the country is warmer and more beautiful and the soil is richer and better the further south one goes; for towards the north the land is more stony and sandy, as I saw when I went to the Freshwater sea for the catch of big fish.

There are several districts or provinces in the country of the Hurons, with different names, just like the different provinces of France. . . . and in this stretch of country there are about twenty-five towns and villages. Some of these are not enclosed or shut in, while the others are fortified by strong wooden palisades in three rows, interlaced into one another and reinforced within by large thick pieces of bark to a height of eight or nine feet, and at the bottom there are great trunks of trees placed lengthwise, resting on strong short forks made from tree-trunks. Then above these palisades there are galleries or watch-towers, which they call *Ondaqua*, and these they stock with stones in war-time to hurl upon the enemy, and water to put out the fire that might be laid against their palisades. The Hurons mount up to them by means of a ladder, very ill-made and difficult to climb, and defend their ramparts with great courage and skill.

These twenty-five towns and villages may be inhabited by two or three thousand warriors at the most, without reckoning the ordinary people who may number about thirty or forty thousand souls in all. The chief town formerly contained two hundred large lodges, each filled with many households; but of late, on account of lack of wood and because the land began to be exhausted, it has been reduced in size, divided in two, and rebuilt in another more convenient locality. . . . There are certain districts where they move their towns and villages every ten, fifteen, or thirty years, more or less, and they do so only when they find themselves too far away from wood, which they have to carry on their backs tied up and attached to

54

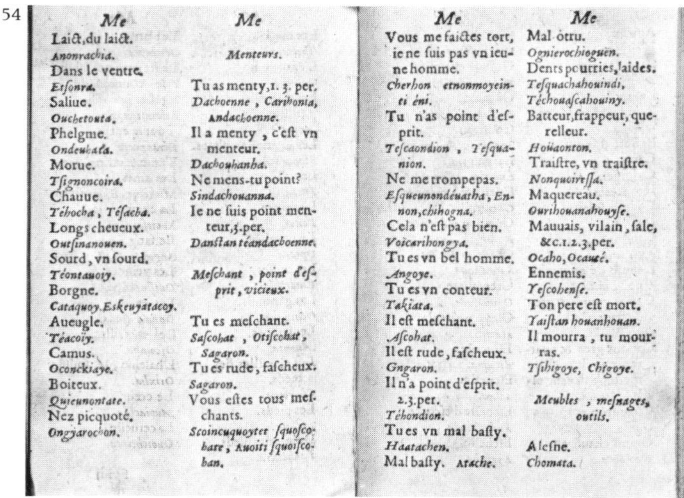

Me

Laict, du laict.
Anonrachia.
Dans le ventre.
Etſonra.
Saliue.
Ouchetouta.
Phelgme.
Ondeuhata.
Morue.
Tſignoncoira.
Chauue.
Téhocha, Téſacha.
Longs cheueux.
Outſinanouen.
Sourd, vn ſourd.
Téontauoiy.
Borgne.
Cataquoy. Eskeuyátacoy.
Aueugle.
Téacoïy.
Camus.
Oconckiaye.
Boiteux.
Quieunontate.
Nez picquoté.
Ongyarochon.

Me

Menteurs.

Tu as menty, 1. 3. per.
Dachoenne, Carihonia, Andachoenne.
Il a menty, c'eſt vn menteur.
Dachouhanha.
Ne mens-tu point?
Sindachouanna.
Ie ne ſuis point menteur, 3. per.
Danſtan téandachoenne.

Meſchant, point d'eſprit, vicieux.

Tu es meſchant.
Saſcohat, Otiſcohat, Sagaron.
Tu es rude, faſcheux.
Sagaron.
Vous eſtes tous meſchants.
Scoincuquoytet ſquoſcohate, Auoiti ſquoiſcoban.

Me

Vous me faictes tort, ie ne ſuis pas vn ieune homme.
Cherhon etnonmoyeinti éni.
Tu n'as point d'eſprit.
Teſcaondion, Teſquanion.
Ne me trompe pas.
Eſqueunondéuatha, Ennon, chihogna.
Cela n'eſt pas bien.
Voicarihongya.
Tu es vn bel homme.
Angoye.
Tu es vn conteur.
Takiata.
Il eſt meſchant.
Aſcohat.
Il eſt rude, faſcheux.
Gngaron.
Il n'a point d'eſprit. 2.3.per.
Téhondion.
Tu es vn mal baſty.
Haatachen.
Mal baſty. *Atache.*

Me

Mal otru.
Ognierochioguen.
Dents pourries, laides.
Teſquachahouindi, Téchouaſcahouiny.
Batteur, frappeur, querelleur.
Hoüaonton.
Traiſtre, vn traiſtre.
Nonquoirreſſa.
Maquereau.
Ourihouanahouyſe.
Mauuais, vilain, ſale, &c. 1. 2. 3. per.
Ocaho, Ocaueé.
Ennemis.
Yeſcohenſe.
Ton pere eſt mort.
Taiſtan houanhouan.
Il mourra, tu mourras.
Tſibigoye, Chigoye.

Meubles, meſnages, outils.

Aleſne.
Chomata.

54 Pages from Gabriel Sagard's dictionary of the Huron language, printed in his *Le grand voyage du pays des Hurons*, 1632.

55

55 Frontispiece from Sagard, *Le grand voyage du pays des Hurons*, 1632.

a collar resting and supported on their forehead; but in winter their custom is to make a kind of sledge which they call *Arocha*, made of long boards of the wood of the white cedar, on which they put their burden, and with rackets tied to their feet draw their load over the snow without any difficulty.

Text used: George M. Wrong (Ed.) and H. H. Langton (Transl.), The Long Journey to the Country of the Hurons by Father Gabriel Sagard, *Toronto, The Champlain Society, vol. 35, 1939, pp. 90-3.*

56 François du Creux. 'Tabula Novae Franciae', 1660.
Published at Paris in 1664, the general map is based on the Sanson map of 1656 (plate 68) as far as the Great Lakes region is concerned. North of the St Lawrence Du Creux attempted to show the various routes which Father Gabriel Druillettes' *Relation* of 1657-8 described as leading from the St Lawrence to James Bay. Although Lake St John (reached by Father de Quen in 1647) is clearly marked, the largest lake of the region, Mistassini, is not shown, and the Labrador peninsula as a whole has a flattened appearance. The most important feature of the map is the inset of Huronia which shows the various mission posts inland from Georgian Bay, possibly as they existed in 1639 when the Jesuits of the Huron missions were known to have drawn a map, since lost. A manuscript map of 1651, now in the Library of Congress, 'Description du Pais Des Hurons', may alternatively have been the basis for the printed map. By this time the mission stations of Huronia had been destroyed by the Iroqouis incursions of the late 1640s, which left the area 'today deserted' ('hodie desertae').

2
Religion and customs of the Hurons

From Father Jean de Brébeuf's letter incorporated in the *Relation* of 1635

Brébeuf was one of the first Jesuit missionaries to reach Canada in 1625. He spent most of his time among the Hurons until his death in 1649 at the hands of the Iroquois. Chief founder of the Huron missions, Brébeuf was an experienced and discriminating observer of the Hurons in the years before they were weakened by disease and war.

If you ask them who made the sky and its inhabitants, they have no other reply than that they know nothing about it. And when we preach to them of one God, Creator of Heaven and earth, and of all things, and even when we talk to them of Hell and Paradise and of our other mysteries, the headstrong savages reply that this is good for our Country and not for theirs; that every Country has its own fashions. But having pointed out to them, by means of a little globe that we had brought, that there is only one world, they remain without reply . . .

They believe in the immortality of the soul, which they believe to be corporeal. The greatest part of their Religion consists in this point. We have seen several stripped, or almost so, of all their goods, because several of their friends were dead,

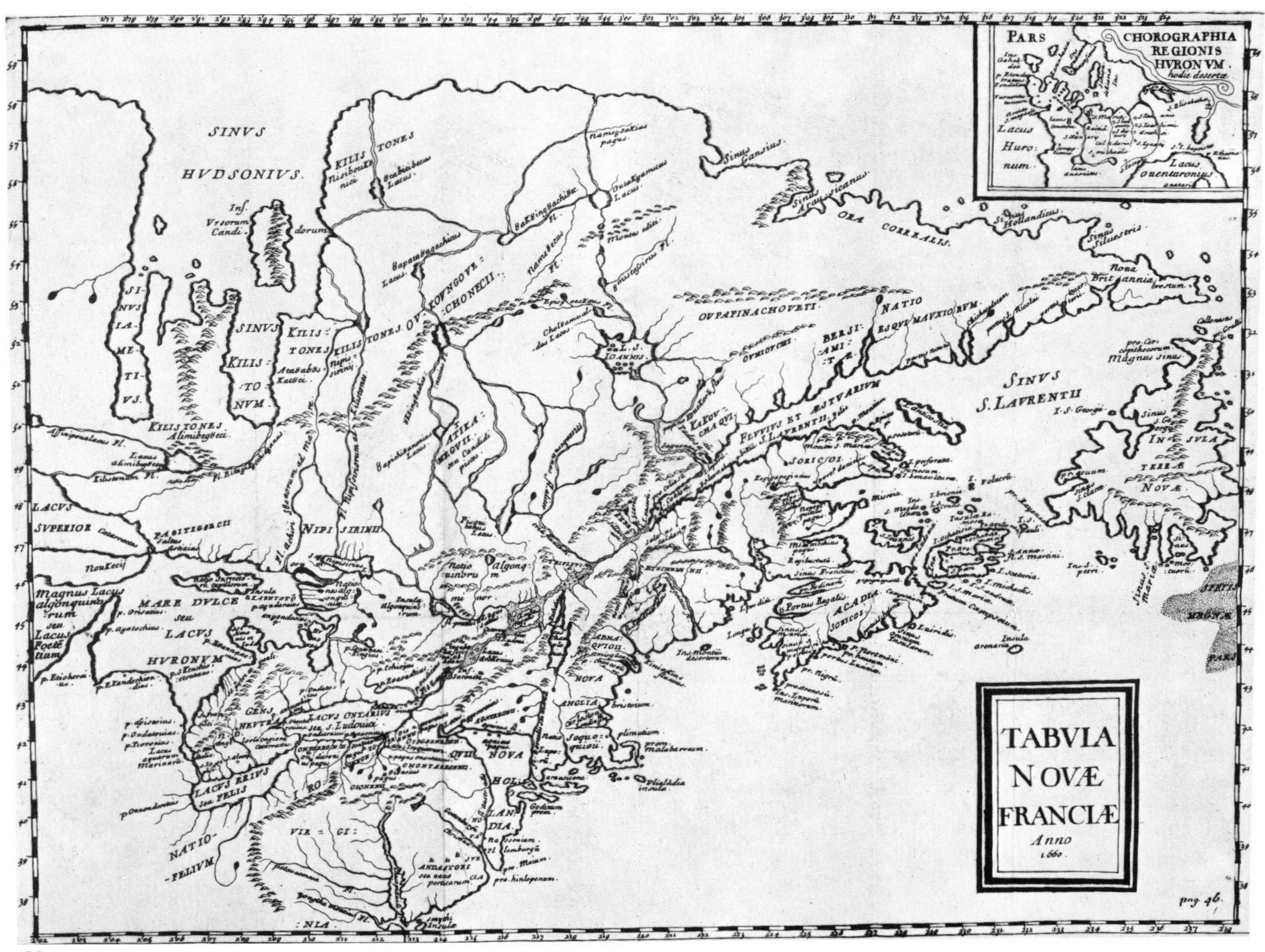

56

57

57 In 1664 the Cramoisy Press in Paris published *Historia Canadensis* by François du Creux. The book was in effect a skilful summary of the Jesuit *Relations*, with some use of Champlain's *Voyages* and other sources. The illustrations are carefully observed, but they lack the spontaneity of Champlain's drawings and there is no evidence that they were drawn anywhere but in Paris. The quotations in this and other captions are taken from the Champlain Society edition of 1951-2.
Huron women. Their dress is described in the text in an extract based on Le Jeune's *Relation* of 1632: '. . . all seasons they wear furs cleverly stitched together at the shoulders and reaching from the neck to the knees; this dress is girt with a cord . . . In spite of their dirt the women have their ornaments, which consist chiefly of wampum necklaces and bracelets, and of belts embroidered with porcupine quills; the women like the men also disfigure their faces with paint'.

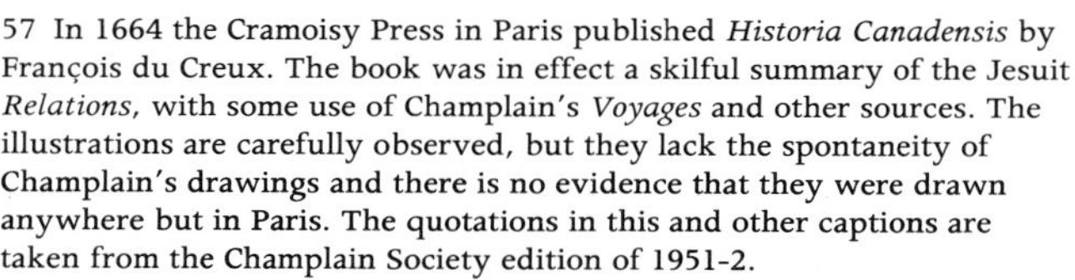

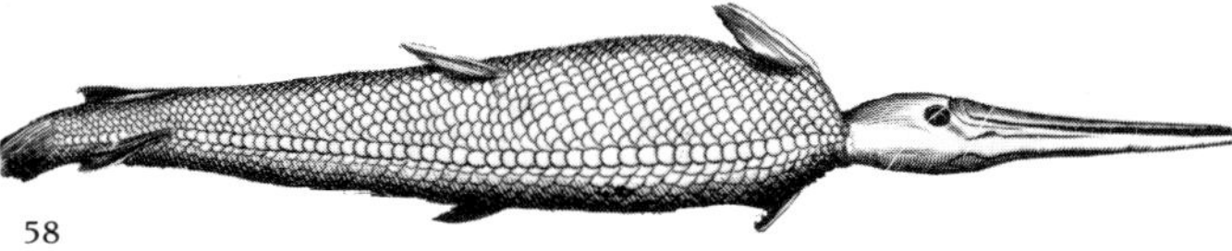

58

58 The gar pike of the Great Lakes, from the *Historia Canadensis*. '. . . it sometimes attains a length of ten feet, is about as thick as a man's thigh and has somewhat the same shape as the pike; its colour is a grayish white. The chausaron is covered with scales, which are so hard and so closely set together that a knife cannot pierce them; the French call it the armour fish . . . the jaws are two and a half feet long . . . it has two rows of very sharp teeth. It has a great appetite, and is not content with devouring other fish; it preys also upon birds.'

to whose souls they had made presents. Moreover, dogs, deer, fish, and other animals have, in their opinion, immortal and reasonable souls. In proof of this, the old men relate certain fables, which they represent as true; they make no mention either of punishment or reward, in the place to which souls go after death. And so they do not make any distinction between the good and the bad, the virtuous and the vicious; and they honour equally the interment of both . . .

As regards morals, the Hurons are lascivious, although in two leading points less so than many Christians, who will blush some day in their presence. You will see no kissing nor

59

59 Birds, from the *Historia Canadensis*. The illustration shows a sea-bird sanctuary in the St Lawrence. In the center is a bird incredibly described by du Creux 'about as large as a hen, which is dun coloured and white and black underneath. One of its feet has talons like the eagle, the other is webbed like a duck; with the latter it swims, with the former it dives into the water and brings out fish to eat, a hitherto unheard of dexterity.'

60 The Moose from the *Historia Canadensis*.' . . . the natives hunt this animal with dogs and then kill it with their arrows or their spears. The right time for hunting the moose is when the snow is hard and deep upon the ground . . . the moose sinks with his own weight and is easily overcome even by a child. But in winter when the snow is not deep, and the rain is continuous the Indians are destitute and in great danger of dying of starvation.'

60

61-5 Huron warriors, from the *Historia Canadensis.* 'They have no set fashion for trimming the hair and each follows his own fancy. Some of them brush their hair straight up to form a crest, the whole of one tribe getting its name from this fashion; others shave the crown and the back of the head and let the hair fall down on both sides of the temples; others shave one side of the head and let the other side grow . . . they paint themselves various colours, a fashion which seems horrible to us, but so beautiful to them, so much do tastes differ. Some of them may be seen with the nose and eyes blue and the eyebrows and cheek black; others with black, red and blue stripes from the ears to the mouth; others with stripes running from ear to ear across the forehead, and three stripes across each cheek; others will blacken the whole face hideously with the exception of the forehead and the point of the chin and a circle round the eyes; one is reminded of the people one sees crazed with drink in France. Even mothers paint the children in this way to make them beautiful.

'The dress of the Indians corresponds to their other barbarous customs; in summer the men wear no clothes at all, except what natural modesty requires, while in other seasons of the year they will fling about them the skins of the beaver, the bear or the wolf, leaving the greater part of the body exposed. Some of them have a more sensible dress, a bear skin that covers the left arm and, passing under the right arm, descends to the knees before and behind . . .'

61 62 63 64 65

immodest caressing; and in marriage a man will remain two or three years apart from his wife, while she is nursing. They are gluttons, even to disgorging; it is true, that does not happen often, but only in some superstitious feasts,—these, however, they do not attend willingly. Besides, they endure hunger much better than we,—so well that after having fasted two or three entire days you will see them still paddling, carrying loads, singing, laughing, bantering, as if they had dined well. They are very lazy, are liars, thieves, pertinacious beggars. Some consider them vindictive; but, in my opinion, this vice is more noticeable elsewhere than here. . . .

What shall I say of their strange patience in poverty, famine, and sickness? We have seen this year [1635] whole villages prostrated, their food a little insipid sagamité [gruel]; and yet not a word of complaint, not a movement of impatience. They receive indeed the news of death with more constancy than those Christian Gentlemen and Ladies to whom one would not dare to mention it. Our Savages hear of it not only without despair, but without troubling themselves, without the slightest pallor or change of countenance. We have especially admired the constancy of our new Christians. The next to the last one who died, named Joseph *Oatij,* lay on the bare ground during four or five months, not only before but after his Baptism,—so thin that he was nothing but bones; in a lodge so wretched that the winds blew in on all sides; covered during the cold of winter with a very light skin of some black animals, perhaps black squirrels, and very poorly nourished. He was never heard to make a complaint, however.

Text used: R. G. Thwaites (Ed.), The Jesuit Relations and Allied Documents. Travels and Explorations of the Jesuit Missionaries in New France 1610-1791, *Cleveland, The Burrows Brothers Company, 1896-1901, vol. 8, pp. 117-25, 127-31.*

3 Nicollet's journey to Green Bay, 1634

From Father Barthelemy Vimont's account in the *Relation* of 1642

Jean Nicollet worked with Champlain from the time of his arrival in Canada in 1618. After Champlain's return to New France in 1633 he sent Nicollet westward to the 'gens de Mer' on a journey, usually dated 1634, which seems to have taken him to Sault Ste Marie, along the northern shores of Lake Michigan to Green Bay, and possibly

66

to meet the Manitouiriniou,—that is to say, 'the wonderful man'. They meet him; they escort him, and carry all his baggage. He wore a grand robe of China damask, all strewn with flowers and birds of many colors. No sooner did they perceive him than the women and children fled, at the sight of a man who carried thunder in both hands,—for thus they called the two pistols that he held. The news of his coming quickly spread to the places round about, and there assembled four or five thousand men. Each of the chief men made a feast for him, and at one of these banquets they served at least six-score Beavers. The peace was concluded; he returned to the Hurons, and some time later to the Three Rivers, where he continued his employment as Agent and Interpreter, to the greater satisfaction of both French and the Savages, by whom he was equally and singularly loved.

Text used: R. G. Thwaites (Ed.), Jesuit Relations, *vol. 23, pp. 277-9.*

67

66-7 Two maps by Jansson both published at Amsterdam in 1636: 'America Septentrionalis' (*top*) and 'Nova Anglia Novum Belgium et Virginia' (*bottom*).
The discrepancies between the Great Lakes area in these two maps issued in the same year by the same cartographer illustrate how far removed from notions of scientific cartography were most of the products of this period. More surprising is the fact that later cartographers often ignored the more authoritative maps of Champlain and his Jesuit successors in favor of one or other of Jansson's representations. See plate 81 for whole of map 67.

some distance up the Fox River. Certainly Nicollet, as agent and interpreter to the Company of New France, penetrated farther west than any other Frenchman of the period.

While in the exercise of this office, he was delegated to make a journey to the nation called People of the Sea, and arrange peace between them and the Hurons, from whom they are distant about three hundred leagues Westward. He embarked in the Huron country, with seven Savages; and they passed by many small nations, both going and returning. When they arrived at their destination, they fastened two sticks in the earth, and hung gifts thereon, so as to relieve these tribes from the notion of mistaking them for enemies to be massacred. When he was two days' journey from that nation, he sent one of those Savages to bear tidings of the peace, which word was especially well received when they heard that it was a European who carried the message; they despatched several young men

4
The Jesuits reach Sault Ste Marie, 1641

From Father Jérôme Lalemant's *Relation* of 1642

Father Isaac Jogues arrived in Canada in 1636, Father Charles Raymbault a year later. The two Jesuits were present at a great concourse of Indians in September 1641 on the shores of Lake Huron where they received an invitation to return with a group of Chippewa Indians to their homeland at Sault Ste Marie. The account which Lalemant obtained from his two colleagues gives us the first description of the Sault.

They started from our house of Ste Marie, about the end of September, and after seventeen days of navigation on the great Lake or fresh-water sea that bathes the land of the Hurons, they reached the Sault, where they found about two thousand Souls, and obtained information about a great many other sedentary Nations, who have never known Europeans and have never heard of God,—among others, of a certain nation, the Nadouessis [Sioux], situated to the Northwest or west of the Sault, eighteen days' journey farther away. The first nine days are occupied in crossing another great Lake that com-

68

mences above the Sault; during the last nine days one has to ascend a River that traverses those lands. These peoples till the soil in the manner of our Hurons, and harvest Indian corn and Tobacco. Their Villages are larger, and in a better state of defense, owing to their continual wars with the Kristinons [Cree], the Irinions [Illinois], and other great Nations who inhabit the same country. Their Language differs from the Algonquin and Huron tongues.

The captains of this Nation of the Sault invited our Fathers to take up their abode among them. . . . But we need Laborers for that purpose; we must first try to win the Peoples that are nearest to us, and meanwhile pray Heaven to hasten the moment of their Conversion.

Text used: R. G. Thwaites (Ed.), Jesuit Relations, *vol. 23, pp. 225-7.*

69

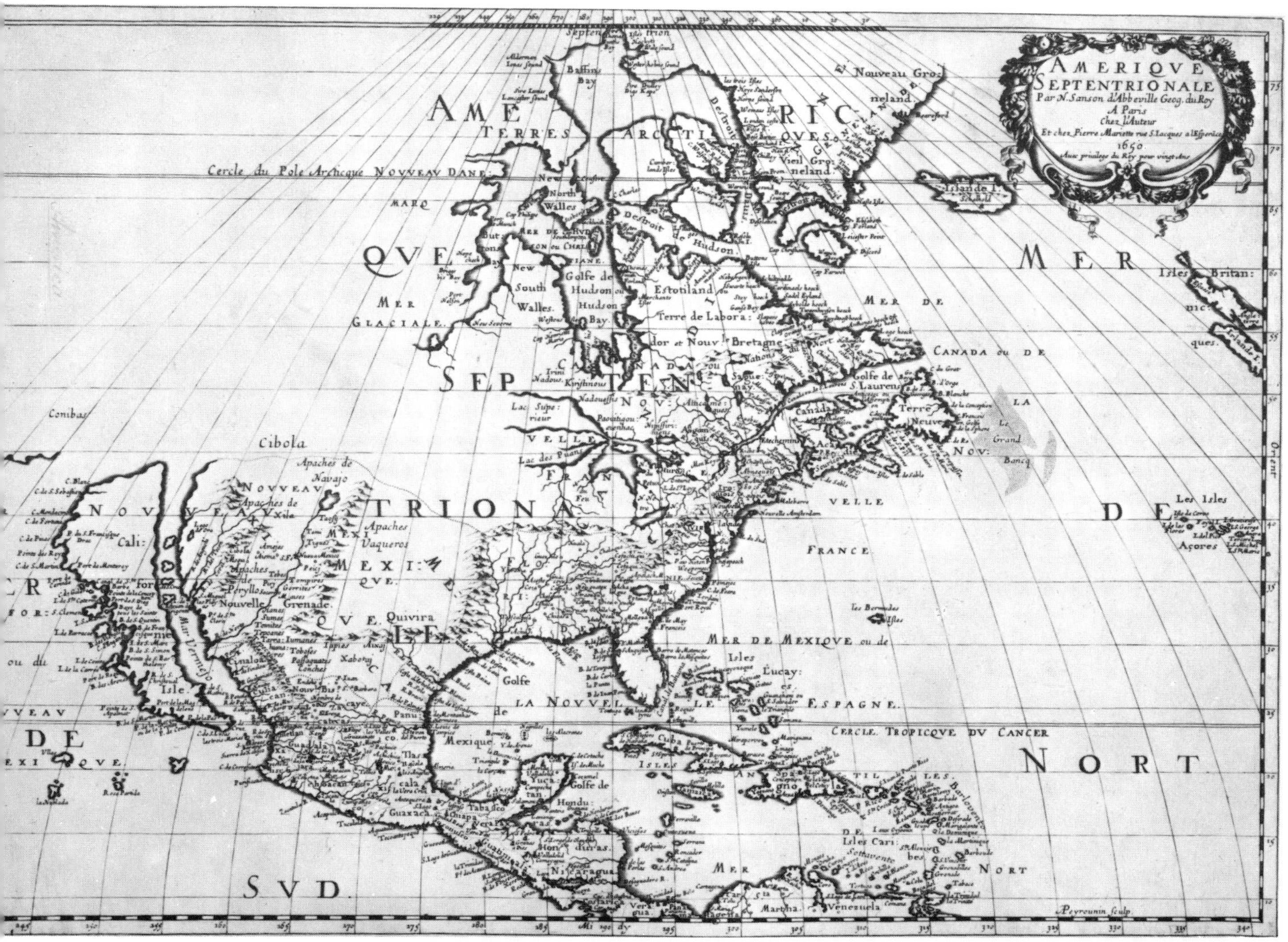

68-9 Two maps by Nicolas Sanson d'Abbeville: 'Le Canada, ou Nouvelle France', 1656 (*top*) and 'Amerique Septentrionale', 1650 (*bottom*).
In these maps by Sanson, heavily dependent on Jesuit reports, all five of the Great Lakes are shown for the first time. Between them, the two maps represent the first major advance on Champlain's map of 1632 (plate 37), and they were reprinted many times, in German and Dutch, as well as French, editions. Erie appears as 'Erie ou Du Chat' ('Lac Derie' had been applied by the French cartographer Boisseau in 1643 to one part of the stretch of water north of the Neutral Nation shown on Champlain's map); the names Supérieur and Ontario are used for the first time; the north-western extremity of Lake Michigan, 'Lac des Puans' or Lake of the Smells (Green Bay), is shown, although it is not differentiated from Lake Michigan; and the true shape of Lake Huron begins to emerge. Farther south the maps are less impressive. They still reflect the sixteenth-century conviction that the rivers emptying into the Gulf of Mexico flowed from a crescent-shaped range of mountains running from Florida to Texas, an error which for long hindered any realistic assessment of the probable length and course of the Mississippi. See also plate 220.

5
The Great Lakes described

From Father Paul Ragueneau's *Relation* of 1647-8

The journeyings of the Jesuits and their interrogation of the Indians among whom they lived had given them by the late 1640s a clear idea of the number and relationship of the westernmost of the Great Lakes. Here, Lake Superior is for the first time mentioned by name ('Ce Lac superieur' in the French original) and its position in relation to Lake Huron and Lake Michigan explained.

The great Lake of the Hurons, which we call 'the fresh-water Sea', four hundred leagues in circumference, one end of which beats against our house of Sainte Marie, extends from East to West, and thus its width is from North to South although it is very irregular in form.

The Eastern and Northern shores of this Lake are inhabited by various Algonquin Tribes . . . [there are] numerous other Algonquin Tribes, still further away, who dwell on the shores of another lake larger than the fresh-water sea, into which it discharges by a very large and very rapid river; the latter, before mingling its waters with those of our fresh-water sea, rolls over a fall that gives its name to these peoples, who come there during the fishing season. This superior Lake extends towards the Northwest, that is, between the West and the North.

A Peninsula, or a rather narrow strip of land, separates that superior Lake from a third Lake, which we call the Lake of the Puants, which also flows into our fresh-water sea by a mouth on the other side of the Peninsula, about ten leagues farther West than the Sault. This third Lake extends between the West and Southwest,—that is to say between the South and the West, but more towards the West,—and is almost equal in size to our fresh-water sea. On its shores dwell other nations whose language is unknown,—that is, it is neither Algonquin nor Huron. These peoples are called Puants, not because of any bad odor that is peculiar to them; but, because they say that they come from the shores of a far distant sea toward the North, the water of which is salt, they are called 'the people of the stinking water'.

Text used: R. G. Thwaites (Ed.), Jesuit Relations, *vol. 33, pp. 149-51.*

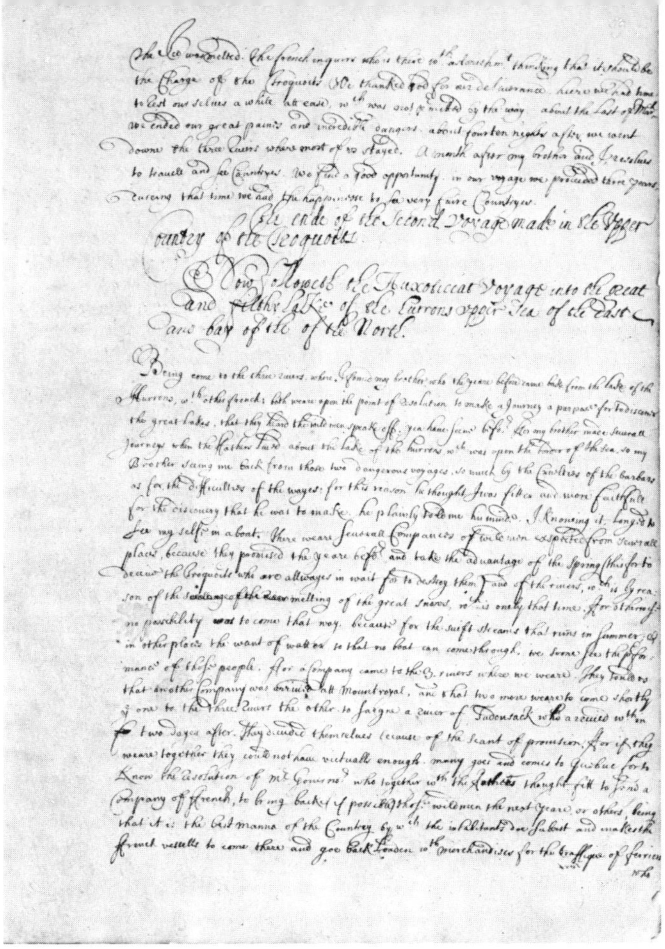
The ende of the Second Voyage made in the Upper Countrey of the Iroquoits

Now followeth the Auxoticiat Voyage into the great and filthy Lakes of the Hurons Upper Sea of the East and bay of the North.

70

70 A page from Radisson's manuscript narrative, *c.* 1669.
Bodleian Library, Oxford, Rawlinson Ms.329.
The narrative was probably written in London in the winter of 1668-9 during Radisson's enforced spell of idleness after his vessel heading to Hudson Bay in company with the *Nonsuch* had been forced to turn back. Its imperfect English and occasional use of French words point to the account having been written or at least dictated by Radisson himself. The manuscript fell into the possession of Samuel Pepys, but after his death was lost together with many other documents from the great collection which Pepys had amassed. Fortunately it was among those manuscripts which were rescued in the mid-eighteenth century by the collector Richard Rawlinson from shopkeepers who were using them as scrap paper. It was published for the first time in 1885. The heading 'Auxoticiat Voyage' on this page puzzled scholars until it was realized that the French had been both misspelt and run together—that the mysterious word consisted of the French prefix 'aux' and a garbled spelling of 'Ottawa', and that Radisson was describing 'A Voyage to the Ottawa [Indians]'.

6
The explorations of Radisson and Groseilliers

From Radisson's narrative of *c.* 1668-9

Of the enterprise and daring of Pierre Esprit Radisson and Des Groseilliers (Médart Chouart) there can be no doubt; but on the precise date and track of their journeys queries multiply on every side. The extracts given here are taken from the 'Auxoticiat Voyage' of Radisson's narrative which has been alternatively dated 1654-6 and 1658-60; if the former, then Des Groseilliers was accompanied by some unnamed Frenchman, not Radisson. The 'delightfullest lake of the world' of the first extract is indisputably Lake Michigan, but the 'salt water' has been interpreted as Hudson Bay by some historians, the Gulf of Mexico by others. In the second extract, speculation that the 'great river that divides' and the 'forked river' are early references to the Mississippi and Missouri may well be correct; but there is no firm evidence that either explorer ever reached those rivers.

i) We embarked ourselves on the delightfullest lake of the world. I tooke notice of their Cottages & of the journeys of our navigation, for because that the country was so pleasant, so beautifull & fruitfull that it grieved me to see y^t ye world could not discover such inticing countrys to live in. This I say because that the Europeans fight for a rock in the sea against one another, or for a sterill land and horrid country, that the people sent heere or there by the changement of the aire ingenders sicknesse and dies thereof. Contrarywise those kingdoms are so delicious & under so temperat a climat, plentiful of all things, the earth bringing foorth its fruit twice a yeare, the people live long & lusty & wise in their way. What conquest would that bee att litle or no cost; what laborinth of pleasure should millions of people have, instead that millions complaine of misery and poverty! . . . We meet wth severall nations, all sedentary, amazed to see us, & weare very civil. The further we sejourned the delightfuller the land was to us. I can say that [in] my lifetime I never saw a more incomparable country, for all I have ben in Italy; yett Italy comes short of it, as I think, when it was inhabited, & now forsaken of the wildmen. Being about the great sea, we conversed wth people that dwelleth about the salt water, who tould us that they saw some great white thing sometimes uppon the water, & came towards the shore, & men in the top of it, and made a noise like a company of swans; wch made me believe that they weare mistaken, for I could not imagine what it could be, except the Spaniard; & the reason is that we found a barill broken as they use in Spaine.

ii) We weare 4 moneths in our voyage wthout doeing any thing but goe from river to river. We mett severall sorts of people. We conversed wth them, being long time in alliance wth them. By the persuasion of som of them we went into ye great river that divides itselfe in 2, where the hurrons wth some Ottanake & the wild men that had warrs wth them had retired. There is not great difference in their language as we weare told. This nation have warrs against those of [the] forked river. It is so called because it has 2 branches, the one towards the west, the other towards the South, wch we believe runns towards Mexico, by the tokens they gave us. Being among these people, they told us the prisoners they take tells them that they have warrs against a nation, against men that build great cabbans & have great beards & had such knives as we have had. Moreover they shewed a Decad of beads and guilded pearls that they have had from that people, wch made us believe they weare Europeans.

Text used: Gideon D. Scull, Voyages of Peter Esprit Radisson, *Boston, The Prince Society, 1885, pp. 150-1, 167-8.*

7 Lake Superior and the routes to the Pacific

From Father Jérôme Lalemant's *Relation* of 1659-60

A section of Lalemant's annual report for 1659-60 is devoted to an account passed on to him by one of the Jesuit missionaries in the field (probably Father Gabriel Druillettes) after the latter had met on the Saguenay River an Indian chief who knew the country as far as Lake Superior. The Indian's description of the great lake is expanded here into a speculative analysis of the lake's function as a portal to the Pacific, a concept graphically illustrated in this period by Sanson's 1656 map of North America.

This lake, which is more than eighty leagues long by forty wide in certain places, is studded with Islands picturesquely distributed along its shores. The whole length of its coast is lined with Algonkin Nations, fear of the Iroquois having forced them to seek there an asylum. It is also enriched in its entire circumference with mines of lead in a nearly pure state; with copper of such excellence that pieces as large as one's fist are found, all refined; and with great rocks, having whole veins of turquoise. The people even strive to make us believe that its waters are swollen by various streams which roll along with the sand grains of gold in abundance—the refuse, so to speak, of the neighboring mines. . . .

But there are riches of another nature. The Savages dwelling about that end of the lake which is farthest distant from us, have given us entirely new light, which will not be displeasing to the curious, touching the route to Japan and China for which so much search has been made. For we learn from these people that they find the Sea on three sides, toward the South, toward the West, and toward the North, so that, if this is so, it is a strong argument and a very certain indication that these three seas, being thus contiguous, form in reality but one sea, which is that of China. For,—that of the South, which is the Pacific sea and is well enough known, being connected with the North sea, which is equally well known, by a third Sea, the one about which we are in doubt,—there remains nothing more to be desired than the passage into this great sea, at once a Western and an Eastern sea.

Now we know that, proceeding Southward for about three hundred leagues from the end of the lake Superior, of which I have just spoken, we come to the bay of St Esprit, which lies on the thirtieth degree of latitude and the two hundred and eightieth of longitude, in the Gulf of Mexico, on the coast of Florida; and in a Southwesterly direction from the same extremity of lake Superior, it is about two hundred leagues to another lake, which empties into the Vermilion sea on the coast of New Granada, in the great South Sea. It is from one of these two coasts that the Savages who live some sixty leagues to the West of our lake Superior obtain European goods, and they even say that they have seen some Europeans there.

Moreover, from this same lake Superior, following a River toward the North, we arrive, after eight or ten days' journey, at Hudson Bay, in fifty-five degrees of latitude.

Text used: R. G. Thwaites (Ed.), Jesuit Relations, *vol. 45, pp. 219-25.*

71

71 Sketches from the *Codex Canadensis*, c. 1700. *Thomas Gilcrease Institute, Tulsa.* Caribou and deer; detail from p. 34.

8 Reports of a great river to the south

i) From Father Jérôme Lalemant's *Relation* of 1661-2

As the Iroquois increased their destructive raids on the surrounding Indian nations so they brought back intriguing reports of distant regions. After describing Indian incursions into Virginia, Lalemant turned to the accounts brought back by an Iroquois war party which had struck farther west, deep into Shawnee territory. They told of fertile lands, probably in the Ohio valley, and of a river which flowed down to the coast in Spanish territory.

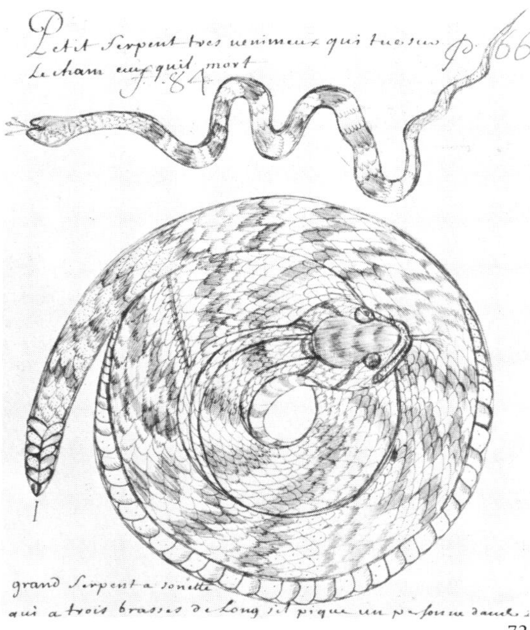

72

72-5 Sketches from the *Codex Canadensis*, c. 1700. *Thomas Gilcrease Institute, Tulsa.* Snakes: detail from p. 66. Magpies: detail from p. 44. Indians fishing, and their implements: p. 15. Fish: detail from p. 58.

It is a country which has none of the severity of our winters, but enjoys a climate that is always temperate—a continual Spring and Autumn, as it were. The soil there is so fertile that one could almost say of it, within bounds, what the Israelite discoverers said of the Promised land; for, to mention the Indian corn only, it puts forth a stalk of such extraordinary thickness and height that one would take it for a tree, while it bears ears two feet long with grains that resemble in size our large Muscatel grapes. No Moose or Beavers are seen there, as they live only in cold countries; but to make up for this, Deer, Buffalo, wild Hogs, and another species of large animal wholly unknown to us, inhabit those beautiful forests, which are like so many Orchards, consisting almost wholly of fruit-trees. In their branches live very peacefully birds of all colors and of every note, especially little Paroquets, which are so numerous that we have seen some of our Iroquois return from those countries with scarfs and belts which they had made from these birds by a process of interweaving. One finds there also a kind of serpent of prodigious size and two brasses in length; but these are harmless Snakes, their venom not being hurtful or their sting injurious. The people are not so inoffensive as the snakes, for they make use of a poison with which they understand perfectly the art of infecting springs, and even whole rivers; and they do it with such skill that the water loses nothing of its fair appearance, although it be tainted throughout. Their villages are situated along a beautiful river which serves to carry the people down to the great Lake (for so they call the Sea), where they trade with Europeans who pray as we do, and use Rosaries, as well as Bells for calling to Prayers. According to the description given us, we judge them to be Spaniards. That Sea is doubtless either the Bay of St Esprit in the Gulf of Mexico, on the coast of Florida; or else the Vermilion Sea, on the coast of New Granada, in the great South Sea.

ii) From Father Claude Dablon's *Relation* of 1670-1

More than thirty years after Jean Nicollet probably reached, but did not explore, the area of the Fox River southwest of Green Bay, the two Jesuit fathers, Claude Dablon and Claude Jean Allouez followed in 1670 the course of the river through the fertile region of eastern Wisconsin. During their travels they collected more detailed information about the Mississippi than the earlier reports provided.

These people are situated in the midst of that beautiful region mentioned by us, near the great river named Missisipi, of which it is well to note here what information we have gathered. It seems to form an inclosure, as it were, for all our lakes, rising in the regions of the North and flowing toward the south, until it empties into the sea—supposed by us to be either the vermilion or the Florida Sea, as there is no knowledge of any large rivers in that direction except those which empty into these two Seas. Some Savages have assured us that this is so noble a river that, at more than three hundred leagues' distance from its mouth, it is larger than the one flowing before Quebec; for they declare that it is more than a league wide. They also state that all this vast stretch of country consists of nothing but treeless prairies,—so that its inhabitants are all obliged to burn peat and animal excrement dried in the Sun,—until we come within twenty leagues of the sea, when Forests begin to appear again. Some warriors of this country who tell us they have made their way thither, declare that they saw there men resembling the French, who were splitting trees with long knives; and that some of them had their houses on the water,—for thus they expressed themselves in speaking of sawed boards and of Ships. They state further that all along that great river are various Tribes of different Nations, of dissimilar languages and customs, and all at war with one another.

Texts used: i) R. G. Thwaites (Ed.), Jesuit Relations, *vol. 47, pp. 145-7; ii) Ibid., vol. 55, pp. 207-9.*

73

9
Life on the trail, 1670

From the narrative of René de Bréhant de Galinée, 1670

One of the most vivid accounts of travel in the North American wilderness came from the pen of a Sulpician missionary, Father Galinée, who spent only three years in Canada. In 1669-70 he accompanied François Dollier de Casson on an exploring expedition from Montreal to the Great Lakes, and on his return wrote an account of his experiences which remained in manuscript form until its discovery and publication in the nineteenth century.

74

Navigation above Montreal is quite different from that below. The latter is made in ships, barks, launches, and boats, because the River St. Lawrence is very deep, as far up as Montreal, a distance of 200 leagues; but immediately above Montreal one is confronted with a rapid or waterfall amidst numerous large rocks, that will not allow a boat to go through, so that canoes only can be used. These are little birch-bark canoes, about twenty feet long and two feet wide, strengthened inside with cedar floors and gunwales, very thin, so that one man carries it with ease, although the boat is capable of carrying four men and eight or nine hundred pounds' weight of baggage. There are some made that carry as many as ten or twelve men with their outfit, but it requires two or three men to carry them.

This style of canoe affords the most convenient and the commonest mode of navigation in this country, although it is a true saying that when a person is in one of these vessels he is always, not a finger's breadth, but the thickness of five or six sheets of paper, from death. These canoes cost Frenchmen who buy them from Indians nine or ten crowns in clothes, but from Frenchmen to Frenchmen they are much dearer. Mine cost me eighty livres. It is only the Algonkin-speaking tribes that build these canoes well. The Iroquois use all kinds of bark except birch for their canoes. They build canoes that are badly made and very heavy, which last at most only a month, while those of the Algonkins, if taken care of, last five or six years . . . They are so frail that to bear a little upon a stone or to touch it a little clumsily is sufficient to cause a hole, which can, however, be mended with resin.

The convenience of these canoes is great in these streams, full of cataracts or waterfalls, and rapids through which it is impossible to take any boat. When you reach them you load canoe and baggage upon your shoulders and go overland until the navigation is good; and then you put your canoe back into the water, and embark again . . . When the weather is fine, after unloading your canoe, you make a fire and go to bed without otherwise housing yourself; but when it is wet, it is necessary to go and strip some trees, the bark of which you arrange upon four small forks, with which you make a cabin to save you from the rain. The Algonkins carry with them pieces of birch-bark, split thin and sewed together so that they are four fathoms in length and three feet wide. These roll up into very small compass, and under three of these pieces of bark hung upon poles eight or nine men can be easily sheltered. Even winter cabins are made with them that are warmer than our houses. Twenty or thirty poles are arranged lengthwise so that they all touch each other at the top, and the bark is spread over the poles, with a little fire in the centre. Under these strips of bark I have passed days and nights where it was very cold, with three feet of snow upon the ground, without being extraordinarily inconvenienced.

As to the matter of food, it is such as to cause all the books to be burned that cooks have ever made, and themselves to be forced to renounce their art. For one manages in the woods of Canada to fare well without bread, wine, salt, pepper, or any condiments. The ordinary diet is Indian corn, called in France Turkey wheat, which is ground between two stones and boiled in water; the seasoning is with meat or fish, when you have any. This way of living seemed to us all so extraordinary that we felt the effects of it. Not one of us was exempt from some illness before we were a hundred leagues from Montreal.

Text used: James H. Coyne (Ed.), Exploration of the Great Lakes 1669-1670 . . . Galinée's Narrative and Map, *Ontario Historical Society, Papers and Records, vol. 4, Toronto, 1903, pp. 9-13.*

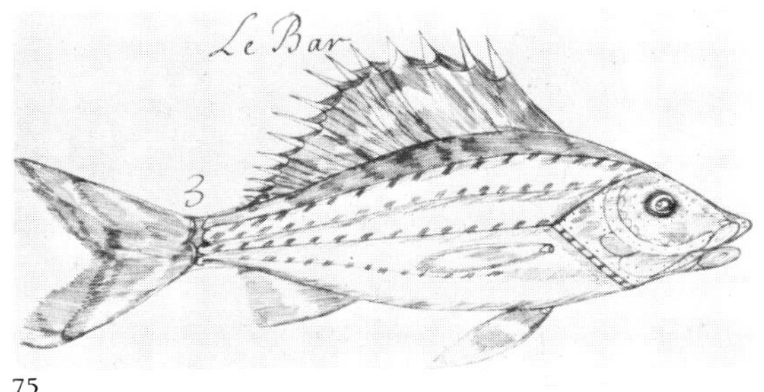

75

10 Jolliet and Marquette discover the Mississippi, 1673

From Father Claude Dablon's *Relation* of 1672-3

Since no original papers have survived from the expedition of 1673 there has been considerable controversy about the authorship of this account, in particular whether Dablon's report was based on oral information given him by Jolliet or on the journal which we know Marquette kept but which was subsequently lost. The amount of detail seems to point to the latter. The narrative was not published at the time because on the orders of Louis XIV the Cramoisy press stopped printing the *Jesuit Relations* with the issue of 1671-2.

Jolliet and Marquette left the mission of St Ignace on the Straits of Mackinac in May 1673, crossed the Fox-Wisconsin portage south-west of Green Bay, and on 17 June reached the Mississippi at Prairie de Chien. The extract given here includes one of the earliest first-hand descriptions of the 'pisikious' or buffalo.

76

76 Buffalo: detail from p. 35 of the *Codex Canadensis*, c. 1700. *Thomas Gilcrease Institute, Tulsa.*

Here we are, then, on this so renowned River, all of whose peculiar features I have endeavored to note carefully. The Missisipi River takes its rise in various lakes in the country of the Northern nations. It is narrow at the place where Miskous [the Wisconsin] empties; its Current, which flows southward, is slow and gentle. To the right is a large chain of very high Mountains, and to the left are beautiful lands; in various Places, the Stream is divided by Islands. On sounding, we found ten brasses of Water. Its Width is very unequal; sometimes it is three-quarters of a league, and sometimes it narrows to three arpents [under 200 yards]. We gently followed its Course, which runs toward the south and southeast, as far as the 42nd degree of Latitude. Here we plainly saw that its aspect was completely changed. There are hardly any woods or mountains; the Islands are more beautiful, and are Covered with finer trees. We saw only deer and cattle, bustards, and Swans without wings, because they drop Their plumage in this country. From time to time, we came upon monstrous fish, one of which struck our Canoe with such violence that I Thought that it was a great tree, about to break the Canoe to pieces. . . . When we reached the parallel of 41 degrees 28 minutes, following the same direction, we found that Turkeys had taken the place of game; and the pisikious, or wild cattle, That of the other animals.

We call them 'wild cattle', because they are very similar to our domestic cattle. They are not longer, but are nearly as large again, and more Corpulent. When Our people killed one, three persons had much difficulty in moving it. The head is very large; The forehead is flat and a foot and a half Wide between the horns, which are exactly like Those of our oxen, but black and much larger. Under the Neck They have a Sort of large Dewlap, which hangs down; and on The back is a rather high hump. The whole of the head, The Neck, and a portion of the Shoulders, are covered with a thick mane Like that of horses; It Forms a crest a foot long, which makes them hideous, and, falling over their eyes, Prevents them from seeing what is before them. The remainder of the Body is covered with a heavy coat of curly hair, almost Like That of our sheep, but much stronger and Thicker. It falls off in Summer, and The skin becomes as soft As Velvet. At that season, the savages Use the hides for making fine Robes, which they paint in various colors. The flesh and the fat of the pisikious are Excellent, and constitute the best dish at feasts. Moreover they are very fierce; and not a year passes without their killing some savages. When attacked, they catch a man on their Horns, if they can, toss Him in the air, and then throw him on the ground, after which they trample him under foot, and kill him. If a person fire at Them from a distance, with either a bow or a gun, he must, immediately after the Shot, throw himself down and hide in the grass; for if they perceive him who has fired, they run at him, and attack him. As their legs are thick and rather Short, they do not run very fast, as a rule, except when angry. They are scattered about the prairie in herds; I have seen one of 400.

In July the two explorers became the first Europeans to sight the mouth of the Missouri.

. . . sailing quietly in clear and calm Water, we heard the noise of a rapid, into which we were about to run. I have seen nothing more dreadful. An accumulation of large and entire trees, branches, and floating islands, was issuing from the Mouth of The river pekistanouï, with such impetuosity that we could not without great danger risk passing through it. So great was the agitation that the water was very muddy, and could not become clear.

Pekitanouï is a river of considerable size, coming from the northwest, from a great distance; and it discharges into the Missisipi. There are many Villages of savages along this river, and I hope by its means to discover the vermillion or California sea.

77 J. B. L. Franquelin. 'Carte du Fleuve St. Laurent dressée sur les Mémoires et observations du Sr. Jolliet en 46 Voyages', 1685. *Service Historique de la Marine, Paris, 126-1-3.*
Contrary to the common assumption that no survey worthy of the name was carried out in the Gulf of St Lawrence until Cook's in 1759, a considerable number of charts were made by French hydrographers before the end of the seventeenth century. Among them were some drawn by Jolliet, who wrote to the Secretary of State, the Marquis de Seignelay, in November 1685 a letter (translated and printed in Delanglez, 1948): 'I have acquired much experience during the voyages I made to the Mississippi River, the Illinois country, the Lake of the Ponteouatami [Green Bay], the country of the Ouenibegons [Winnebago], Lake Superior in the Ottawa country, Baye du Nord [Hudson Bay], Anticosti, Percee Island, Belle Isle and Newfoundland, always with dividers or compass in hand, noting every cape and spit, as well as the bearings from one to the other. This experience emboldens me, my Lord, to present to you this map which is [the result of] my work during the past six years . . . I inserted in the final draught the information and the noteworthy details observed during forty-six voyages on a bark and three in a canoe.' The existence of this version of Jolliet's work by Franquelin is explained in note to Seignelay by Governor Denonville three days later: 'I have had Sieur Franquelin make drawings of Sieur Jolliet's sketches. The latter is seriously interested in his work and has made a thorough study of the river.'

77

Judging from The Direction of the course of the Missisipi, if it Continue the same way, we think that it discharges into the Mexican Gulf. It would be a great advantage to find the river Leading to the Southern Sea, toward California; and, as I have said, this is what I hope to do by means of the Pekitanouï, according to the reports made to me by the savages. From them I have learned that, by ascending this river for 5 or 6 days, one reaches a fine prairie, 20 or 30 leagues long. This must be crossed in a northwesterly direction, and it terminates at another small river,—on which one may embark, for it is not very difficult to transport Canoes through so fine a country as that prairie. This 2nd River Flows toward The southwest for 10 or 15 leagues, after which it enters a Lake, small and deep, which flows toward the West, where it falls into The sea. I have hardly any doubt that it is The Vermillion Sea, and I do not despair of discovering It some day, if God grant me the grace and the health to do so, in order that I may preach the Gospel to all The peoples of this new world who have so Long Groveled in the darkness of infidelity.

Text used: R. G. Thwaites (Ed.), Jesuit Relations, *vol. 59, pp. 109-13, 141-3.*

78

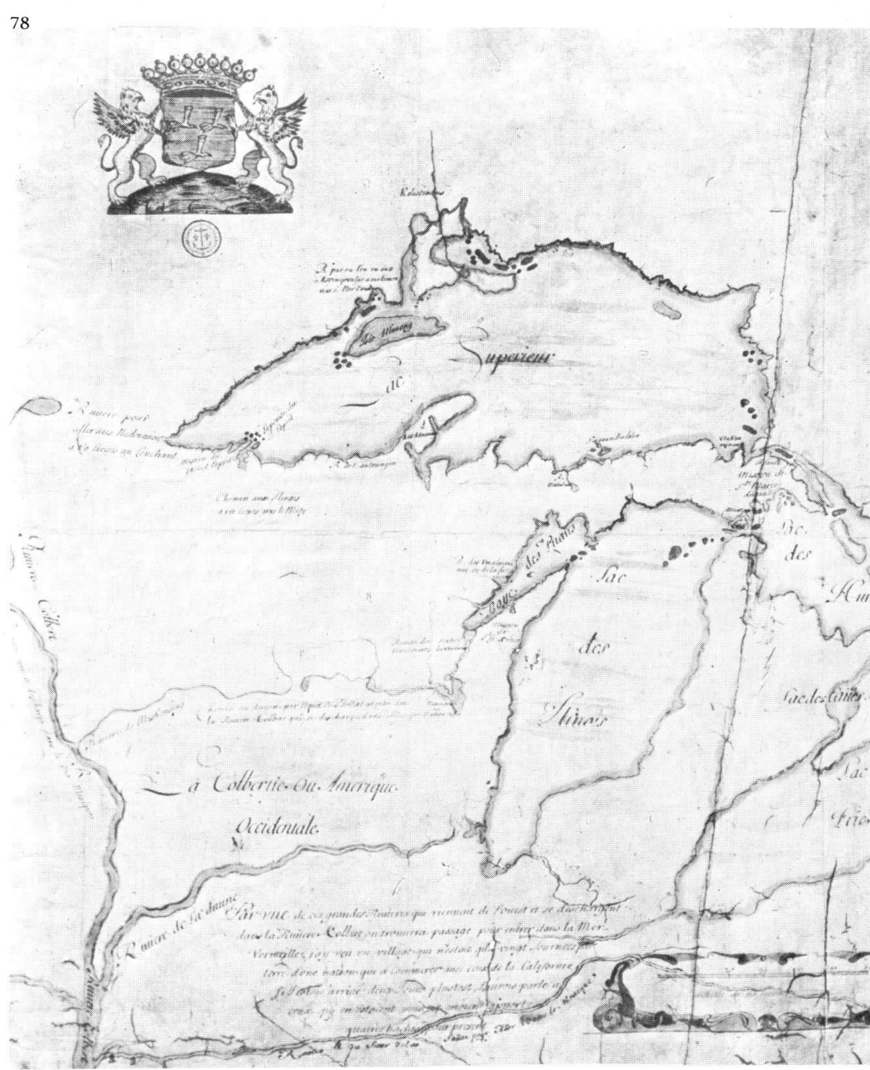

78 [?J. B. L. Franquelin]. 'Carte de la descouverte du Sr Jolliet . . .' [?1675]. *Service Historique de la Marine, Paris, Recueil 67, carte No. 39.*
This appears to be another copy of Jolliet's lost map of 1674 (see plates 15, 46-7). The intention seems to have been to emphasize the ease of water-communication between the Great Lakes and the Mississippi, a point which Frontenac had stressed in his letter to Colbert of November 1674. But the most controversial feature of the map is the interpolation on it of the course of the Ohio with the inscription, 'Route du Sieur de la Salle pour Aller dans le Mexique'. This is in a different, clumsier handwriting—neither Franquelin's nor Jolliet's—and is clearly a later addition to the map. Although regarded by some historians as evidence of La Salle's 'discovery' of the Ohio *c.* 1670 it hardly survives critical examination; nor does Jolliet mention the subject in his dedicatory letter to Frontenac which this map also carries.

11
La Salle reaches the mouth of the Mississippi, 1682

From the manuscript memoir of Henri de Tonty, 1693

Tonty was an Italian who had served with the French army in Europe (and lost a hand during the wars), and became one of La Salle's most trusted subordinates. His account of the expedition of 1682 is succinct and dispassionate, and includes his reflections on the potentialities of the region revealed by La Salle's explorations.

. . . We proceeded on our course, and after going forty leagues, arrived at the sea on the 7th of April.

M. de La Salle sent canoes to inspect the channels. Some went to the channel on the right hand, some to the left, and M. de La Salle chose that in the centre. In the evening each made his report, that is to say, that the channels were very fine, wide, and deep. We encamped on the right bank, erected the arms of the King, and returned several times to inspect the channels. The same report was made.

This river is 800 leagues long, without rapids, to wit, 400 from the country of the Sioux, and 400 from the mouth of the Islinois River to the sea. The banks are almost uninhabitable, on account of the spring floods. The woods are chiefly poplar, the country one of canes and briars and of trees torn up by the roots; but a league or two from the river, is the most beautiful country in the world, prairies, open woods of mulberry trees, vines, and fruits that we are not acquainted with. The savages gather the Indian corn twice in the year. In the lower course of the river, the part which might be settled, is where the river makes a course north and south, for there, in many places, every now and then it has bluffs on the right and left.

The river is only navigable for ships as far as the village of Nadesche, for above that place the river winds too much; but this would not prevent one's setting out from the country above with pirogues [sailing barges] and flatboats, to proceed from the Ouabache [Ohio] to the sea. There are but few beavers, but to make amends, there is a large number of buffaloes or bears, large wolves, stags, *sibolas*, hinds, and roe deer in abundance; and some lead mines, with less than one-third refuse. As these savages are stationary, and have some habits of subordination, they might be obliged to make silk in order to procure necessaires for themselves, if the eggs of silkworms were brought to them from France, for the forests are full of mulberry trees. This would be a valuable trade.

As for the country of the Islinois, the river runs 100 leagues from Fort St Louis, to where it falls into the Mississipy. It may be said to contain the finest lands ever seen. The climate is the same as that of Paris, though in the 40th degree of latitude . . .

I should not know how to describe the beauty of all the countries that I have mentioned, and, if I had worked them, I would say for what purposes they might be utilized. As for the Mississipy, it might produce every year peltries to the amount of 2,000 crowns, and abundance of lead and of timber for ships. Commerce in silk might be established there, and a port to harbor ships and form a base for the Gulf of Mexico. Pearls will be found, and even if wheat could not be had below, the upper river would furnish it, and one could furnish the [West Indian] islands with what they need, such as lumber, vegetables, grain, and salt beef.

Text used: L. P. Kellogg (Ed.), Early Narratives of the Northwest 1634-1699, *New York, Barnes & Noble, 1959 reprint of 1917 edn., pp. 302-3, 322.*

79 Louis Hennepin. 'Carte d'un tres grand Pais Nouvellement découvert dans l'Amerique Septentrionale', Amsterdam, 1697.

Although on this map Hennepin avoids the great westward bulge in the lower Mississippi shown by Franquelin (see plate 53) and other cartographers of the period, he misplaces the river far enough west to bring it near the mouth of the Rio Grande ('R. de la Magdelaine'). The sources of the Mississippi, and other western streams, are marked close together near a group of mountains in the western interior—another concept which was to persist long in the maps of the region. Not until the maps of Claude and Guillaume de l'Isle early in the next century did the Mississippi appear in its correct position.

79

2 EXPLORATION WESTWARD FROM THE NORTHEASTERN SEABOARD

In addition to exploring the regions around the Great Lakes and in the Mississippi Valley, the French were deeply involved in the northeast of the continent. They were the first to make a serious claim to the area and unknown Frenchmen were probably the earliest visitors to the interior of Nova Scotia. In their search for furs and souls, however, they moved into the interior and abandoned the northeast to the English, who had undertaken some exploration there before 1630. By that date, when John Winthrop led the first of a great wave of settlers over to New England, colonies were well established by the Puritans at Plymouth and by the Dutch at New Amsterdam and other, more transitory communities could be found scattered along the coasts of New England and Nova Scotia. Although the area had many advantages for settlement (stressed by the promoters who frequently portrayed New England as an irresistible combination of the Garden of Eden before the Fall and the Promised Land of the Israelites), there were drawbacks which were to influence the whole pattern of exploration and settlement up to the Revolution.

The northeast coastline is rocky and hostile but it does contain many good harbors which provided havens for the earliest visitors. Along the shore where the land was low were salt marshes covered by high grass and, farther inland occasionally reaching to the sea edge, was the American forest. Some clearing had been undertaken by the Indians to facilitate hunting[1] but, in general, the earliest travellers thought the forest dense and impenetrable. The river valleys became the primary routes for travel and communication, and in trying to go west the first explorers were confronted with the harsh facts of geography. In the north almost all the rivers flow south to the sea and none, with the exception of the Hudson-Mohawk, which creates a route to the Great Lakes, provides a way into the interior. Farther south the river valleys give more easily negotiated access to the west but only as far as the foothills of the mountains. From New York to Pennsylvania the Appalachian Mountains are formed from a series of ridges, the most prominent of which is the Alleghenies, which separate eastern Pennsylvania from the Ohio Valley. The mountains created the major physical barrier to early exploration and expansion.

The other barrier to westward movement was human. The Indians of northeast America came from two major cultures. In the coastal regions lived Algonkians, represented by such tribes as the Delawares in Pennsylvania and New York and the Narragansetts, Wampanoags and Connecticuts to the north. Of these tribes the Delawares, estimated to have a population of 8,000, were the most numerous.[2] In New England a great plague in 1616-17, probably the result of the introduction of some European disease, decimated the total native population to a figure of around 15,000 to 18,000.[3] These Indians, living along the coast and in the river valleys, were mainly sedentary, subsisting mostly by agriculture and fishing rather than by hunting and trapping, unlike the second main group, the Iroquois. The five nations of the Iroquois (later, six, with the introduction of the Tuscaroras in 1722) were greater in number, had stronger political ties and fighting ability and were, in consequence, more powerful than the Algonquins. The hunting grounds of the Iroquois extended north to the St Lawrence River and east to Lake Champlain and it was this tribe who controlled the route between the coastlands and the Great Lakes. To the English and the Dutch they were a natural counter-weight to the French-dominated Hurons to the north and had the additional attraction of supplying furs. The push of settlement west was bound to cause conflict, as first manifested in clashes with the Algonkians, such as King Philip's War in New England.

English attitudes to exploration were conditioned by the physical and human barriers which confronted them but there were other factors which dissuaded explorers. New England was settled primarily as a haven from religious persecution. The colonial leaders intended to plant a compact, closely regulated community and, consequently, the inhabitants were not encouraged to search for routes to the Pacific Ocean or for precious metals as in the more southerly colonies. It was believed that exploration would inevitably lead to expansion of settlement away from the main centers of orthodoxy. This would lessen religious fervor and threaten the moral well-being of the settlers. In modern New York the only possible path to the west, other than through the mountains, was by the Mohawk Valley, a route controlled by Albany fur interests which saw exploration as a threat to their virtual monopoly of the trade.

By the late seventeenth century, English attitudes were changing and restraints were breaking down. The vision of New England as a second Canaan was tempered by the appearance of less altruistic men whose chief aim was their own enrichment by exploitation of furs and fish. Others came into the area for more intellectual purposes. These were the scientists, eager to search for new species of plants and animals in an exciting virgin land. The ambitions of these two groups of men led to exploration of much of the area. Gradually the mountain barrier was breached. Among the first Englishmen into the region beyond the Appalachians were probably traders from Pennsylvania, the nearest British equivalent to the *coureurs de bois*. Their activities in the Susquehanna Valley provoked New York into expressing an interest in the area, which had largely been ignored by the French, and it was the latter who provided the greatest spur to English exploration. To prevent French dominance in the continent, it was necessary to expand and consolidate English influence in the trans-Appalachian region and in doing this the British had one great advantage. Although their exploration was slower and less spectacular than that of their rivals, it was followed almost directly by settlement and was therefore more substantial. The English, unlike the French, had provided their empire with the 'flesh and blood' of population.

1 Exploration in New England and Nova Scotia to 1730

New England and adjoining Nova Scotia are bounded to the north by the Gulf of St Lawrence, to the south by Long Island Sound, to the west by the Appalachians and to the east by the sea. Exploration within them was necessarily limited but there were a few people who attempted overland treks in the period up to 1730. Unfortunately written records of their adventures were rare. At the same time, in southern New England population and settlement rapidly increased; the farmers and traders followed hard on the heels of the first explorers.

Some of the earliest explorers were colonists looking for fresh territory in which to build settlements. Various factors caused people to move inland and along the coast: the pressure exerted on the land by a rapid increase in population, the search for better soil to cultivate and the desire for freedom to worship as each community wished. In 1636 Roger Williams and his followers, expelled from Massachusetts Bay, trekked overland to the largely unknown Narragansett region, thus laying the foundations for the colony of Rhode Island.

Expansion of settlement, however, was largely confined to the coastal areas and the lower river valleys. The settlers at first showed little inclination to move into the interior beyond the reach of easy communication, and the leaders did not encourage such initiative. The frontier areas were regarded as the 'dark and dismal Western Wood, the Devil's Den'. A different incentive was needed to provide a spur to more adventurous exploration.

The earliest visitors to the New England shores had remarked on the abundance of fur-bearing animals, notably the beaver which provided the raw material for the hats then currently fashionable. The search for furs led directly to the exploration of the Connecticut Valley and traders were among the first inhabitants of the Narragansett Country. The initial encouragement to advance into the Connecticut came with the visit of Waghinnacut, the chief of the Mohegan Indians, to Boston in 1631. John Winthrop recalls the visit in his journal: 'Waghinnacut, a sagamore upon the River Quonehtacut which lies west of the Naragancet . . . was very desirous to have some Englishmen to come plant in his country, and offered to find them corn, and give them yearly eighty skins of beaver, and that his country was very fruitful, etc. . . .'[4] The Pilgrims were the first to respond to invitations of this kind, sending Edward Winslow and William Holmes up the Connecticut River, and establishing a small trading post at Hartford. The first overland trip from New England was made by John Oldham in 1633. He followed the 'Old Connecticut' path from Watertown through Waltham and Wayland, to Cochituate Pond (near Framingham), thence southwest to the Connecticut via Oxford. He obtained some beaver and came back with glowing reports of the fertile valley bottoms.[5] His favorable descriptions encouraged others to mount trading expeditions to the Connecticut. One of these was William Pynchon, the founder of Springfield, and Oldham himself followed his first visit by a later one. Meanwhile other traders were investigating the region north from Boston. In 1635 Simon Willard led a party of settlers seventeen miles inland to found Concord. Here he could intercept furs from the Pawtucket and Nashaway Indians coming down the Merrimac River and later, during the 1640s, he extended his activities up stream. At the same time Thomas King and his associate John Prescott were pushing west from Concord, and in 1645 Prescott established a trading post at Lancaster. Various groups of New Englanders attempted to share in the trade of the Dutch on the Hudson and the Swedes on the Delaware without much lasting benefit. Not surprisingly, the traders did not care to advertise their discoveries, for the settlers' advance was detrimental to their trade: it thrust back the Indians, destroyed the forest and game, and they were forced to move on. Hence they left very few accounts of their adventures as the first inland explorers in many areas of New England. But news of their journeys and descriptions of the fresh lands and peoples they encountered was inevitably circulated among their fellow colonists who were eager to know all they could about their new homeland. The perception was sometimes faulty but images of the northeast were very strong.

80 Beaver, from the *Codex Canadensis*, c. 1700. *Thomas Gilcrease Institute, Tulsa.*

North of the Merrimac River, including Nova Scotia, there was no such dramatic increase in population. The boundary between the French in Acadia (Nova Scotia) and the British in northern New England was ill-defined. Both nations claimed the area between the Ste Croix and Kennebec Rivers. The lack of stable government and society in any of these frontier lands made them less appealing to the immigrant than the better organized colonies to the south. Throughout the seventeenth century the sparse population was scattered along the coast, occasionally moving inland into the river valleys. In Nova Scotia, between 1632 and 1654 there were only about 200 or 300 people living around the Bay of Fundy. Later settlement spread from Port Royal to the north and east along the main lines of communication, invariably the rivers. 'The American frontier moved far more rapidly than did that of the Acadians which, in a century and a half, had pushed only as far as the estuarine marshland areas of the northern and eastern extremities of the Bay of Fundy except for very small outliers . . .'[6]

The attractions of the northern area were chiefly fur, fish and especially timber, as areas were opened up, particularly in the eighteenth century, to provide an alternative source of timber to the Baltic for the British navy. Groups from the south came to the northern coasts to fish and to explore, activities which often caused friction with the local inhabitants. The visitors had a very low opinion of the locals, 'for the most part fishermen and share in their wives as they do in their boats'. As elsewhere in the northern regions of the continent, the search for furs also prompted exploration. The principal object of the Laconia Company, established by John Mason, Sir Ferdinando Gorges and others in 1629, was to discover a direct communication to Lake Champlain for opening up trade. Waltar Neale, an early governor of the company, was sent on several trips inland along the Piscataqua River in the early 1630s and he claimed to have made great discoveries to the west. He left no record of his adventures, but since the Piscataqua River runs north-south and the mountains bar a route to Lake Champlain, his allegations must be treated with

81

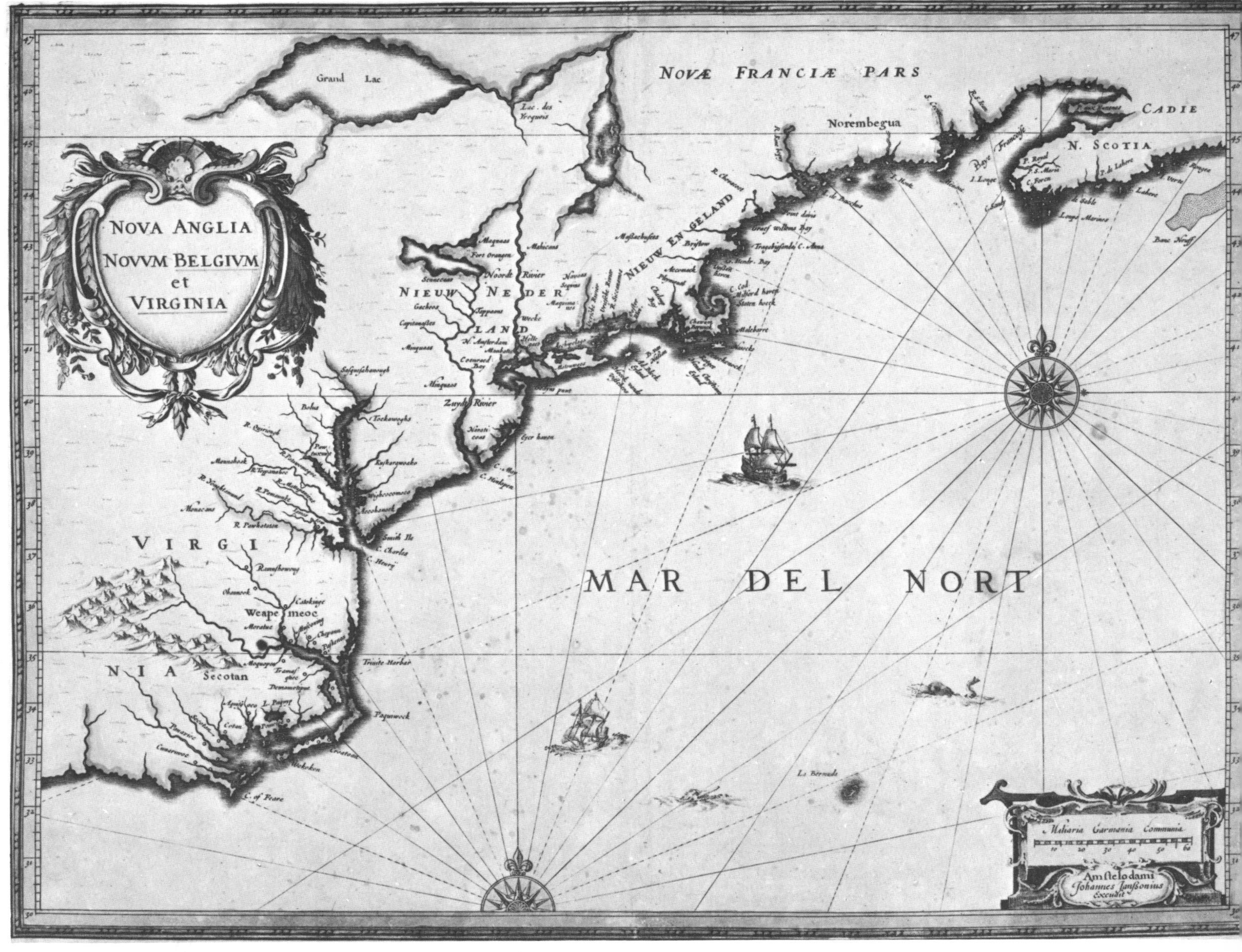

81 Jan Jannsson. 'Nova Anglia Novum Belgium et Virginia', this version published 1660.
This is a close and slightly enlarged copy of an important prototype map for the region prepared to illustrate a work by Johannes de Laet (1630). It is the first map in a general atlas to include a number of important New England names, copied from John Smith's map of the area published over thirty years earlier. It is the first printed map to show New Amsterdam, Fort Orange, the Hudson ('Noordt River') and the Delaware ('Zuydt River'). For more than a century after its publication, this map provided the basis for many others of the area. Additions were made as the region became better known, until the later maps appear cluttered in comparison with the simplicity and clarity of Jansson's original.

some scepticism. John Winter, writing to Robert Trelawny from Richmond Island, Maine, in 1634 described several trips inland along the Saco River: '. . . for the planters heare aboutes, if they will have any bever must go 40 or 50 myles Into the Country with their packes on their backes . . .'[7] He gives no additional details of such exploration. Further attempts were made to find a lake to the west. In 1642 Darby Field explored the White Mountains, the first European in the area[8]. Accompanied by two Indians, he travelled overland and began his ascent of the mountains some 100 miles from the settlement of Saco. He maintained that from the summit he could see to the north a great expanse of water (probably the Gulf of St Lawrence) and to the west other waters which he judged to be the lake out of which flowed the Canada River (St Lawrence). Field's report of shining stones in the area encouraged others to travel there, including Thomas Gorges and Richard Vines of Maine who ascended the Saco River and thought they had found the sources of the Connecticut, Saco, Androscoggin and Kennebec Rivers but little else (see selection 1)[9].

Expansion and exploration in New England and Nova Scotia were to lead to confrontations between England and France. Eventually, in the eighteenth century, rival forts were built at Halifax (plate 82) and Louisburg. Earlier they led to friction between individual colonies. There was conflict between Connecticut and New York, Connecticut and Rhode Island, Rhode Island and Plymouth, over the problem of ownership of the Narragansett country and the question of the jurisdiction of the commonwealth of Massachusetts Bay over Maine. Confusion led to the examination of charters which proved to be very vague on the matter of boundaries. Maps were drawn up and expeditions sent to run boundary lines. Such activities had two incidental results, the development of cartography in the colonies and the first systematic exploration of some of the areas under dispute. Massachusetts was undoubtedly the

82 Des Barres. 'A View of the Town and Harbour of Halifax, from Dartmouth Shore', *c.* 1773, from the *Atlantic Neptune*.
Des Barres was employed by the British government to survey the coast of North America. He lived in Halifax between 1763 and 1773 and not only made surveys but also drew many views of the coast.
The naval base and fortress of Halifax was established by the British on the eastern shore of Nova Scotia in 1749 to counter the French threat to the English colonies, symbolized by their base at Louisburg.

main adversary in the inter-colony conflict as her leaders insisted upon strictly interpreting the boundaries laid down in the 1629 charter. Several expeditions were authorized in the 1650s to discover the northern line of the colony at the source of the Merrimac and the corresponding latitude on the coast. In October 1652 two of the explorers, John Sherman and Jonathan Ince, reported that they had discovered the source of the Merrimac at Aquedahian, 'where it issues out of Lake Winnapusseakit, upon the first of August'.[10] As a result, Massachusetts decided that her charter gave her the right to annex Maine, an action taken in 1652. She was not so lucky with New Hampshire which was established as a separate colony in 1679.

Another consequence of expansion was conflict with the Indians. In the first two decades of settlement the main tribes in New England, Narragansetts and Wampanoags, were well disposed towards the colonists, encouraging white expansion as a counter to the hostile Pequots who had retreated east under the pressure of the Mohawk advance. This caused friction with the militant Pequots and a short, but bloody struggle ensued during which the Pequots were almost destroyed. The Puritans attempted to control relations with the Indians whom at first they judged to be, not savages, but heathens who deserved to be converted. Missionaries were sent out amongst them with only a limited success compared with French achievements. The trade in furs, always an excuse for malpractice, was run by a system of government-controlled truck houses to which Indians brought their skins; such an arrangement seems to have given the Indians a fair deal. Similarly controlled was the purchase of land and many New Englanders felt obliged to pay for land taken over from the Indians, although this was by no means general practice. Expansion of settlement continued and the establishment of new townships inevitably caused friction with the Indians. They began to feel insecure and none more so than King Philip, chief of the Wampanoags, who felt his power was being undermined by the encroachment of the English. Similar resentment was felt among the Narragansetts and in 1675 both tribes attacked and provoked the most ferocious Indian war of the seventeenth century. The Indians frequently raided outlying settlements and took many prisoners who, however involuntarily, were explorers often anxious to record their experiences. Among these was Mrs Mary Rowlandson, wife of the minister at Lancaster, Massachusetts. She was taken prisoner and travelled around northern New England, first southwest and then north to the borders of New Hampshire, Vermont and Massachusetts and along the Connecticut River to Chesterfield in New Hampshire. Here she spent several days before the Indians retraced their steps as far as Princeton near Lancaster where negotiations were begun for her release. Eventually she was rescued by her husband. During her captivity she was able to observe, and later to write vivid descriptions of the Indians and their customs (see selection 2). Bitter reprisals were taken by the colonies. Many Indians were killed, many were sold into slavery in the West Indies and others 'encouraged' to live in enclaves. The way was now open for further expansion into the interior, but the next major step in exploration was to take place west of the Appalachians.

83 Chief Ninigret. Oil painting; artist unknown; believed to have been painted in 1647 for John Winthrop, the first governor of Massachusetts Bay. *Museum of Art, School of Design, Providence, Rhode Island.*
Chief of the Eastern Niantics, one of the allied tribes in New England (the Narragansett Bay area), which fought with the British against the Pequots in 1637. In the following two decades Ninigret became regarded as a trouble maker by the New England governments. Since he was supplied with arms from New Amsterdam, it was thought that the allied tribes would aid the Dutch in a war against the British colonies. In 1654 the government of Massachusetts Bay raised an army against the Niantics. The threat was sufficient to engineer the submission of Ninigret, although he continued to be regarded with the greatest suspicion.

84 King Philip of Mount Hope, 1772, by Paul Revere, from Thomas Church, *The entertaining history of King Philip's war*, 2nd edition.
Famed for his midnight ride in 1775, Paul Revere was also a competent artist and engraver. King Philip was chief of the Wampagnoags in the Plymouth area of New England and in 1675 led an uprising against the colonists. After initial success, the Indians gradually succumbed to the settlers and in August 1676 King Philip was trapped and killed. He became part of American folklore and was still popular 100 years later when Revere engraved this portrait.

85 Burial ceremony of the Iroquois, from P. Lafitau, *Moeurs des sauvages Ameriquains*, 1724.
The person to be buried (looking remarkably alive!) is sitting to the left of an open grave. Near him is a collection of his belongings, notably a bow and arrow and food, to defend and sustain him on the journey to the next world. In the background a chief is giving out prizes to the Indians. These gifts appear to be greatly valued, since a recipient is being challenged.

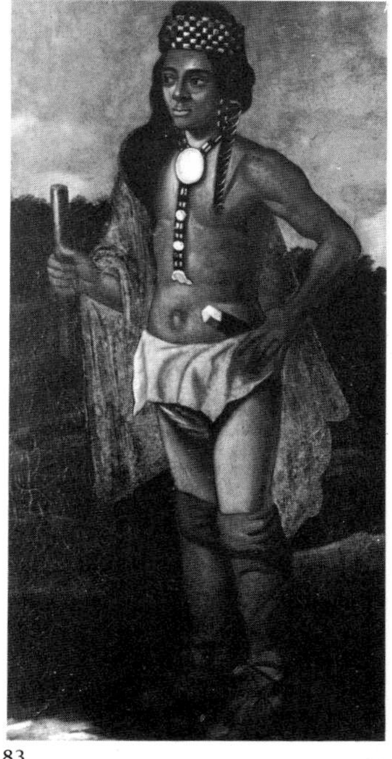

83

84

85

2 New York to 1730

The fur trade was the dominating reason for the exploration of New York. It encouraged the Dutch to penetrate inland from the settlement of New Amsterdam and influenced British policy towards exploration, the Indian and, ultimately, the French. Almost as soon as the Hudson was explored in 1609, the Dutch arrived to trade in furs, establishing two important posts at Fort Orange (Albany) and at Fort Nassau where the Schuylkill enters the Delaware, near the site of Philadelphia. It was the Iroquois who early on became the central figures in the New York fur trade. They supplied the Dutch at Fort Orange with peltry, first from their own territories and then by sending hunting parties north beyond Lake Ontario. With Dutch and English help they became the dominant nation in the northeast colonies. Their friendship was ceaselessly cultivated and an incidental result was the exploration of the area they dominated. Prior to 1634 several Dutchmen had ventured into the region west of Fort Orange and in 1616 two men crossed from the Mohawk River to Otsego Lake, and went down the Susquehanna into the area now occupied by Pennsylvania.[11] They left no record of their adventures but a journal kept on an expedition which set out in 1634 gives a good account of Indian tribes and customs in the north. In that year the Dutch heard reports that the Mohawk had concluded a truce with the Canadian tribes in order to trade with the French. They were alarmed and dispatched three men to investigate. The journey took place in the depths of winter, the men leaving on 11 December 1634, with five Mohawk Indians as guides. The party went along the valley of the Mohawk passing through the country of the Mohawks and the Oneidas and enjoying the hospitality of the Indians at their townships (the chief settlement of each tribe was known as a 'castle'). On 30 December they arrived at the Oneida Castle and stayed until 12 January. They observed with curiosity several Indian customs, including the driving out of devils. They saw evidence of trade with the French and listened to complaints against the Dutch. The Indians claimed they were paid a poor price for their skins, suggested a reasonable increase, and promised that if the Dutch agreed, they would be granted a monopoly of the trade. The visitors undertook to pass on these grievances and proposals. On the return journey they were treated once more to Indian hospitality, arriving back at Fort Orange on 21 January (see selection 3).

Other attempts to ensure lasting friendship with the Iroquois were made by missionaries, such as Johannes Megapolensis in the 1640s. In 1642 the first formal treaty between the Dutch and the Iroquois was concluded by Arent van Curler. The traders, however, seldom ventured very far west of Fort Orange and the Iroquois did not encourage long journeys through their territories. Dutch expansion was slow, concentrating on the upper Hudson Valley and along the Jersey shore, although in 1661 a discontented group of settlers from Beverwyck, alongside Fort Orange, trekked west. Led by Arent van Curler, they founded a settlement at Schenectady, a site he had discovered when making peace with the Indians in 1642. One of the main reasons for the slow expansion of the Dutch in New Amsterdam, and an important factor in their overthrow by the English in 1664, was a low rate of immigration, expecially when compared with the colonies to the north.

86 Arnoldus Montanus. *Nieuwe Weereld*, 1671.
The map at the beginning of Arnoldus Montanus' description of the New World was based on Jansson's map 'Nova Anglia Novum Belgium et Virginia' (plate 81). It included this original cartouche which illustrates the Dutch attitude to North America. In their view the Indian chief was highly placed and his people occupied themselves by hunting various animals, notably the beaver. In the background are shown European soldiers and a stone-built fort, illustrating the power of the white settlers and explorers.

86

87

87 View of New Amsterdam, from Carolus Allard, *Orbis habitabilis*, no. 79, 1680.
The view of the town is relegated to the background by a symbol of the fur trade: one Indian is handing a beaver to another. The Dutch emphasized the importance of the trade on which they hoped, in vain, to build an empire in North America.

The chief legacy of the Dutch was the well-established fur trade centered on Albany, and amicable relations with the Iroquois. The English concluded their first Indian treaty in the year they took over New York. Albany was by this time at the intersection of two of the most important lines of communication in North America. To the north ran the route through the Hudson and Lake Champlain to Canada and to the west stretched the path to the Great Lakes and the Mississippi Valley through the Mohawk Valley. Albany was the base from which expeditions and individuals set off into the nearer and farther wilderness. Its traders, however, in order to guard their monopoly, prevented their private competitors, explorers and settlers, from travelling west for fear of upsetting the Iroquois and the source of fur; up to 1712 Schenectady was still the most western township in New York. In many ways the policy followed by Albany was short-sighted. Greater encouragement to the western tribes and the *coureurs de bois* to bring their furs directly to Albany could have radically undermined French influence on the continent. Certainly the latter were worried about the strength and influence of the Albany fur trade. La Salle's plans for the exploration and settlement of the west and the establishment of Fort Frontenac on the northeast shore of Lake Ontario in 1673 were prompted partly by the fear that the English would rob the French of the Canadian fur trade. The 1680s brought an intensification of Anglo-French rivalry in trade which became part of the wider struggle between the two powers. Late in the decade Governor Frontenac returned to America, determined to remove the Anglo-Iroquois threat and to conquer New York. Combined raiding parties of Indians, *coureurs de bois* and French soldiers attacked outlying settlements. They descended on Schenectady in 1690, almost destroying the settlement and causing the survivors to flee to Albany and down the Hudson. As so often, expansion was influenced by politics, the frontier moved forwards and then retreated for a time, and it became increasingly clear that New York would have to adopt a more positive attitude to the west.

Since 1675 New York had been governed in the main by men with wide vision who comprehended the importance of trying to control the west. Governor Thomas Dongan encouraged the distant tribes to bring their furs directly to Albany. Earlier, Governor Andros had sent out messengers to the Iroquois to request their presence at conferences and had even gone to their castles himself in 1675. Dongan extended this practice to the more western tribes and the office of interpreter was gradually institutionalized. In 1682 there is first mention of a regular interpreter, Akus Cornelius. Others included a woman, Hilletie van Olinda, who was half Indian, and Arnout Viele who was present at every important Indian transaction between 1682 and 1692. Viele travelled extensively in the west, often for long periods, observing the Indians, but unfortunately has left no record of his journeys. There are only occasional references in the colonial records. His farthest trip was in 1692-4 as an independent trader. He left Albany with some Delaware and Shawnee Indians, went south to New Jersey and west to the Susquehanna, down the Ohio and explored as far west as the Wabash. He traded with the Miami Indians, attempted to enlist them on the side of the British, and spent some time in the country of the western Shawnee between the Cumberland and the Ohio Rivers. He eventually arrived back at Albany in the summer of 1694.[12] Viele penetrated farther inland than any New Yorker up to that time.

From 1684 Governor Dongan also began to issue passes for traders to visit the far western tribes. They reached the heart of the Great Lakes area, exchanging goods with the Huron and Ottawa and other distant Indians. Even before this, in 1683, Le Febvre de la Barre, governor of New France, wrote that the English had hired a great number of French deserters to show them the way to the Ottawa country.[13] In 1685 Joannes Roseboom, an Albany trader, led a party as far as Michilimackinac (Mackinac at the junction of Lakes Huron and Michigan). Dongan was delighted with this success and included a short account of the expedition in a report of 1687: '. . . last year [1685] some of our people went a trading among the farr Indians called the Ottawais, inhabiting about three months journey to the West and N.W. of Albany from whence they brought a good many beavers'.[14] The following year more elaborate plans were made. Two parties were sent west; the first led by Roseboom left Albany in September to spend the winter in the Seneca country. The second, commanded by Captain Patrick McGregory, was to leave in the spring, catch up with Roseboom and together they would journey to the Ottawas. Unfortunately they were captured by the French who would not allow such adventurous trading by the English in an area which they had explored and dominated for the past fifty years.[15]

The policy of Dongan was continued by Governor Bellomont (1698-1701) who took up many proposals from the Secretary for Indian Affairs, Robert Livingstone. He recruited a company of *boschloopers*, independent fur traders and the Dutch equivalent of the *coureurs de bois*, to extend English influence in the west as well as licensing traders. Among these was Samuel York who had been taken prisoner by the French at Casco Bay in 1690. He was carried to Canada and lived there until his escape in 1700. He reported to Bellomont:

'I have been about three years ar severall times in the Ottowawas country ahunting with the French, in which country they [the French] had two palisado'd forts. There is excellent hunting there for beaver and all sorts of wild beasts as Deer Moose, &c. The

88 Benjamin Furley. Map of Pennsylvania and New Jersey, c. 1700. *British Museum, London, Add. Ms. 5414, Roll 28.*
This map was probably drawn around 1700 and certainly after the settlement of Philadelphia, but it does not give much detail which would suggest that the author had any first-hand knowledge of the country to the west, which is at the top of the page.

Pennſylvania
Philadelphia
Lacus
NEW JERSEY
STATEN ISLAND
Part of Long Island
New York
Hudsons River

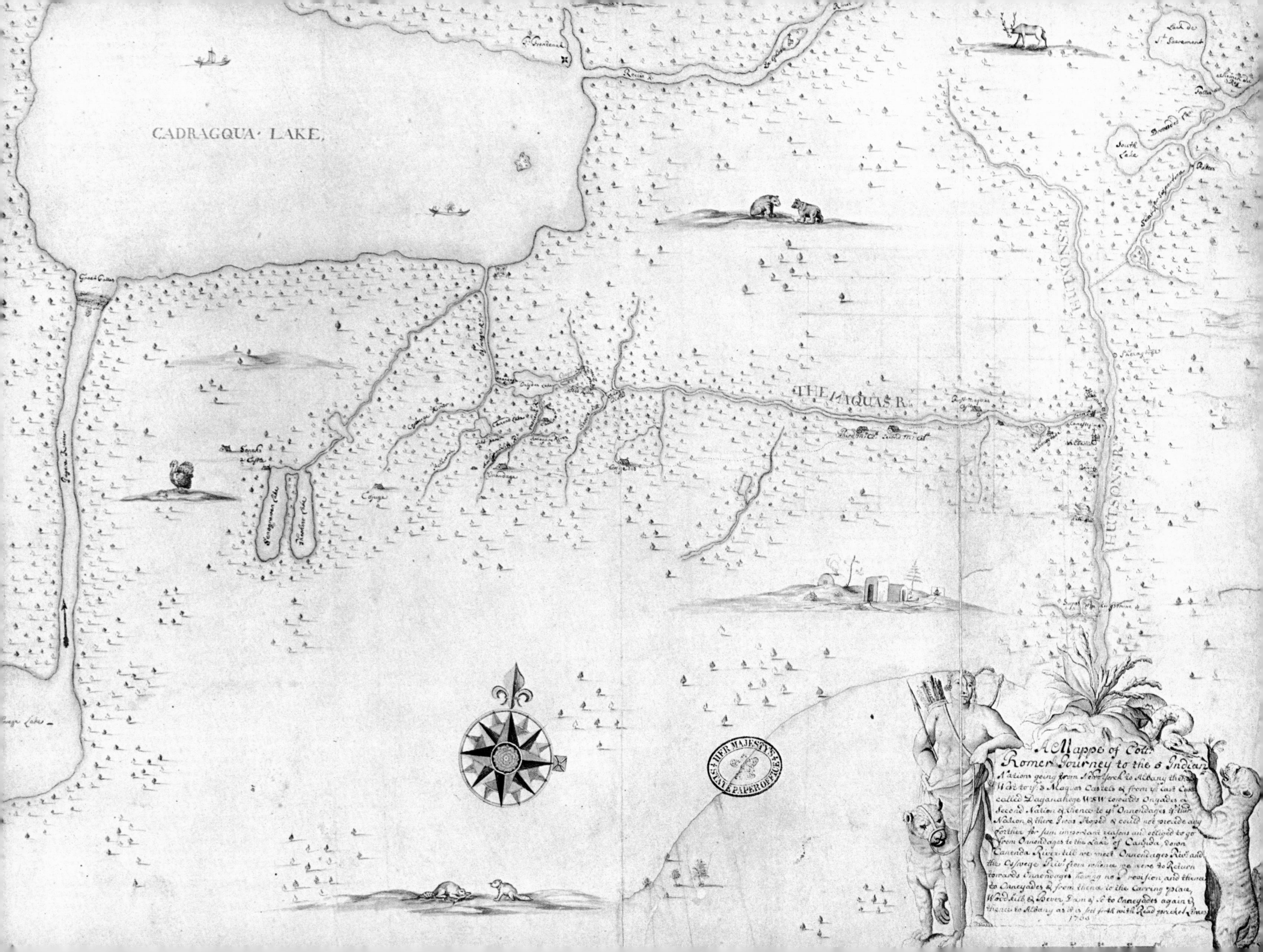
A Mappe of Coll.
Romers Journey to the 5 Indian
Nations going from New-York to Albany thence
West to ye 3 Maquas Castels & from ye last Castle
called Daganahoge W.S.W. towards Onyades ye
Second Nation & thence to ye Onnondages ye third
Nation, & there I was stoped & could not procede any
further for sum important reasons and obliged to go
from Onnondages to the Lake of Canada, down
Canenda River till we meet Onnondages River and
the Oswege River from whence we were to Return
towards Onnondages having no Provision, and thence
to Onneyades & from thence to the Carring place,
Woodkill & Bever Dam & c to Onneyades again &
thence to Albany as it is sett forth with Read pricked Lines
1700
CADRAGQUA LAKE
THE MAQUAS R.
HUTSONS R.
HUTSONS R.
South Lake
HER MAJESTY'S STATE PAPER OFFICE

Ottowawas are a very numerous people, their country very fine and pleasant affording great plains very fruitful and well water'd. I have gone round a Lake in the Ottowawas country, called by the French Le Lac des Hurons which is 400 leagues in circumferance upon the sides of which Lake live severall Nations, vizt the Chusturios, the Ochipoy, Kescacons, Towecenegos, the Hurons &^{c}. I have been also round another Lake called the Meshigans, which is about 300 leagues round, on the sides whereof live severall Nations vizt Les Puants, Les Sachi, Puotwatemi, Les Miami.'[16]

He also confirmed Indian reports that the Ottawas were dissatisfied with the French and they and the *coureurs de bois* were eager to make contact with Albany because they considered that the goods supplied by the British in exchange for furs were more varied and of a better quality than those of the French. Bellomont accepted York's offer to lead a party of traders and Indians to the west. However they were stopped in Onondago country, west of Lake Owasco, by the Iroquois who declared that it was too dangerous to continue since they were at war with the far Indians. They 'bade these men return to Albany unless they meant to be knocked on the head by the French or Indians'.[17] Whilst at the Onondago's Castle, York encountered a party of three men sent out by Governor Bellomont. Vital to Dongan's plans for securing the English frontier against the French, had been the erection of a line of forts in the west and Bellomont took up the idea, hoping to be able to construct an English fort and trading post at Detroit. But the area had yet to be explored properly and the party at Onondago were to select a suitable site. One of the three, Colonel Wolfgang Römer, had the additional task of making a survey of the land between Albany and the Seneca lands (the Western Finger Lakes). He was to take particular notes of the carrying places between rivers and lakes. The other two, Hendrick Hansen and Major Peter van Brugh, kept a journal of the trip which illustrates perfectly the problems encountered in any dealings with the Indians. Their friendship and cooperation were essential on the expedition for the selection of a site and the construction of a fort and such help was not forthcoming. The Five Nations were at the time negotiating with the French and described in great detail their treatment in Canada. After delays at Onondago Castle while trying to procure canoes and a guide necessary for any further exploration between Lake Oneida and Lake Ontario, the party eventually reached the Lake of Canada (Lake Ontario) but could not find a suitable site there, although one was found close to Lake Oneida (see selection 4). Meanwhile Römer made a survey and prepared a map (plate 89). Bellomont used his findings as a basis for a report to the Board of Trade in London on the state of the frontier defenses. Money was needed for repairs and for new building but little was forthcoming. Although traders continued to go to Lake Ontario and beyond, there was, as yet, no consistent policy towards the west.

3 Pennsylvania and the push west to 1776

From the beginning William Penn was determined to attract as many useful settlers to Pennsylvania as possible. To achieve this he hired Thomas Holme as surveyor general to draw up elaborate plans for the distribution of the land as well as maps of the area. Penn himself wrote numerous promotional tracts to stimulate immigration. He also encouraged good relations with the Indians by supervising the fair and voluntary purchase of their lands, and his description of the local natives shows a sympathetic attitude (see selection 5). His benevolent approach succeeded, the Indians treating him with respect. Equally satisfying were the increasing numbers of settlers who arrived not only from Britain but also from Germany and Switzerland. Expansion along the Delaware and Schuylkill was swift. Almost as soon as he arrived in the colony, Penn became interested in the Valley of the Susquehanna, first explored by a Frenchman, Etienne Brûlé, in 1616.[18] He encouraged traders to go west and in 1683 dispatched two men, James Graham and William Haig, to Albany to investigate the possibilities of purchasing land on the Upper Susquehanna from the Iroquois in order to attract furs. By 1688-9 a map drawn by Benjamin Chambers showed a path leading from the Delaware to the Susquehanna.[19] These activities aroused the suspicion of the other colonies, notably New York. In 1691 the governor and council, in an address to the King, complained of the claims of Penn to the Susquehanna and his attempts to draw the fur trade to Pennsylvania. They maintained that the area had belonged to New York for some time.[20] Undoubtedly a significant quantity of peltry was carried into Pennsylvania, although the Iroquois refused to sell any land.

The region to the west of Pennsylvania, from the Susquehanna to the Maumee and Wabash Rivers, had largely been ignored by the French, and, in the seventeenth century, supported very few Indians. It was through this area that Arnout Viele, interpreter, travelled in 1692-4. By the early eighteenth century, however, several tribes such as the Delawares were retreating into the region, away from the expanding white settlements. Traders followed the Indians, establishing trails across the Susquehanna and the mountains which separated that valley from the Ohio, a journey of about fourteen days through country which was largely forested and inhabited by wolves, panthers and various species of large birds, such as eagles and black ravens. James le Tort, who set up stores on the Susquehanna, was one of the first traders to reach the Ohio by 1727. He traded with the Mingoes, Delawares, Shawnees, Wyandots (Hurons) and as early as 1728 was preparing for an expedition to the country of the Miamis on the southern shore of Lake Michigan. At the same

89 Römer. 'A Mappe of Coll. Romer his Journey to the 5 Indian Nations going from New Yorck to Albany', 1700. *Public Record Office, London, CO 700, New York, 13A.*
During his visit to the lands of the Onondago Indians in 1700, Römer surveyed the lands between Albany and the Western Finger Lakes. This resulting map shows the Mohawk ('Maquas') from its junction with the Hudson west to the territory of the Oneida Indians. Römer's most detailed work was around Lake Oneida where he indicates the settlements of the Oneidas ('Onyedes'), Onondagos ('Onondage'), Cayugas ('Cajuge') and Senecas ('Seneks 2 castle'). Afterwards he explored west from Lake Oneida along the Oswega to Lake Ontario ('Cadragqua') to search for a suitable site for a fort.

90 Thomas Holme. A Portraiture of the City of Philadelphia in the Province of Pennsylvania in America, 1682, issued 1683. *New York Public Library.*
This plan, by the surveyor general of Pennsylvania, was made the basis on which land was to be allotted within the city. Penn intended to make grants here as a bonus to purchasers of land elsewhere. He envisaged an orderly and spacious city, with streets twice the width of any in London. He also made provision for five open spaces and squares for gardens.

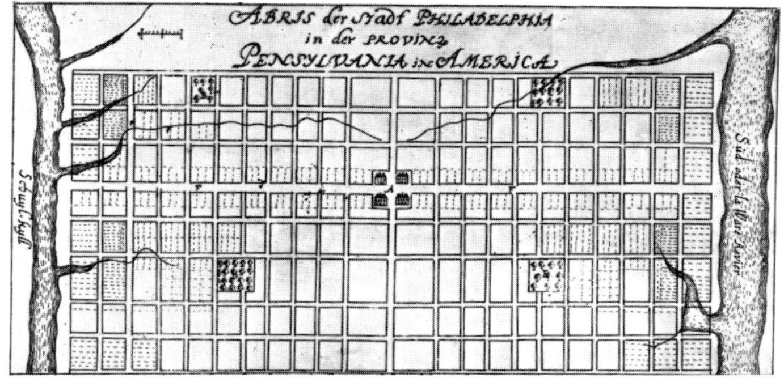

90

91

92

91-2 Thomas Pownall, an Englishman who served as governor of Massachusetts in the mid-eighteenth century, showed a great interest in the geography of America. He went on several tours of the northern colonies, writing about and sketching what he saw. He wrote *A topographical description . . . of North America*, 1776.
The sketches were later painted by Paul Sandby, engraved and published in Britain.

91 View of Bethlehem, the Great Moravian Settlement in the Province of Pennsylvania, London, 1761.
In 1739 the German Moravian immigrants were granted land at the junction of the Delaware and Lehigh Rivers in western Pennsylvania. Here they built the towns of Nazareth and Bethlehem. The Moravians were a tightly built religious community with all the goods and even the buildings owned by the church. Their towns became flourishing centers of agriculture and industry in the wilderness.

92 View of the Great Cahoes Falls on the Mohawk River, London, 1761.
The Falls are situated just above the mouth of the Mohawk River.
They greatly impressed the earliest travellers. Pownall described the sound of the waters 'like the roar of a storm at sea heard from the land in the dead of night' (*A topographical description*, p. 35). Because of the falls, westbound travellers were forced to enter the river by means of an overland route from Albany rather than by taking a boat from its mouth.

time competitors from the colonies to the south, notably Virginia, were exploring the same area.[21] By 1750 the trading frontier was near to the Wabash and Miami Rivers. The Miami or Twightwee Indians welcomed traders such as George Croghan, operating from Pennsylvania, at the town of Pickawillany some 100 miles up the Miami River and 500 miles west of Philadelphia. It has been estimated that by the mid eighteenth century there were about 300 traders in the Ohio country, some nearly as far north as Lake Erie. Little record of what they found was registered but stories from expeditions must have been passed round and stimulated followers, and their activities opened up the region for others.

Both diplomats and missionaries were sent out amongst the Indians to cultivate their friendship. Perhaps the best known of the former was Conrad Weiser who had moved south from New York along with other Palatine Germans. His knowledge of Indian languages gained him a job as interpreter in 1731. Five years later he travelled north along the Susquehanna to the Onondago's Castle near Syracuse and in 1748 led the first embassy to the Indians beyond the Alleghenies. Missionary activity among the Indians was undertaken mainly by the Moravians. It was from Bethlehem, Pennsylvania, the town they built on land granted in 1739, that Christian Post set out northwest to the Wyoming Valley in 1758-9, where he also acted as a diplomat. Most of these emissaries into the far country left accounts of their experiences which included descriptions of the land and the natives. After his first expedition of 1758 to the Delaware and Shawanee Indians on the Ohio, near Fort Duquesne, Post commented on the Indian character:

'There is not a prouder, or more high minded people, in themselves than the Indians. They think themselves the wisest and prudentest men in the world; and that they can over-power both the *French* and the *English* when they please. The white people are, in their eyes, nothing at all. They say, that through their conjuring craft they can do what they please, and nothing can withstand them. In their way of fighting they have this method, to see that they first shoot the officers and commanders: and then, they say, we shall be sure to have them. They also say, that if their conjurers run through the middle of our people, no bullet can hurt them.'[22]

Weiser's picture of the Susquehanna and the Endless Mountains at the time of his winter journey to Onondago in 1737 is the first real account of the district that has been preserved.

Another description of the area was made by John Bartram, a man who looked at America with an eye different from most. Throughout the colonial period scientists were corresponding with their counterparts in England and Bartram, of Pennsylvania, sent specimens of North American flora and fauna across the Atlantic, where they found their way into the collections of individuals like Sir Hans Sloane.[23] His collecting trips took him north to the Falls of the Mohawk and later to Florida and Carolina. In 1743 he travelled to the Onondago country, accompanied by Conrad Weiser and the cartographer Lewis Evans. They kept journals and Evans drew a map (plate 93). Bartram's account is the liveliest and the most complete. Leaving the Schuylkill River on 3 May, they followed the Swatara Creek through the Blue Mountains then west to the Susquehanna and spent a few days at the important Indian town of Shamokin (Sunbury) at the forks of the Susquehanna. They finally reached Onondago on 21 July. Whilst Weiser engaged in the negotiations with the Indians, Bartram made a trip to Fort Oswego. The return journey followed the same route. Bartram described several Indian customs in a very human and amusing style and discussed the flora and fauna of the area from the point of view of a naturalist (see selection 6).

At the same time as the traders and explorers were moving west, immigrants were settling farther inland and up into the

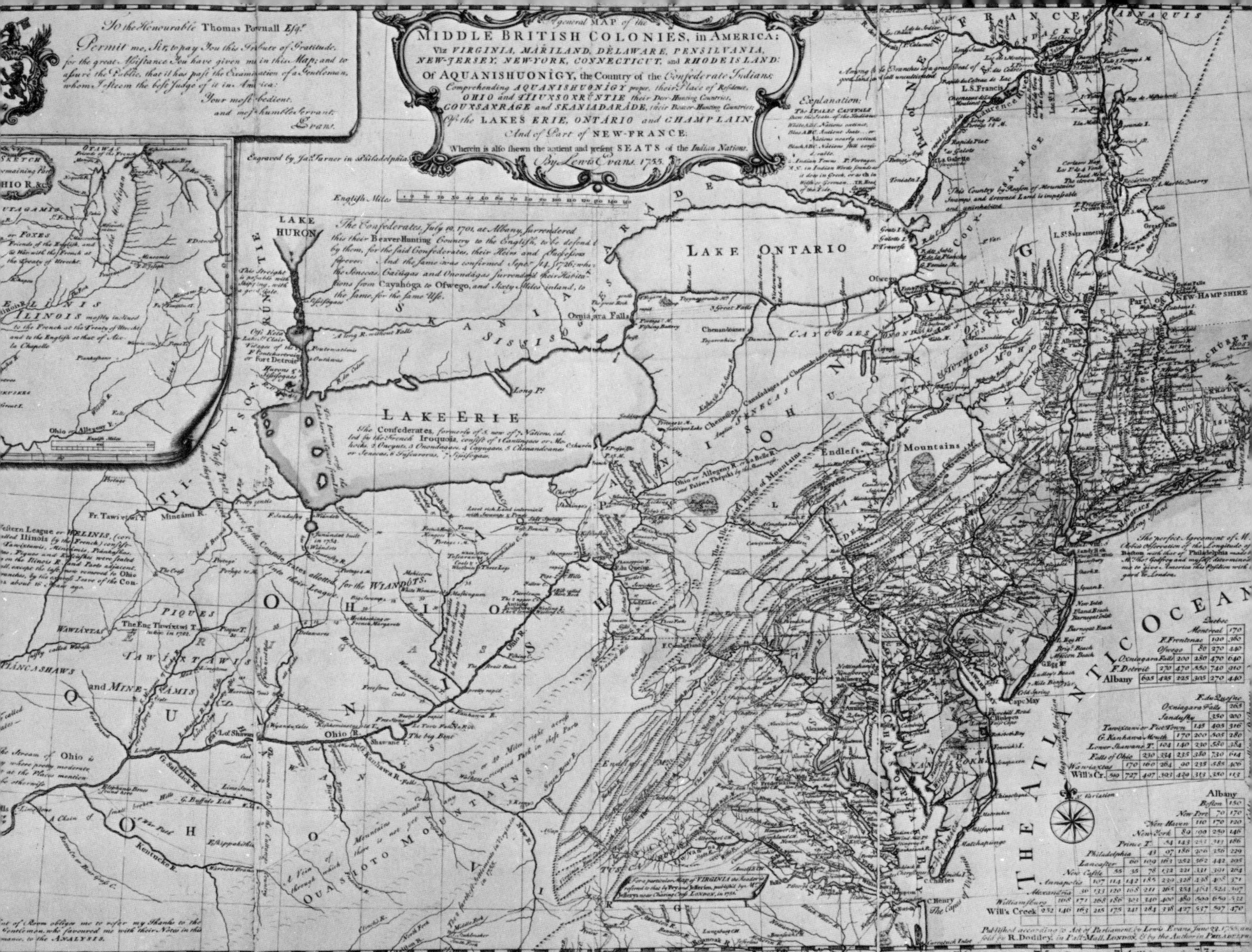

93

93 Lewis Evans. 'A general map of the Middle British Colonies, in America', 1755. *British Museum, London.*
One of the few great maps of the colonial period, Evans's work was the product of extensive geographical, scientific and political study and insight. In 1750 Evans, who had been north to Onondago with John Bartram in 1743, was commissioned by the assembly of Pennsylvania to produce a map of the province. He took four years to draw up the surveys, the work being done in secret because of French interest in the region. The map was published in 1755 together with an analysis written by Evans in which he described the face of the country in considerable detail and accuracy. In this he stressed the need for permanent settlements in the border areas rather than posts established by itinerant traders. The map itself has been classed as being far superior to the other English maps of the period, and was long used as an authority for settling boundary disputes. The most striking contribution to cartography is found in the region of the Ohio, the delineation of which was based on information gained by George Croghan in his various expeditions to the west.

Alleghenies and Pennsylvania and New York. Excited by the activities of the Pennsylvania traders, New York once more began to take an active interest in the west. Sir William Johnson, superintendent of Indian Affairs, New York, established a post at Oghwaga on the Susquehanna in 1740 from which agents were sent out along the network of trails, meeting the Indians in their own country. At the same time there was more activity west of the post at Oswego. By 1750 Albany had ceased to have influence over trade and expansion. In New England men such as John Sargeant and David Brainerd left their missions near Stockbridge, Massachusetts, to visit the settlements of the Oneidas and other Indians, along the Susquehanna Valley. Their journals omit descriptions of the land through which they travelled but include records of the Indians and their customs. In 1745 Brainerd visited the Delawares who lived at Juniata on the Susquehanna near Sunbury. He noted that they were probably the most ungodly of all the tribes he had encountered and described the antics of a 'conjurer' who can be compared with John Bartram's Indian 'hobgoblin': 'He made his appearance in his pontifical garb, which was a coat of bears skins, dressed with the hair on, and hanging down to his toes, a pair of bearskin stockings, and a great wooden face, painted the one half black, and the other tawny, about the colour of an Indian's skin, with an extravagant mouth, cut very much awry; the face fastened to a bear-skin cap, which was drawn over his head.'[24]

However, a far greater threat than the Indians served to unite the colonies. The French kept a watchful eye on English westward expansion into areas which they had claimed many decades before. To protect their interest, the French constructed a line of forts in the back country stretching from Crown Point on Lake Champlain to Fort Duquesne on the site of Pittsburg. The declaration of war in Europe in 1744 was the signal for renewed hostilities which were virtually continuous until the French were defeated in 1760. The war had two main effects on expansion and exploration. First the frontier retreated as the settlers turned east for greater pro-

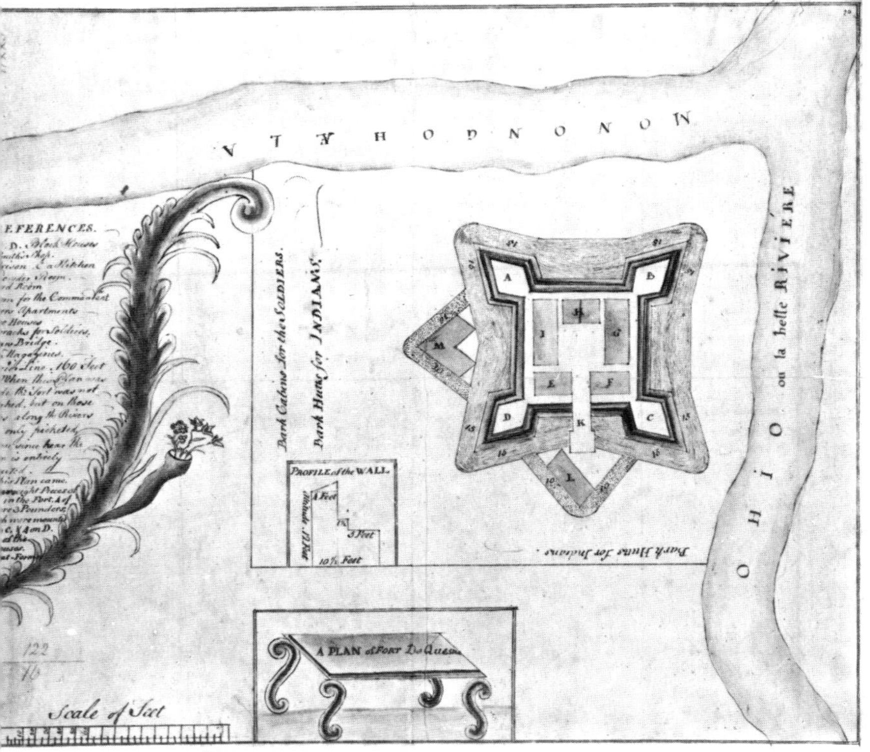

94

95 James Hunter. 'A View of Ticonderoga from a Point on the North Shore of Lake Champlain', 1777. *British Museum, London.*
Ticonderoga fort, on the far side of the lake, was built by the French in 1755 between Lake George and Lake Champlain in New York. It saw some of the bloodiest action in the French and Indian War. An attack of the British in July 1758 was repulsed by the French, leading to the disgrace and replacement of General Abercromby, the British commander. Although the fort fell to General Amherst the following year, the French destroyed most of it in their retreat. It was held by the British until 1775 when it was captured by the colonists. The British regained it without a fight in 1777 but the Americans later retook it by surprise. It has now been restored, following the old French plan, and houses a museum.

96 'The Country between Crown Point and Albany being the Great Pass from the English to the French Settlements in North America', 1758. *British Museum, London, Maps 69917(8).*
Although the area depicted in this anonymously drawn map was the most convenient route from the British areas to the St Lawrence, it was jealously guarded by the French. In 1731 they constructed a fort at Crown Point on the shore of Lake Champlain from which attacks could be launched on the country behind New England and New York. Thus the British regarded the region as a wilderness until the French vacated the forts in 1758 and explorers and settlers moved in from the south and east.

97 Cyprian Southack. 'The Harbour and Islands of Canso, Part of the Boundaries of Nova Scotia', 1720. *Public Record Office, London, CO 700, Nova Scotia 6.*
An early attempt at a survey of the coast of North America. Its main purpose appears to have been chiefly to point out the hazards to shipping, both merchant vessels and fishing fleets, in an area economically dependent on the sea. It looks primitive when compared with Des Barres's chart of the same area, drawn up fifty years later (plate 98).

95

tection and outlying trading posts, such as Pickawillany, were either destroyed by the French or deserted. At the same time, war was a spur to expansion. Exploration became a military necessity, instead of being left in the hands of fur and other traders and missionaries. Army expeditions were official, organized and meant that soldiers like Major Robert Rogers gained an almost unrivalled knowledge of conditions

94 'A plan of Fort DeQuesne', 1758; sketched prior to its destruction by the French in the same year. *British Museum, London.*
British activity in Western Pennsylvania and beyond aroused French interest in a region which they hitherto ignored. In 1754 a strong French force expelled a party of British from the strategically important Forks of the Ohio and constructed Fort Duquesne, named after the governor of New France. The following year an English party under General Braddock attempted to remove the French but suffered a shattering defeat ten miles from the fort. However, in 1758 a force led by General John Forbes marched towards the Forks of the Ohio but the French deserted the fort and destroyed it before the British arrived. Fort Pitt, later Pittsburg, was built on the same site. See also plates 172, 173.

96

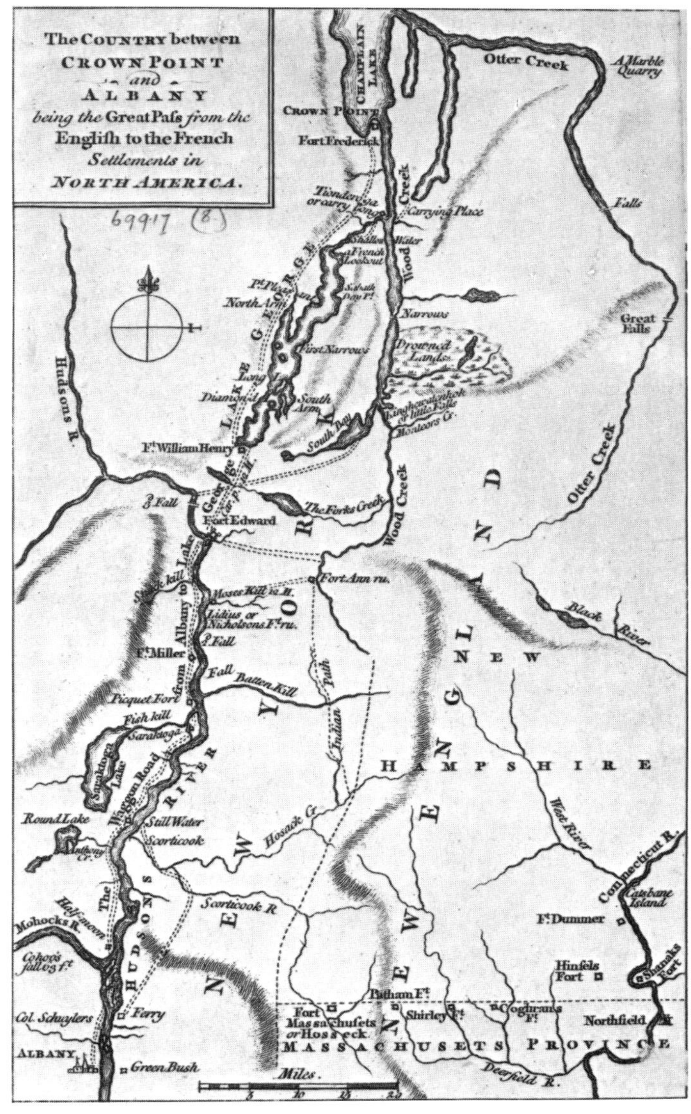

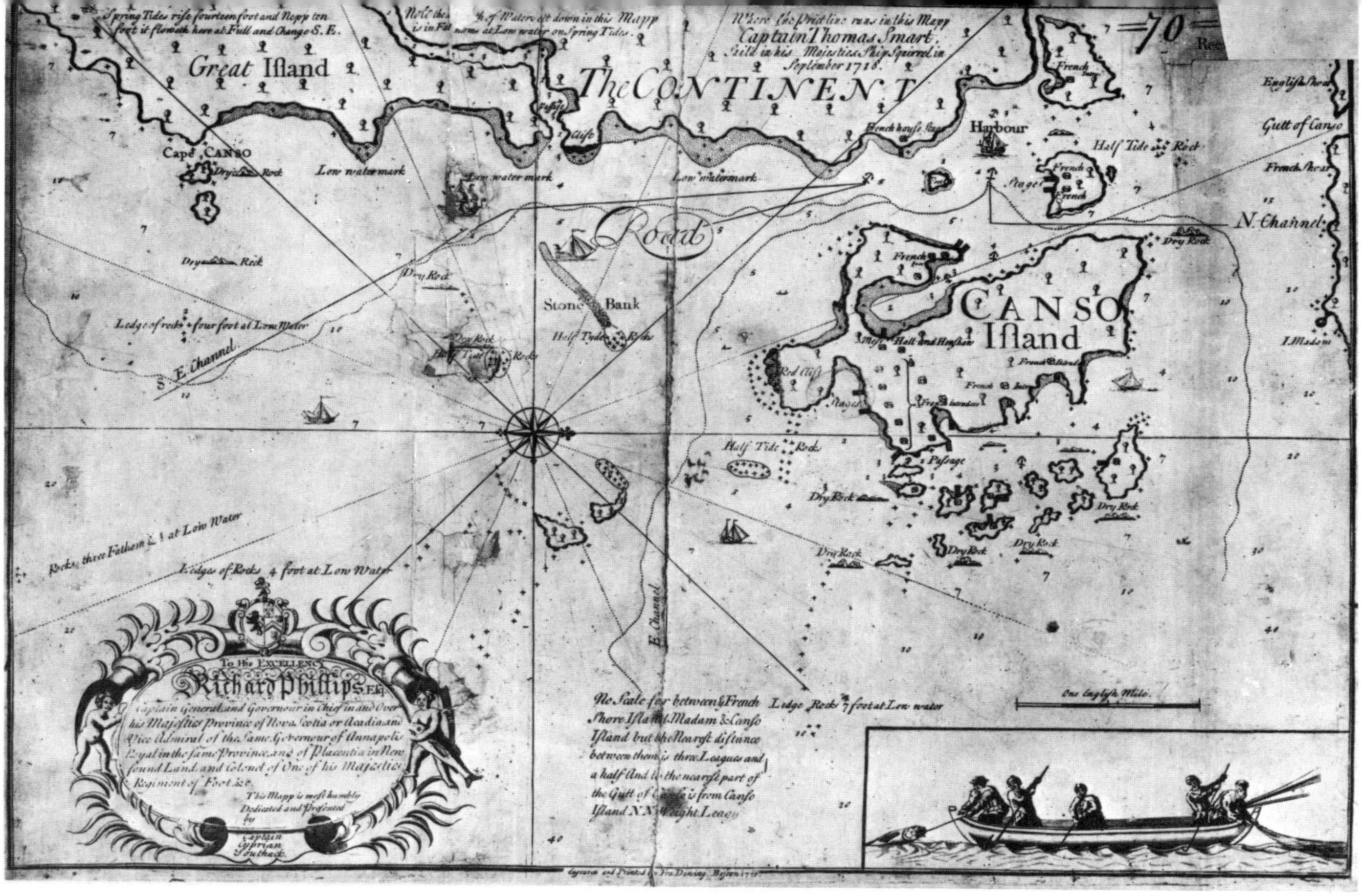

97

in the west. There was an increase in the number of diplomatic parties visiting the Indians, whose friendship was also cultivated by traders and missionaries.

Others explored less willingly. As in earlier wars, the Indians descended on outlying settlements and took captives for ransom. Several, following the example of Mary Rowlandson, wrote narratives of their adventures which included descriptions of their captors and the country through which they were escorted. Peter Williamson, living near the forks of the Delaware in Berkshire County, Pennsylvania, was taken prisoner by Delaware and Shawanee Indians in the autumn of 1754. He was carried into the Appalachians and beyond, to the winter quarters of the Indians. During his cold, winter sojourn, he observed their appearance and customs of dress:

'That they in general, wear a white blanket, which in War-time they paint with various Figures; but particularly the Leaves of Trees, in order to deceive their Enemies when in the Woods. Their Mogganes are made of Deer Skins, and the best sort have them bound round the Edges with little Beads and Ribbands on their Legs they wear Peices of blue Cloth for Stockings, something like Soldiers Spatter-dashes; they esteem them very easy to run in[.] Breeches they never wear, but instead thereof, two Peices of Linen, one before and another behind. The better Sort have Shirts of the finest Linen they can get, and to these some wear Ruffles; but these they never put on till they have painted them of various Colours, which they get from the Pecone Root, and Bark of Trees, and never pull them off to Wash, but wear them, till they fall in Peices.'[25]

By 1760 British forces were in control of the country from Cape Breton to the Upper Mississippi but, although the French threat had been removed, there were still barriers to free movement west. One of these was the rebellion of the Illinois led by Pontiac. For years the natives had been accumulating grievances against the malpractice of the British traders and land speculators and Pontiac managed to channel this discontent into a concerted effort. Fort Detroit and Fort Pitt were attacked in May 1763 and one by one the western forts were taken, causing a panic among the frontier settlers. Eventually Indian resistance was crushed by Colonel Bouquet at Bushy

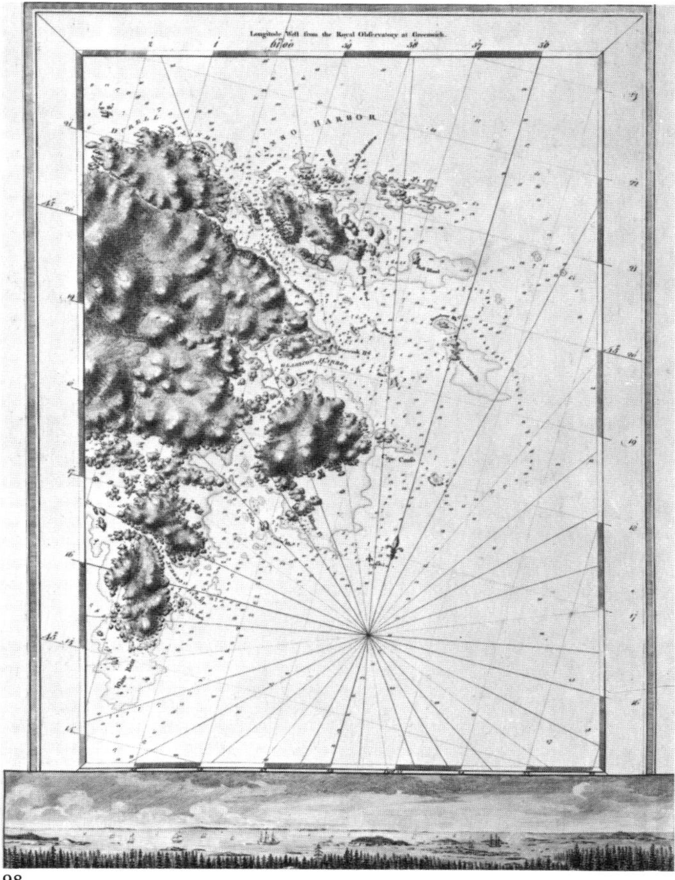

98

98 Des Barres. 'Canso Harbor, Port George, Glasgow Harbor and a view', plate 28 from the *Atlantic Neptune*.
One of many maps made as a result of Joseph des Barres's surveys between 1763 and 1773. Less decorative than Southack's earlier map (plate 97), it is far more accurate and of much greater value to the mariner.

99

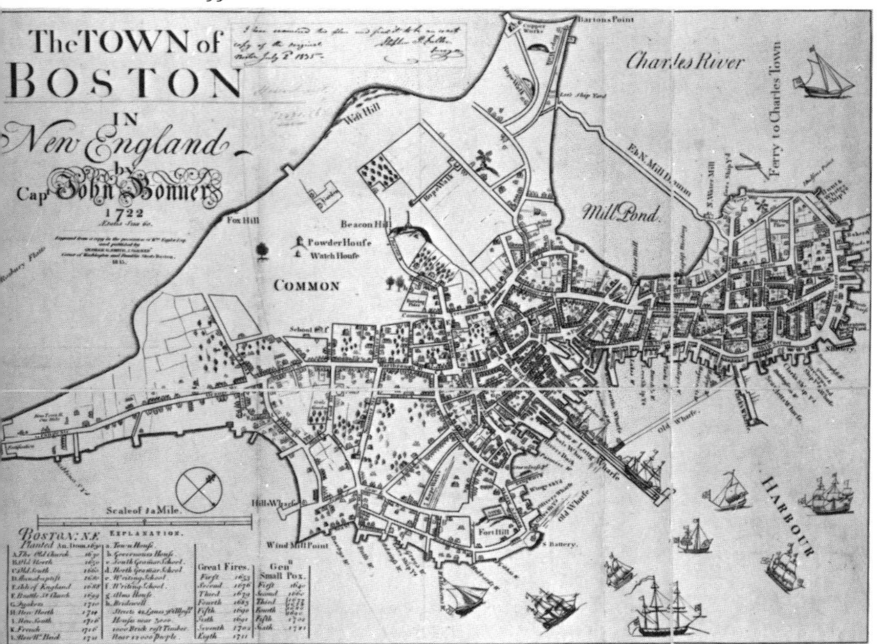

99 'The Town of Boston in New England', by John Bonner, 1722. *British Museum, London.*
Although the area of exploration had moved much farther west by 1722, Bonner's plan illustrates a secondary stage of exploration: the settlement and development of an area. It is the earliest and most important plan of the town, giving information found nowhere else.

Run west of the Ohio but peace was not concluded until 1765 when George Croghan went into the Illinois country and negotiated with Pontiac. Croghan had been one of the most active traders and diplomats in the west for over twenty years. He learned various Indian dialects and spent several months of each year exchanging goods with the tribes between the Ohio region and Lake Erie, returning with furs to his storehouses in the Ohio country. In 1750-1 he accompanied Christopher Gist to the towns of the Twightwees on the Miami River.[26] Because of his knowledge of the Indians and their country, he was the obvious choice to lead an embassy to Pontiac. Leaving Fort Pitt on 15 May 1765, he was joined by Seneca, Delaware and Shawnee Indians, and together they proceeded down the Ohio River, arriving at the mouth of the Scioto River on 23 May. After negotiating with the Indians there, he moved down the Ohio and into a region to which few Englishmen had ventured and about which even fewer had written. Near the mouth of the Wabash the party was attacked by Illinois, several members were killed, and Croghan himself 'got the stroke of a hatchett on the Head, but my Scull being pretty thick the hatchett wou'd not enter, so you may see a thick Scull is of service on some occasions'.[27] The prisoners were then force marched across country to Port Vincennes, a French post on the Wabash, and to the Indian settlement of Ouitenon. Croghan describes in some detail the country they passed through. At the settlement the natives, fearing reprisals from the Iroquois, released the survivors and Croghan was free to set out for the Illinois River. En route he met Pontiac and peace was concluded. There was now no cause to go farther west and Croghan headed back east by way of Detroit and Ontario (see selection 7). Because of Croghan's expedition in 1765 and another the following year the Illinois country was now clear for English occupation even though it might still be a largely unknown and perhaps not very comfortable area.

The other barrier to free westward movement after 1763 was constructed by the attitude of the British government. There were two opposing views on expansion in America itself. The traders, supported by mercantilists, wished the west to become a permanent Indian reservation, a source of supply for goods and the raw materials for industry. They were against expansion of settlement because it disturbed the Indian and disrupted trade, whereas the land speculators wanted to open up the west for settlement. Representatives of both opinions lobbied the government in England and official policy vacillated between complete closure of the west, with strict control over the fur trade, and one of gradual expansion. Despite this uncertainty the flow of population into the west continued. In New York there was some movement into the area around Lake George and Lake Champlain. New Englanders began to penetrate Nova Scotia, along the coast of Maine and up the Kennebec River. The greatest expansion was into the Susquehanna region, both from New York and from the middle colonies. Land speculation was rife and grandiose plans were formulated for the creation of new colonies in the west. Governor Franklin of New Jersey and Sir William Johnson planned a colony in the Illinois region and asked for a grant of 63,000,000 acres from Lake Erie to the Mississippi. Many such expansionist schemes were rejected by a more cautious British government. At the same time trading companies, including Baynton, Wharton and Morgan in which George Croghan was prominent, were winning and losing fortunes in trade to the west. They established posts, sometimes through agents, as far west as Lake Winnipeg and the Sioux lands beyond the Mississippi.

The removal of the French and Indian threat also encouraged exploration of the newly acquired regions. The longest journey in the period between 1763 and 1775 was undertaken by Jonathan Carver.

100

100 The Indians talking to Colonel Bouquet in 1764, from William Smith, *An historical account of the expedition against the Ohio Indians*, 1766.
Expansion to the west after the defeat of the French in 1763 was halted temporarily by an Indian revolt of the same year led by Pontiac. The Indians terrorized the frontier settlements, taking many captives. Eventually resistance was crushed by Colonel Bouquet at Bushy Run in 1764.

101

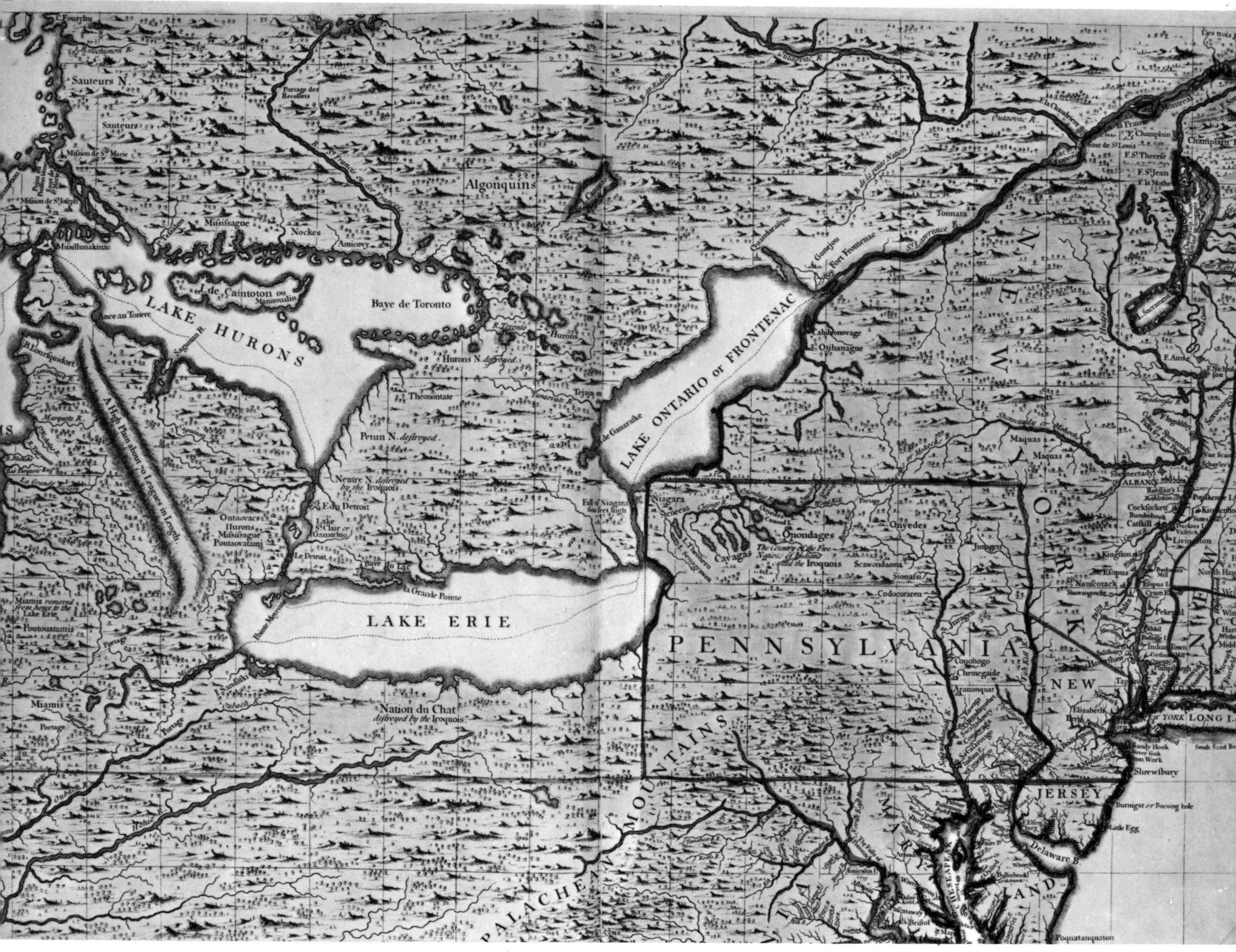

101 Henry Popple. Map of the Northern Colonies, 1733, map no. 6 from *The British Empire in America. British Museum, London.*
This detailed map illustrates the growth of knowledge about the interior of northeast America by the first third of the eighteenth century. There is much information given of places and Indians in the areas of the Great Lakes, as a result of trading expeditions from New York. It still contains many geographical inaccuracies which do not appear on French maps of the same period, errors such as the southwest-northeast alignment of Lake Ontario. In 1733 the British were still some way behind the French in their knowledge of the interior.

Historians are sceptical that he was the author of the journal that was published after his journey. However there is no evidence to suggest that he did not travel to the west of the Great Lakes, even if he did not visit all the areas he describes. Carver was probably the source rather than the author of the narrative.[28] A captain in the army, he was employed by Major Robert Rogers to explore west of the post of Michilimackinac (Mackinac) at a fee of eight shillings a day plus expenses. Leaving Boston, he arrived at Mackinac on 6 September 1766, and from there, accompanied by traders and Indians, went to Green Bay on the western side of Lake Michigan, down the Fox River to the carrying place that linked it with the Wisconsin River. He reached the Mississippi by way of the Wisconsin on 15 October, turned north along the river, describing the country and, as he passed, an Indian burial cave and the Falls of St Anthony (see plate 108). He went as far north as the St Francis River. Around the site of St Paul, he mused on the possibility of constructing a waterway between there and New York by way of the Great Lakes. He alleges he spent the winter with the Indians on the Ste Croix River, although this claim is open to doubt.[29] Whether or not he spent the winter with the Indians, he probably returned to Mackinac by way of the Chippeway River and then across country to Lake Superior, which he rounded on the north side as far as the Falls of St Marie (see selection 8). Carver's account of the expedition, together with the maps he drew of the area, greatly increased knowledge of the mid-west. However this was still not as accurate as French understanding of the same region. Other trips were mooted, but all plans for exploration and expansion were interrupted by the Revolution, disputes over control of the west being one of the major factors that contributed to the outbreak of hostilities. The increased knowledge of the area bequeathed by early explorers was accompanied by problems which, it appeared to the colonists of 1775, could only be resolved by violence.

1
Expedition to the White Mountains, 1642

From the *Journal of John Winthrop*, Hartford, Conn., 1790

No original accounts have survived of early exploration by the English in northern New England in the 1640s. John Winthrop, recounting events in the first years of settlement, notes that there were two expeditions into the White Mountains (modern northern New Hampshire) in June 1642.

One Darby Field, an Irishman, living about Piscataquack, being accompanied with two Indians, went to the top of the white hill. He made his journey in 18 days. His relation at his return was, that it was about one hundred miles from Saco, that after 40 miles travel he did, for the most part, ascend, and within 12 miles of the top was neither tree nor grass, but low savins, which they went on top of sometimes, but a continual ascent upon rocks, on a ridge between two valleys filled with snow, out of which came two branches of Saco river, which met at the foot of a hill which was an Indian town of some 200 people. Some of them accompanied him within 8 miles of the top, but durst go no further, telling him that no Indian ever dared to go higher, and that he would die if he went. So they staid there till his return, and his two Indians took courage by his example and went with him. They went divers times through the thick clouds for a good space, and within 4 miles of the top they had no clouds, but very cold. By the way, among the rocks, there were two ponds, one a blackish water and the other reddish. The top of all was plain about 60 feet square. On the north side there was such a precipice, as they could scarce discern to the bottom. They had neither cloud nor wind on the top, and moderate heat. All the country above him seemed level, except here and there a hill rising above the rest, but far beneath them. He saw to the north a great water which he judged to be about 100 miles broad, but could see no land beyond it. The sea by Saco seemed as if it had been within 20 miles. He saw also a sea to the eastward, which he judged to be the gulf of Canada: he saw some great waters in parts to the westward, which he judged to be the great lake which Canada river comes out of. He found there much muscovy glass [mica], they could rive out pieces of 40 foot long and 7 or 8 broad. When he came back to the Indians, he found them drying themselves by the fire, for they had a great tempest of wind and rain. About a month after he went again with five or six in his company, then they had some wind on top, and some clouds above them which hid the sun. They brought some stones which they supposed had been diamonds, but they were most crystal . . .

Field's report on the country and the 'diamonds' encouraged others to travel in the area. Winthrop takes up the story.

Amongst others, Mr Gorge and Mr Vines, two of the magistrates of Sir Ferdinand Gorge his province, went thither about the end of the month. They went up Saco river in birch canoes, and that way, they found it 90 miles to Pegwagget [Pigwacket, now Fryeburg, Maine], an Indian town, but by land it is but 60. Upon Saco river, they found many thousand acres of rich meadow, but there are ten falls, which hinders boats etc. From the Indian town, they went up a hill (for the most part) about 30 miles in woody lands, then went about 7 or 8 miles upon shattered rocks, without tree or grass, very steep all the way. At the top is a plain about 3 or 4 miles over, all shattered stones, and upon that is another rock or spire, about a mile in height, and about an acre of ground at the top. At the top of the plain arise four great rivers, each of them so much water, at the first issue, as would drive a mill; Connecticut river from two heads, at the N.W. and S.W. which join in one about 60 miles off, Saco river on the S.E., Amascoggen which runs into Casco Bay at the N.E., and Kennebeck, at the N. by E. The mountain runs E. and W. 30 or 40 miles, but the peak is above the rest. They went and returned in 15 days.

Text used: James K. Hosmer (Ed.), Winthrop's Journal, *New York, 1906, vol. II, pp. 62-3, 85-6.*

2
Mary Rowlandson travels with the Indians, 1675-6

From *A Narrative of the Captivity and Restauration of Mrs. Mary Rowlandson*, Cambridge, Mass., 1682

During King Philip's War in New England, the Indians attacked several of the outlying villages, killing many of the inhabitants and taking prisoners who were carried round the country. When Lancaster was attacked in 1676, Mary Rowlandson was captured and travelled round the northern border of Massachusetts and in the New Hampshire area. The relation of her experiences was first published in 1682 and commanded more attention than any other contemporary publication in America. She recounts her travels with the Wampanoags and comments on their appearance and behavior.

On the tenth of February 1675 [1676], come the Indians with great numbers upon Lancaster: Their first coming was about sunrising; hearing the noise of some Guns, we looked out; several Houses were burning, and the Smoke ascending to Heaven. There were five persons taken in one house, the Father, and the Mother and a sucking Child, they knockt on the head; the other two they took and carried away alive. Their were two others, who, being out of their Garison upon some occasion were set upon; one was knockt on the head, the other escaped: Another their was who running along was

102-4 Three drawings by William Bartram. *Knowsley Hall, Prescott, Nos. 46, 117, 186.*
William Bartram was the son of the Pennsylvania naturalist, John Bartram. Although he is best known for his work on the flora and fauna of the southern colonies, his first work was done in his native colony. Before his trip to Georgia and Florida in 1765, he sent many drawings to Peter Collinson, the British naturalist. Forty of these have been collected in a volume, now in the collection of the Earl of Derby at Knowsley Hall near Liverpool. (See also plates 187-9 and others in Chapter 4.)

102 Iris. Several naturalists in America sent over seeds to their British colleagues. These were carefully cultivated and, if they flourished in the British climate, were gradually introduced into the gardens of others.

103 Composite drawing of an unnamed bird perched on a spray of swamp cornus and a sprig of *Galega*, a pink flowering plant. Bartram completed several of these composite drawings which were greatly valued by naturalists in Britain. They were eager to identify any new species of plant or animal which might be found in the American colonies, and it helped identification if the artist placed the fauna in their natural environment.

104 The great mud tortoise from Pennsylvania. According to the British naturalist and artist George Edwards, who corresponded with William Bartram and some of whose own drawings are reproduced in plates 291-3, this was a 'very fearsome' beast.

102

by Wm Bartram
Philadelphia
Flower'd in my Garden at Mill-Hill
May 1760 — P Collinson

103

Galega
Swamp Cornus femina

104

The great Mud Tortoise from
Pennsylvania
Called the Snaping Turtle
WB

T. 27.

Cornus mas &c.

Turdus minor &c.
The Mock-bird.

105a

58

Coluber fasciatus

Lilium &c.

Anguis &c.

105b

shot and wounded, and fell down; he begged of them his life, promising them Money (as they told me) but they would not hearken to him but knockt him in head, and stript him naked, and split open his Bowels. Another seeing many of the Indians about his Barn, ventured and went out, but was quickly shot down. There were three others belonging to the same garison who were killed; the Indians getting up upon the roof of the Barn, had advantage to shoot down upon them over their Fortification. Thus these murtherous wretches went on, burning, and destroying before them.

Mrs Rowlandson was taken as far north as an area around Chesterfield, New Hampshire. After spending a few days in this location, the Indians retraced their steps south to Princeton near Lancaster. Here she observed several Wampanoag customs, including an exhortation to their warriors before a battle and some kind of celebration, as she negotiated for her release.

Before they went to that fight, they got a company together to *Powaw*; the manner was as followeth. There was one that kneeled upon a Deerskin, with the company round him in a ring who kneeled and striking upon the ground with their hands, and with sticks, and muttering or humming with their mouths; besides him who kneeled in the ring, there also stood one with a Gun in his hand: Then he on the Deer-skin made a speech, and all manifested assent to it: and so they did many times together. Then they bade him with the Gun go out of the ring, which he did, but when he was out, they called him in again; but he seemed to make a stand, then they called him the more earnestly, till he returned again: Then they all sang. Then they gave him two Guns, in either hand one: and so he on the Deer-skin began again; and at the end of every sentence in his speaking, they all assented, hummering or muttering with their mouthes, and striking upon the ground with their hands. Then they bade him with the two Guns go out of the ring again; which he did, a little way. Then they called him in again, but he made a stand; so they called him with greater earnestness; but he stood reeling and wavering as if he knew not whither he should stand or fall, or which way to go. Then they called him with exceeding great vehemency, all of them, one and another: after a little while he turned in, staggering as he went, with his Armes stretched out, in either hand a Gun. As soon as he came in, they sang and rejoyced exceedingly a while. And then he upon the Deer-skin, made another speech unto which they all assented in a rejoicing manner: and so they ended their business, and forthwith went to Sudbury-fight . . . Mr Hoar [John Hoar of Concord, a representative of the government of Massachusetts, who negotiated for her release] called them [the Indians] betime to Dinner, but they ate very little, they being so busie in dressing themselves, and getting ready for their Dance: which was carried on by eight of them, four Men and four Squaws: My master and mistress [Quinnapin, a chief of the Wampanoags, and his wife Weetamoo, to whom Mrs Rowlandson acted as a servant] being two. He was dressed in his Holland shirt, with great Laces sewed at the tail of it, he had his silver Buttons, his white Stockins, his Garters were hung round with Shillings, and he had Girdles of Wampom upon his head and shoulders. She had a Kersey Coat, and covered with Girdles of Wampom from the Loins upward: her armes from her elbows to her hands were covered with Bracelets: there were handfulls of Necklaces about her neck, and severall sorts of Jewels in her ears. She had fine red Stokins, and white Shoos, her hair powdered and face painted Red, that was alwayes before Black. And all the Dancers were after the same manner. There were two other singing and knocking on a Kettle for their musick. They keept hopping up and down one after another, with a Kettle of water in their midst, standing warm upon some Embers, to drink of when they were dry. They held on till it was almost night, throwing out Wampom to the standers by. At night I asked them again, if I should go home? they all as one said No, except my husband would come for me. When we were lain down, my Master went out of the Wigwam, and by and by sent in an Indian called James the Printer, who told Mr Hoar, that my Master would let me go home to morrow, if he would let him have one pint of Liquors. Then Mr Hoar called his own Indians, Tom and Peter, and bid them go and see whether he would promise it before them three: and if he would, he should have it; which he did, and he had it. Then Philip smeling the business cal'd me to him, and asked me what I would give him, to tell me some good news, and speak a good word for me, I told him, I could not tell what to give him, I would any thing I had, and asked him what he would have? He said, two Coats and twenty shillings in Mony, and have a bushel of Seed Corn, and some Tobacco. I thanked [him] for his love: but I knew the good news as well as the crafty Fox. My Master after he had had his drink, quickly came ranting into the Wigwam again, and called for Mr Hoar, drinking to him, and saying, He was a good man: and then again he would say, Hang him Rogue: Being almost drunk, we would drink to him, and yet presently say he should be hanged. Then he called for me. I trembled to hear him, yet I was fain to go to him, and he drank to me, shewing no incivility. He was the first Indian I saw drunk all the while that I was amongst them. At last his Squaw ran out, and he after her, round the Wigwam, with his mony jingling at his knees: But she escaped him: But having an old Squaw he ran to her: and so through the Lords mercy, we were no more troubled that night.

Text used: Charles H. Lincoln (Ed.), Narratives of the Indian Wars, 1675-99, *New York, 1913, pp. 118, 152-3, 156-8.*

105A Mark Catesby. The Mock-Bird, from *Hortus Europae Americanus*, 1767. 'They are familiar and sociable Birds, usually perching on the tops of Chimneys or Trees, amongst the Inhabitants, who are diverted with their tuneful Airs most part of the Summer. Their food are Haws, Berries and Insects. In winter, when there is less variety and plenty, they will eat the berries of Dogwood.' Part of Catesby's comment.

105B Mark Catesby. The Wampum Snake and Red Lilly, from *Hortus Europae Americanus*, 1767.
'This snake receives its name from the Resemblance it has to *Indian* Money called Wampum, which is made of Shells cut into regular Pieces and strung with a mixture of Blue and White. . . . They are found in *Virginia* and *Carolina*.' See plate 119 for further information on Catesby.

3
A Dutch trip into the Mohawk country, 1634-5

From 'The narrative of Harmen Meyndertez van den Bogeart', *Independent*, XLVII.1317, 1895

The identity of the author of this narrative has caused some debate; it is now thought that it was penned by Van den Bogeart, the surgeon at Fort Orange and one of the three Dutch members of the expedition sent to investigate the possibilities of trading with the Mohawks. The narrative is important as it presents the first description of the life of the Iroquois by any European who travelled amongst them. Going along the Mohawk Valley in December 1634, they passed through the country of the Mohawks and the Oneidas until they came to the Oneida Castle (or chief settlement), between modern Utica and Syracuse.

Without anything to eat we went to the Sinnekens' castle, and after marching awhile the savages showed me the branch of the river that passes by Fort Orange and past the land of the Maquas. A woman came to meet us, bringing us baked pumpkins to eat. This road was mostly full of birches and beautiful flat land for sowing. Before we reached the castle we saw three graves, just like our graves in length and height; usually their graves are round. These graves were surrounded with palisades that they had split from trees, and they were closed up so nicely that it was a wonder to see. They were painted with red and white and black paint; but the chief's grave had an entrance, and at the top of that was a big wooden bird, and all around were painted dogs, and deer, and snakes, and other beasts. After four or five leagues' marching the savages still prayed us to fire our guns, and so we did, but loaded them again directly, and went on to the castle. And we saw to the northwest of us, a large river, and on the other side thereof tremendously high land that seemed to lie in the clouds. Upon inquiring closely into this, the savages told me that in this river the Frenchmen came to trade. And then we marched confidently to the castle, where the savages divided into two rows, and so let us pass through them by the gate, which was—the one we went through—3½ feet wide, and at the top were standing three big wooden images, carved like men, and with them I saw three scalps fluttering in the wind, that they had taken from their foes, as a token of the truth of their victory. This castle has two gates, one on the east and one on the west side. On the east side a scalp was also hanging; but this gate was 1½ feet smaller than the other one. When at last we arrived in the chief's house, I saw there a good many people that I knew; and we were requested to sit down in the chief's place where he was accustomed to sit because at the time he was not at home, and we felt cold and we were wet and tired. They at once gave us to eat, and they made a good fire. This castle likewise is situated on a very high hill, and was surrounded by two rows of palisades. It was 767 paces in circumference. There are 66 houses, but much better, higher, and more finished than all the others we saw. A good many houses had wooden fronts that are painted with all sorts of beasts. There they sleep mostly on elevated boards, more than any other savages. In the afternoon one of the council came to me, asking the reason for our coming into his land, and what we brought for him as a present. I told him that we did not bring any present, but that we only paid him a visit. He told us that we were not worth anything, because we did not bring him a present. Then he told us how the Frenchmen had come thither to trade with six men, and had given them good gifts, because they had been trading in this river with six men in the month of August of this year. We saw very good axes to cut the under wood, and French shirts and coats and razors; and this member of the council said we were scoundrels, and were not worth anything because we pay not enough for their beaver skins. They told us that the Frenchmen gave six hands of seawan for one beaver, and all sorts of things more. The savages were pressing closely upon us, so that there was hardly any room for us to sit. If they had desired to molest us, we could hardly have been able to defend ourselves; but there was no danger.

The Dutch stayed with the Indians at the Oneida Castle until January 12 and observed several Indian customs including the driving out of devils.

Two savages came, inviting us to come and see how they used to drive away the devil. I told them that I had seen it before; but they did not move off, and I had to go, and because I did not choose to go alone I took Jeronimus along. I saw a dozen men together who were going to drive him off. After we arrived the floor of the house was thickly covered with the bark of trees for the hunters of the devil to walk upon. They were mostly old men, and they had their faces all painted with red paint—which they always do when they are going to do anything unusual. Three men among them had a wreath on their heads, on which stuck five white crosses. These wreathes are made of deer hair that they had braided with the roots of a sort of green herb. In the middle of the house they then put a man who was very sick, and who was treated without success during a considerable time. Close by sat an old woman with a turtle shell in her hands. In the turtle shell were a good many beads. She kept clinking all the while, and all of them sang to the measure; then they would proceed to catch the devil and trample him to death; they trampled the bark to atoms so that none of it remained whole, and whenever they saw but a little cloud of dust upon the maize, they beat at it in great amazement and then they blew that dust at one another and were so afraid that they ran as if they really saw the devil; and after long stamping and running one of them went to the sick man and took away an otter that he had in his hands; and he sucked the sick man for awhile in his neck and on the back, and after that he spat in the otter's mouth and threw it down; at the same time he ran off like mad through fear. Other men then went to the otter, and then there took place such foolery that it was quite a wonder to see. Yes; they commenced to throw fire and eat fire, and kept scattering hot ashes and red-hot coal in such a way that I ran out of the house.

Text used: 'Journey into the Mohawk Country' in J. F. Jameson (Ed. and trans.), Narratives of New Netherland, *New York, 1909, pp. 148-9, 152-3.*

4 Hansen, van Brugh and Colonel Römer visit Onondago in 1700

From *The Journal of the Expediciôn of Col. Römer, Major Van Brugh and Henrick Hansen for Onnondage*, 1854

The three men had been sent by Governor Bellomont to search for a suitable site for a fort on the shores of Lake Ontario and to survey the land between Albany and the Western Finger Lakes. They were delayed for some time at the Onondago Castle, west of Lake Owasco, by the uncooperative mood of the Iroquois who persistently refused to lend them the canoes essential for any further exploration.

We came to Onnondage where a house was made ready for us, where we lodged & heard that Decanissore and some other Sachems were abroad, &, as they told us, were sent for to hear what news the Indians brought from Canada, & had newes that they were near at hand; so we staid till the next day.

27 d° [September] We sent for the Sachems together & asked them whether there was a canoe at Canaida [Lake Ontario], for our use to go in that Lake & so down the River till where the river comes in that runs out of the Lake of Oneyde. They answered there was no Canoe, but that there would be one or more to day or to morrow, & also said that they could not talk about till all the Sachems were come, wch they expected home to day.

The Indians persisted in their tactics for another few days, but insisted on telling their visitors of the good relations that they had with the French. The three men tried again to obtain help.

This afternoon we heard that the messenger ordered to go for Decanissore was not gone, because it rained & snowed all this day.

Oct. 1st We hired an Indian wch we sent to Decanissore wch in the afternoone came to the Castle with Decanissore & we desired Decanissore that he would call the Sachems together wch he did, and when they assembled Col. Römer desired that they would make a Canoe for him to go to Schenectade with, & a canoe or two to lend us now to go in Canainda Lake as farr as where the river comes in, that comes out of the Lake of Oneyde & two of their own men to go along with us to look for ye best place to build a Fort, & also when their people would be ready to work at ye Fort again. Whereupon they said they would answer early the next morning.

The following day, negotiations were reopened, but first they had to hear again the treatment of the Indians by the French and a conference that they had held together in Canada. Eventually the Indians got round to discussing the request of the English.

They also answered to what we desired to them yesterday, & said, that there were two Canoes ready at Canainda to go thro' the Lake & go up and down the river, but they desired that they being poor that we would pay them for it, and when we returned from Canainda they would tell us whether there should be a Canoe made for Col. Römer to go home in, but desired they might be paid for it. Which we promised. They also engaged us two men to go wth us to Canainda & one Sachem among them.

3do [October] We went to Canainda, but the Sachem that was appointed to go with us was drunck, & so did not go, but we got another in his roome at Canainda and so we went in the Canoe thro' the Lake of Canainda until a river that runs out of the lake of Oneyda, but found no fitt place to build a Fort; so we were advised to go to Quiehook the Creek that runs out of the Lake of Oneyda, & so returned to the Castle of Onnondage.

6do We went with Decanissore, Sinniquanda, both Sachems, for Quiehook by the Ledge called Kagnewagrage about 1½ Dutch mile from the Lake of Oneyda where we saw a very fitt place and good wood to erect a Fort.

7do We returned to the Castle and when we came nigh it we heard that our people that had a passe to go to the remote nations of Indians were come thither. We ordered them to come to us, & we heard that they were wholly discouraged to go further; also our Sachems desired to know on what intencôn those people were come; which we told them & desired them to send a man or two with them; wch they said did not sute them; because but tenn or 11 dayes ago, some of the Sinnekes [Senecas] were taken prisoners & they would send no people into the fire, for they looked on them as dead that went thither.

8do We asked our people that had the passe what they would do, to go further or return back, but there was not one that said he would go further. Then we asked the Mahikanders that were to go with them what they would do, who said they would return, for said they if we proceed we are dead people. Whereupon Col. Römer resolved forthwith to depart for Oneyde. The Sachems of Onnondage were not well pleased about that passe, because my Lord [Governor Bellomont of New York] had not acquainted them therewith & said that our people had run a great hazard of their owne people for those that were a hunting knew not of any of Corlaers people being abroad, & therefore feared that our own people would kill them as well as by their enemies. Whereupon those people that were to go to the farr Nations resolved to return home.

Text used: E. B. O'Callaghan and B. Fernow (Ed. and trans.), Documents relative to the Colonial History of the State of New York, *vol. IV, New York, 1856-87, pp. 802-6.*

5
William Penn describes the Delaware Indians, 1683

From *Penn's Letter to the Society of Traders of Pennsylvania*, London, 1683

By 1683 William Penn had been in his colony for almost a year and had time to observe the land and its possibilities. In this extract he gives a valuable early picture of the appearance and customs of the Delaware Indians.

The *Natives* I shall consider in their Persons, Language, Manners, Religion and Government, with my sence of their Original. For their Persons, they are generally tall, streight, well-built, and of singular Proportion; they tread strong and clever, and mostly walk with a lofty Chin: Of Complexion, Black, but by design, as the Gypsies in England: They grease themselves with Bears-fat clarified, and using no defence against Sun or Weather, their skins must needs be swarthy; Their Eye is little and black, not unlike a staight-look't Jew: The thick Lip and flat Nose, so frequent with the East-Indians and Blacks, are not common to them; for I have seen as comely European-like faces among them of both, as on your side the Sea; and truly an Italian Complexion hath not much more of the White, and the Noses of several of them have as much of the Roman.

Of their Customs and Manners there is much to be said; I will begin with Children. So soon as they are born, they wash them in Water, and while very young, and in cold Weather to chuse, they Plunge them in the Rivers to harden and embolden them. Having wrapped them in a Clout, they lay them on a straight thin Board, a little more than the length and breadth of the Child, and swadle it fast upon the Board to make it straight; wherefore all Indians have flat Heads; and thus they carry them at their Backs. The Children will go very young, at nine moneths commonly; they wear only a small Clout round their Waste, till they are big; if Boys, they

106 Huron women, from François du Creux, *Historia Canadensis*, 1664. Note the baby swaddled to a board and propped against a tree.

106

go a Fishing till ripe for the Woods, which is about Fifteen; then they Hunt, and after having given some proofs of their Manhood, by a good return of Skins, they may Marry, else it is a shame to think of a Wife. The Girls stay with their Mothers, and help to Hoe the Ground, plant Corn and carry Burthens; and they do well to use them to that Young, they must do when they are Old; for the Wives are the true Servants of their Husbands: otherwise the Men are very affectionate to them.

When the Young Women are fit for Marriage, they wear something upon their Heads for an Advertisement, but so as their Faces are hardly to be seen, but when they please: the Age they Marry at, if Women, is about thirteen and fourteen; if Men, Seventeen and Eighteen; they are rarely elder.

These poor People are under a dark Night in things relating to Religion, to be sure, the Tradition of it; yet they believe a God and Immortality, without the help of Metaphysicks; for they say, There is a great King that made them who dwells in a glorious Country to the Southward of them, and that the Souls of the good shall go thither, where they shall live again. Their Worship consists of two parts, Sacrifice and *Cantico*. Their Sacrifice is their first Fruits; the first and fattest Buck they kill, goeth to the fire, where he is all burnt with a Mournful Ditty of him that performeth the Cremony, but with such marvellous Fervency and Labour of Body, that he will even sweat to a foam. The other part is their *Cantico*, performed by round-Dances, sometimes Words, sometimes Songs, then Shouts, two being in the middle that begin, and by Singing and Drumming on a Board direct the Chorus: Their Postures in the Dance are very Antick and differing, but all keep measure. This is done with equal Earnestness and Labour, but great appearance of Joy. In the Fall, when the Corn cometh in, they begin to feast one another; they have been two great Festivals already, to which all come that will: I was at one my self; their Entertainment was a green Seat by a Spring, under some shady Trees, and twenty Bucks, with hot Cakes of new Corn, both Wheat and Beans, which they make up in a square form, in the leaves of the Stem, and bake them in the Ashes: And after that they fell to Dance. But they that go, must carry a small Present in their Money, it may be six Pence, which is made of the Bone of a Fish; the black is with them as Gold, the white, Silver; they call it all *Wampum*.

Text used: Albert C. Myers (Ed.), Narratives of Early Pennsylvania, West New Jersey and Delaware, 1630-1707, *New York, 1912, pp. 230-1, 234.*

6
John Bartram visits Onondago, 1743

From his *Observations*, London, 1751

In 1743 John Bartram, the naturalist, travelled north along the mountains from Pennsylvania to New York. His journal of the trip contains many amusing incidents and descriptions both of the Indians and of the countryside. On the journey north, he and his companions, Conrad Weiser and Lewis Evans, were treated to Indian hospitality.

. . . we lodged within about 50 yards of a hunting cabin, where there were 2 Men, a Squaw, and a child, the men came to our fire and made us a present of some venison, and invited Mr *Weisar*, *Shickcalamy* and his son, to a feast at their cabin. It is incumbent on those who partake of the feast of this sort, to eat all that comes to their share or burn it: now *Weisar* being a traveller was intitled to a double share, but he being not very well, was forced to take the benefit of a liberty, indulged him, of eating by proxy, and called me, but being unable to cope with it, *Lewis* came to our assistance, notwithstanding which we were hard set to get down the neck and throat, for these were allotted to us; and now we had experienced the bounds of their indulgence, for *Lewis* ignorant of the ceremony of throwing the bone to the dog, tho' hungry dogs are generally nimble, the *Indian* more nimble, laid hold of it first, and committed it to the fire, religiously covering it over with hot ashes. This seems to be a kind of offering, perhaps first fruits to the Almighty power to crave future success in the approaching hunting season.

During their stay at Onondago, Bartram observed another Indian ceremony which totally bewildered him.

At night, soon after we were laid down to sleep, and our fire almost burnt out, we were entertained by a comical fellow, disguised in as odd a dress as *Indian* folly could invent; he had on a clumsy vizard of wood colour'd black, with a nose 4 or 5 inches long, a grining mouth set awry, furnished with long teeth, round the eyes circles of bright brass, surrounded by a larger circle of white paint, from his forehead hung long tresses of buffaloes hair, and from the catch part of his head ropes made from the plated husks of *Indian* corn; I cannot recollect the whole of his dress, but that it was equally uncouth: he carried in one hand a long staff, in the other a calabash with small stones in it, for a rattle, and this he rubbed up and down his staff; he would sometimes hold up his head and make a hideous noise like the braying of an ass; he came in at the further end, and made this noise at first, whether it was because he would not surprise us too suddenly I can't say: I ask'd *Conrad Weiser*, who as well as myself lay next the alley, what noise that was? and *Shickalamy* the *Indian* chief, our companion, who I supposed, thought me somewhat scared, called out, lye still *John*. I never heard him speak so much plain *English* before. The jackpudding presently came up to us, and an *Indian* boy came with him and kindled our fire, that we might see his glittering eyes and antick postures as he hobbled round the fire, sometimes he would turn the Buffaloes hair on one side that we might take the better view of his ill-favoured phyz, when he had tired himself, which was sometime after he had well tired us, the boy that attended him struck 2 or 3 smart blows on the floor, at which the hobgoblin seemed surprised and on repeating them he jumped fairly out of doors and disappeared.

On the return trip to Pennsylvania, Bartram brings his naturalist's eye to describe the countryside between Sunbury and the western branch of the Susquehanna and has another encounter with strange Indian customs.

I took a fancy to ascend 2 thirds of the height of a neighbouring hill, in the way I came to abundance of loose stones, and very craggy rocks, which seemed to threaten impending ruin, the soil was black and very rich, full of great wild stinging nettle, as far as I went I rolled down several loose stones to make a path for my more expeditious return. This I found the *Indians* much disturbed of, for they said it would infallibly produce rain the next day, I told them I had sufficient experience, it signified nothing, for it was my common practice to roll down stones from the top of every steep hill, and could not recollect that it ever rained the next day, and that I was almost sure to morrow would be a very fair day.

11th August We got out before sun rise, and rode over very good bottoms of *Linden Poplar*, and Elm, we killed a rattle snake, and soon after found a patch of *Chamerododendron*, at 8 we came to a creek winding between the mountains on the left, then along a level to another from the right, which we crossed to our former cabin. Quickly after we reached a bad hill, where I first found the *Ginseng* in this journey, the soil was black and light, with flat stones facing the east, there we passed by 9, then over a bottom of laural and pine to a creek we had several times crossed, when obstructed as frequently we were by hills, keeping close to the water on the side we were riding. At 10 we left this creek for the sake of a shorter way than we came, for this purpose we kept a S. course to the top of a high but very poor hill, which we reached about a qr. after eleven, and had a prospect still to a gap we were to pass to the river; the northside of this hill was clothed with tall spruce, while pine and beech, the top with chesnut, scrubby oak, and huckle berries, the S. side with shrub, honeysuckles &c. Our way was now over a poor pebbled stone vale of laurel, spruce firr, pine, chestnut, and huckle berries, to a *Run* of water; where we dined on parched meal mixed with water. We left that place at half an hour after one, and soon found ourselves much distressed by the broad flat stones on the side of the hill our way lay over. Our horses could hardly stand, but even slipt on their sides on our left a rivulet rushed from a precipice, and the mountains were so steep and close to its sides, that we were oblidged to climb to the top of that on the west; here we suffered our horses to rest while we gathered huckle berries to eat, we travelled on the top a good way all stony to the point, which was very narrow, and the flat stones on each ride turned up like the ridge on a house, this reminded me of *Dr. Burnets Theory*, and his ingenious *Hypothesis*, to account for the formation of mountains. The descent was moderate, the land middling, oak, chestnut and huckle berries: we found a *Run* here and reposed ourselves for this night, having supped on venison, shot by our *Indians* who left us on the hill that evening. It was fair and pleasant, and the great green grass-hopper began to sing (*Catedidist*) these were the first I observed this year. Before day break it began to rain, it lasted about an hour and then ceased. The Indians insisted that it was caused by the stones I rolled down 2 days ago, I told the *Antecoque Indians* if their observations had any truth it should have been the day before, which was remarkably fair. To this he cunningly replyed, that our *Almanacks* often prognosticated on a day, and yet the rain did not come within two days.

Text used: John Bartram, Observations on the Inhabitants . . . and other matters . . . made by Mr John Bartram, in his Travels from Pensilvania to Onondago, Oswego and the Lake Ontario, in Canada, *London, 1751, pp. 23-4, 43-4, 68-70.*

107 Sr Robert de Vaugondy. 'Partie de l'Amerique Septentrionale, qui comprend le Cours de l'Ohio, la Nlle. Angleterre, la Nlle York, le New Jersey, la Pensylvanie, le Maryland la Virginie, la Caroline', 1755. *Public Record Office, London, CO 700, NAC, Gen 9.*
The impressive extent of French knowledge of northeast North America in the mid eighteenth century demonstrated on this map can be compared with the details on Lewis Evans's map of the Middle British Colonies of the same year (plate 93). From the two it can be seen that the French were much more familiar with the Great Lakes area and the far west in the region of the junction of the Ohio and Mississippi Rivers because of their extensive exploration of the interior.

107

7
George Croghan meets Pontiac in the Illinois country, 1765

From 'Croghan's Journal', *The Monthly Journal of American Geology*, December 1831

After defeat had been inflicted on the Indians by Colonel Bouquet in 1763, George Croghan was chosen to lead a mission west into Illinois Country to meet and negotiate terms for peace with the native leader, Pontiac. Croghan went down the Ohio River as far as the mouth of the Wabash, where his party was attacked by hostile Indians.

8th [June]—At day-break we were attacked by a party of Indians, consisting of eighty warriers of the *Kiccapoos* and Musquattimes [allied Algonquin tribes], who killed two of my men and three Indians, wounded myself and all the rest of my party, except two white men and one Indian; then made myself and all the white men prisoners, plundering us of everything we had. A deputy of the Shawneese who was shot through the thigh, having concealed himself in the woods for a few minutes after he was wounded—not knowing but they were Southern Indians, who are always at war with the northward Indians—after discovering what nation they were, came up to them and made a very bold speech, telling them the whole northward Indians would join in taking revenge for the insult and murder of their people; this alarmed those savages very much, who began excusing themselves, saying their fathers, the French, had spirited them up, telling them that the Indians were coming with a body of southern Indians to take their country from them, and enslave them; that it was this that induced them to commit this outrage. After dividing the plunder (they left great part of the heaviest effects behind, not being able to carry them), they set off with us to their village at Ouattonon, in a great hurry, being in dread of pursuit from a large party of Indians they suspected were coming after me. Our course was through a thick woody country, crossing a great many swamps, morasses, and beaver ponds. We travelled this day about forty-two miles.

During this forced march Croghan had time to observe and comment on the countryside along the Wabash River and that surrounding the Indian settlement of Ouitenon.

18th and 19th [June]—We travelled through a prodigious large meadow, called the Pyankeshaw's [a Miami tribe] Hunting Ground: here is no wood to be seen, and the country appears like an ocean: the ground is exceedingly rich, and partly overgrown with wild hemp; the land well watered, and full of buffalo, deer, bears, and all kinds of wild game.

20th and 21st—We passed through some very large meadows part of which belong to the Pyankeshaws on Vermilion River; the country and soil are much the same that we travelled over for these three days past, wild hemp grows here in abundance; the game very plenty: at any time, in half an hour we could kill as much as we wanted.

22nd—We passed through part of the same meadow as mentioned yesterday; then came to a high woodland, and arrived at Vermilion River, so called from a fine red earth found here by the Indians, with which they paint themselves. About half a mile from the place where we crossed this river, there is a village of the Piankeshaws, distinguished by the addition of the name of the river. We then travelled about three hours, through a clear high woody country, but a deep and a rich soil; then came to a meadow where we encamped . . . The country hereabouts is exceedingly pleasant, being open and clear for many miles; the soil very rich and well watered; all plants have a quick vegetation, and the climate very temperate through the winter. This post has always been a very considerable trading place. The great plenty of furs taken in the country, induced the French to establish this post [Port Vincennes], which was the first on the Ouabache [Wabash], and by very advantageous trade they have been richly recompensed for their labor. On the south side of the Ouabache runs a big bank, in which are several fine coal mines, and behind this bank, is a very large meadow, clear for several miles. It is surprising what false information we have had respecting this country: some the mention the spacious and beautiful meadows as large and barren savannahs. I apprehend it has been the artifice of the French to keep us ignorant of the country. These meadows bear fine wild grass, and wild hemp ten or twelve feet high, which, if properly manufactured would prove as good, and answer all the purposes of the hemp we cultivate.

Whilst at the village Croghan and his party were released and he made his way to meet Pontiac.

18th [July]—I set off for the Illinois with the Chiefs of all those Nations when by the way we met with Pondiac together with the Deputies of the Six Nations, Delawares & Shawanese, which accompanied Mr Frazier & myself down the Ohio & also Deputies with speeches from the four Nations living in the Illinois Country to me & the Six Nations, Delawares & Shawanese, on which we return'd to Ouiatonon and there held another conferance, in which I settled all matters with the Illinois Indians—Pondiac & they agreeing to every thing the other Nations had done, all which they confirmed by Pipes & Belts, but told me the French had informed them that the English intended to take their Country from them, & give it to the Cherokees to settle on, & that if ever they suffered the English to take possession of their Country they would make slaves of them, that this was the reason of their Opposing the English hitherto from taking possession of *Fort Chartres* & induce them to tell Mr. La Guttrie & Mr Sinnott [an interpreter and an agent sent out previously] that they would not let the English come into their Country. But being informed since Mr Sinnott had retired by the Deputies of the Six Nations, Delawares & Shawanese, that every difference subsisting between them & the English was now settled, they were willing to comply as the other Nations their Brethren had done and desired that their Father the King of England might not look upon his taking possession of the Forts which the French had formerly possest as a title for his subjects to possess their Country, as they never had sold any part of it to the French, & that I might rest satisfied that whenever the English came to take possession they would receive them with open arms.

Text used: Journal of George Croghan, who was sent, after the peace of 1763, by the government to explore the country adjacent to the Ohio River in Reuben G. Thwaites (Ed.), Early Western Travels, 1748-1764, *vol. I, Cleveland, 1904, pp. 135, 138-9, 143-5, 147-8.*

109 'A plan of Captain Carvers Travels in the interior Parts of North America in 1766 and 1767', from Jonathan Carver, *Travels through the interior parts of North-America*, 1778.
Carver included this map to illustrate the account of his travels. As with the narrative itself, it is possible that Carver was not the author of the map. However, he almost certainly travelled in the area shown here, that is from Mackinac, at the junctions of Lakes Huron and Michigan, west to the Mississippi and to the area northwest of the Rum River.

8
Jonathan Carver visits the Mississippi, 1766-7

From *Carver's Travels through the Interior Parts of North America . . .*, London, 1778

Jonathan Carver was employed by Major Robert Rogers to explore west of the British post at Mackinac. He went down the Fox River, across the portage, into the Wisconsin River which led him to the Mississippi. He went up that river, describing the land as he passed.

On the first of November I arrived at Lake Pepin, which is rather an extended part of the River Mississippi, that the French have thus denominated, about two hundred miles from the Ouisconsin. The Mississippi below this lake flows with a very gentle current, but the breadth of it is very uncertain, in some places it being upwards of a mile, on others not more than a quarter. This River has a range of mountains on each side throughout the whole of the way; which in particular parts approach near to it, in others lie at a great distance. The land betwixt the mountains, and on their sides, is generally covered with grass with a few groves of trees interspersed, near which large droves of deer and elk are frequently seen feeding. In many places pyramids of rocks appeared, resembling old ruinous towers: at others amazing precipices: and what is very remarkable, whilst this scene presented itself on one side, the opposite side of the same mountain was covered with the finest herbage, which gradually ascended to its summit. From thence the most beautiful and extensive prospect that imagination can form opens to your view. Verdant plains, fruitful meadows, numerous islands, and all these abounding with a variety of trees that yield amazing quantities of fruit, without care or cultivation, such as the nut tree, the maple which produces sugar, vines loaded with rich grapes, and plum-trees, bending under their blooming burdens, but above all, the fine River flowing gently beneath and by reaching as far as the eye can extend, by turns attract your admiration and excite your wonder . . .

About thirty miles below the Falls of St. Anthony, at which I arrived the tenth day after I left Lake Pepin, is a remarkable cave of an amazing depth. The Indians term it Wakon-teebe, that is, the Dwelling of the Great Spirit. The entrance into it is

108 The Falls of St Anthony, 1766, from Jonathan Carver, *Travels through the interior parts of North-America*, 1778.
First discovered by Louis Hennepin during his wanderings on the upper Mississippi in 1680-1, the falls were described by Carver (see page 80).

108

109

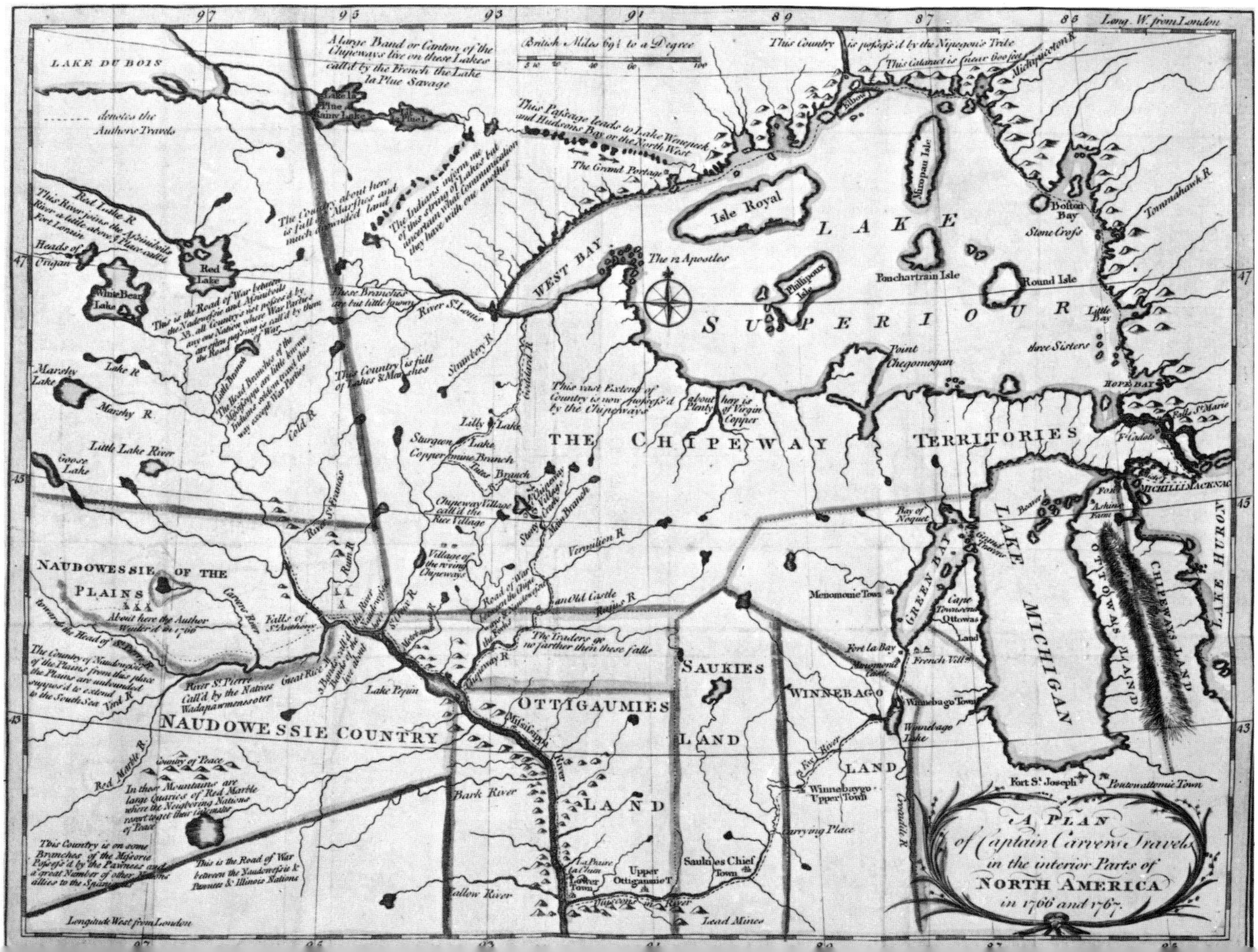

about ten feet wide, the height of it five feet. The arch within it is near fifteen feet high and about thirty feet broad. The bottom of it consists of fine clear sand. About twenty feet from the entrance begins a lake, the water of which is transparent, and extends to an unsearchable distance; for the darkness of the cave prevents all attempts to acquire a knowledge of it. I threw a small pebbel towards the interior parts of it with my utmost strength: I could hear that it fell into the water, and notwithstanding it was so small a size, it caused an astonishing and horrible noise that reverberated through all those gloomy regions. I found in this cave many Indian

110

110 A man and woman of the Naudouessie (Sioux), from Jonathan Carver, *Travels through the interior parts of North-America*, 1778.

hieroglyphicks, which appeared very ancient, for time had nearly covered them with moss, so that it was with difficulty that I could trace them. They were cut in a rude manner upon the inside of the walls, which were composed of a stone so extremely soft that it might easily be penetrated with a knife: a stone every where to be found near the Mississippi. The cave is only accessible by ascending a narrow, steep passage that lies near the brink of the river. . . . The Falls of St. Anthony received their name from Father Louis Hennepin, a French missionary, who travelled into these parts about the year 1680, and was the first European ever seen by the natives. This amazing body of waters, which are above 250 yards over, form a most pleasing cataract; they fall perpendicularly about thirty feet, and the rapids below, in the space of 300 yards more, render the descent considerably greater; so that when viewed at a distance they appear to be much higher than they really are. . . .

In the middle of the Falls stands a small island, about forty feet broad and somewhat longer, on which grow a few cragged hemlock and spruce trees; and about half way between this island and the eastern shore, is a rock, lying at the very edge of the fall, in an oblique position, that appeared to be five or six feet broad, and thirty or forty long. These falls vary much from all the others I have seen, as you may approach close to them without finding the least obstruction from any intervening hill or precipice.

The country around them is extremely beautiful. It is not an uninterrupted plain where the eye finds no relief, but composed of many gentle ascents, which in the summer are covered with the finest verdure, and interspersed with little groves, that give a pleasing variety to the prospect. On the whole, when the Falls are included, which may be seen at a distance of four miles, a more pleasing and picturesque view cannot, I believe, be found throughout the universe. I could have wished that I had happened to enjoy this sight at a more seasonable time of the year, whilst the trees and hillocks were clad in nature's gayest livery, as this must have greatly added to the pleasure I received; however, even then it exceeded my warmest expectations. I have endeavoured to give the reader as just an idea of this enchanting spot as possible, in the plan annexed: but all description, whether of the pencil or the pen, must fall infinitely short of the original.

At a little distance below the falls stands a small island, of about an acre and half, on which grow a great number of oak trees, every branch of which, able to support the weight, was full of eagle's nests. The reason that this kind of birds resort in such numbers to this spot, is that they are here secure from the attacks of either man or beast, their retreat being guarded by the Rapids, which the Indians never attempt to pass. Another reason is, that they find a constant supply of food for themselves and their young, from the animals and fish which are dashed to pieces by the falls, and driven on the adjacent shore.

Having satisfied my curiosity, as far as the eye of man can be satisfied, I proceeded on, still accompanied by my young friend [a prince of the Winnebago Indians], till I had reached the River St. Francis, near sixty miles above the Falls. To this River Father Hennepin gave the name of St. Francis, and this was the extent of his travels, as well as mine, towards the north-west. As the season was advanced, and the weather extremely cold, I was not able to make so many observations on these parts as I otherwise should have done.

Text used: Jonathan Carver, Travels Through the Interior Parts of North-America in the Years 1766, 1767 and 1768, *London, 1778, pp. 54-5, 63-5, 69-72.*

111 Mark Catesby's Pennsylvania magnolia from *Hortus Europae Americanus*, 1767. Reproductions of his work in the southern colonies are to be found in Chapter 3.

111

3 THE SOUTHERN COLONIES: WESTWARD FROM THE COAST, 1640-1730

During the seventeenth century the interior of the continent remained unknown territory for most of the colonists along its southeastern coast. The hunters and traders who began to penetrate westward from the tidewater settlements in the latter half of the seventeenth century in increasing numbers left few records of their explorations. Their activities were undertaken initially without special authorization and sometimes, in the sale to the Indians of rum and firearms, against the wishes and laws of the government. They were often illiterate; many 'married' and remained among the Indians, returning occasionally to sell their furs and to renew their supplies for barter. Nor was the merchant who furnished them with goods and frequently underwrote their expeditions concerned in publishing for others what he learned about his trade territory.

The English colony which began at Jamestown in 1607 and spread slowly along the river banks and estuaries owed its very survival to the development of farms and plantations which provided food for the settlers and a highly marketable commodity for the mother country. The cultivation of tobacco, not the fur trade, became the economic basis of the colony and its most important export.[1] The Virginia Company in London and the royal governor deplored such dependence on the 'vicious, scurvy weed' and tried to introduce other staples and industries, but with little success.[2] These planters were absorbed in their farms and did little exploring.

As farther north, the hostility of the Indians surrounding the settlements was also an inhibiting factor in the apparent lack of enterprise in exploration among the Virginia settlers. The great massacre of 1622 nearly wiped out the colony; the menace to the safety of the colony did not end until comparative peace followed a major Indian uprising of 1644. Serious interest by the Virginians in finding out about the extent and nature of the land beyond the tidewater was dormant in the first half of the century. Indians had told Captain Christopher Newport, who brought the first settlers in 1607, of high mountains to the west; Captain John Smith drew these 'hills' rather vaguely on his 1612 map of Virginia, and marked with an X the points he had reached up the tidal rivers off Chesapeake Bay in his navigations of 1608. For several decades little knowledge was added to the information on Smith's map and to reports by his contemporaries. One of them, William Strachey, in his *Historie of travell into Virginia Britania*, wrote 'we wot not how farre' the continent extends beyond the falls of the rivers.[3]

Several powerful motives, however, eventually encouraged probings beyond the Fall Line. Alliances with local tribes for common protection against marauding Indians led to short military expeditions. Friendly relations, which promoted barter with more distant tribes, encouraged the opening of trade routes. Land-hunger, which for some colonists who wished to expand their estates became an insatiable drive, led to a search for additional arable territory. These desires and aims were not mutually exclusive; when supported by wealthy colonists or by officials in power, they led to action.

112 W. Hollar. Virginia Indian, aged 23, 1645. Copperplate engraving. *British Museum, London.*

112

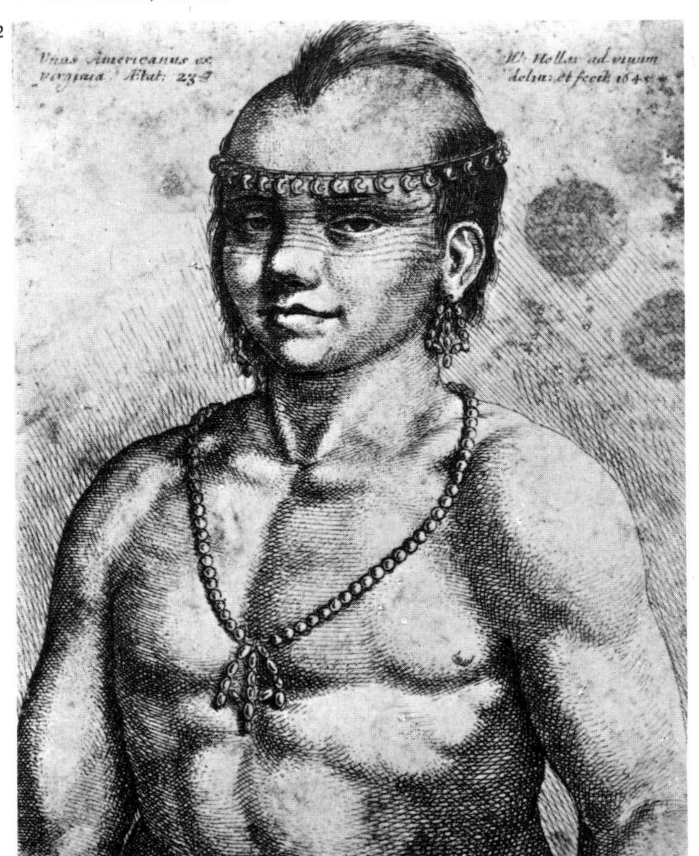

1 Explorations from Virginia, 1650-1716

In 1650, over forty years after the arrival at Jamestown, two prominent colonists, Edward Bland and Captain Abraham Wood, made an exploration south and west from the falls on the Appomattox River, the present site of Petersburg, Virginia. Edward Bland, an English merchant who came to Virginia in 1634, had acquired a plantation of 8,000 acres in Charles City County, on the north bank of the James River. Abraham Wood, also a large landowner, was commander of Fort Henry at the falls of the Appomattox; he was later to become a major general, below the governor only in military rank, and to serve for twenty-two years as member of the Council, the highest court in the colony. Bland and Wood, accompanied by an Indian guide and two companions, crossed the Nottaway and Meherrin Rivers. They reached the Hocomowananck (Roanoke) River below the falls, probably near Roanoke Rapids.[4] There the Indians brought them 'roasting eeres and Sturgeon'; the next day, September 1, they went 'to the place where they kill sturgeon six miles up the River running Northerly, and all exceeding rich land . . . this place where they kill sturgeon also are the Falls'.[5]

Bland, who published an account of their journey the following year, *The Discovery of New Britaine*, describes enthusiastically the fertile open fields 'in which Tobacco will grow larger and in more quantity' in a 'more temperate

113

113 Sasquehanok Indian village, from Arnoldus Montanus, *America*, 1671.

114 Farrer. 'A Mapp of Virginia', 1651. *Huntington Library, San Marino, California.*
John Farrer, an official of the Virginia Company in England, shows on this map a still vigorously held belief that the Pacific Ocean was not far beyond a narrow range of hills west of tidewater Virginia. A westward passage by the Hudson River and the St Lawrence, that join at 'A Mighty great Lake', is blocked on later editions of this popular map by an extension of the peninsula across the lake. The unsuccessful grant to Sir Robert Heath in 1629 of Carolina to the south of Virginia and the short-lived plantation of the Swedes on the Delaware River are also delineated; the map is a fascinating combination of fact and fiction. The legend on Sir Francis Drake indicates the claim which the English felt they had on the Pacific Coast, wherever that might be.

The map was republished several times with numerous additions made by Virginia, daughter of John Farrer. North is at the right.

Climate than the English now inhabite' with two crops of grain a year. He wrote with the eye of a colonizer: 'the Land is Champion, very rich levell, and very convenient for Hogs and Cattle' near to 'timber trees five feet over, whose truncks are a hundred foot in cleare timber' and of easy access to supplies in Virginia.[6] Wood's interest, as he told the Indians whom he encountered, was 'to trade in the way of Friendship and [he] desired the great men that what Wares or Skins the Town did afford might be brought to our Quarters'. There is some evidence that Wood's approach may have opened up a significant trade with the Indians from his store at Fort Henry.[7] The journey to the 'Country of New Britaine' was more important for stirring interest in the interior and its possibilities than for actual discovery and achievement.

The hope for a direct westward route to the Pacific, across a continent thought to be much narrower than it actually is, was as persistent among the English as among the French farther north. Such a route, with goods transported for a short distance by land, would make Virginia merchants the middle-men for the wealth of the Indies to the markets of Europe. 'What opulency does China teeme with which shall not be made our owne by the Midwifry of this virtuall passage?' wrote Edward Williams in his *Virgo triumphans* in 1650.[8] What lay on the other side of the mountains west of the coastal settlements? It stood to reason, they believed, that a great bay or sea of the Pacific, similar to the Gulf of Mexico, extended eastward toward the mountains bordering Virginia. Verrazano had reported seeing the South Sea across the narrow isthmus of the Outer Banks in 1524; the Roanoke colonists rowed up the Roanoke River to find the westward passage, but turned back from lack of food; Captain John Smith, on orders from London, looked in vain for a strait to the Pacific from Chesapeake Bay. Edward Bland reported on the title page of his volume that he had found a westward flowing

114

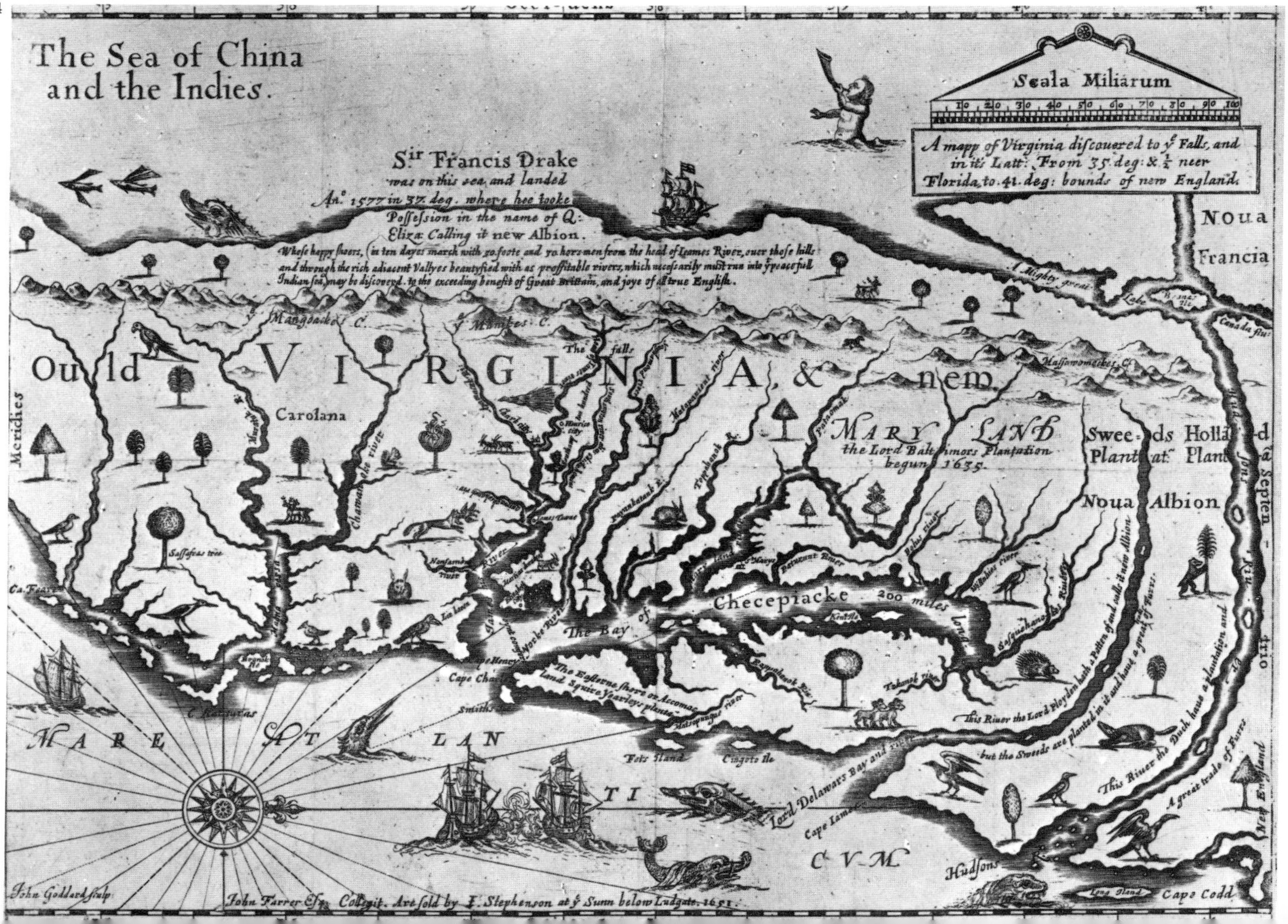

river; in his text he suggested that it flowed around the base of the great mountains southwest and then northward.[9] Governor William Berkeley, who arrived in Virginia in 1642, believed from Indian reports that over the mountain range were 'great Rivers that run into a great sea . . . it must prove a passage to the South Sea' and was 'preparing fifty Horse and fifty Foot, to go and discover this thing in person'; this news from Virginia was published in 1649 in *A perfect description of Virginia,* attributed to John Farrer, an official of the Virginia Company.[10] Farrer drew and published a map in 1651 (plate 114) which showed graphically this conception of the South Sea washing the shores of Sir Francis Drake's 'New Albion', just over the Virginia mountains. Governor Berkeley, probably hampered by the colony's financial difficulties and by Indian disturbances, did not make his intended expedition, but the hope of such a discovery remained with him; some twenty years later he commissioned a German scholar and adventurer, John Lederer, to find out what was beyond the mountains.

Lederer, a young surgeon from Hamburg, had recently arrived in the colony. He was interested in the natural resources of the country, in Indian trade, and in the culture and religious beliefs of the native tribes. In 'three several Marches' that he made, he was a pioneer explorer of the Blue Ridge and of the North Carolina Piedmont.

On his first 'march', begun on 9 March 1670, he followed the South Anna River and reached the Blue Ridge near Swift Run Gap, northwest of Charlottesville, Virginia. The bitter cold and a vista of even higher mountains stretching on before him discouraged further search, and he returned.

Lederer's second journey was his most important (see selection 1 for his first and second journeys); it opened the way for the Virginia fur trade with the Cherokee Indians of the southern Appalachians. On 20 May 1670 he set out with a party of twenty colonists on horseback and five Indians, led by Major William Harris of Abraham Wood's militia regiment. The party bushwhacked their way directly west from the falls of the James River for eight days through dense forests and over stony terrain. They reached the James River again and Major Harris declared it was 'an arm of the Lake of Canada';[11] exhausted and discouraged, they tried angrily to force Lederer to return with them. He showed them his personal commission from Governor Berkeley and they left him, 'a prey to Indians or savage beasts'. Lederer continued with Jacksetavon, a Susquehanna Indian, who accompanied him the rest of the way. For four days they travelled a southerly trail without meeting an Indian, an indication of the contemporary sparseness of native population in that area. Finally they reached a Saponi village on a branch of the Roanoke. There an Indian gave Lederer instructions on how to avoid the Appalachian barrier; these directions, as present topographical knowledge shows, were to take Indian trails skirting the southern end of the Appalachian range in northern Georgia. This was the route found later in the century by traders from Charles Town on their way to the Mississippi Valley. Lederer reached the Akenatzy (Occaneechi) island settlement on the Roanoke River at present Clarksville, Virginia. He described accurately the high southern banks of the river and the fertile bottom lands and fields to the north; the fierce and treacherous Occaneechi themselves lived on the island, 'fix'd here in great security, being naturally fortified with Fastnesses of Mountains and Water on every side'. Lederer continued southwest, across Piedmont North Carolina, noting the location and customs of the Indians he found. On the Catawba near present Rock Hill, South Carolina, he reached the Ushery or Esaw Indians. There Lederer made a geographical error which has plagued his memory. Most continental map-makers since the Mercator-Hondius map of Virginia and Florida in 1606 had incorrectly placed a large lake in that area.

115

116

115 Blaeu. A new description of the southern part of Virginia and the eastern part of Florida and of the regions between them, 1640, from W. J. and J. Blaeu, *Le Théâtre du Monde*, Amsterdam, II, 1640, between pp. 28 and 29.
Although based on the Mercator-Hondius 'Virginia and Florida (1606)', Blaeu's map makes numerous changes that show an attempt to incorporate new geographical information. Two great cusps or bays expand the South Carolina coast; and Jamestown on the Powhatan (James) River is added west of an enlarged Chesapeake Bay.

The great lake of unknown size below the 'Apalatcy' mountains, found on most maps at this time, is the lake which John Lederer was expecting to find and thought he had reached in 1670.

116 Lederer. '. . . his three marches', from *The discoveries of John Lederer*, 1672.
Lederer was a keen observer of Indian customs and he helped to open the lucrative Virginia fur trade with the Indians of western Carolina. The details on his map, with their inaccuracies, long influenced European map-makers.

Lederer, possibly wishing to show how far he had been, said that three miles from the Ushery village where he stayed was a lake about ten leagues broad.[12] European cartographers seized upon this apparent confirmation of Mercator's lake to fill the otherwise blank interior, and the non-existent lake, with other details from Lederer's own map (plate 116), became a feature of subsequent maps of America for many years.

Lederer returned to Virginia by a more eastern route, crossing the pine barrens of North Carolina in July, which he called the Arenosa Desert, and visiting the Toskiroro (Tuscarora) Indians, who played an important part in the later history of the Carolina colony.

Lederer was not exhausted either in spirit or energy by his attempts to find a pass across the mountains. A month later, on 20 August 1670, he started from the falls of the Rappahannock in Northern Virginia with ten Englishmen and five Indians in another attempt to find great rivers over the hills that flowed into the Pacific. They climbed the Blue Ridge only to view beyond 'a prodigious Mountain' surrounded by others 'high and inaccessible'. Discouraged by this evidence that the South Sea was not at hand, they drank a toast to the King, named the mountain peak they had reached King Charles, and returned. Lederer left Virginia for Maryland and eventually sailed back to Germany.

If Lederer did not succeed in finding a pass over the Alleghenies, he made several valuable contributions to the exploration of the southeast. He was the first European to record journeys in the southern Piedmont. He wrote of the location, names, government, manners, and religious beliefs of the native tribes he met; thus he preserved important archaeological and historical information about these Indians. He helped to open the great Indian trading path southwest from Virginia to the Catawba and Cherokee.

The success of Lederer initiated a series of exploratory parties by Abraham Wood, Captain William Byrd I, Governor Berkeley, and perhaps others. On 1 September 1671 Wood sent out from his trading post at Appomattox Thomas Wood, probably his relative who died on the expedition, Captain Thomas Batts, a well-to-do colonist, and Robert Fallam, who kept a journal of the expedition.[13] Perecute, an able and courageous Appomattox chief, accompanied them with seven Indians of his tribe. The group crossed the Blue Ridge and descended into the beautiful Valley of Virginia, where they were welcomed at a Totero village near the present city of Roanoke. Acquiring a Totero guide, they pushed on over the eastern continental divide with its endless vista of high

117

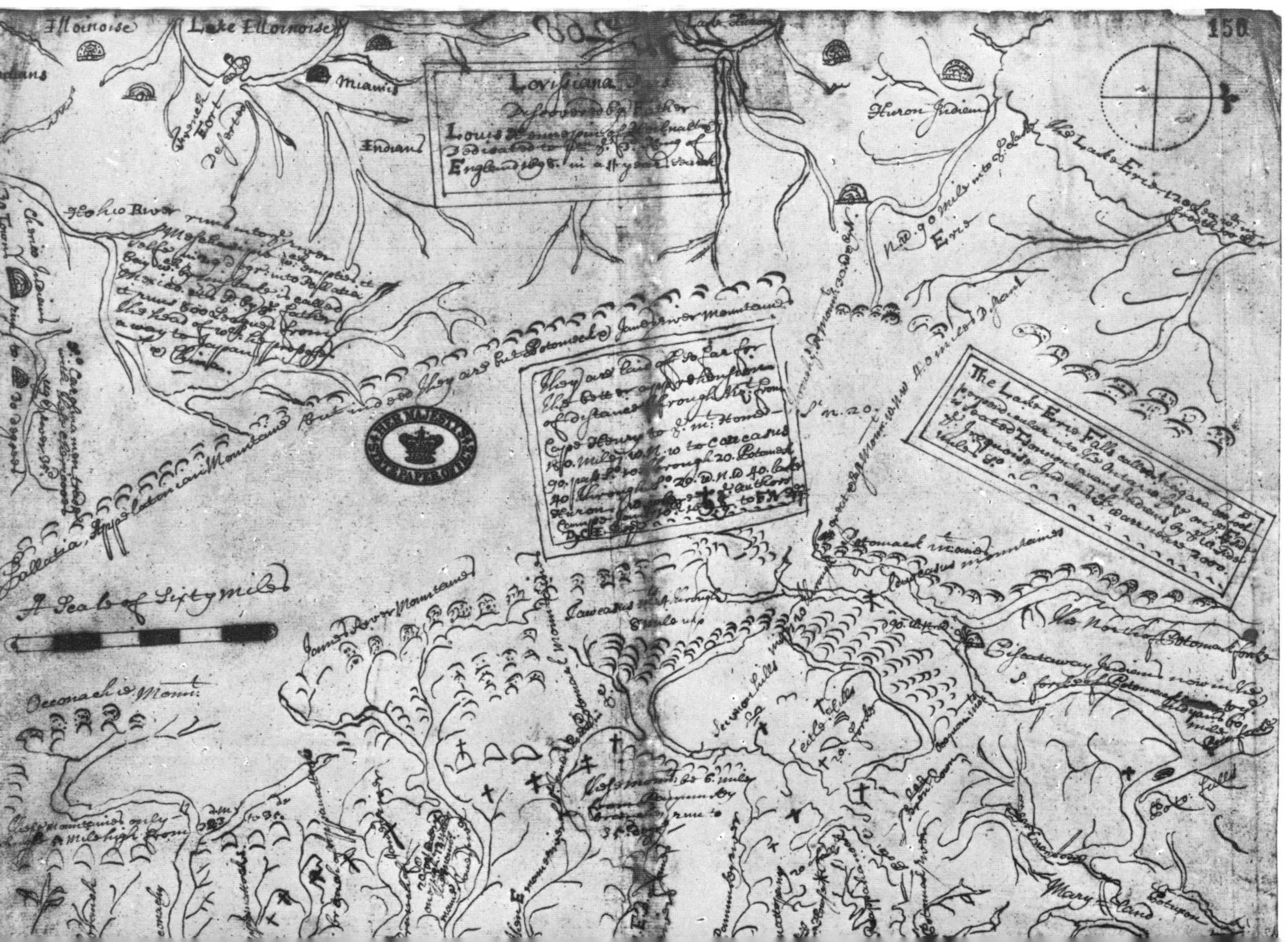

117 Cadwallader Jones. 'Louissiana Pars', Virginia and Louisiana, 1699. *Public Record Office, London, CO5/1350, p. 250.*
Cadwallader Jones, a Virginian planter and explorer, here attempts to relate his knowledge of Virginia to the trans-Appalachian region and the Great Lakes as shown on Father Hennepin's map of Louisiana, published in England in 1698. Jones shows a better conception of Virginia from the headwaters of navigation to the valley of Virginia beyond the Blue Ridge than any previous map-maker, though the limits of his knowledge and accuracy are soon reached. Eighteen crosses, only one beyond the Blue Ridge on the Shenandoah River, indicate 'where ye Author Camp'd'. To the southwest (the top left of the map) 'Hohio River runs into ye river Meschasipie, which flows into Pallatia Bay, wch he [Hennepin] proposes [as] a way to Japan and China'. Jones's chief thesis is that a viable route lies across the three ranges to the Great Lakes, especially to Lake Erie; he notes the distances, though not lucidly, as far as Lake Huron. The map with its numerous legends supports Jones's far-sighted and just thesis in his *Memorial* that trade with the Indians is feasible and very profitable, that the valleys are rich and fertile, and that military protection against invasion is needed.

118

118 Hennepin. 'America Septentrionalis', 1698, from Louis Hennepin, *A New Discovery of a Vast Country*, 1698.
This is a detail from Hennepin's map of North America, which appeared first in a Dutch edition of his work published in Amsterdam in 1697. Hennepin never reached the mouth of the Mississippi, as he claimed, and his narrative and map include information, often distorted, which he gathered from the accounts of other explorers.

His work excited much interest in England and in the colonies concerning the possibilities of trade and expansion in the Mississippi Valley. Cadwallader Jones's map (plate 117) and the proposals in his *Memorial* were strongly influenced by Hennepin.

mountains, 'a pleasing tho' dreadful sight' to Fallam. They followed the New River to where it breaks through a range at Peter's Falls on the West Virginia line. A little farther they found some meadows where they camped; they convinced themselves that the river ebbed and flowed with the tide and that from a hilltop nearby they caught a reflected glimmer of the Western Sea! They took possession in the name of King Charles.[14]

They did not know that a few months before, on 14 June 1671, at Sault Ste Marie between Lake Superior and Lake Huron, Daumont de Saint-Lusson, surrounded by a group of Frenchmen, some in splendid attire of silk and velvet and others in the black gowns of Jesuit fathers, planted a huge wooden cross and took possession 'of all countries, rivers, lakes, and streams . . . bounded on one side by the seas of the North and of the West, and on the other by the South Sea' for and in the name of Louis XIV of France.[15] Here began the conflict of claims for the interior valley of North America that foreshadowed the mighty struggle initiated at Fort Duquesne eighty-four years later.[16]

On their return to the Totero village Batts and Fallam heard of a 'great company' led by William Byrd I that had passed by on its discoveries a few days before. Captain Byrd was soon to become one of the great merchants in the Indian fur trade; so distant and prompt were his sources of information that he had already in that year heard of a French settlement 'in the back of Virginia', possibly La Salle's on the Illinois, and was apprehensive of the damage to the Virginia fur trade by Indian activities.[17] Batts and Fallam reached Appomattox 'hungry, wet, and weary' on the first of October.

In the years until his death about 1680, Abraham Wood was one of the most active and powerful men in Virginia. To his great trading post at Fort Henry on the Appomattox came Indians to barter and delegations of tribal chiefs to be entertained and to make alliances; from Fort Henry he commanded the militia that protected the frontier against hostile Indian incursions; and from Appomattox he sent his traders hundreds of miles to gather the furs which he shipped to England.

One of the most illuminating accounts of Indian traders and Indian captivity comes from a letter from Abraham Wood to his friend John Richards in London. In May 1673 he sent two of his agents, the experienced trader, James Needham, and a bright but illiterate lad, Gabriel Arthur, on a mission to establish relations with the Tomahitans, a branch of the Yuchi Indians who probably lived on the Hiwassee River in present Cherokee County, western North Carolina.[18] From the Occaneechi island on Roanoke River the two, accompanied by a band of Tomahitans, followed the route of Lederer to the Trading Ford on the Yadkin. There they turned west along the Catawba River valley until they reached the escarpment of the Blue Ridge, rising suddenly two thousand feet above the Piedmont hills. Entering through a gap into the valley of the French Broad, the present site of Asheville, North Carolina, they crossed 'five shallow rivers' through deep gorges below the towering mass of the Great Smoky Mountains. At the Tomahitan town on the Hiwassee, or possibly some other tributary of the Little Tennessee River, Needham left Arthur to learn the language and develop friendly relations. Near the Trading Ford on his return Needham was murdered by John Hasecoll, an Occaneechi Indian. 'Soe died this heroyick English man', wrote Wood, 'whose fame shall never die if my penn were able to eternize it which had adventured where never any English man had dared to attempt before and with him died one hundered forty-foure pounds starling of my adventure with him. I wish I could have saved his life with ten times the vallue'.[19] The Occaneechi had already prevented an earlier attempt by Wood to by-pass their jealously guarded and profitable position as middlemen in the fur trade; Hasecoll incited the Tomahitans accompanying Needham to fear and hatred of the English.

Arthur, on their return, barely escaped torture and death; he was saved by the timely return of the Tomahitan chief, who befriended him. For nearly a year young Gabriel accompanied the Tomahitans on their expeditions; the far-ranging activities of an Indian war party are impressively shown by the account he gave to Wood on his return (see selection 2) in June 1674 after escaping from an Occaneechi ambush.

Another Virginian, Cadwallader Jones, was only twenty-one years of age when Wood sent Needham and Arthur on their expedition in 1673, but he was soon to become one of the most vigorous proponents of the fur trade and expansion across the mountains. During his twenties Jones acquired extensive patents to land in northern Virginia, fought marauding Indians, was in charge of the fort on the Rappahannock with the rank of lieutenant colonel, had 'an inland trade about four hundred miles from here S.S.W.' with Indians in Carolina, and may have crossed the Blue Ridge while exploring the headwaters of the Rappahannock River in 1682.[20] After a tempestuous eight or nine years as governor of the Bahama Islands, Jones returned to Virginia in 1698. In January 1699 he submitted to Governor Francis Nicholson of Virginia 'An Essay: Louissiania and Virginia Improved', stimulated by his reading Father Louis Hennepin's *A new discovery of a vast country in America*, published in London the previous year. Jones urged in his 'Essay' the expansion of trade and settlements across the mountains, as 'a trade from hence Settled would answer with those Indians. From our Cawcasean Mountains [Blue Ridge], which is now to me well known, Cannot rationally be above one hundred miles into Louissiana Country.'[21] Jones's map (plate 117) illustrates clearly the geographical ignorance of the English and French at this time as well as recent increases in their knowledge. Both Jones and Hennepin drew upon what other reports and maps were available to them.

119 Mark Catesby lived in Virginia from 1712 to 1719, where he made drawings of the flora and fauna. His most productive period was during his second visit, from 1722 to 1725 in the Carolinas.
Red-winged starling [blackbird]. Watercolor, *c.* 1724. Nests 'always over the water, among the reeds or sedge'—Catesby. *Royal Library, Windsor Castle.*

119

120

120 Mark Catesby. Goat-sucker of Carolina. Watercolor, *c.* 1724. Probably a chuck-will's widow, although the drawing combines some elements of the eastern night-hawk with this bird. 'Swiftly mounting . . . they make a hollow and surprizing noise . . . like the wind blowing into a hollow vessel'—Catesby. *Royal Library, Windsor Castle.*

The significance of Cadwallader Jones's essay and map is that at long last the mirage of a near and easy way to the Pacific had faded; the faint possibility only remained of a passage hundreds of miles beyond the Blue Ridge. On the other hand, as Jones argued urgently, beyond those mountains was a vast territory with many Indian tribes open to trade; action was necessary to divert the great potentialities of this area from the French. Leadership in Virginia to implement Jones's proposals, however, was lacking; Governor Nicholson forwarded his essay to London, where it gathered dust in the files of the Lords of Trade.

A vigorous new lieutenant governor, Alexander Spotswood, came to Virginia in 1710 and sent out exploring parties to the mountains within a few months after his arrival. Spotswood may have read Jones's essay; like him, he recommended formation of a Virginia Company to promote trade with the Indians and proposed the construction of a series of forts along the frontier.[22] In 1716 he personally organized a party of Virginia gentlemen, accompanied by servants and rangers, to explore beyond the Blue Ridge. Reaching the top, where they named a peak Mount George, they descended to the Shenandoah River before starting back. With the governor was a Huguenot visitor, the Rev. James Fontaine, who left a record of the event in his autobiography: 'We crossed the river, which we called the Euphrates . . . I went a swimming in it . . . We had a good dinner, and after it we got the men together, and loaded all their guns, and we drank to the King's health in Champagne, and fired a volley—the Princess's health in Burgundy, and fired a volley, and all the rest of the Royal Family in claret, and fired a volley. We drank the Governor's health and fired another volley. We had several sorts of liquor, viz. Virginia red wine and white wine, Irish usquebaugh, brandy, shrub, two sorts of rum, champagne, canary, cherry, punch, water, cider, &c'.[23]

If some of the gentlemen regarded the expedition only as a festive bibulous outing, the governor's purpose was serious. He was the first important colonial official of the British government to perceive fully the value of the tramontane territory and to act upon that understanding. But it was the fur traders and expansionists of Carolina, not Virginia, who led the way west, around the southern end of the Appalachians, where they confronted the French established on the Mississippi.

2 Carolina and Florida, 1650-1700

Between Virginia and the Spanish outposts hundreds of miles to the south, the coast and the land behind it had been little troubled by European colonizers. Around 1650, however, English settlers in Virginia began to show an interest in the area southward from Chesapeake Bay. In September 1653 a young Virginian, searching for a sloop he had lost, sailed with some companions through Currituck Inlet 'and so went to Rhoanoke island; where, or near thereabouts, they found the great commander of those parts with his Indians a hunting, who received them civilly, and showed them the ruins of Sir Walter Ralegh's fort'.[24] The young man brought the Indian chief to the house of Col Francis Yeardley of Lynnhaven, a prominent member of the House of Burgesses from Lower Norfolk, who entertained him and sent carpenters who built the 'king' an English house, furnished with 'utensils and chattels'. Yeardley also arranged for the purchase of 'three great rivers', probably at the head of Albemarle Sound. In 1654 or 1655 Yeardley also had a twenty-foot square house, with a chimney, built for a Nathaniel Batts on Salmon Creek at the head of Albemarle Sound, probably for use both as residence and trading center.[25] Batts was given 'special priveleges' by the General Assembly of Virginia, for the 'discovery of an inlet to the southward' in 1657. In 1672 Batts was still using the house or living there, since in that year the peripatetic George Fox, founder of the Society of Friends, canoed across Chowan River from Edenton to visit him. Fox asked him to read a paper to 'the Emperor and his thirty Kings under him of the Tusroures [Tuscaroras]' and referred to Batts as, 'the Old Governor' and 'Nathaniel Batts, who had been Governor of Roan-oak. He went under the name of Captain Batts, and had been a rude, desperate man'.[26] (See plate 164.)

Interest in what was soon to be the province of Carolina was stirring the imagination of persons farther afield than Virginia. In New England a 'committee for Cape Faire at Boston', supported by merchants and motivated at least in part by diminishing open land in the Massachusetts Bay Colony, sent the *Adventure* under an experienced sea captain, William Hilton, 'for the discovery of Cape Feare and more South parts of Florida'.[27] After being driven far off her course by a late summer hurricane, the *Adventure* made her way over the shoals into the Cape Fear River on 4 October 1662 (see plate 121). In their long boat the voyagers explored 'thirty leagues' (probably nearer fifty miles) up the river. 'There are abundance of vast meadows', they reported on their return to Boston, 'besides upland fields, that renders the contry fit to be called a land for Catle . . . and greatt swamps laden with varieties of great Oakes and other trees of all Sorts.'[28] With undue optimism they noted that they saw but few mosquitoes and no rattlesnakes and that the Indians were very courteous. A colonizing attempt from Boston in the spring of 1663 followed the enthusiastic description brought back by the *Adventure*; but the settlers soon returned, discouraged.

In England, meanwhile, events were occurring which affected the future history not only of the southern coast but of the entire North American continent. Charles II had, by letters patent on 20 March 1663, granted to eight of his courtiers the Province of Carolina, which extended, roughly, from Virginia to the Florida peninsula, and westward from the Atlantic coast to the Pacific Ocean. Two years later, with royal generosity in bestowing land which he did not own,

121 Nicholas Shapley. Hilton's discoveries along the Carolina coast, 1662. *British Museum, London, Add. Ms. 5415, c. 4.*
Hilton left a glowing account of his explorations, which has recently been found and published by Professor Louise Hall, and this map on which names record eponymously Hilton's companions and events on their expeditions.

121

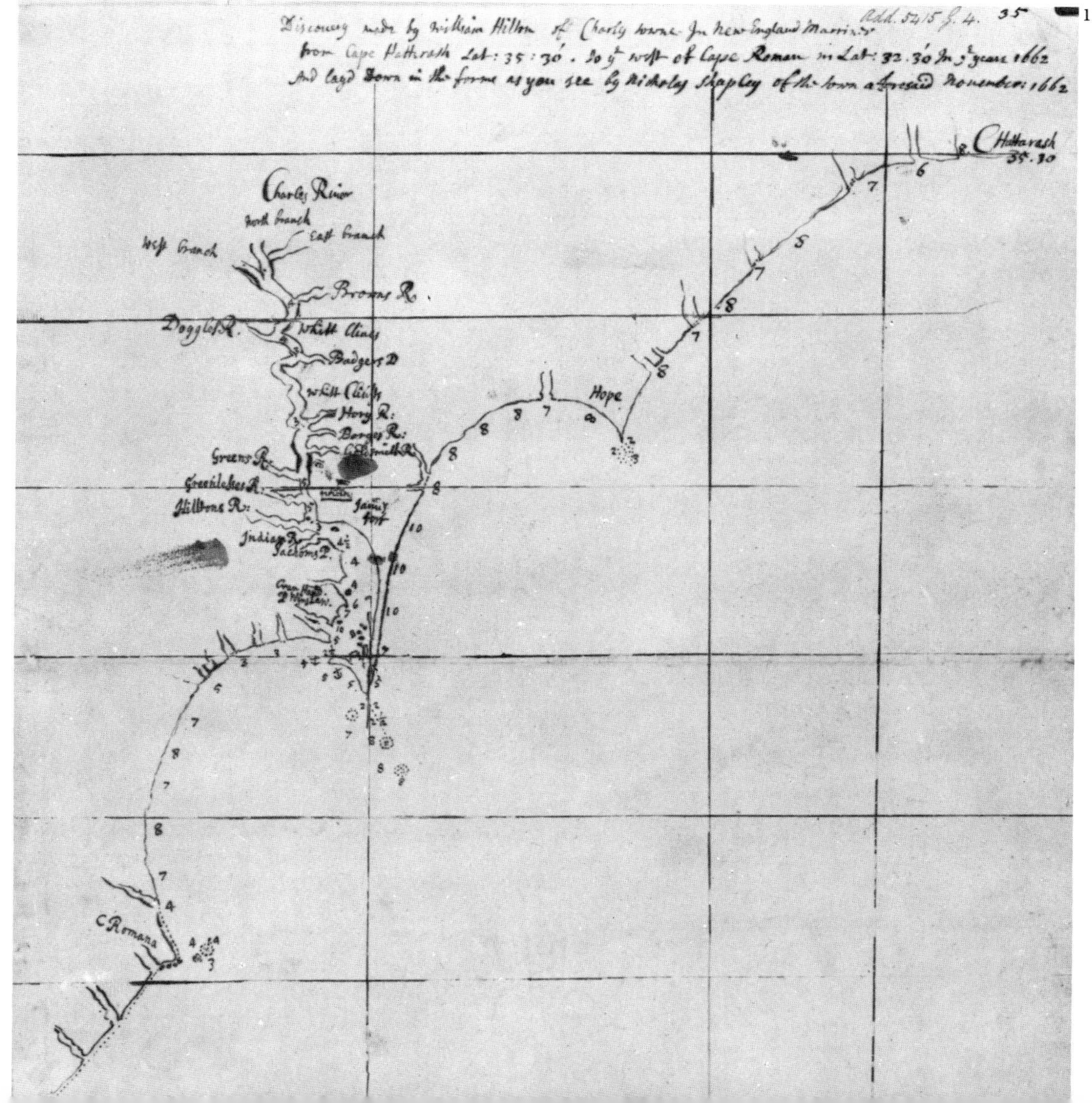

122

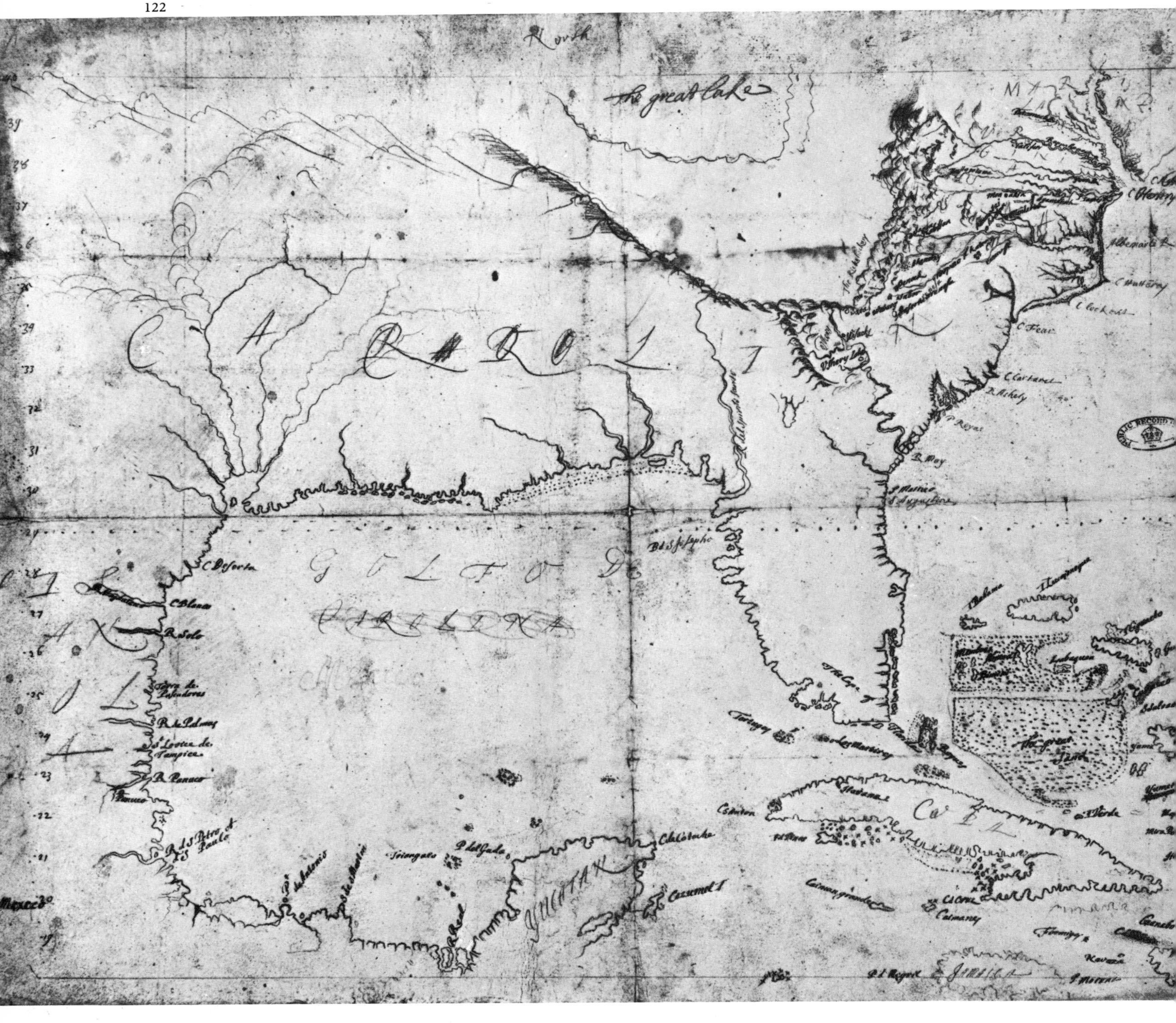

he extended the bounds granted to the eight Proprietors of Carolina north from 30° to $36\frac{1}{2}^\circ$ and south from 30° to 29°; the southern limits thus included St Augustine, which Pedro Menéndez de Avilés had founded in 1565 and which, with its outposts, the Spanish had occupied ever since. With the approval of the new Proprietors a group of 'adventurers' from the Barbadoes initiated a series of exploratory voyages along the coast which led eventually to permanent settlement. In the fall of 1663 they sent William Hilton for a second trip which extended as far south as Port Royal, where he named Hilton Head, an island which still bears his name.[29] In 1664 a settlement was made on the Cape Fear River at Charles Town, sometimes confused with the later Charles Town in South Carolina.[30] The next year its governor, Sir John Yeamans, made another coastal voyage 'south and west', and in 1666 Lt Col Thomas Sandford, an official of the Cape Fear colony, visited the Indian cassique or chief at Port Royal, 'leaving an English man . . . for learning their language; and to that

122 Locke. Map of Carolina, 1671. *Public Record Office, London, MPI/11.* This manuscript map, endorsed by John Locke, philosopher and secretary to Lord Ashley, one of the most active of the Lords Proprietors and Chief Justice of the province, is apparently based on a Spanish map, with English names added. Along the Carolina coast is 'R. Ashely'; to the interior are the savanna, Ushery Lake, and 'Deserta Arenosa' of John Lederer's explorations in 1670, described in the journal of Lederer which Sir William Talbot had just brought to England from Maryland. On the back are the notes for a Carolina promotion essay in Locke's hand. John Ogilby had requested maps of Carolina from Locke; this may be the rough draft which Ogilby used for the First Lords Proprietors' map: the endorsed notes are similar to the account of Carolina published in Ogilby's English edition of *America*, London, 1671, in which the map was inserted.

123 Mark Catesby. Summer red bird. Watercolor, *c.* 1724. *Royal Library, Windsor Castle.*

56
Summer Redbird
Muscicapa Americana rubra.
Platanus Occidentalis.

123

Tricolor.
Ligurinus
44
Linaria Cærulea

purpose one of my company Mr. Henry Woodward, a Chirurgeon, had before I sett out assured mee his resolution to stay with the Indians if I should think convenient'.[31] Dr Woodward did not remain long at Port Royal. The Spanish, who kept a vigilant eye on English activities, were alerted to his presence. They seized and took him to St Augustine. From there he escaped when the English buccaneer Captain Robert Searle raided the town in 1668; he served as surgeon aboard a privateer until it was wrecked in a hurricane off Nevis, one of the Leeward Islands.

Woodward was there when the fleet under Governor Joseph West, bound for Carolina, stopped at the island in December 1699. Instead of returning to England to report to the Lords Proprietors, as he had intended, he volunteered to accompany the colonists, was accepted, and from the first became energetic in promoting the colony's affairs by his knowledge of the Indians and influence among them. The colonists wisely chose to make their first settlement in the Kiawah country some distance north of Port Royal, which they felt was 'in the very chaps of the Spaniard'. There two rivers, named the Ashley and Cooper, the names of one of the Lords Proprietors, flowed into a spacious bay with an entrance more easily defended than that of Port Royal. Their first settlement on the Ashley, which they called Charles Town, was moved in a few years to the peninsula formed by the two rivers.

Within a few weeks after landing Woodward began a series of intrepid explorations to the interior that opened the way to trade and alliances with the natives. 'I have discovered a Country soe delicious & fruitfull', he wrote to Sir John Yeamans, whom he had known as governor of the unsuccessful colony on the Cape Fear River, 'that were it cultivated doutless it would prove a second Paradize'.[32] To reach it he had travelled west and north an eight days' journey to the Wateree, a branch of the Santee River.[33] 'I there contracted a leauge with the Emperour & all those petty Cassekas [chiefs] betwixt us & them', Woodward wrote. The 'Emperour' sent furs back with Woodward to Governor William Sayle; and some weeks later, when the colony was in dire need of food, he supplied it with welcome provisions.

In July 1671 Woodward opened a land route from Charles Town to Virginia on a secret trading mission for Sir John Yeamans, who had recently arrived in Charles Town.[34] He probably retraced his way up the Santee and Wateree to the 'Esaugh' (Catawba) tribe below present Charlotte, North Carolina, and from there followed the path to General Wood's Fort Henry traversed the previous year by John Lederer.

A far more important mission was Woodward's contact with the small but greatly feared Westo tribe on the Savannah River. Some Westo Indians appeared at Lord Ashley's plantation to barter furs in early October 1674; Woodward, who was the special agent of Lord Ashley, the Earl of Shaftesbury, met them and agreed to return with them to their head town. His purpose was to achieve a friendly contact with them on behalf of the province, to establish trade relations for the benefit of the Lords Proprietors, and to explore the country. He gave a brief but instructive account of his journey (see selection 3), which established a route followed by later traders to the Creek, Cherokee, and Chicasaw Indians.

The Charles Town colonists, however, were antipathetic to the Westo alliance because they disliked the trading monopoly it gave to the Proprietors and because the Westos continued their attacks on friendly neighboring Indians. The Carolinians encouraged a war against the Westos by the Savannah Indians; without 'much Blood shed or money spilt' by the English, the Westos were defeated and within ten years

125

126

124 Mark Catesby. Painted finch. Watercolor, *c.* 1724. *Royal Library, Windsor Castle.*

125 Gascoigne. 'A New Map of the Country of Carolina' [1682]. *British Museum, London.*
Joel Gascoigne's Carolina is the Second Lords Proprietors' map of the province and it shows the great increase of geographical knowledge since Ogilby's First Lords Proprietors' map was published ten years before (see plate 122). The route of Lederer's 1670 journey, with its widely copied geographical misconceptions (see plate 116), has disappeared entirely; the southeasterly course of the rivers from the Appalachian Mountains is correctly drawn, and the rapid increase of settlements on the Ashley and Cooper Rivers is evident, both on the map and the inset.

Woodward furnished much of the detail for the interior through his visits to the Westo Indians on the Savannah River (here incorrectly identified as the May River (St John's), settled by the French in 1564), Cotifaciqui on the Santee, and Esaw (Catawba Indians) on the Wateree. The Wateree is a tributary of the Santee, however, not an independent river flowing into the sea. Gascoigne's was the best printed map of the province of Carolina until well into the eighteenth century. West is at the top.

126 Native king with his attendants, from J. Ogilby, *America*, 1671. This engraving may be based upon the drawing, by the French artist and colonist, Le Moyne, of King Saturiba, in De Bry, *Florida*, plate 39, 1591.

after Woodward's journey not more than fifty of them remained, scattered and eventually absorbed by the Creek Indians. An ominous increase in the Indian slave trade accompanied the Westo War of 1680; it also broke the monopoly of trade with the interior tribes which the Proprietors had attempted to establish. The way was open to further exploration by enterprising Carolina traders.[35]

It was again the indefatigable Woodward who led the way. While on a trip to London in 1682, Woodward was given a commission which Professor Verner Crane called 'a noteworthy document in the history of English exploration'.[36] It enlarged on the benefits to the King and to the Proprietors of having 'the Inlands of our Province of Carolina well discovered and what they do containe and also a passage over the Apalatean Mountains found out'. Armed with his commission, in the summer of 1685 Woodward reached the Chattahoochee River, the present boundary line between Georgia and Alabama. At that time the chief villages of the Lower Creek Indians, Coweta and Kasihta, were on its banks. At Coweta, the 'war town' of the Creeks, Woodward met the head chief of the Ochese tribe, formed a cordial relationship, and arranged for a trading center which was to develop into a stronghold for English interests. While the Indians were building a stockade under the direction of English who accompanied Woodward, the news reached Lieutenant Antonio Matheos at the fort of Apalache, an outpost of St Augustine near the Gulf coast. He immediately marched north with 250 Indians and a small contingent of Spanish troops. Woodward prudently vanished into the forest but left a letter to be delivered to the Spaniards. After explaining his proprietary mission, he ended pointedly: 'I am very sorry that I came with so small a following that I cannot await your arrival. Be informed that I came to get acquainted with the country, its mountains, the seacoast, and Apalache. I trust in God that I shall meet you gentlemen later when I have a larger following, September 2, 1685. Vale'.[37]

Hardly had the Spanish left, after burning the stockade and appropriating the trading goods, than the defiant Woodward returned with the English to trade. It was, however, his last appearance on the Chattahoochee; he was carried back by the Indians to Charles Town on a stretcher, very ill, followed by 150 warriors laden with peltry. For nearly twenty years, since Sandford had left the young surgeon at Port Royal in 1666, Dr Henry Woodward had played the chief role in making first contacts with the Indians and in inland exploration. 'He was', writes Professor Crane, 'the first English settler in South Carolina, the first interpreter and Indian agent, the first Englishman to penetrate the western wilderness beyond the Chattahoochee, the pioneer, in a word, of English expansion in the lower South'.[38]

If Woodward did not return to the Chattahoochee, however, the Carolina traders did, despite determined Spanish opposition and punishment of the Indians who received the English. An important trading post developed near the head of navigation on the Savannah River. There merchandize from and deerskins to Charles Town were transported by water or carried overland by the path Woodward had opened in his Westo journey of 1674. A fort and warehouse were built with the active approval of the Lords Proprietors and by 1692 the English were stretching out their tentacles of trade as far as the Indians of Mobile Bay, inland from the Gulf coast.[39]

Before the end of the century they were going farther. The rivers running north from the gulf were to prove an easy and natural transportation route for the French after 1700. They were an impediment to the English but not a serious one; by trails through the rolling upper foothills and at ford crossings where many hospitable tribes had their villages, the traders built stockhouses or 'factories' among the Alabama, Talapoosa, Abihka, and other tribes. In 1698 Captain Thomas Welch, a Carolina trader, reached the Mississippi River and crossed it to the Quapaw village at the mouth of the Arkansas.[40] He opened relations with the powerful and warlike Chickasaw in the northeastern part of what is now the state of Mississippi; they became firm allies of the English and, supplied with firearms, raided the unarmed neighboring tribes for slaves which they sold to the traders. The English alliance with the Chickasaws was the major obstacle which prevented the French from complete achievement of their design to control the lower Mississippi Valley.[41] In May 1699 Bienville, who had just established the first French settlement at Biloxi, heard from the Bayagoula Indians that two Englishmen with a large band of Chickasaws had surprised an Acolapissa village on the Pearl River two days before and had carried off a great number of men as slaves.

The ever-present lure of mines and sudden wealth also drew the Carolinians westward. The first recorded exploration of the Appalachian mountains from Charles Town was made in 1690 by Surveyor General Maurice Mathews and James Moore, planter and slave-trader, who 'journied over the Apalathean mountn's for inland discovery and Indian trade' and also for mines and ore. After their return Mathews took several specimens to England for assay.[42]

Not all the exploration was westward. Some years before the end of the century, Jean Couture, a *coureur de bois*, made his way from the Mississippi up the Tennessee and across the Appalachians to Carolina and opened up an important new route. It was Couture whom Tonty had left at a stockaded post near the mouth of the Arkansas on the return from his unsuccessful search for La Salle, who heard the story of La Salle's murder from Cavelier, Douay, and Joutel, and who first informed Tonty of his master's death. Couture, who may have run foul of strict French trade regulations, was a man of ability, enterprise—and considerable imagination. He told attentive listeners in Carolina of finding gold 'not far from the branch of a navigable river', a journey in a canoe down the Mississippi, across the Gulf, up the Rio Grande, down another river to California, and back to Canada. Couture's tale of this fifteen-thousand mile junket, writes Father Jean Delanglez, became 'one of the most fantastic in all the literature of mythical travels'.[43] In 1699 Governor Blake of South Carolina employed Couture to lead a group of traders from the Savannah River down the Tennessee on a significant mission to establish trade and control of the Mississippi River. By February 1700 they were alienating Quapaw Indians on the Arkansas from the French, according to a Jesuit report, and by 1701 renegade French *coureurs de bois* were buying cheap English goods in Carolina and returning to 'French' territory to sell them to the Indians.[44] Bienville found five of these renegade Frenchmen near Biloxi; in 1699, he turned back an armed English ship on the Mississippi sent by Dr Daniel Coxe to establish a colony in 'Carolana'.[45] In December 1699 James Boyd, a French trader who had arrived in London from Carolina, informed the Lords for Trade and Plantations that 'the English Indian Traders inhabiting there, had made many Journeys through the Country westward to above 1000 or 1200 miles distance'.[46] Throughout the southeast scores of traders were exploring the network of Indian trails with their pack horses and transporting goods up and down rivers and streams by canoe in unrecorded journeys which were opening the land to competing interests.

The mighty and inevitable conflict between the French and English was already well under way in the first years of the new century. Still farther south the Spanish looked with justifiable apprehension on the most recent intrusions into what they regarded as territory over which they possessed sole legal and divinely bestowed right.

3 Activity in seventeenth-century Florida

The Spanish at St Augustine, established there since the destruction of the French colony in 1565, had long kept an uneasy and wary eye upon the activities of the French and especially of the English. The chief functions of this outpost of the empire was to protect the Spanish treasure fleets, to be a haven for the survivors of vessels wrecked along the coast, and to serve as a base for the supervision and supply of missions among the Indians. For over a century mere survival was a problem; exploration was the last of their concerns.

During most of the seventeenth century the Franciscan fathers labored zealously to convert the natives and to establish missions along the Guale (Georgia) and Orista (South Carolina) coast, in spite of Indian uprisings, French and English pirates who ravaged the settlements, and inadequate support from their own countrymen. The missions at Santa Elena on Parris Island, Santa Catarina on St Catherine's, and elsewhere had military protection. By the middle of the seventeenth century St Augustine was the base for thirty-five missions served by seventy friars and protected by several presidios or military outposts. The Apalache Indians in northwest Florida had repeatedly called for missionaries; a mission was established at San Luis (now Tallahassee) which grew into nine flourishing churches in the area and later extended its work among the Apalachicola (the Lower Creeks of the English) up the Chattahoochee River nearly to its falls by 1679.[47]

Occasionally rumors of 'gente blanca a caballo', probably traders with packhorses, came to the governor at St Augustine, who sent small parties of soldiers and Indians to search for intruders. In 1661, after more rumors, Don Luis de Rojas sent an expedition clear across Georgia from the coast to the Apalachicolas on the Chattahoochee in a fruitless journey. The Spanish were spurred into renewed activity and concern by rumors of French interest in the Gulf coast after La Salle's attempted colonization at Matagorda Bay. In February 1686 a vessel sent from Havana, under the command of Enriquez Barroto, rediscovered Pensacola over a century and a quarter after Tristan de Luna landed there in 1559. Juan Jordán, an officer aboard, described the bay as 'the best I have ever seen . . . The Panzacolas brought forth and gave us Tortillas of corn, and we presented them with glass beads. They were delighted with these'.[48] Such favorable reports on the bay as a harbor resulted in a naval approach by Admiral Andrés de Pez in 1693 accompanied by the able Mexican scientist Sigüenza, who surveyed and mapped the harbor.

This voyage was followed by a land expedition under Laureano de Torres y Ayala, who was ordered before assuming his office as governor of Florida to sail to the port of Apalache and march from there to Pensacola and Mobile. He reached Pensacola to find not a single Indian in the vicinity and 'learned that all the Apalachicolas have withdrawn more than sixty miles north, that they are pagan, and that they are carrying on a considerable trade with the English at San Jorge [Charles Town]'.[49] Torres did his best to impress his superiors in Spain with the 'indomitable fortitude and determination' required in his march through forests and swamps, an achievement which the great conquistadors would have regarded as a routine trek. In spite of his 'obdurate determination' to fulfill orders, he and his men decided that the difficulties in traversing the sixteen leagues to Mobile Bay by land were insuperable; yet Luna in 1559 merely mentioned in passing that he sent some of his captains with the expedition's horses over the same route.[50]

Another and better side to Torres's character is shown in his humane treatment of an unfortunate group of English who were captured by Indians after being shipwrecked near modern Palm Beach during a hurricane in September 1696. The ship, bound for Philadelphia from Jamaica, was carrying several Quakers, including the merchant Jonathan Dickinson,

127

128

127 Fort Carolina, from J. Ogilby, *America*, 1671. After the destruction of the French colony in 1565, the Spanish renamed Fort Caroline San Matheo. The Spanish continued to keep a small garrison and a mission there; but English raids into Florida in the early years of the eighteenth century forced withdrawal from many outposts, including San Matheo.

This engraving of Arx Carolina on the River May is an elaboration of Le Moyne's drawing, found in De Bry's *America*, plates 9 and 10, 1591.

128 Vander Aa. Shipwreck of Dickinson and his party in 1696 [1707], from Johann L. Gottfried, *De Aamerkenswaadigste . . . Landreisen*, Leyden, 1706-27, ix. 6.
This engraving by Pieter vander Aa, the prolific Dutch engraver and publisher, first appeared in Aa's *Naaukerige Versameling der . . . Reisen* in 1706. It shows the capture by Indians of the Dickinsons' shipwrecked party on the east Florida coast. Like many other engravings by Aa, including the other scenes reproduced in plates 143-5, it lacks first-hand authenticity and is derived from the narrative. There are no hills on the Florida coast.

with his wife and babe of six months, and the eminent Quaker missionary, Robert Barrow. Dickinson's account of the perils and tribulations, *Gods protecting providence*, is one of the most graphic in the literature of Indian captivities (see selection 4).[51] It also offers a vivid picture of the east coast of Florida such as is given in no Spanish narrative. Dickinson describes the Indians encountered, their villages and manner of life, and the pathless way through boggy marshes, over burning sands, and across the impediments of inlets in their long struggle to reach St Augustine. Clad chiefly in breech-cloths made from pages of a Bible tossed to them by an Indian, they endured baking sun by day and, as the middle of November approached, the more deadly cold of nights below freezing. Only when they reached St Augustine did they find a welcome in Governor Torres's house.

The Spanish attitude toward the Indians in Florida at this time was on the whole benevolent. The Franciscan friars at their missions encouraged agriculture, which supplied the Spanish with food. The Spanish opposed the sale of firearms to the natives. Since both the English and, later, the French trading policy encouraged the sale of guns, the Spanish Indians were comparatively helpless against the aggressive onslaughts of their northern foes. With the development of a general expansionist policy by the English in the early years of the eighteenth century the effect on the Indian population of the Florida peninsula was destructive.

4 Trade expansion and the empire builders, 1700-30

An aggressive policy of trade expansion, accompanied by military action against the Spanish and French and their Indian allies, characterized a group of 'empire builders' in Charles Town during the early years of the eighteenth century. Such activities and attitudes were not restricted to this period; but they resulted in extensive exploration and in knowledge of the southeast.

Among these merchants and planters who increased geographical information about the region were James Moore, Senior, his son Governor James Moore, 'Tuscarora Jack' Barnwell, and Thomas Nairne. The great merchant houses of Charles Town sent out their representatives with goods; and scores of independent traders travelled the Indian trails to ever remoter villages for deerskins, exploring the land between the Atlantic and the Mississippi and establishing homes with native 'wives' and children in tribal settlements which were centers for their activities. 'The English trade for cloath alwayes atracts and maintains the obedience and friendship of the Indians', wrote Thomas Nairne, the South Carolina provincial Indian agent, in his *Memorial* of 10 July 1708 to the Earl of Sunderland, secretary of State; 'They Effect them most who sell best cheap'.[52] English traders were successful among the Indians because they usually undersold the Spanish and French and provided better goods.

An especially powerful instrument employed against the French and Spanish colonies was 'the notorious traffic in Indian slaves by which', as Professor Crane comments, 'South Carolina achieved a bad eminence among the English colonies'.[53] The expansionists like James Moore, Sr, and Thomas Nairne themselves led Indian allies against the French and Spanish forts and went on far-ranging slave-hunting expeditions. The captured Indians were usually sent to the West Indies for sale, where they brought a handsome profit; Indians kept on the Carolina plantations did not make as docile slaves as imported Africans and could easily escape. Nairne in his *Memorial* stated that the policy of exterminating or removing French Indian allies by encouraging tribal raids was important to the policy of westward penetration and colonial expansion. He drew the extraordinary conclusion that 'the good prices the English traders give them [the Upper Creeks and Chickasaws] for slaves encourage them to this trade extreamly, and some men think that it lessens their numbers before the French can arm them and it is a more Effectuall way of Civilising and Instructing, then all the Efforts used by the French Missionaries'.[54] Nairne himself went on a slave-hunting expedition by the St John's River to the Everglades. A map by Herman Moll shows this journey, the earliest delineation of a trip into the Everglades recorded by English or Spanish (see plate 129). Nairne's own map of the southeast, accompanying his *Memorial* and printed in 1711 (plate 130) has the revealing phrase, curving southward from Pensacola, 'No Inhabitants from here to the Point of Florida'.

An even more driving force than Nairne's for western trade and colonization and a shrewder ambassador to the Indians appeared on the South Carolina scene about 1713. Pryce Hughes, a gentleman of property and education from Mont-

129 Moll. 'A New Map of the North Parts of America claimed by France', 1720, in Herman Moll, *The world described*, London 1708-20, No. 9. Thomas Nairne made a slave-hunting expedition with a group of Yamassee Indians about 1702 as shown on this map. Other raids followed with devastating effect on the Indian population. Below Florida on Moll's map is an account of Nairne's expedition. 'Explanation of an Expedition in Florida Neck, by Thirty-Three Iamesee Indians accompany'd by Capt. T. Nairn. A. The Place where the Indians leave their canoes to go a slave-hunting, it is 6 days Rowing from St. Whan's Rivers Mouth. B. Large inland Lakes, some of them joyned together. C. The Furthermost place where ye Indians have gone with Canoes. E. The Path they took to go a Slave Catching. F. Cacenta Town. G. Large Pond where was one house. H. Place where they swam over a Deep River. I. The same River is here Brackish. K. Place where they took 29 slaves. L. Here they took 6 Slaves. M. Here they took and killed 33 Men at 1 a Clock ye same day a very Numerous body of Indians came against them, they beeing but 33 men. yet put them presently to Flight; they having no Armes but Harpoos, made of Iron and Fishbones; they were all Painted. N. Fresh water Creek.'

Most of this information is found on a large manuscript map now in the Public Record Office, CO 700, Carolina North and South 3.

129

130

130 Nairne. 'A Map of South Carolina', 1711.
This is the first printed map to show the explorations of the Charles Town traders and expansionists west to the Mississippi River. It appears as an inset in Edward Crisp's 'A Compleat Description of the Province of Carolina', an important map which shows the location and plantations of over 250 settlers in coastal South Carolina at the end of the first decade of the eighteenth century.

gomeryshire, Wales, had arrived with a plan for a Welsh settlement at Port Royal; but he soon had larger visions. In 1713 he was in the Cherokee country, where he rescued two Frenchmen from Indian captivity on the Tennessee River. These he persuaded to attempt to turn the Illinois Indians and 'seven numerous nations' beyond the Mississippi on the Missouri to English trade. His plan was to secure the upper valley fur trade and to cut the French great river route between Canada and Louisiana. 'I've been a considerable way to the Westwd. upon the branches of the Mesisipi', he wrote to his brother-in-law, John Jones, late in 1713, 'where I saw a country as different from Carolina as the best parts of our country are from the fens of Lincolnshire . . . with many fine navigable Rivers, pleasant savannahs, plenty of coal, lead, iron, lime and freestone wth several salt springs . . . and as fine timber as the largest I ever saw in England'.[55]

In 1714 the success of Hughes's activities became alarmingly clear to the French. 'He was an engineer, a geographer, a man of spirit', wrote Governor Cadillac of 'Master You'.[56] By midsummer Hughes had visited the centers of trade in the Indian country of the southeast and made a map of the area (plate 131) which Governor Spotswood of Virginia copied about 1720 and sent to the Board of Trade. Hughes himself Spotswood described as 'an English Gent., who had a particular fancy of rambling among the Indians'.[57]

But as Hughes's plans ripened and the southeast, both Spanish and French, seemed to be falling into English hands, the whole grand design of the Carolina imperialists crashed in disaster.

In the winter of 1714 Hughes was firmly ensconced among the Natchez planning to win the lower Mississippi tribes to alliance, to visit, even farther west, the Indians of the Red River, and to establish a Welsh colony on the Mississippi. But Bienville had alerted his lieutenants; in the spring of 1715 Hughes was captured while voyaging down the Mississippi and taken to Mobile for questioning. Bienville released him; but on the way to the Alabamas, alone and unprotected, he was murdered by a band of Tohome Indians who had suffered, in Cadillac's bitter phrase to Governor Craven protesting about Carolina incitement of natives, from 'these English trafficking in human flesh'.[58] Already the terrible Yamassee-Creek war had begun which threatened the very survival of Carolina. Thomas Nairne, 'the ablest frontiersman of his day in the South', was captured at the outset by the Indians and died by slow and excruciating torture.[59] The rapacity, knavishness, and tyranny of some traders, too often double-dealing after plying the Indians with rum, brought a terrible punishment on them as well as on innocent settlers living on farms and outlying plantations. Peace of a fashion came after 1717, but intrigues by Spanish and French colonial governments and vacillations in allegiance among the different native tribes and their chiefs continued.[60]

In 1725 and 1726 the Carolina Assembly sent two agents of considerable diplomatic skill on missions into the Indian territory, Colonel George Chicken to the Cherokees and Tobias Fitch to the Creeks. The journals of their travels give a vivid picture of Indian councils and negotiations though little description of the country they traversed. Their talks, however, eased tensions and opened trade routes.[61]

Different in background from Fitch and Chicken and far more grandiose in his plans was Sir Alexander Cuming. A brilliant but erratic young Scots baronet and lawyer, he arrived in Charles Town in December 1729. At the end of a brief stay he made an astonishing month's trip of almost a thousand miles, from 13 March to 13 April 1730, to the Cherokee country, gathering minerals, herbs, and 'natural curiosities' for his collection as a scientific explorer and member of the Royal Society. On this expedition he evolved a bizarre yet surprisingly effective plan to pacify the Cherokee, who were showing disturbing signs of turning to French allegiance, and to persuade them to acknowledge the sovereignty of the king of England. Appearing suddenly before an Indian council at Keowee 'with three cases of Pistols, a gun and a sword under a Great Coat' in complete

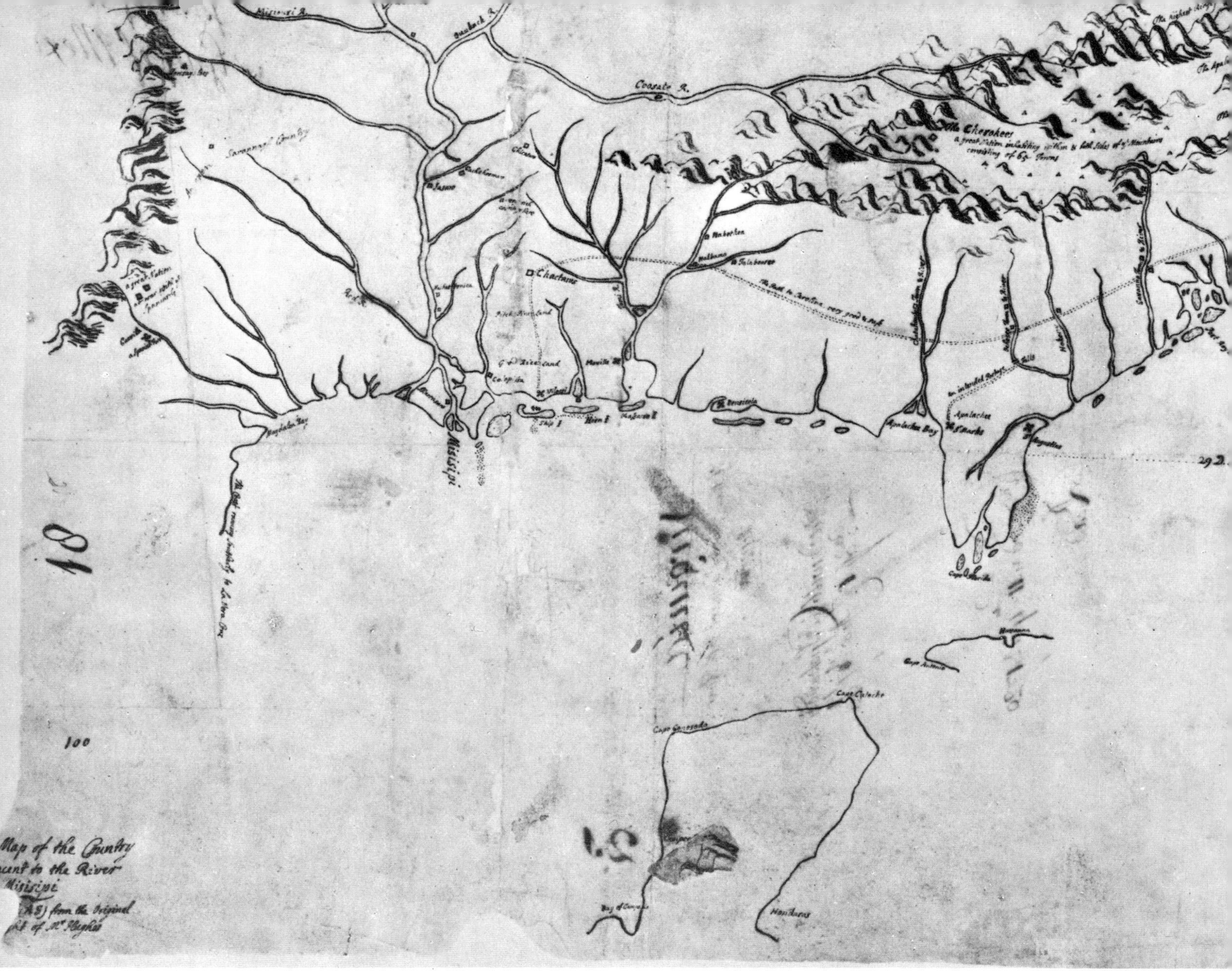

131

131 Hughes. 'A Map of the Country adjacent to the River Misisipi' [1713] *c.* 1720. *Public Record Office, London, CO, Virginia 2.*
The ambitious Pryce Hughes produced a map in 1713 which shows 'The Path to Carolina, very good & safe' from the French capital at Biloxi, through the Choctaw villages to Charles Town and a 'portage' from the Ochesee (?Ocmulgee) River to Spanish San Marco on the Gulf. By the time of his death in 1715 Hughes must have learned much more in his expeditions than he shows on this 'draught'.

disregard of protocol and decorum at an Indian assembly, he overawed and won the Indians to acknowledge English 'sovereignty' by his dramatic personality and actions. He also won the chief Moytoy to firm allegiance by engineering his election as emperor of the Cherokees in a subsequent assembly at Nequasse. Sir Alexander's shrewdest and most far-reaching ploy was an invitation for six chiefs to accompany him to England. The Indian 'Princes' and 'Generals' were the talk of London and the sensation of the press, which published Cuming's journal and reported the events of their stay. They were received by the King and maneuvered by the Board of Trade into signing a solemn treaty. The sequel for Sir Alexander was not a happy one; relegated immediately to the background by the government, he soon fell into obscurity and into debt, spending nearly thirty years a prisoner in the Fleet. For the province of Carolina, however, the alliance with the powerful Cherokee nation and its chiefs was strongly established, and in the friendship of 'Little Carpenter', the great chief Attakullakulla, who had accompanied Cuming to London, the English found an ally whose adherence to them remained constant through the vicissitudes of following decades.[62]

5 Later journeys within the Carolinas, 1700-30

Exploration of the still unsettled parts in the Carolinas during the early years of the eighteenth century resulted in some of the most informative accounts of the period. Three men, Lawson, Catesby, and Byrd, each with a different background, dominant interest, and perspective, left behind records of their observations.

In 1700 John Lawson, a young man of ability, education, and private fortune, set sail in order to see the New World. Leaving England the first of May, he landed in Charles Town and by December received an appointment from the Lords Proprietors to make a reconnaissance survey of the back country of the Carolinas, a region vaguely mapped and

132

133

only partly known to traders along Indian trails. He began a journey from Charles Town on 28 December 1700 in a large canoe with an Indian guide and five other Englishmen, only one of whom continued with him to the end. He made the fifty-nine day journey of some six hundred miles or more to an English settlement on Pamlico River through territory which so delighted him that he built a house on the Neuse River near the future site of New Bern. In 1708 he was appointed surveyor general of North Carolina. The next year he was in London seeing the Lord Proprietors and attending to the publication of his *New voyage to Carolina*, a work still valuable for its comments on the flora and fauna of the region and for its history of the province as well as for the journal of his first expedition to the interior. In London Lawson met Baron Christoph von Graffenried and Franz Louis Michel, organizers of a Swiss and Palatine colony, who purchased from the Lords Proprietors land on the Neuse and Trent rivers. They asked Lawson, who accompanied the first contingent of colonists, to lay out the plan for New Bern near his own house. In 1711 Graffenried and Lawson were captured by Tuscarora Indians while they were exploring a way to Virginia. Incensed by the increasing occupation of land by settlers, the Indian war council condemned both to death. Graffenried managed to persuade the Indians to forego his execution and, after six weeks' imprisonment, to free him. Lawson, according to a report heard by Christopher Gale, chief justice of the province, was tortured to death by the Indians *à petit feu*, a process in which the Indians, according to Lawson's own earlier description, 'split the Pitch-Pine into Splinters, and stick them into the Prisoner's body yet alive. Thus they light them which burn like so many Torches; and in this manner they make him dance round a great Fire, every one buffeting and deriding him, till he expires'.[63]

Lawson, during his years in Carolina, gathered specimens of plants, animals, and insects which he sent to James Petiver, a London apothecary who was one of the chief botanical collectors of his time.[64] Lawson's 'Natural History of Carolina', which is included in his *New voyage to Carolina*, is the most complete treatment of the subject which had appeared and is enriched with his own personal observations.

The year after Lawson's untimely death another Englishman, Mark Catesby, arrived in Virginia and later spent several years in the Carolinas gathering specimens of the flora and fauna of the region and making drawings of them. In the short but charming autobiography which Catesby prefixed to the first volume of his *Natural history of Carolina, Florida, and the Bahama Islands* he describes the purpose of his coming to America. 'The early Inclination I had to search after Plants and other Productions in Nature being much suppressed by

132 Seven Cherokee chiefs in London, 1730. *British Museum, London, Department of Prints and Drawings.*
Sir Alexander Cuming succeeded in his plan to impress a mission of Cherokee chiefs, whom he took to London, with British greatness and power. In a picturesque and unusual ceremony the Board of Trade consummated a treaty with the seven chiefs. The British claimed that it established the King of England as sovereign of the Cherokees and of their land. Ukwaneequa, the young lad at 4 in Isaac Basire's engraving, became the great chief Attakullakulla, the powerful friend of the English for a generation.

133 Michel. Tuscarora Indian tribunal, *c.* 1711. *Burgerbibliothek, Bern, Mül. 441 (1).*
A major organizer of the Palatine colony, Franz Louis Michel, made this pen drawing with black wash of the captivity of Von Graffenried, Lawson and their negro servant in his *Relations du voyage d' Amèrique que le Baron de Graffenried a fait en y amenant une colonie Palatine et Suisse, et son retour en Europe.*

134 Michel. Three Americans, post-1704. *Burgerbibliothek, Bern, Ms hist. helv. X. 152.*
Franz Louis Michel made a watercolor drawing of three southern Algonkian (?Powhatan) Indians during his two visits to the country between 1702 and 1704. His original account, *Kurze Americanische Reisbeschreibung* (1702) is lost; this contemporary copy was made by his brother, John Louis Michel.

134

my residence too remote from London . . . my Curiosity was such that I soon imbibed a passionate Desire of viewing as well the Animal as Vegetable Productions in their Native Countries; which were Strangers to England. Virginia was the Place (I having Relations there) suited most with my Convenience to go to, where I arrived the 23d of April 1712'.[65] (See selection 6.)

For several years Catesby observed and sent specimens back to England before returning there. Inspired in London by the botanist Dr William Sherard to continue a more careful study, supported by the Royal Society, and financed by contributions of Governor Francis Nicholson of South Carolina and others, he arrived in Charles Town on 23 May 1722 after a long voyage. For almost a year Catesby gathered specimens in the coastal plain while staying at the homes of wealthy plantation owners. He then extended his investigations to the interior with Fort Moore on the Savannah River as a base, gathering seeds and the more spectacular plants for shipment to his subscribers in England. For several months he made his most extensive explorations toward the mountains. He left no journal with exact accounts of the directions and distances of his trips; but the comments and notes which accompany his drawings show that he followed an unusual bird into untrodden woodland or hunted a new species of tree or flower in unfrequented territory. He was an explorer of rocks and soil, of seeds and nuts, of animals and fishes, and their haunts. On the trip he saw a run of sturgeon on the Savannah: 'Twenty Miles above Savannah Fort, on the Savannah River, where the Cataracts begin, three of us in two days killed sixteen, which to my Regret was left rotting on the shore, except that we regaled our selves with at the Place, and two we brought to the Garrison'.[66] Except for short excursions inland Catesby spent the next two years in the lowlands.

Early in 1725 Catesby went to the Bahama Islands as the guest of Governor George Phenny.[67] This was his last year as a field naturalist; he returned to England in 1726 to devote the rest of his life to horticulture, authorship, and scientific illustration. If Catesby lacked formal training as a naturalist and began his work as an amateur artist, he had a critical intelligence, imagination, and natural artistic ability. He also had enormous pertinacity; unable to pay for professional engravers, he learned to engrave himself. He spent over twenty years engraving and coloring more than two hundred plates and writing for them nearly three hundred pages of commentary. His study of birds in their native habitat enabled him to show them in their natural environment with appropriate trees, flowers, and insects; in this he was an innovator, followed by William Bartram and John James Audubon.[68] His original drawings, bound in three volumes of his *Natural history* with his printed commentaries, have recently been identified in the Royal Library at Windsor Castle; some of them are here reproduced from the original water colors for the first time (plates 136-41, 147-8, 154-5). How these original paintings came to the Royal Library is unknown.

Unlike Lawson and Catesby, Col William Byrd was born in America; Virginia was his home and his first love. Although long periods of his life were spent in London for education and as agent of the colony, he enjoyed the beauty of the pristine wilderness and the rugged frontier. His explorations were not made with the scanty equipment of a frontiersman, however, who carried only a gun, ammunition, and perhaps a few accessories on a packhorse. Byrd was a Virginia gentleman of the eighteenth century, one of the wealthiest and most powerful members of a small group that governed the colony. He travelled with servants and with a plentiful supply of food and drink. Nor did his most memorable journey follow the trails of the hunter or trader; it was a direct and undeviating path of some 241 miles from the Atlantic Ocean westward to the foothills of the Blue Ridge, most of it beyond the bounds of settlement and impeded by swamps, rivers, and other obstacles. Byrd was one of the Virginia commissioners appointed to run the boundary line between Virginia and North Carolina in 1728. For the most part the commissioners accompanied the surveyors. When they came to the morass of the Great Dismal Swamp, however, the commissioners circumambulated it while the surveyors ploughed through with enormous difficulty. Byrd's account of the expedition is one of the classics of American literature (see selection 7).

Byrd's accounts of the survey are much more than a narrative

136

136 Mark Catesby. Largest Carolina moth. Watercolor, *c.* 1724. *Royal Library, Windsor Castle.*

135 Mark Catesby used the drawings made during his visits to North America and the Bahama Islands to prepare plates for the great work he produced on his return to England, the *Natural history of Carolina, Florida, and the Bahama Islands,* 1731-43. He engraved and colored the plates, adding a few more from specimens and from the work of others like John White. For a few plates he mentions the time or circumstances of the first painting; for most, the exact date is unknown.
Angel fish, *c.* 1724, from *Natural history,* II, 31. 'Esteemed in Carolina an excellent eating Fish. . . . The form of this fish is so odd and singular that . . . it would be difficult to give an idea of it by words only'—Catesby.

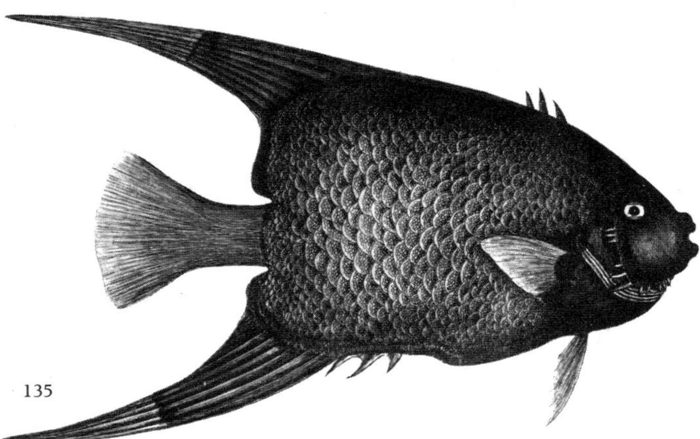

135

137 Mark Catesby. Humming bird. Watercolor, *c.* 1724. *Royal Library, Windsor Castle.*

65
Bignonia Fraxini folijs coccineo
flore minore

of events and a geographical description. He includes the howling of wolves in 'Treble, Tenor, and Bass' that followed them at night; the buffaloes, bears, deer, and wild turkeys that they encountered and killed for food; and the impediments to their progress of great beaver dams, almost impenetrable cane thickets, and swollen rivers. The value of Byrd's *Histories* is in the wealth of information with which he was able to illumine what he saw. The crossing of the Indian Trading Path, along which his father William Byrd I used to send his traders, brings to mind the caravans of a hundred horses, laden with deerskins, that used to return from trafficking with distant tribes. A 'Prodigious Flight of Wild Pigeons' is the occasion for a description of the sky-darkening migrations of passenger pigeons, who would break down the branches of oak trees when they roosted for the night in immense numbers and who would make 'vast Havoc' by laying 'waste whole Forrests in a short time, stripping them of everything edible'.[69] Byrd's satiric comments on the shiftless human population along the border is one of the first characterizations of a type of pioneer too prone to foul its own nest and later known as 'po' white trash'. In the 'Lubberland' of North Carolina, he writes, 'these People live so much upon Swine's flesh that it . . . makes them extremely hoggish in their Temper, & many of them seem to Grunt rather than to speak . . . tis a thorough aversion to Labor that makes People file off to N. Carolina'.[70]

After passing the Indian Trading Path near Moniseep Ford

138 Mark Catesby. Bison. Watercolor, *c.* 1724. *Royal Library, Windsor Castle.*

139 Mark Catesby. White-bill woodpecker [ivory-billed woodpecker]. Watercolor, *c.* 1724. *Royal Library, Windsor Castle.*

139

140

140 Mark Catesby. Red-headed woodpecker. Watercolor, *c.* 1724. *Royal Library, Windsor Castle.*

141

141 Mark Catesby. Pol-cat [skunk]. Watercolor, *c.* 1724. *Royal Library, Windsor Castle.*

on the Roanoke River, the surveyors entered territory not before seen but by Indians and occasional hunters. When they reached the Dan River, a branch of the Roanoke 149 miles from the coast, the North Carolina commissioners, whose food supply was exhausted and who believed that the survey would be sufficient for 'an Age or Two', refused to go farther.[71] The Virginia surveyors continued for another seventy-two miles, to Peter's Creek.

Byrd's insistence on a continuation was soon justified. By 1749 the rapid advance of settlements made necessary the extension of the line to a point near the Watauga River valley in present Tennessee; by 1779 another survey reached Cumberland Gap, through which frontiersmen and their families were pushing into Kentucky.

1
Lederer reaches the Virginia Blue Ridge and explores the Carolina piedmont, 1670

From *The Discoveries of John Lederer*, London, 1672

Though unknown traders may have preceded him, the German traveller John Lederer is the pioneer explorer of the Blue Ridge and Carolina Piedmont. On his first trip he followed a tributary of York River and reached the crest of the Blue Ridge near Hawk Bill or Swift Run Gap in March 1670.

The fourteenth of March, from the top of an eminent hill, I first descried the Apalatæan Mountains, bearing due West to the place I stood upon: their distance from me was so great, that I could hardly discern whether they were Mountains or Clouds, until my Indian fellow travellers prostrating themselves in Adoration, howled out after a barbarous manner, Okéepœze, i.e. God is nigh.

The fifteenth of March, not far from this hill, passing over the South-branch of Rappahanock river, I was almost swallowed in a Quicksand. Great herds of Red and Fallow Deer I daily saw feeding; and on the hill-sides, Bears crashing Mast [nuts] like Swine. . . . The Wolves in these parts are so ravenous, that I often in the night feared my horse would be devoured by them, they would gather up and howl so close round about him, though Tether'd to the same tree at whose foot I myself and the Indians lay: but the Fires which we made, I suppose, scared them from worrying us all. Beaver and Otter I met with at every River that I passed; and the Woods are full of Grey Foxes. . . .

The height of this Mountain was very extraordinary: for notwithstanding I set out with the first appearance of light, it was late in the evening before I gained the top. . . . To the North and West, my sight was suddenly bounded by Mountains higher than that I stood upon. Here did I wander in Snow, for the most part, till the Four and twentieth day of March, hoping to find some passage through the Mountains; but the coldness of the Air and Earth together, seizing my Hands and Feet with numbness, put me to a *ne plus ultra*; and therefore having found my Indian at the foot of the Mountain with my Horse, I returned back by the same way that I went.

On his second trip, Lederer followed the James River for a distance before turning southwest to cross the Roanoke near present Clarksville, Virginia, where he found the treacherous Occaneechi Indians on an island.

The fifth of June [1670], my Company and I parted good friends, they back again, and I with one Sasquesahanough-Indian, named Jackzetavon, only, in pursuit of my first Enterprize, changing my course from West to Southwest & by South, to avoid the Mountains. . . .

From hence, by the Indians instructions, I directed my course to Akenatzy, an Island bearing South & by West, and about fifty miles distant, upon a branch of the same River, from Sapon. The Countrey here, though high, is level, and for the most part a rich soyl, as I judged by the growth of the Trees; yet where it is inhabited by Indians, it lies open in spacious Plains. . . .

The next day after my arrival at Akenatzy, a Richohockan Ambassadour, attended by five Indians, whose faces were coloured with Auripigmentum (in which Mineral these parts do much abound) was received, and that night invited to a Ball of their fashion; but in the height of their mirth and dancing, by a smoke contrived for that purpose, the Room was suddenly darkned, and for what cause I know not, the Rickohockan and his Retinue barbarously murthered. This struck me with such an affrightment, that the very next day, without taking my leave of them, I slunk away with my Indian Companion. . . .

I travelled til the nineteenth of June; and then after a two days troublesome Journey thorow Thickets and Marish [marshy] grounds, I arrived at Watary above fourty miles distant and bearing West-Southwest to Shakor. This Nation differs in Government from all the other Indians of these parts: for they are Slaves, rather than Subjects to their King. Their present Monarch is a grave man, and courteous to strangers: yet I could not without horrour behold his barbarous Superstition, in hiring three youths, and sending them forth to kill as many young women of their Enemies as they could light on, to serve his son, then newly dead, in the other world, as he vainly fancyed. These youths during my stay returned with skins torn off the heads and faces of three young girls, which they presented to his Majestie, and were by him gratefully received.

Lederer continued southwest, until he reached the Ushery (Esaw or Catawba) Indians on the Catawba River near present Rock Hill, South Carolina. No lake existed in this region except on the contemporary European maps; Lederer describes Ushery Lake and its 'brackish water' vaguely but does not actually state that he saw it. On his return he took a more easterly route, crossing the Carolina pine barrens in the heat of July.

The six and twentieth of June, having crossed a fresh River which runs into the Lake of Ushery, I came to the Town, which was more populous then any I had seen before in my March. . . .

These miserable wretches are strangely infatuated with illusions of the devil: it caused no small horrour in me, to see one of them wrythe his neck all on one side, foam at the mouth, stand bare-foot upon burning coals for near an hour, and then recovering his senses, leap out of the fire without hurt, or signe of any. This I was an eye-witness of. . . .

To avoid Wisacky-Marish, I shaped my course Northeast; and after three days travel over hilly ways, where I met with no path or road, I fell into a barren Sandy desert, where I suffered miserably for want of water; the heat of the Summer having drunk all the Springs dry, and left no signe of any, but the Gravelly chanels in which they run. . . . In this distress we travelled till the twelfth of July, and then found the head of a River, which afterwards proved Eruco; . . . after we had crossed the River twice, we were led by it upon the fourteenth of July to the Town of Katearas, a place of great Indian Trade and Commerce, and chief Seat of the haughty Emperour of the Toskiroro's, called Kaskusara, vulgarly Kaskous. His grim Majestie, upon my first appearance, demanded my Gun and Shot; which I willingly parted with, to ransom my self out of his clutches: for he was the most proud imperious Barbarian that I met with in all my Marches.

Lederer reached Appomattox, Virginia, on 18 July 1670. His advice to traders includes an interesting list of things for which Indians bartered their pelfry.

If you barely designe a Home-trade with neighbour-Indians, for skins of Deer, Beaver, Otter, Wild-Cat, Fox, Racoon, &c. your best Truck is a sort of course [coarse] Trading Cloth, of which a yard and a half makes a Matchcoat or Mantle fit for their wear; as also Axes, Hoes, Knives, Sizars [scissors] and all sorts of edg'd tools. Guns, Powder and Shot, &c. are Commodities they will greedily barter for: but to supply the Indians with Arms and Ammunition, is prohibited in all English Governments. . . .

To the remoter Indians you must carry other kinds of Truck, as small Looking-glasses, Pictures, Beads and Bracelets of glass, Knives, Sizars, and all manner of gaudy toys and knacks for children, which are light and portable. For they are apt to admire such trinkets, and will purchase them at any rate.

Text used: William P. Cumming (Ed.), The Discoveries of John Lederer, *Charlottesville, Va., 1958, pp. 17-22, 24-5, 28-33, 41-2.*

2 Gabriel Arthur's trans-Allegheny journeys with the Tomahitan Indians, 1673-4

From a letter by Abraham Wood to John Richards, 22 August 1674, in the Public Record Office, London, Shaftesbury Papers, section ix, bundle 45, no. 94

In May 1673 Major General Abraham Wood sent two of his traders, the experienced James Needham and a lad, Gabriel Arthur, on a southwestern exploration. Reaching the Tomahitan Indians on a branch of the Tennessee River, Needham left Arthur to establish friendly relations. On his return journey with a band of Tomahitans, Needham was murdered by John Hasecoll.

My poore man Gabriell Artheur all this while ecaptivated all this time in a strange land, where never English man before had set foote, in all likelihood either slaine, or att least never likely to returne to see the face of an English man, but by the great providence and protection of God allmighty still survives. . . .

The Tomahittans hasten home as fast as they can to tell the newes the King or chife man not being att home, some of the Tomahittans which were great lovers of the Occheneechees went to put Indian Johns command in speedy execution and tied Gabriell Arther to a stake and laid heaps of combustible canes a bout him to burne him, but before the fire was put too the King came into the towne with a gunn upon his shoulder and heareing of the uprore for some was with it and some a gainst it. The King ran with great speed to the place, and said who is that that is goeing to put fire to the English man. A Weesock borne started up with a fire brand in his hand said that am I. The King forthwith cockt his gunn and shot the wesock dead, and ran to Gabriell and with his knife cutt the thongs that tide him and had him goe to his house and said lett me see who dares touch him.

Arthur then went on a series of raids with the Indians.

Now after the tumult was over they make preparation for to manage the warr for that is the course of theire liveing to forage robb and spoyle other nations and the king commands Gabriell Arther to goe along with a party that went to robb the Spanyarrd, promising him that in the next spring hee him selfe would carry him home to his master. Gabriell must now bee obedient to theire commands. in the deploreable condition hee was in was put in armes, gun, tomahauke, and targett and soe marched a way with the company, beeing about fifty. they travelled eight days west and by south as he guest and came . . . within sight of the Spanish town, walld about with brick and all brick buildings within. . . . A Spanniard [passed] in a gentille habitt, accoutered with gunn, sword and pistoll. one of the Tomahittans espieing him att a distance crept up to the path side and shot him to death. In his pockett were two pices of gold and a small gold chain. which the Tomahittans gave to Gabriell, but hee unfourtunately lost it in his venturing. . . .

They rested but a short time before another party was commanded out a gaine and Gabrielle Arther was comanded out a gaine, and this was to Porte Royall, Here hee refused to goe saying those were English men and he would not fight a gainst his own nation, he had rather be killd . . . the King sware by the fire which they adore as theire god they would not hurt them soe they marched a way over the mountains and came upon the head of Portt Royall river in six days . . . At lengeth they brought him to the sight of an English house, and Gabriell with some of the Indians crept up to the house side and lisening what they said, they being talkeing with in the house, Gabriell hard one say, pox take such a master that will not alow a servant a bit of meat to eate upon Christmas day, by that meanes Gabriell knew what time of the yeare it was, soe they drew of secretly and hasten to the Indian town, which was not above six miles thence. about breake of day stole upon the towne. The first house Gabriell came too there was an English man. Hee hard him say Lord have mercy upon mee. Gabriell said to him runn for thy life. Said hee which way shall I run. Gabriell reployed, which way thou wilt they will not meddle with thee. Soe hee rann and the Tomahittans opend and let him pas cleare there they got the English mans snap-sack with beades, knives, and other petty truck in it. They made a very great slaughter upon the Indians.

On a raid which was an extension of a friendly visit to the Monetons on the Great Kanawha River, the Tomahitans attacked unsuccessfully a hostile tribe, possibly Shawnees on the Ohio River.

Now the king must goe to give the monetons a visit which were his frends, mony signifing water and ton great in theire language Gabriell must goe along with him They gett forth with sixty men and travelled tenn days due north and then arived at the monyton towne sittuated upon a very great river att which place the tide ebbs and flowes. Gabriell swom in the river severall times, being fresh water. . . . This river runes north west and out of the westerly side of it goeth another very great river about a days journey lower where the inhabitance are an inumarable company of Indians, as the monytons told my man which is twenty dayes journey from one end to the other of the inhabitance, and all these are at warr with the Tomahitans. when they had taken theire leave of the monytons they marched three days out of thire way to give a clap to some of that great nation, where they fell on with great courage and were as curagiously repullsed by theire enimise.

And heare Gabriell received shott with two arrows, one of them in his thigh, which stopt his runing. . . . They tooke Gabriell and scowered his skin with water and ashes, and when they perceived his skin to be white they made very much of him and admire att his knife gunn and hatchett they tooke with him. They gave those thing to him a gaine. . . . Whilst he was there they brought in a fatt beavor which they had newly killd. Gabriell made signes to them that those skins were good a mongst the white people toward the sun riseing. they would know by signes how many such skins they would take for such a knife. He told them foure and eight for such a hattchett and made signes that if they would lett him return, he would bring many things amongst them. they seemed to rejoyce att it and carried him to a path that carried to the Tomahittans gave him Rokahamony for his journey.

142

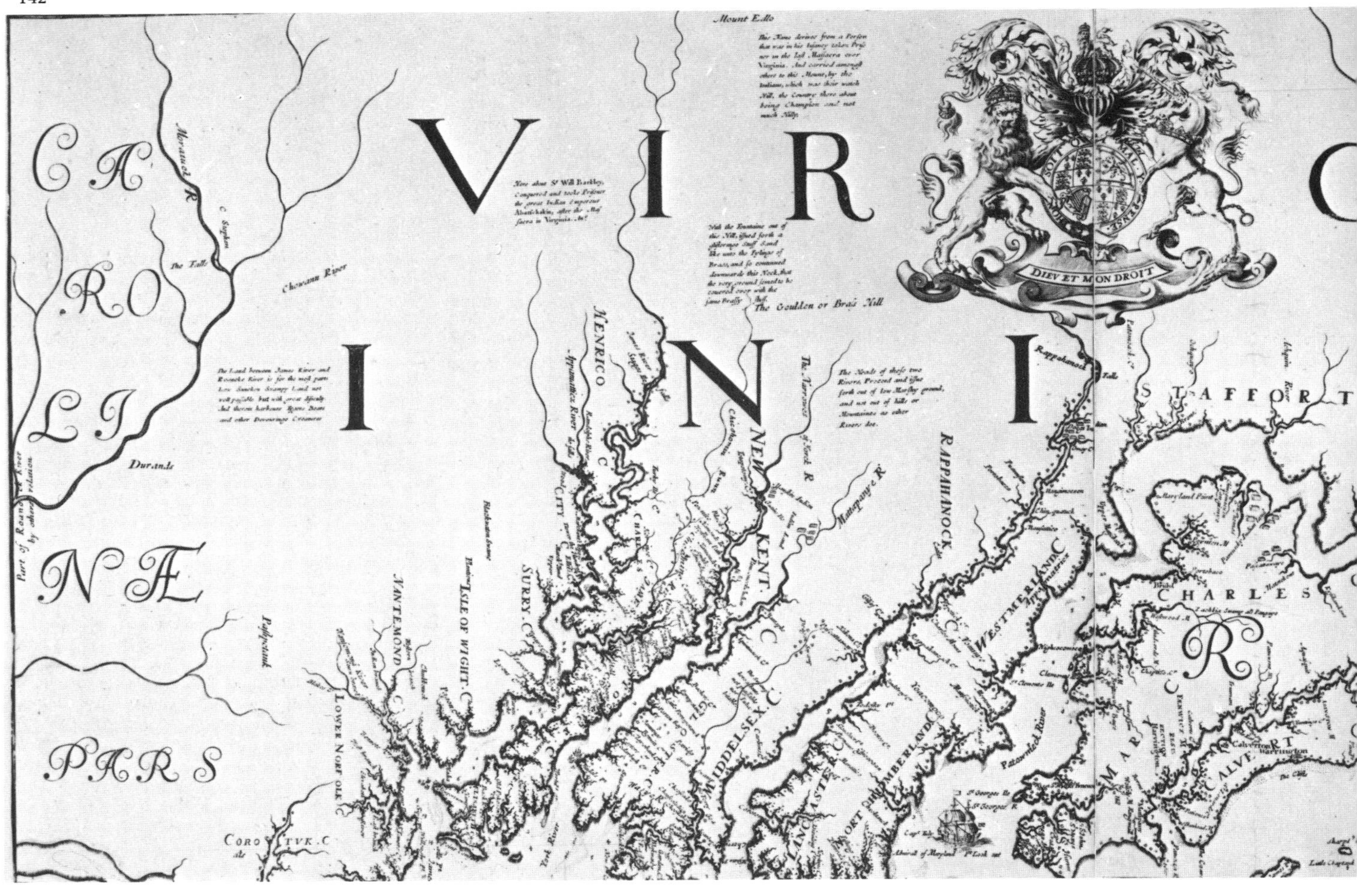

After a hunting and fishing expedition with the Tomahitans, Arthur evaded attempted capture by the Occaneechi and reached Wood's store at Fort Henry 18 June 1674.

Text used: Clarence W. Alvord and Lee Bidgood, The First Explorations of the Trans-Allegheny Region, *Cleveland, Ohio, 1912, pp. 216, 218, 220-1, 222-3.*

3
Henry Woodward's visit to the Westo Indians, 1674

From 'a ffaithfull relation of my Westoe voiage, by Henry Woodward Carolina: Decbr 31: 1674'. *Public Record Office, London, Shaftesbury Papers*

Dr Woodward, an important agent in promoting Indian alliances and trade for the newly established settlement of the Lords Proprietors in Carolina, learned that some strange Indians, who proved to be of the Westo tribe on the Savannah River, had arrived at the Earl of Shaftesbury's plantation near Charles Town. Woodward returned with them and wrote a letter to the earl, selections from which are given below.

We travelled the remaining part of that afternoon West and by North thorough your Lordships land towards the head of Ashley River, passing divers tracks of excellent oake and Hickery land, with divers spatious Savanas, seeming to the best of my judgment good Pastorage. As we travelled this day I saw (as divers other times likewise in my journey) where these Indians had drawne uppon trees (the barke being hewed away) the effigies of a bever, a man, on horseback and guns, Intimating thereby as I suppose, their desire for freindship, and comerse with us. . . . Thursday wee tooke our journey dew West, passing many large pastorable Savanas, the other land promising very well. This day wee shott two Bucks. The best of both with a fatt Turkey wee carried along with us, for our better accomodation at night. Fryday wee traveled West and by South, haveing towards three the afternoon a sight of the mountaines, which bore northwest of us, passing the head of Port Royall river over a tree, where the river intricately runs through large vallies of excellent land, at the beginning of the adjoyning Hills, along whose banks in a mighty thicke wood wee tooke up our Quarters. The ensuing day wee went over many fattigous hills, the land especially the vallies being excellent good, our course West a little Southwardly.

Woodward found the Westos seated on the west bank of the Savannah River near present Augusta, Georgia. They evidently had trade relations with Virginia, whence they may have been driven earlier in the century.

We came in sight of the Westoe towne, alias the Hickauhaugau which stands uppon a poynt of the [Savannah] river uppon the Westerne side soe that the river encompasseth two-thirds thereof. When we came within [sight] of the towne I fired my fowling peece and pistol which was answered with a hollow and imediately thereuppon they gave mee a vollew of fifty or sixty small arms. Here was a concourse of some hundred of Indians, drest up in their anticke fighting garbe. Through the midst of whom being conducted to their cheiftaines house, the which not being capable to containe the crowd that came to see me, the smaller fry got up and un-

142 Herrman. Virginia and Maryland, 1673. *British Museum, London.* This detail of the western half of Augustus Herrman's fine map of Virginia and Maryland shows how little was known of the continent beyond the coastal plain after over half a century of English settlement.

The plantations and houses along the banks of the tidal rivers are continuous and frequent; the country beyond is blank, with stylized river courses. West of the James River is Mount Edlo, a reputed Indian 'watch hill, the Country thereabout being Champion and not much Hilly'. West of the Potomac Herrman reports 'mighty High and great Mountains . . . Supposed to be the very middle Ridg of Northern America . . . as Indians reports from the other side Westwards doe the Rivers take their Originall issuing out into the West Sea.'

On the other side of these mountains, writes Herrman, is the Spaniard, 'possessed with great store of Minneralls'. Neither he nor the English colonists knew how many thousand miles away the Spaniards were, nor that Marquette and Jolliet were exploring the Mississippi that same year for France. West is at the top.

couvered the top of the house to satisfy their curiosity. The chiefe of the Indians made long speeches intimateing their own strength (and as I judged their desire of freindship with us). This night first haveing oyled my eyes and joynts with beares oyl, they presented mee divers deare skins, setting beforee me sufficient of their food to satisfy at least half a dozen of their owne appetites. Here takeing my first nights repose, the next day I veiwed the Towne, which is built in a confused maner, consisting of many long houses whose sides and tops are both artifitially done with barke, uppon the topes of most whereof fastened to the ends of long poles hang the locks of haire of Indians that they have slaine. The inland side of the towne being duble Pallisadoed, and that part which fronts the river haveing only a single one. Under whose steep banks seldom ly less than one hundred faire canoes ready uppon all occasions. They are well provided with arms, amunition, tradeing cloath and other trade from the northward for which at set times of the year they truck drest deare skins furrs and young Indian Slaves. In ten daies time that I tarried here I viewed the adjacent part of the Country. They are Seated uppon a most fruitfull soyl. . . . The 6th of [November] in safety I arrived at your Honors Plantation at the Head of Ashley River.

Text used: Collections of the South Carolina Historical Society, V, *1897, pp. 456-62.*

4
Dickinson describes shipwreck and Indian captivity on the east Florida coast, 1696

From Jonathan Dickenson, *Gods Protecting Providence . . . evidenced in the remarkable deliverance of divers persons from the devouring waves of the sea. . . . And also from the more cruelly devouring jawes of the inhumane canibals of Florida,* Philadelphia, 1699

Dickinson (Dickenson), his wife and baby, and fellow Quakers, voyaging from Jamaica to Philadelphia, were shipwrecked in a tropical hurricane at Hoe-Bay (Jupiter Island), near the present Jonathan Dickinson Florida State Park, north of Palm Beach.

143 Vander Aa. Indians strip Dickinson's party of clothes after looting the ship, from Johann L. Gottfried, *De Aamerkenswaadigste . . . Landreisen*, ix, 14, 1707.

About one o'clock in the morning we felt our vessel strike some few strokes, and then she floated again for five or six minutes before she ran fast aground, where she beat violently . . . but the wilderness country looked very dismal, having no trees, but only sand hills covered with shrubby palmetto, the stalks of which were prickly, that there was no

144

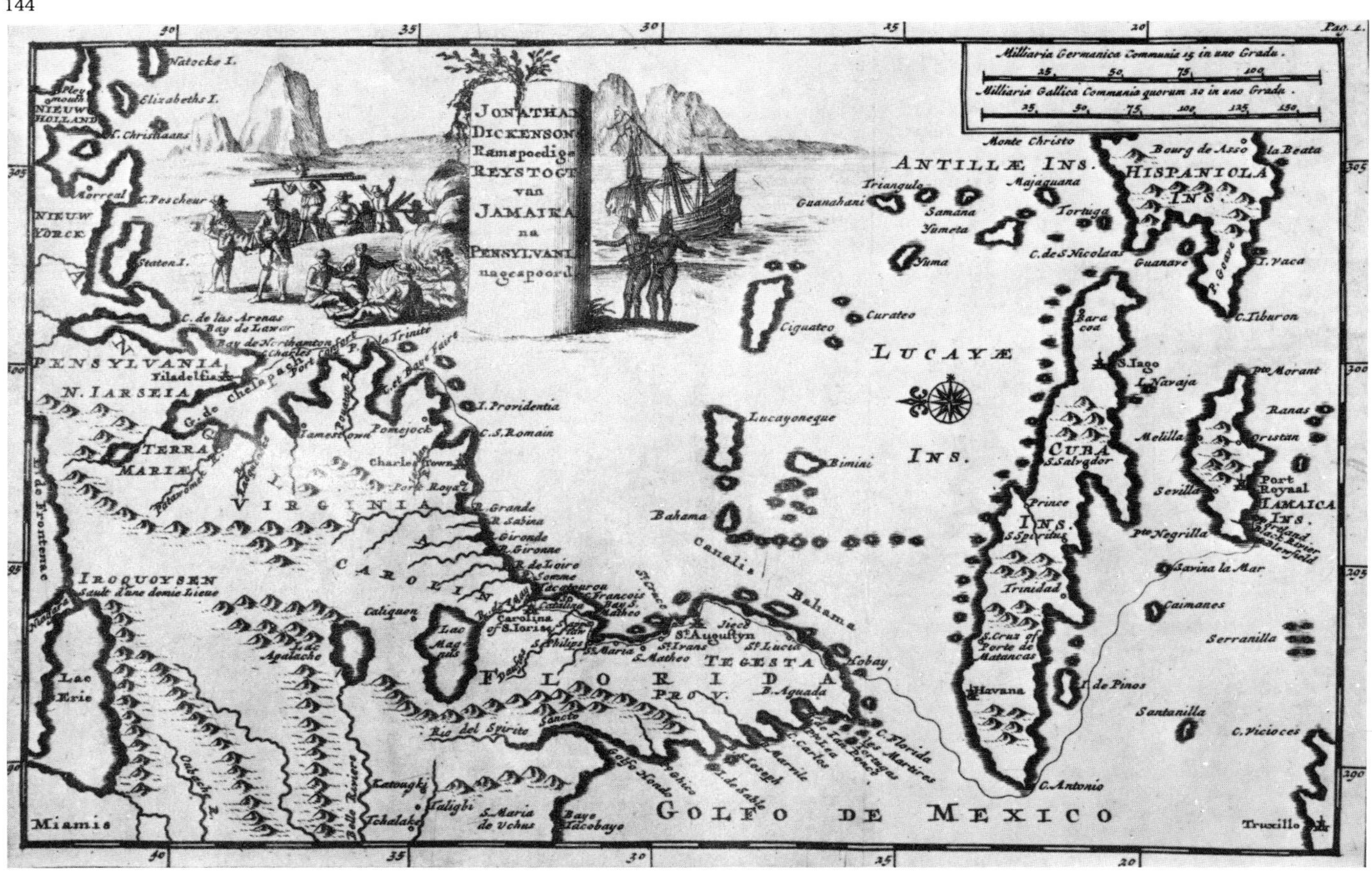

145

144 Vander Aa. Jonathan Dickinson's Journey, 1707, from Johann L. Gottfried, *De Aamerkenswaadigste . . . Landreisen*, Leyden, 1706-27.
This map draws a line showing the journey of Dickinson, his family, and surviving fellow passengers on a voyage from Jamaica to Philadelphia. Their ship weathered two hurricanes; the third drove the vessel ashore at Hoe Bay. From St Augustine they sailed to Philadelphia, incorrectly shown on this map at the head of Chesapeake Bay, via Charles Town, South Carolina.
Dickinson's journal was first published in Philadelphia in 1698 and was very popular; Pieter vander Aa published a Dutch translation in 1706 which was reprinted several times. East is at the top.

145 Vander Aa. Dickinson's party straggles into St Augustine, where they are hospitably treated, from Johann L. Gottfried, *De Aamerkenswaadigste . . . Landreisen*, ix, 26, 1707.

walking amongst them. I espied a place almost a furlong within that beach being a bottom; to this place I with my Negro soon cut a passage, the storm and rain continuing. Thither I got my wife and sick child being six months and twelve days old, also Robert Barrow an aged man, who had been sick about five or six months, our master, who some days past broke his leg, and my kinsman Benjamin Allen, who had been very ill with a violent fever most part of the voyage. . . .

About the eighth or ninth hour came two Indian men (being naked except a small piece of platted work of straws which just hid their private parts, and fastened behind with a horsetail in likeness made of a sort of silk-grass) from the southward, running fiercely and foaming at the mouth having no weapons except their knives: and forthwith not making any stop; violently seized the two first of our men they met. . . . And while these two (letting the men loose) stood with a wild, furious countenance, looking upon us I bethought myself to give them some tobacco and pipes, which they greedily snatched from me, and making a snuffing noise like a wild beast, turned their backs upon us and run away. . . .

Within two or three hours after the departure of the two Indians, some of our people being near the beach or strand returned and said the Indians were coming in a very great number all running and shouting. . . . The Indians went all to the vessel taking forth whatever they could lay hold on, except rum, sugar, molasses, beef and pork.

But their Casseekey (for so they call their king) with about thirty more came down to us in a furious manner, having a dismal aspect and foaming at the mouth. Their weapons were large Spanish knives . . . they rushed in upon us and cried *Nickaleer Nickaleer.*

The cacique, persuaded that they were not Nickaleer (English), prevented their slaughter. The Jobeses Indians, after stripping the castaways of their clothes and possessions, forced them to their village.

The Casseekey told us that it [St Lucie] was about two or three days' journey thither and that when we came there, we should have our throats and scalps cut and be shot, burnt and eaten. . . .

Returning in a short time with some of his men with him, and afresh they went greedily to stripping my wife and child, Robert Barrow and our master who had escaped it till now. Thus were we left almost naked, till the feud was something abated and then we got somewhat from them which displeased some of them. We then cut our tents in pieces, and got the most of our clothing out of it: which the Indians perceiving, took the remains from us. We men had most of us breeches and pieces of canvas, and all our company interceded for my wife that all was not taken from her.

The party eventually were allowed to start north for St Augustine. Passed on from tribe to tribe, they were maltreated by Indians, refused aid by Spanish soldiers and tormented by thirst, hunger, insects, and freezing cold without clothing. The survivors reached St Augustine on November 15, where they were kindly treated and given transportation to Charles Town, South Carolina. Dickinson and his family reached Philadelphia 1 April 1697.

Text used: E. W. and C. M. Andrews (Ed.), Jonathan Dickinson's Journal, *London, Oxford University Press, 1945, pp. 28-9, 32-3 (reprint of first edition).*

5
Lawson's 'thousand-miles' travel to and from piedmont North Carolina, 1700-1

From John Lawson, *A New Voyage to Carolina,* London, 1709

Leaving Charles Town, South Carolina, in a large canoe on December 28, Lawson and his companions paddled along the coast and reached the Santee River 10 January 1701.

The next Day we enter'd Santee-River's Mouth, where it is fresh Water, occasion'd by the extraordinary Current that comes down continually. With hard Rowing, we got two Leagues up the River, lying all Night in a Swampy Piece of Ground, the Weather being so cold all the Time, we were almost frozen ere morning, leaving the Impressions of our Bodies on the ground. We set forward early in the Morning, to seek better Quarters. . . .

As we went up the River, we heard a great Noise, as if two Parties were engaged against each other, seeming exactly like small shot. When we approach'd nearer the Place, we found it to be some Sewee Indians firing the Canes Swamps, which drives out the game, then taking their particular stands, kill great Quantities of both Bear, Deer, Turkies, and what wild Creatures the Parts afford.

Soon leaving the canoe, Lawson journeyed along the Santee, Wateree, and Catawba rivers, describing the Indian tribes and individuals met, such as medicine-men and their practices. After reaching the Esaw Indians, on the Catawba River, the southernmost tribe visited by Lederer thirty years earlier, he followed the Indian Trading Path, along which he met traders from Virginia. Lawson viewed the country for its colonizing values; but it was another thirty years before the settlements reached that far. At the famous Trading Ford on the Yadkin, Lawson was tempted to buy an offered square mile of 'clear Field' on 'a most pleasant River, keeping a continual pleasant warbling noise, with its reverberating on the bright Marble Rocks.' From there the company journeyed to the Keyauwee Town on Carraway Creek near Hillsborough.

146

146 Frontispiece from J. Lawson, *Allerneuste Beschreiben,* Hamburg, 1712.
Buffalo: 'Indians spin the hair into Garters, Girdles, Sashes, and the like, it being long and curled, and often of a chestnut or red color'—Lawson.
Terrapin: 'The Land-Terrebin . . . is an utter Enemy to the Rattle-Snake, for when the Terrebin meets him, he catches hold of him a little below his Neck, and draws his Head into his Shell . . . soon dispatches him, and there leaves him'—Lawson.
Rattler and blacksnake: 'The long, black snake . . . kills the Rattle-Snake, wheresoever he meets him, by twisting his Head about the Neck . . . and whipping him to death with his Tail'—Lawson.
Possum: 'If a Cat has nine lives, this Creature surely has nineteen; for if you break every Bone in their Skin and mash their skull, leaving them for dead, you may come back an hour after, and they will be gone quite away, or . . . creeping away'—Lawson.
Deer and wildcat: 'The wildcat takes most of his Prey by surprize, get up the Trees, which they pass by or under, and thence leaping directly upon them . . . and fastens his teeth in their shoulders . . . till they fall down for want of strength'—Lawson.
Rattlesnake: 'They have the Power, or Art (I know not which to call it) to charm Squirrels, Hares, Patridges, or any such thing, in such a manner, that they run directly into their Mouths'—Lawson.
Raccoon: 'He goes to a Marsh, where standing on the Land, he lets his Tail hang in the Water. This the Crab takes for a Bait, and fastens his Claws therein, which as soon as the Racoon perceives, he . . . springs forward a considerable way, on the Land'—Lawson.
Bear: 'I prefer their Flesh before any Beef, Veal, Pork, or Mutton'—Lawson.

Next day, we had 15 Miles farther to the Keyauwees. The Land is more mountainous, but extremely pleasant, and an excellent Place for the breeding Sheep, Goats, and Horses; or Mules, if the English were once brought to the Experience of the Usefulness of those Creatures. The Valleys are here very rich. . . .

They are fortify'd in, with wooden Puncheons, like Sapona, being a People much of the same Number. Nature hath so fortify'd this Town, with Mountains, that were it a Seat of War, it might easily be made impregnable; having large Corn-Fields joining to their Cabins, and a Savanna near the Town, at the Foot of these Mountains, that is capable of keeping some hundred Heads of Cattle. And all this environ'd round with very high Mountains. . . . Those high Clifts have no Grass growing on them, and very few Trees, which are very short, and stand at a great Distance one from another. The Earth is of a red Colour.

After crossing the Haw River, they reached an Occaneechi town near present Durham, where they met a friendly Indian, Enoe-Will.

We got safe to the North-side of the famous Hau-River [so called] from the Sissipahau Indians, who dwell upon this Stream, which is one of the main Branches of Cape-Fair, there being rich Land enough to contain some Thousands of Families; for which Reason, I hope, in a short time, it will be planted. . . . Here is plenty of good Timber and the Land is extraordinary Rich, no Man that will be content within the Bounds of Reason, can have any grounds to dislike it. . . .

The Country, thro' which we pass'd, was so delightful, that it gave us a great deal of Satisfaction. About Three a Clock, we reach'd the Town, and the Indians presently brought us good fat Bear, and Venison, which was very acceptable at that time. Their Cabins were hung with a good sort of Tapestry, as fat Bear, and barbakued or dried Venison; no Indians having greater Plenty of Provisions than these. The Savages do, indeed, still possess the Flower of Carolina, the English enjoying only the Fag-end of that fine Country. We had not been in the Town 2 Hours, when Enoe-Will came into the King's Cabin; which was our Quarters. We ask'd him, if he would conduct us to the English, and what he would have for his Pains; he answer'd, he would go along with us, and for what he was to have, he left that to our Discretion. . . .

Our Guide and Landlord Enoe-Will was of the best and most agreeable Temper that ever I met with in an Indian, being always ready to serve the English, not out of Gain, but real Affection; which makes him apprehensive of being poison'd by some wicked Indians, and was therefore very earnest with me, to promise him to revenge his Death, if it should so happen. He brought some of his chief Men into his Cabin, and 2 of them having a Drum, and a Rattle, sung by us, as we lay in Bed, and struck up their Musick to serenade and welcome us to their Town. And tho' at last, we fell asleep, yet they continu'd their Consort till Morning. These Indians are fortify'd in, as the former, and are much addicted to a Sport they call Chenco, which is carry'd on with a Staff and a Bowl made of Stone, which they trundle upon a smooth Place, like a Bowling-Green, made for that Purpose.

From here Lawson left the Trading Path, passing through Tuscarora villages to Pamlico River, where he settled and became a co-founder of Bath.

Text used: John Lawson, A New Voyage to Carolina, *Hugh T. Lefler (Ed.), Chapel Hill, N.C., 1967 (reprint of 1709 edition), pp. 16, 17, 60, 61, 62.*

6
Catesby explores the southern colonies as a naturalist, 1722-5

From Mark Catesby, *The Natural History of Carolina, Florida, and the Bahama Islands: Containing the Figures of Birds, Beasts, Fishes, Serpents, Insects, and Plants,* 2 vols, London, 1731-43, vi-xi

Catesby reached Charles Town on 23 May 1722. He gives an account of his journeys in Carolina and his methods of gathering specimens and drawing them.

The inhabited Parts of Carolina extend West from the Sea about 60 miles, and almost the whole Length of the Coast, being a level, low Country. In these Parts I continued the first Year searching after, collecting and describing the Animals and Plants. I then went to the Upper uninhabited Parts of the Country, and continued at and about Fort Moore, a small Fortress on the Banks of the River Savanna, which runs from thence a Course of 300 Miles down to the Sea, and is about the same Distance from its Source, the Mountains.

I was much delighted to see Nature in these Upper Parts, and to find here abundance of Things not to be seen in the Lower Parts of the Country; this encouraged me to take several Journeys with the Indians higher up the Rivers, toward the Mountains which afforded not only a Succession of new vegetable appearances, but most delightful Prospects imaginable, besides the Diversion of Hunting Buffello's, Bears, Panthers, and other Wild Beasts. In these Excursions I employ'd an Indian to carry my Box, in which, besides Paper and materials for Painting, I put dry'd specimens of Plants, Seeds, &c.—as I gathered them. To the Hospitality and Assistance of these Friendly Indians, I am much indebted, for I not only subsisted on what they shot, but their First Care was to erect a Bark Hut, at the approach of Rain to keep me and my Cargo from Wet.

I shall next proceed to an account of the Method I have observed in giving the Natural History of these countries; to begin therefore with Plants, I had principally a Regard to Forest-Trees and Shrubs, shewing their several Mechanical and other uses, as in Building, Joynery, Agriculture, and others used for Food and Medicine.

There being a greater Variety of the feather'd Kind than of any other Animals (at least to be come at) and excelling in the Beauty of their Colours, besides having oftenest relation to the Plants on which they feed and frequent; I was induced cheifly (so far as I could) to compleat an Account of them, rather than to describe promiscuously, Insects and other Animals; by which I must have omitted many of the Birds, for I had not time to do all.

Of Beasts there are not many Species different from those in the old World, most of these I have Figur'd.

Of Serpents very few I believe have escaped me.

Of Fish I have not described above Five or Six from Carolina.

As I was not bred a Painter, I hope some faults in Perspective, and other Niceties, may more readily be excused . . . In designing the Plants, I always did them while fresh and just gather'd: And the Animals, particularly the Birds, I painted them while alive (except a very few) and gave them their gestures peculiar to every kind of Bird, and where it would

147 Mark Catesby. Pied-bill dopchick. Watercolor, c. 1724. *Royal Library, Windsor Castle.*

148 Mark Catesby. Bald eagle with fish. Watercolor, c. 1724. *Royal Library, Windsor Castle.*

The Pyed bill Dopchick Podiceps minor rostro vario 91

147

148

AMERICÆ nova Tabula.
Auct: Guiljelmo Blaeuw.
Septentrionalissimas Americæ partes, Groenlandiam puta, Islandiã et adjacentes, quod Americæ tabulæ commodè comprehendi non potuerint, peculiari hac tabella Spectatoribus exhibendas duximus.
MAR DEL NORT
OCEANUS ATLANTICUS
MAR DEL ZUR
OCEANUS PERUVIANUS
MARE PACIFICUM
CIRCULUS ÆQUINOCTIALIS
Tropicus Cancri
Tropicus Capricorni
AMERICA SEPTENTRIONALIS
AMERICA MERIDIONALIS
NOVA FRANCIA
AFRICÆ PARS
EUROPA
HISPANIA
HAVANA
S. DOMINGO
CARTAGENA
MEXICO
CUSCO
POTOSI
LA MOCHA in Chili
RIO JANEIRO
OLINDA in Phernambuco

admit of, I have adapted the Birds to those Plants on which they fed. Fish which do not retain their Colours when out of their Element, I painted at different times, having a succession of them procur'd while the former lost their colours.

At my return from America, in the Year 1726, I had the Satisfaction of having my Labours approved of . . . I alter'd my Design of going to Paris or Amsterdam where I first proposed to have them done . . . The Expence of graving would make it too burthensome an Undertaking . . . At length by the kind Advice and Instructions of that inimitable Painter Mr. Joseph Goupy, I undertook and was initiated in the way of Etching them myself.

Catesby concludes his Preface with an explanation of his method of nomenclature and comments on the problems of colors, particularly green, fading in his specimens during his drawing them.

150

149 Blaeu. 'Americae nova Tabula', 1635 [1640], from W. J. Blaeu, *Le théâtre du monde*, II, 106, 1640. *British Museum, London.*
This new map of America by Willem Janszoon Blaeu (1571-1638), one of the foremost cartographers of his time and map-maker of the Dutch East India Company, shows the general European conception of the western hemisphere at the end of the first third of the seventeenth century. The delineation of the coast and the nomenclature on both the Pacific and the Atlantic coasts are Spanish in origin and follow the maps of Ortelius and Wytfliet. To these Blaeu has inserted on the east coast the English names given by the Roanoke colonists to 'Virginia' and by Frobisher, Davis and Hudson to the far north; he has added the French names in Florida and along the St Lawrence.

European geographers still had no knowledge of the extent of the Mississippi River; from the narratives of the De Soto expedition (1539-43) they believed in a range of mountains east-west above the Gulf which would preclude a great river. The Great Lakes system was not yet known, although Champlain had reached Huron by the Ottawa River, had heard of other lakes from the Indians, and in 1632 published a remarkable map with several of the Great Lakes on it (plate 37). Blaeu had apparently not seen this last map by Champlain. He gives equal prominence to the Ottawa River and the St Lawrence above their juncture.

150 Mark Catesby. Flying squirrel. Watercolor, *c.* 1724. *Royal Library, Windsor Castle.*

151 Mark Catesby. 'A Map of Carolina, Florida and the Bahama Islands, from *Natural history of Carolina* . . ., 1731-43.
This map is largely derived from that of Henry Popple, 'Map of the British Empire', 1733 (plate 101), but it does show the areas in which Mark Catesby worked to produce a magnificent and delightful record of the flora and fauna.

151

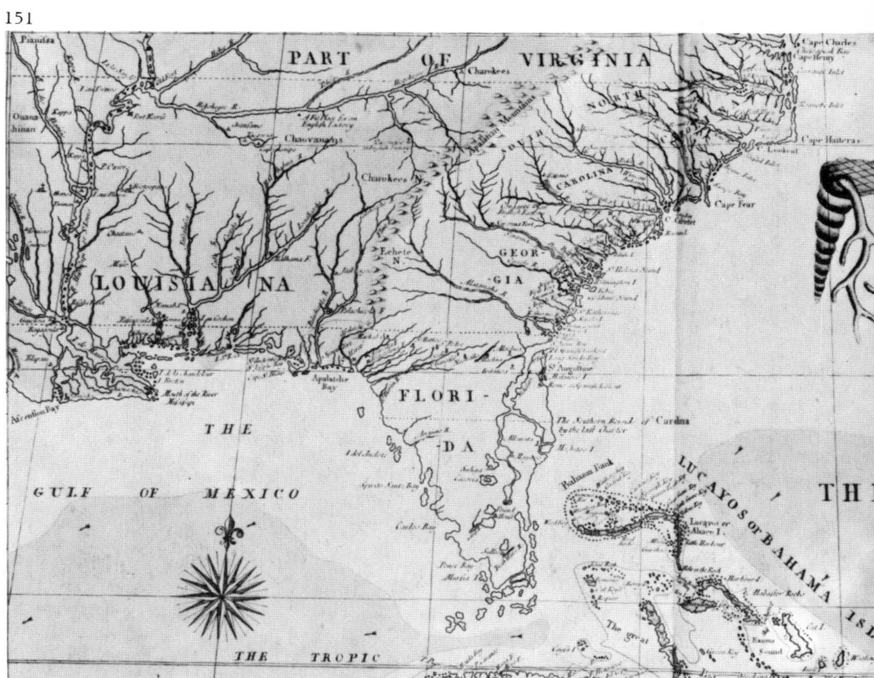

7
William Byrd describes the Great Dismal Swamp and helps run the Virginia-North Carolina dividing line, 1728

From William Byrd, *The History of the Dividing Line*, first published in *The Westover Manuscripts* . . ., Petersburg, Va., 1841. The manuscript of the *Secret History* is in the American Philosophical Society, Philadelphia.

Byrd was appointed a Virginia commissioner to oversee the survey of the disputed boundary line. His *History*, not published until 1841, and *Secret History*, unpublished until 1929, written with sophistication and with humorously caustic comments on the character and manners of the North Carolinians he observed, give a picture of frontier conditions and of unexplored land beyond the Indian Trading Path which crossed the Roanoke River at Monyshop (Moniseep) Ford. The Great Dismal Swamp, only twenty-two miles from the beginning of the Line at the coast, is here described in the *Secret History*.

The Surveyors described the Dismal to us in the following Manner. That it was in many places overgrown with tall Reeds interwoven with large Briars in which the Men were frequently intangled. And that not only in the Skirts of it, but likewise towards the Middle. In other places it was full of Juniper Trees, commonly so call'd, tho' they seem rather to be white Cedars. Some of these are of a great Bigness: but the Soil being soft & boggy, there is little hold for the Roots, & consequently any high Wind blows many of them down. By this means they lye in heaps, horsing upon one another, and brittling out with Sharp Snaggs, so that Passage in many places is difficult and Dangerous. The Ground was generally very quaggy, & the Impressions of the Men's feet were immediately fill'd with Water. So if there was any hole made it was soon full of that Element, & by that Method it was

NOVA SCOTIA
Bay of Fundy
Ste Croix R
Belle Isle
Table Mountain
Cape Breton
Cape Breton I
Halifax
St Francis R
St John R
MAINE
Richmond Is
Kennebec R
Androscoggin R
White Mtns
Fryeburg
Casco Bay
Saco R
Saco
L Winnapusseakit
Piscataqua R
Aquedahian
Portsmouth
Merrimac R
Massachusetts Bay
NEW HAMPSHIRE
VERMONT
Connecticut R
Salem
Boston
Cape Cod
Concord
Lancaster
Framingham
Chesterfield
Oxford
MASSACHUSETTS
RHODE ISLAND
Narragansett Region
Springfield
CONNECTICUT
Berkshire Hills
Long Island
New York/New Amsterdam
Hudson R
L Champlain
Ticonderoga
L George
NEW YORK
Schenectady
Albany
Fort Orange
Mowhawk R
Schoharie R
Utica
Otsego L
Oswego R
L Oneida
Syracuse
L Owasco
Irondequoit
Seneca
Seneca L
Oghwaga
Owegy
Susquehanna
Fort Frontenac
Lake Ontario
Mackinac
Fort Le Boeuf
Detroit
Fox R
Maumee R
Wisconsin R
Mississippi R
Delaware R
Bethlehem
Burnett's Hills
Blue Mountains
Sunbury
Schuylkill R
Philadelphia
Fort Nassau
Wilmington
PENNSYLVANIA
Juniata R
Susquehanna R
MARYLAND
Wills Creek
Potomac R
Logstown
Pittsburg
(Fort Duquesne)
(Fort Pitt)
Youghoigheny R
Gist's Settlement
Monongahela R
Ohio R
Massanuten Mts
Shenandoah R
Shenandoah
Rappahannock R
Port Royal
Chesapeake Bay
Swift Run Gap
Rapidan R
S Anna R
Charles City
Williamsburg
Jamestown
Charlottesville
James R
Fort Henry
North R
Appomattox R
Petersburg
Great Dismal Swamp
Albemarle Sound
Roanoke I
Cape Hatteras
Natural Bridge
Nottaway R
Chowan R
VIRGINIA
Meherrin R
Occaneechi
Moniseep Ford
Bath
Pamlico R
Roanoke
Roanoke R
(Staunton R)
Clarkesville
ALLEGHENY MOUNTAINS
Twightwee
Pickawillany
Scioto R
Miami R
Gt Kanawha R
New River
Coal R
Peter's Falls
Ohio R
Wabash
Neuse R
New Bern
Hillsborough
Durham

Fig 2 The east

152

153

154

that our People supply'd themselves with drink. Nay if they made a Fire, in less than half an Hour, when the crust of Leaves & Trash were burnt thro', it wou'd sink down into a Hole, & be extinguish't. So replete is this Soil with Water, that it cou'd never have been passable, but in a very dry Season. And indeed considering it is the Source of 6 or 7 Rivers, without any Visible Body of Water to supply them, there must be great Stores of it under Ground. Some part of this Swamp has few or no Trees growing in it, but contains a large Tract of Reeds, which being perpetually green, & waving in the Wind, it is call'd the Green Sea. Gall-Bushes grow very thick in many parts of it, which are ever green Shrubs, bearing a Berry which dies a Black Colour like the Galls of the Oak, & from thence they receive their Name.

Abundance of Cypress Trees grow likewise in this Swamp, and some Pines upon the Borders towards the firm Land, but the Soil is so moist & miry, that like the Junipers a high wind mows many of them down. It is remarkable that towards the middle of the Dismal no Beast or Bird or even Reptile can live, not only because of the softness of the Ground, but likewise because it is so overgrown with Thickets, that the Genial Beams of the Sun can never penetrate them. Indeed on the Skirts of it Cattle & Hogs will venture for the Sake of the Reeds, & Roots, with which they will keep themselves fat all the winter. This is a great Advantage to the Bordering Inhabitants in that particular, tho' they pay dear for it by the Agues & other distemper occasion'd by the Noxious Vapours the rise perpetually from that vast Extent of Mire & Nastiness. And a vast Extent it is, being computed at a Medium 10 Miles Broad, & 30 Miles long, tho' where the Line past it, 'twas compleatly 15 Miles broad. However this dirty Dismal is in many parts of it very pleasant to the Eye, tho' disagreeable to the other Sences, because there is an everlasting Verdure, which makes every Season look like the Spring. The way the Men took to Secure their Bedding here from moisture, was, by laying Cypress Bark under their Blankets, etc which made their Lodging hard, but much more wholesome.

By October 7 the surveyers had run the line 169 miles. The North Carolina commissioners declared in writing that it would be 'an age or two' before settlements reached so far, and left, together with one of Byrd's fellow Virginia commissioners. Byrd continued the survey seventy-two miles; within twenty years frontier settlements required an extension of another ninety miles. The following extract from *The History* describes the end of Byrd's survey at Peter's Creek on the border of Stokes County, North Carolina.

The Hills beyond that River [Peter's Creek] were exceedingly lofty, and not to be attempted by our Jaded Palfreys, which could now hardly drag their Legs after them upon level Ground. Besides, the Bread began to grow Scanty, and the Winter Season to advance apace upon us.

We had likewise reason to apprehend the Consequence of being intercepted by deep Snows, and the Swelling of the many Waters between us and Home. The first of these Mis-

152 Mark Catesby. Orchids growing out from a tree branch, with a butterfly, *c.* 1724, from *Natural history*, II, 88. Catesby's engraving from drawings made in the Bahamas of a plant and insect also found on the mainland.

153 Mark Catesby. Head of a Hooping [Whooping] crane, *c.* 1724, from *Natural History*, I, 75. 'Early in the Spring, great multitudes of them frequent the lower parts of the Rivers near the Sea, and return to the Mountains in the Summer'—Catesby. Now almost extinct.

154 Mark Catesby. Turkey buzzard. Watercolor, *c.* 1724. 'Their food is carrion . . . They have a wonderful sagacity in smelling'—Catesby. *Royal Library, Windsor Castle.*

155 Mark Catesby. Carolina paroquet. Watercolor, *c.* 1724. Now almost, if not entirely, extinct. 'The only one of the Parrot kind in Carolina'— Catesby. Also the cypress, described as 'aquatic'. *Royal Library, Windsor Castle.*

156 Byrd. The dividing line between Virginia and Carolina, *c.* 1738. *Bodleian Library, Oxford, Rawlinson Copperplate No. 29.*
The upper part of this engraving shows the boundary line run by the Virginia and North Carolina commissioners in 1728. The lower half gives a detail of the eastern part of the line with illustrations of various creatures: 1, a flying fish, probably *prionotus carolinus,* with a squirrel descending a tree; 2, a six-foot rattlesnake, apparently a diamondback, although this species is not today found so far north; 3, an opossum with young: 4, a female Indian; 5, a frigate bird (coastal) or swallowtailed kite (Dismal Swamp); 6, a passenger pigeon.

In July 1737 Byrd wrote Peter Collinson, the English naturalist, that he was expecting to finish his *History of the dividing line* in 1738 for publication, and, as he was intending to describe some of the wild life of the frontier, he asked Collinson to make arrangements for some plates. Byrd did not publish the manuscript but this plate was evidently prepared for it.

155

156

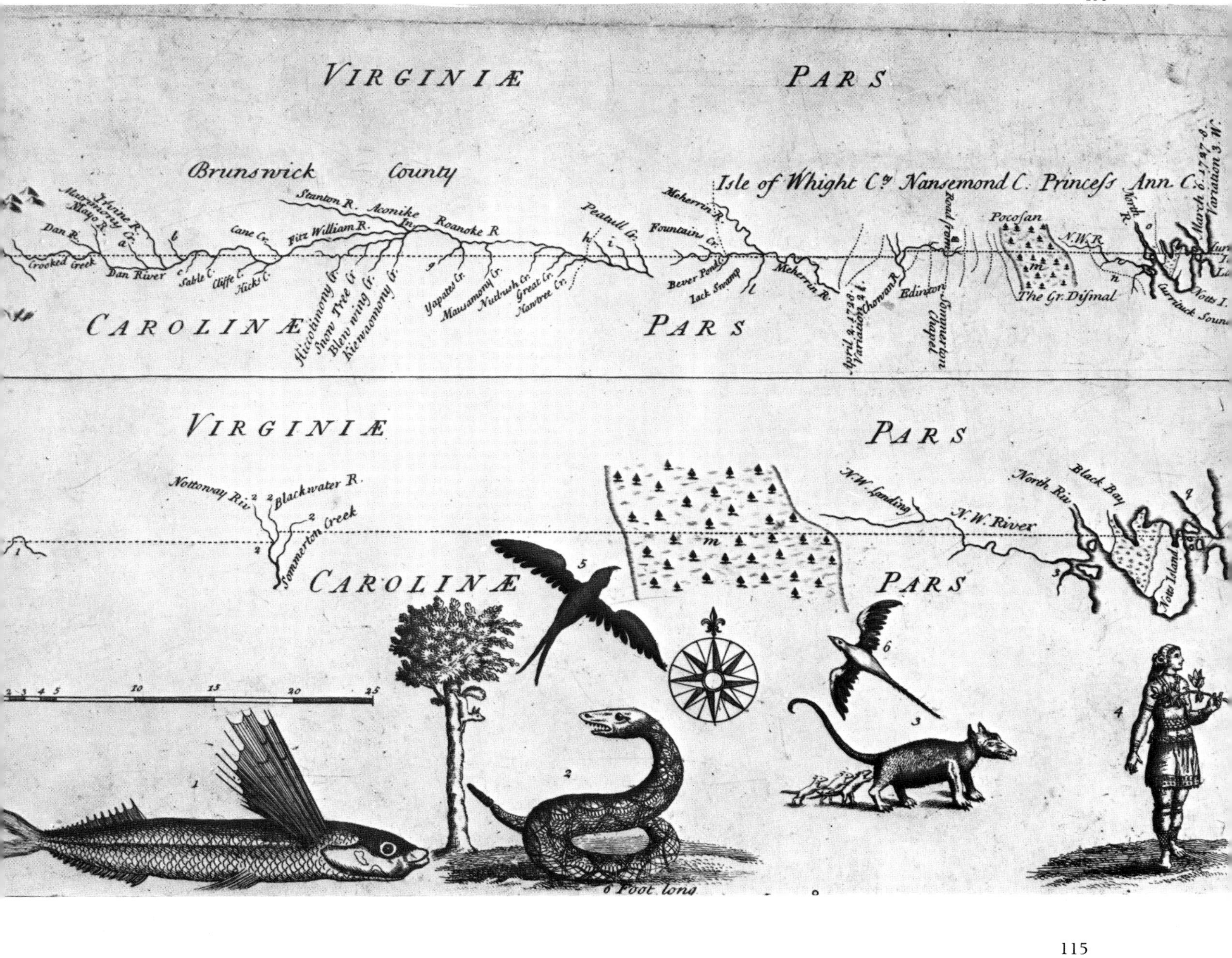

fortunes would starve all our Horses, and the Other ourselves, by cutting off our Retreat, and obliging us to Winter in those Desolate Woods. These considerations determin'd us to Stop short here, and push our Adventures no farther. The last Tree we markt was a Red Oak, growing on the Bank of the River; and to make the Place more remarkable, we blaz'd all the Trees around it.

We found the whole Distance from Corotuck Inlet to the Rivulet Where we left off, to be, in a Strait Line, Two Hundred and Forty-one Miles and Two Hundred and Thirty Poles. And from the Place where the Carolina Commissioners deserted

157

us, 72 Miles and 302 Poles. This last part of the Journey was generally very hilly, or else grown up with troublesome Thickets and underwoods, all which our Carolina Friends had the Discretion to avoid.

Text used: William Byrd's Histories of the Dividing Line, *William K. Boyd (Ed.), Raleigh, NC, 1929, pp. 85-6, 234.*

157 Byrd. 'My Plat of 20,000 Acres in N° Carolina, 1733, from William Byrd, *History of the dividing line* (Ed. T. H. Wynne, II, 37, 1866). Byrd purchased this tract, which he called 'The Land of Eden' for its supposed fertility, from the North Carolina boundary line commissioners, who received it in payment for their services. In 1733 the tract was far beyond the frontier settlements, although in twenty years the Great Wagon Road from Philadelphia to the Yadkin, fifteen miles to the west, was in operation. Byrd's model communities never developed. The original plat is among Byrd's Westover Papers.

158 Eden in Virginia, 1736, from *Neu-gefundenes Eden,* Bern, p. 96. *John Carter Brown Library, Providence, Rhode Island.*

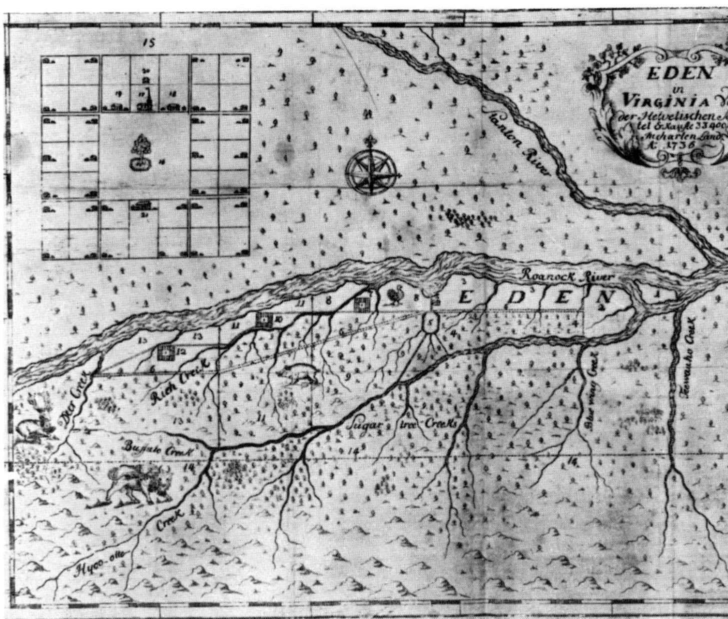

158

4 THE SOUTHEAST: PENETRATING THE MOUNTAIN BARRIER, 1732-75

For the trader with his heavy burdens and the frontiersman searching for a way by which his family and cattle might travel to establish a new settlement, the discovery of possible routes was of vital importance. Long before the coming of the white man, an intricate complex of trails, made by buffaloes seeking pasturage or returning to a favorite salt lick and by Indians going on their hunting expeditions, crisscrossed the land. The knowledge of river systems and the location of carrying places for canoes, if less used than in Canada, was also important. For this reason early explorers like Lederer and Needham used Indian guides who knew the trails and the portages or who by long training could follow the single-file paths through almost impenetrable cane thickets, laurel slicks, and dense forests which concealed the traveller from the sight of an enemy beyond a few yards. Such concealment was necessary for those using the Indian war paths, among the most famous of which were the Great Indian War Path through the Valley of Virginia and the Warriors' Path between the Cherokee in eastern Tennessee over the Cumberland Gap north to the Ohio and the Shawnee and Iroquois regions. This Warriors' Path had many ancillary trails and extensions branching out from it, as did the other main routes.[1] The wise traveller used caution; Daniel Boone, after being captured twice by hostile Indians, made his night's rest off the path and hid his tracks. When settlers began moving their families and goods to the frontier, the major trails were widened and cleared. The most important of these during the colonial period was 'The Great Wagon Road from Philadelphia to the Yadkin' in North Carolina, which turned south from the Cumberland range in Pennsylvania through the Valley of Virginia and crossed to the east of the Blue Ridge at Staunton River. Radiating from and beyond these trails and roads, explorer-settlers cut new paths.

Complex political and economic conditions during the first half of the eighteenth century in Europe caused large numbers of emigrants to leave their lands and homes, often devastated or destroyed. From Germany came the Palatines under Joshua von Kocherthal and Conrad Weiser, and the Moravians under Count Nicolaus Ludwig von Zinzendorf and Bishop August Spangenburg. The twelve Moravian brethren who made their way from Bethlehem, Pennsylvania, to Bethabara, North Carolina, and cleared the way for their wagon south from the Staunton River left a moving and graphic account of their difficulties. In their diary of 1753 they recorded the problems of crossing rivers and swamps, of tying trees to the wagon to hold it back on slopes so dangerously steep that 'we thought at times that it could not possibly be done without accident, but in spite of stump and stone we got down safely'.[2]

The Scotch-Irish from Ulster formed the largest group of emigrants from the British Isles; inured to privation, stubborn and tenacious, independent and hardy, they made ideal frontiersmen. Usually they arrived without sufficient money to buy fertile land, or any land; trained in a hard school, it was said that they 'kept the Sabbath and everything else they could lay their hands on'. These and smaller groups of English, Welsh, Huguenot, French, and Swiss landed only to find the good farming areas of the coastal plain already taken. They pushed west from Philadelphia to the Cumberland Valley in

159

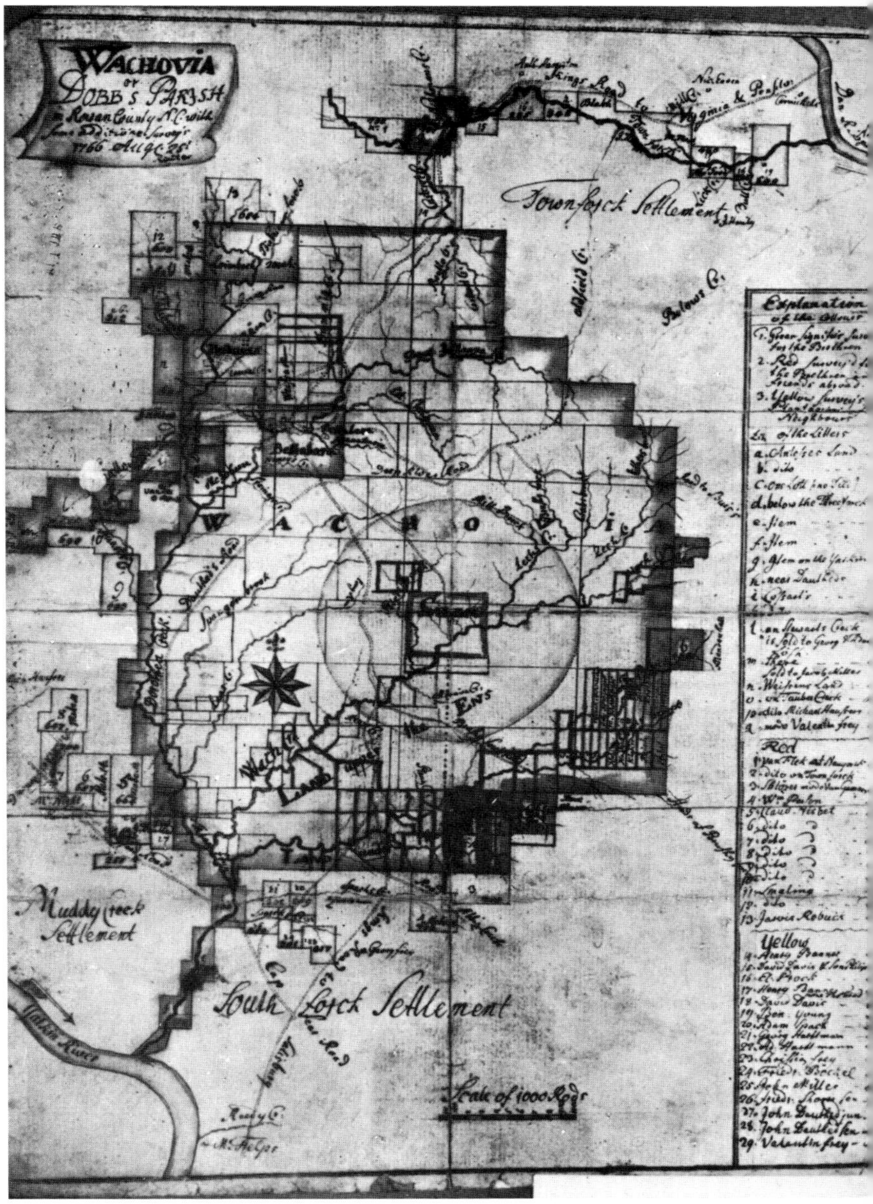

159 C. G. Reuter. Wachovia, Dobbs Parish, North Carolina, 1766.
Moravian Archives, Winston-Salem, NC.
Soon after Bishop Spangenburg arranged for the purchase from Lord Granville's agent of a 100,000-acre tract of land on the North Carolina frontier in 1752, the Moravians came from their settlement in Bethlehem, Pennsylvania, by the 'Great Wagon Road' through the Valley of Virginia to the Yadkin River. Industrious, methodical, and skilled, they soon carved out settlements in the wilderness. Christian Gottlieb Reuter, an experienced surveyor, followed careful instructions from church authorities in Bethlehem in his work.

160

161

Pennsylvania and from Chesapeake Bay along the upper Potomac in Maryland. Around 1730 individual families and small groups began to enter the Shenandoah Valley of Virginia from Pennsylvania. In 1741 John Peter Salley's farm on the James River was the vanguard of settlements to the southwest; at his death in 1754 the Great Wagon Road from Pennsylvania to the Yadkin in North Carolina passed west of his house and settlers were living on the Holston River a hundred miles down the Valley.[3]

1 Westward from Virginia and North Carolina

On 16 March 1742, John Howard and four companions stood on the banks of Cedar Creek, looking at the magnificent arch of Natural Bridge in the Valley of Virginia that towered over 200 feet above them (plate 200). They had gathered that morning at the cabin of John Peter Salley (Salling, Sally), five miles away at the forks of the James River and North River in the Valley, and were at the beginning of a hazardous and extraordinary journey of exploration across the mountains to the Mississippi. Howard had received from the Virginia Council permission in 1737 to make 'discoveries toward the River Mississippi' and had offered his companions shares in the 10,000 acres of land promised him by the Council.[4]

160 American stage wagon, 1798, from Isaac Weld, *Travels through . . . North America*, 1799.
'The coachee', wrote Weld, who travelled in Virginia after his arrival in 1795, 'is a carriage peculiar, I believe, to America; the body of it is rather longer than a coach but of the same shape. In the front it is left quite open down to the bottom, and the driver sits on a bench under the roof of the carriage. There are two seats in it for the passengers, who sit with their faces toward the horses. . . . On each side of the doors, above the panels, it is quite open.'

161 C. G. Reuter. Bethabara, 1766. *Moravian Archives, Winston-Salem, NC.*
When the dozen Moravians arrived in Bethabara, a few pioneers like Gist and Boone were temporary neighbors a few miles up the Yadkin, and the Moravians themselves explored and hunted farther west. Through the streets of the little settlement later passed scores of frontiersmen with their families, pushing to and over the Blue Ridge in spite of danger from marauding Indians.

162 G. von Redeker. 'A View of SALEM', 1787. *Moravian Archives, Winston-Salem, NC.*
This contemporary painting gives a picture of what a frontier town looked like. The Moravian houses were often built of brick and stone, more solidly than the usual frontier dwelling. Now part of Winston-Salem, many of the buildings from the 1760s in and around Salem still remain.

163 Beaufort, South Carolina, c. 1798. *Beaufort County Library, SC.*
This charming primitive painting by an unknown artist is a copy of an original by thirteen-year-old John Barnwell, a descendant of 'Tuscarora Jack' Barnwell. Barnwell, a leader against the Spanish and Indian foes of the colony and a diplomatic representative in London in the successful effort to make the colony a royal province, is buried here in the cemetery of St Helena's church.
Beaufort, laid out in 1710, was an important outpost in the Indian trade and a center for plantation development south of Charles Town. Near here in 1666 Dr Henry Woodward was left by an official of the Cape Fear colony to learn the language and ways of the Indians, and in 1670 Governor William Sayle landed his colonists before deciding to move northward to a safer location at Charles Town.

164 Comberford. 'The south part of Virginia now the north part of Carolina', 1657. *New York Public Library.*
'Batts House' on Fletts Creek (now Salmon Creek) at the head of Albemarle Sound was built in 1654-5 by Colonel Francis Yeardley as a trading post for Nathaniel Batts, an early explorer, landowner and settler. The map records for the first time many names still in use; some of them, such as 'Battis Pointe' on Pamlico River, were probably given by Captain Batts. '. . . the north part of Carolina' in the title was added in a later hand some time after the grant of Carolina in 1663.
Nicholas Comberford is one of a recently identified group of London chart-makers on vellum. They used similar colors, patterns and techniques and have come to be called the Thames School. See also plate 294.

162

163

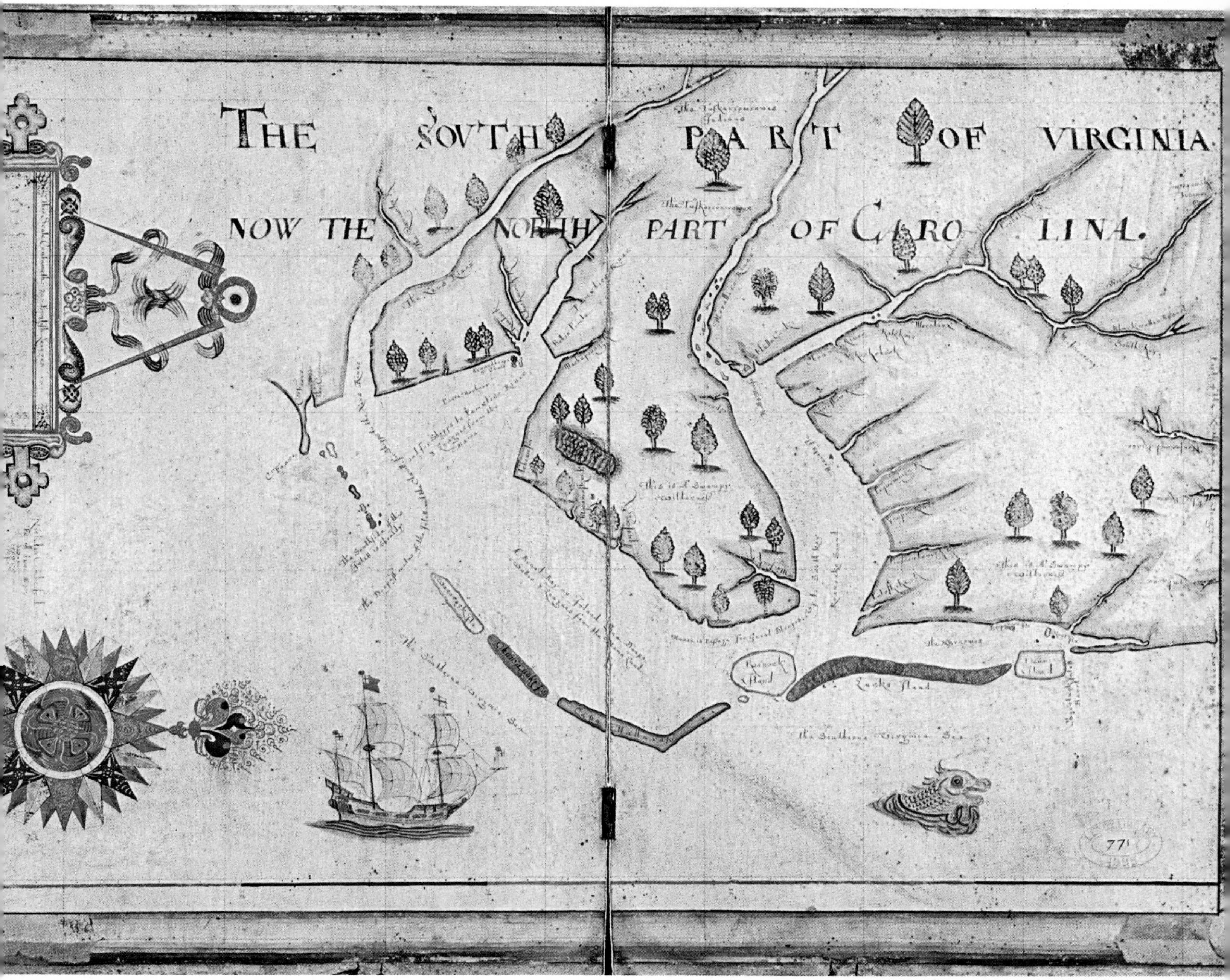

THE SOUTH PART OF VIRGINIA NOW THE NORTH PART OF CAROLINA.

164

165

167

166

168

Salley, whose journal is the fullest record of the expedition (see selection 1), had brought his family down the Valley from Pennsylvania the previous year. According to local tradition, Salley had been captured a number of years before by some Cherokees, adopted by them as Menou (the Silent), again captured by Illinois on a Cherokee hunting expedition north of Tennessee, carried a prisoner to Kaskaskia on the Mississippi and there adopted by a squaw whose son had been killed. Taken to Canada by the French at Kaskaskia, he was finally set free.[5]

Salley's journal relates in detail the 1742 trip across the mountains and, in a hastily constructed boat, down the New or Wood's River beyond the camping place reached by Batts and Fallam seventy years before; down the Great Kanawha past the present site of Charleston, West Virginia, and Coal River, which they so named because of the coal they saw in the bordering mountains; and down the 'Allegany' (Ohio) to the Mississippi, which they reached on 7 June 1742. Descending the Mississippi, they were taken prisoners by a French convoy on its way to New Orleans. There they were closely examined by Bienville, then governor, who wrote to the authorities in France, 'these rash men shall not return home to bear witness of what they have learned among us. I shall send them to the fort at Nachitoches, whence I will have them escorted to the mines of New Mexico'.

Two years later the five were still languishing in a New Orleans prison. Salley and Baudran, a fellow prisoner who knew the country well and was highly respected by the Choctaws, escaped with one or two others. They made a boat from the hides of two bulls they killed and used the shoulder blades tied to sticks as paddles to cross Lake Pontchartrain. Aided by the Choctaws and others, Salley reached Charles Town; after further misadventures, including capture by a French privateer off the Carolina coast, he reached home and family on 17 May 1745 after an absence of over three years. Salley's journal is preserved in a copy made by Peter Jefferson, who used it in preparing his 'Map of Virginia' (1751).[6]

In the period following Salley's journey not only traders, hunters, and settlers explored the passes over the ranges west of the Valley of Virginia. Land speculators and partners in the great land companies also flourished; they were usually of a different social and economic class from the frontiersmen and farmers who actually settled the land, although at certain levels their purposes and methods merged. The holders of high public office, the wealthy merchants, and the leading planters planned with wide vision; their ambition extended to thousands, even hundreds of thousands, of acres. It was the enterprise of these men, their political power and influence, and their willingness, however selfishly motivated, to risk large financial sums, that made possible exploration and settlement of land beyond the Blue Ridge.[7] Virginia was a colony particularly suitable for speculators in large land grants. She made territorial claims, based upon her charters, to all land from her southern boundary west to the Mississippi and north to the Great Lakes, back of Pennsylvania.

165 Mark Catesby. Rock rose of Pennsylvania, from *Hortus Europae Americanus or a Collection of 85 curious trees and shrubs, the produce of North America, 1767.*

166 Mark Catesby. Yellow jessamin, from *Hortus Europae Americanus*, 1767. The Carolina (yellow) jessamine is the state flower of South Carolina.

167 Mark Catesby. Laurel tree of Carolina, from *Hortus Europae Americanus*, 1767. 'This stately tree perfumes the woods . . . from May till November, producing first its fragrant and ample blossoms, succeeded by its glittering fruit'—Catesby, *Natural history*, 1731-43.

168 Mark Catesby. Water tupelo or black gum, from *Hortus Europae Americanus*, 1767.

169

169 Virginia farmhouse, *c.* 1800. *National Gallery of Art, Washington, Garbisch Collection.*
A detail of a rural scene from a painting by an unknown artist, *End of the Hunt*, a Virginia fox-hunting picture.

The conflict of these claims with those of France, which included all land extending to the headwaters of tributaries of the Mississippi, was largely theoretical as long as Virginia's active interests remained east of the Blue Ridge; this was still true in the early years of the century, when large grants and purchases of land were being made in the Piedmont. West of the Blue Ridge, however, the possibility of settlers from Pennsylvania excited interest in the rich and beautiful valley among land-hungry Virginians. As a result grants and patents in land over the Blue Ridge were given to individuals and companies from the 1730s onwards. One company, the Loyal Land Company, founded in London in 1749, secured a grant of 800,000 acres north of the North Carolina line and west of the Alleghenies in that year. Other proposals and petitions followed. In February 1754 Governor Dinwiddie of Virginia, a militant opponent of French claims, proclaimed that 200,000 acres 'on the East side of the River Ohio shall be laid off and granted' to volunteers in the colonial troops; George Washington later became much interested in securing the rights of Virginia soldiers under claims based on this proclamation.[8] (See plate 170.)

The Loyal Land Company of London moved with dispatch. It sent its representative in Virginia, Dr Thomas Walker, to explore the country and find suitable places for settlement. Dr Walker, a man of considerable learning, good judgment, and enterprise, believed in western expansion, both financially and as a counter to French control of the region. In 1748 he had explored the upper Holston as far as present Kingsport, Tennessee, with John Finley (Findlay), an experienced hunter, and with two influential landowners in the Valley, Colonel James Patton and Colonel John Buchanan. After reaching the forks of the Holston River on his second trip, Walker struck west (see selection 2). He reached a break in the long, narrow, precipitous ridge of the Cumberland mountains, a pass which he later named Cumberland Gap after the Duke of Cumberland, commander-in-chief of the British army. On its southern approach Dr Walker noted the interesting cave and the clear stream bordered with rhododendrons; on the north side were almost impenetrable thickets and a salt lick where he saw a hundred buffalo. This was the pass over which thousands of settlers from Pennsylvania and North Carolina poured into Kentucky in the latter half of the eighteenth century; its discovery as a viable route by Walker was his greatest achievement. His journey of four months and a week was filled with adventures; the explorers were blocked by unscalable cliffs, shot a charging buffalo, were attacked by a bear, and found frequent rattlesnake bites the greatest hazard

170

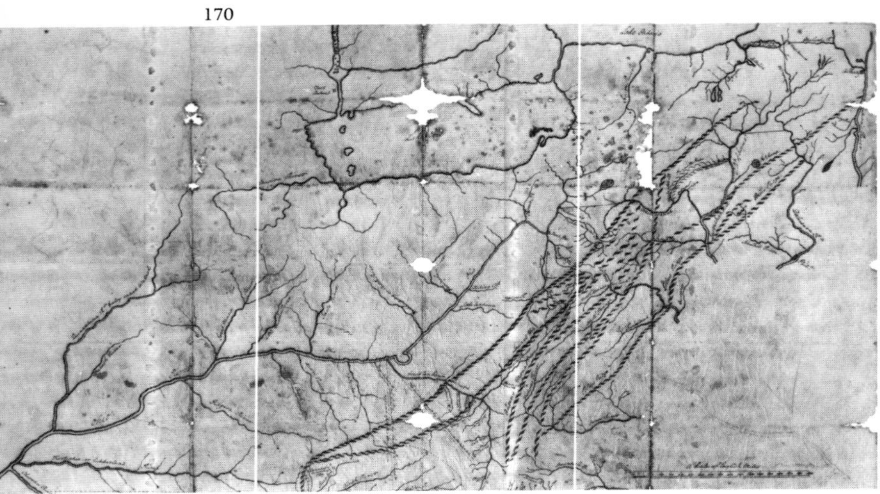

to their horses.[9] The Loyal Land Company's plans never materialized, though Dr Walker fought against counterclaims, such as those of Judge Richard Henderson's Transylvania Company, for many years and in 1779 was a Virginia Commissioner on the survey which extended the 1749 boundary line between North Carolina and Virginia to Cumberland Gap.

The French had reinforced their claim to the land adjacent

170 The Walker-Washington Map, *c.* 1770. *Library of Congress, Washington.*
This holograph map in George Washington's hand is endorsed 'Aligany Copied from a Map of Doc. Walkers laid before the Assembly'. It is evidently a copy of the map Dr Walker presented to the Virginia House of Burgesses on 13 December 1769 and was made by Washington in preparation for his survey of the land promised him and his regiment in the Great Meadows campaign in 1754 by Governor Dinwiddie. The grant lay between the Little and Great Kanawha Rivers in little known territory; but Dr Walker's explorations and surveys west of the Valley of Virginia had begun in 1750. At the lower center of the map are lines showing various treaties with the Cherokee Indians, some of which conflicted with the Virginia cession which Washington surveyed in the fall of 1770.

171 John Mitchell. A Map of the British Colonies in North America (detail of southeast), 1755. *British Museum, London.*
Mitchell's work is the most important map in North American colonial history. Diplomatically, it was the basis for territorial boundaries drawn in the treaties concluding the French and Indian War and the American Revolution. Geographically, it incorporated knowledge derived from the analysis of reports, journals, and maps available in the files of the British Board for Trade and Plantations. Its numerous legends and notes on Indians, settlements, and trails still provide a valuable source for historical and ethnological study.

For the southeastern area Mitchell relied chiefly on Colonel John Barnwell's map, made about 1721. He traces the route of Thomas Welch to the Quapaw Indians at the mouth of the Arkansas River, notes the location of the Upper, Middle, and Lower Cherokee towns, and marks the battle sites of Carolinian victories over the Spanish. Following Barnwell, however, he makes the mistake of placing the Tennessee River too far north. He used the journals and maps of Dr Walker, Gist, and other English explorers and traders for the Ohio Valley. By necessity he drew upon French sources for Canada and much of the Mississippi Valley.

Dr John Mitchell was born in 1711 in Lancaster County, Virginia, and returned to practice there after his medical education, probably at Edinburgh University. By 1746 he was well known as a naturalist; in that year he went to England because of his health. There he began intensive preparation for his map of North America and soon received official support.

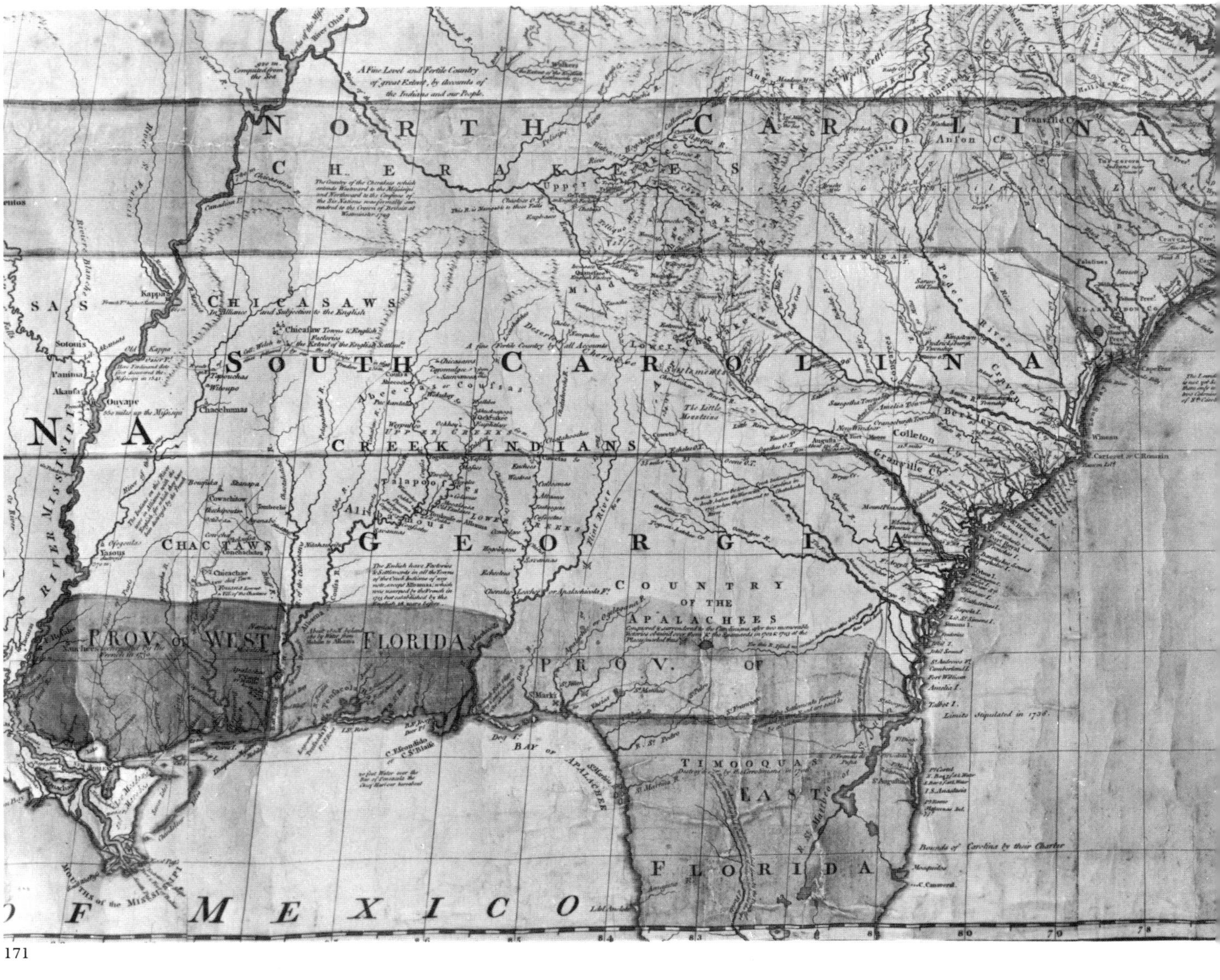

171

172 Gist. 'The Draught of Gen!. Braddock's Route towards Fort Duquesne', 1755. *John Carter Brown Library, Providence, Rhode Island.*
Christopher Gist had already acquired a knowledge, extraordinary for the time, of the course of the Ohio and its tributaries in the complex ranges of the Alleghenies. He was the natural choice as scout in Braddock's disastrous march in 1755. This map also shows detail away from the route taken by the army.

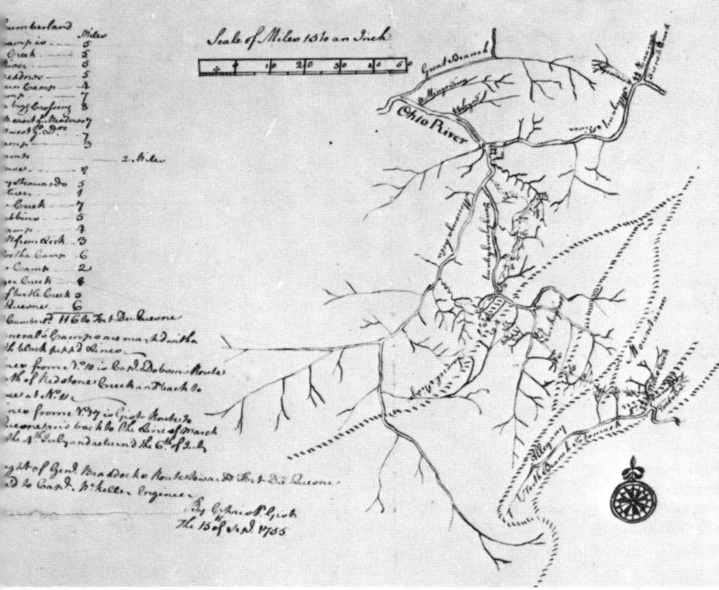

173

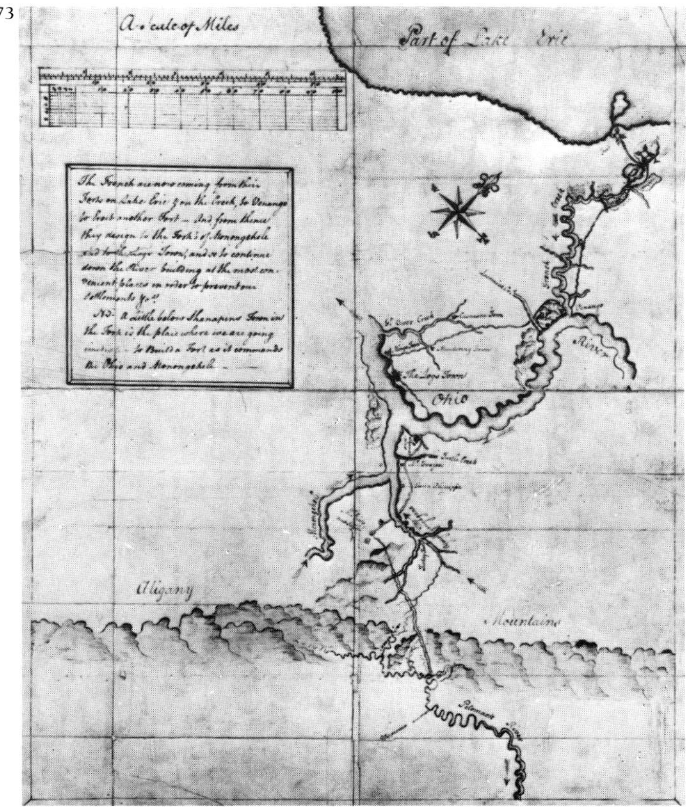

173 Washington. Sketch of journey to Fort Le Boeuf [?1754]. *Public Record Office, London, MPG 118.*
George Washington's map of the route he took on his mission to Fort Le Boeuf in the winter of 1753-4 is entirely in his own hand; it shows the country he passed through from the Potomac at Wills Creek, by the new home of his guide Christopher Gist, to the forks of the Monongahela and Ohio Rivers, and up French Creek to his encounter with the French commander. Both Washington and Gist were excellent surveyors and keen observers, as this map of their journey shows. Washington's plan to build a fort, which he notes in the legend at left center, was thwarted by the French, who drove away his workmen from the strategic site of present Pittsburgh, and erected Fort Duquesne there in 1754. See also plate 94.

to the Ohio by right of La Salle's discoveries (see page 40) and its former ownership by their allies the Shawnees; De Lery, chief engineer of Canada, made a topographical survey of the Allegheny and upper Ohio rivers in 1729, and Captain Céleron de Bienville in 1749 went down the Ohio and its tributaries with 200 soldiers, planting lead plates with suitable inscriptions to show French possession. Céleron's force warned, expelled, captured, or killed the English traders they met and confiscated their goods.[10] The English, on their part, claimed the territory by cession from their allies, the Iroquois, at the treaty of Lancaster in 1744. A major confrontation of the two colonial powers was approaching.

The French had explored the Ohio and its major branches; the English knew the Valley only from traders' accounts. In 1749 another company, with strong financial and political backing in Virginia and in England, the Ohio Company, sent beyond the Alleghenies several men who soon returned with little success; they had met hostility both from Indians and from Pennsylvania traders.[11] The Company then turned to Christopher Gist, a native of Maryland, in whom they found a remarkable frontiersman, hardy, skilled as a surveyor, sagacious in Indian relations, and honest. His instructions were extensive and complex; accompanied only by one inexperienced negro lad and a pack horse he accomplished much of his mission successfully. He was to map the rivers, find the mountain passes, survey suitable lands for settlement, and ascertain the size and trade possibilities of Indian tribes in the entire Ohio Valley as far as the falls at present Louisville, Kentucky, an area far beyond the grant made to the Ohio Company.[12]

When Gist received his instructions in September 1750, he was living with his family on his farm on the north bank of the Yadkin River on the North Carolina frontier. He started his journey on 31 October 1750 from Old Town on the Potomac in Maryland (see selection 3), where Thomas Cresap, an important member of the Ohio Company, was living. Going north by the War Path to Juniata River in western Pennsylvania, he turned west to Logstown on the Ohio, where he found the Indians suspicious and hostile. Gist found it advisable thereafter to conceal his real purpose and to emphasize his mission as an envoy from the Virginia government to improve trade. Crossing the mountains until he reached the Scioto River, he met George Croghan, trader and emissary of the Pennsylvania government. Together they went north to Twightwee Town on the upper Miami River; with skillful diplomacy they persuaded a large conference of Indians there to meet at Logstown the following year, turning their sympathies toward the English. Here were laid the foundations for the Logstown treaty of 1 June 1752, at which Gist was present and which granted English settlement rights east of the Ohio River.[13] Gist returned to the Ohio from Twightwee and crossed over the river into present Kentucky, taking a great curved swing south and then east through virgin territory of blue grass meadows and coal-bearing mountains. Information he gathered was soon used in new maps; Joshua Fry, a commissioner at the Logstown treaty, drew Gist's route on the revised edition of 'Virginia' which he was preparing. Gist provided invaluable knowledge for the military, political, and territorial activities of the English during the remainder of the colonial period.

Gist soon became involved in events more important than the affairs of the Ohio Land Company. To them he made a report on a journey to the upper Ohio country in 1751-2. In 1752 he also moved from the Yadkin to establish 'Gist's Settlement' on a southern branch of the Youghiogheny River, in frontier Pennsylvania. It was natural therefore that young Major George Washington should engage Gist as guide on his historic mission in 1753 to Fort Le Boeuf, the French post

174

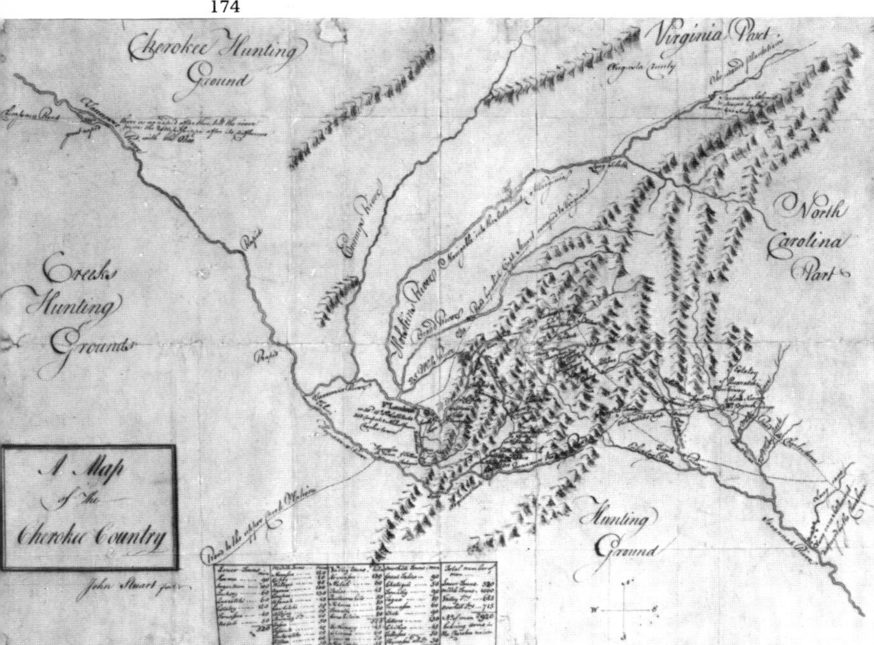

175

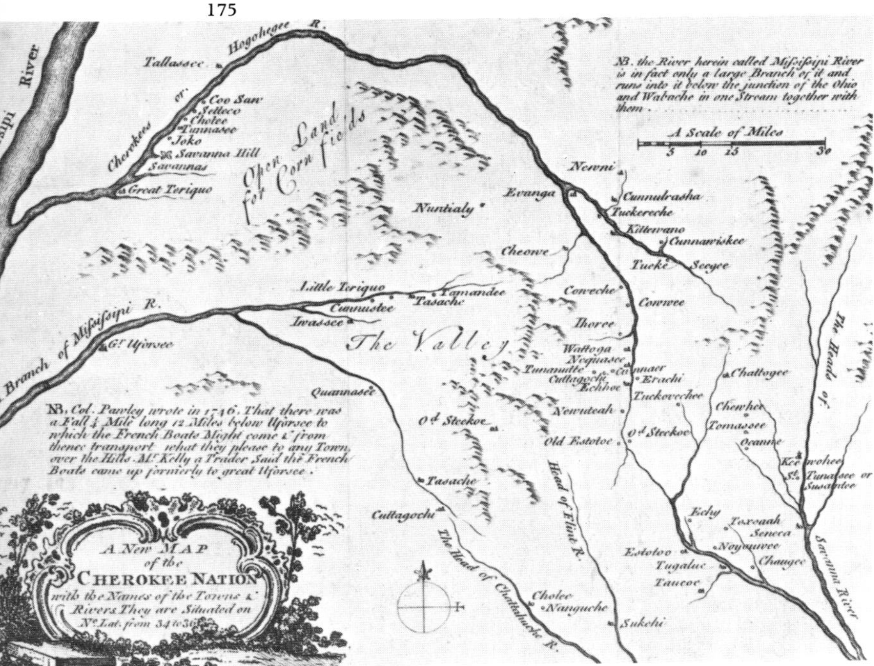

174 John Stuart. 'A Map of the Cherokee Country', *c.* 1761. *British Museum, London, Add. Ms. 14036.e.*
Stuart, captured in the Cherokee massacre of the reatreating garrison from Fort Loudoun on 10 August 1760, escaped through the aid of his friend Attakullakulla. The map shows 'The Road by which Capt. Stuart escaped to Virginia' as well as the roads to South Carolina and the location of forts and Cherokee Indian settlements. In 1764 Stuart was appointed superintendent of Indian affairs for the Southern District, a position which he held with skill and effectiveness until his death in 1779.

175 Kitchin. 'A New Map of the Cherokee Nation', 1760. *British Museum, London.*
Thomas Kitchin, a prolific map-publisher and later hydrographer to George III, made this map for the *London Magazine,* XXIX (1760). It has new and detailed information about the Cherokee settlements and an interesting note on French commercial navigation up to Uforsee (Muscle Shoals). Kitchin has confused the course and direction of the Little Tennessee River, however, making it flow independently into the Ohio above the Tennessee.

at the head of a tributary of the Ohio. Washington's delivery of Lieutenant Governor Robert Dinwiddie's letter asserting English claims to the Ohio Valley and the polite but firm repudiation made by Legardeur de St Pierre, the officer in charge of the fort, is regarded as an incipient action of the French and Indian War. 'Gist's Settlement' was the location of Washington's stand before his retreat to the hastily constructed Fort Necessity at Great Meadows, where he capitulated on 4 July 1754. The French burned Gist's and the neighboring houses; this ruined Gist financially. In 1755 he was General Edward Braddock's scout on the march to Fort Duquesne (present Pittsburgh); he knew the terrain well, and on a dangerous but successful scouting mission approached to within half a mile of the French fort. After the British defeat, he recruited a company of scouts as its captain. With his death in 1759 ended the career of one of the great frontiersmen of the colonial period.[14]

An account of a canoe trip down the Holston River from Virginia to the Cherokees, made at the end of the French and Indian War, is given in the *Memoirs* of Lieutenant Henry Timberlake. He made a sympathetic study of Cherokee culture as well as giving a careful description of their land and settlements. The Cherokees, allies of the English at the beginning of hostilities, had by 1760 turned bitterly against them and had killed or made captive the soldiers at Fort Loudoun at the mouth of the Little Tennessee. In 1761 they sued for peace and requested Lt Col Adam Stephen of the Virginia forces to send an officer to visit their towns and cement a renewal of friendship. Young Timberlake, at the time an ensign who had seen service under Washington and General John Forbes, volunteered. He took with him Sergeant Thomas Sumter, later General Sumter of Revolutionary War fame, a servant, and John McCormack, an interpreter. From Fort Robinson at Long Island on Holston River (Kingsport, Tennessee) they made their way by canoe to the upper Cherokee settlements in southeastern Tennessee. It was a trip of considerable danger from enemy Indians, bears, rapids, and accidents. They found a cave on the Holston with stalagmites (one near Three Springs Ford, Hamblen County, Tennessee?) where they almost lost their canoe and possessions:

'[We saw an] amazing quantity of buffaloes, bears, deer, beavers, geese, swans, ducks, turkeys and other game, till we came to a large cave; we stopped to examine it, but after climbing, with great difficulty, near 50 feet almost perpendicular, to get to it, we saw nothing curious, except some pillars of the petrified droppings, that fell from the roof, of a prodigious size. I could not, indeed, penetrate very far, for want of light.'[15]

On 20 December 1761 they reached Tommotly, and were there greeted by Outacity (Mankiller), the commander-in-chief. He took them to Chote, the chief Over-the-Hill Cherokee town, where the headsmen assembled to hear the articles of peace read at the great meeting house.

'The town-house,' wrote Timberlake, 'in which are transacted all public business and diversions, is raised with wood, and covered over with earth, and has all the appearance of a small mountain at a little distance. It is built in the form of a sugar loaf, and large enough to contain 500 persons, but extremely dark, having, besides the door, which is so narrow that but one at a time can pass, and that after much winding and turning, but one small aperture to let the smoak out, which is so ill contrived, that most of it settles in the roof of the house. Within it has the appearance of an ancient amphitheatre, the seats being raised one above another, leaving an area in the middle, in the center of which stands the fire; the seats of the head warriors are nearest it.'[16]

The Cherokees accepted the peace terms. After three months, during which Timberlake observed the customs of the Indians, won their high regard, and made an excellent map of the Little Tennessee River and the location of Cherokee towns, he returned to Williamsburg, Virginia, with Ostenaco, Outacite, and their followers. Governor Fauquier agreed to implement Ostenaco's wish to meet the Great White Father in London. Thomas Jefferson, then a student at William and Mary College, described the scene before departure.

'I knew much of the great Outassete, the warrior and orator of the Cherokees. He was always the guest of my father on his journeys to and from Williamsburg. I was in his camp when he made his great farewell oration to his people the evening before he departed for England. The moon was in full splendour, and to her he seemed to address himself in his prayers for his own safety on the voyage and that of his people during his absence. His sounding voice, distinct articulation, animated action, and the solemn silence of his people at their several fires, filled me with awe and veneration, although I did not understand a word he uttered.'[17]

Timberlake accompanied Ostenaco and two other Indians to England, where the Cherokees made a public sensation, met the King, and sat for a portrait by Sir Joshua Reynolds.[18]

The Treaty of Paris in 1763 gave the sovereignty over all North America east of the Mississippi to the English. The government in London soon after announced the Proclamation Line of 1763, which reserved the territory west of the Allegheny watershed to the Indians, forbidding white settlement there. Private exploration, however, continued, and several

177

178

177 Ostenaco, from an engraving after Reynolds, 1762.
Ostenaco was the head of one of two rival parties among the Cherokee; he evinced bravery and integrity. He was not, however, the equal in intelligence and diplomatic skill of Attakullakulla, the other great Over-the-Hill Cherokee chief at this time. De Brahm lists in his *Report* (Ed. De Vorsey, p. 109, 1971) the various military ranks among the Cherokee, which are tattooed on them by symbols: Gun-Men, or Boys, is the lowest, before achieving a certain number of scalps; then Raven; and next Man-killer 'much as a Colonel'; and Warrior, the highest rank 'much as a General'.

178 Cunne Shote, from an engraving after Parsons, 1762.
An engraving by James M. Ardell of Francis Parsons's painting of Cunne Shote, chief and great warrior of the Cherokees. The original oil on canvas is now in the Thomas Gilcrease Institute, Tulsa.

176 Timberlake. 'A Draught of the Cherokee Country', 1765, from the *Memoirs* of Lieut Henry Timberlake, opp. p. 160, 1765.
This is the most accurate map of the Little Tennessee River and of the Over-the-Hill Cherokee settlements along its banks made during the colonial period. Timberlake made the surveys and gathered the information for it during his peace mission to the Cherokees from Virginia in the winter of 1761-2.

176

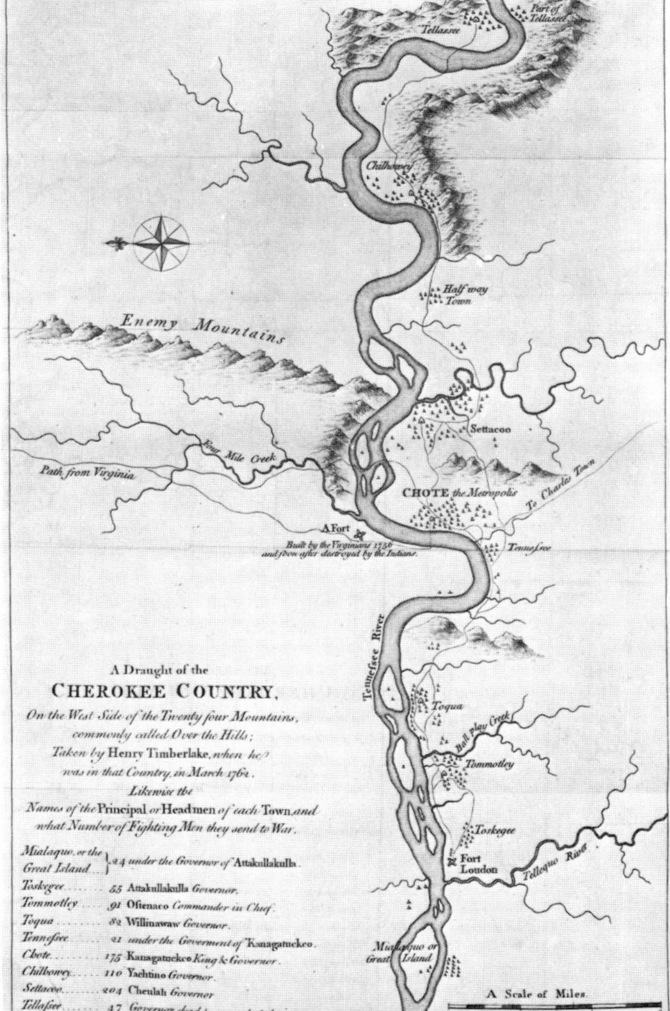

179

179 Three Cherokee chiefs in London, 1762.
A copperplate engraving, probably from a painting which the St James *Gazette* of 3 July 1762 states Joshua Reynolds was making of the Cherokee chiefs. 1 Their interpreter who was poisoned. '2 Outacite or Man-Killer, who Sets up the War-Whoop, as Woach, Woach, ha, ha, hoch, Waoch.
3 Austenaco or King, a great Warrior who has his Calumet or Pipe.
4 Uschesees, Ye Great Hunter, or Scalpper.'

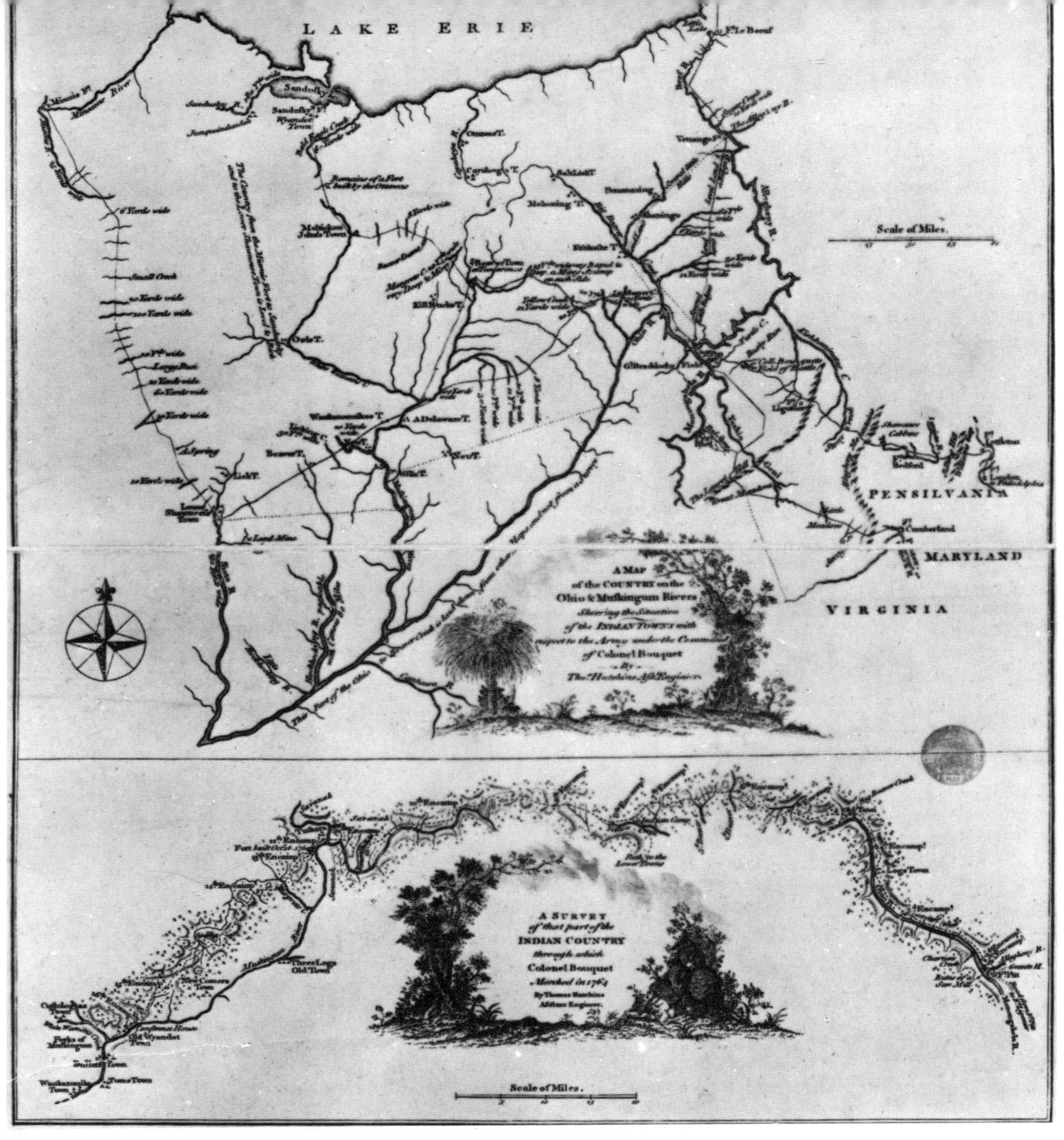

180

180 Hutchins. 'A Map of the Country on the Ohio & Muskingum Rivers', 1766, from William Smith, *An historical account of the expedition against the Ohio Indians*, 1766.
This is one of the most accurate colonial maps of the region west of the Ohio, as well as one of the most attractively designed engraved maps of the period. Thomas Hutchins records on the lower map the route of Colonel Henry Bouquet in 1764, and on the upper map the larger area which Hutchins had traversed and explored as Indian agent, trader, and engineer.

things led to increased official expeditions. The government needed to know more about its new possessions; pro-French tribes had to be pacified and borders protected by new forts; and Indian trade required encouragement. In 1764 Colonel Henry Bouquet led the first English army west of the Ohio to pacify Pontiac's supporters (see pages 67/8). The accounts of his campaign were published, with illustrations by the Philadelphia artist, Benjamin West, and with maps of the region by Thomas Hutchins, whose varied services as engineer, surveyor, map-maker, guide, and interpreter gave him extraordinary knowledge of the country.[19] Two years after serving with Bouquet, Hutchins accompanied Captain Harry Gordon, whom General Gage ordered to make a careful survey of the Ohio, the Mississippi, and the Gulf coast, to Pensacola in West Florida. Gordon's journal is a mine of information about the geography along his route, as well as Indian trade and fortifications. At the mouth of the Ohio he met Captain Philip Pittman, who was on a similar mission surveying the Mississippi from its mouth to the Illinois River. Pittman's published report formed the first English observations on European settlements along the river.[20]

While Gordon, Hutchins, and others were surveying the Ohio River and some of its tributaries, scores of hunters and traders from the frontier settlements were following the trails across the mountain ranges into present Kentucky and bringing back exciting reports of great rolling grasslands beyond, where deer and elk abounded and herds of buffalo gathered at the salt licks. In 1766 Benjamin Cutbird, who had married Daniel Boone's niece, and John Stuart, Boone's brother-in-law, left the Yadkin in North Carolina, crossed the mountain passes and reached the Mississippi.[21] In the same year Captain James Linville, his son James, and sixteen-year old John Williams were ambushed by Indians while sleeping near the Watauga River in eastern Tennessee; the Linvilles were killed, but Williams, his thigh fractured by a bullet, dragged himself to a horse which he mounted. His bone broke in his escape; but he rode east for five days to the Yadkin settlements and lived to a ripe old age.[22] In June 1766 Captain James Smith with four others went on a trip along the Cumberland River to the Ohio and mouth of the Tennessee; Smith's slow return, hampered by a painful leg wound, is told with some vivid details in one of the few journals preserved from such trips in these years.[23]

For some the freedom of life in the forests, unfettered by the restraints even of frontier society, and the lure of adventure, with the excitement of the chase and the encounters with hostile Indians, seemed the ideal existence. This was the period of the famous Long Hunters, so called because their absences in the wilderness extended a year or two.[24] The Long Hunters went in groups well provided with two or

181 The conference between Bouquet and the Indians on the Muskingum River, 1764; in William Smith, *An historical account of the expedition against the Ohio Indians*, 1766.
Colonel Henry Bouquet's brilliant campaign to pacify the Indians after the Pontiac Conspiracy concluded with their capitulation and promise of restitution. An important secondary effect was the opening of the Ohio Valley to further exploration and settlement. At Bushy Run in August 1764, against apparently overwhelming odds, Bouquet had shown himself superior in Indian warfare to his opponents at their wiliest. The return of English captives taken by the Indians in their devastating raids on border settlements and garrisons resulted in happy reunions. Many children, however, had become so attached to their foster parents that they did not want to rejoin their forgotten relatives.

Bouquet, who was rewarded by promotion to the command of the Southern Department as brigadier general, died soon after reaching Pensacola, Florida. See also plate 100.

three horses each which carried supplies necessary on the outward journey and returned, good fortune and Indians permitting, laden with skins. The most famous of these expeditions, organized by James Knox in southwest Virginia in 1770, included expert and long-experienced backwoodsmen like Kasper Mansker. One day, deep in the woods, they heard an extraordinary and unidentifiable sound; fearing Indian ambush, Mansker stealthily reconnoitered and found Daniel Boone, lying on his back on a deerskin and zestfully singing.[25] Boone joined the Long Hunters for a while; but not for long, since he loved solitude and was developing interests other than hunting. By 1771 there was no other white man who knew the country between the Cumberland and the Ohio as well as Boone. He had followed old trails and made new ones with the skill of an experienced woodsman, had explored the river valleys and the rich rolling grasslands with the eyes of a practical farmer and amateur surveyor, and had learned how to survive hunger, the attacks of wild animals, and Indian captivity.

May of 1769 proved to be a turning point in Boone's life; he set out on a two years' odyssey of exploration of the Kentucky Country (see selection 4). Inspired by a visit from John Finley, who earlier that spring had related stories of a terrestrial paradise he had seen south of the Ohio in 1767, Boone, in company with Finley, Boone's brother-in-law John Stuart, and three other men, crossed the Cumberland Gap.[26] Twice Boone was captured by Indians; he escaped, though with the loss of the skins he and his friends had collected. The first winter he remained and explored alone; the second year he was joined by his brother Squire. This was the greatest period of Boone's wide-ranging wanderings. He learned the land from the Cumberland Gap to the Ohio and from the mountains to the falls of the river where Louisville now stands. For a person with Boone's temperament it was an idyllic land and way of life: game in abundance, beautiful and endless vistas of country which he might dream one day to own and settle; and freedom from legal troubles, taxes, and annoying neighbors. At last Daniel and Squire, their packhorses loaded with pelts, started back to the Yadkin. In May 1771, as they neared Cumberland Gap, they were set upon and overpowered by Indians who did not kill them but left them stripped of their possessions.[27] It was a severe blow financially and must have tried Boone's famous humor and fortitude in disaster.

In the years that followed Boone was the leader of groups that crossed the mountains to establish homes and to build frontier communities. In 1773 he organized and led several families, forty persons in all, who started off with cattle, swine, horses, and necessary equipment. They reached the approach to Cumberland Gap in the Powell River valley before the Indians struck. Several were killed; two young lads, one of them Boone's son James, were slowly tortured to death. The would-be settlers returned to the Holston Valley.[28] In 1775 a plan of Judge Richard Henderson of North Carolina to establish a new independent colony, under the name of the Transylvania Company, matured. At a great council held in March 1775 at Sycamore Shoals on the Watauga River, with 1,200 Cherokees whom Boone had persuaded to come, Henderson and his associates displayed to them £10,000 in sterling and in clothing, utensils, and fire-arms. These the Company offered in exchange for over 20 million acres in the Cumberland and Kentucky River valleys. The Indians ceded the land and the chiefs signed the treaty.[29] Boone had already gathered a force of woodsmen; on March 10, a week before the signing of the treaty, they began cutting the trees and clearing the way west from Long Island on the Holston River for what became known as the Wilderness Road. They reached their destination, Big Lick on the Red River, a tributary of the Kentucky, in less than a month; by April five men were staking their claims around the proposed capital of Transylvania, Boonesborough. The settlement was subjected to repeated attacks by Indians from the North during the Revolution; Boone's skill and leadership saved Boonesborough repeatedly from destruction or abandonment. Once, carried captive by the Shawnees across the Ohio, he escaped when he learned of an impending attack; he rode a horse to the Ohio and after crossing it made the rest of the journey afoot through territory he knew well. He reached Boonesborough in time to warn and prepare the settlers successfully against surprise.

Many, like Christopher Gist, may have possessed equal or better woodlore than Boone, and others like George Rogers Clark and Richard Henderson had more far-sighted wisdom and sagacity. But even in his own lifetime he became the romantic ideal of the American frontiersman, independent, intrepid, wily, honest, extraordinary in stamina, expert in marksmanship, who explored the 'dark and bloody land' west of the Alleghenies and forged the way for later comers.

After 1775, Boone became less the explorer than the settler. The Proclamation of 1763, reserving the western lands to the Indians (see page 125), was being increasingly disregarded by the colonists. This led to bitter conflict. The Indian tribes had areas which were their hunting grounds; for their way of life, nomadic as well as agricultural, they needed vast regions to kill game and, later, to secure the skins which were necessary for barter. The land was tribal in ownership; they were often savagely resentful of intruders. To the European, the land belonged to the sovereign, who granted individual ownership under certain restrictions. Personal property, from the immemorial past, had been acquired through deeds, patents, and purchases. In America the King had given charters to colonies or proprietors; the colonists' attitude toward Indian property rights varied widely from William Penn and the Quakers, who bought land conscientiously from Indian tribes, to those who saw only an endless wilderness stretching toward the Pacific, occasionally crossed by wandering Indians. Their right to the land, they felt, was better than that of the natives, who might be used and kept pacified or driven away and exterminated. In the British colonies, treaties with the Indians made by crown or colonial representatives, even when designed or intended to keep the native allies friendly or at peace, in fact kept pushing the boundaries of settlement farther west; of this the Indians were well aware. Even more disruptive were purchases of land beyond the settlements by groups of colonists, in flagrant violation of English colonial policy. Boone understood this conflict of attitudes, but like Judge Richard Henderson, George Washington, and most colonials, believed in the right and inevitability of western expansion by the English.

2 Explorations of and from South Carolina, Georgia and Florida, 1732-75

In the new colony of Georgia, chartered in 1732 and settled 1 February 1733, General James Oglethorpe's policy of equitable payment to the Indians for their land and regulations for justice in trading relations bore profitable fruit. One of Oglethorpe's successful moves was his taking a delegation of Yamacraw Indians to England in 1734. Tomo-chi-chi, the mico of the Yamacraws, a Creek tribe, with his wife, nephew, and several warriors, were well housed in London, taken to Hampton Court, entertained at Windsor Castle, laden with gifts and returned with reports of the power, greatness, and liberality of the English which spread quickly and widely among the Indians.

Georgia had been planned not only as a haven for 'worthy indigents' but also as a bulwark between the English of South Carolina and the Spanish of Florida. Oglethorpe founded the town of Savannah on a bluff eighteen miles up the river and built outlying forts. At a meeting with fifty chiefs of the Creek Indians soon after his arrival, they agreed to a treaty granting the Trustees of Georgia all the land between the Savannah and Altamaha Rivers to their fall lines. At the head of navigation on the Savannah, the town of Augusta was marked out in 1735 as a trading post. It was on the old path from Charles Town to the Creek and Cherokee towns and soon became a great storage depot for goods in the Indian trade and a shipping place for furs and skins to Charles Town.

182

For the Indians the Augusta factories or storehouses held brightly colored cloth and blankets, guns and ammunition, shirts, hoes, axes, and all the trinkets the Indians loved, at reasonable prices. One of the bitterest complaints of the Indians was the unscrupulous business practices of the Charles Town traders, who too often charged what the traffic would bear and used false weights and measurements. Accompanying the treaty which the Trustees approved was a long list of barter prices: a gun for ten buck-skins, a blue blanket for five buck-skins, one large hatchet for three doe-skins, brass kettles at a buck-skin per pound.[30] From Augusta, one might see single traders with three or four packhorses setting out for villages hundreds of miles away, or occasionally great caravans of traders with their Indian helpers leading long strings of horses. To Augusta came Indians bringing peltry and food, or a delegation of chiefs to make a new treaty of alliance or land cession.

Despite the wide-ranging activity of the Indian trader, the literature of the middle years of the eighteenth century is sparse in accounts of exploration in the South. The colonial Indian agents made regular reports of visits to distant

182 Tomo Chachi Mico or King of the Yamacraw and Tooanahomi his Nephew, Son to the Mico of the Etchitas, *c.* 1734. Engraving.
Tomo Chachi, or Tomo-chi-chi, headed a delegation of Creek Indians to London. He presented George II with some eagle feathers at a formal ceremony in Windsor Castle. He said: 'These feathers are a sign of Power in our Land, and have been carried from Town to Town there; and we have brought them over to leave with you, O Great King, as a sign of everlasting Peace.'

183 Mark Catesby. Trumpet flower, from *Hortus Europae Americanus*, 1767.

184 Mark Catesby. Tulip tree, from *Hortus Europae Americanus*, 1767.

185 Mark Catesby. Dogwood, from *Hortus Europae Americanus*, 1767.
The flowering dogwood, whose flowers vary from white to pink, is now the state flower of North Carolina and Virginia.

186 Mark Catesby. Pellitory or 'tooth-ache tree', from *Hortus Europae Americanus*, 1767. Catesby notes that this tree, or its root, was used by people along the Virginia and North Carolina seacoast; it is still an ingredient for dentifrice.

83

185

84

186

187

188

189

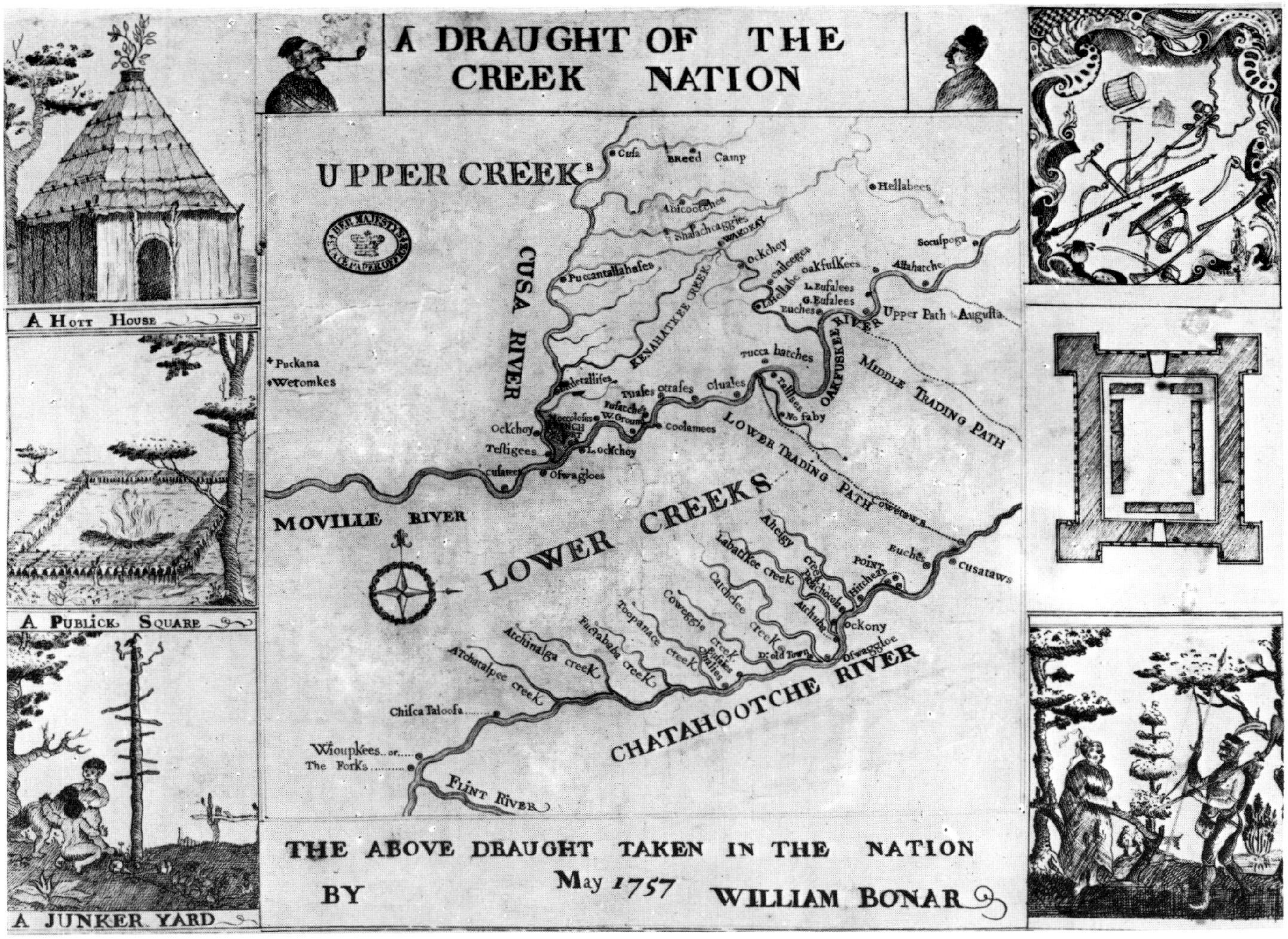

193

193 Bonar. 'A Draught of the Creek Nation', 1757. *British Museum, London.*
This charming manuscript map, with its bordering sketches of a Creek host house and other drawings, shows the location of the Upper and Lower Creek settlements at a time when both French and English were vying for Creek alliance.

William Bonar, an aide to Samuel Pepper, South Carolina Indian agent, entered Fort Toulouse early in 1757, disguised as a packhorseman, and brought back important information about French fortifications and strength. Shortly after, the French captured him; but while he was being taken to Mobile an Upper Creek band, at Pepper's persuasion, rescued him. In recognition of his contributions Bonar was made lieutenant and was placed in command of Fort Johnston in 1759.

194

194 The governor's house in St Augustine, 1764. *British Museum, London, K. Top. CXXII.86.2.a.*
John Bartram visited and dined with Governor James Grant of East Florida in 1766. 'The Governor's residence,' De Brahm, surveyor general of East Florida, wrote in his *Report of the general survey*, 'has both sides piazzas, viz., a double one to the south, and a single one to the north; also a Belvidere and a grand portico.'

alarmed the English, who captured and clapped him in prison, where he soon conveniently died.[32] After several months Bonnefoy escaped and reached a French outpost.

At the end of the colonial period two able observers and writers, both naturalists, explored the southern provinces with a new approach. John Bartram and his son William, like Catesby forty years before them, were not looking for trade routes or new lands to settle; their journeys through terrain not yet reported were less important than their discoveries of a new world seen with the eyes of a scientist. When John Bartram left Philadelphia, where Bartram's Botanical Garden on the Schuylkill River was already famous, for a trip to Florida in 1765, he visited his brother, Colonel William Bartram, on the Cape Fear River (see also Chapter 2). There also was his son William, who had come in 1761 and set up a trading store. John Bartram, who had just been appointed botanist to His Majesty George III, took his son with him as assistant and companion on the trip. Although Peter Collinson had published two of William's drawings in the *Gentleman's Magazine* as early as 1758,[33] it was on this trip through the Carolinas, Georgia, and Florida that William, under his father's tutelage, received the technical training and developed the knowledge of natural history that were to direct his future interests and contributions. The father and son were aided in their journeys

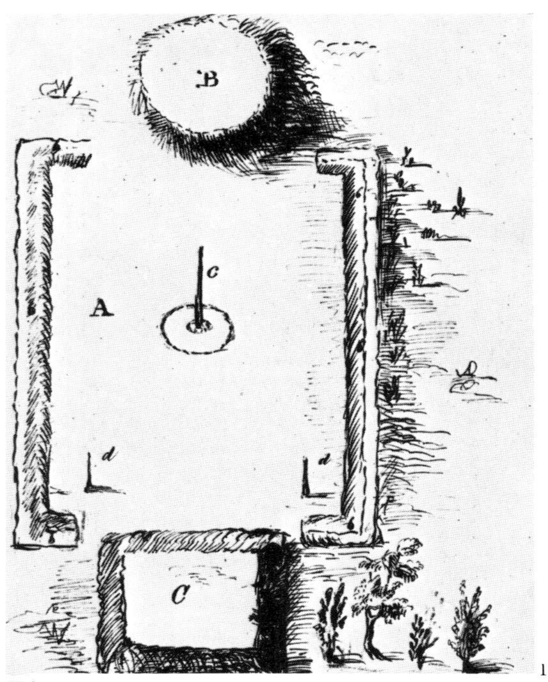

195 William Bartram. Plan of the ancient chunky-yard, 1789.
Historical Society of Pennsylvania, Philadelphia.
This plan is found in John Howard Payne's manuscript copy of William Bartram's answers to Benjamin S. Barton's queries about Indians.

The chunky or chungke game (from Catawba *chenco*) is played by hurling a round stone disk on its edge across the playing area; the players then throw sticks or poles to see which will be closest to the disk when it stops. Lawson describes the sport (see Chapter 3, selection 5), and James Adair gives a fuller account in *History of the American Indians*, London, 1775.

by the governors of South Carolina and Florida; but their entertainment by the wealthy planters of Charles Town contrasted with the primitive conditions and equipment of their expeditions in the wilderness, far from the shelter of a settler's cabin, with negligible protection from drenching rains and swarming insects. John Bartram's detailed diary of his nine months' journey, often no more than a series of abbreviated jottings, is nevertheless filled with botanical discoveries and gives vivid vignettes of scenes and events he observed. He was present with Governor James Grant at the Treaty of Picolata between the English and Lower Creek Indians on the St John's River on 15-16 November 1765, and gives the only known description, so far east, of the calumet ceremony of the Creek chiefs there.[34] He was the first European to explore the upper sources of the St John's River, reached before, if at all, by unrecorded Spaniards or English Indian-slave hunters like Captain Nairne. There, on 15 January 1766, near Lake Jessup, 'our hunter killed a large he-bear supposed to weigh 400 pounds . . . we found it to our surprise to be very mild and sweet, above all four-footed creatures, except venison. . . . We had a fat young buck and three turkeys fresh shot at the same time but we chose the [bear] for its sweetness and relish'.[35]

William Bartram returned with his father to Philadelphia. His genius in drawing aroused the admiration of the wealthy London physician and collector Dr John Fothergill, who commissioned him to make another trip south to collect specimens and make drawings. The sketches and water-color paintings which resulted, now in the Fothergill collection in the Natural History Museum in London, are notable for the vitality and character which he gives to his delineations, especially of birds.[36] (See plates 187-9, 202, 212-16.)

Bartram landed in Charles Town in the spring of 1773 and did not return to Philadelphia until January 1777. During these years he travelled extensively in Florida, made two trips to the Cherokee country in northern Georgia and North Carolina, and visited the Creeks and Choctaws on his way to the Mississippi and back. He deplored the devastation of native resources by farmers and planters which he observed along the river settlements; but most of his trips were through landscapes but little disturbed by white men. Such descriptions as exciting escapes from attacking alligators and confrontation by two bears on a narrow peninsula are dramatic; his pictures of his beloved Alachua savanna, of idyllic mountain scenery in the southern Blue Ridge are not surpassed by any other colonial writer.[37]

Bartram's achievement is that he combined the eye of a poet and literary artist with that of a scientific observer. His description of nature and of the people he met influenced profoundly the writers and poets of the Romantic Period. Soon after Bartram published his *Travels through North & South Carolina, Georgia, East & West Florida* in 1791, Coleridge read his beautiful description of Salt Springs in Florida, where 'just under my feet was the inchanting and amazing crystal fountain, which incessantly threw up, from dark, rocky caverns below, tons of water every minute' and wrote,

'Where Alph, the sacred river, ran
Through caverns measureless to man
Down to a sunless sea.'[38]

Professor Lowes has shown the pervasive influence of the *Travels* in 'Kubla Khan' and 'The Rime of the Ancient Mariner'. William Wordsworth, Robert Southey, Thomas Campbell, Percy Shelley, and other English poets show Bartram's influence and through Chateaubriand's use of his descriptions it was multiplied in Europe to an extent difficult to ascertain.[39] Many readers of the Romantics, without knowing it, have looked at nature through Bartram's eyes.

At the end of the colonial period, just before the American Revolution, a number of able writers and cartographers recorded their explorations and observations of the south and of the Indians. James Adair, who lived and traded for forty years (1735-75) among the Catawba, Cherokee, and Chickasaw nations, gave in his *History of the American Indians* (1775) first-hand information about life and conditions among

196 Sea oats (*Avena aquatica Sylvestris*), from Bernard Romans, *A concise natural history*, 1775.

197

197 Choctaw busts, from Bernard Romans, *A concise natural history*, 1775.
'Both sexes mark their faces and bodies, particularly the women, with indelible blue figures of fancy, among which is a great deal of voluted work of vast variety'—Romans.

198

198 Choctaw burial stage, from Bernard Romans, *A concise natural history*, 1775.
'As soon as the deceased is departed, a stage is erected and the corpse is laid on it and covered with a bear skin; if he be a man of note, it is decorated and the poles painted red with vermillion and bears' oil . . . at this stage the relations come and weep, asking many questions of the corpse, such as, why he left them? did not his wife serve him well? was he not contented with his children? had he not earnt enough? . . . was he afraid of his enemies? etc. and this accompanied by loud howlings'—Romans.

the Indians east of the Mississippi, with an account of his own experience.[40] William Gerard de Brahm, a trained engineer and surveyor, led 156 German Protestant settlers to Georgia. His exceptional abilities led to his appointment by George III as surveyor general of the Southern District of North America, to the planning and construction of military fortifications, and to extensive surveying. His first important work was his 'Map of South Carolina and a Part of Georgia' (1757); probably no area so extensive in the British colonies had been delineated before with such accuracy and professional skill. In 1773 he submitted to the King his *Report of the general survey in the southern district* in two volumes which included not only maps and geographical information of the rivers and coasts he had surveyed but also voluminous notes on the history of the region, the interior of the country and its inhabitants, and a glossary of the Cherokee language.[41] Bernard Romans, an educated Dutchman who was for a while assistant to De Brahm, in 1775 published *A concise natural history of East and West Florida*;[42] in it he gives a perceptive account of his travels, though neither in style nor scientific knowledge does he equal William Bartram. John Stuart, the superintendent of Indian affairs in the southern district (1764-79), compiled with his assistants a series of large wall maps for the British government which attempted to incorporate the geographical information gathered from every source available to him. [43]

Stuart's maps are an impressive achievement not only in themselves but in their visual demonstration of knowledge gained by the English in a century of exploration. In 1673 Herrman's 'Virginia' showed little knowledge west of the coastal plain; south of Virginia John Ogilby, the royal geographer, filled the interior of the First Lords Proprietors' map of Carolina (*c.* 1672) with such non-existent misconceptions as a desert, a marshy savanna below the Blue Ridge, and a great lake of unknown size. When Stuart's great wall maps were made about 1775, not all of the southeast had been surveyed; but its chief boundaries, coasts, river systems, mountain ranges, and settlements, both English and Indian, had been explored, reported, and mapped.

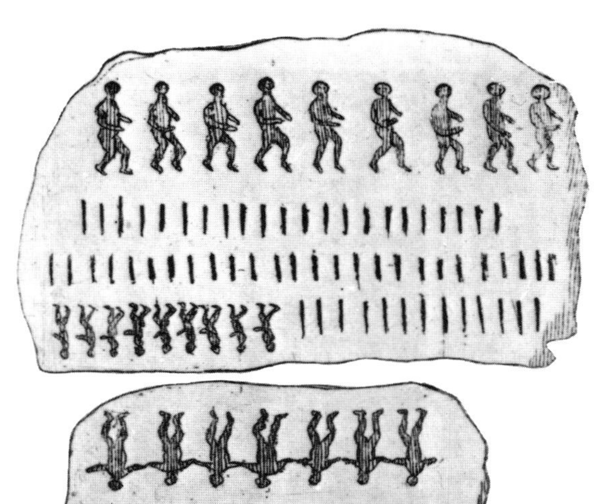

199

199 Choctaw and Creek hieroglyphics, from Bernard Romans, *A concise natural history*, 1775.
'To give an idea of Indian hieroglyphick painting, I have subjoined the two following cuts; the first is chactaw, and means that an expedition by seventy men . . . killed nine of their enemies and that the place . . . was the first public place in their territories where they arrived with their scalps. The Creek . . . means that ten of that nation of the Stag family came in three canoes . . . that six of the party near . . . a brook had met two men and two women with a dog, that they lay in ambush . . . killed them . . . and went home with the four scalps'—Romans.

1
Salley's trip from Virginia to the Mississippi, 1742

From a copy of Salley's *Brief Account*, made by Peter Jefferson, in the Public Record Office, London, C.O. 5/1327

Salley, whose land at the forks of the James and North Rivers was then at the southern limits of settlement in the Valley of Virginia, accompanied John Howard, his son, and two others on discoveries toward the Mississippi. This is the first known description of the Natural Bridge, later surveyed by George Washington and purchased for thirty shillings in 1774 by Thomas Jefferson, who called it 'the most sublime of Nature's works'.

On the sixteenth of March, 1742, we set off from my House and went to Cedar Creek about five miles, where is a Natural Bridge over said Creek, reaching from the Hill on the one side to the Hill on the other. It is a solid Rock and is two hundred and three feet high, having a very large Spacious arch, where the Water runs thro', we then proceeded as far as Mondongachate, now called Woods River, which is eighty-five Miles, where we killed five Buffoloes, and with their hides covered the Frame of a Boat, which was so large as to carry all our Company, and all our provisions and Utensels, with which we passed down the said River two hundred and fifty-two miles as we supposed, and found it very Rocky, having a great many Falls therein, one of which we computed to be thirty feet perpendicular and all along surrounded with inaccessible Mountains, high precipices, which obliged us to leave said River. We went then a south west course by Land eighty five Miles, where we came to a small River [northeast fork of Coal River], and there we made a little Boat, which carried only two men and our provisions. The rest travelled by Land for two Days and then we came to a large River, where we enlarged our Barge, so as she carried all our Company, and whatever Loading we had to put into her. Where we came to this River the Country is mountainous, but the farther down the plainer in those Mountains, we found great plenty of Coals, for which we named it Coal River. Where this River and Woods river meets the North Mountains end, and the Country appears very plain and is well water'd, there are plenty of Rivulets, clear Fountains and running Streams and very fertile Soil. On the sixth day of May we came to Allegany [Ohio] which we supposed to be three Quarters of a mile [wide], and from here to the great Falls [at Louisville, Ky.] on this River is well watered abounding with plenty of Fountains small streams and large Rivers; and is very high and fertile Soil. At this Time we found the Clover to be as high as the middle of a man's leg. The Falls mentioned above are three miles long in which is a small Island, the body of the Stream running on the North side, through which is no passing by reason of great Rocks and large Whirlpools, by which we went down on the south side of said Island without

200

201

200 Natural Bridge, Virginia, 1798, from Isaac Weld, *Travels through the states of North America*, London, 1799.
This is one of the earliest drawings of the Natural Bridge. Weld made his observations on and drawings of American scenery and American manners in 1795, 1796, and 1797.

201 'View of Long-Reach' (1796), from V. Collot, *A journey in North America*, Paris, 1826, pl. 15.
General Collot, who had been in America during the Revolution, made a return visit in 1795-6 at the request of Adet, the French Minister to the United States. He travelled extensively and journeyed down the Ohio and Mississippi to New Orleans. Long-Reach is a stretch of the Ohio River a few miles above present Marietta, Ohio.

202

202 William Bartram. 'Alligator mississipiens', *c.* 1766. *Natural History Museum, London, Fothergill Album.*
'The Alegator of St. Johns. Fig. 1. Represents the action of this terrable monster when they bellow in the Spring Season. they force the water out of their throat which falls from their mouth like a Cataract & a steam or vapour from their Nostrals like smoke. Fig. 2. Represents them rising up out of the water when they devour the fish &c.'—Bartram.

much Danger or Difficulty and in time of a Fresh in the River, men may pass either up or down, they being active or careful. On the seventh day of June we entered into the River Mississippi, which we computed to be five miles wide, and yet in some places it is not above one mile over, having in most places very high Banks, and in other places it overflows. The current is not swift but easy to pass either up or down, and in all our passage we found great plenty of Fish, and wild fowl in abundance.

Salley mentions salt springs and a lead mine used by the French near the forks of the Ohio and Mississippi. He then gives one of the earliest accounts of an English voyage down the Mississippi.

From the Falls mentioned above in the River Allegany to the mouth of said River is four Hundred fifty Miles, from thence to the Town of New Orleans is One Thousand four Hundred and ten Miles, and is Uninhabited excepting fifty Leagues above New Orleans. It is a large spacious plain Country endowed with all the natural Advantages, that is a moderate healthy Climate, Sweet water, rich Soil, and a pure fresh Air, which contribute to the Benefit of Mankind. We held on our passage down the River Mississippi [until] the second day of July, and about nine o' the Clock in the Morning we went on Shore to cook our Breakfast. But we were suddenly surprised by a Company of Men, Viz[t]. to the Number of Ninety, Consisting of French men Negroes, & Indians, who took us prisoners and carried us to the Town of New Orleans, which was about one Hundred Leagues from us when we were taken, and after being examined upon Oath before the Governor [Bienville] first separately one by One, and then All together, we were committed to close Prison.

After two years in prison, Salley and some companions escaped, finally reaching Charles Town. Salley's notes and journal had been taken from him; the present 'Narrative' was written soon after reaching home.

On the Eighteenth Day of April, we left Charles Town, the second time, and travelled by Land, and on the seventeenth Day of May, 1745, we arrived at my House, having been absent three years Two Months and one Day, from my family, having in that time by the nicest Calculation I am able to make, travelled by Land and Water four thousand six hundred and six Miles since I left my own House till I returned Home again.

John Peter Salley.

Text used: Fairfax Harrison, 'The Virginians on the Ohio and the Mississippi in 1742', Virginia Magazine of History and Biography, *30, 1922, pp. 213-17 passim, 222.*

2
Dr Thomas Walker crosses Cumberland Gap, 1750

From the manuscript journal of Dr Thomas Walker

Dr Walker left his home, Castle Hill, south of Charlottesville, Virginia, to inspect the country granted to the Loyal Land Company of London. He went to the forks of Holston River at present Kingsport, Tennessee, and from there turned west across Clinch and Powell Rivers to Cave Gap, which he later called Cumberland Gap.

Having, on the 12th of December last, been employed for a certain consideration to go to the Westward in order to discover a proper Place for Settlement, I left my house on the Sixth day of March, at 10 o'clock, 1749-50, in Company with Ambrose Powell, William Tomlinson, Colby Chew, Henry Lawless & John Hughs. Each man had a horse and we had two to carry the baggage . . .

29th. Our Dogs were very uneasie most of the Night.

30th. We kept down Reedy Creek, and discover'd the tracks of about 20 Indians, that had gone up the Creek between the time we Camped last Night, and set off this Morning. We suppose they made our Dogs so restless last Night. We Camped on Reedy Creek [a tributary of Holston River].

March 30th. We caught two young Buffaloes one of which we killed, and having cut and marked the other we turn'd him out.

31st. We kept down Reedy Creek to Holston where we measured an Elm 25 feet round 3 feet from the Ground. We say [saw] young Sheldrakes, we went down the River to the North Fork and up the North Fork about a quarter of a mile to a Ford and then crossed it. In the Fork between Holston's and the North River, are five Indian Houses built with loggs and covered with Bark, and there were abundance of Bones, some whole Pots and Pans, some broken and many pieces of mats and Cloth. On the West Side of the North River, is four Indian Houses such as before mentioned, we went four miles Below the North River and Camped on the Bank of Holston's, opposite to a large Indian Fort.

April 1st. The Sabbath. We say [saw] Perch, Mullets, and Carp in plenty, and caught one of the large Sort of Cat Fish. I marked my Name, the day of the Month, and date of the year on several Beech Trees . . .

April 13th. We went four miles to large Creek, which we called Cedar Creek, being a Branch of Bear-Grass, and from thence Six miles to Cave Gap, the land being Levil. On the North side of the Gap is a large Spring, which falls very fast, and just above the Spring is a small Entrance to a large Cave, which the Spring runs through, and there is a constant Stream of Cool air issuing out. The Spring is sufficient to turn a Mill. Just at the foot of the Hill is a Laurel Thicket, and the Spring Water runs through it. On the South side is a plain Indian Road. The Mountain on the North Side of the Gap is very Steep and Rocky, but on the South side it is not So. We called it Steep Ridge. At the foot of the hill on the North West Side we came to a Branch, that made a great deal of flat Land. We kept down it 2 miles, Several other Branches Coming in to make it a large Creek, and we called it Flat Creek [Yellow Creek]. We camped on the Bank where we found very good Coal. I did not Se any Lime Stone beyond this Ridge. We rode 13 miles this day.

Walker reached the Cumberland River a few miles below Barbourville, Kentucky. While he was examining land up the river, two of his men remaining behind built a cabin, possibly as proof of occupancy or as a shelter for later agents. The first recorded house in that region, it was noted on later maps as 'Walker's Settlement'.

[April] 28th. We kept up the River to our Company whom we found all well, but the lame Horse was as bad as we left him, and another had been bit in the Nose by a Snake. I rub'd the wounds with Bears oil, and gave him a drench of the same and another of the decoction of Rattle Snake root some time after. The People I left had built an House 12 by 8, clear'd and broke up some ground, & planted Corn, and Peach Stones. They also had killed several Bears and cured the meat. This day Colby Chew and his Horse fell down the Bank. I Bled and gave him Volatile drops, & he soon recovered.

Returning by a northerly route, he crossed Kentucky River south of its Red River branch, eventually reaching habitations at Hot Springs, Virginia, where he 'found Six Invalides there'. He left his men at Staunton, the Augusta County Court House. The following paragraph ends his journal:

[July] 13th. I got home about Noon. We killed in the Journey 13 Buffaloes, 8 Elks, 53 Bears, 20 Deer, 4 Wild Geese, about 150 Turkeys, besides small Game. We might have killed three times as much meat, if we had wanted it.

Text used: J. Stoddard Johnston (Ed.), First Explorations of Kentucky, *Louisville, Ky., 1898, pp. 8-9, 43-4, 48-50, 55, 75.*

3 Christopher Gist explores the Ohio Valley, 1750-1

From the *Journals* of Christopher Gist in the Public Record Office, London

Gist was appointed agent of the Ohio Land Company, with instructions to explore the Ohio River and its tributaries and to survey areas suitable for settlement. From Thomas Cresap, an important member of the Company, he received orders to negotiate with Indians encountered, who were generally hostile to settlement. Crossing the mountains, Gist reached the Ohio and came to an important trading center, Logstown, eighteen miles below present Pittsburgh.

Sunday Nov 25. The People in this Town, began to enquire my Business, and because I did not readily inform them, they began to suspect me, and said, I was come to settle the Indian's Lands and they knew I should never go Home again safe; I found this Discourse was like to be of ill Consequence to me . . . and told them I had a Message to deliver the Indians from the King, by Order of the President of Virginia, & for that Reason wanted to see M Montour: This made them all pretty easy (being afraid to interrupt the King's Message) and obtained me Quiet and Respect among them, otherwise I doubt not they would have contrived some Evil against me. . . .

Monday 26. Tho I was unwell, I prefered the Woods to such Company & set out from the Loggs Town down the River NW 6 M to great Beaver Creek . . . The Bottoms upon the River below the Logg's Town very rich but narrow, the high Land pretty good but not very rich, the Land upon Beaver Creek the same kind; From this Place We left the River Ohio to the SE & travelled across the Country.

Exploring the country and tributaries north of the Ohio, with many conferences with Delaware and Shawnee Indians, he journeyed to Twightwee at the forks of Miami River, in company with George Croghan, trader and Indian agent for Pennsylvania.

Sunday 17 [February, 1751]. Crossed the little Miamee River, and altering our Course We went SW 25 M, to the big Miamee River, opposite the Twigtwee Town. All the Way from the Shannoah Town to this Place (except the first 20 M which is broken) is fine, rich level Land, well timbered with large Walnut, Ash, Sugar Trees, Cherry Trees &c, it is well watered with a great Number of little Streams or Rivulets, and full of beautiful natural Meadows, covered with wild Rye, blue Grass and Clover, and abounds with Turkeys,

203 Charleston harbor, South Carolina. Watercolor by Bishop Roberts painted before 1739. *Colonial Williamsburg.*
The artist lived and worked in Charleston from 1735 until his death four years later. This is his only known work.

204 Mark Catesby. The Baltimore-Bird, from *Hortus Europae Americanus*, 1767. Also the tulip-tree.
'This Gold-colour'd Bird I have only seen in *Virginia* and *Maryland*; there being none of them in *Carolina*. It is said to have its Name from the Lord Baltimore's Coat of Arms, which are Paly of Six Topaz and Diamond, a Bend, counterchang'd; his Lordship being a Proprietor in those Countries.
It breeds on the Branches of tall Trees, and usually on the Poplar or Tulip-Tree. Its Nest is built in a particular manner, supported only by two Twigs fix'd to the Verge of the Nest, and hanging most commonly at the Extremity of a Bough.' The above is Catesby's comment.

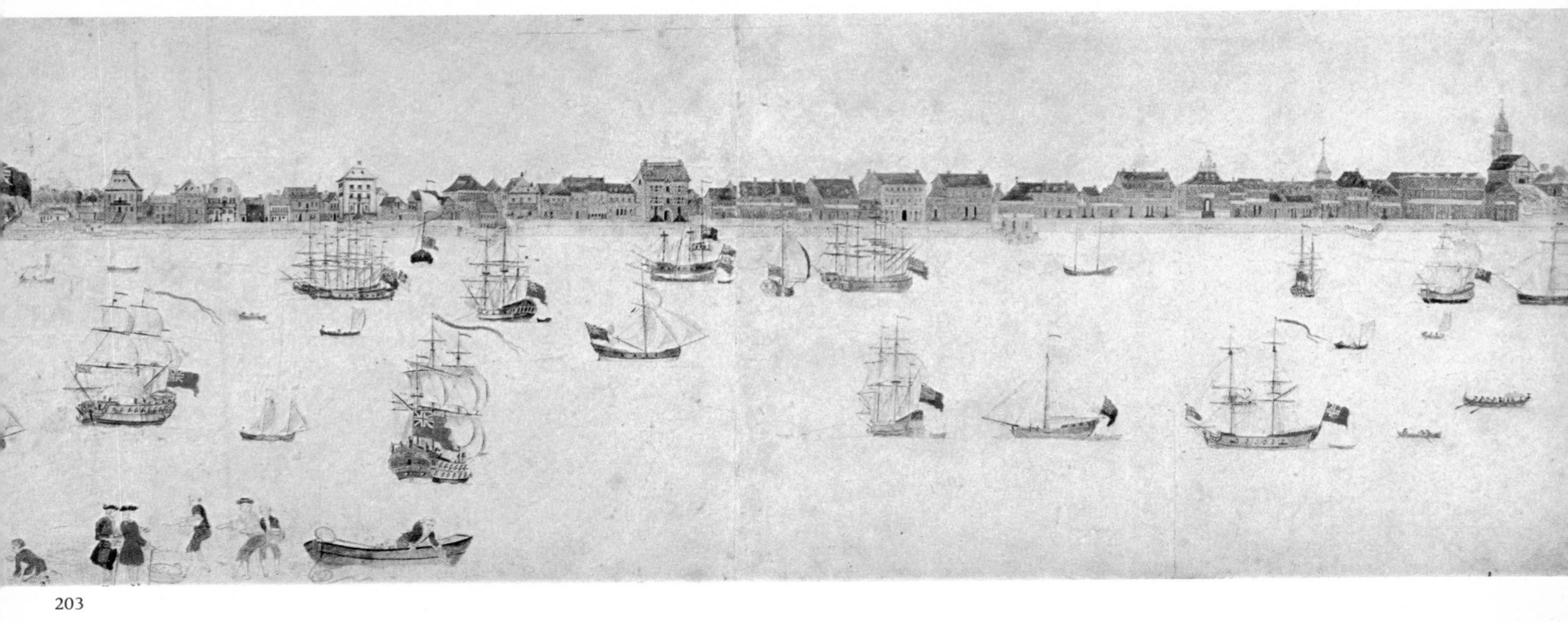

203

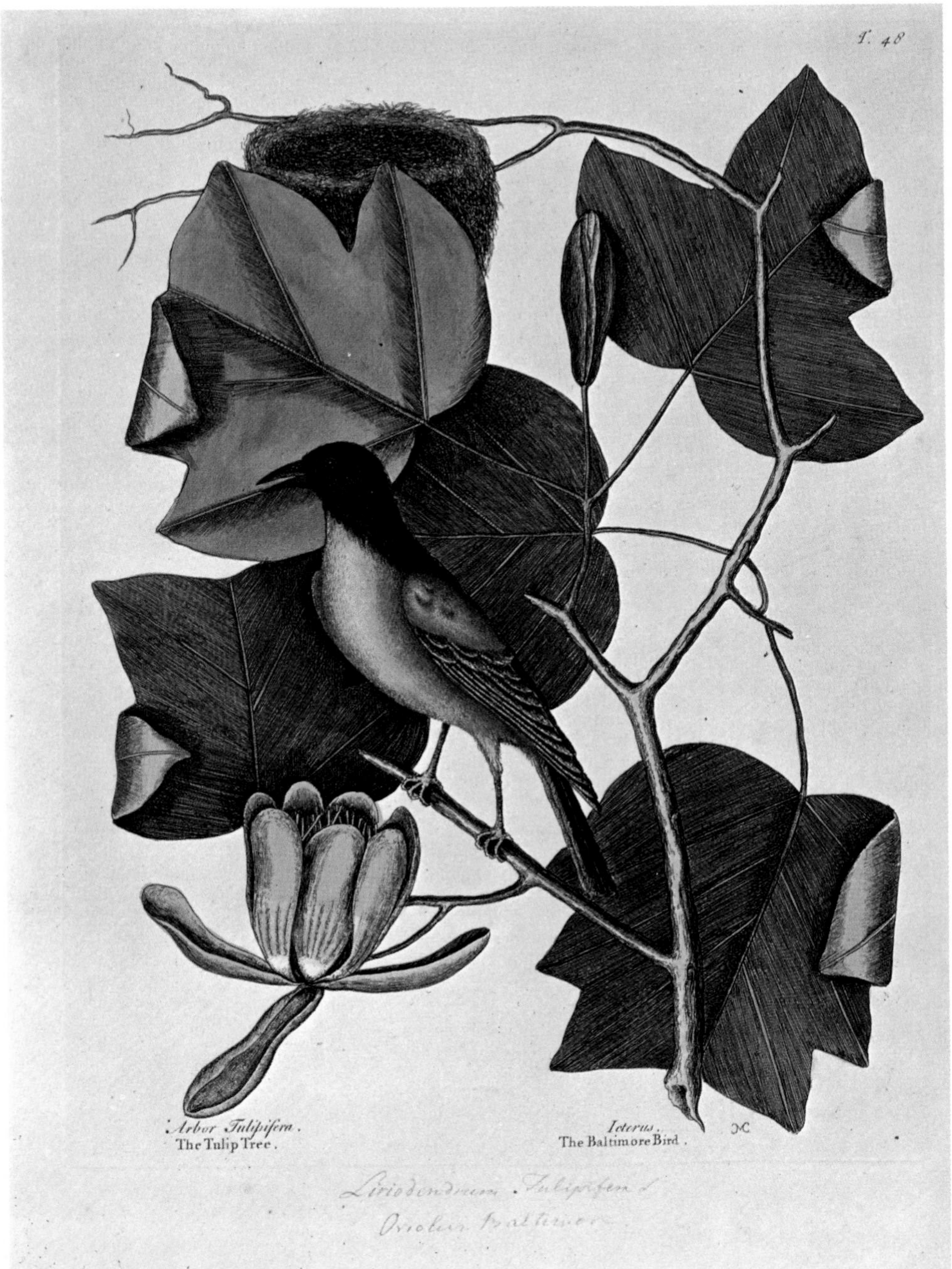
T. 48
Arbor Tulipifera.
The Tulip Tree.
Icterus.
The Baltimore Bird.
MC
Liriodendrum Tulipifera
Oriolus Baltimore

204

206

205

207

Deer, Elks and most Sorts of Game particularly Buffaloes, thirty or forty of which are frequently seen feeding in one Meadow: In short it wants Nothing but Cultivation to make it a most delightfull Country—The Ohio and all the large Branches are said to be full of fine Fish of several Kinds, particularly a Sort of Cat Fish of a prodigious Size; but as I was not there at the proper Season, I had not an opportunity of seeing any of them.

After important diplomatic meetings which turned the Indians toward a friendly alliance with the English, Gist crossed the Ohio at the mouth of the Scioto. The mammoth bones he describes were from Big Bone Lick (Boone County, Kentucky), near the Ohio twenty-five miles below the mouth of Big Miami River and eighty-five miles above the Falls.

Wednesday [March] 13. We set out S 45 W, down the said River on the SE Side 8 M, then S 10 M, here I met two Men belonging to Robert Smith at whose House I lodged on this Side the Miamee River, and one Hugh Crawford, the said Robert Smith had given Me an Order upon these Men, for two of the Teeth of a large Beast, which they were bringing from towards the Falls of Ohio, one of which I brought in and delivered to the Ohio Company—Robert Smith informed Me that about seven Years ago these Teeth and Bones of three large Beasts (one of which was somewhat smaller than the other two) were found in a Salt Lick or Spring upon a small Creek which runs into the S Side of the Ohio, about 15 M, below the Mouth of the great Miamee River, and 20 above the Falls of Ohio—He assured Me that the Rib Bones of the largest of these Beasts were eleven Feet long, and the Skull Bone six feet wide, across the Forehead, & the other Bones in Proportion; and that there were several Teeth there, some of which he called Horns, and said they were upwards of five Feet long, and as much as a Man could well carry: that he had hid one in a Branch at some Distance from the Place, lest the French Indians should carry it away—The Tooth which I brought in for the Ohio Company, was a Jaw Tooth of better than four Pounds Weight; it appeared to be the furthest Tooth in the Jaw, and looked like fine Ivory when the outside was scraped off—I also met with four Shannoah Indians coming up the River in their Canoes, who informed me that there were about sixty French Indians encamped at the Falls.

Gist turned south before reaching the Falls; from the Red River branch of the Kentucky he turned east. After reaching Pound Gap in the coal country at the West Virginia line near Whitesburg, Ky., he found food scarce and 'the country being still rocky mountainous, & full of Laurel Thickets, the worst traveling I ever saw'. He crossed the Valley of Virginia and entered North Carolina at a pass near Galax, Virginia.

Monday April 1. Set out the same Course about 20 M. Part of the Way We went along a Path up the Side of a little Creek, at the Head of which was a Gap in the Mountains, then our Path went down another Creek to a Lick where Blocks of Coal about 8 to 10 In: square lay upon the Surface of the Ground, here We killed a Bear and encamped.

Tuesday 2. Set out S 2 M, SE 1 M, NE 3 M, killed a Buffaloe. . . .

Saturday [May] 18. Set out S 20 M to my own House on the Yadkin River, when I came there I found all my Family gone, for the Indians had killed five People in the Winter near that Place, which frightened my Wife and Family away to Roanoke about 33 M nearer in among the Inhabitants, which I was informed of by an old Man I met near the Place.

Sunday 19. Set out for Roanoke, and as We had now a Path, We got there the same Night where I found all my Family well.

First printed in part by Thomas Pownall, A Topographical Description . . . of North America, *London, 1776, Appendix vi.*
Text used: William M. Darlington (Ed.), Christopher Gist's Journals, *Pittsburgh, 1893, pp. 34-5, 47, 57-8, 61, 65-6.*

4
Daniel Boone explores Kentucky, 1769-75

Filson's 'The Adventures of Col. Daniel Boon', read and signed as accurate by Boone himself on 12 May 1784, is found in a small volume that described the 'Kentucke' wilderness and its settlement. Filson, a schoolteacher who underwent hardships in his wanderings to collect first-hand testimony, wrote in a 'Johnsonese' style in humorous contrast to the few surviving examples of Boone's own terse, semi-literate, but effective frontier writing.

It was on the first of May, in the year 1769, that I [Daniel Boone] left my family and peaceable habitation on the Yadkin River, in North-Carolina, to wander through the wilderness of America, in quest of the country of Kentucke, in company with John Finley, John Stewart, Joseph Holden, James Monay, and William Cool. We proceeded successfully, and after a long and fatiguing journey through a mountainous wilderness, in a westward direction, on the seventh day of June following, we found ourselves on Red-River, where John Finley had formerly been trading with the Indians, and, from the top of an eminence, saw with pleasure the beautiful level of Kentucke. At this place we encamped, and made a shelter to defend us from the inclement season, and began to hunt and reconnoitre the country. We found every where abundance of wild beasts of all sorts, through this vast forest. The buffaloes were more frequent than I have seen cattle in the settlements, browzing on the leaves of the cane, or croping the herbage on those extensive plains, fearless, because ignorant, of the violence of man. Sometimes we saw hundreds in a drove, and the numbers about the salt springs were amazing. In this forest, the habitation of beasts of every kind natural to America, we practised hunting with great success until the twenty-second day of December following.

This day John Stewart and I had a pleasing ramble, but fortune changed the scene in the close of it. In the decline of the day, near Kentucke river, as we ascended the brow of a small hill, a number of Indians rushed out of a thick cane-brake upon us, and made us prisoners. The time of our sorrow

205 Jacquin. *Poinciana pulcherrima,* or Barbados pride, from N. J. Jacquin, *Selectarum Stirpium Americanarum Historia,* 1780. *British Museum, London.* A tall tree with scarlet blossoms, the French call it 'Fleurs de Paradis'. It grows commonly in the Caribbean; in India it is the flame tree; it is prevalent in Florida, called royal poinciana.

Baron Nicolas-Joseph Jacquin went to the West Indies and South America in 1755. *Selectarum* was first published in 1763. The 1780 edition, in six volumes, of which fewer than twenty-five copies are known, was published with plates drawn and colored by hand.

206 Jacquin. *Passiflora quadrangularis,* or passion flower, from N. J. Jacquin, *Selectarum,* 1780. *British Museum, London.* This flower 'made an extraordinary impression upon the early explorers of America. They saw in this the crown of thorns of the crucifixion. Three styles suggested nails. . . . Five stamens five wounds. Ten parts of the perianth the Apostles, Peter and Judas excluded'—H. W. Rickett, *Wild flowers of the United States; the South Eastern States, New York, 1967.*

207 Jacquin. Tree orchid: *Epidendrum altissimum,* from N. J. Jacquin, *Selectarum,* 1780. *British Museum, London.*

Jacquin (1727-1817), a celebrated Dutch naturalist, was professor of botany and chemistry at the University of Vienna before he left to visit the New World.

208

209

208 Daniel Boone, by Chester Harding, from a photograph in the *Wisconsin Historical Society, Madison, Draper Collection.*

209 Daniel Boone's beaver trap. Photograph by Steve Ladish of original in the *West Virginia State Museum, Charleston, West Virginia.*

210 Flat-bottom boat, 1796, from V. Collot, *A journey in North America,* 1826. Although such river traffic was not common on the Ohio until after the Revolution, French traders and miners on the Mississippi had long before developed boats with the shallow draught needed to float heavy cargoes down to New Orleans.

was now arrived, and the scene fully opened. The Indians plundered us of what we had, and kept us in confinement seven days, treating us with common savage usage. During this time we discovered no uneasiness or desire to escape, which made them less suspicious of us; but in the dead of night, as we lay in a thick cane brake by a large fire, when sleep had locked up their senses, my situation not disposing me for rest, I touched my companion and gently awoke him. We improved this favourable opportunity, and departed, leaving them to take their rest, and speedily directed our course towards our old camp, but found it plundered, and the company dispersed and gone home.

While Judge Richard Henderson was concluding the treaty of the Transylvania Company with the Cherokee in March, 1775, Boone gathered a company of woodsmen at Long Island on the Holston River and cleared a pioneer route, the famous Wilderness Road.

I undertook to mark out a road in the best passage from the settlement through the wilderness to Kentucke. I soon began this work, having collected a number of enterprising men, well armed. We proceeded with all possible expedition until we came within fifteen miles of where Boonsborough now stands, and where we were fired upon by a party of Indians that killed two, and wounded two of our number; yet, although surprised and taken at a disadvantage, we stood our ground. This was on the twentieth of March, 1775. Three days after, we were fired upon again, and had two men killed, and three wounded. Afterwards we proceeded on to Kentucke river without opposition; and on the first day of April began to erect the fort of Boonsborough at a salt lick, about sixty yards from the river, on the S. side.

Text used: James Filson, The Discovery . . . of Kentucke, *Wilmington, Del., 1784, pp. 50-2, 59.*

5
Bonnefoy's journey up the Tennessee as Cherokee captive, 1741-2

From Bonnefoy's journal in Paris, Archives Nationales, Colonies F. 3: 24, ff. 361-71.

Antoine Bonnefoy, a French soldier in a large convoy going upstream from New Orleans, was in a pirogue or dugout canoe which became separated from the main convoy near the mouth of the Ohio River. On 15 November 1741 his pirogue was attacked by 80 Cherokee Indians; five survivors were taken captive, although in sight of the main convoy across the Mississippi.

When we had been bound with these collars the savages, having found in our boat what had been intended for our breakfast, brought it to us to eat, and gave us to understand by signs that no harm should come to us, and that we should be even as themselves. They then unloaded our boat, and distributed the goods equally among the 80 men of the party. . . . The party took up its course, paddling without making the least noise, along the River Ouabache [Ohio] till six o'clock

210

the next morning, then rested about two hours, during which time they broiled some meat they had found in our pirogue when we were captured. They gave us (as they always did) a portion equal to theirs, after which they resumed their paddles, and gave us each one, after having made us each drink, as with the first meal, the evening before, a cup of rum. I bathed a wound I had received in the knee, from a musket-shot in that first discharge; after which I was not further troubled by it.

In the course of this river [Tennessee] which I estimate as 450 leagues from the Oaubache to the first village of our savages, there are three waterfalls. The first is situated about half way up. The portage is about one-quarter of a league. The second is eight days' journey further up. The portage amounts to a good league. At this place the river is two leagues broad, and rolls its waters like a cascade, a league long, in the shape of a hill, like that of the portage which we were obliged to make. The third, at which we arrived on the first of February, has a portage of only about 100 paces. The river at this place is extremely rapid, and generally is so, more and more, from this uppermost fall to the place where we left it, February 3, to make the rest of our journey by land. The savage who had adopted me gave me, before setting out upon the march, a gun, some powder, and some bullets.

They reached Tellico, an important Cherokee Town on the Tellico River, a branch of the Little Tennessee, on 7 February 1742.

At the first sight of our savages, all the men ran out to the place where we then were, for the ceremony customary among this nation. Our clothes were taken off, and a stock was made for each of us, without, however, putting us in it; they merely put on us our slave's-collar. Then the savages, putting in each one's hand a white stick and a rattle, told us that we must sing, which we did for the space of more than three hours, at different times, singing both French and Indian songs, after which they gave us to eat of all that the women had brought from the village, bread of different sorts, sagamité (corn porridge), buffalo meat, bear meat, rabbit, sweet potatoes, and graumons [grapes]. Then they buried at the foot of the tree a parcel of hair from each one of us, which the savages had preserved for that purpose from the time when they cut our hair off. After this march was finished they brought us into the council-house, where we were each obliged to sing four songs. Then the savages who had adopted us came and took away our collars. I followed my adopted brother who, on entering into his cabin, washed me, then, after he had told me that the way was free before me, I ate with him, and there I remained two months, dressed and treated like himself, without other occupation than to go hunting twice with him. We were absent thirteen days the first time and nine days the last.

The journey up the Tennessee took nearly three months. About three months later Bonnefoy with two companions escaped the Indians' tolerant and loose supervision and descended the river on a raft. Bonnefoy alone reached an Alabaman village friendly to the French; he was taken to Fort Toulouse at the junction of the Coosa and Tallapoosa Rivers. He reached the fort on 1 June 1742; his captain 'did not recognize me . . . so much was I disfigured'.

Text used: Translation by J. Franklin Jameson in N. D. Mereness, Travels in the American Colonies, *New York, 1916, pp. 243-6.*

6
Bartram describes alligators in St John's River and the beauties of the Cherokee country, 1774 and 1775

From William Bartram's *Travels Through North & South Carolina . . .*, Philadelphia, 1791

Bartram, camping alone in 1774 on a little promontory where the St John's flows into Lake Dexter, was preparing fish for his supper.

Raising my head, I saw before me, through the clear water, the head and shoulders of a very large alligator, moving slowly toward me; I instantly stepped back, when, with a sweep of his tail, he brushed off several of my fish. It was certainly providential that I looked up at that instant, as the monster would probably, in less than a minute, have seized and dragged me into the river . . .

211

211 A log cabin, 1796, from V. Collot, *Voyage dans l'Amerique Septentrionale*, 1826.
The frontiersman cleared the land around his house, building it of the logs that he had felled. The house was usually near a spring or stream. Collot's journey and drawings were made some years before this engraving; the cabin can be considered characteristic of many eighteenth-century pioneer homes.
Collot, who fought under Rochambeau during the Revolution and became governor of Guadeloupe, returned to North America for a visit in 1796.

Shortly after, he witnessed a sight similar to those later observed by Audubon and others.

I was again alarmed by a tumultuous noise, however, I soon accounted for the prodigious assemblage of crocodiles at this place. The river from shore to shore, and perhaps near half a mile above and below me, appeared to be one solid bank of fish, of various kinds, pushing through this narrow pass of St Juans into the little lake, on their return down the river, and that the alligators were in such incredible numbers, and so close together from shore to shore, that it would have been

212

212 William Bartram. Alligator hole, 1774. *Natural History Museum, London, Fothergill Album.*
'View of the Alegator Hole in Istmus Florida. . . . It is one of those vast circular sinks, which we behold everywhere about us as we traversed these forests, after we left the Alachua savanna. . . . The surface of the water [is] six or seven feet below the rim of the funnel. . . . The water is transparent, cool, and pleasant to drink, and well stored with fish; a very large alligator at present is lord or chief'—Bartram, *Travels,* 1791. Probably this is Blue Sink, a mile north of Newberry, Florida.

213 William Bartram. Eastern coach-whip, *c.* 1774. *Natural History Museum, London, Fothergill Album.*
'Coach-whip snake. . . . Head & Neck dark brown, with a mixture of yellow all the remaining part of his body white except upperside which is a light cream colour. . . . They run fast & are found in the Sandhill of E[as]t Florida'—Bartram.

214 William Bartram. Various specimens from Cape Fear, North Carolina, *c.* 1770. *Natural History Museum, London, Fothergill Album.*
Toad flax; ruby throated hummingbird; great stone crab; sea shell.
Below: golden corydalis; false garlic. 'All from the seacoast of Cape Fear No Carolina'—Bartram.

easy to have walked across on their heads, had the animals been harmless. What expressions can sufficiently declare the shocking scene that for some minutes continued, whilst this mighty army of fish were forcing the pass? During this attempt, thousands, I may say hundreds of thousands of them were caught and swallowed by the devouring alligators. I have seen an alligator take up out of the water several great fish at a time, and just squeeze them betwixt his jaws, while the tails of the great trout flapped about his eyes and lips, ere he had swallowed them. The horrid noise of their closing jaws, their plunging amidst the broken banks of fish, and rising with their prey some feet upright above the water, the floods of water and blood rushing out of their mouths, and the clouds of vapour issuing from their wide nostrils, were truly frightful. This scene continued at intervals during the night, as the fish came to the pass.

On his second trip to the southern Appalachians, in May 1775, Bartram visited the Cherokee town of Cowee, near present West's Mill, Macon County, North Carolina.

I arrived at Cowe about noon; this settlement is esteemed the capital town; it is situated on the bases of the hills on both sides of the river, near to its bank, and here terminates the great vale of Cowe, exhibiting one of the most charming natural mountainous landscapes perhaps any where to be seen; ridges of hills rising grand and sublimely one above and beyond another, some boldly and majestically advancing into the verdant plain, their feet bathed with the silver flood of the Tanase, whilst others far distant, veiled in blue mists, sublimely mount aloft, with yet greater majesty lift up their pompous crests and overlook vast regions. The vale is closed at Cowe by a ridge of mighty hills, called the Jore mountain, said to be the highest land in the Cherokee country, which crosses the Tanase here . . .

[We] continued through part of this high forest skirting on the meadows; began to ascend the hills of a ridge which we

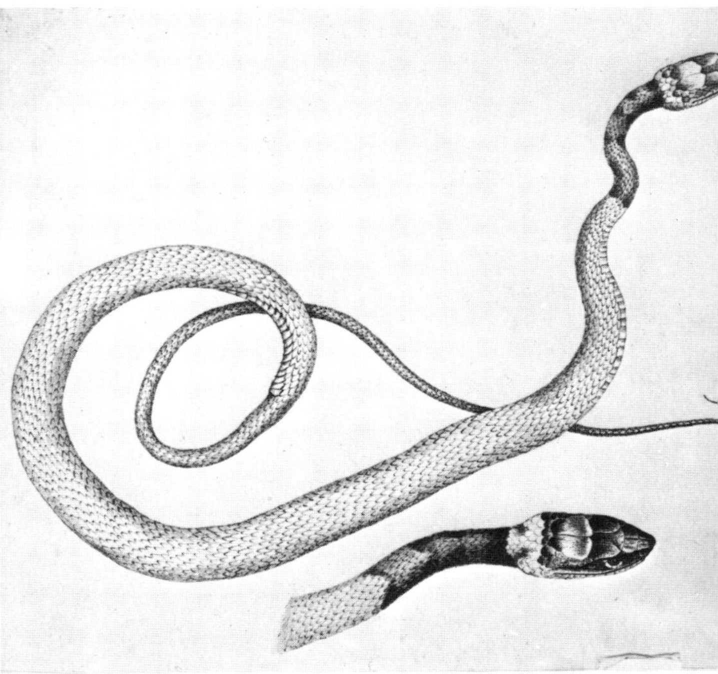

213
214

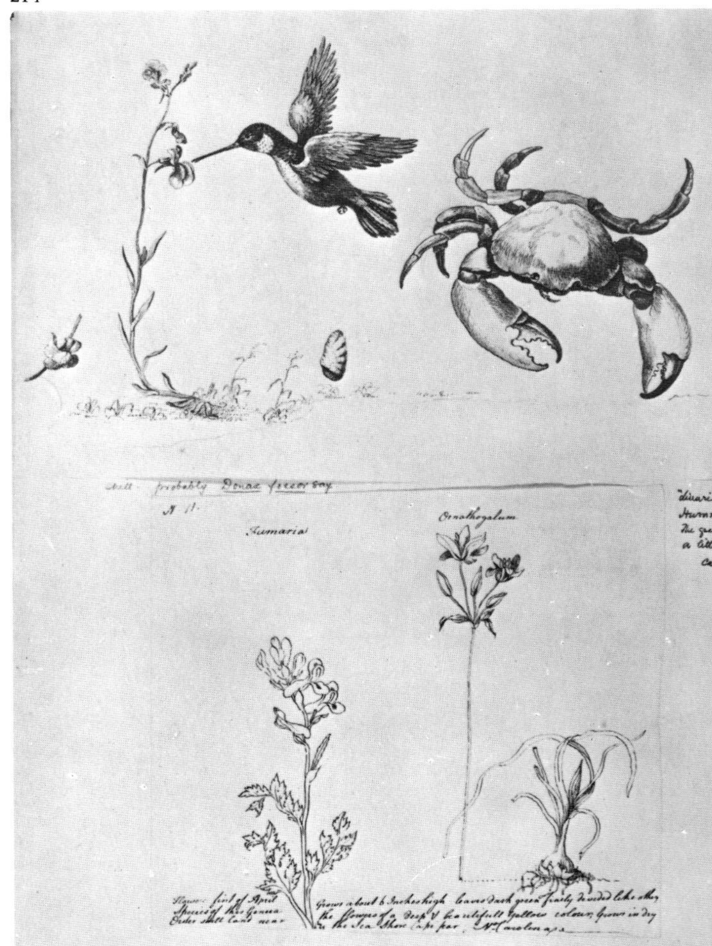

were under the necessity of crossing, and having gained its summit, enjoyed a most enchanting view, a vast expanse of green meadows and strawberry fields; a meandering river gliding through, saluting in its various turnings the swelling, green, turfy knolls, embellished with parterres of flowers and fruitful strawberry beds; flocks of turkeys strolling about them; herds of deer prancing in the meads or bounding over the hills; companies of young, innocent Cherokee virgins, some busily gathering the rich fragrant fruit, others having already filled their baskets, lay reclined under the shade of floriferous and fragrant native bowers of Magnolia, Azalea, Philadelphus, perfumed Calycanthus, sweet Yellow Jessamine and cerulian Glycine frutescens, disclosing their beauties to the fluttering breeze, and bathing their limbs in the cool fleeting streams.

Text used: William Bartram, Travels Through North & South Carolina, Georgia, East and West Florida, *Philadelphia, 1791, pp. 121, 123, 353, 356-7.*

215

216

215 William Bartram. Myrtle warbler and flycatcher, *c.* 1770. *Natural History Museum, London, Fothergill Album.*
Shown in this drawing are La[u]rus cerasus (?chokecherry); Myrtle warbler, Yellow rump flycatcher (Catesby's nomenclature) chasing insect; early flowering Red lychnis or fire pink. 'All from North Carolina WB 1769'—Bartram. Bartram evidently drew these in 1770 while at 'Ashwood', his Uncle William's plantation on the Cape Fear River, North Carolina; he was residing in Pennsylvania in 1769.

216 William Bartram. Cardinal, 1772. *Natural History Museum, London, Fothergill Album.*
Devil-wood, which Bartram found on the northwest branch of the Cape Fear River; cardinal, 'red bird or Virginia nightingale'; crab apple; a fish; and coral honeysuckle at top right.

5 LOUISIANA AND THE SOUTHWEST: SPANISH AND FRENCH EXPLORATION

1 Seventeenth-century Spanish exploration from New Mexico and the Rio Grande

In the mid-seventeenth century, while the English strengthened their colonies along the Atlantic seaboard and began to push west and south across and around the mountain ranges, and while the French extended their St Lawrence holdings, their missions and trade, west and north into the Great Lakes region and beyond, the northern tip of the empire of New Spain lay sleeping in the sun along the upper Rio Grande. Ogilby, in his *America* (1671), describes the extent of Spain's wealthy central and South American colonies, and then adds as an afterthought, 'besides a great part which lies to the Northward, behind inaccessable Mountains and Wildernesses'.[1] The sixteenth-century design for a great northern invasion under Coronado and then Oñate had faded, and even the geography of this region of mountains and pueblos had been largely forgotten. To Father Benevides, fighting his way up the Rio Grande in 1625 to inspect the churches and install the Inquisition, the intense cold and heat came as a surprise, and he tried, in his *Memorial* of 1634, to give his readers some idea of where this province of New Mexico might be.[2] The little capital of Santa Fé, which Bolton called 'a sentinel on the very rim of European civilization',[3] was there to give him a reception; a few other small settlements of Spaniards, a few valiant Franciscan missionaries in the outlying pueblos, were there as well. All seemed at peace, and the good father's words glow with accomplishment, as he tells of the miraculous mass conversions, or reconversions, which he effected.

Father Benevides went not only to the pueblos near Santa Fé, such as Taos, where he says he was able to train a 'marvellous choir' and to uproot polygamy,[4] and southwest to Acoma, high on its rock, where the church was where Coronado had placed it,[5] but north and east to settlements of the Apaches, an increasingly intransigent set of tribes. From the Xila and Navaho Apaches, he sent Fathers de Salas and Lopez southeast, to the Apaches Vaqueros, a wandering tribe on the great plains who depended on the buffalo for livelihood,[6] and finally to the Jumanos, on an upper branch of the Nueces River, in what is now Texas. Here they received confirmation of the miraculous visits of Mother Maria de Jésus, the famous nun of Agréda in Spain, who was convinced that she had been many times bodily transported to North America, where she preached to the heathen Indians and prepared them for the coming of the friars. The Jumanos had sent embassies demanding baptism, saying that a holy nun wandered among them, preaching in their language. Now they came to meet the Spaniards with a flower-decked cross, which they said the nun had helped them decorate.[7] Father Benevides, after his return to Spain in 1629, visited Mother Maria de Jésus in Agréda, and became an implicit believer.[8] He pleaded for missionaries. Father de Salas did reach the Jumanos again a few years later, and in 1650, Captains Martin

217

218

217 Mother Maria de Jésus de Agréda preaching to the Chichimecos of New Mexico, from Father Alonso de Benevides, *Tanto, que se saco de una carta,* Madrid, 1631
An engraving of the miraculous nun in whose supernatural visits to the North American Indians she herself, and many others, devoutly believed.
For the second time, in 1689, the Jumanos approached the Spanish on the Rio Grande asking to be baptized; it was Father Massenet's intense desire to find confirmation of the miraculous visits of Mother Maria which encouraged the De Léon expedition, after the discovery of the La Salle colony, to the founding of the first Spanish mission in Texas, San Francisco de los Texas, four miles west of the Neches River.

218 Deer hunt, from Le Page du Pratz, *Histoire de la Louisiane,* 1758.
This Indian method of 'surrounding' a stag was also used by Spanish explorers on the Mendoza-Lopez expedition of 1684.

and Castillo took a small trading expedition east to the Jumanos and beyond to the Tejas (Texas) Indians.[9] A modest trade with these Texan tribes thus began from New Mexico. 'Texas' was a word meaning 'friends' or 'allies', which the Spanish used in place of the tribal name 'Hasinai' or 'Assinais'.[10]

Texas was also beginning to be entered, in the latter half of the seventeenth century, from another part of New Spain. Settlement of what is now northern Mexico had been extended with the establishment of the provinces of Nueva Léon and Coahuila, with frontiers along the lower Rio Grande. Father Larios, a Franciscan missionary working there, began to long for conversions on the other bank. In Spanish exploration the priest was usually the pioneer, as was the trader for the French and English. In 1675, Governor Barcarcel of Coahuila sent Lieutenant del Bosque and a group of soldiers with Fathers Larios and San Buenaventura on the first missionary expedition into present Texas (selection 1). They reached the Ona River, a branch of the Nueces, and were met by numbers of Indians who declared they wanted to become Christians and learn to live in pueblos. Yet one Indian spoke to the Spaniards more prophetically than they knew, saying that the young might embrace the new ways, but the old would hold to the ways of their fathers.[11]

In 1680 Indian resentment, partly against the new religion, burst into furious flame and, led by Popé, the pueblos struck all at once, aided by distant tribes. Two thousand eight hundred Spaniards were massacred; one thousand were besieged in Santa Fé; the survivors fled desperately south down the Rio Grande, and settled finally near El Paso. For twelve years, New Mexico belonged to the Indians. They looted and burned, and the old ways prevailed.[12]

When the refugee colony had been settled at El Paso for about three years, they were approached by a delegation led by Juan Sabeata, a Jumano, asking for a resumption of trade with his people, for missions, and for help for them and the Texas against the marauding Apaches. In 1684, Governor Cruzate sent an expedition under Captain Mendoza, with Fathers Lopez and Zavalete.[13] Crossing the Rio Grande at La Junta, its junction with the Conchos, they pushed into rough, unknown country, often camping without water. In his diary, Mendoza writes one evening, with surprise, 'In the midst of so much evil, there is a little spring of fresh and kindly water, and, as an exquisite thing I had it noted with particular care'.[14] Food was scarce, and they found the Jumanos starving, too. They were able to 'surround' some deer, and when they killed their first buffalo, it was a great relief. They crossed the Pecos, and were met by Sabeata with a great number of Indians, who begged them to make war on the Apaches. Finally, at San Clemente on the Colorado, they built a small bastion with two rooms, one a chapel (selection 2). Twice they beat off Apache attacks; the Texas failed to arrive; they were forced to return, exploring another route.[15]

The retaking of New Mexico, in 1693 by Governor Vargas of El Paso, is as dramatic a story as that of its loss. After a preliminary expedition in 1692, when he recaptured the lower pueblos, Vargas marched boldly on Santa Fé, through eerie, deserted country, with only forty Spaniards and fifty Indian allies, and entered the city practically alone. With bravado and skill, he met and came to agreement with his Indian adversary, El Picuri, and went with him to subdue the outlying pueblos, whose allegiance he had lost.[16] Spain held New Mexico once more.

219

220

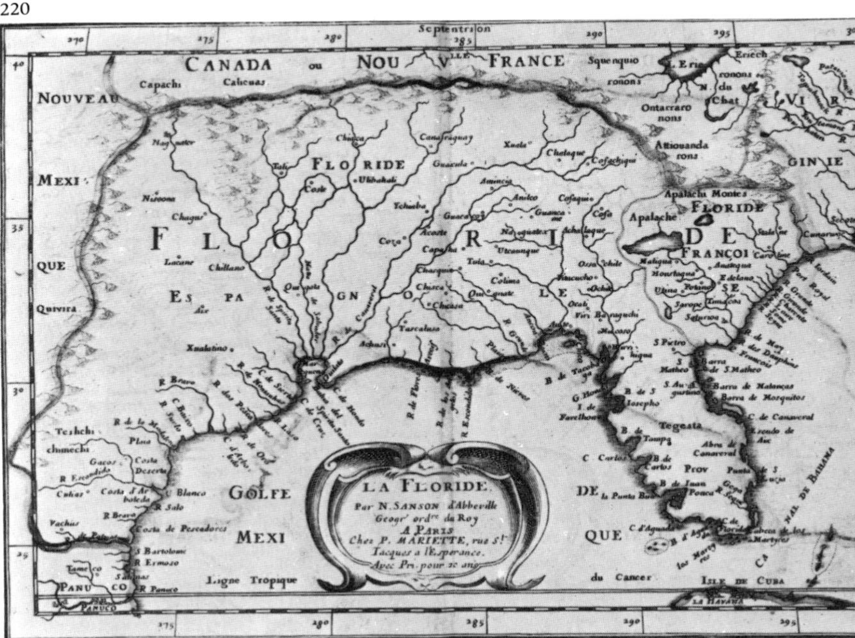

219 Robert, Cavelier de la Salle, in ?1685, from an engraving preserved in the *Bibliothèque Municipale de Rouen*. Rouen was La Salle's early home.

220 Sanson. 'La Floride', 1657, from N. Sanson, *L'Amérique*, plate 4, 1657. This influential map of southeastern North America was copied by many later European geographers. Nicolas Sanson d'Abbeville, le père (1600-67), was the royal geographer of Louis XIV and founded a famous family of French cartographers. In designing this map he followed an earlier map of Johannes de Laet, 'Florida et Regiones Vicinae' (1630), but added new details and names. 'Floride Françoise', occupying present Georgia and South Carolina, has 'R. de May' (St John's River) too far north by two degrees; this caused its later confusion with the Savannah River, as in Gascoigne's map of 1682 (see plate 125). North of the Gulf of Mexico Sanson perpetuated a still greater geographical misconception; four great rivers, hemmed in by mountains, flow into the Bahia del Spirito Santo. Marquette, Jolliet, and La Salle, in journeying down the Mississippi, helped to alter this conception. Decades were to pass before the great river system of the Mississippi, with its delta projecting into the Gulf, was to be identified.

2 La Salle's Gulf Coast colony and the consequent French explorations

Before she completed the retaking of her New Mexican outpost, Spain received news which made her fear for her whole northern possession. The French had entered the Gulf Coast area. The Jesuit father Marquette and the trader Jolliet in 1673 made the first voyage down the Mississippi as far as the Arkansas (see page 36), and in 1682 La Salle confirmed their suspicions that the great river led not to the Pacific, but to the Gulf of Mexico, by making the whole journey to the mouth. He claimed the vast central valley of North America for France. Spain knew nothing of these voyages, but was made uneasy by reports that the renegade governor Peñalosa, expelled from New Mexico by the Inquisition, had in 1678 begun to treat with French officials.[17] Using 'the mines of New Biscay' as lure, he submitted a number of proposals for the French conquest of 'Quivira and Teguayo', to which he said he had journeyed,[18] from a base on the Gulf Coast.

La Salle returned to France from his exploration of the Mississippi convinced that the French should enter its mouth from the sea and confirm possession. He was influenced by Peñalosa, and began to include in his proposals the conquest of Spanish mine territory, showing a map in which the Mississippi inclined temptingly to the west.[19] Peñalosa fell into obscurity, but La Salle was sent in 1684, with four vessels and a colony of settlers, to the coast of the Gulf of Mexico. The King's commission gave him the right 'to command . . . from the Saint-Louis on the river of the Islinois to New-Biscaye'.[20]

The tragic story of the La Salle colony has had many tellers. Here its importance is chiefly in the exploration of unknown areas which it engendered. The causes of the disaster lie further back than the voyage, in the double ambitions to invade New Spain as well as to find the Mississippi; in the resentment between La Salle and Captain Beaujeu, given command of the little fleet at sea, but not even informed of their destination; in the secretive and difficult side of the nature of the brilliant and courageous La Salle, who could

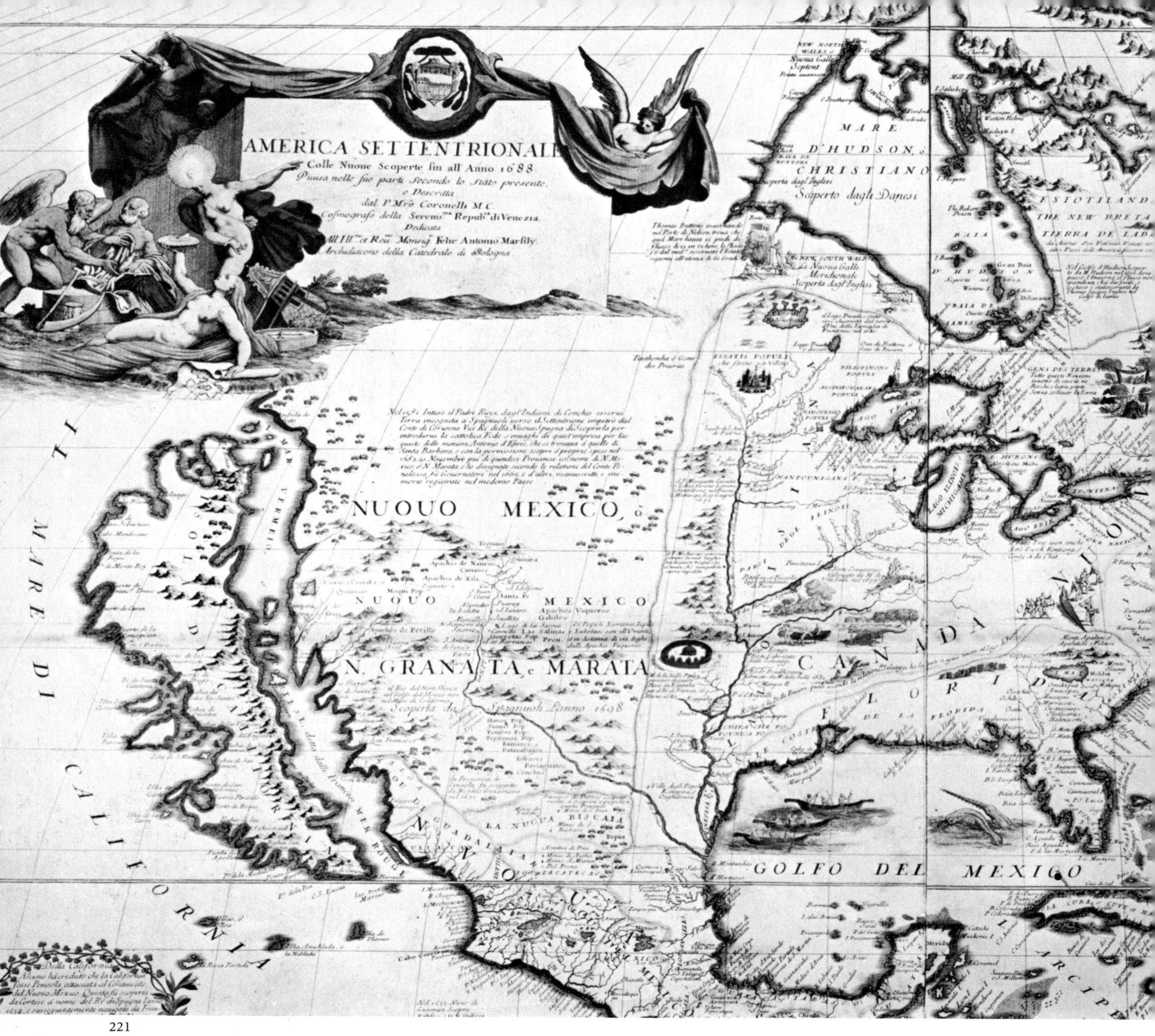

221

221 Coronelli. 'America Settentrionale', 1689, from Vincenzo M. Coronelli, *Atlante veneto*, 1690 (detail).
Although Coronelli continued to gather information for this beautiful and influential map until 1688, according to the title cartouche, he does not include mention of La Salle's Gulf settlement and his death. These were known in France after the return of Cavelier, La Salle's brother, in 1687. Official cosmographer to the Republic of Venice and map-maker to Louis XIV, Coronelli had access in France to the maps and official reports of explorers as well as valuable accounts of Jesuit missionaries supplied to him by friends. He notes the voyages of Marquette (1673) and La Salle (1682) on the Mississippi River, but was apparently influenced by Franquelin's map to place its mouth some six hundred miles too far west, near the Rio Grande. He places the Ohio River too far south and draws it again as the Ouabache. California is drawn as an island, although he notes that it may be a peninsula. 'Carolina' has the same boundaries and names as Sanson's French Florida, 1657 (plate 220), on which it is based. Some of the illustrations which beautify the map he derived from De Bry, such as the killing of the alligators (misplaced in the central Mississippi Valley!) and making a dugout.

Coronelli's prolific output of some four hundred maps was nevertheless accompanied by careful preparation and study. His delineation of the Great Lakes is the best and most accurate on a general map before the eighteenth century.

command, but seldom win or give friendship or affection. They sailed from Rochelle on 24 July 1684, in the flagship *Joly*, a smaller armed vessel, a store-ship, and a ketch. These carried a hundred soldiers, artisans and laborers, thirty volunteers, several families, and some unmarried girls.[21] Six missionary priests were aboard, three Sulpicians, including La Salle's brother, Cavelier, and three Recollets, Fathers Membré, Douay, and LeClerc, the last two of whom became chroniclers of the adventure. Two of La Salle's young nephews went, as did the engineer and map-maker Minet. The most reliable journal of the whole affair was kept by the volunteer Joutel, one of the few survivors.[22]

From the first, the voyage was plagued with misfortune. On New Year's Day, 1685, after crossing the Gulf of Mexico, and surviving several disasters, La Salle, his brother and Joutel cast anchor off a marshy, rush-covered plain. A thick fog descended; when it lifted, Captain Beaujeu and the *Joly* had disappeared.[23]

What happened next is a matter of some controversy;

Parkman, on the basis of his study of all the documents, collected by Margry, the French authority, supports the account of Joutel.[24] La Salle was seeking the mouth of the Mississippi; although he had once been there, and observed its latitude, he knew little about its longitude. The state of the currents made him think their landfall as far east as the Bay of Apalache; they therefore sailed west along the coast, straining for any sight of the great river. On January 8 they did descry an opening, and the sea was discolored. La Salle wished to explore, but the captain objected, and La Salle, Joutel says, 'too lightly altered his design to avoid giving offense to brutish people'.[25] He and Joutel were both convinced, later, that this had been a mouth of the Mississippi; Parkman, however, produces evidence that they were already well beyond it.[26] Thinking the *Joly* ahead to the west, La Salle followed the coast, which was flat, muddy, uninviting. Finally, La Salle turned to retrace his course, when to his relief, the *Joly* appeared. Now ensued more controversy. La Salle wanted to go back eastward to find the Mississippi; Beaujeu wanted to sail for France, with provision for the voyage. Joutel, sent ashore with 120 men, explored eastward, found game and water, and finally what he called 'a great river',[27] actually the entrance to present Matagorda Bay, 400 miles west of the Mississippi delta.

Here La Salle took decisive action. He declared that this was a mouth of the Mississippi, the place to which he had been sent; he landed his soldiers and colonists beside the inlet, and gave orders for the *Aimable* and the *Belle* to enter the harbor. Later, after the *Aimable* lost most of her priceless stores when she was wrecked on a reef, the *Joly* sailed for France, leaving the little colony of sick and homesick people alone with the Indians, little knowing how far they were from help in a hostile and unexplored land.[28]

The small group did what they could. They built a flimsy fort on the shore, around which the Indians often howled at night. They hunted game, speared fish, found salt. Once a Spanish ship sailed past. La Salle explored, and was convinced at last that he was not on any part of the Mississippi. He moved the colony to good, high ground, which Bolton has established was on Garcitas Creek.[29] Heat almost destroyed the crops; the wood supply was a scorching journey across the plains. With great difficulty they made a simple building, naming both fort and harbor St Louis. Many sickened and died.[30] Joutel recorded throughout his careful and sensitive observation of the new scene (selection 3).

Meanwhile, Tonty, La Salle's faithful lieutenant, left in command of the fort among the Illinois, started in February, 1685, to descend the Mississippi in an attempt to meet La Salle at the mouth. The journey, by canoe, took him until Holy Week. Though he sent his canoes in every direction, no trace could they find of La Salle. His *Memoir* of 1693 gives a note on the blithe optimism concerning American geography of even such a realist as Tonty. He proposed to his men that 'if they would trust me to follow the coast as far as Manhatte, . . . we should arrive shortly at Montreal; that we should not lose our time, because we might discover some fine country, and might even take some booty on our way'.[31] His men were opposed, however, so they reascended the Mississippi, leaving a letter for La Salle among the friendly Bayagoulis Indians. Ten of Tonty's men remained on the Arkansas River, where they built a little house.[32]

Knowing nothing of this, La Salle set out on a series of desperate explorations to find the Mississippi, his only hope of communication and return. In October, 1685, he and his men explored the shore, the *Belle* following, and they then turned inward. They found Indians who had had contact with the Spaniards. They found a great river, not the Mississippi, and returned in March in tattered condition. Joutel, left in command, had learned to hunt buffalo, kept all at work, and received the elder Duhaut, lost from La Salle's party. He brought word of the butchering of the *Belle*'s crew by Indians; she herself was wrecked on the opposite shore of the bay, destroying the last means of escape except on foot, overland.[33]

La Salle now decided that he must reach, not only the Mississippi, but Illinois and Canada. He set out again in April 1686, leaving Joutel in command; he returned in October with only eight of his twenty men. They had seen much beautiful territory filled with game, crossed flooded rivers on rafts, struggled through canebrakes. Toward the east, they had reached the Cenis Indians, who received them kindly and sold them horses. 'Cenis' is a shortened form of 'Assinais', also called 'Texas'.[34] Here they met Comanches, with loot from the Spaniards. 'The Sieur de la Salle', says Father Douay, 'made them [the Cenis] draw a map of their country, of that of their neighbors, and of the River Colbert, or Mississippi, with which they are acquainted. They reckoned themselves six days' journey from the Spaniards'.[35] The survivors struggled back to Fort St Louis.

Now of the original 180, only 45 colonists remained, and a feeling of total abandonment settled over them. La Salle still had his courage, but found it hard to communicate it to his followers, many of whom had developed deep resentment toward him and bitter antagonisms toward each other. After a grim Christmas, he split his sad little group in two, and in January 1687, prepared to make the only attempt left to reach Canada and succor. This time he took Joutel, and left Le Sieur Barbier, one of the few remaining leaders of the expedition and father of a child born at Fort St Louis, in command of those who remained. Joutel's account of the trek is the fullest and most dependable. Across the Brazos and near the Trinity River, the crisis came. Duhaut, Liotot, and Hiens, in a hunters' camp, were berated by Moranget for their handling of the buffalo meat. That night they killed

222 Buffalo hunt, from Le Page du Pratz, *Histoire de la Louisiane*, 1758. Joutel and the colonists on Matagorda Bay learned hunting methods from observing the Indians.

223 An Indian holds the feather-trimmed peace pipe, or calumet, an important symbol and object of veneration. In the background is the Mississippi.

Father Douay accompanied La Salle on one of his attempts to reach Canada and also made the journey back with Joutel and the Abbé Cavelier. He left a description of the great peace ceremony of the Cenis, the calumet dance. *A new discovery of a vast country in America*, published by Father Hennepin in 1698, includes this and other pictures, much fact, and a great deal of fiction.

222

223

224

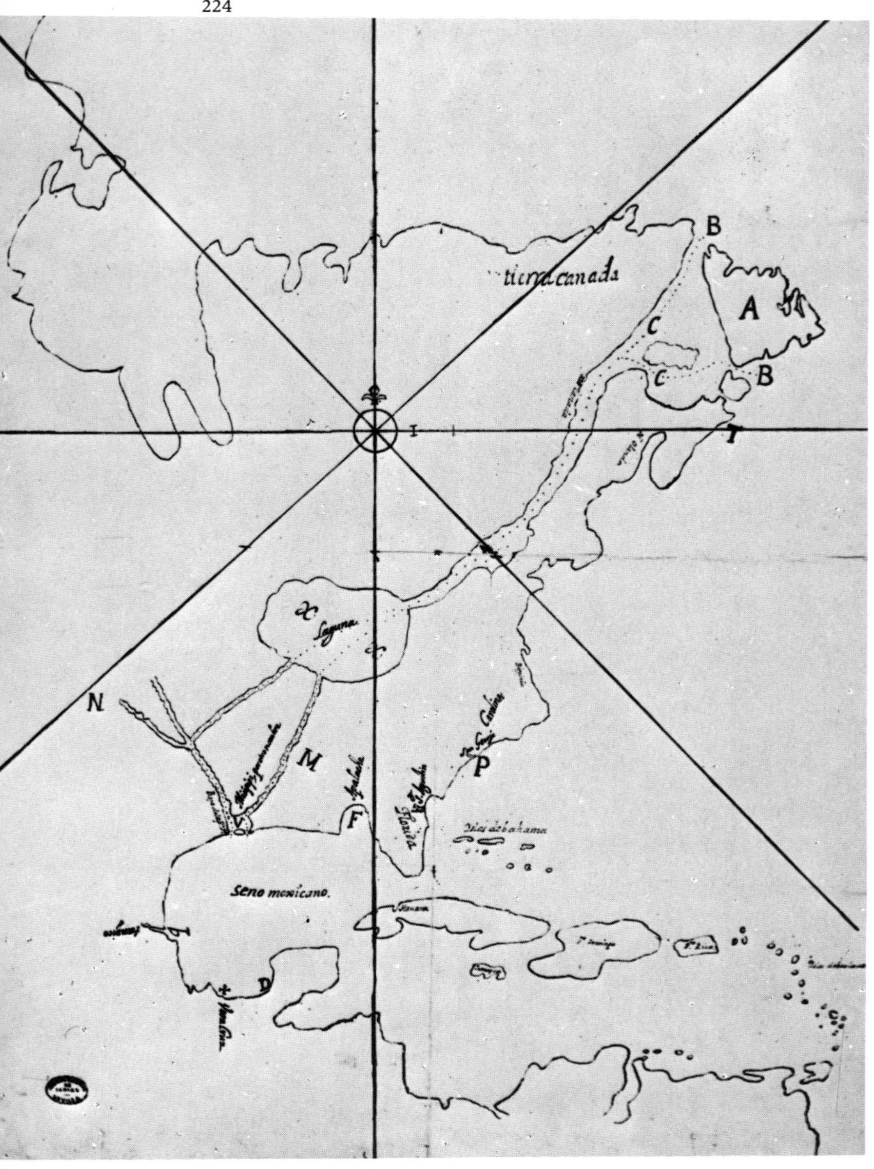

224 'Mapa de las Costas de Golfo de Mexico', 1686, by Captain Martin de Echagaray. *Archivo General de Indias, Seville, Mexico, 61-6-20(1).* Echagaray, a pilot and naval captain stationed at St Augustine, Florida, sent a memorial to the Spanish government in 1684, offering to explore the Gulf coast, especially the 'Bay of Espíritu Santo'; he said the Indians reported that 'two great rivers flowed into it, one leading to the region called Movila, and the other to New Mexico.' When the Spanish learned, in 1685, of La Salle's colony, they commissioned Echagaray, then in Cadiz, to draw this map of what he thought the region looked like. The two great rivers both run from the same large lake, into which flows the St Lawrence. Spanish ignorance of coast and interior is here graphically illustrated.

him, Nika, La Salle's Indian follower, and Saget, his servant. L'Archevêque, Teissier, and De Marle were also compromised. La Salle and Father Douay went to look for Moranget; L'Archevêque drew La Salle into an ambuscade, and Duhaut and Liotot murdered him.[36] Thus died one of the greatest of the explorers of the North American continent.

At this point, the assassins took command of the survivors loyal to La Salle: Joutel, the Abbé Cavelier, Father Douay, the younger nephew of the Caveliers, and two other boys. They decided to make for the Cenis villages. Joutel, sent ahead to treat for corn, describes amusingly the first three Indians they encountered: on horseback, two completely naked, and one fully apparelled in Spanish clothes. In the great lodges of the Cenis, Joutel was left to trade while the others returned to Duhaut's camp (selection 4). He found Ruter, Grollet, and a third Frenchman, deserters from La Salle's former expedition, tattooed and living like the savages.[37] Back at the camp, Duhaut wished to build a ship and try for the West Indies; Joutel and his party wanted to escape to Canada, which the murderers opposed. The dilemma was resolved like the previous crisis, by murder, and Joutel, who had had no hand in the tragic events, and his party were allowed to depart for Canada, with supplies, four horses, and two Indian guides.[38]

The subsequent journey of this little troop was one of the most remarkable explorations of the period. They travelled over rivers and among tribes completely unknown to them, some of whose customs were surprising, such as the bodily carrying of the heavy Joutel, or the attempt to present two young wives at once to the Abbé Cavelier. They covered a vast territory, passed among the Assonis, a branch of the Caddo tribe of the western Red River. Finally they reached the banks of the Arkansas; of this tremendous moment, Joutel wrote: 'Looking over to the further side, we discovered a great cross, and at a small distance from it, a house built after the French fashion. It is easy to imagine what inward joy we conceived at the sight of that emblem of our salvation. We knelt down, lifting up our hands and eyes to heaven. . . . We spied several canoes making toward us, and two men clothed coming out of the house. . . . who, the moment they saw us, fired each of them a shot to salute us'.[39] These were Couture and DeLaunay, two of Tonty's men who had remained here in 1686 when he made his attempt to meet La Salle. They welcomed the weary travellers, wept over La Salle's death, and supplied them with a heavy wooden canoe. In this they descended the Arkansas, and came at last to the long-sought Mississippi. Travel upstream was not easy, but now at last they had a known way. They entered the Illinois River, and reached a happier Fort St Louis on 14 September 1687.[40]

The King of France sent no ship to the relief of La Salle's little colony on the Gulf, when the returned Cavelier at last told the truth; but when Tonty learned it, he set off to try to rescue them. Sharing La Salle's dream, he hoped to reach the Spanish and plunder their mines. In February 1690, he arrived at the later site of Natchitoches on the Red River, and travelled west toward the Cadodoquis.[41] Here he was deserted by all his men, save one Frenchman and an Indian. He pushed on, fearlessly exploring, and turned south to 'Naoudiché'. In crossing a stream he says his French companion's 'bag slipped off, and thus all our powder was lost, which very much annoyed me'.[42] This is the nearest approach to rage in the journal of the self-controlled Tonty. He learned that Hiens and his companions had been murdered by these Indians. Now, bereft of ammunition, deserted even by his guide, he had to turn back. Near the Mississippi, he encountered a terrible flood, in which his sufferings were extreme. He returned to Illinois in September 1690 (selection 5).[43]

3 Spanish exploration into Texas and defensive action against the French inspired by the search for the La Salle colony, 1685-99

For the little that is known of the fate of La Salle's sad 'lost colony' on the Gulf of Mexico, it is necessary to return to Spanish archives. In July 1685, a corsair was captured off Mexico, and a young man found on board who had deserted La Salle on his way to the Gulf. From him, Spain first learned of La Salle's descent of the Mississippi in 1682, and of the

225

225 The *Joly*, commanded by Captain Beaujeu, flagship of the small fleet which transported La Salle and his colony to the Gulf Coast in 1684. *Archivo General de Indias, Sevillle.*
One of the only three known relics of the La Salle colony, perhaps drawn by Jean de L'Archevêque, who collaborated in both La Salle's murder and that of his assassins. He made his way back to Texas, was found there by the Spanish, and taken to Santa Fé.

226 Lawrence van den Bosh. Mississippi River and adjacent Gulf coast, 1694. *Newberry Library, Chicago, Ayer Collection No 59.*
This remarkable manuscript map shows a knowledge of the lower Mississippi Valley exhibited on no Spanish or French map before the eighteenth century. Neither the exploration nor the explorer providing the information has so far been identified. Numerous legends in English are apparently based on second-hand sources: 'Floating Island four Leagues from ye mouth of Messisippi River which hideth[?] the Mouth of ye said River, in which Island there be both Oysters and Birds The Island is not noted in earlier Maps'; 'The town of the Rich Spaniards'; 'Mountains of Silver & Gold Mines'; 'Lossaing where Monsr De la Salle was killed'.

This map accompanies a letter which is dated 'From North Sassifrix, the 19th of October . . . 1694' and which states that Bosh received his information of the region 'on the left side of the Messacippi River from a French Indian'. The map and letter in the Ayer Collection are contemporary copies of the originals.

226

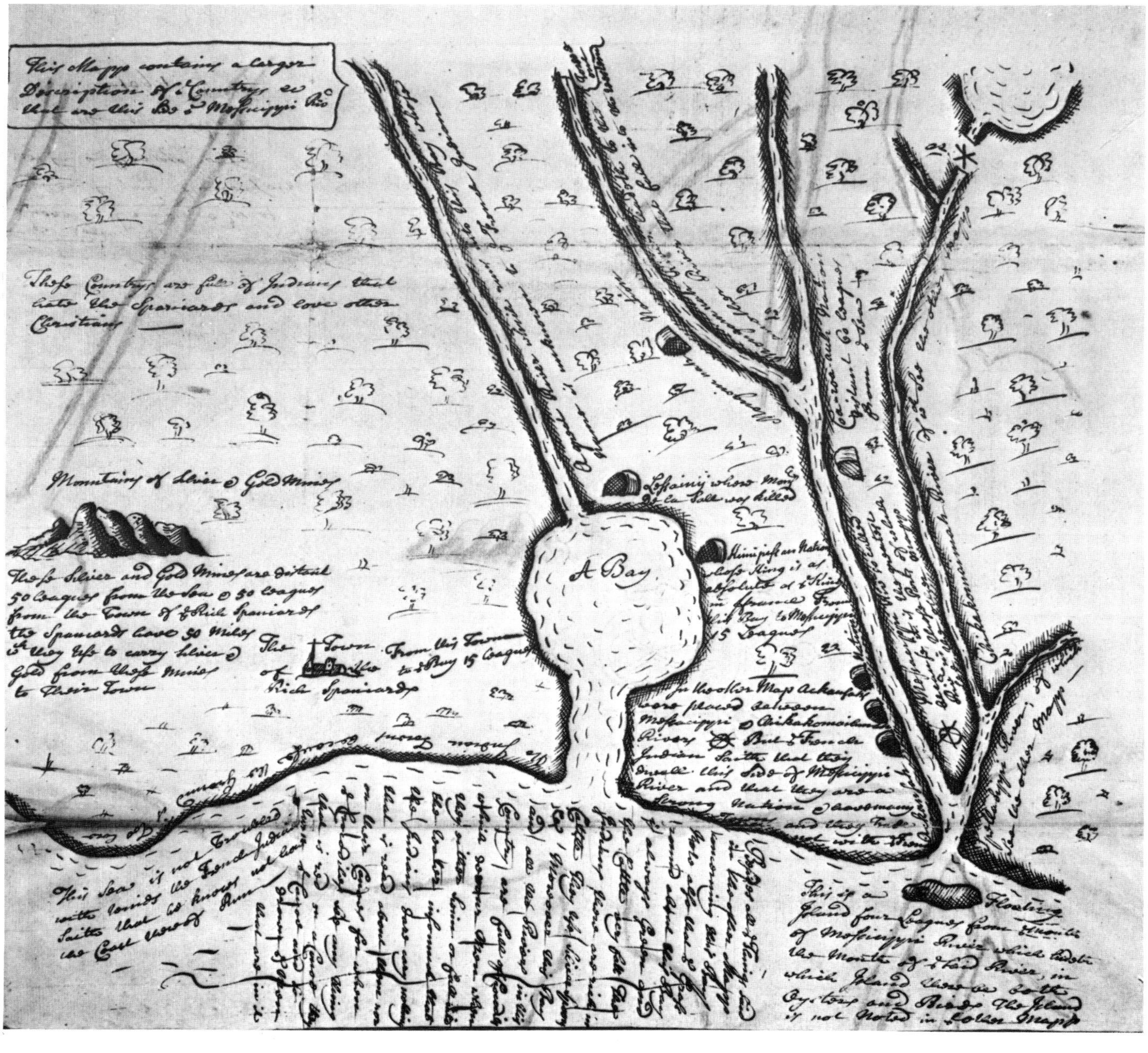

227

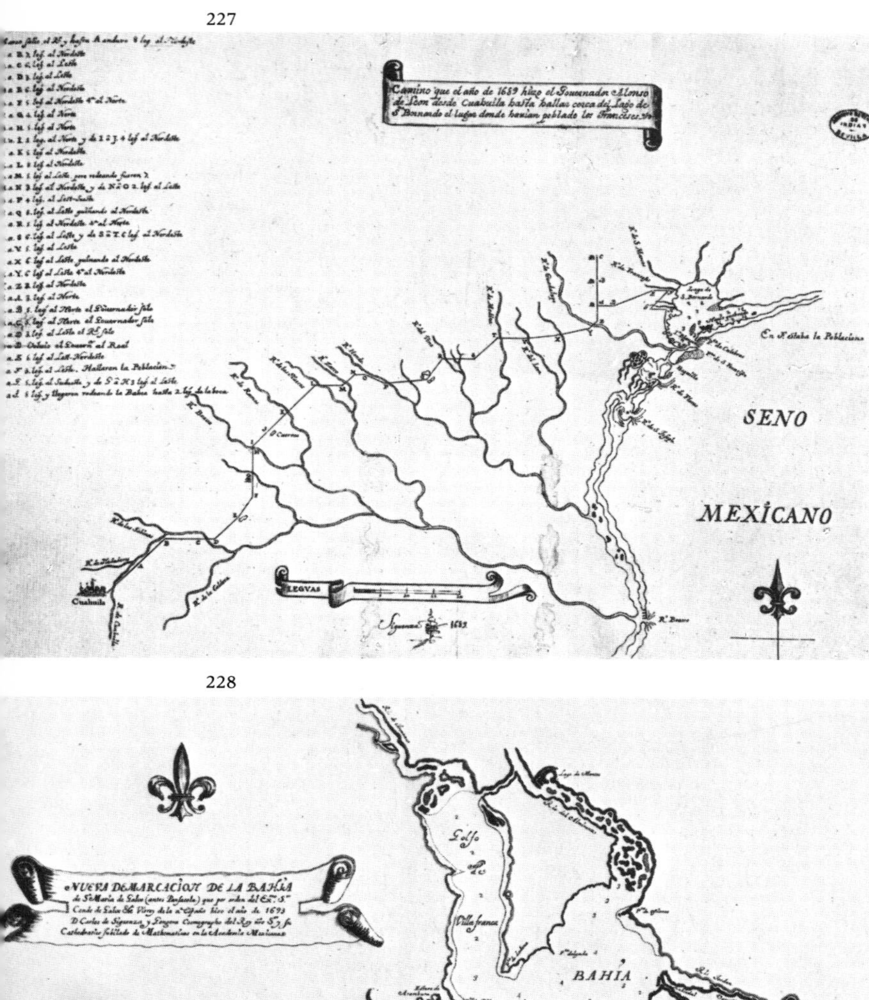

228

227 Sigüenza y Gongora. Map of the route of Governor Alonzo de Léon, 1689. *Archivo General de Indias, Seville, Mapas y Planos Mexico 86.*
De Léon's journey in search of the La Salle colony. At Garcitas Creek they found 'six houses, not very large, built with poles plastered with mud, and roofed over with buffalo hides', and 'a wooden fort made from the hulk of a wrecked vessel'. Just down the creek lay San Bernardo (present Matagorda) Bay. All was deserted, but a few French were found among neighboring Indians. This map is signed 'Siguenza'; Father Massenet had addressed his long account of the trip to this Mexican scholar.

228 Sigüenza y Gongora. Map of the Bay of Santa Maria de Galve, or Pensacola Harbor, 1693. *Archivo General de Indias, Seville, JGI, Mapas y Planos, Florida y La., 25.*
Sigüenza, who accompanied Andrés de Pez to Pensacola Bay in 1693, kept a journal of their shore explorations into western Florida. In 1698, with rumors of a new French threat, a small bastion, the Presidio de San Carlos de Austria, was established on the Bay, just in time for Captain Arriola to deny entrance to Iberville and his little fleet in 1699.

present French colony, which he thought at the mouth of the Mississippi. Alarm was intense; it was believed the French were moving in force, and everything possible must be done to 'pluck out the thorn that had been thrust into the very heart of America'.[44]

Eleven exploratory expeditions were sent out from New Spain between 1685 and 1699 in the search and in resultant defensive action.[45] Four were by sea: one west from Florida, and three east from Mexico. By sea, they explored the coast and discovered harbors; all failed either to identify the mouth of the Mississippi behind its debris, or to find the colony, then still inhabited, although they did see the wrecks of the *Aimable* and the *Belle* near the mouth of what they called San Bernardo Bay. By land, Captain Delgado searched northwest from Apalache, and learned from the Mobilas Indians that a canoe of white men had once descended the Mississippi. Captain Alonzo de Léon, at El Paso, followed the Rio Grande to the sea, and searched along the coast.[46] Fear was dying down when, in 1688, Jean Géry was captured, ruling over a rancheria across the Rio Grande. He was a deserter from the La Salle colony, but his tale was full of confusion and inconsistencies. However, the search was resumed. Sabeata, the chief of the Jumanos, reported 'other Spaniards' near the Texas Indians, and 'wooden houses by the sea'. Captain Retana was sent from Conchos; Sabeata met him, declared the French destroyed, and gave him the only known relics of the colony, still existing in the Archives of the Indies in Seville: a piece of a journal in French, a picture of the *Joly*, and a poem by L'Archevêque.[47]

Now in 1689 came the expedition which ended the search, captained by Alonzo de Léon and sparked by the missionary zeal of Father Massanet. With fifty soldiers, many horses and mules, Jean Géry, and Indian guides whom he knew, they pushed east to the Nueces River, crossed it, and descended the Guadalupe. Suspense heightened as they began to find bits of French clothing on the Indians, and to hear reports of a few survivors still in the villages. Two of these proved to be L'Archevêque and Grollet. Finally, three leagues downstream on Garcitas Creek, there it lay:[48] a tiny, pathetic, ruined settlement, devastated by smallpox and Indians, which had set both French and Spanish exploring for hundreds of weary miles. Down the creek, they reached the empty shores of the bay, silent in the heat.[49]

Though Father Massanet wished to find the French colony, he was even more anxious to reach again the Texas Indians, and hunt for confirmation of the miraculous visits to them of Mother Maria de Jésus. This he achieved, twenty-five leagues north of the Guadalupe.[50] He promised the Texas a mission, and did return in 1690 with Alonzo de Léon and a mission colony. They met the chief of the Texas with all his people assembled, and founded, with elaborate ceremony, the first Spanish mission in the territory, San Francisco de los Texas, four miles west of the Neches. Father Massanet was hotly opposed to a garrison; De Léon was forced to leave the mission unprotected.[51] In 1691, Téran de los Rios was appointed Governor of the new Texas territory, and started east, hoping to found more missions. He reached and named present San Antonio, and met Sabeata and the Jumanos. At San Francisco de los Texas, Father Massanet was holding on in the face of floods, sickness, and lack of converts. Téran, fighting the snow, explored as far as a Cadodacho settlement on the Red River. Provisions failing, he had to return, and Father Massanet himself applied the torch to San Francisco de los Texas. With fear of the French allayed, the great territory was abandoned for a time to the Indians.[52] No Spanish expedition since De Soto had reached the Mississippi.

An important Spanish settlement was made, however, as a result of the sea searches for the La Salle colony: these voyages rediscovered Pensacola Bay. In 1693, it was explored by Captain de Pez, mapped, and described by Sigüenza y Gongora, the distinguished Creole cosmographer.[53] It was not, however, until 1698, with rumors of a new French threat, that the Presidio de San Carlos de Austria, a small fort, was established on Pensacola Bay.

4 Exploration in the first years of French Louisiana; interaction with the Spanish, 1699-1718

'At the beginning of the 18th Century', writes Louise Kellogg, 'France had the most magnificent opportunity that has ever been offered to a colonizing power. The Mississippi Valley lay open for occupation and exploitation. Nowhere else in the world is there such a valley; extending through twenty degrees of latitude with all the climates of the temperate zone, protected by high mountains on the east and west, drained by the longest river in the world, the Mississippi Valley was a prize worthy of struggle and sacrifice'. It contains fifty-four subordinate navigable rivers.[54] France was not fully aware of this opportunity, although with her post on the Illinois and the voyages made on the Mississippi, she knew far more about what La Salle had claimed for her than the other colonizing nations. Still, the loss of La Salle's gulf colony made the King hesitant. It was rumors of an English claim, that of Dr Daniel Coxe, including part of the Mississippi, that persuaded him to move. It was also the eloquence of a Canadian leader, Pierre le Moyne d'Iberville, who offered the King access to the fur trade, rich lands, an approach to the buffalo herds, and a base for the conquest of the always alluring Spanish mines.[55]

Iberville sailed from Brest on 24 October 1698, with four ships, and about 400 people equipped to set up a colony. With him were his brother Bienville, M. Sauvole de la Villantray, Father du Ru, and Father Douay, who had been with La Salle and made the tremendous journey back. Iberville had had access to the manuscript journal of Joutel.[56] On 25 January 1699 they came to anchor off a low-lying sandy island at the entrance of a promising harbor. Having been warned off Pensacola by the Spanish, they anchored off Ship Island, and soon made contact with the Biloxi and Bayagoula Indians.[57]

In March, 1699, Iberville succeeded in penetrating the maze of the delta (selection 6). With him were Bienville, Sauvole, Father Douay, and a few men, in two longboats and two bark canoes.[58] The forests were uninhabited. Finally, at sixty-four leagues up the river, they reached the village of the Bayagoulas. Here at last Iberville could prove he was on the Mississippi: he found a chief of the Mongoulachas wearing a blue serge cloak which had been given him by Tonty. Bienville had a rare ability to acquire Indian languages, and could already communicate. They continued up the river through the strange, tropical country, to the village of the Houmas, where stood a 'large post, thirty feet high, . . . ornamented with carved designs of fishes'.[59]

Iberville was hunting for a branch of the Mississippi which he had found described in Le Clercq's *Établissement de la Foi*; he finally found the small river, later named the Iberville, and explored it eastward with the two canoes, discovering Lakes Maurepas and Pontchartrain, and passing through them to the coast. The boats, with Bienville and Sauvole, he sent back down the mainstream, to obtain from the Mongoulachas

229 Pierre le Moyne d'Iberville, founder of Louisiana, from an engraving in Margry, *Découvertes*, IV, reproduced in J. Winsor, *Narrative and critical history of America*, V, 15, 1884-9.

230 Jean-Baptiste le Moyne de Bienville, from an engraving in J. Winsor, *Narrative and critical history of America*, 1884-9.
Bienville was the brother of Iberville, four times governor of Louisiana, and the founder of New Orleans.

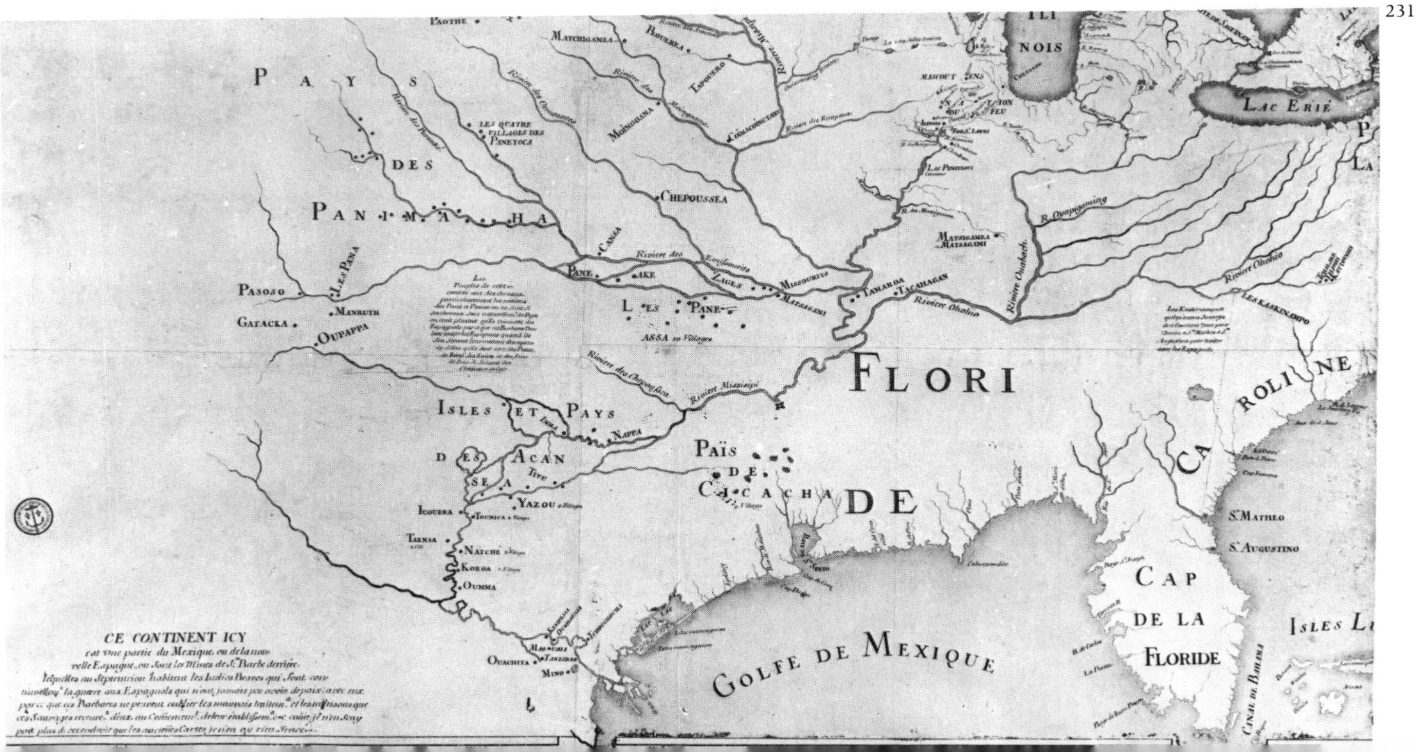

231 Franquelin. 'Carte de l'Amerique Septent.le', 1687. *Service Historique de la Marine, Paris, SHM66 (8-9-10-11)*.
This Mississippi Valley detail of Franquelin's large map of North America is significant because it is based on La Salle's report of his expedition to the mouth of the river from Canada in 1682 and includes the latest information about the river's tributaries and about the Indian tribes of the region. It shows how far west La Salle thought the Mississippi entered the Gulf; it helps to explain why he sailed so far west in his search for the mouth in 1684; and it clarifies his repeated insistence in his *Memorial* to Seignelay and elsewhere that the river flowed from Canada near to the Spanish mines and would make them easily available for seizure and exploitation.

Jean-Baptiste Franquelin sent the first draft for this map, which was dedicated to Pontchartrain, French minister of finance, to Paris where De la Croix drew the finished copy. It is similar in many details to Franquelin's lost map of 1684, of which there are several tracings (*cf.* J. Winsor, *Narrative and critical history of America*, IV, pp. 228-9, 1884-9). See also plate 53.

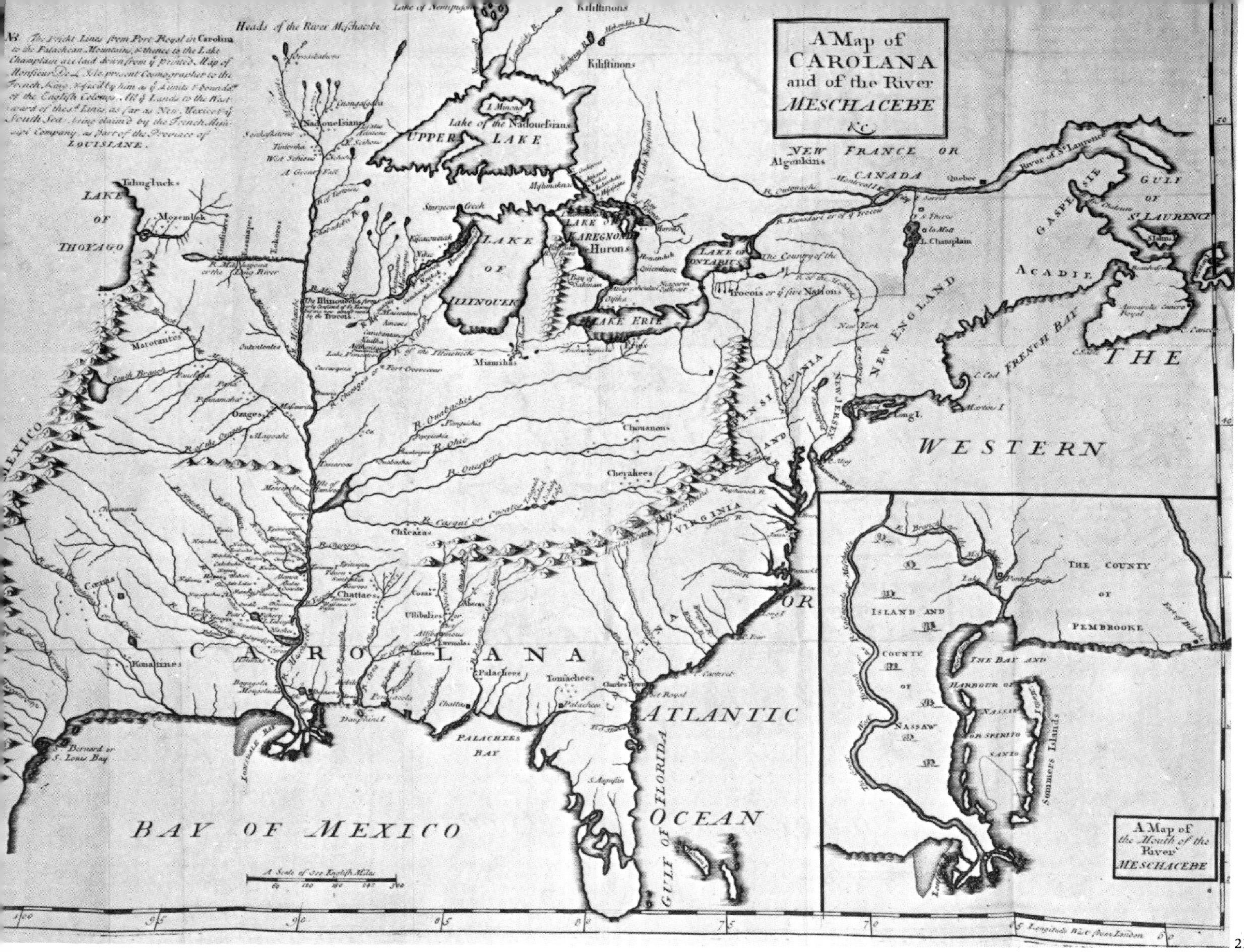

232

232 Coxe. 'A Map of Carolana and the River Meschacebe', 1722, from Daniel Coxe, *A description of the English province of Carolana*, opp. p. 1, London, 1722.
This map and the work in which it appears present the claims of Dr Daniel Coxe, (1640-1730), physician to Charles II and to Queen Anne, to Carolana, the territory granted by Charles I to Sir Robert Heath in 1629. The King with his council had voided Sir Robert's Carolana charter when he made the 1663 Carolina grant to eight Lords Proprietors; but Dr Coxe, who had extensive and determined colonial plans, raised legal questions after he had acquired the earlier 'rights' about 1692.

Coxe's map is based on French and British maps, with additional information gathered for him by English colonials. He left the boundaries of Carolana undefined; diplomatically Coxe wished to avoid conflict with the established coastal settlements of Carolina. He placed the Overhill (or Over-the-Hill) Cherokee Country on the Little Tennessee to the west of Virginia instead of in Southeast Tennessee and South Carolina (see plate 176). Four rivers, possibly the Miami, Ohio, Cumberland, and Tennessee, empty into a great (non-existent) lake before flowing into the Mississippi. 'S. Bernard or S. Louis', site of La Salle's abortive colony on Matagorda Bay, is placed far to the west on the Gulf. The geography of the northwest corner is highly imaginative; west of Lahontan's River of the West, beyond the mountains, is a non-existent Lake of Thoyago. East of the Mississippi in the inset are the proposed counties of Nassau and Pembroke.

How much actual exploration Dr Coxe promoted is unknown; but he stimulated continued English interest in the land beyond the Appalachians.

233

233 The carrying of the Great Sun of the Natchez, from Le Page du Pratz, *Histoire de la Louisiane*, 1758.
The Natchez had great reverence for the sun, and kept a perpetual fire burning in their temple. They called their ruler 'Le Grand Soleil', and observed many reverential customs toward him and other exalted persons.

the clinching piece of evidence of the identity of the river of which the Bayagoulas had told him. Bienville had the immense satisfaction of putting into his brother's hands the very letter left by Tonty for La Salle in 1686. One can imagine the solemn hush, in that wild setting, in which they read his words. 'Although we have neither heard news or seen signs of you, I do not despair that God will grant success to your undertakings. I wish it with all my heart; for you have no more faithful follower than myself, who would sacrifice everything to find you'.[60] A spot was chosen on Biloxi Bay, and a small wooden fort erected, where Sauvole was placed in command of a garrison. Bienville, then only eighteen, was given second rank. Iberville sailed for France in May, 1699, to seek supplies, and to report to the King that his mission was accomplished.[61]

234

235

234 General dance of the Natchez Indians, from Le Page du Pratz, *Histoire de la Louisiane*, 1758.
The Natchez Indians lived on high land on the eastern shore of the Mississippi, north of the entrance of the Red River. From the time when Iberville reached them on one of his first explorations to their final tragic downfall, the French of Louisiana were impressed by the strength and individuality of the Natchez. 'Of all the savages, they are the most civilized nation,' wrote Pénicaut. Le Page du Pratz went to live among them, and described in detail their customs and beliefs. He considered the Natchez War of 1729, and the consequent extermination and deportation of the tribe, the result of French stupidity.

235 Alexandre de Batz. Savage in winter dress, *c.* 1732, *Peabody Museum, Harvard University, Bushnell Collection.*
Alexandre de Batz, son of the French settler A. Batz, drew several valuable sketches of Indian life about 1730, as well as making architectural drawings of buildings in New Orleans.

The next months found Bienville exploring and acquiring his great diplomatic skill with the Indians, while Sauvole literally and painfully held the fort. One day, about twenty-three leagues from the mouth of the Mississippi, Bienville was suddenly confronted by an armed English ship sailing up the river. This was the *Carolina Galley*, under Captain Bond, sent out by Dr Daniel Coxe to claim his grant of 'Carolana'. The dauntless young Bienville hailed and boarded her, and persuaded the captain that the French were already seated and in possession. This bend in the river has been known ever since as English Turn.[62] Bienville increased his Indian allies, often using their fear of the Chickasaws, friends of the English. Sauvole, in the little fort at Biloxi, struggled against heat, drought, floods and famine; dysentery and yellow fever; mosquitoes, snakes and crocodiles. When the missionary Fathers de Montigny and St Cosme made the appalling trip down the Mississippi and along the gulf shore from their missions among the Taensas and the Tamarois to visit Biloxi, Sauvole was sadly unable to feed them.[63]

In January, 1700, Iberville returned from France with more

236 Guillaume de l'Isle. 'Carte du Mexique et de la Floride', 1703. *British Museum, London.*
This important map of Mexico and Florida, of which a detail only is reproduced,is the basis in content and area covered for many later maps by European geographers during the eighteenth century. For the first time on a printed map the mouth of the Mississippi River, with its delta, is delineated with some accuracy. A great body of information, reported in France since Coronelli prepared his map in 1689 (see plate 221), was available and used in the preparation of this map.

The survivors of La Salle's colony, Joutel, Cavelier, and others had crossed new country; Tonty had made several trips down the Mississippi and visited the Choctaw Indians; Bienville, with St Denys and Pénicaut, had explored the beginnings of the Red River; Le Sueur in 1700, searching for mines, had gone up beyond the Illinois River into the Sioux country; and Father Gravier and other Jesuit priests had descended the river. Above all Iberville on his first voyage explored the coast, entered the delta in 1699, returned to his base at Biloxi by Lake Pontchartrain, and on his second voyage went up the Mississippi again to the Natchez.

Father Jean Delanglez, SJ, an authority on the early cartography of the Mississippi, has shown that this map and the preserved manuscript drafts that preceded it were the result of careful research by the geographer Claude de l'Isle, the father of Guillaume. Claude read the log which Iberville kept on his first voyage and wrote a series of questions on moot points for Iberville to answer. Guillaume de l'Isle, whose name appears on the map as its author, probably designed and drew it. He was a pioneer in scientific cartography, making use when available of celestial observations to locate correct longitude and leaving blank the regions on his map for which information was undependable. His productions were therefore not as beautiful as those of seventeenth-century geographers like Blaeu, who filled such spaces with swash lettering and pictorial embellishments.

236

237

237 Guillaume de l'Isle. 'Carte de la Louisiane et du Cours du Mississippi', 1718 [*c.* 1735]. *British Museum, London.*
Geographically, politically, and historically this is one of the most important maps of the Mississippi Valley. Quickly copied, widely referred to, it was the chief authority for the Mississippi River for over fifty years, although exploration continued to add to the knowledge of the tributaries and adjacent regions.

In its preparation de l'Isle studied the reports and maps available to him. He uses, and gives credit to, the maps and memoirs of Le Maire; he records the expeditions of St Denys in 1714 (erroneously 1713 on the map) and 1716 to the Rio Grande and the establishment of Natchitoches on the Red River in 1718; and attempts with some success to interpret the often conflicting reports about the tributaries of the Mississippi River. His tracing of the route of the De Soto-Moscoso 1539-43 expedition, the first on a 'modern' map, parallels in general the findings of the exhaustive *Final report of the United States de Soto expedition commission* (1939). In his delineation of areas surrounding the Valley, de l'Isle is often not so successful. The southern half of Florida appears as a great archipelago, a misconception found on Nairne's map of 1711 (see plate 130) as well as on some later French and English maps until 1770. Between Lake Erie and Lake Michigan is a long, narrow, high plateau, found on the Morden-Berry 'English Empire' (1695), 'A Plaine like a Terras Walk about 200 miles in length'. Lake Michigan is too wide. In the west de l'Isle profited by a careful report to him on the Missouri by De Bourgmont; but the upper reaches of the Missouri and Rio Grande were unknown and erroneously drawn.

Politically the map was aggressive and provocative; it pushes French Louisiana west to a tributary of the Rio Grande and east to the Appalachians, laying a basis to a claim to Carolina. Angry protests by British colonial officials and a cartographical war resulted.

De l'Isle later added 'Nouvelle Orleans', founded in 1718, to his map; Covens and Mortier made a new and slightly larger copy of the map between 1733 and 1741, which is here reproduced.

settlers. They built a fort on the Mississippi, eighteen leagues from the sea. Tonty came down the river to visit. Iberville went up as far as the high lands of the Natchez, and was struck by the unique culture of this tribe,[64] well described by Father Gravier, with its Great Sun, its Stung Serpent, its perpetual fire,[65] and its sacrifice of victims to accompany dead leaders. Bienville and St Denys explored along the Red River; Bienville travelled on foot north to a Ouachita village (present Oklahoma), reached the Yatasses, and heard of the Cadadoquis.[66] Another member of the colony, Pierre Le Sueur, had come with the understanding that he might explore for mines along the upper Mississippi north of the Illinois. He made the mighty journey up in 1700 and back in 1702, accompanied by the carpenter Pénicaut. Very successful in his relations with the Sioux, he found in Minnesota copper and lead, and mines of 'blue earth', of which he brought back samples to Louisiana.[67] Soon after the death of Sauvole in 1700, Iberville moved the fort to Mobile Bay. Tonty came again, exploring north into Alabama to use his skill to make peace between the Chickasaws and the French-allied Choctaws. In 1706, Iberville, returning once more from France, died in the West Indies of the dreaded yellow fever, and soon the faithful and heroic Tonty also was dead. It was the end of an era.[68]

The little colony was strengthened by new arrivals, grants were taken up and trading posts founded on the lower Mississippi and its branches, and agriculture helped by the importation of African slaves.

It was the intrepid St Denys who accomplished the next notable westward exploration, in search of Spanish trade, and who triggered, as had La Salle, a defensive Spanish reaction leading to eastward exploration into Texas. In 1711, Father Hidalgo, a Franciscan at San Juan Batista on the lower Rio Grande, decided on a bold step. He had been with Father Massanet at the founding of the first Spanish Texas mission in 1690, and had ever since regretted its abandonment. He sent three letters to Louisiana, urging the French to take under their protection the Assinais, or Texas, Indians. The letter reached Cadillac, governor of the Mississippi colony, who gave St Denys the ostensible commission to find and assist Father Hidalgo and to purchase livestock, and the secret commission to open what trade he could.[69]

St Denys started off from the Red River in 1714, where he had built the beginnings of the important post of Natchitoches, fortified in 1717. With him went Pénicaut, the carpenter and journal keeper,[70] and about twenty-five men. They travelled on foot across the vast plains and rivers of Texas, finding the country largely depopulated,[71] and they arrived at San

238 Father Antonio Margil de Jésus, ?1714. *Iconographia Colonial, Museo Nacional, Mexico.*
Father Margil was a leader among the Spanish explorer missionary priests who clung to the attempt to hold Spanish territory in Texas in the eighteenth century and to Christianize and settle Indian tribes. Native of Valencia, a founder of the College of Zacatecas in Mexico, he helped in 1716 to re-establish San Francisco de los Texas, Father Massanet's abandoned mission on the Nueces.

This reproduction is from a photograph of the original in the Bancroft Library, University of California, Berkeley, California.

239 Le Buteaux. View of the camp on the concession of Monseigneur Law at New Biloxi, on the Louisiana coast, 1720. *Newberry Library, Chicago, Ayer Collection.*
The headquarters of John Law's Company of the Indies was at this 'camp' east of the projected, but never built, fort at New Biloxi, across the bay from Old Biloxi. In 1722 the capital was moved from New Biloxi to New Orleans. Law's main concession was on the Arkansas River.

Jean Baptiste Michel le Buteaux's black-and-white wash drawing, made at the order of Elias Huteus, director-general of the company, on 10 December 1720, gives in vivid detail the activities of a frontier post.

238

Juan Batista in Coahuila on the Rio Grande, to the utter amazement of the Spanish. Father Hidalgo was away, but Captain Ramon, commanding the presidio, received his French visitor cordially. St Denys made himself very agreeable, especially to Ramon's charming granddaughter, Manuela Sanchez.[72] In June 1715, he went to Mexico City, where the Duke of Linares promised him a commercial treaty in return for his help in settling Spanish missions among the Assinais. On his return he married Manuela, and kept his promise.[73] He led a large expedition with Captain Ramon's son, and Fathers Hidalgo, Espinosa and Margil, to found four missions and a garrison near the Neches and Angelina Rivers; he exhorted his friends the Assinais to receive the Spaniards gladly. He sold the goods he had brought, and purchased stock. Captain Ramon was warmly received in Natchitoches and Mobile.[74] However, although the Spanish had liked St Denys, they had been frightened by his demonstration of their accessibility to the French. Again official Spain responded by a spurt of mission establishment, its way to confirm a frontier. In 1716, Ramon and Father Margil founded the mission at Nacogdoches, and in 1717, the easternmost one, Los Adaes, only fifteen miles from Natchitoches. There were now six missions and a small presidio in Texas, with consequent exploration of that territory.[75]

Concerning St Denys's second journey to the Rio Grande in 1716, there were many contemporary points of view. To many he was a dashing hero-explorer, helping Spain to help the Indians, furthering peace. To some French, he was a pro-Spanish renegade; to some Spanish, a dangerous threat, forcing open the gates Spain always closed against foreign trade. He did have with and following him several 'associates' with goods to sell. On his arrival in San Juan, he found the authorities alarmed and the climate changed. His goods were seized; he set off for Mexico City to protest, and was clapped in prison. In 1717, he was freed, and allowed to return to San Juan. Threatened with reimprisonment or deportation, he dismounted a horseman, seized his steed, and made one more dramatic exploratory journey back to Natchitoches in 1719.[76]

In the meantime, in 1718, the Spanish had sent the new governor of Texas, Alarcón, with Father Olivares, to strengthen Spanish Texas. Since they were to found both missions and two villas, they had with them seventy-two people, seven families, 'cattle, sheep, goats, chickens, six droves of mules, and 548 horses'.[77] With this troop they crossed the trailless country and bridgeless rivers of Texas in a summer which Captain Domingo Ramon described as the wettest he had ever experienced (selection 8).[78] Fray Céliz, diarist of the expedition, described the 'thunder peeling like harquebus shots in battle'.[79] Their chief achievement was the founding of the mission of San Antonio de Valero, later known as the Alamo, and the nearby Villa de Béjar. Thus began San Antonio, the most durable Spanish post in Texas, which became a great modern city. They reached San Bernardo (Matagorda) Bay with great difficulty, visited and supplied the missions founded by Ramon and St Denys, even as far east as Los Adaes, and explored north to the Cadadoquis before their return.[80] Once more, Spanish exploration and frontier settlement had been stimulated by belief in a French threat.

5 Exploration resulting from conflict and the pursuit of trade in the north, 1719-30

When St Denys returned to French Louisiana in 1719, he found many new developments. The colony had been a pawn of royal finance, until Law's 'Mississippi bubble' burst of its own weight of inflated paper money (see plate 239). Boisbriant was now governor, Bienville commandant-general; he had firmly put down the first rising of the Natchez. Population had markedly increased; recent émigrés included Bénard de la Harpe and Le Page du Pratz, who became explorers and

239

240

240 Lassus. View and Perspective of New Orleans, 1726. *Archives Nationales, Section outre-mer, Dépôt des Fortifications des Colonies, Paris, Louisiane, No. 71.* Jean Pierre Lassus made this watercolor drawing of which only a detail is reproduced, of the new settlement of New Orleans, with its backdrop of vast stretches of cypress swamps, from the Algiers side of the Mississippi. The first smaller clearing had been made in 1718; the military engineers Le Blond de la Tour and Adrien Pauger planned and laid out streets in 1721. At the left of the enlarged clearing is a windmill, designed by Pauger and built in 1724 on a levee. Back of the parade ground and the church of St Louis is the clearing of the portage leading to Lake Pontchartrain. Flights of geese are on the horizon; in the foreground men are clearing ground, for planting, and on the river's edge one is spearing an alligator.

Jean Lassus and his brother Joseph arrived from France in February 1725 with commissions as surveyors to Louisiana for the Company of the Indies. They ran into conflict with Pauger, the engineer-in-chief; the elder Lassus was dismissed in 1728 but Joseph married and remained in New Orleans for fifteen years.

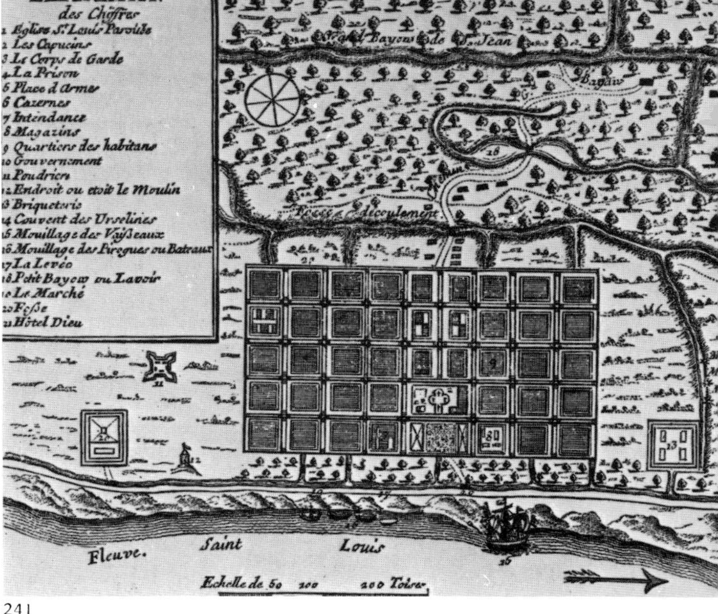

241

241 Sérigny. View of New Orleans in 1719, from reproduction in J. Winsor, *Narrative and critical history of America,* V. 39, of an inset in M. de Sérigny's 'Carte de la Côte de la Louisiane en 1719 et 1720'. Bienville had founded the little town on an island along the east bank of the Lower Mississippi in 1718, at a place where the Indians portaged their canoes from the river to Lake Pontchartrain, by way of the Bayou St Jean. Le Sieur Périer was sent out from France to plan and build the fort and the town, but died on the way. He was replaced by Le Blond de la Tour, who worked first at New Biloxi, and was transferred, with his assistants Pauger and Boispinel, to New Orleans in 1722.

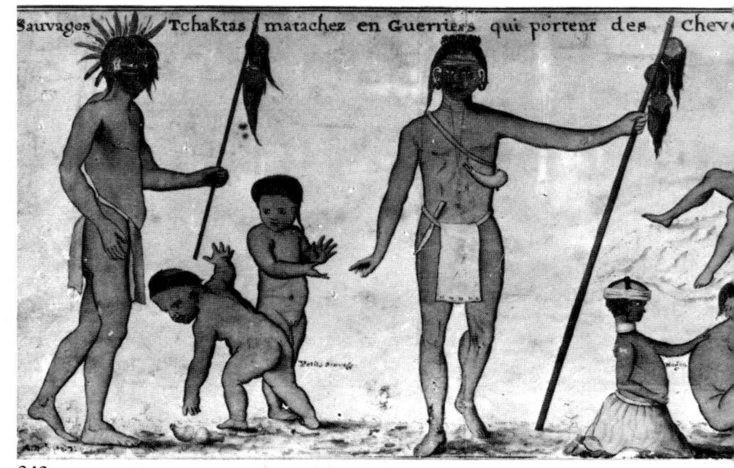

242

242 Alexandre de Batz. Choctaw Indians equipped as warriors and carrying scalps, c. 1732. *Peabody Museum, Harvard University, Bushnell Collection.* The Choctaws, east of the Mississippi in present Alabama, early became allies of the French, as the Chickasaws were of the English. The French, from the days of Tonty onward, worked to keep these tribes at peace, the English, to foment war between them.

important chroniclers. In 1718, Bienville had founded New Orleans on its island along the lower river.[81] Many negroes were imported; farming began in earnest on the grants. That of La Harpe was eighty leagues west of Natchitoches, among the Nassonite Indians, requiring real exploration to reach it. He fortified his post, and attempted trade with the Indians and even the Spaniards.[82] Le Page du Pratz settled at Natchez, Diron d'Artaguiette, previously intendant at the colony, at Baton Rouge.[83] On the eastern side of the Mississippi, the effort to counter the English traders had led to exploration into present Alabama and the establishment of Fort Toulouse. About 1727, Le Page du Pratz left the river and took a

243

243 Northern savages going hunting in the winter with their families, from Le Page du Pratz, *Histoire de la Louisiane*, 1758.
Le Page du Pratz describes this dog transport in his account of De Bourgmont going up the Missouri to make peace with the Padoucas (Comanches) in 1724:

'On the 24th of July, at six in the morning, this little army set out, consisting of three hundred Warriors, including the Chief of the Canzas, three hundred women, about five hundred young people, and at least three hundred dogs. The women carried considerable loads, to the astonishment of the French, unaccustomed to such a sight. The young women were also well loaded for their years; and the dogs were made to trail a part of the baggage, and that in the following manner: The back of the dog was covered with a skin, with its pile on, then the dog was girthed round, and his breast-leather put on; and taking two poles of the thickness of one's arm, and twelve feet long, they fastened their two ends half a foot asunder, laying on the dog's saddle the thong that fastened the two poles; and to the poles they also fastened, behind the dog, a ring, or hoop, lengthwise, on which they laid the load.' Du Pratz, *History of Louisiana*, II, 109-110, 1763.

short trip into Tennessee with some of his Natchez Indians.[84]

Now another European war altered colonial life, this time between France and Spain, and by 1721, all inhabitants of all the Spanish Texan missions were withdrawn to San Antonio. St Denys probably helped in the consequent demolition of the missions, which was bitterly resented in Spain. The result was one of the last great Spanish exploratory expeditions into Texas, that of the Marquis of Aguayo, between 1719 and 1722, with 500 men and droves of animals. Father Peña, his chaplain, describes the terrible winter crossing of the rivers, the rough, abandoned country through which they forged a new route. On the Neches, St Denys arrived, and swam his horse across to arrange a truce. Aguayo left ten missions, always poorly supplied and harrassed by Apaches; four presidios, which lasted until Spanish dominion ended in 1836; and a real settlement at San Antonio.[85]

244

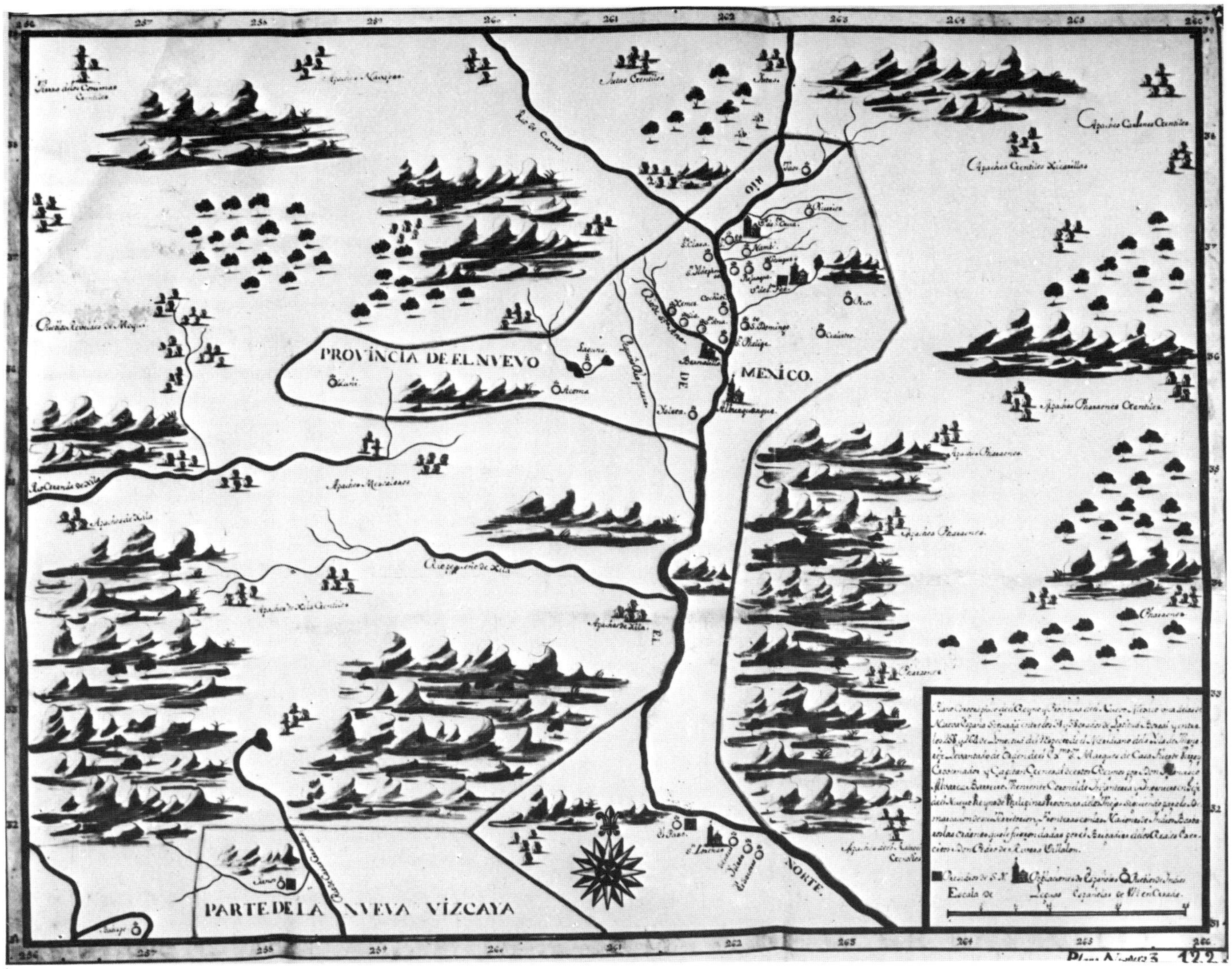

244 Barreiro. 'Plano cosmographico de . . . Nuevo Mexico', *c.* 1727. *Archivo General de Indias, Seville, Mexico No. 122.*
This important map shows the settlements around the Rio Grande. Presidios with garrisons are at El Paso and Santa Fé; Spanish settlements on the upper Rio Grande, marked by a church, are at Albuquerque, Bernalillo, Santa Fé, and Santa Cruz; and native Christianized pueblos, such as Zuni, Acoma, Taos, and Pecos, are indicated by a cross above the circle. Surrounding them are groups of small houses, denoting ominous hostile Apache tribes and, to the extreme north, the Wutahs from which Utah later derived its name.

245

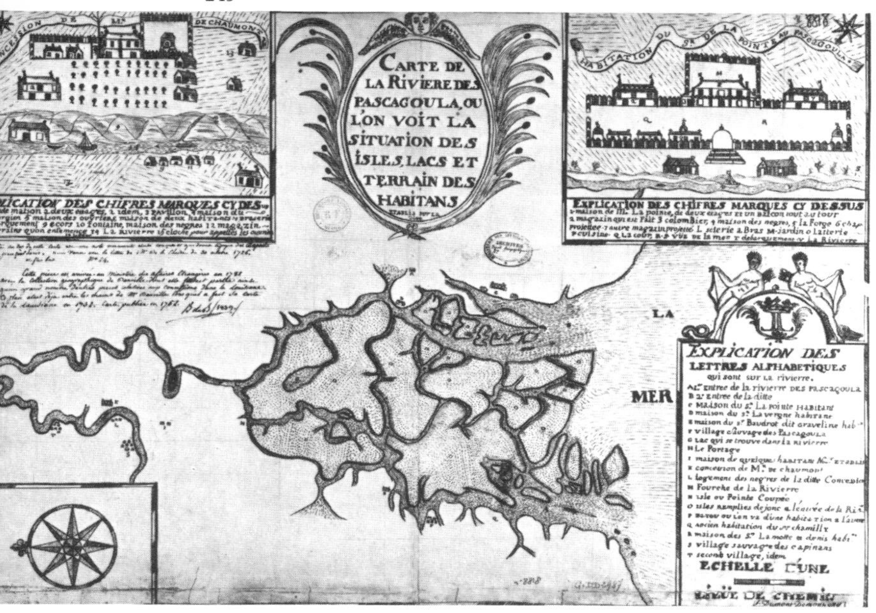

245 Dumont. Chart of the Pascagoula River, 1726. *Bibliothèque Nationale, Paris.*
François Dumont de Montigny's drawings of the De la Pointe and Chaumont concessions show interesting architectural details of early plantation houses. Unlike the early single-story structures in New Orleans, these are galleried, two-storied buildings. The Pascagoula, halfway between Biloxi and Mobile, flows past numerous islands into the Gulf.

Significant exploration, still motivated by French-Spanish rivalry and the desire of the French to open and the Spanish to resist mutual trade, now moved to the rivers of the north. La Harpe ascended the Red River and explored north into present Oklahoma (selection 9), seeking the Comanches who were known to trade with the Spaniards, and encountering the Osages and the Panis.[86] La Harpe quotes a letter from Du Tisné, who was sent by Bienville to the Osages. Du Tisné had founded a small post for furtrading called Fernandina among the Caddoan Indians of the middle Arkansas.[87] In 1719, he reached the Osage River, a branch of the Missouri, where he traded. He went on to the Panis in Oklahoma, and across buffalo plains to the Padoucas, or Comanches, 'a very brave and warlike nation'.[88] Even farther north, the French were beginning to explore the great Missouri. It had fascinated them ever since Marquette and Jolliet, in 1673, had seen its turbulent flood pouring into the Mississippi, and Marquette had written, 'I hope by means of it to make the discovery of the Vermilion Sea and California'.[89] The most notable of the early explorers of the Missouri was Étienne de Bourgmont. He fell in love with a Missouri Indian girl, and lived among her tribe from 1712-18. He explored up the Missouri as far as the Niobrara, and wrote 'The Route one must keep to ascend the Missouri River' for the cartographer De l'Isle. Rewarded by Bienville in 1718 for his explorations, he went to France and married a rich widow.[90]

Once more the Spanish reacted in dread to exaggerated rumors of French advance on the northern rivers. In 1720, Governor Valverde of New Mexico was ordered to build a presidio at El Cuartelejo, an Apache rancheria in present western Kansas. Then a rumor came of a French settlement on the South Platte. Captain Villasur was sent with a troop to rout this out, and establish a defensive post. Curiously enough, one of his lieutenants was 'Juan de l'Archibeque', now a respected craftsman of Santa Fé. It was Bandelier, the great archaeologist and scholar, who found the archives of the Spanish Franciscans in the pueblo of Santa Clara, superstitiously guarded by the Indians, and learned from them that this man was l'Archevêque, who had conspired to kill La Salle.[91] Now he himself met a tragic fate, as the Villasur expedition, encamped on the North Platte, was set upon by Comanches and practically annihilated. There is dispute as to whether any Frenchmen were with the Indians;[92] however, Governor Boisbriant was startled and horrified when Comanches made their way to his presence, and presented to him the sacred vessels of the Mass, taken from the Villasur expedition, in a sort of grotesque dance.[93]

Now the French were alarmed, fearing the Spanish meant to occupy the Platte and block their trade. De Bourgmont was brought back from France and made commander on the Missouri. In 1723, he built Fort Orléans on the north bank, near the center of the present state of Missouri. It was supplied from New Orleans, and hopefully destined for the Santa Fé trade; first, intertribal wars had to be quelled, and the friendship won of the Comanches (Padoucas), the fierce, horse-riding tribe which dominated Kansas and Colorado. De Bourgmont showed his skill, making alliances with the intermediate tribes, and taking representatives with him up the Kansas River to treat with the Comanches. He returned their captured slaves, achieved a treaty, and the French flag now flew only 300 miles from the Spanish.[94] Fort Orléans was abandoned in 1727. The Santa Fé trail had not been opened, but a lively trade was sending furs down the rivers to New Orleans.

These were the major journeys of exploration into new territory in the seventeenth and first thirty years of the eighteenth centuries, initiated by the French of Louisiana and the Spanish of New Mexico and the Rio Grande. Yet, throughout this period, every journey eastward into Texas and Oklahoma with their predatory Apaches, every venture north into Alabama with its hostile English and Chickasaws, every

246 Indian canoe; French sailboat, from the *Codex Canadensis*, c. 1700. *Thomas Gilcrease Institute, Tulsa.*

246

laborious voyage in canoes and piraguas up and down the enormous, winding Mississippi and its tributaries, was an exploration. To traders, missionaries, colonizers, and officials, the land appeared fresh, fascinating, and demanding of extremes of courage and endurance. 'On the Mississippi', wrote Nancy Miller Surrey, 'the voyagers found enormous floating trees, with dangerous currents near them, sandbars, driftwood matted into wooded islands, "planters" or almost submerged tree trunks into which boats would crack, "sawyers", logs fastened to the bottom which appeared and and disappeared with the current.' The horseshoe meanderings doubled time and distance, while heavy rains, tornadoes, scarcity of food and water, flies and mosquitoes beset them.[95] Often while trying to hunt bear or buffalo on the shore, men became lost; d'Artaguiette, making his laborious voyage of inspection in 1722, picked up two on a raft.[96] He, like many others less famous, lived on wild meat and camped in floods. Father Charlevoix, one of the most descriptive historians of French Louisiana, descending the Mississippi in 1721-2 in a 'pettiaugre', was very uneasy about 'these savages who are not yet reconciled to us', and also about the huge 'caymans' or alligators, with their fearsome rumbling. He describes the beauty and great possibilities of the land, especially around Natchez, mentions 'very fine cotton upon the tree', indigo, and tobacco. He questioned the importation of negro slaves, however, 'who are only attached to us by fear, and for whom the very land where they were born has not the dear name of mother country!'[97] Perhaps the most appealing account of all the pioneer journeys is that of Marie-Madelaine Hachard or Sister Saint-Stanislaus, a very young, gentle girl from Rouen who came in 1727 with a group of Ursuline nuns under Mother Tranchepain to teach the daughters of New Orleans, and also some of the 'sauvagesses et negresses'. Their journey in a little 'chaloupe' through the rough Mississippi delta, their camping out each night on the banks, sewed into cloth two by two to keep off the swarms of mosquitoes and the scorpions, are most vividly recounted by Madelaine. She found unexpected politeness in New Orleans, but religion in sad neglect.[98]

So the French of Louisiana and the Spanish of New Mexico and Texas explored and possessed their land, before the growing conflict with the encroaching English threatened and altered both.

6 Spanish and French exploration just before the American Revolution, 1730-76

'They who are possessed of the Mississippi will command the continent', wrote the English translator of Le Page du Pratz's *History of Louisiana* in 1763.[99] In the latter eighteenth century, we see the loss of the great basin and the southwest, by French and Spanish, to the English, and to their children, the new Americans. One of the causes of the weakening of French Louisiana was that the good relations with the Indians created by gifted leaders such as Tonty, Bienville, St Denys and De Bourgmont were not maintained. Some say that France moved the tribes too much, concentrated them dangerously in dependence on French centers. Le Page du Pratz, living in one such center, Natchez, could not see why it was not possible to live well with the Indians. He had a great respect for them, studied and praised in his history their method of raising children, and recorded many conversations with his wise friend the Stung Serpent (selection 10).[100] He had gone far to repair relations after the first Natchez uprising; he and Bienville were both away when Governor Chopart,

247

247 'Carte de la Louisiane', 1757, from Le Page du Pratz, *Histoire de la Louisiane*, I, 1758.
Le Page du Pratz was not himself an important explorer, although he was a keen observer and recorded information collected from reports of earlier colonists and from the Natchez and other natives. On this map he gives the location of many Indian tribes and of the mines on the upper Mississippi. He made use of a Spanish map captured by the Comanches when Villasur was slain in 1720. 'From this map it appears,' wrote Le Page, 'that we ought to bend the Red River, and that of the Arkansas, somewhat more, and place the source of the Missisipi more westerly than our geographers do.' The accuracy of Le Page's map was not improved by his following the Spanish.

248 Alexandre de Batz. Savage adorned as a warrior, having taken the scalps of three Natchez men. Drawn from life on the spot, 1732
Peabody Museum, Harvard University, Bushnell Collection.
This is Buffalo Tamer, chief of the Tonicas. The Natchez had killed his predecessor the year before. The woman is the widow, the child the son, Jacob, of the dead chief.

248

249

249 A view of New Orleans taken from the opposite side of the River Mississippi, 1765. *Louisiana State Museum, New Orleans.*
This unsigned sketch was found in England. It shows the river front of the town at the end of the French colonial period, and was probably made by a British officer, sent in 1765 to survey the river. The British were taking over the part of Louisiana east of the Mississippi which had been ceded to England at the end of the French and Indian War.

with selfish stupidity, demanded the land of a whole Natchez village. The result was a coordinated uprising like the war with the Pueblo Indians in 1680, and fierce French reprisals. This weakened the whole structure of the colony just as France was taking on the burden of the French and Indian War with England.

Nevertheless, Louisiana planters maintained their homes, and French traders continued to explore new territory for some time to come. Fort Cavagnolle replaced Fort Orléans on the Missouri. In 1741, Bienville was visited by brothers, Pierre and Paul Mallet, who astounded him by saying that they had been to Santa Fé. They had started in 1739 opposite the fort on the Missouri, with a small group of companions, and ascended it to the Panimahas on the Niobrara River. Then they had struck southeast to the Platte and ascended that to the Padouca or Loup. Then southwest to the Republican River. They kept crossing rivers to the south. The plains were bare. They passed through Comanche territory unharmed. Finally they came to the upper waters of the Arkansas; from there, with Indian guidance, they reached Taos and Santa Fé. The astonished Spaniards received them well. One of their companions married there; one was hanged for inciting the Indians. Seven left after nine months. They realized now they need not go north; they used the Pecos, Canadian, and Arkansas Rivers. Some went to the Panis to trade; the rest built canoes from the bark of elms, and floated down to New Orleans.[101] The Santa Fé trail had been opened.

The decades of the 1740s and 50s were a time of contraband trade, between the French, the Spanish, and the intermediate Indians.[102] English traders were also beginning to penetrate the west, with their annoying ability to undersell the French. 'By 1753', writes Nasatir, 'Frenchmen, be they voyageurs, traders, trappers, explorers . . . had penetrated the whole trans-Mississippi West country, and . . . made known the country contained in the watershed of the Mississippi-Missouri Rivers. They had set foot on most of the territory lying between the Mississippi and the Spanish border; they had reached the Rocky Mountains'.[103] After this great achievement, a war-weakened France secretly ceded Louisiana to Spain in 1762 to keep it out of English hands. French-initiated trade and exploration practically ceased. The Indian tribes became hostile again; the Santa Fé trail was forgotten, and had to be rediscovered by the Americans in the nineteenth century.[104]

There was, however, a large part of the Spanish domain, to the west and north of Santa Fé and also to the east in Texas, which remained unexplored in this century because it was controlled by the most intransigent of the Indian tribes, the Apaches, called by Bolton 'the Ishmael of the plains'.[105] They were nomadic, horse-riding, tricky, and savage in customs. One of their strongholds was in the mountains north of San Antonio. Again it was a priest, Father Santa Ana, who insisted on an attempt to found a mission for them. After the collapse of this, Captain Rabago urged a new try on the San Saba River. Some Apaches in San Antonio promised that the Indians would come. Governor Parilla went himself on the expedition, in 1757, with Father Terreros. They marched straight north for nine days and, in the mountains now, they reached the river and built two missions and a fort. Suddenly, 3000 Apaches appeared and camped nearby, but would not enter the missions. After disappearing and returning several times they finally massacred practically the whole company of friars and settlers, and destroyed fort and missions.[106]

Because of the secret cession of French Louisiana in 1762, it was Spain, and not England, which with some difficulty with unwilling French colonists took possession when the Peace of Paris ended the French and Indian War in 1763. Border defenses between Louisiana and Texas were withdrawn. The mission method of the Spanish was replaced by the trader method of the French. Much was now accomplished by a gifted Indian agent, Athanaze de Mezières, who became a Spanish subject and worked to unify the whites and for better relations with the Indians. From his headquarters at Natchitoches, he tried to stop the slave trade in the Red River Valley, halt English infiltration, and get back 'white men shamelessly living among the red'. He did a great deal

250 Alexandre de Batz. Sacred tree near the Natchez temple, possibly an Osage orange, 1732. *Peabody Museum, Harvard University, Bushnell Collection.*

 250

of exploring, opening a route from Natchitoches to San Antonio, and travelling to the upper Brazos and 300 miles beyond, fighting off Apaches. But the whole route from San Antonio to Santa Fé was not found until Pedro Vial travelled it in 1786.[107]

In 1766-8 the last great exploratory journey of this period was undertaken by Spanish officials in North American New Spain, now extending to the Mississippi. France as enemy had disappeared; England loomed in the east. But the real enemy which had halted Spanish advance, and caused the abandonment of much, was unconquered and unassimilated Indian tribes, especially Apaches and Comanches, from the Gila River in lower Arizona on the west to the borders of Louisiana on the east. Therefore the viceroy, Cruillas, sent the Marqués de Rubí, Captain de Lafora of the Royal Engineers, José de Gálvez, visitador general, and José de Urrútia, cartographer, with a troop, on a journey of inspection of the frontiers, which lasted twenty-three months and covered 7,600 miles.[108] (See plate 364.)

The expedition began to encounter the depredations of the Apaches even in northern Mexico. The region around El Paso was devastated. On the 250-mile journey up the Rio Grande to Santa Fé, they passed through uninhabited territory, harassed by the Apaches all the way. Rubí recommended a presidio halfway up.[109] Returning to El Paso, they explored to the west, finding the Jesuit missions in Pimeria Alta in somewhat better condition. Back at El Paso, they crossed the Rio Grande in dugouts, and set out into Texas, travelling 175 miles north to the site of the San Saba mission. The small presidio near there was moved to San Antonio, the largest and best establishment, with a presidio, a municipality, and five

251

251 Apache and Comanche Indians, *c.* 1775. *National Library of Mexico.* Reproduced in Morfi, *History of Texas*, 1781 (Ed. C. E. Castañeda), opp. p. 88, 1935.
This is a pen drawing from life, one of few by the Spanish. The artist, Fray Vincente de Santa Maria, a missionary, accompanied Rubí on his great inspection. The drawing comes from the late period of weakening Spanish hold on Texas, when missionary attempts were made to reach the ever more aggressive Apaches and Comanches. The subject is the fiesta or dance of the Comanche and Apache Indians. There are two victims undergoing the 'petit feu' torture, by the fire.

252

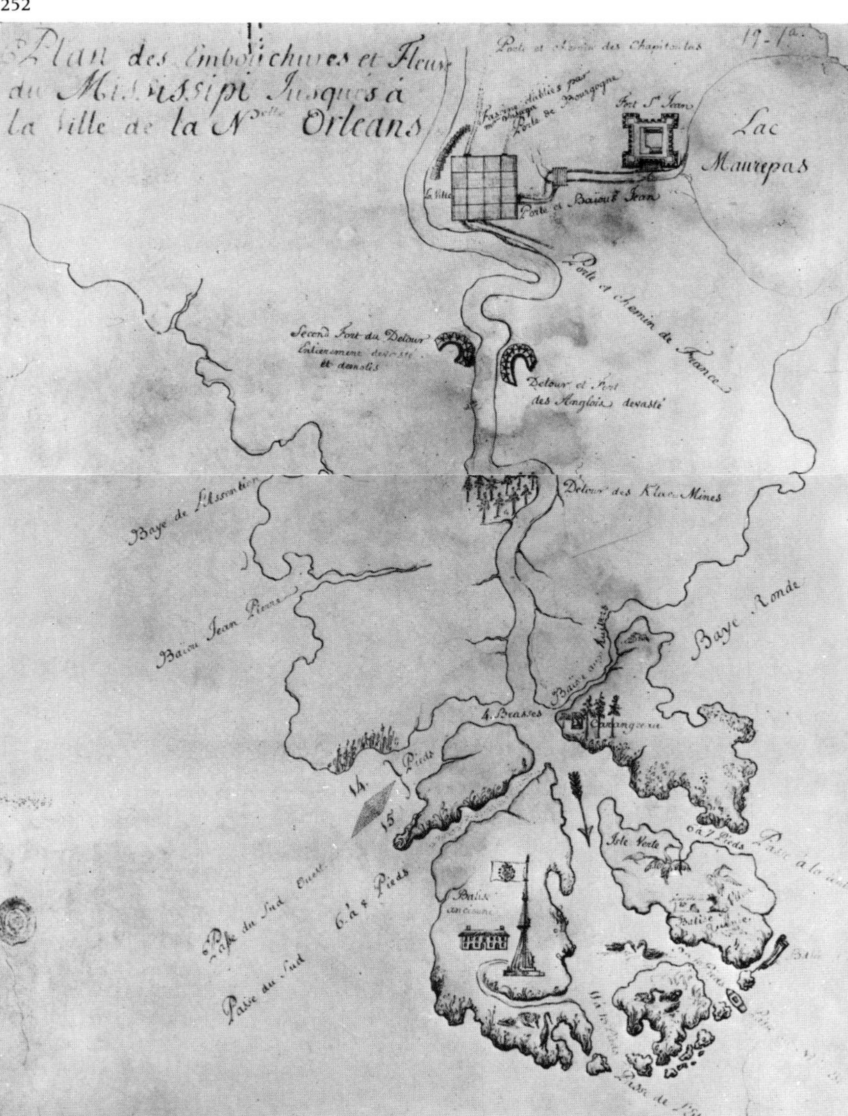

252 'Plan des Embouchures et Fleuve du Mississipi Jusquès á la ville de la N.elle Orleans', *c.* 1762. *Biblioteca Nacional, Madrid.*
This French map of the Mississippi from its mouth to New Orleans must have been taken by or given to the Spanish after the cession of Louisiana by France in 1762. A sentry stands at duty in the gateway of Old Balise, across East Pass from the ruined fort on Isle Verte; several men are stationed on the high observation flagstaff nearby, from which they can see a ship entering Northeast Pass.

missions. They went east, finding not one Indian convert at Nacogdoches, Ais, or Los Adaes. Rubí decided that these eastern posts should be abandoned. He went south to the coast, deciding to hold Lareto, near Matagorda Bay. River crossings were no easier than a hundred years before for De Léon.[110] De Lafora's diary is scornful of the poverty, lack of missionary success, and poor defense of his own nation.[111] Bolton rightly reminds us, however, that North America was always a difficult outpost for Spain; her success as a colonizing power can only be judged fairly by the West Indies, Central and South America. Rubí's sensible recommendations for a smaller ring of better defenses were largely followed;[112] but Bonilla, in his *Brief compendium of the history of Texas*, 1772, still found it beset by 'an immense number of warlike nations of heathen Indians, who may work its ruin and desolation'.[113] When Spanish Louisiana was ceded to Napoleon in 1800, and sold to the United States of America in 1803, all the authorities of the time were hard put to it to define its boundaries.

1
The Bosque-Larios expedition into Texas, 1675

From the diary of Fernando del Bosque, in a manuscript in the Archivo de la Secretariá de Gobierno del Estado de Coahuila, Mexico

On the first missionary journey from Mexico into what is now Texas, Father Larios, Lieutenant del Bosque, and their troop crossed the Rio Grande. They moved west into buffalo country; the Spaniards were still astonished at the appearance of the buffalo.

I arrived at a very copious and very wide river, with a current more than four hundred varas across, which the Indians said was called Rio del Norte. On its banks it is very pleasing, and it had many fish, such as catfish, piltontes, very large turtles, and eels.

Having travelled northward apparently about four leagues, I arrived at an arroyo between hills, where I found fifty-four adult heathen Indians of the Yorica and Jeapa nations, loaded with tierces of jerked buffalo meat. The meat is very savory. The form of the buffalo is very ugly. Although large, they resemble cows and bulls. Their hair is shaggy. The withers are very high, making them appear humpbacked, and their necks are large. The head is short and very shaggy, so that the wool covers the eyes and prevents them from seeing well. The horns are small and thick, but like those of the bull. The hips and haunches are like those of a hog, and the tail is bare except at the end, where there are long bristles. The hoofs are cloven, and at the knees and from there up to the shoulder there is much bristle-like hair, like he-goats. The females are of the same sort and have four teats. They gaze at the people sidewise like wild hogs, with hair abristle.

Translation used: H. E. Bolton, of 'Autos de la conquista de la Prov^{e} de Coahuila' (manuscript in the Archivo de la Secretariá de Gobierno del Estado de Coahuila, legajo no. 1, Años 1688 á 1736).
Text used: H. E. Bolton (Ed.), Spanish Exploration in the Southwest, 1542-1706, *New York: Scribner, 1916, pp. 296, 298.*

2
The Mendoza-Lopez expedition to the Jumanos, 1684

From the 'Itinerary of Juan Dominguez de Mendoza', in a manuscript in the Archivo General y Publico, Mexico City

This expedition, requested by Sabeata, penetrated much farther eastward than those before. On the (Texan) Colorado River, they built the first tiny Spanish chapel in Texas, in the buffalo country.

We arrived at the said place of San Clemente on the 16th of the month of March. . . . The San Clemente River [Colorado] flows toward the east. The bottom lands of the river are luxuriant with plants bearing nuts, grapes, mulberries, and many groves of plums; with much game, wild hens, and a variety of animals, such as bear, deer, and antelopes, though few, but the number of buffalo is so great that only the divine Majesty, as owner of all, is able to count them. The stay in this place was to await forty-eight nations—not counting those who were present with us, who were sixteen—besides many others whom, through their ambassadors, I was awaiting.

We were in said place, as already stated, from the 16th of March to the 1st of May. Every day the holy sacrifice of the mass was celebrated, for which purpose I built a bastion with two rooms; the one below served as a chapel where they celebrated mass, and they celebrated all the service of Holy Week, singing it, many Christian Indians who were among so many barbarous nations assisting in everything. All those present in our company asked to become Christians. The other room of the bastion served as a safeguard against the aforesaid enemies, because it was on a hill, where it served as great security both for all the camp and for the horses.

Translation used: H. E. Bolton, of 'Alsamiento Gral. de los Indios de Nueva Mexico en 1680' (manuscript in the Archivo General y Publico, Mexico, Provincias Internas, vol. 37).

Text used: H. E. Bolton (Ed.), Spanish Exploration in the Southwest, 1542-1706, *New York: Scribner, 1916, pp. 338, 339.*

3
Joutel describes the country around La Salle's colony on Matagorda Bay, 1685

From Henri Joutel, *Journal Historique.* Manuscript in the Dépôt des Cartes, Plans, et Journaux de la Marine, Paris

Joutel, left in command of the Gulf Coast colony when La Salle made his first two explorations in search of the Mississippi, was a sensitive and accurate observer of the flora and fauna about him in Texas.

We were near the bay of St. Louis and the bank of the river aux Boeufs, on a little hillock, whence we discovered vast and beautiful plains, extending very far to the westward, all level and full of greens, which afford pasture to an infinite number of beeves and other creatures.

Between a little hill and our dwelling, was a sort of marsh, and in it abundance of wild fowl, as curlews, water hens and other sorts. In the marsh there were little pools full of fish. We had also an infinite number of beeves, wild goats, rabbits,

253 Wild turkey, from the *Codex Canadensis*, c. 1700. *Thomas Gilcrease Institute, Tulsa.*

253

254

254 The grandgosier (or pelican); the flamant (or flamingo), from Le Page du Pratz, *Histoire de la Louisiane*, 1758.
The flamingo, without its long legs and down-curved beak, is inaccurately drawn.

255 Tufted duck or hooded morganser; pelican with fish in its mouth; wild swan, from the *Codex Canadensis*, c. 1700. *Thomas Gilcrease Institute, Tulsa.*
Father St Cosme, one of the Jesuit explorers who made the long canoe trip down the Mississippi to visit the Biloxi colony in 1700, wrote of the pelican: 'We found a certain bird, as large as a swan, which has the bill about a foot long, and the throat of extraordinary size, so large in some, they say, that it would hold a bushel of wheat. . . . They say that this bird gets in the current, and opening his large bill [takes the fish] that thrust themselves into his gullet.'

256 Indian customs, from the *Codex Canadensis*, c. 1700. *Thomas Gilcrease Institute, Tulsa.*
33: savage sacrificing to the moon; 34: head of the god of the earth with a worshipper, and a skin cabin with a skin offered as a sacrifice; 35: a baby in its cradle; 36: a child in its hammock; 37: a mortar.

255

turkeys, bustards, geese, swans, fieldfares, plovers, teal, partridges and many other sorts of fowl fit to eat, and among them one called le grand gosier, or the great gullet, because it has a very large one; another as big and fleshy as a pullet, which we called the spatula, because its beak is shaped like one, and the feathers of it being of a pale red, are very beautiful. The river supplied us with abundance of other fishes, whose names we know not. The sea afforded us oysters, eels, trout, a sort of red fishes and others, whose long, sharp and hard beak tore all our nets. We had plenty both of land and sea tortoises, whose eggs served to season our sauces. The land tortoises differ from those of the sea, as being smaller, round, and their shell more beautiful. They hide themselves in holes they find or make in the earth.

There are abundance of creeping vines, and others that run up the bodies and to the tops of trees, which bear plenty of grapes, fleshy and sharp, not to compare to the delicacy of ours in Europe; but we made verjuice of them, which was very good in sauce. Mulberry trees are numerous along the rivers.

Nothing is more beautiful than to behold those vast plains when the blossoms appear. I have observed some that smelt like a tuberose, but the leaf resembles our borage. I have seen primroses having a scent like ours, African gilliflowers, and a sort of purple wind flowers.

Text used: B. F. French (Ed. and trans.), Historical Collections of Louisiana and Florida, *New York, 1846-53, vol. I, 1846, pp. 120, 121, 123.*

256

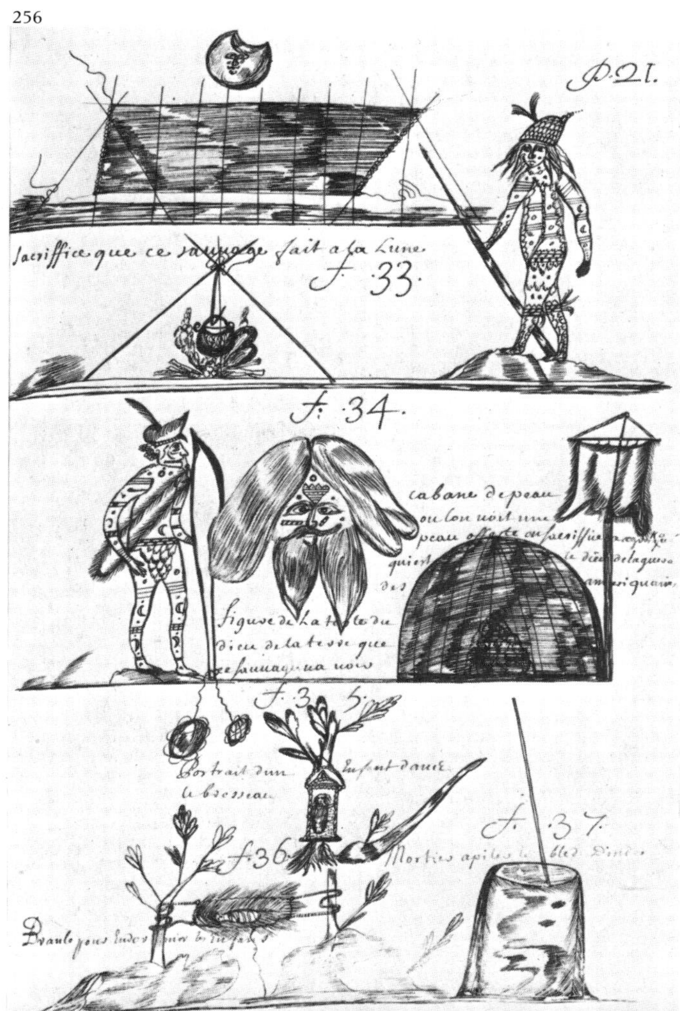

4

Life in the lodges of the Cenis Indians, as Joutel saw it, 1687

From Henri Joutel, *Journal Historique*. Manuscript in Dépôt des Cartes, Plans, et Journaux de la Marine, Paris

After the death of La Salle, the murderers decided to go to the Cenis villages, on the Trinity River, where La Salle and his party had been hospitably received on a former expedition. Joutel was sent ahead with a few others to treat for corn. As always, he observed carefully.

The cottages that are inhabited, are not each of them for a private family, for in some of them there are fifteen or twenty, each of which has its nook or corner, bed and other utensils to itself; but without any partition to separate it from the rest. However, they have nothing in common besides the fire, which is in the midst of the hut, and never goes out. It is made of great trees, the ends whereof are laid together, so that when once lighted, it lasts a long time, and the first comer takes care to keep it up.

The cottages are round at the top, after the manner of a bee-hive, or a rick of hay. Some of them are sixty feet diameter. In order to build them they plant trees as thick as a man's thigh, tall and straight, and placing them in a circle, and joining the tops together from the dome or round top, then they lash and cover them with weeds. When they remove their dwellings, they generally burn the cottages they leave, and build new on the ground they design to inhabit.

257 Savage of the nation of the Onneiothehage, from the *Codex Canadensis*, c. 1700. He smokes tobacco in honor of the sun, whom he adores as his particular god. *Thomas Gilcrease Institute, Tulsa.*

257

Their moveables are some bullocks' hides and goat skins well cured, some mats close wove, wherewith they adorn their huts, and some earthen vessels which they are very skilful at making, and wherein they boil their flesh or roots, or sagamise, which, as has been said, is their pottage. They have also some small baskets made of canes.

Tillage consists in breaking up just the surface of the earth with a sort of wooden instrument, like a little pickaxe, which they make by splitting the end of a thick piece of wood, that serves for a handle, and putting another piece of wood sharp pointed at one end into the slit.

The Indians are generally handsome, but disfigure themselves by making scores or streaks on their faces, from the top of the forehead down the nose to the tip of the chin; which is done by pricking the skin with needles, or other sharp instruments, till it bleeds, whereon they strew fine powder of charcoal, and that sinks in and mixes with the blood within the skin. They also make, after the same manner, the figures of living creatures, of leaves and flowers on their shoulders, thighs, and other parts of their bodies, and paint themselves, as has been said before, with black or red, and sometimes both together.

None of them having any places of worship, ceremonies or prayers, to denote the divine homage, it may be said of them all, that they have no religion, at least those that we saw.

Text used: B. F. French (Ed. and trans.), Historical Collections of Louisiana and Florida, *New York, 1846-53, vol. I, 1846, pp. 148, 149, 151.*

5

Tonty, attempting to rescue La Salle's colony, encounters a great flood, 1690

From Henri de Tonty, Mémoire adressé au Comte de Pontchartrain, 1693

When, in 1689, Tonty finally learned about La Salle's death, he set off to try to reach and aid the colonists left at Matagorda Bay. He reached the Cadodoquis on the Red River, and Naoudiché, farther south; but there, deserted by guides and out of ammunition, he had to turn back. Near the Mississippi, he met a terrible flood.

When our guide was gone I told the Chaganon to take the lead; all he said in answer was, that that was my business; and as I was unable to influence him, I was obliged to act as guide. I directed our course to the southeast, and after about 40 leagues' march, crossing seven rivers, we found the River Coroas. We made a raft to explore the other side of the river, but found there no dry land. We resolved to abandon our horses, as it was impossible to take them on upon account of the great inundation. In the evening, as we were preparing to depart, we saw some savages. We called to them in vain—they ran away, and we were unable to come up with them. Two of their dogs came to us, which, with two of our own, we embarked the next day on our raft. We crossed 50 leagues of flooded country. The water, where it was least deep, reached halfway up the legs; and in all this tract we found only one little island of dry land, where we killed a bear and dried its flesh. It would be difficult to give an idea of the trouble we had to get out of this miserable country, where it rained night and day. We were obliged to sleep on the trunks of two great trees placed together, and to make our fire on

258

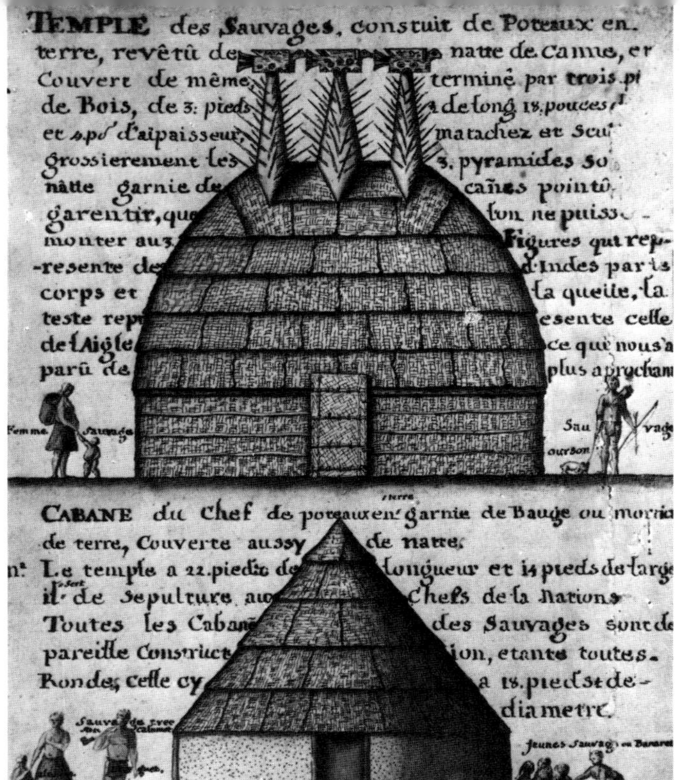

258 Alexandre de Batz. Temple and house of the chief of the Acolapissas, 1732. *Peabody Museum, Harvard University, Bushnell Collection.*
De Batz made these interesting sketches on 15 April 1731 in a village of the 'Colas-Pissas' (Acolapissas) who were said by Pénicaut to have moved in 1718 from the north shore of Lake Pontchartrain to the Mississippi, thirteen leagues above New Orleans. Bienville had reached this friendly tribe, of Choctaw lineage, during his first year of exploration of the coastal lakes.
The small figures of Indians give the scale, and there is interesting detail, such as the bear cub (ourson). Many similarities can be noted between this architecture and that of the round lodges of the Cenis (Assinais, Texas) in present Texas, described by Joutel.

the trees, to eat our dogs, and to carry our baggage across large tracts covered with reeds; in short, I never suffered so much in my life as in this journey to the Mississippi, which we reached on the 11th of July.

Text used: B. F. French (Ed. and trans.), Historical Collections of Louisiana and Florida, *New York, 1846-53, vol. I, 1846, pp. 77, 78.*

6
Iberville enters the Lower Mississippi, 1699

From *Historical Journal; or Narrative of the Expeditions made . . . to colonize Louisiana under . . . M. Pierre Le Moyne d'Iberville, Governor-General.* Manuscript in Office of the Ministère de la Marine et des Colonies, Paris

Iberville anchored his ships off Ship Island, and, with a party of his men, set out in two longboats and two canoes to find and enter the Mississippi.

At this moment we perceived a pass between two banks, which appeared like islands. We saw that the water had changed; tasted, and found it fresh, a circumstance that gave us great consolation in that moment of consternation. Soon after we beheld the thick, muddy water. As we advanced, we saw the passes of the river, three in number, and the current of the stream was such that we could not ascend it without difficulty, although the wind was fair and favorable.

The coast consists of nothing more than two narrow strips of land, about a musket shot in width, having the sea on both sides of the river, which flows between these two strips of land, and frequently overflows them. At four o'clock, after having ascended the river one league and a half, we landed in a thick cane-brake, which grows so tall and thick on both banks of the river, that it is difficult to see across, and it is impossible to pass through without cutting it down. Beyond the canes are impenetrable marshes. The banks are also bordered by trees of prodigious height, which the current of the river draws down to the sea, with their roots and branches. At five leagues from the mouth, it [the river] is not more than a musket-shot wide. There are bushes on each side, especially on the starboard side; as you ascend, the banks appear more and more submerged, the land being scarcely visible. We saw a great quantity of wild game, such as ducks, geese, snipe, teal, bustards, and other birds. We also saw a Mexican wolf, and a

259 Cypress, from Le Page du Pratz, *Histoire de la Louisiane*, 1758.
Very tall cypress trees, growing out of black swamp water, are a conspicuous feature of the American deep South.

260 Sweet gum, or copalm, from Le Page du Pratz, *Histoire de la Louisiane*, 1758.

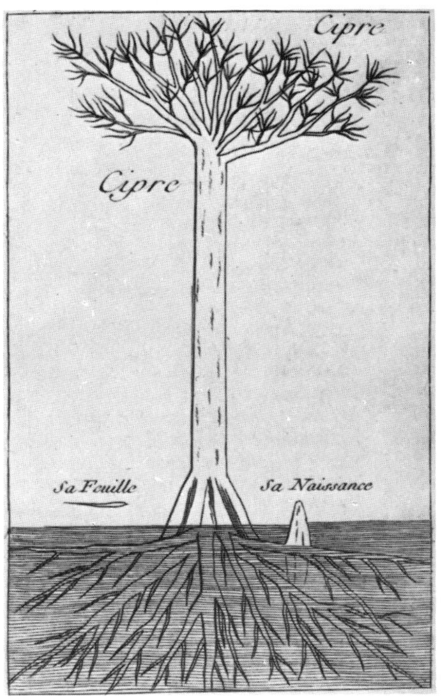

259

260

species of rat [pouched rat] which carried its young in a sack under its belly.

We saw some small canoes, each made from three bundles of cane, bound with thin wooden straps. The Indians make use of these in the chase, in crossing from one side of the river to the other. At six o'clock we landed and encamped. On ascending a tree we could discern the sea at a distance of about a league and a half from us. At this point we found the rapidity of the current stronger than usual.

When Iberville and his party neared the village of the Mongoulachas, the Indians met them with the calumet of peace.

These ceremonies and the feasting continued until six o'clock, at which hour the chief made the young men sing, each one

262

261

263

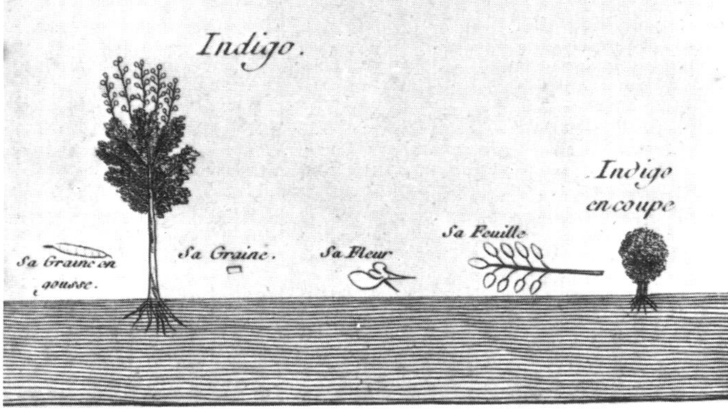

261 Noyer noir, or black walnut, from Father Pierre de Charlevoix, SJ, *Histoire et description generale de la Nouvelle France*, II, opp. p. 49, 1744. This engraving is from the second volume of Father Charlevoix's *Histoire* which contains the *Journal historique d'un voyage fait par ordre du Roi*, a series of letters addressed to the Duchess of Lesdiguières. They give the observations of this very perspicuous Jesuit father, made on his adventurous trip by canoe from Illinois to the mouth of the Mississippi in 1721-2.

262 Sassafras, from De Charlevoix, *Histoire . . . de la Nouvelle France*, II, opp. p. 10, 1744. Sassafras was sought for medicinal purposes by explorers from earliest times.

263 Indigo: plant, seed, flower, leaf, from Le Page du Pratz, *Histoire de la Louisiane*, 1758.

holding in his hand a gourd filled with small grains. They shook them in cadence, which accorded well with their voices; at the end of each song, which is short, they make the most frightful yells; which can be heard at the distance of a league, reverberating through the woods. This ceremony having lasted two hours, the chief bid us adieu, after his manner. We gave him to understand that on the morrow we were going to his village. The Indians then lighted their flambeaux, which consisted of dried reeds tied up in bundles, and stuck in the ground and set on fire, giving out a brilliant light. Four of them began to dance around these lights, clapping their hands and touching together their feet, for about an hour. After this last dance all of them retired with the exception of four or five who remained with us.

Text used: B. F. French (Ed. and trans.), Historical Collections of Louisiana and Florida, *New York, 1846-53, vol. VI, 1875, pp. 55-9, 69, 70.*

7
Father Gravier explains the calumet, 1700

From *Relation . . . du Voyage de R. P. Jacques Gravier de la Compagnie de Jésus en 1700 . . .*; manuscript in the possession of the Society of Jesus, Paris

Father Gravier takes his place among the authors of the famous *Jesuit Relations* as a fearless missionary-explorer, and a sensitive observer. Here he explains the importance to the Indians of the calumet, the pipe of peace, and the dances and ceremonies that attended it. He travelled in 1700 from Illinois to Biloxi and back by canoe, to assist Father du Ru, who came with Iberville.

As I have here mentioned the calumet, you will be pleased to have me tell you something of it here. There is nothing among these Indians more mysterious or commendable. No such honor is paid to the crowns and sceptres of kings as they pay to it. It seems to be the god of peace and war, the arbiter of life and death. To carry and show it enables you to march with assurance amid enemies who in the heat of the combat lay down their arms when it is shown.

There is a calumet for peace and one for war, which are distinguished simply by the colour of the feathers with which they are trimmed. The red is a mark of war; they use it also to settle their disputes, to confirm alliances and to speak to strangers. It is a kind of pipe to smoke tobacco, made of a red stone polished like marble and pierced so that one end serves to receive the tobacco and the other fits on the handle. This is a hollow piece of wood, two feet long, and as thick as an ordinary cane. It is by reason of this that the French have styled it Calumet, corrupting the word *Chalumeau*, because it resembles a pipe, or rather a long flute. It is embellished with the head or neck of various birds, whose plumage is very beautiful. They add also large red or green or other coloured feathers, with which it is all trimmed. They esteem it especially because they regard it as the calumet or pipe of the sun, and in

264 March of the calumet of peace, from Le Page du Pratz, *Histoire de la Louisiane*, 1758.
The ceremony of the calumet, or peace pipe, here drawn as used by the Natchez, was practised in different forms but always with impressive seriousness by all the tribes of the Mississippi Valley.

264

fact they proffer it to him to smoke when they wish to obtain calm, rain or fair weather. They would scruple to bathe in the beginning of hot weather, or to eat new fruits till after they had danced the calumet, that is to say, the chief holds it in his hands singing airs, to which the others respond, dancing and making gestures in time with the sound of certain instruments of the fashion of small drums.

Text used: J. G. Shea (Ed. and trans.), Early Voyages Up and Down the Mississippi, *Albany, 1861, pp. 129, 130.*

8
The expedition of Governor Alarcón into Texas, 1718-19

From Fray Francisco Céliz, untitled diary in Archivo General de la Nación, Mexico City

After the alarm caused by the arrival of St Denys on the Rio Grande, Governor Alarcón was sent with a large expedition to strengthen Spanish Texas against the French, in a terribly rainy season. The diarist of his expedition displays something rare in the annals of the explorers, a sense of humor. They reached a ford on a river near New Braunfels, Texas.

It so happened that, twenty-four buzzards having come to tarry close to where we were stopping, the governor asked the chaplain, 'Father, what are those birds looking for?' To which the father replied, 'They may have come to make happy over the funeral rites of somebody present,' at which the anguish was even greater, even before entering the water. He began, therefore to cross with great difficulty, and the greatest fatality would have befallen us that can be imagined had not God and the most holy Virgin extended the arms of their omnipotence and mercy to protect and favor the governor against the extremely dangerous situation in which he found himself. He, having started to cross on the strongest horse that could be found, carried on the haunches the sergeant of the company. Upon arriving at the opposite bank, he reined the horse back, and, the current catching its haunches, it was swept downstream with both riders submerged and grasping the horse, for about half the distance of a musket-shot. At this place they came up still holding on to the horse, and, going down again, they lost their grasp on the horse, and the water carried them submerged for more than another half the distance of a musket-shot where they again arose. The anxiety they experienced may well be imagined, especially since the governor, who was dressed, did not know how to swim. And, although the said sergeant knew how to swim well, this would not have enabled him to rescue himself, because of the great force of the water, if here God had not performed a miracle through the intercession of His most pure Mother who provided them with two savin [cypress] branches to which they held on, and from there, because of the great depth, they were rescued by ropes. After this miraculous occurrence, I have asked the governor several times about the case, and he has always assured me that he does not know how he went [down the stream], whether under the water or over the water. The truth is that those who saw him say that he went downstream motionless, all of which proves that it was entirely a miracle, because the rescue could not have been attributed to natural causes, especially when the horse with the saddle nevermore turned up and the governor lost the buttons off his pants, thus forming a sort of ball and chain on his feet. [For all of this] we thank unceasingly only God and His most holy Mother, and, moreover, we invoke their favor in the furtherance of this expedition and [place the] conquest under their charge. Furthermore, although [the governor] carried in his pocket a small silver box with the rosary and the prayer book in which the most holy Virgin is praised, they not only did not fall into the water when his pants came down, but the prayer book did not even get wet.

265

266

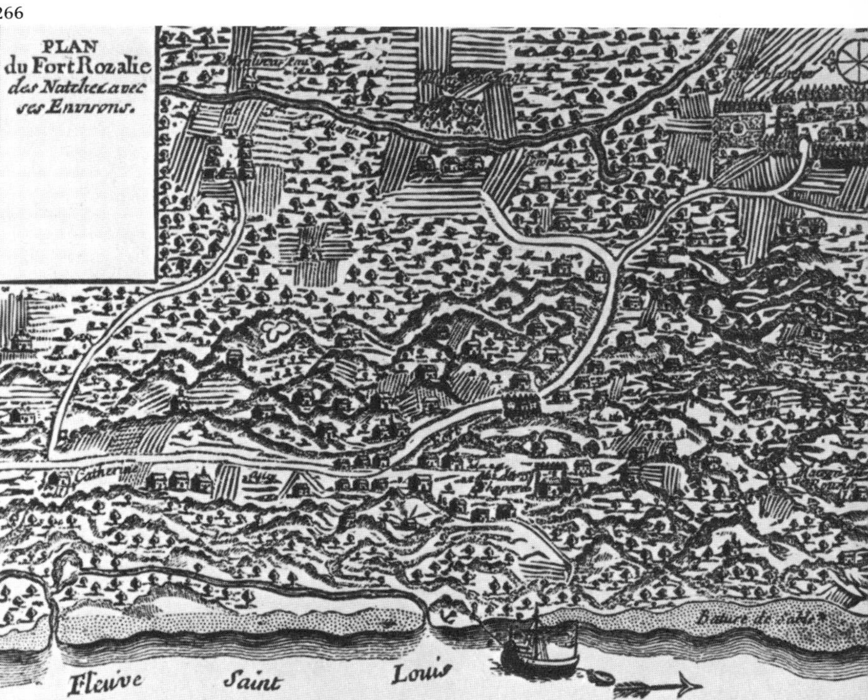

265 Alexandre de Batz. Savages of several nations, 1735. *Peabody Museum, Harvard University, Bushnell Collection.*
Illinois, Fox (Reynards) and Atakapa Indians. The hand of the chief at the left is resting on the head of a domesticated whooping crane. The two barrels contain candle tallow; the smaller box, bear oil.

266 Plan of Fort Rozalie of the Natchez with its surrounding territory, from Dumont de Montigny, *Mémoires*, II, p. 94. Reproduced in J. Winsor, *Narrative and critical history of America*, V, p. 47, 1884-9.
This fort was built in 1716 after the first Natchez war. Bienville insisted that the Indians build it themselves, on their own territory. The Natchez lands were high and fertile, and popular with colonists. Le Page du Pratz had his concession here.

Dumont de Montigny was a lieutenant stationed at Fort Rozalie at the time of the second Natchez uprising; his wife was captured and enslaved by the Natchez.

This same day we traveled about six leagues to a high hill where we stopped. On the 17th, we arrived at the river of San Antonio, where the villa named Bexar stands.

On the 22d, we continued our journey in the direction of southeast, and at about seven leagues we stopped to rest. It happened that on this day, from noon until the evening prayers, the governor lay on a large snake at this place, without the reptile having moved, in spite of its known ferocity. This occurrence was taken to be almost a miracle.

Text used: F. L. Hoffmann (Ed. and trans.), Diary of the Alarcón Expedition into Texas, 1718-1719, *Quivira Society Publications, vol. V, Los Angeles, 1935, pp. 53, 54, 55, 64.*

267 La Harpe. 'Carte Nouvelle de la Partie de L'Oüest de la Louisianne' [1720]. *Manuscript Division, Library of Congress, Washington DC.*
Bénard de la Harpe shows his explorations from the command post that he built at Natchitoches on the Red River, together with other contemporary French expeditions in the early eighteenth century west and northwest of the Mississippi. He delineates his trips up the Red River, to the Osage Indians on the Arkansas, and to the Wabash, where he found Indian villages with '4000 persons'. He shows the routes of St Denys to the Rio Grande in 1717, of Du Tisné to the upper tributaries of the Arkansas in 1719, and of Villasur's ill-fated Spanish expedition in 1720. La Harpe's own final journey to the Padoucas before his return to France in 1723 came after he drew this map, although he notes the territory they occupy.

9
La Harpe travels northwest into Oklahoma, 1719

From La Harpe, *Journal Historique concernant l'établissément des Français à la Louisiane,* 1723. Copy of manuscript in library of the American Philosophical Society, Philadelphia

Bénard de la Harpe, a distinguished French officer and colonist, arrived in Louisiana in 1718. He built the fort at Natchitoches, and settled and fortified his outpost among the Nassonites, where he traded with both Indians and Spanish. In 1719 he undertook the northwestern exploration into southern Oklahoma described here.

M. de la Harpe believed it to be the interest of the company to explore the country which had been pointed out to him in the northwest, and by this means to effect an entrance, by treating with the Indians, into New Mexico.

For this purpose he took with him an escort of two officers, three soldiers, two negroes, and several Indians who spoke the language of the country, and set out on the 11th August. On the 21st he travelled forty-nine leagues through a fine

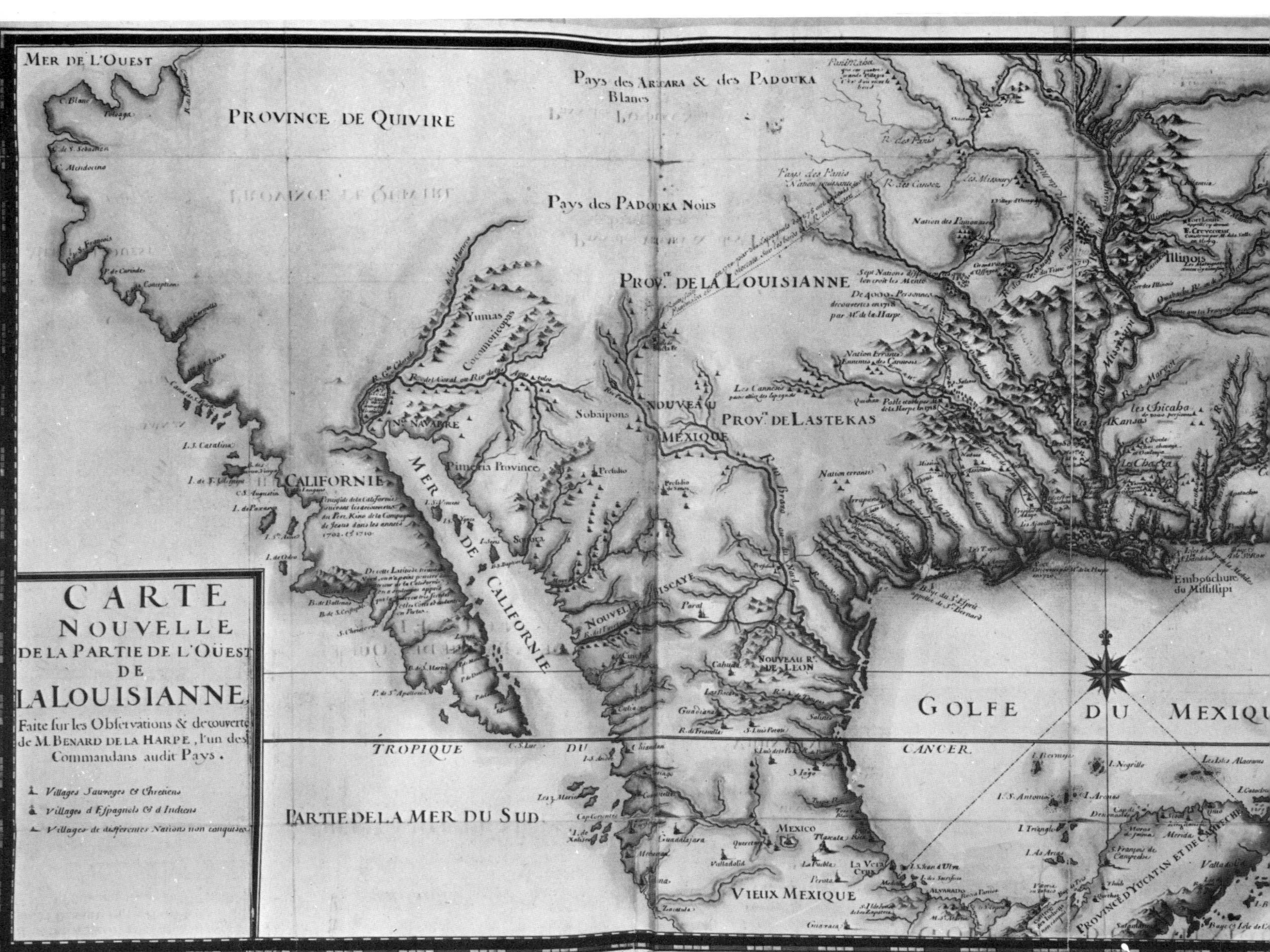

267

268

269

country, with sloping hills and prairies, abounding in game. He met a party of Natsoo Indians who had been on a hunting expedition, and had killed forty-six buffaloes and cows. On the 22d he passed several prairies, and a little river which emptied into Red River. He then entered into an extensive prairie, surrounded by mountains. On the 26th he had gone eighteen leagues further, when he met with a party of Osage Indians who seemed disposed to attack him, but yet suffered him to pass on. On the 27th he travelled six leagues further, over a beautiful prairie country filled with deer and buffalo, and entered the mountains, where he found a number of Indian huts. Travelling six leagues further he met with a party of Kansas, who were encamped on the banks of the Ouachita with forty warriors, and going in pursuit of the Tancaros. On the 28th he passed a beautiful prairie, interspersed with hills, and a large herd of buffaloes followed by a pack of wolves as large as those of France. On the 29th he travelled three leagues further, to a branch of the Ouachita river, which had about two feet of water in it. On its banks we met a party of Nacodoches, who were occupied in smoking meat. On the 31st he travelled six leagues further, to a river which is a branch of the Arkansas. On the 2d September he advanced fifteen leagues through prairies and over hills, when he came to several lead mines. Six leagues further on he met six chiefs of nations who had come to meet him near a village called Imaham, lat. 37° 45′, and to assure him of their friendship.

Text used: B. F. French (Ed. and trans.), Historical Collections of Louisiana and Florida, *New York, 1846-53, vol. III, 1851, p. 73.*

270

268-70 Hand-colored plates from the luxurious 1780 edition of Baron Nicolas-Joseph Jacquin's *Selectarum Stirpium Americanarum Historia.*

268 *Portlandia grandiflora.* This is a fifteen-foot shrub which Jacquin saw in Jamaica, but which also grows in southern North America.

269 *Epidendrum coccineum.* Tree orchid, plentiful in Florida.

270 *Plumeria alba.* The common name for this tree, with its beautiful, very fragrant, white flowers, is *frangipani.* It grows in Florida.

10
Le Page du Pratz lives among the Natchez and observes the country, 1718-23

From Le Page du Pratz, *Histoire de la Louisiane . . .*, Paris, 1758. 3 vols

A tropical tornado was a terrifying experience.

Some time after my return from New Orleans to the Natchez, towards the month of March 1722, a phenomenon happened, which frightened the whole province. Every morning, for eight days running, a hollow noise, somewhat loud, was heard to descend from the East, and that with an incredible quickness; and tho' the noise seemed to bear on the water, yet without agitating it, or discovering any more wind on the river than before. This frightful noise was only the prelude of a most violent tempest. The hurricane, the most furious ever felt in the province, lasted three days. But in the places, where the force or height of the hurricane passed, it overturned everything in its way, which was an extent of a large quarter of a league broad; so that one would take it for an avenue made on purpose, the place where it passed being entirely laid flat, whilst everything stood upright on each side. The largest trees were torn up by the roots, and their branches broken to pieces and laid flat to the earth, as were also the reeds of the woods. In the meadows, the grass itself, which was then but six inches high, and which is very fine, could not escape, but was trampled, faded, and laid quite flat to the earth.

271

The Stung Serpent, highly honored by the Natchez, explained to Le Page du Pratz the Indian point of view.

'Why', continued he, with an air of displeasure, 'did the French come into our country? We did not go to seek them: They asked for land of us, because their country was too little for all the men that were in it. We told them, they might take land where they pleased, there was enough for them and for us; that it was good, the same sun should enlighten us both, and that we should walk as friends, in the same path; and that we would give them of our provisions, assist them to build, and to labour in their fields. We have done so; is not this true? What occasion, then, had we for Frenchmen? Before they came, did we not live better than we do, seeing we deprive ourselves of a part of our corn, our game, and fish, to give a part to them? In what respect, then, had we occasion for them? Was it for their guns? The bows and arrows, which we used, were sufficient to make us live well. Was it for their white, blue, and red blankets? We can do well enough with buffalo skins, which are warmer; our women wrought feather-blankets for the winter, and mulberry-mantles for the summer; which indeed were not so beautiful; but our women were more laborious and less vain than they are now. In fine, before the arrival of the French we lived like men who can be satisfied with what they have; whereas at this day we are like slaves, who are not suffered to do as they please.'

To this unexpected discourse I know not what answer another would have made; but I frankly own, that if at my first address he seemed to be confused, I really was so in my turn.

A sample of Le Page du Pratz's careful description of Louisiana flora is his account of the Spanish moss, still prevalent today.

The other excrescence is commonly found upon trees near the banks of rivers and lakes. It is called Spanish beard, which name was given it by the natives, who, when the Spaniards first appeared in their country about 240 years ago, were greatly surprised at their mustachios and beards. This excrescence appears like a bunch of hair hanging from the large branches of trees, and might at first be easily mistaken for an old perruque, especially when it is dancing with the wind. As the first settlers of Louisiana used only mud walls for their houses, they commonly mixed it with the mud for strengthening the building. When gathered it is a grey colour, but when it is dry its bark falls off, and discovers black fila-

271 Death and convoy of the Stung Serpent of the Natchez, from Le Page du Pratz, *Histoire de la Louisiane*, 1758.
The Stung Serpent, a high-ranking noble among the Natchez, was a friend of Le Page du Pratz, who reported his conversation with respect. In this plate is shown the winding route by which he is carried to the temple after death, and the victims about to be strangled who will accompany him on his journey to another world. This barbarous custom of the admirable Natchez horrified the French, who tried vainly to dissuade them.

272 Devin. Map of the coast of Louisiana, c. 1720. *Bibliothèque Nationale, Paris, No. 8802.*
In 1719 and 1720 Devin made a detailed survey of the coast from the Bay of St Louis (Matagorda Bay) to St Joseph Bay and Apalachicola River in west Florida, with the soundings, shoals and reefs. The eastern part only of the map is here reproduced.

273 De Crenay. 'Carte De partie de la Louisianne', 1733. *Archives Nationales, Section outre-mer, Paris, DFC Louisiane 1A.*
Baron de Crenay, royal lieutenant and commandant at Mobile, founded Fort Rozalie in 1731 and traversed many of the trails shown on this map in counter-moves against the attempts of English agents and traders to disrupt and destroy the French tribal alliances. Of primary importance to the French system was the continued loyalty of the Choctaws. The detailed information concerning the location of Indian villages and of trading paths covers most of modern Mississippi and Alabama.

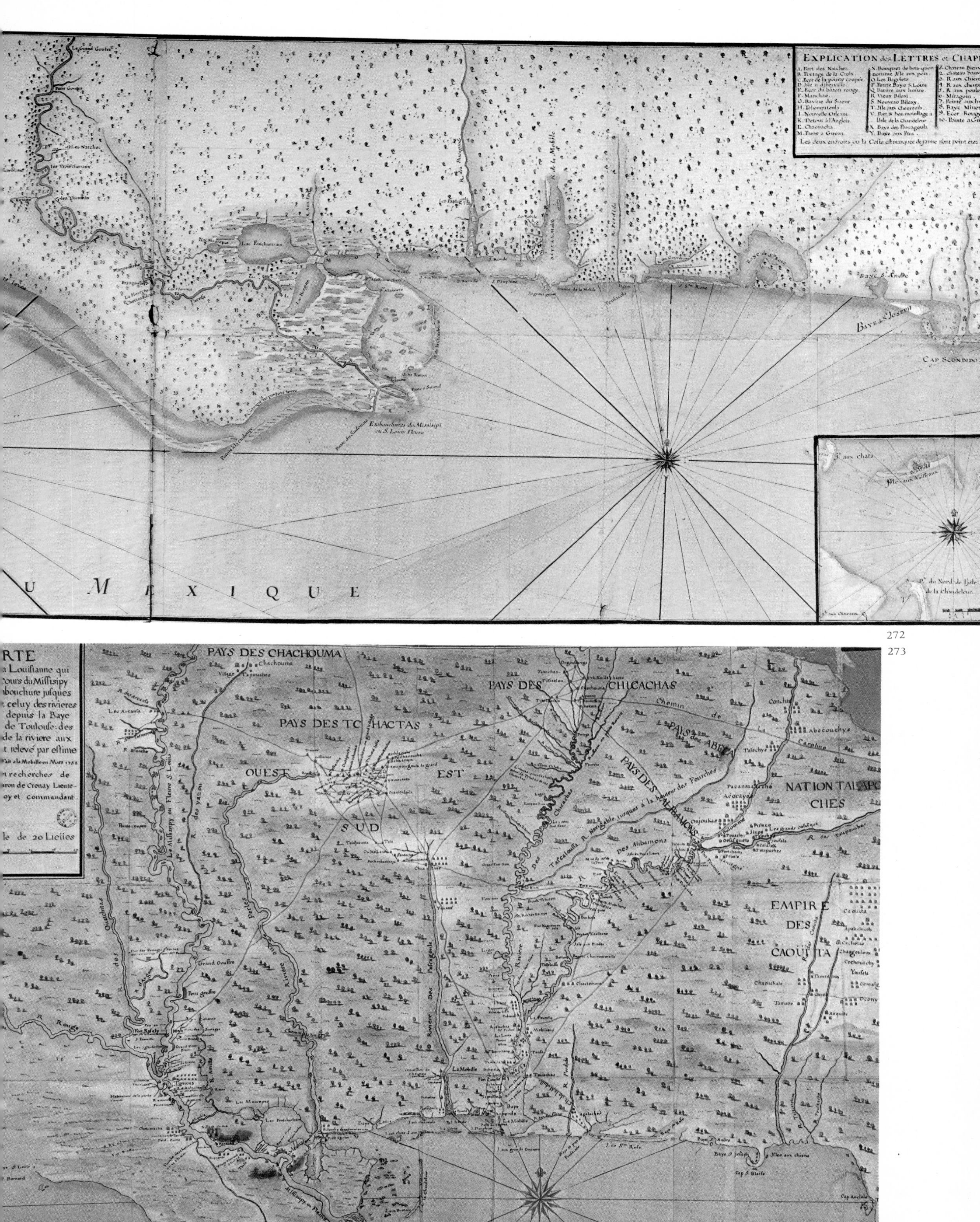
EXPLICATION des LETTRES et CHAPITRE
A. Fort des Natchez.
B. Portage de la Croix.
C. Ecor de la pointe coupée
D. Isle a d'Iberville.
E. Ecor du bâton rouge.
F. Manchac.
G. Ravine du Sueur.
H. Tchoupitoula.
I. Nouvelle Orleans.
K. Detour à l'Anglois.
L. Chaouacha.
M. Passe a Guyon.
N. Bouquet de bois qu'on nomme Isle aux pois.
O. Les Rigolets
P. Petite Baye S. Louis
Q. Bature aux huitre.
R. Vieux Biloxi.
S. Nouveau Biloxy.
T. Isle aux Chevreuils.
V. Port & bon mouillage a Isle de la Chandeleur
X. Baye des Pascagoula
Y. Baye aux Pins.
Z. Chateau Bienville
2. chateau Sauvage
3. R. aux Chiens.
4. R. aux chevreuils
5. R. aux poules.
6. Miragoin.
7. Pointe aux huitres.
8. Baye Minet.
9. Ecor Rouge.
10. Pointe a Guillory.
Les deux endroits ou la Coste est marquée de jaune n'ont point étez levez
Lac Pontchartrain
Embouchures du Missisipi ou S. Louis Fleuve
BAYE de St JOSEPH
CAP SCONDIDO
U MEXIQUE
PAYS DES CHACHOUMA
PAYS DES CHICACHAS
PAYS DES TCHACTAS
OUEST
EST
SUD
PAYS des ABEKA
PAYS DES ALIBAMONS
NATION TALAPO CHES
EMPIRE DES CAOUITA
LFE DU
MEXIQUE

274

275

276 277

ments as long and as strong as the hairs of a horse's tail. I dressed some of it for stuffing a mattress, by first laying it up in a heap to make it part with the bark, and afterwards beating it to take off some small branches that resemble so many little hooks. It is affirmed by some to be incorruptible: I myself have seen of it under old rotten trees that was perfectly fresh and strong.

Translation used: Le Page du Pratz, The History of Louisiana, *(no trans. or ed. given), London, 1763, pp. 55, 56, 74, 75, 37, 38.*

274-5 Original paintings of birds which formed the basis for the splendid plates in George Edwards, *A natural history of birds*, III, 1750. *British Museum, London.*
The two birds represented here and in plates 291-3 were drawn from specimens brought home from Hudson Bay by James Isham who, as Edwards explained in the text: 'has obliged me extremely by furnishing me with more than thirty different Species of Birds, of which we have hitherto had little or no Knowledge, the far greatest Part of them being Non-descripts . . . Mr. Isham has been emply'd for many Years in the Service of the Hudson's-Bay Company, and has, for some Years past, been Governor under them at different Times, of several of their Forts and Settlements in the most Northern habitable Parts of America; where at his leisure Times, his commendable Curiosity led him to make a Collection of all the Beasts, Birds, and Fishes of those Countries, as well as the Habits, Toys and Utensils of the native Americans. The Furs of the Beasts, and the Skins of the Birds were stuffed, and preserved very clean and perfect, and brought to London in the Year 1745.'

274 'The Ash-colour'd Heron from North-America': possibly the Sandhill Crane, *Crus canadensis tabida* (Peters).

275 'The Blue-Winged Goose': probably the lesser snow goose, *Chen caerulescens caerulescens* (Linnaeus). 'This Bird was brought from Hudson's-Bay by Mr. Isham, and I believe, hath never been described. It is there a Bird of Passage, continuing in that Country so long as the Waters are unfrozen, and returning into Southern Countries when the Frost shuts up its Subsistance. My Friend, Mr. Light [another Hudson's Bay Company factor] has told me, there is a Goose which comes in summer to Hudson's Bay, having its Forehead as it were scorched with Heat, and that the Natives firmly believe, that these Geese to avoid the Winter's Cold, fly toward the Sun, and approach so near that it singes its Forehead against his Orb. It is hard to convince these Savages that there are Climates on this Earth warmer than their own, to which Birds may fly for Food and Shelter during their rigid Winters. The above described, I think, must be the Bird of which the Natives hold this Opinion.'

276-7 Two engravings from Le Page du Pratz, *Histoire de la Louisiane*, 1758, illustrating his views on the contentment of the Indians (before the coming of the Europeans) and the thoughtful and gentle manner in which the Natchez brought up their children.

278 Plan of the fort; prisoner on the fire-frame; scalping scene, from Le Page du Pratz, *Histoire de la Louisiane*, 1758.
Cruelty to prisoners, which the French deplored among the river tribes, was found by the Spanish in extreme forms among the dreaded Apaches.

11
Lafora describes the Apaches and the province of Texas, as he and Rubí make the last Spanish inspection, 1766-8

From Nicolas de la Fora, *The Frontiers of New Spain*. Diary of expedition with Marqués de Rubí, 1766-68. Mss in Madrid, Mexico City, partial one in Bancroft Library

With its fierce climate, its vast stretches of impenetrable forest, and its powerful and hostile Indians, La Fora could see little hope for Spanish Texas, even after two hundred years of occupation.

The temperature of this country ranges to extremes of heat and cold. The rivers and arroyos which I have mentioned in the diary are impassable when it rains. This is the reason why the immense distance between San Antonio de Béjar and the vicinity of Nacogdoches is inhabited during the winter only by numberless bear, coyote, deer, and bison. Nor can many birds live there, with the exception of wild turkeys which travel in flocks and many owls, whose cry suits perfectly the lugubrious nature of the country. The unending forest of pine, live-oak, and oak makes it more dismal. The trees are so tall and thick that in some places it is difficult to see the sky.

278

Moreover, there are immense numbers of walnut, mulberry, plum, chestnut, and medlar trees which offer a supply of wild fruit to travelers.

The Apaches are a single nation, but are under different names. These groups differ little in language and not at all in their arms which are bows and arrows. Neither do they differ in the extreme cruelty toward the conquered. They tear off their living flesh and eat it. They shoot arrows into them and, in short, inflict every imaginable cruelty upon them. They are extremely indolent and plant little or nothing. Thus they are compelled to steal their food.

The Apaches habitually go naked, with only a breechclout. When they are going to war they paint their bodies and faces with many different colors made from several kinds of herbs. They call this 'painting red'.

To the shame and dishonor of the Spaniards, the provinces of Coahuila and Texas suffer daily at the hands of the Apaches. They receive from them a thousand injuries, which are gradually bringing their unhappy subjects to ruin.

Text used: Nicolas de la Fora, The Frontiers of New Spain, 1766-1768. *Lawrence Kinnaird (Ed. and trans.), Quivira Society Publications, vol. XIII, Berkeley, California, 1958.*
(Reprint used: New York, 1967), vol. I, pp. 79, 80, 184, 185.

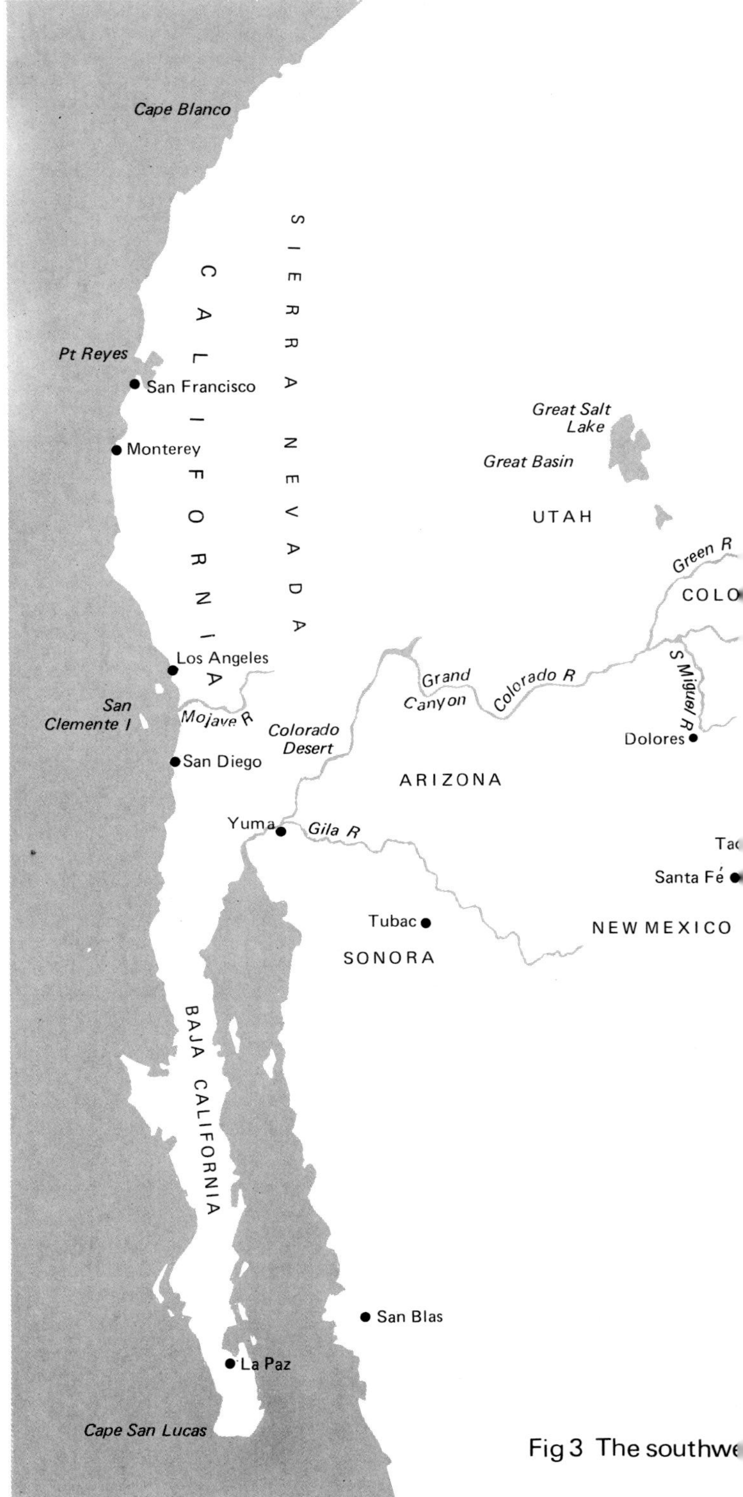

Fig 3 The southwe

6 THE FUR TRADE AND EXPLORATION: NORTH TO THE ARCTIC AND WEST TO THE ROCKIES

1 Discovery and trade in Hudson Bay, 1660-1713

While on the eastern seaboard and more southerly areas of North America the task of exploration and settlement proceeded in a steady rather than spectacular fashion, far away to the north and northwest Europeans were making lengthy probes of continental dimensions. As in Champlain's day these explorations were closely associated with the demands of the fur trade, and to a lesser extent with the continuing hope that a passage might yet be found to the western ocean. During their perilous search in the sixteenth century for a navigable sea route through the North American continent to Asia, European seamen had discovered the 'mighty overfall' of Hudson Strait, which they confidently assumed was the gateway to the Pacific. The detailed explorations of the early seventeenth century banished these hopes as a succession of expeditions forced their way through the strait and into the great bay beyond, only to find their path westward barred by an icebound coast. Nor did the disappointed explorers find compensation in commercial benefits; Hudson Bay and its hinterland appeared a desolate, uninhabited wilderness, and after the voyages of Foxe and James in 1631-2 no ship from Europe passed through Hudson Strait for almost forty years.

The first gradual appreciation of the importance of Hudson Bay came from the French in Canada, who hesitantly identified the sea to the north of which their Indian traders spoke with the bay discovered and then abandoned by English explorers. As the French *coureurs de bois*, notably Radisson and Groseilliers (see Chapter 1), travelled among the Indians west of the St Lawrence they heard more about the source of many of the furs brought down to the French posts. The Huron traders reported that they received their beaver from the 'Christinos' or Cree Indians, who lived near 'the Bay of the North Sea'. After the fashion of all good traders, Radisson and Groseilliers determined to bypass the middlemen and trade direct with the Cree. These Algonkian Indians, 'the best huntsmen of all America' Radisson later described them, were considered by both French and English to be among the most cooperative, intelligent and physically attractive of the Indian peoples of the northeast. They lived in the hinterland of James Bay, extended east as far as Lake Mistassini, and to the west were pushing along the southwestern shores of Hudson Bay, past the Nelson and Churchill river systems into northern Saskatchewan and the plains country. Radisson and Groseilliers returned from their westward wanderings which took them to Lake Superior in 1659-60 (though probably not to Hudson Bay itself, as Radisson asserted) with a splendid haul of furs (see selection 1). Radisson reported the excited reaction of the fur merchants in Quebec:

'In which country have you been? From whence do you come? For wee never saw the like. From whence did come such excellent castors? Since your arrival is come into our magazine near 60,000 pounds tournois [gold coin] of that filthy merchandize which will be prized like gold in France. Them were the very words they said to me.'[1]

279

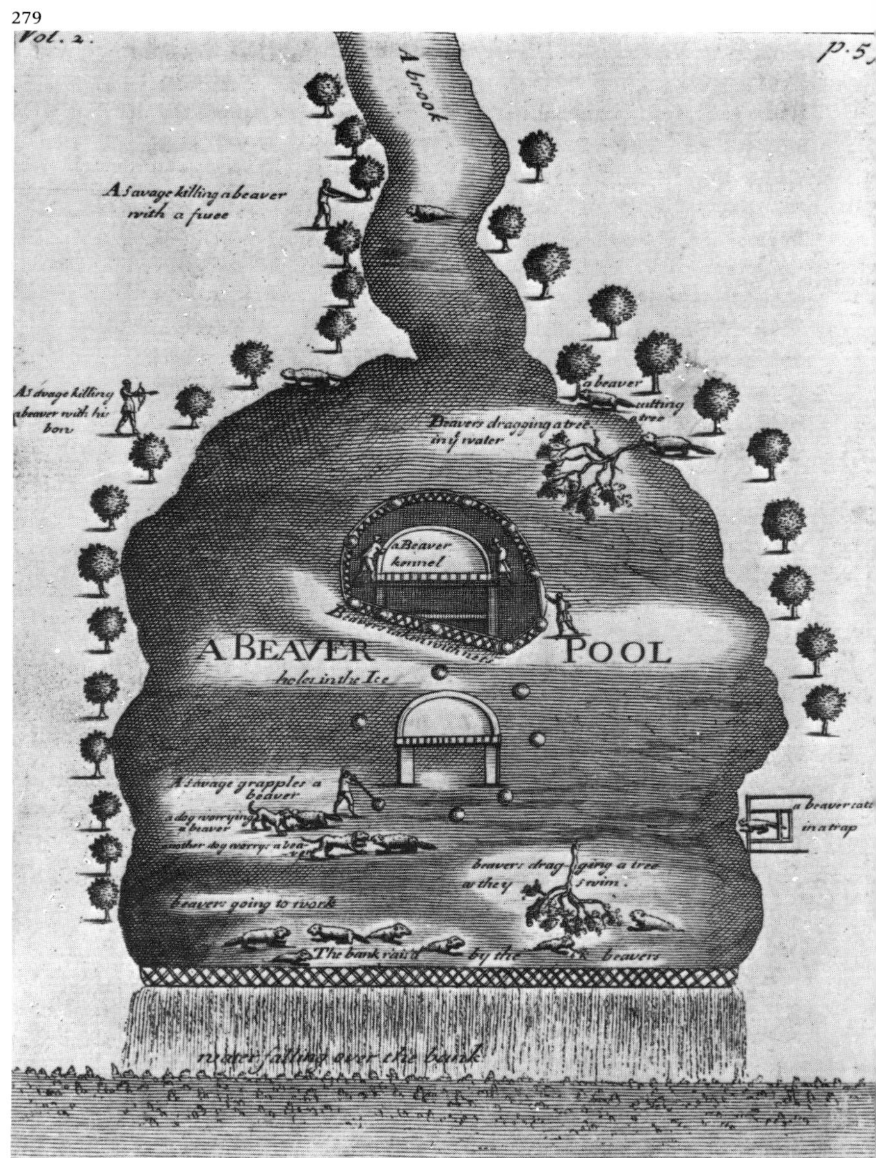

279 Beavers, from Lahontan, *New voyages*, 1703.
Lahontan shows the different methods of hunting beaver: by traps, with nets stretched over holes in the ice, by shooting. Another method, not depicted here, was 'by making a great hole under their Banks, by which they drain all the Water out of their Lakes, and then the Beavers being left on dry Ground the Savages kill them . . .'

Radisson and Groseilliers brought back more than a cargo of fine furs; they returned with a revolutionary concept of the future of the northern fur trade. Their discovery that the real center of the Indian trade lay far beyond Lake Superior convinced them that the most direct way to bring furs from the country of the Crees was not by the long and tortuous canoe route to the St Lawrence, but by the much shorter carry down to the shores of Hudson Bay, and then out by

280

281

281 The Hudson's Bay Company's charter of 1670 begins with this initial surrounding the miniature of Charles II, by whom it was granted. *Hudson's Bay Company Archives.*

280 Indian canoes, from P. Lafitau, *Moeurs des sauvages Ameriquains,* 1724.

282 Wreck of the *Pélican* off Nelson River, Hudson Bay, in 1697, from Bacqueville de la Potherie, *Histoire de l'Amérique Septentrionale,* 1722. The survivors from the French vessel landed a few miles from the Hudson's Bay Company's York Fort.

283 The French attack on York Fort, 1697, from La Potherie, *Histoire,* 1722. Note the French mortar bombs in mid-air, and the Canadian skirmishers (D). After a day's rather perfunctory bombardment the fort surrendered, and was retained by the French until 1714.

ocean-going ships. In their proposals lay the origin of the English Hudson's Bay Company, and of a rivalry between the St Lawrence and Hudson Bay approaches to the fur country of the west which was to last 150 years, and eventually take the competing traders to the Pacific in their quest for furs. For these ideas the two men found little enthusiasm in New or Old France. The reaction of French officialdom at Quebec was frosty disapproval of their unauthorized venture of 1659–60, while the failure of expeditions to reach Hudson Bay from the St Lawrence proved the difficulty of the overland route. The Jesuit Father De Quen had seen Lake St John on the Saguenay in 1647, and in 1661 Fathers Dablon and

2

283

Druillettes reached Lake Necouba in an attempt to find a route from Tadoussac to Hudson Bay; but when they turned back they were only halfway to their destination across some of the most difficult country the French had yet encountered. Nor was the task made easier by the reluctance of the dominant Montagnais Indians to let Frenchmen through to make direct contact with the tribes farther north.

Frustrated and resentful, Radisson and Groseilliers turned to England. They arrived in London in 1665 claiming that they had passed through Hudson Bay to the South Sea, and returned, all within a matter of weeks. More credible than this nonsense was their detailed analysis of the potentialities of the northern fur trade, and in 1668 the *Nonsuch* ketch sailed for Hudson Bay, financed by a consortium of businessmen and courtiers, and carrying Groseilliers on board. Discovery, settlement, minerals and furs were all mentioned in the instructions, but the last clearly predominated. Whereas the captains were vaguely advised 'to have in yor. thoughts the discovery of the Passage into the South Sea and to attempt it as occasion shall offer', they were under firm orders to sail 'to such place as Mr. Gooseberry [sic] and Mr. Radisson shall direct . . . in ordr. to trade with the Indyans there.'[2] The appointed place turned out to be Rupert River in James Bay, the southernmost part of Hudson Bay, or the 'Bottom of the Bay' as it was to become known—and there the vessel wintered. Beaver was plentiful, it was reported on the expedition's return, and in 1670 some of the original subscribers, together with other investors, were granted a royal charter which incorporated them as the Hudson's Bay Company. The new company was given a monopoly of commercial and governmental rights over the seas, straits and lands within the entrance of Hudson Strait—a grant which since no specific boundaries were defined was apparently limitless. The company established additional posts at the mouths of Moose River and Albany River, and in 1682 built York Fort, farther northwest at Port Nelson near the mouth of the Nelson and Hayes rivers. Here for the first time it moved outside the James Bay catchment area to tap the rich fur trade of the west whose potentialities Radisson and Groseilliers had glimpsed many years before. Already operations had settled into a routine in which the company kept permanent garrisons at the Bayside posts, which were visited each summer by the Indians of the interior with their canoes loaded with furs, and by annual ships from England which came through the Strait as the ice cleared.

In Canada the French had from the beginning shown a nervous concern about these activities, and in 1671 a party led by Paul Denis, Sieur de Saint-Simon, and including the Jesuit Father Albanel, at last succeeded in making the arduous overland journey from the St Lawrence to James Bay by way of the Saguenay River and Lake Mistassini. It took two summers to cover the relatively short distance, and Albanel's report illustrated the difficulties of the journey even for a small party travelling light (see selection 2). In 1674 and 1679 the journey was made again, on the second occasion by the Mississippi explorer Louis Jolliet who arrived at the Bay 'after having travelled 343 leagues because of detours, although the distance is only 160 leagues in a straight line, and after 127 portages, some long and some short. . . .'[3] Behind these reconnaissance probes lay the growing French realization that the Bay posts were not only attracting Indians who had previously traded with Canada, but that they were better placed to bring in the fine coat beaver of the north, so much in demand by the hatters of Europe. A decision by French mercantile interests to challenge the English position in Hudson Bay was made easier by the worsening relations in Europe between the French and English governments; and in 1683 there began in Hudson Bay hostilities which lasted, in sporadic fashion, for almost thirty years. Posts were attacked, captured and restored, land and sea expeditions were mounted, diplomatic arguments waxed fierce—and the fur trade suffered.

During this long period of war and uncertainty it is not surprising that the English company devoted few of its limited resources to exploration of the interior. Yet it was in 1690–2 that one of the most remarkable journeys in North America by an English explorer was made, a journey whose

284 Encounter in Hudson Strait between one of D'Iberville's ships and a band of Eskimos, from La Potherie, *Histoire*, 1722. Under figure C the French, drawing on their knowledge of Canadian Indian practice, are presenting the Eskimos with a calumet or pipe of peace.

285 A French Canadian of D'Iberville's force of 1697 prepared for winter warfare, from La Potherie, *Histoire*, 1722.

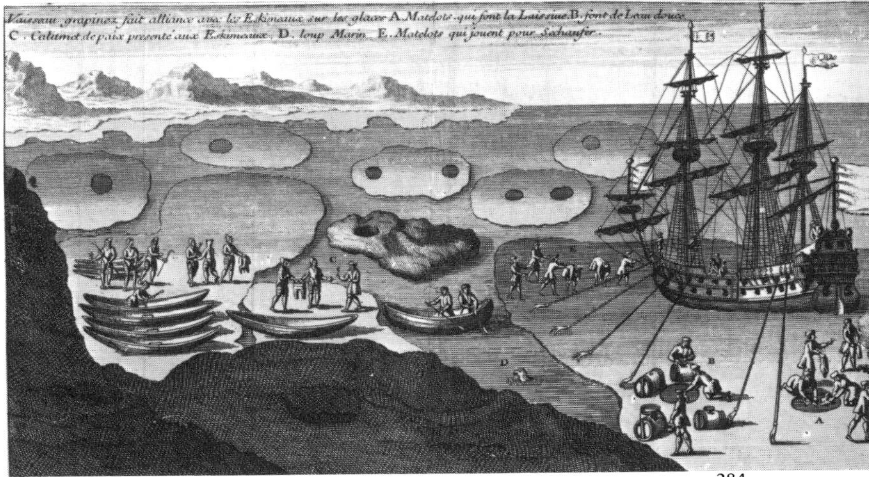

284

285

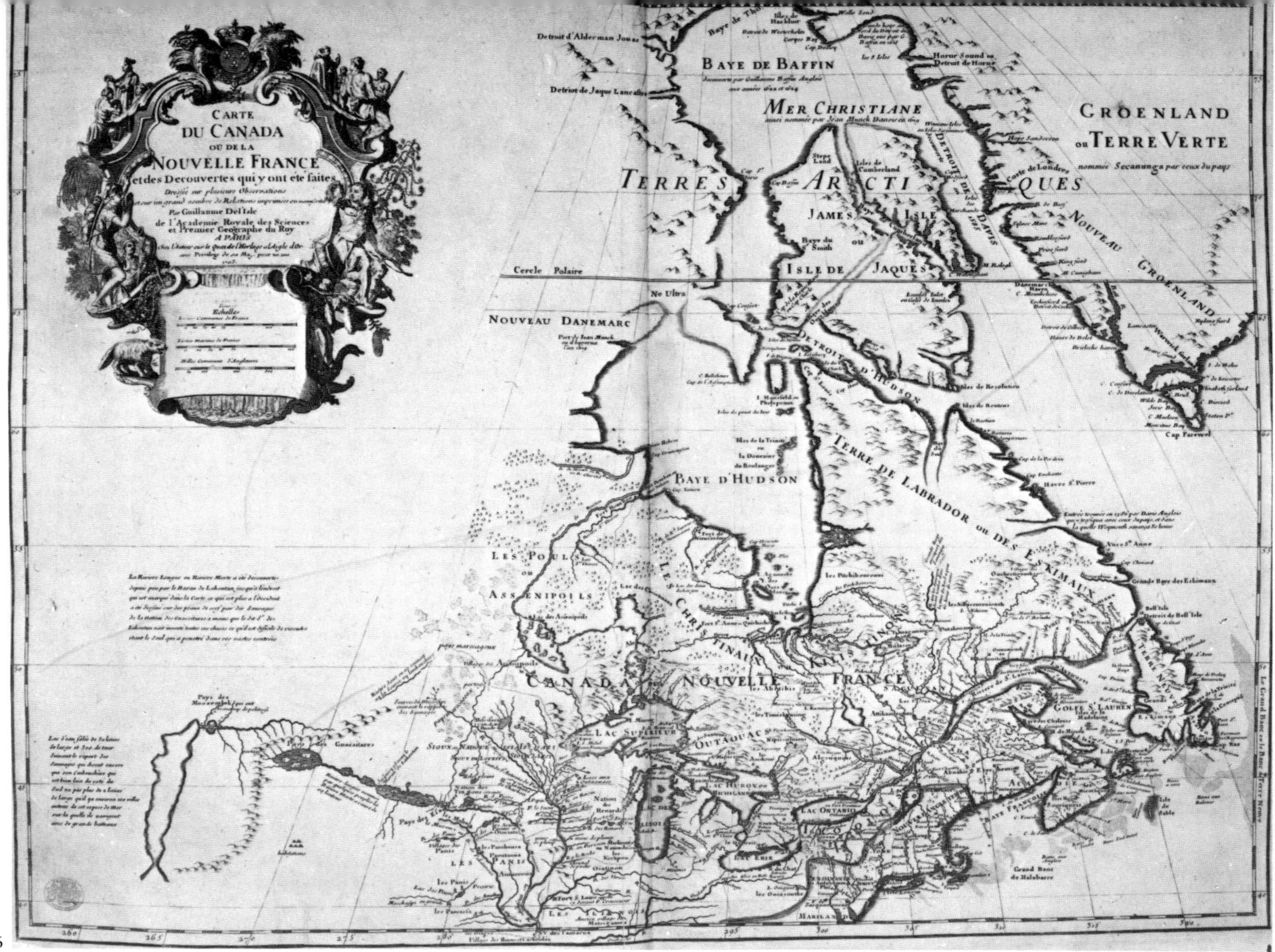

286

286 Guillaume de l'Isle. 'Carte du Canada ou de la Nouvelle France', Paris, 1703.
One of the many maps produced by the distinguished family of French cartographers (and owing more to the father, Claude de l'Isle, than to his more famous son, Guillaume), this is of particular interest because of its early attempt to incorporate Lahontan's imaginary geography west of the Mississippi (see plate 289). Farther north Lake Winnipeg ('Lac des Assenipoils') is shown with its water communication down to Hudson Bay, but this was from Indian report rather than from European discovery, and there is as yet no knowledge of the Saskatchewan River. In the southeast the Ohio is shown in more accurate fashion than usual but its nomenclature is still confused with the Wabash, of which river there is as yet no substantial indication. Detroit is shown, only two years after its founding by Cadillac.

full extent has been revealed only in documents discovered in the present century (see selection 3). These show that in 1690 Henry Kelsey, 'a very active Lad, delighting much in Indians Company', left York Fort for a journey inland which lasted almost two years. Insofar as he had official instructions from his superior at York they were 'to call, encourage, and invite, the remoter Indians to a trade with us'.[4] Travelling always with Indians, Kelsey seems first to have paddled with his Cree companions to the Saskatchewan, that great waterway of the Indian trade, and then to have gone on foot to the northern plains, covered with 'short Round sticky grass'. In the summer of 1691 Kelsey struck out in a different direction, following with the Cree the track of the Assiniboine Indians southwest across the Saskatchewan and Red Deer rivers, and on to the great plains of western Canada. Kelsey was the first European to reach this area, thick with herds of buffalo, and with an Indian population far more numerous than any Hudson's Bay man had encountered. Here Kelsey met not only the Siouan-speaking Assiniboine of the plains but also the mysterious 'Naywatanee Poets'—probably Atsina, members of the Blackfoot group of tribes—whose chief proved too apprehensive of the Cree and their muskets to agree to Kelsey's proposal that they should bring down their furs direct to the Bay posts.

Kelsey's journey was an extraordinary achievement, based as it was on his ability to live and travel safely with the Indians. He was the first white man to visit the northern plains, to see the buffalo herds and the grizzly bear, and to observe the Indians of the prairies in their home environment. But for long his discoveries were obscured by the failure of the company to publish or even preserve his notes. No evidence of Kelsey's explorations appeared on contemporary maps; his journey was an isolated and soon-forgotten feat in an era when Englishmen were reluctant to move away from the familiar surroundings of the Bayside posts. The lack of the essential birch and cedar for canoes as far north as York, the determination of the London Committee to exercise a tight control over its servants in the Bay, and its disapproval of cohabitation with Indian women (Kelsey almost certainly had an Indian 'wife' with him), all reinforced the company's established policy of relying on the quality and reliability of its goods to attract the Indians down to the Bay to trade, rather than following the French example of pushing far inland to make contact with the Indian hunters and trappers in their own country.

2 French exploration to the Missouri and the Saskatchewan

On the inland routes west from Lake Superior and beyond the Winnipeg basin it was the French who followed Kelsey's path. In 1688 Jacques de Noyon had canoed from the farthest west of the French posts at Lake Nipigon to Rainy Lake, and the next year probably reached Lake of the Woods. But here

287 'Cours des Rivieres, et fleuve, courant a L'ouest du nord du Lac Superieur . . .' 1728-9. *Service Historique de la Marine, Paris, Recueil 67, carte No. 87.*
This manuscript map was prepared, perhaps by the French engineer Gaspard Chayssegros de Léay at Montreal or Quebec, from the sketches drawn for La Vérendrye by the Cree Indian Auchagach and others. It shows the latest information and rumors about the west available to La Vérendrye before he began his explorations in the 1730s. From Lake Superior on the righthand side of the map, the two main routes westward are shown: the one from Fort Kaministiquia ('Kamanestigonia'), the other farther south along Grand Portage. From Lake of the Woods ('Lac des Bois') westward the map is dominated by the River of the West shown flowing across the prairies, with Cree country to the north and the Sioux and Assiniboine of the great plains to the south. Beyond Lake Winnipeg ('Ouinipigon') the river continues its straight westward course, past the mountain of shining stone which figures so prominently in the Indian reports of this period, and on towards the western sea (as is explained more fully in the caption). Although this is the earliest appearance of Lake Winnipeg on a map drawn from first-hand report, and its shape bears some resemblance to actuality, its line, size and location are hopelessly wrong. Towards the bottom of the map the Mississippi is correctly shown as having its source near the height of land south of Lake Winnipeg—instead of the usual assumption that the great river rose in a group of lakes—though here again the relationship of the Upper Mississippi to the Lake Winnipeg/Lake of the Woods region is inaccurate, and suffers from the same distortion as the rest of the map.

287

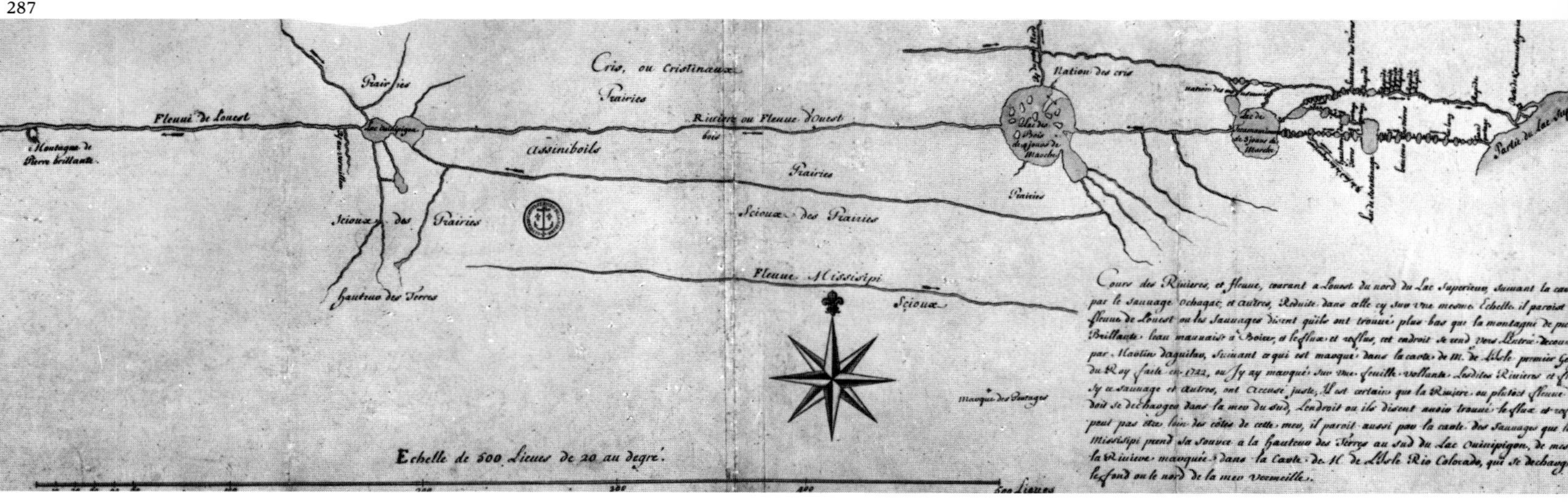

288 Guillaume de l'Isle. 'Mer de l'Ouest', *c.* 1700, Paris, 1752.
Published by de l'Isle's son-in-law, Philippe Buache, a half-century after its alleged construction, this map has remained a source of debate and controversy. There is no evidence to support Buache's claim that de l'Isle put the famous Mer de l'Ouest on a manuscript globe of 1697, nor that de l'Isle ever drew the map shown here; instead, there is some suspicion that Buache used the name of his dead father-in-law to gain publicity and credence for his own theories about the geography of northwest America. The map represents the great inland sea in simple and dramatic form, stretching as it does from California into the heart of the American continent, and connecting with the equally celebrated and mythical Rivière de l'Ouest. On the sea's southern shores are those other will-o'-the-wisps of western geography—the fabulous cities of Cibola and Quivira.

288

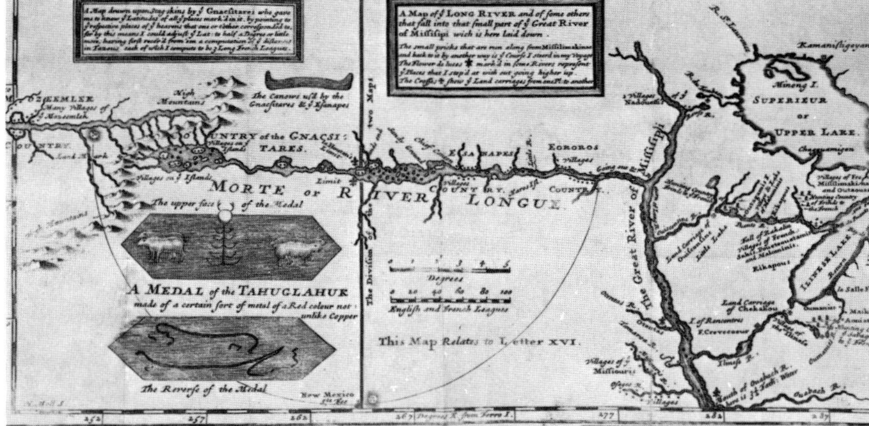

289

289 The fabulous Long River or Riviere Longue of Lahontan, from his *New Voyages*, 1703.
Here is depicted a purely imaginary waterway flowing into the Mississippi from a distant ridge of mountains, on the reverse side of which another river whose banks were dotted with sizeable cities and towns ran westward into a great salt lake nearly a thousand miles in circumference. Despite the incredible nature of Lahontan's assertions, the features shown on this map were copied by many geographers during the first half of the eighteenth century, among them such respected cartographers as Guillaume de l'Isle (see plate 286).

the westward movement halted and even receded as French energies were diverted by the long years of war during which they seized the most important of the Hudson Bay posts at York (renamed Fort Bourbon) and held it from 1697 to 1714. The French never made full use of this vantage point for tapping the western fur trade, and by the terms of the Treaty of Utrecht (1713) the post was returned to the Hudson's Bay Company. With the situation back to its prewar normality the French once more took up the task of westward expansion along the labyrinth of lakes and rivers beyond Superior. During De Noyon's travels in this region he had met Assiniboine as well as Cree, and had heard that at the far end of the Lake of the Woods a river (the Winnipeg River) flowed into the western sea (no doubt Lake Winnipeg). On this substratum of geographical fact his Indian informants built a bizarre fantasy of tribes of dwarfs, of white, bearded men on horseback, and great stone cities—all solemnly related by Bégon, the intendant of New France, in a memorandum he wrote in 1716 to justify expeditions to follow De Noyon's old track.[5]

290

290 Section of 'Amerique', Sieur le Rouge, Paris, 1746.
The map is notable for its apparent ignorance of the explorations of the La Vérendrye family in the 1730s and 1740s, and its reliance instead on earlier Indian reports which represented a great River of the West flowing from the Lake of the Woods and Lake Winnipeg towards the Pacific. It is further evidence of the timelag between exploration and publication. Even when new geographical facts were known some publishers continued for reasons of economy to use existing copperplates for many years after the maps they depicted were out-of-date, simply altering the date.

The first step was to strengthen the French hold on the western end of Lake Superior, where in 1717 Kaministiquia was re-established on the thickly forested shores of the northwest corner of the lake, and Chequamegon on the southwest shore in 1719. This was in conformity with general French policy in Canada in the years after the ending of formal hostilities in 1713: at Niagara far away to the southeast, in the lush valleys of the Ohio and the Illinois, at the vital base at Mackinac, the French were busy establishing, reoccupying or strengthening the strategic posts of their expanding empire. 1720 saw the return to North America of the Jesuit scholar, Father Charlevoix, sent by the French government to collect from the traders, missionaries and Indians of the 'upper country' all the information he could about the lands to the west. Dominating Charlevoix's resultant memoir of 1723 was his conviction that not far to the west lay a great interior sea. This concept of the western sea or *mer de l'ouest* was to obsess French explorers throughout this period. It was usually envisaged as a North American Mediterranean, connected to the Pacific by a strait, and linked in some indeterminate way on its other shore with the river and lake network west of the Great Lakes—or perhaps west of the Missouri. Since the whole idea rested on theoretical geography unsupported by actual exploration, no two maps showed the inland sea in quite the same shape or position. In support of it stood a wild array of reports and rumors: the alleged discovery in 1592 by the old Greek pilot Juan de Fuca of a large inlet along the Pacific coast between latitudes 47°N. and 48°N.; the great river supposedly seen farther south in latitude 41°N. by Martín Aguilar while on Vizcaíno's expedition along the Californian coast in 1602–3; Lahontan's fabulous Long River twisting westward across a mysterious landscape (plate 289); Indian stories of salt water and white men somewhere over the horizon. This imaginary interior sea distorted all attempts to represent the geography of the western half of the continent; for it could not coexist with a massive north-south range of mountains, and so no indication of the reality of the Rockies appears on maps until the second half of the eighteenth century. Instead, a height of land was visualized not far distant from the western edge of French knowledge, and from this the Mississippi and Missouri ran down to the Gulf of Mexico on one side and a great westward-flowing river on the other. Charlevoix himself placed the western sea to the southwest of the Lake of the Woods, and suggested that an approach to it through Sioux country would pay for itself through fur trade profits. On this understanding a new fur trading association, the Company of the Sioux, established in 1727 a post, Fort Beauharnois, at Lake Pepin on the Upper Mississippi where Nicolas Perrot had first established a temporary base forty years earlier. The persistent hostility of the nearby Fox Indians made the post untenable, but in any event the quest for the western sea was about to move farther north where (also in 1727) there arrived to take command of the *postes du nord* Pierre Gaultier de Varennes, Sieur de la Vérendrye. Forty-three years old, a veteran of war in Europe and America, he was the last of the great explorers of New France.

Like his predecessors, La Vérendrye was a trader as much as an explorer. Historians have disputed interminably and inconclusively over his order of priorities,[6] but the facts of the political and economic situation are clear enough. The French government was not willing to subsidize discovery expeditions; they were expected to pay their way from fur trade profits, and the most the government was prepared to do was to grant La Vérendrye a trading monopoly in the Lake Winnipeg area which might finance his search for the western sea. There was nothing new about this: since Champlain's time exploration and the fur trade had been interwoven. The search for furs was the most persistent element in the westward drive; conversely, the assumption that discovery could be financed by the fur trade had distracted and diverted explorers since the early seventeenth century. Discovery 'for its own sake' was not yet fashionable; behind the explorations of both French and English in North America lay the motive forces of national rivalry and economic incentive, and it is within this context that the explorations of La Vérendrye and his contemporaries must be set.

La Vérendrye's first stay at the *postes du nord* (Nipigon and

291-3 George Edwards. Illustrations from *A natural history of birds*, III, 1750. *British Museum, London.*

291 'The speckled Diver, or Loon': probably the Arctic loon, *Gavin arctica* (Linnaeus).

292 'The Hooping-Crane from Hudson's-Bay': *Crus american* (Linnaeus).

293 'The Bittern from Hudson's-Bay': American bittern, *Botaurus lentiginosus* (Rackett).

291

293

292

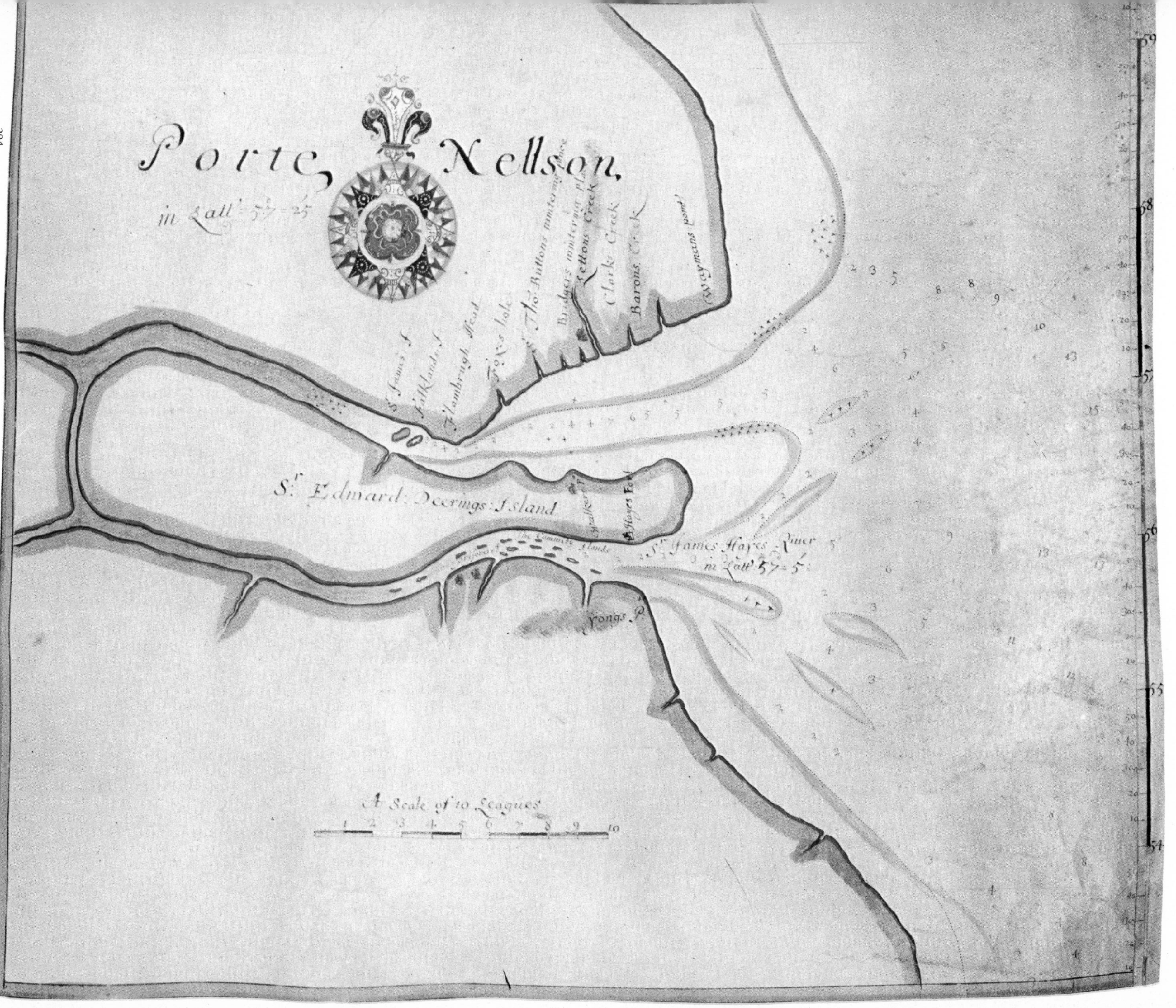
Porte Nellson
in Latt 57—25
St James I
Falklands I
Flambrugh Head
Foxes hole
Sr Tho. Buttons watering place
Bridgers watering place
Settons Creek
Clarks Creek
Barons Creek
Waymans point
Sr. Edmund Deerings Island
Walkers P
Hayes Fort
St James Hayes River
in Latt 57—5
Yongs P
A Scale of 10 Leagues

294 John Thornton. Inset of 'Port Nelson' from a larger map of Hudson Bay, 1685. *British Museum, London, Add. Ms. 5414(20).*
Thornton, one of a school of chart-makers working in London under the auspices of the Drapers' Company (see Campbell, 1973), was commissioned by the Hudson's Bay Company in about 1680 to draw charts for its ship-masters. This beautifully-colored map on vellum is typical of the elaborate style of the school. Although soundings are shown, the real purpose of the map was to confirm the Company's claim to the area around the mouth of the Nelson and Hayes Rivers by demonstrating that the names used were English (or Indian). An entry in the Company records for 20 March 1685 (OS) notes: 'Mr. John Thorneton haveing Drawen out very curiously the Map of Hudsons Bay upon parchment Ordered he shall have a reward of £4 for the same.' The site was an important one, for although Thornton's map suggests the difficulty of the shallow sea approach, the twin rivers of the Nelson (the more northerly) and the Hayes formed an important trade artery between Hudson Bay and the rich fur-trapping areas of the Lake Winnipeg basin and the country to the northwest.

295 'Carte Physique des Terreins les plus élevés de la Partie Occidentale du Canada', by Philippe Buache, Paris, 1754.
The 'Auchagach map' (see plate 287) is shown but with a distortion which has compressed the area between Lake Winnipeg and Lake of the Woods to insignificant proportions, and greatly prolonged the distance from Lake of the Woods to Lake Superior. It is inferior in almost every respect to La Vérendrye's manuscript map of 1740 (plate 331). The upper Mississippi and Red River are shown with a pronounced east-west direction; La Vérendrye's route of 1738 to the Mandans ('Ouachipouanes') is marked, but the Mandan villages are shown on the banks of a rather unimpressive River of the West which flows only a short distance before reaching the Sea of the West. To the north, although the region between Lake Winnipeg and Hudson Bay is better proportioned than on the La Vérendrye manuscript maps, the Nelson water-communication with York is shown flowing, not from the Lake Winnipeg basin, but from a large lake hundreds of miles to the north.

Kaministiquia) brought him information from the Indians which, though now almost standard in form, never failed to excite. Crees told him that 'they had been beyond the height of land and reached a great river which flows straight towards the setting sun, and which widens continually as it descends . . . much lower down there is a small mountain, the stones of which sparkle night and day.'[7] In preparation for his intended exploration La Vérendrye steadily extended his organization westward from Lake Superior. In 1731 he opened a new and easier route to Rainy Lake by way of Pigeon River and Grand Portage; in 1732 he built a strong, palisaded depot at Fort St Charles on the western shores of the Lake of the Woods; and in 1734 his sons established Fort Maurepas just south of Lake Winnipeg on the Red River. These moves had far-reaching implications for the fur trade. The French were at last outflanking the redoubtable Sioux, and were poised on the fringe of the plains country of the Assiniboine. Here they could make direct contact with the Indian trappers of the

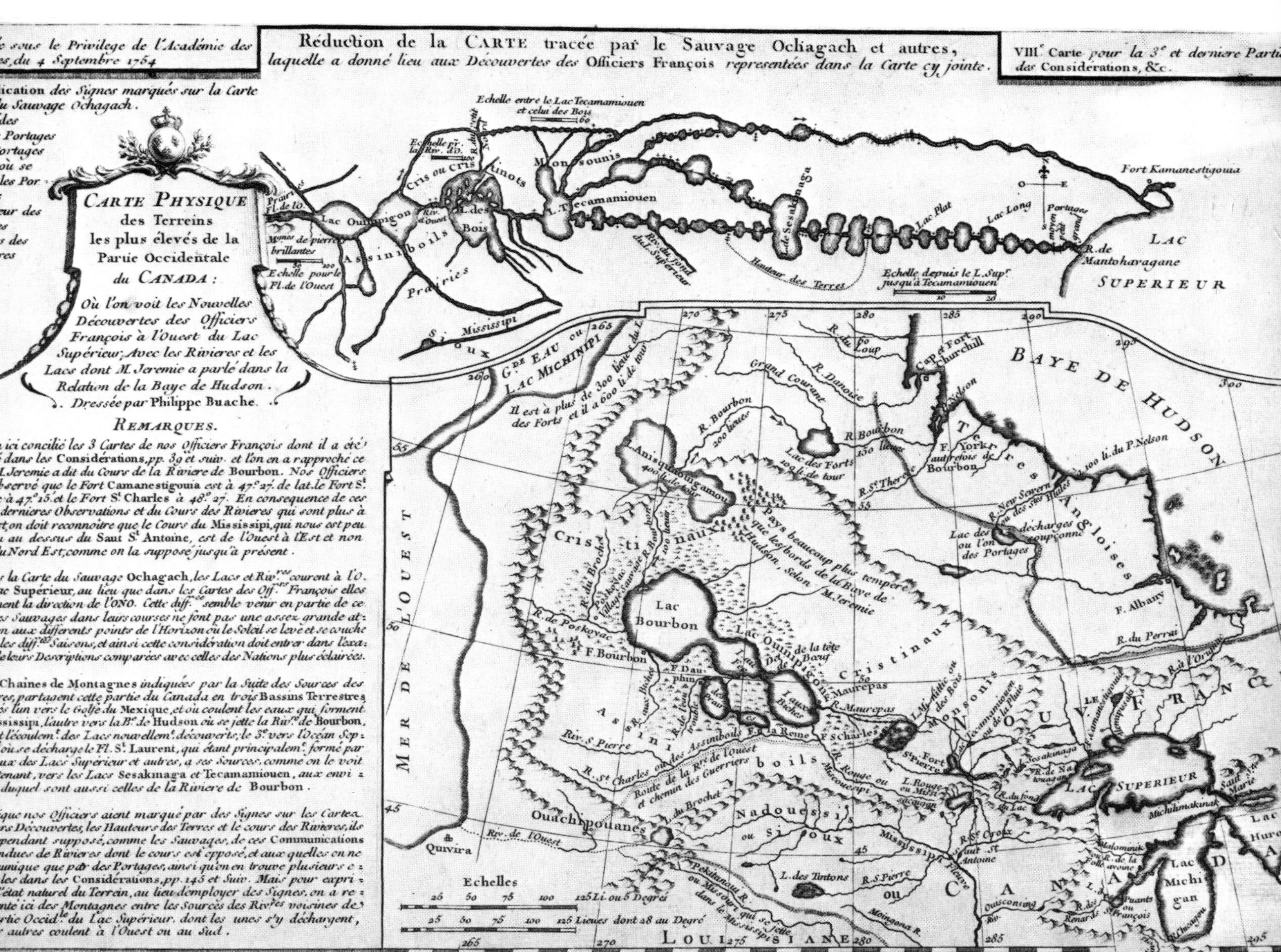

295

plains, and block or divert the trade routes which took furs down the rivers to the English posts on Hudson Bay. And always there was the lure of Indian reports of great rivers and the sea, and now persistent rumors about light-skinned, bearded people of advanced civilization who lived along the banks of the River of the West and were called 'Mantannes'. Often enough these reports had a factual basis. In the stories about great rivers to the west can be discerned the misty outlines of the Missouri and the Saskatchewan; an Indian tribe of Mantannes or Mandans did exist, and certainly differed from the Cree or Assiniboine to the north; yarns of horses and white, bearded men clad in steel may well have reached halfway across the continent from New Spain. And if the Indians embroidered or inflated their reports they were only meeting the insistent demands of the white man for news about the lands and seas to the west.

By 1738 La Vérendrye was ready to lead an expedition to the country of the Mandans. For years he had been delayed by involvement in Sioux-Cree hostilities, and by the necessity to explain and justify his intentions to his merchant associates in Montreal, to the governor of New France, Beauharnois, at Quebec, and to the secretary of state, Maurepas, in Paris. After establishing Fort La Reine at Portage-la-Prairie on the newly discovered Assiniboine River, La Vérendrye and his party had to leave the woods, waterways and birchbark canoes, and strike out across the plains on foot. They were accompanied by well-disciplined Assiniboine warriors, who killed buffalo to ensure a steady meat supply as the party kept southward across the prairies. In December 1738 the first Mandan village was reached. It was a fortified village with spacious dwellings, set in a fertile river-plain, and inhabited by a hospitable, affluent people; but they were unmistakably Indian, if lighter-skinned than most, and La Vérendrye's disappointment is plainly recorded in his journal entries (see selection 6). A little farther on other Mandan villages lay on the banks of a wide, muddy river which flowed swiftly southwest (in fact, a local, misleading twist of the Missouri), and here La Vérendrye left two of his party. The next summer this pair met Indians from the west who used horses, and whose reports of white men living on the shores of a great sea were more convincing than usual, for their chief wore a crucifix and seemed to have a smattering of Spanish. In a final effort to follow the route of these Indians and discover the western sea, two of La Vérendrye's sons returned to the Mandan villages in 1742 and crossed the Missouri to trek southwest in a fruitless quest for the sea. Ironically, they were crossing one of the most arid stretches of the continent—the Badlands of North Dakota. They travelled part of the way with 'Bow Indians' (probably Cheyenne), stayed with Arikara Indians, and heard of other tribes to the west which may have included Comanche, Crow and Kiowa. The Frenchmen's dependence on the Indians forced them to turn back in early 1743 when within sight of mountains from whose summits, they believed, they would have sighted the sea. Whether these were the Black Hills of Dakota or the Big Horn Range of Wyoming (and therefore arguably part of the Rocky Mountains) is uncertain; even if the latter, the Frenchmen were still a thousand miles distant from the Pacific, and between them and the ocean lay some of the highest, most rugged terrain in the whole continent.

On neither of these long journeys had the La Vérendryes found the River of the West or the western sea; and La Vérendrye clearly believed that the river of the Mandans was the Missouri and therefore flowed in the wrong direction (see, for example the map of 1740, plate 331). Nor had the explorers found much potential for easy profit; merely further indication of the immense width of the continent in its middle latitudes. All this turned La Vérendrye's attention back to the north, and in particular to the 'Rivière Blanche' (the Saskatchewan) which flowed into the western end of Lake Winnipeg. The process of fort-building moved on to the new river, at Cedar Lake and then at Basquia (The Pas). One of La Vérendrye's sons, the Chevalier, reached the Forks of the Saskatchewan in 1739, and in the absence of any contemporary knowledge of Kelsey's earlier travels in this region must be presumed the effective discoverer of the river, one of the most important arteries of the fur trade. Upriver the Crees told him that it flowed 'from a height of land where there were very lofty mountains, and that beyond those mountains they knew of a great lake the water of which was not good to drink.'[8] Whether springing from the imagination or derived from genuine information, here was a realistic indication of the geography of the western half of the continent; but the geographers of Europe, with their maps bursting with westward-flowing rivers, straits and inland seas, could not assimilate the depressing concept of a great mountain range lying between the French and the ocean.

It was along this route to the west that La Vérendrye intended to make his final journey, but he died (in 1749) before he could attempt it, and the effort was made under the direction of Jacques Legardeur de St Pierre. In a memoir of 1751 he claimed that his lieutenant, De Niverville, had followed the Saskatchewan a thousand miles beyond The Pas as far as the Rocky Mountains ('Montagnes des Roches' in the French original) where he even established a post, Fort la Jonquière.[9] Although the distances are roughly correct, there is no corroborative evidence for this story, and the assertion that a post was founded, in an area so remote from any other Europeans, is frankly incredible. Of more practical import was the fact that chiefly through the efforts of the La Vérendrye family the French now controlled the rich fur area of the Lower Saskatchewan. In 1753 the new commandant of the western posts, the Chevalier de la Corne, built a post (Fort la Corne) near the Forks, and French domination of the interior routes seemed complete. Their presence across the Indian canoe routes down to Hudson Bay menaced the very existence of the Hudson's Bay Company.

3 Coastal and inland exploration from Hudson Bay, 1713-74

The English company was slow to react to the threat posed by these French moves. Its London Committee, shrewd, cautious, unimaginative, preferred to rely on its traditional policy of attracting the Indians down to its bayside posts. For a half-century after Kelsey's journey of 1690-2 the only noticeable flurry of exploring activity from the Bay was prompted by an enterprising company governor at York Fort, James Knight, who received the post back from the French in 1714. The journals he kept in the next few years contain, besides the routine accounts of daily events, elaborate explanations of his plans regarding the expansion of Company trade and the discovery of the Northwest Passage. To Knight that elusive strait promised a way to a land of treasure, an El Dorado on the Pacific coast of North America, rumors about which had reached him in England, and prompted him to take to York 'Cruseables, Melting Potts, Borax &C for the Trial of Minerals'.[10] Obsessed by reports of gold, white men and a western ocean which his interrogation of Chipewyan ('Northern') Indians from the northwest seemed to reveal (see selection 4), Knight sent William Stuart inland in 1715-16. Dependent on Indians for guidance and support, and without any surveying instruments except a compass, Stuart's report on his return was vague and confused.[11] Although his own guess that after travelling a thousand miles he had reached latitude 67°N. was clearly an over-estimate, he was certainly the first European to cross the Barrens, and he probably reached the vicinity of Great Slave Lake. In Knight's journals and letters can be dimly discerned a whole medley of Athapaskan tribes stretching far away into the sub-Arctic northwest, Slave, Dogrib, Yellowknife Indians, and some glimmering of the mineral potentialities of the area. In a further attempt to tempt the Chipewyan down to the bay, Knight established in 1717 a new company post to the north at the mouth of Churchill River, near the edge of Chipewyan territory. He then returned to England to persuade the company to fit out a sea expedition to the west coast of Hudson Bay, and although almost eighty years old commanded it in person. The venture turned into one of the tragedies of Arctic exploration, for Knight's hopes of finding a short passage to the land of gold and furs which lay somewhere to the west foundered on the barren, treeless shores of Marble Island in Hudson Bay where his two vessels, the *Albany* and *Discovery* sloop, were trapped in 1719. Every member of the expedition died, and the last sight we have of Knight's men comes from oral tradition later in the century among the Eskimos of the area. Its reliability is open to question, but it gives a moving description of the plight of the dwindling band of survivors, who in the summer of 1720 'frequently went to the top of an adjacent rock, and earnestly looked to the South and East, as if in expectation of some vessels coming to their relief'.[12]

News of the disaster confirmed the reluctance of company servants to venture away from the posts, and the next attempt to find a Northwest Passage through Hudson Bay was the work of a critic of the Hudson's Bay Company, Arthur Dobbs. The company's lack of interest in his enthusiastic projects for northern discovery aroused Dobbs to a suspicious investigation of the company's own record in this field. His conclusions were summarized in the words of one of his associates, Joseph Robson, a former employee of the company, who complained that 'The Company have for eighty years slept at the edge of a frozen sea'.[13] This cutting criticism was not altogether justified; the company's refusal to expand inland was based on a careful estimate of the potentialities of the fur trade and a recognition of the limitations of its own servants. But Dobbs was correct in seeing that the steady French westward expansion of the 1730s and 1740s was cutting across the hinterland of the company's most profitable posts at York and Churchill, and in a more general way fencing off the shorebound English from the great central plains of North America. Whatever his deficiencies as a geographer and economist, Dobbs was at least capable of

296

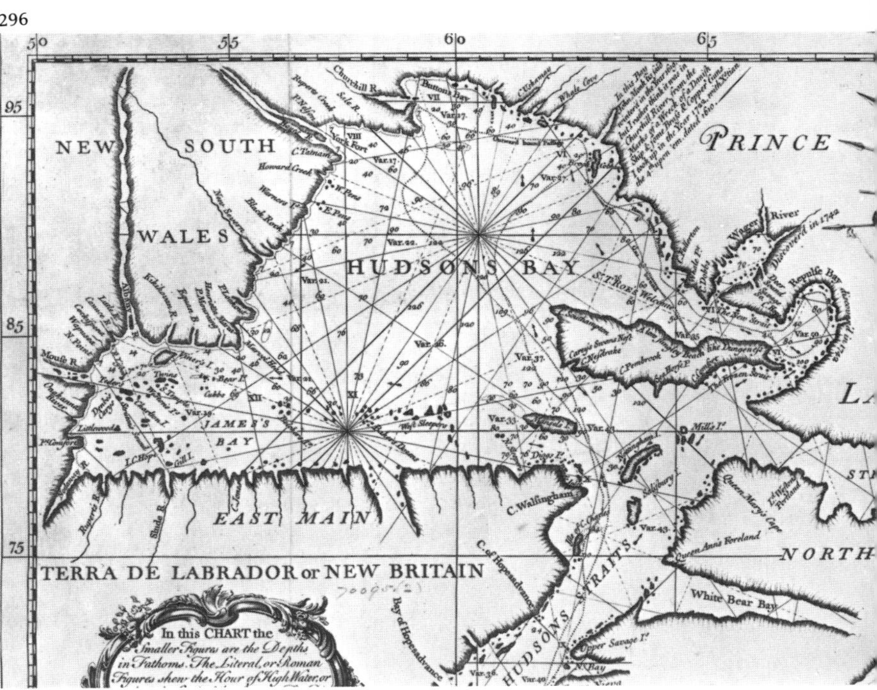

297

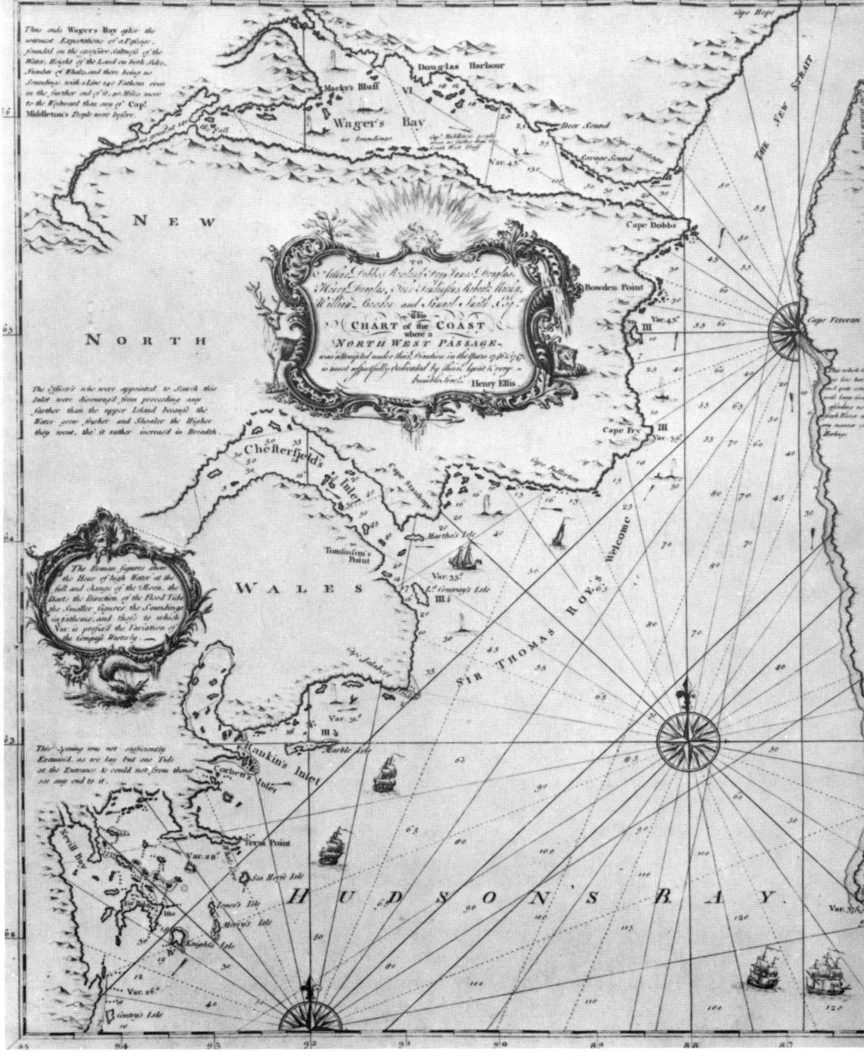

296 Christopher Middleton. 'Chart of Hudson's Bay and Straits. . . .', London, 1743. (North is at the right.) *British Museum, London.*
This map, together with two color plates 325 and 326, neatly sums up the controversy in England about Middleton's explorations of 1741-2. Middleton's map marks an unbroken coastline north from Churchill, the newly discovered Wager as a river, and to the north the tide flowing down the west coast of Hudson Bay through the Frozen Strait.

297 Henry Ellis. 'The Chart of the Coast where a North West Passage was attempted . . . in the Years 1746 and 1747', London, 1748.
This map by the agent on William Moor's expedition of 1746-7 shows the Wager as closed, not a strait as had been hoped; it also marks the discovery of Chesterfield Inlet up which a longboat sailed for four days until the water became shallower and fresher.

298

298-301 Scenes from the Moor expedition of 1746-7, from Henry Ellis, *Voyage to Hudson's Bay*, 1748.

298 The *Dobbs-Galley* and the *California* laid up for the winter (of 1746-7) in a creek about five miles from York Fort.

299 Half a mile away were the wintering quarters of the discovery crews, the men in log huts similar to those described by Isham (see plate 333), the officers in a double-storied building taken out in frame, and named Montagu House after one of the subscribers to the expedition, the Duke of Montagu.

299

300

301

300-1 The discovery vessels anchored in Douglas Harbor, Wager Bay, while the upper part of the Wager was explored in light boats, including the fall funnelling through a passage 60 yards wide, 150 miles from the entrance of the Wager. The fall was passed on 2 August 1747, but the next day the boats found they could get no farther west.

thinking continentally, and reports reaching Britain about the French search for the River of the West heightened his apprehensions that his plans for finding a Northwest Passage would be anticipated by a French discovery of a more southerly route to the Pacific.

Prodded by Dobbs, the Admiralty sent a discovery expedition to Hudson Bay in 1741 commanded by Christopher Middleton, a former company captain, which wintered at Churchill. Though stricken with scurvy, it explored the west coast of Hudson Bay in the summer of 1742, discovering and naming Wager River or Inlet, and tracing Roe's Welcome in the northwest corner of the Bay to its final, frozen extremity (see selection 7). The question first put by Foxe a century earlier, and resurrected by Dobbs, had finally been answered—the Welcome, although stretching farther north than the maps indicated, was not the entrance of the Northwest Passage, and Middleton in his disappointment named its northern point Repulse Bay. Middleton's map of the expedition's discoveries, 1743 (plate 296), was the first attempt at an accurate survey of the west coast of Hudson Bay, and was a notable advance on the rough sketches of the region produced by earlier cartographers. Though on a small scale, and not showing the detail which a closer examination of the coast would have revealed, it included all the main features of the west coast except Chesterfield Inlet; for Middleton mistook the entrance of the inlet, masked by its screen of sheltering islets, for a deep bay. Within a few months of the expedition's return Dobbs embarked on an unscrupulous campaign to discredit the unfortunate Middleton. His motives in doing this were revealed in a letter of early 1743 to the captain in which he argued that if Middleton would admit that a passage might still exist then 'the Presumption will be a great Inducement to open the Trade to the Bay'.[14] Henceforth the Northwest Passage was part of a wider scheme to abolish the monopoly of the Hudson's Bay Company, and to further this end Dobbs organized a private expedition of trade and discovery under William Moor which sailed for Hudson Bay in 1746. After wintering near the company post at York, the expedition followed in the summer of 1747 Middleton's track along the west coast of the Bay, but apart from discovering and partially exploring Chesterfield Inlet, it added little to his surveys (see plate 297).

Dobbs's attempts to overthrow the company by a Parliamentary attack on its charter also failed (although Parliament supported him in 1745 to the extent of offering a £20,000 reward for the discovery of a navigable Northwest Passage); but the long controversy focused public, mercantile and official opinion on Hudson Bay and its hinterland in an unprecedented way. Dobbs and Middleton were involved in a long and scabrous pamphlet war against each other; Dobbs produced in 1744 *An account of... Hudson's Bay* which collected a great deal of material on the area, and outlined the alleged discoveries of Admiral de Fonte between the Pacific and Hudson Bay (see Chapter 7, selection 4); books were written by members of the 1746-7 discovery expedition; and in 1749, as the attack on the company reached its climax, it was forced to release documents about its activities, and to answer questions from a Parliamentary Committee which demolished the barrier of close secrecy behind which it had long sheltered. The discovery ventures of the period, although they had not found the Northwest Passage, had accomplished useful exploratory work in Hudson Bay; and all in all an impressive amount of material about a neglected area of North America had been released. This had happened within a decade, for as late as 1741 the second edition of John Oldmixon's *The British*

Empire in America had noted that despite the author's 'pressing instance' he had been able to obtain no information about Hudson Bay or the company's activities there since 1714. It is true that few of the new publications were in any sense authoritative, as the company men were quick to point out. Dobbs's *Account* was condemned by one of them as 'so erronius, so superficial, and so trifling in almost every respect . . . all the monstrous fables of antiquity can hardly parrellel his absurdities.'[15] But the comment was confided to a private journal, and did nothing to deflate the hopes raised by Dobbs that if the trade of Hudson Bay were thrown open an expansion would follow which would take the English to the Upper Mississippi and beyond, 'by which means', he wrote, 'the Inland Trade of that vast Northern Continent, much greater than Europe, would in time be wholly enjoy'd by Britain, independent of any other European power.'[16]

The crisis at home had occurred at the very moment when French movements in the hinterland of the company's Bayside posts were reaching menacing proportions. The factor at York, James Isham (see selection 8), had written home as early as 1743, 'what is the most Concer'n is to see us sitt quiet & unconcern'd while the french as an old saying, not only Beats the Bush, but run's away with the Hair [hare] also.'[17] In the 1750s, faced with mounting criticism from its Bay factors, and sensitive to criticism in England that it neglected exploration, the company at last began to move. Efforts were made to explore and exploit the forbidding mass of the Labrador peninsula with a series of coastal expeditions along the 'East Main' which produced the first reasonable surveys of the east coast of Hudson Bay and established a new post at Richmond Gulf near the country of the Naskapi Indians. On the opposite side of the Bay the company sent sloops along the coast north from Churchill to trade with the little-known and feared Eskimos (see selection 10), and to complete the surveys made by the Middleton and Moor expeditions. Of more far-reaching importance, Isham was encouraged to probe inland from York, and this resulted in the second major journey into the interior by a Hudson's Bay man, Anthony Henday. His explorations exceeded Kelsey's both in penetration and commercial significance, although his objectives and method of travelling were much the same. He intended to accompany a party of returning Cree inland as far as the country of the 'Archithinue' Indians (Atsina), whom he hoped to persuade to come down to the Bay to trade. Living, as Kelsey had done, with an Indian woman, Henday followed the Cree along their canoe route from York on to the Lower Saskatchewan and past the French post at The Pas. From here Henday's party travelled

302

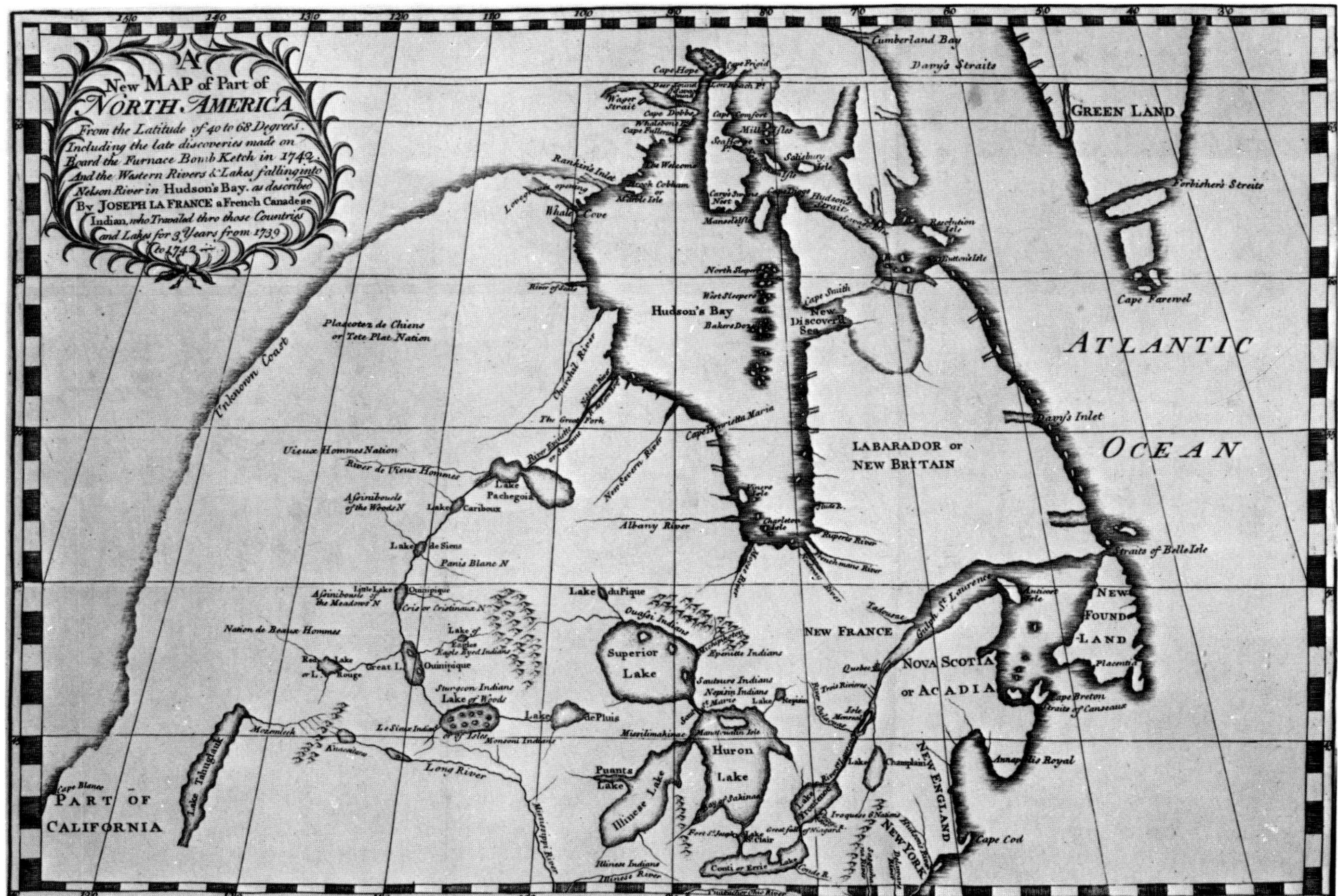

302 'A New Map of Part of North America', 1744, from Arthur Dobbs, *An account of the countries adjoining to Hudson's Bay*, 1744.
This map was based largely on the travels of Joseph la France, a *coureur de bois* who made a long, wandering journey from Lake Superior past Lake Winnipeg and down the Nelson River to York Fort, where he arrived in 1742. He then sailed to England where he met Dobbs, who was busy collecting information about Hudson Bay, described the regions he had seen and helped Dobbs to construct a map of his journey. A friend of Dobbs, Walter Bowman, described how he and Dobbs met La France, who 'gave this Description in my Dineing Room at the Golden fleece in New Bondstreet, when on the floor we chalkt out this map, till he was Satisfied it corresponded to the Idea of his Travels'. When Dobbs published the map in 1744 he made additions to it to support his campaign to launch an expedition to search for a Northwest Passage through Hudson Bay. The Pacific coast is shown swinging northeast from California towards Hudson Bay, while farther south some Lahontan-type apocryphal geography appears.

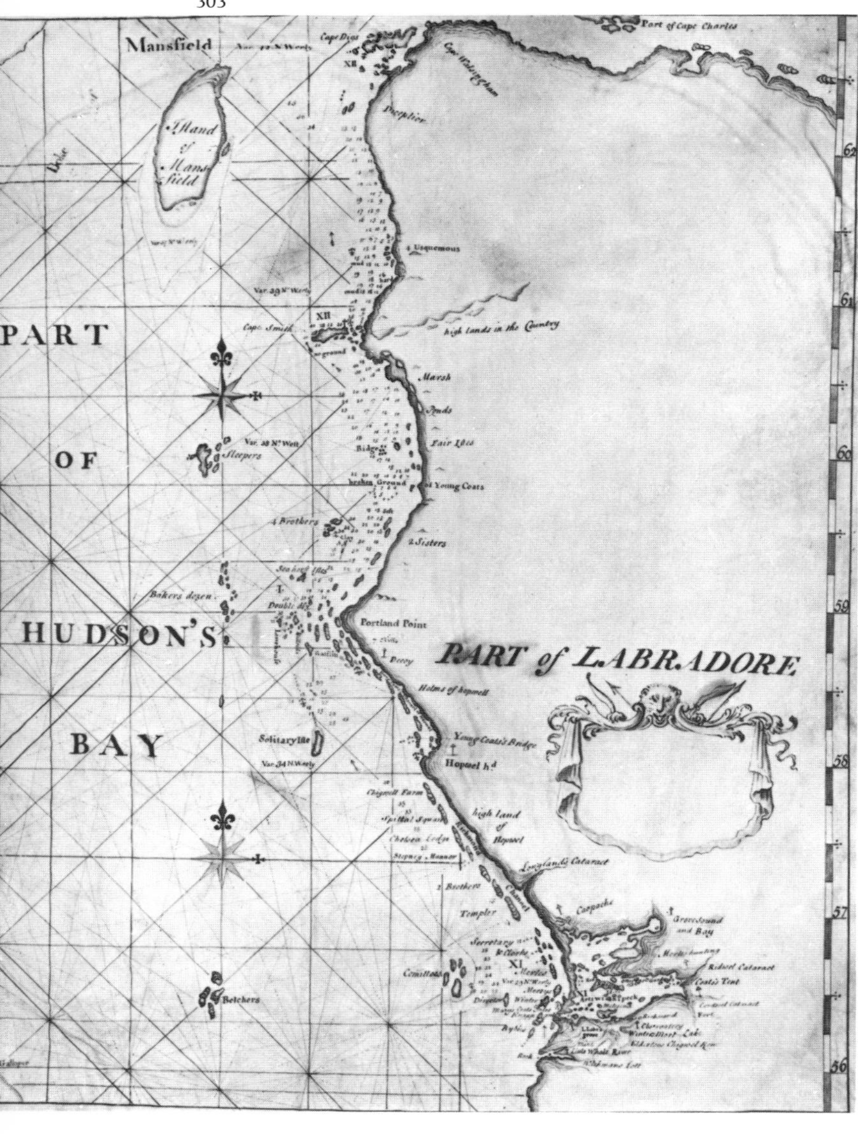

303 The east coast of Hudson Bay, by William Coats, 1750. *Hudson's Bay Company Archives, G. 1/14.*
In 1749 Captain Coats led a Hudson's Bay Company discovery expedition along the little-known east coast of Hudson Bay (the East Main) from Cape Digges at the entrance of Hudson Strait south to Little Whale River, and produced several manuscript maps of his survey. From a technical point of view these maps leave much to be desired. The pattern of rhumb-lines on them shows that Coats relied on the running-traverse system of coastal surveying. This was a quick method of charting a coast from the sea, but its accuracy depended on a true measurement of the ship's speed, and since only prominent points were fixed by compass intersection (and the rest of the coastline was sketched in by eye) errors were frequent. Few of the islands off the coast can be identified, and a 10′ or 15′ error in latitude occurs in several places. Even so, the map represents a considerable step forward (as comparison with Middleton's chart of 1743 shows, plate 296); and it is the first detailed map of the East Main, with soundings, currents and tides marked along a 500-mile stretch of coastline. But, like so many maps drawn by Company explorers in this period of commercial secrecy and rivalry, those by Coats were never published, and not until Aaron Arrowsmith's maps in the last decade of the century did the east coast of Hudson Bay appear in recognizable form on printed maps.

across the South Branch of the Saskatchewan, over prairie country to the North Branch, and then west and southwest searching for the 'Archithinues'. In the fall of 1754 Henday gazed for the first time on the immense buffalo herds of the plains, 'grazing like English cattle, and of the same size, and black having a hump between their shoulders, and short black horns', so numerous that when the Indians killed them they took only the tongue and other delicacies and left the vast carcass to rot or be devoured by wolves.[18]

By mid-October, somewhere south of Red Deer River, Henday at last came across the horsed Atsina of the plains (see selection 9). Their camp was an impressive sight, two hundred tents pitched in rows through which mounted Indians escorted Henday to the tent of the 'great Leader'. The obvious self-sufficiency of these plains Indians, and Henday's failure to persuade them to come down to the Bay posts in person make it worth stressing that the impact of the fur trade on the North American Indian varied according to the area and period involved. It was, in any case, quite different from the impact of the settler. Basically, the Indian and the settler could not co-exist; but to the fur traders, always fewer in number and usually more vulnerable than the clusters of settlers, the Indian trappers and hunters were essential. The relationship was one of mutual dependence. Even so, the coming of the European fur trade brought profound changes to many Indians. The Cree were transformed into a new category of trading Indians, using their firearms to dominate the neighboring tribes, and acting as middlemen in the fur trade both to the St Lawrence and to Hudson Bay. Some, the 'home Indians' attached to trading posts, became completely dependent on the white man, losing their old skills which kept them alive in the wilderness. Nicolas Jérémie, governor at York during the French occupation in the early eighteenth century, described how the failure of European supplies to arrive led to starvation and cannibalism among the Indians who came in to trade, 'for they had lost their skill with the bow since Europeans had supplied them with firearms'.[19] Even those who lived far from the trading posts felt their influence. Muskets replaced bow and spear as hunting weapons; metal tools were used instead of implements of stone or bone; iron or copper kettles and pots took the place of stone and earthenware utensils at the cooking fires; skins were discarded in favor of duffels and blankets. Deep in the interior, tribes which had never seen a white man were affected by his material culture as they began to trade furs through the Assiniboine or Cree for firearms, tools or tobacco. Commercial intercourse quickened among the Indian tribes in the face of the insistent European demand for furs, and with it came cultural changes and shifts in the power balance between the various Indian nations. Indians in closer contact with the roaming Canadian traders were often degraded by the white man's alcohol, or killed by his diseases. Nor must it be forgotten that except in the bleakest regions of the north the fur trader was the forerunner of the settler and the official, the land speculator and the soldier; in more ways than one his appearance marked the end of the Indians' traditional way of life.

The fur traders' journals, where they survive, reveal these

304-5 The interior of Hudson Bay on two maps probably by Andrew Graham, *c.* 1772. *Hudson's Bay Company Archives, G.2/15, G.2/17.*
Together, these maps reveal the extent of the Hudson's Bay Company's knowledge of the interior just before its decision to move inland and establish posts in direct competition with the Canadian traders. Their defects are obvious: the longitudes generally, the distorted outline of Lake Winnipeg ('Frenchman's Lake or Little Sea'), tilted on its axis and stretching more than twice its actual length, the erroneous river route between Albany Fort (on the coast of James Bay) and Lake Winnipeg. Yet they also show how much farther the Company's knowledge extended than the Bayside posts, and in particular the importance of the information brought back by Tomison, Cocking and other servants from their recent reconnaissance journeys inland. On map 305 the extent of Tomison's wanderings around and to the south of Lake Manitoba ('Mantouapau Lake') are shown, and, more striking perhaps, Cocking's westward journey past the forks of the Saskatchewan, and as far as the Eagle Hills near the South Branch. On both maps Canadian posts are shown as far west as 'Basquia' or The Pas (approximately long. 102°W. on the map)—a fact which explains the insistence of the Company factor, Andrew Graham, in 1772 that an inland post must be established near The Pas.

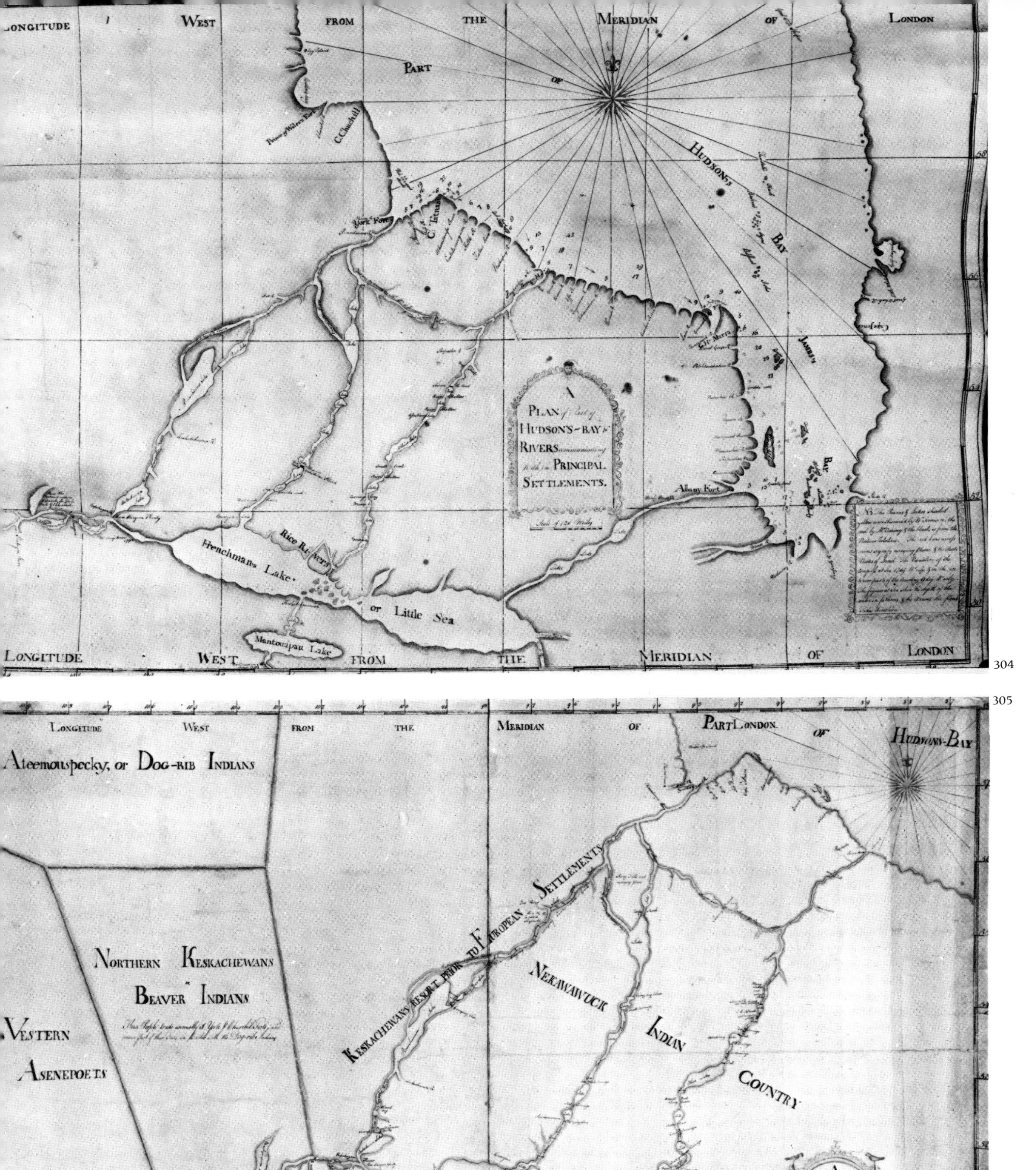

LONGITUDE WEST FROM THE MERIDIAN OF LONDON
PART OF HUDSONS BAY
Prince of Wales's Fort
C.Churchill
York Fort
Albany Fort
JAMES BAY
A PLAN of Part of HUDSON'S-BAY & RIVERS communicating with the PRINCIPAL SETTLEMENTS.
Rice Rivers
Frenchman's Lake or Little Sea
Mantoupau Lake
LONGITUDE WEST FROM THE MERIDIAN OF LONDON

304

305

LONGITUDE WEST FROM THE MERIDIAN OF LONDON
PART OF HUDSONS-BAY
Ateemouspecky, or Dog-rib Indians
Northern Keskachewans or Beaver Indians
Western Asenepoets
Keskachewans Resort Prior to European Settlements
Nehawawuck Indian Country
Eastern Asenepoets
Southern Keskachewans
A PLAN OF PART OF HUDSONS-BAY, & RIVERS, COMMUNICATING WITH YORK FORT & SEVERN
Rice Rivers
Frenchmans Lake
Little Sea
Mantoupau Lake
LONGITUDE WEST FROM THE MERIDIAN OF LONDON

306

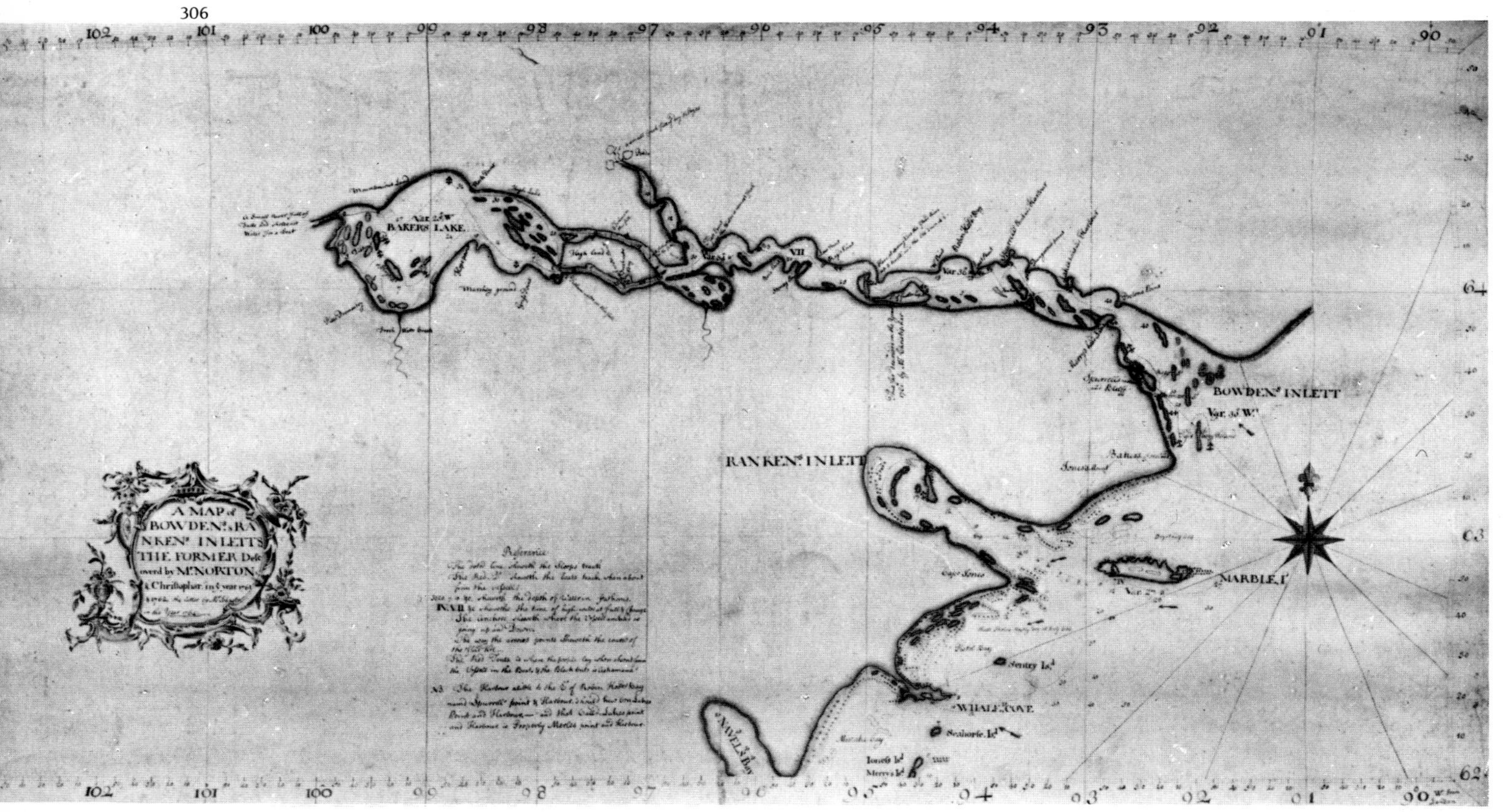

306 The west coast of Hudson Bay, *c.* 1764. *Hudson's Bay Company Archives, G.2/9.*
The map shows contemporary notions of that stretch of the west coast of Hudson Bay visited by the Hudson's Bay Company sloops on their annual trading voyages among the Eskimos, and along which some optimists in England still hoped a Northwest Passage might be found. Despite the claim implicit in the map's title, most of the 150 miles of coastline shown were known before the Company's discovery voyages of the early 1760s, both through the regular slooping voyages north from Churchill (which lies 230 miles south of Navel's Bay), and the explorations of Middleton (1741-2) and Moor (1746-7). The map's most important feature is the full representation of Chesterfield Inlet ('Bowden's Inlett'), discovered by the Moor expedition in 1747, but not thoroughly explored until Company discovery sloops entered it in 1762. Although the map was the most detailed of the area produced up to this time, it had few pretensions to modern standards of cartographical accuracy. Its longitudes show inaccuracies of between 1° and 2°, and its latitudes have smaller and more consistent errors of about 10′.

changes for the most part indirectly. For example, Henday was with Indians closely related to those seen by Kelsey more than sixty years earlier, and the lack of any mention in Kelsey's notes of the horses which figure so prominently in Henday's narrative lends weight to those who date the acquisition of horses by the Blackfoot of the northern plains to the 1740s. After their encounter with the Atsina, Henday's party wandered farther west, and since it was in the Bow River and Red Deer River area (somewhere near the site of modern Calgary) should have been within sight of the Rocky Mountains. It is one of the several puzzles of Henday's journals that they nowhere mention this stupendous mountain barrier in unambiguous terms. Although his only surveying equipment consisted of a compass and some paper, Henday is known to have drawn a 'Draft' of his travels, but of this map no trace remains. Just as in the case of the La Vérendrye brothers in 1742-3 and Niverville on the Saskatchewan in 1751, conclusive evidence of the first European sighting of the northern Rockies is lacking.

On his return journey to York in 1755 with a fleet of sixty or more Indian trade canoes, Henday had to run the gauntlet of the French posts on the Lower Saskatchewan, which lured away many of the best furs. The point was not missed by Henday: he had not only revealed the farflung and complex network of the Indian fur trade of the interior, but had discovered that the French western posts were creaming off the best of that trade, leaving the company posts at the Bayside with only the heavier, less valuable skins. His explorations provided strong arguments for a serious rethinking of company policy, but before the London Committee had reached any decision on the question of inland posts the Seven Years War brought dramatic changes in North America. The French in Canada were first distracted and then crippled by the constant campaigning, and the Montreal-based fur trade suffered in consequence. The conquest of Canada in 1759 and 1760 led to the abandonment of the western posts, and as the war drew to a close the fur trade of an immense area stretching as far as the Rockies seemed about to fall into the hands of the Hudson's Bay Company. Farther south too British traders and officials took over the fur trade of the Great Lakes and the Upper Mississippi area from the French, and among them were men who seemed to have inherited the French enthusiasm for western discovery. The ranger leader Robert Rogers proposed an expedition which would cross the continent near the headwaters of the Mississippi and then proceed down the westward-flowing river 'called by the Indians Ouragan'.[20] One of his lieutenants, Jonathan Carver,

307 Samuel Thornton's map of Hudson Bay, 1709. *Hudson's Bay Company Archives, G.2/2.*
This map by John Thornton's son illustrates the two rival routes to Hudson Bay: the seaborne approach used by the English through the narrow corridor of Hudson Strait, and the French overland approach from the St Lawrence by way of Lakes St John and Mistassini (the latter much elongated here). With its suggested boundary between the English and French running through the middle of the Labrador peninsula, the map was intended to support the contention of the Hudson's Bay Company during the peace negotiations of this period that the whole of the Hudson Bay area was British—despite the fact that York Fort had been in the hands of the French since 1697.

Hudsons Bay
James Bay
Hudsons Straits
Ruperts East Land
Laboradore
Nova Britania
New France
New South Wales
Canada
Sleepers Isles
Bakers Dozen
C. Churchill
Port Nelson
C. Smith
C. Jones
Charlton
Ruperts River
Moose
Albany
Grimingtons I.
Baffins Isles
C. Elizabeth
Isl Resolution
The grand Lake
Lake St. John
Anticosti
not to Goe to the Westward of this Line
not to Come to the Eastward of this Line
The French
The English
Made by Saml Thornton at the Signe of the Platt in the Minories London Anno 1709

308

309

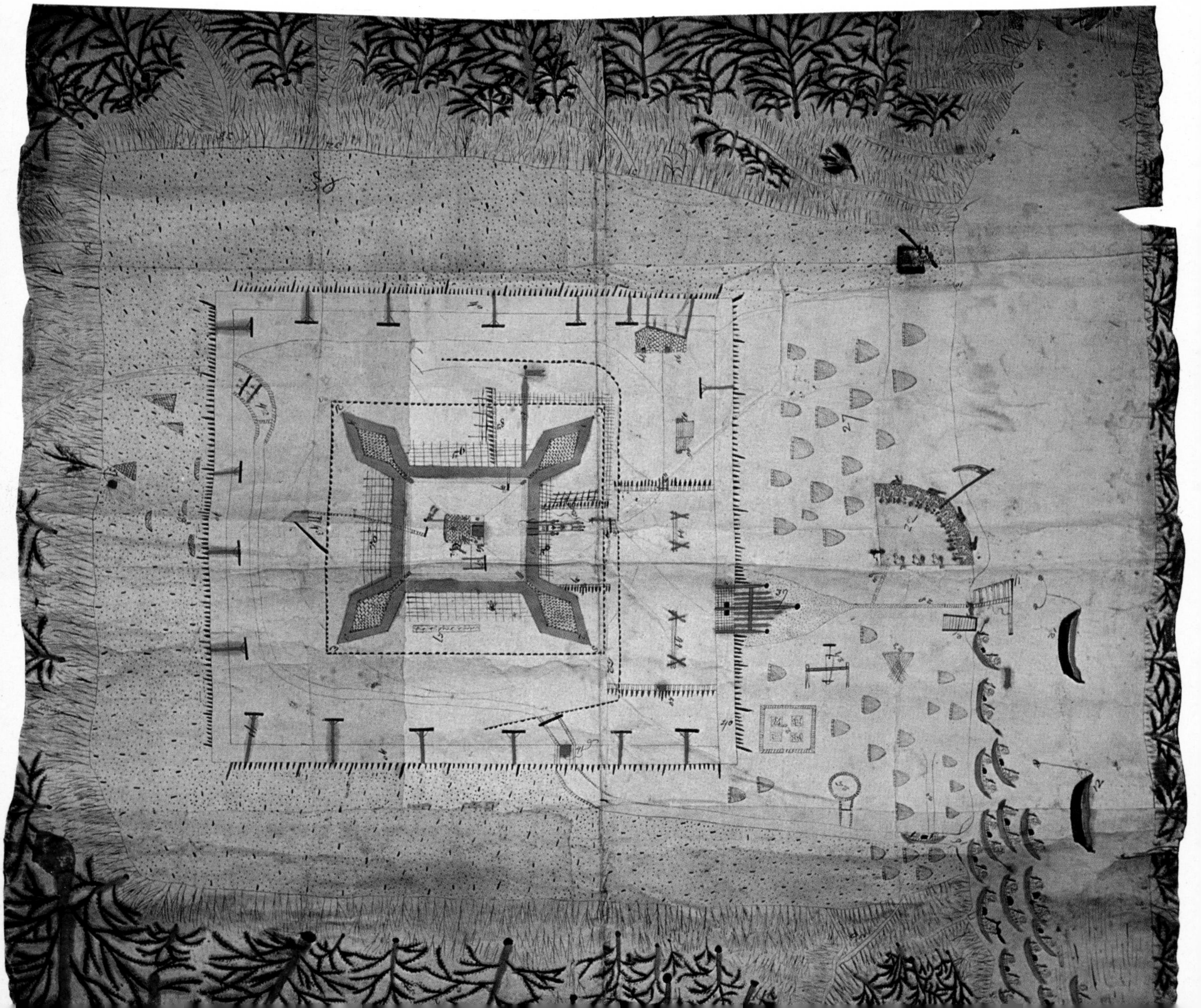

journeyed in 1766 and 1767 in the country between the Upper Mississippi and Lake Superior (see Chapter 2), and later published an account of his travels in which the old symmetrical concepts of North American geography appeared in revised form. He postulated a great north-south range of mountains in the center of the continent from which rivers flowed to all points of the compass, but it ended—conveniently—in about latitude 47°N. or 48°N. to leave room enough for a Northwest Passage. Although Carver's was an anglicized version of the French theoretical geography which had dominated the maps of North America for so long, he was one of the first to commit himself in print to an assessment of the barrier which lay between explorers coming from the east and the Pacific: 'This extraordinary range of mountains is calculated to be more than three thousand miles in length, without any very considerable intervals, which I believe surpasses any thing of the kind in other quarters of the globe.'[21]

The hopes of the Hudson's Bay Company that it would take over the western fur trade by default were short-lived, for the old French routes out of Montreal were soon in use again, this time by traders whose resources were far greater than those of the company's old rivals. Many of the French canoemen and interpreters remained, but they were now supported at Quebec, Montreal and Michilimackinac (Mackinac) by business men from Britain and the American colonies who possessed ample capital and organizing ability. By 1766 the Bay factors were complaining that the Indians were arriving with only the poorer furs, the coveted coat beaver and marten having gone to 'the English pedlars inland'.[22] By 1770 the 'pedlars' (who turned a term of contempt into one feared by their competitors) had reached beyond Lake Winnipeg, and established themselves at The Pas and at the other French sites of the pre-conquest years. Reconnaissance probes from Hudson Bay revealed the menacing extent of this new and formidable threat. William Tomison headed inland from the company post at the mouth of the Severn River to make in 1766-7 a circular journey around Lake Winnipeg in which he observed 'the English and French pedlars daily taking what furs the natives catches'.[23] In 1772-3 Matthew Cocking, despite his lack of surveying instruments and skills, struck deeper inland than any Hudson's Bay man since Henday, reaching well beyond the Forks of the Saskatchewan to the Eagle Hills; and everywhere he found the Canadian traders active. In 1773 the London Committee, reviewing the reports and maps sent home by Andrew Graham, its intelligent and articulate factor at York, decided to fight the Canadian

308 Indians hunting beaver, by James Isham, 1743. *Hudson's Bay Company Archives, E.2/2, fo 12.*
In his accompanying text Isham provided a key to this detailed sketch which, though not of much artistic merit, was drawn from first-hand observation by the Hudson's Bay Company factor.
(1) A Beaver house; (2) the tickness made of stone, mudd, & wood &c.; (3) where the Beaver Lyes within the house; (4) when the Beaver are Disturb'd, or hear a noise they make into the water, from 3 and 6; (5) where their food Lyes; (6) the half Beaver or small Beaver Lyes; (7) a Indian breaking the house op'n with a Chissel, tied to a Long stick; (8) the Beaver making out of the house hearing a noise and makes to the Vaults; (9) netts sett in the Creek with a string and a stick at the End to catch the Beaver as they come out of the house; (10) a Indian sitting by a fire watching a Nett, with a stick by him to Kill them as he hauls them out; (11) Dam's made by the Beaver, that the water shou'd not Run too fast upon them; (12) Vaults the Beaver makes into when Distur'd. out of the house, they Run abt. 12 or 14 foot in Land (i.e.) and abt. 2 foot under the Ground, a foot Square & a foot Deep; (13) a Beaver hawling a tree by the teeth into the water; (14) a stop'age made by Inds. with stakes to Keep the Beaver from going into the River; (15) a Beaver cutting a tree Downe with his teeth, wch. Lean's over the water; (16) the stump where cutt Down; (17) the tail of a beaver; (18) the Castor under wch. Lyes the oyly stones or 2 bladder's; (19) the penis and stones; (20) the Gutts or Interials; (21) the heart and Liver; (22) the Lights; (23) the fore feet; (24) Inds. tent in the woods; (25) a Indian going a hunting; (26) willows on the Edge of the creek; (27) a flock of partridges; (28) thick woods; (29) a stick Lying by the Indn. to Kill Beaver &c.; (30) the Creek which Run's into the Large Rivers &c.

309 Plan of York Fort, by James Isham, *c.* 1750. *Hudson's Bay Company Archives, G.2/5.*
Unfortunately the key to this numbered plan is lost. The wooden fort is shown here on the north bank of the Hayes River, surrounded by an outer stockade pierced by a single gate. Outside the stockade the wood has been cleared to give a clear view and field of fire. On the banks of the river a battery of cannon commands the river approach, where a flotilla of Indian canoes is shown arriving with their cargoes of furs. The plan is full of fascinating detail, such as the half-hidden figure in the top right-hand corner of a Company servant shooting geese from a pit in the ground. Isham's successor, Andrew Graham, described York as 'a handsome, well-built Fort, log on log and plastered on the outside, consisting of four bastions with sheds between them, and a breast work on which are mounted twelve small carriage guns, and good close quarters with a double row of strong palisadoes at proper distances round the fort, and on the bank's edge abreast the fort are two fascine batteries with a good planked platform on which are mounted thirteen heavy cannon.'

310

310 Three Hudson's Bay Company ships, 1769; wash drawing by John Hood. *Hudson's Bay Company Archives.*
The vessels were the *King George, Prince Rupert* and *Sea Horse*, all of about 200 tons, and they are seen here leaving Gravesend on their annual voyage to the posts in Hudson Bay with supplies and trade goods.

311

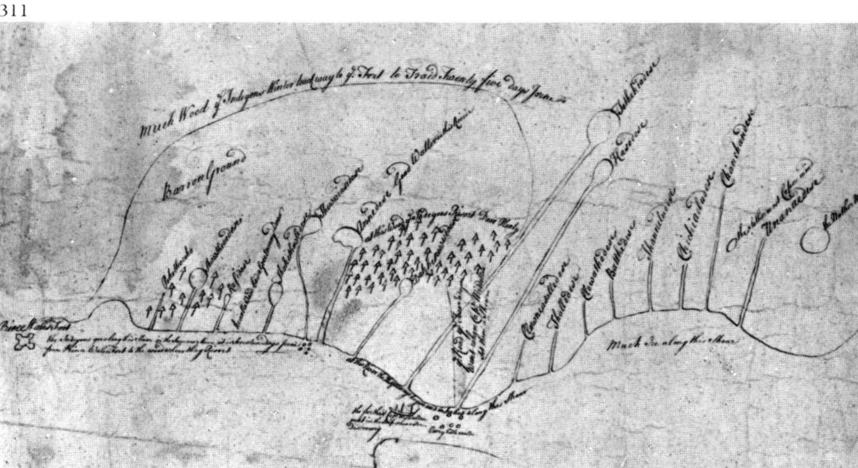

311 Indian map of the region between Prince of Wales Fort, Churchill, and the Coppermine River, *c.* 1767. *Hudson's Bay Company Archives, G.1/19.*
This map, with north to the right and drawn on parchment, represents the optimistic information about the coast to the north of Churchill brought back to the fort by two Chipewyan Indians, Idotliaze and Mattonabee, who had been sent northward in 1762 to investigate the rumored river of copper. Middleton's Frozen Strait (about 600 miles north of Churchill) is shown approximately halfway along the coastline, and the copper mines about the same distance farther on again. In reality, the coast north of Hudson Bay bends round Melville Peninsula at right angles, and then runs more than 1000 miles westward to the ice-choked mouth of the Coppermine River.

312

313

312 Prince of Wales Fort, Churchill River, Hudson Bay, 1777, from Samuel Hearne, *A journey to the Northern Ocean*, 1795.
The farthest north of the establishments of the Hudson's Bay Company in the eighteenth century, Churchill was founded in 1719 and then rebuilt as a stone fortress in the 1730s and 1740s. It was the only one of the Company posts to resemble a European-style fortification rather than a wilderness stockade, but despite its outward show of strength it was not kept on a war footing and it fell an easy prey to a French naval force in 1782, when Hearne was in command.

313 'Athapuscow Lake' (Great Slave Lake), from Samuel Hearne, *A journey to the Northern Ocean*, 1795.
Hearne reached the lake in December 1771 on his homeward journey, and described it as 'about one hundred and twenty leagues long from East to West, and twenty wide from North to South. The point where we crossed it is said to be the narrowest. It is full of islands; most of which are clothed with tall poplars, birch, and pines, and are well stocked with Indian deer. On some of the large islands we also found several beaver. . . .

competition at close quarters, and sent Samuel Hearne orders to establish a post near The Pas.

Hearne was an interesting rather than obvious choice, for although he had never commanded a company post he had lately returned from a notable journey to the Arctic Ocean which provided ample evidence of his toughness of mind and body. This northern expedition was essentially a continuance of efforts made by the Hudson's Bay Company since the 1750s to discover a navigable passage along the west coast of Hudson Bay which would lead it to the copper mines persistently reported somewhere north of Churchill, enable it to expand its Chipewyan and Eskimo trade, and silence criticism in England about its alleged lethargy in searching for the Northwest Passage. By 1764 intensive explorations by company sloops sailing out of Churchill had failed to find such a strait or passage, but an overland venture would not be restricted to the short ice-free navigable season available for coastal surveying. The factor at Churchill, Moses Norton, brought to London in 1768 a copy of 'a rude sketch, drawn with charcoal on a deer's skin, of a map of the country to the northward of Churchill', made by two Chipewyan Indians, Idotliaze and Mattonabee, who had spent five years hunting and exploring to the northwest (see plate 311). At their farthest point they claimed to have found a river which ran between copper mines in a country abounding in wood and furs. Impressed by this news, the London Committee authorized Norton to send Samuel Hearne, mate of one of the sloops at Churchill, on an overland journey in search of the copper mines and the Northwest Passage.

After two false starts Hearne carried out his task in 1770-2 with the aid of a group of Chipewyan Indians led by Mattonabee. They travelled, mainly on foot, across the bleak and featureless Barrens of the northern tundra. 'The land throughout that whole track of country,' Hearne wrote, 'is scarcely any thing but one solid mass of rocks and stones. . . . The surface it is very true, is in most places covered with a thin sod of moss . . . but under it there is in general a total want of soil.'[24] The Chipewyans and other Athapaskan Indians lived on fish and caribou; the streams, though numerous, were usually too shallow for canoes, and the best time for travelling was in winter when the frozen land gave a reasonable surface for snow-shoes and sledges. In July 1771 Hearne at his farthest north became the first European to sight the northern coastline of the American continent, but he found the Coppermine River, the object of so much attention since Knight's time, a sad disappointment (see selection 11). It was shallow and unnavigable, and the reputed mines of copper dwindled to a few scattered lumps. Hearne placed the mouth of the river in latitude 71° 54′N., almost four degrees too far north—a gigantic error which is a reminder that many of the inland explorers of this period were handicapped by their lack of training in survey work. The northwest was soon to be reached by a different school of explorer, versed in the intricacies of the scientific cartography that had developed in Europe in the second half of the eighteenth century. Philip Turnor, Peter Fidler, David Thompson: these were men who, with their sextants and chronometers, not only explored but surveyed, and whose journeys were thereby made immeasurably more valuable to those who followed. But Hearne's single latitude, incorrect though it was, shattered current theories about the Northwest Passage. He had crossed the unknown northeast corner of the continent without finding a strait or even a river of any note. News of the expedition was passed by the company to the British government, soon to send James Cook to the North Pacific to look for the western entrance of the Northwest Passage, and Hearne's own account was published (unlike earlier company journeys), although not until 1795. His book is a classic of northern travel. It reveals Hearne as a percipient observer of the Chipewyan Indians, hitherto little known even to Hudson's Bay men, and a superb if untrained naturalist whose notes on the wild life of the Canadian north were the best to appear in print during the whole century.

Hearne's task in setting up the Hudson's Bay Company's first genuine inland post at Cumberland House on Pine Island Lake (sixty miles beyond The Pas and just north of the Saskatchewan) in 1774 was less spectacular than his northern journey but equally challenging. Four hundred miles inland from York as the crow flies, nearer seven hundred by canoe, the little post could offer only feeble resistance to the Canadian traders as they bypassed it on their way westward. Individual explorers and traders of the toughness and flamboyance of Alexander Henry (see selection 12), Peter Pond and Alexander MacKenzie seemed to typify the energetic ruthlessness of the Northwest Company—as the most important association of the Canadian traders soon became known—in comparison

314-5 Two northern animals from Thomas Pennant, *Arctic zoology*, I, 1784.

314 The Moose, *Alces alces* (Linnaeus), whose European race is the Elk. A live Moose was sent to England from Hudson Bay in 1767, and others later; but Pennant seems to have based this illustration on a portrayal of the European Elk by the celebrated English painter, George Stubbs.

315 The Muskox, *Ovibos moschatus* (Zimmerman). The Cow is shown full-length, the Bull by its head only. Pennant owed both his account and illustration of this little-known animal (whose habitat stretched away into the bleak regions northwest of Hudson Bay) to Samuel Hearne, who sent a complete skin to England from the Hudson's Bay Company post at Churchill in 1783. Earlier descriptions of the Muskox by Jérémie and other writers had been brief and incomplete.

314

315

with which the Hudson's Bay Company often appeared sluggish and unenterprising. But appearances were deceptive. In its own dogged way the English company continued the move inland, set in motion by Hearne. Cumberland House was the first in a long chain of inland posts; and it was the symbol of the Company's new policy. Its establishment marked the beginning of a half-century of direct and often violent competition in the fur trade which was to take the rival organizations from Hudson Bay and the St Lawrence westward into Athapaska, across the Rockies and finally on to the Pacific slope.

Fig 4 Hudson Bay to the Rockies

1
The 'Bay of the North', 1659-60

From Radisson's narrative of *c.* 1668-9

One of the several controversial aspects of Radisson's narrative concerns the alleged journey which he and Groseilliers made from the Lake Superior region to Hudson Bay. Although it is difficult to see how the expedition can be fitted into the known chronology of the movements of the two men, Radisson's description has an authentic ring; and as far as the future development of the fur trade was concerned it is immaterial whether the Frenchman was speaking from first-hand knowledge or from Cree information.

We went away wth all hast possible to arrive the sooner att ye great river. We came to the seaside, where we finde an old howse all demollished and battered wth boulletts. We weare told yt those that came there weare of two nations, one of the wolf, the other of the long-horned beast. All those nations are distinguished by the representation of the beasts or animals. They tell us particularities of the Europians. We know ourselves, and what Europ is, therefore in vaine they tell us as for that.

We went from Isle to Isle all that summer. We pluckt aboundance of Ducks, as of all other sort of fowles; we wanted nor fish nor fresh meate. We weare well beloved, and weare overjoyed that we promised them to come wth such shipps as we invented. This place hath a great store of cows [caribou]. The wildmen kill them not except for necessary use. We went further in the bay to see ye place that they weare to passe that summer. That river comes from the lake and empties itself in ye river of Sagnes, called Tadousack, wch is a hundred leagues in the great river of Canada, as where we weare in ye Bay of ye north. We left in this place our marks and rendezvous . . .

This [the Cree] is a wandring nation, and containeth a vaste countrey. In winter they live in ye land for the hunting sake, and in summer by the watter for fishing. They never are many together, ffor feare of worrying one another. They are of a good nature, & not great whore masters, having but one wife, and are [more] satisfied then any others that I knewed. They cloath themselves all over with castors' [beavers'] skins in winter, in summer of staggs' skins. They are the best huntsmen of all America, and scorns to catch a castor in a trappe.

Text used: Gideon D. Scull (Ed.), Voyages of Peter Esprit Radisson, *The Prince Society, Boston, 1885, pp. 224-6.*

2
The French and the overland route to Hudson Bay, 1672

From Father Claude Dablon's *Relation* of 1671-2

The arrival of the *Nonsuch* in Hudson Bay in 1668, the incorporation of the Hudson's Bay Company in 1670, and the second wintering by

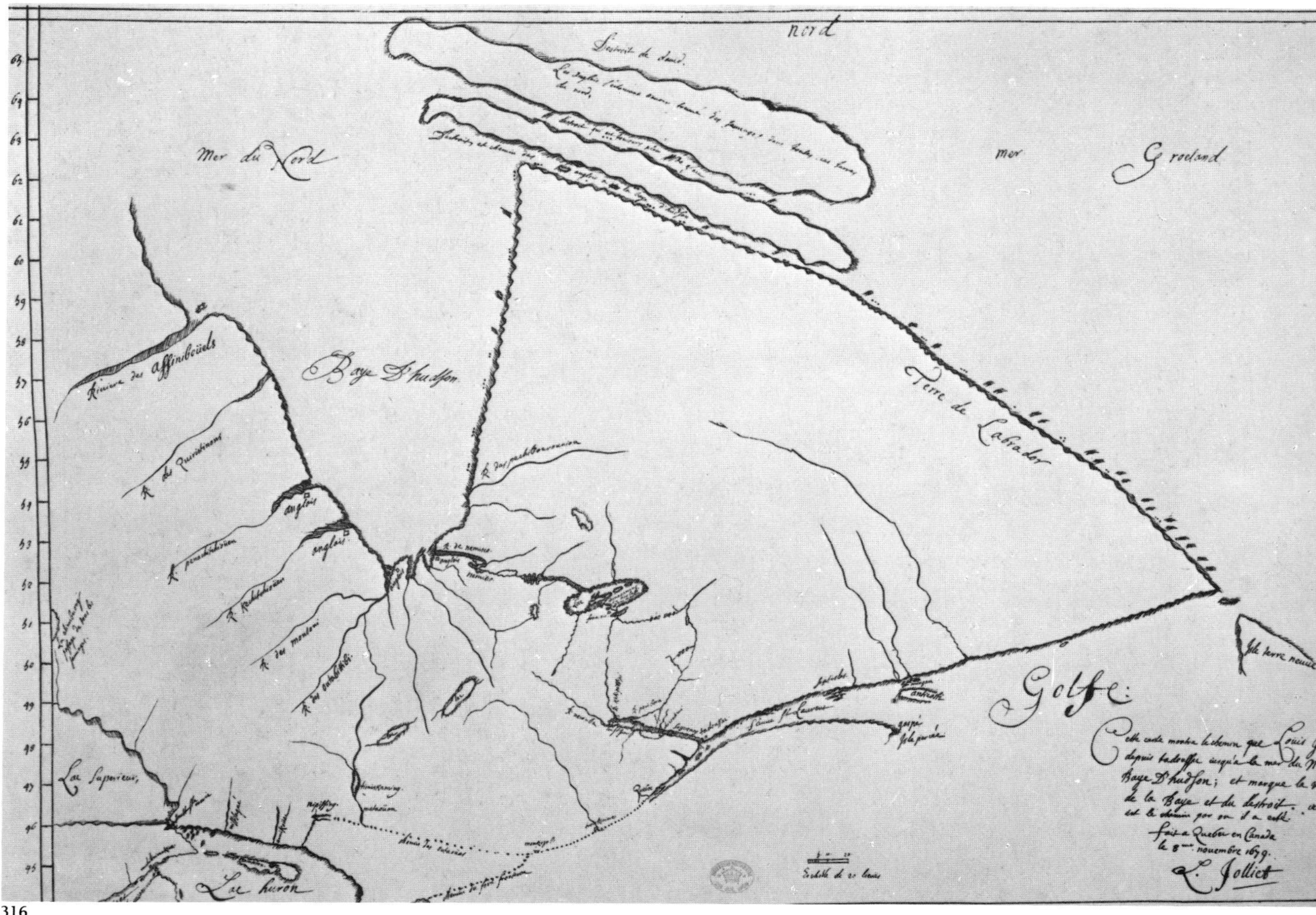

316

the English at Rupert River in 1670-1, caused considerable concern among the French in Canada. In 1671-2 a party which included the Jesuit Father Albanel journeyed overland from the St Lawrence to Fort Charles on Rupert River, wintering on the way. Dablon's *Relation* introduced the journey, and then included an account of the expedition as given by Albanel.

The sea to the North of us is the famous bay to which Hutson gave his name; it has long been stirring our Frenchmen's curiosity to discover it by land, and learn its situation with reference to ourselves, its distance, and what tribes dwell on its shores. The wish to gain a knowledge of this sea has increased since we learned through our Savages that very recently some ships made their appearance there, and even opened a trade with those Nations, who have always been represented to us as populous, and rich in peltries. . . .

On the first of June, 1672, we set out from Nataschegamiou to continue our journey, our party numbering nineteen, of whom sixteen were Savages and three Frenchmen, in three canoes. We had six days' journey of rapids, where we were obliged to propel the canoes almost constantly against the current. Very often we had to land and walk through the woods,—climbing over rocks, leaping into ditches, and again scrambling up steep heights through clumps of trees whose branches tore our clothes; while, with all that, we were very heavily burdened. After this, we were delayed two days by rains.

The ninth tried our patience severely by reason of an extremely difficult portage, both on account of its length, which some place at four leagues, and because of the bad travelling. One must always be in the water half-way to his knees, and at times even to his waist, in crossing and recrossing streams that flow through the midst of a vast Plain which must be traversed to gain the river Nekoubau, to the Southwest of the one left behind. Even the Savages dread this journey, as one full of fatigues and peril. . . .

On the 28th. [June], scarcely had we proceeded a quarter of a league when we encountered, in a small stream on our left, a hoy of ten or twelve tons, with its rigging, carrying the English flag and a lateen sail. A musket-shot's distance thence, we entered two deserted houses. A little farther on, we found that the Savages had wintered near there, and had recently taken their departure. We pursued our course, accordingly, as far as a point of land six leagues distant from the house of the Europeans. There, the tide being low and the wind against us, we withdrew, the mud up to our waists, into a little river on our right, flowing towards the Northeast. Here, upon turning and looking around, we found two or three cabins and an abandoned dog, showing us that the Savages were near, and had decamped only two days before. All that evening we remained there, firing loud musket-shots to make ourselves heard, and amusing ourselves with watching the sea which we had so long sought, and that famous Hutson's bay. . . .

316 Louis Jolliet. 'Carte des regions entre le Saint-Lawrent et la baie d'Hudson . . .', 1679, from A. L. Pinart, *Recueil de cartes, plans et vues . . .*, 1893.
The map, in Jolliet's own hand, shows the arduous route which he followed in 1679 from Tadoussac, along the Saguenay River, past Lake Mistassini, then down to James Bay and the 'anglois' at the mouth of Rupert River. Other Hudson's Bay Company posts at Moose and Albany are also marked; the one shown farther north is probably Severn, which was not in fact established until 1686, although the possibility of a post there was being discussed at the time of Jolliet's visit to the Bay.

317

318

319

317-19 Indian treatment of captives, from P. Lafitau, *Moeurs des sauvages Ameriquains*, 1724.
These illustrations show:
317 the prisoners staked out for the night by their captors;
318 the three bound prisoners running a gauntlet of blows as they approach an Indian village;
319 one of the prisoners being burnt to death on a frame.

Hitherto this journey has been deemed impossible for the French, who had already thrice attempted it, but, unable to overcome the obstacles in its way, had been forced to abandon it in despair of success. . . . It is true this journey is extremely difficult, and all that I write about it is but half of what the traveler must endure. There are 200 saults, or waterfalls, and consequently 200 portages, where both canoe and luggage must be carried on the back. There are 400 rapids, where a long pole must be constantly in hand in order to surmount them. I say nothing of the difficulties to be encountered on foot; they must be experienced to be understood. But one takes courage when he thinks how many souls can be won to Jesus Christ. Going and returning, the distance is 800 leagues; we covered 600 in less than forty days. Our rule was to start early in the morning, and encamp very late. Setting forth as soon as the dawn allowed us to catch but a glimpse of the rocks in the river, we continued until, for lack of light, we could no longer distinguish them.

Text used: R. G. Thwaites (Ed.), Jesuit Relations, *vol. 56, pp. 149, 169, 185-7, 213.*

3
Kelsey journeys inland, 1690

From Henry Kelsey's journal, 1690-1

Until the present century the only description of Kelsey's inland travels from York Factory in 1690-2 was a fragmentary journal for the months July to September 1691 which was printed in 1749. In 1926 a collection of manuscripts which had belonged to Arthur Dobbs, the eighteenth-century critic of the Hudson's Bay Company, was found to contain a volume inscribed 'Henry Kelsey his Book . . .' which included not only a fuller version of the 1691 journal but also a rhyming prologue which described Kelsey's travels in 1690, and established that his perplexing Dering's Point must be at or near The Pas on the Lower Saskatchewan.

320

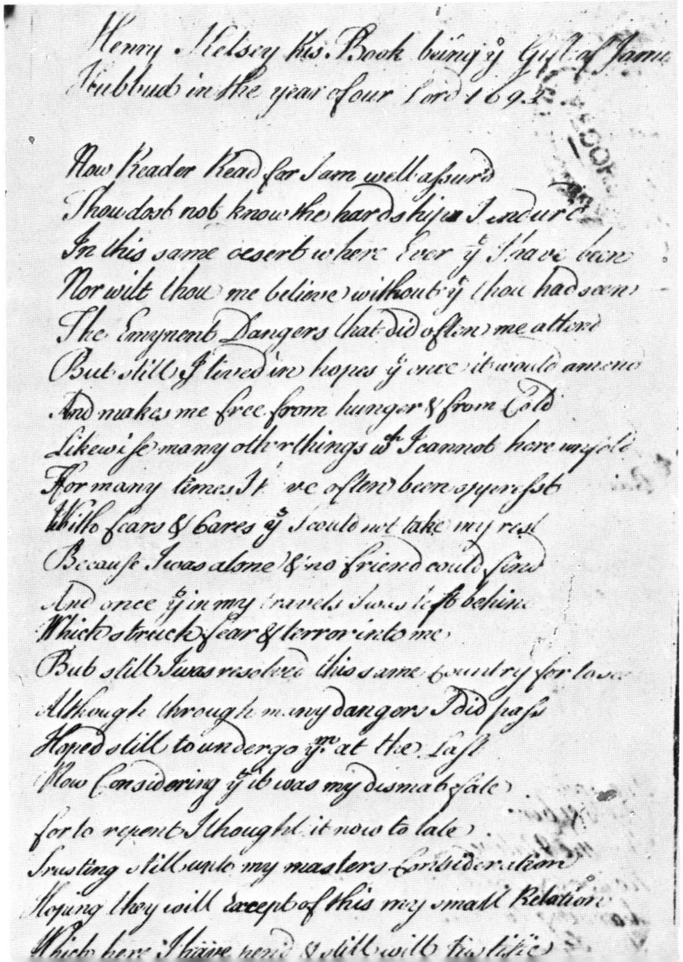

321

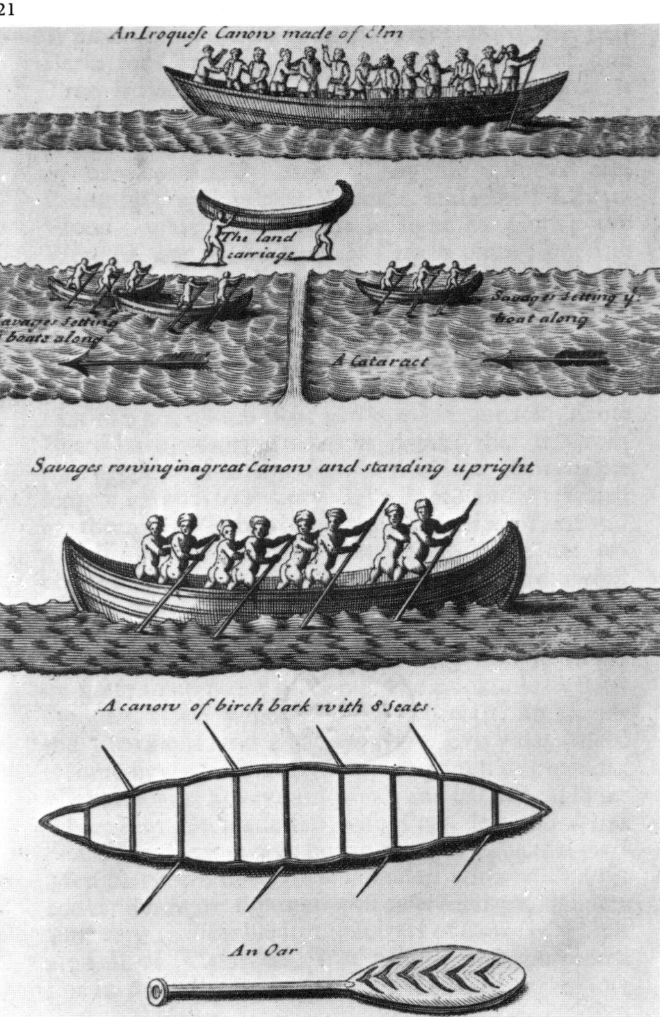

320 The first page of Henry Kelsey's journal, 1690-1. *Public Record Office of Northern Ireland, Belfast, DD162/7.*

321 Indian birch-bark canoes, from the English edition of Lahontan's *New voyages*, 1703.
'. . . the least of all hold but two Persons set upon their Breech, as in a Coffin; and are apt to over-set, if the Passengers move to one side or t'other: But those of a larger size will easily afford stowage for fourteen Persons; tho' they are commonly mann'd only with three Men, when they are imploy'd in transporting Provisions and Merchandize; and even then they'll carry twenty hundred weight . . . they are so light, that two Men carry 'em upon their shoulders with ease. This conveniency of lightness and easie carriage, renders 'em very serviceable in the Rivers of *Canada*, which are full of Cataracts, Water-falls, and Currents. . . .'

Now Reader Read for I am well assur'd
Thou dost not know the hardships I endur'd
In this same desert where Ever yt I have been
Nor wilt thou me believe without yt thou had seen
The Emynent Dangers that did often me attend
But still I lived in hopes yt once it would amend
And make me free from hunger & from Cold
Likewise many other things wch I cannot here unfold
For many times I have often been oppresst
With fears and Cares yt I could not take my rest
Because I was alone & no friend could find
And once yt in my travels I was left behind
Which struck fear & terror into me
But still I was resolved this same Country for to see
Although through many dangers I did pass
Hoped still to undergo ym, at the Last
Now Considering yt it was my dismal fate
For to repent I thought it now to late

Trusting still unto my masters Consideration
Hoping they will Except of this my small Relation
Which here I have pend & still will Justifie
Concerning of those Indians & their Country
If this wont do farewell to all as I may say
And for my living i'll seek some other way
In sixteen hundred & ninety'th year
I set forth as plainly may appear
Through Gods assistance for to understand
The natives language & to see their land
And for my masters interest I did soon
Sett from y house ye twealth of June
Then up ye River I with heavy heart
Did take my way & from all English part
To live amongst ye Natives of this place
If god permits me for one two years space
The Inland Country of Good report hath been
By Indians but by English not yet seen
Therefore I on my Journey did not stay
But making all ye hast I could upon our way
Gott on ye borders of ye stone Indian Country
I took possession on ye tenth Instant July
And for my masters I speaking for you all
This neck of land I deerings point did call
Distance from hence by Judgement at ye lest
From ye house six hundred miles southwest
Through Rivers wch run strong with falls
Thirty-three Carriages five lakes in all
The ground begins for to be dry with wood
Poplo & birch with ash thats very good
For the Natives of that place wch knows
No use of Better than their wooden Bows
According to ye use & custom of this place
In September I brought these Natives to a peace
But I had no sooner from these Natives turned my back
Some of the home Indians came upon their track
And for old grudges & their minds to fill
Came up with them Six tents of wch they kill'd
This ill news kept secrett was from me
Nor none of those home Indians did I see
Untill that they their murder all had done
And the Chief acter was he yts called ye Sun
So far I have spoken concerning of the spoil
And now will give accot. of that same Country soile
Which hither part is very thick of wood
Affords small nutts wth little cherryes very good
Thus it continues till you leave ye woods behind
And then you have beast of severall kind
The one is a black a Buffillo great

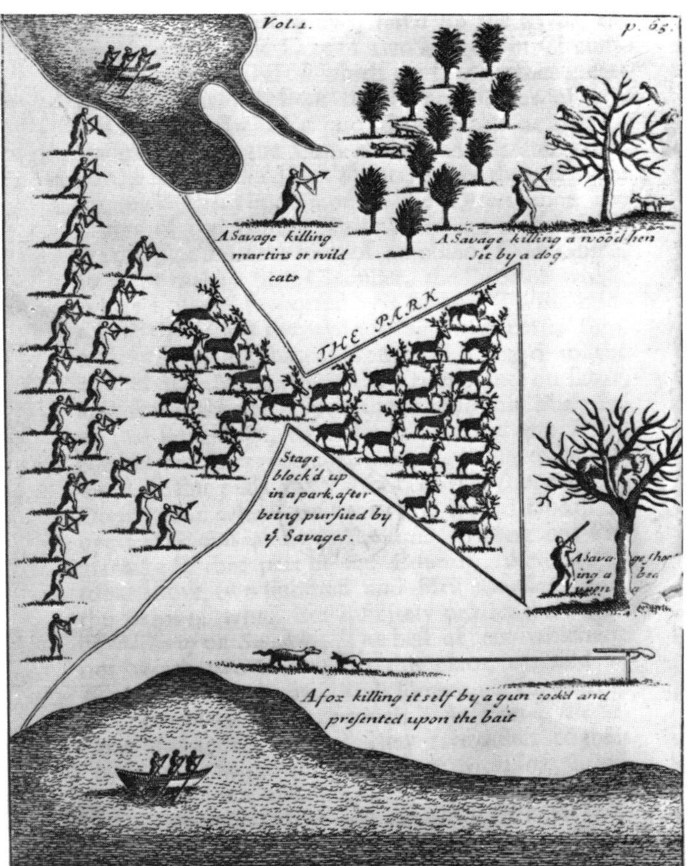

322

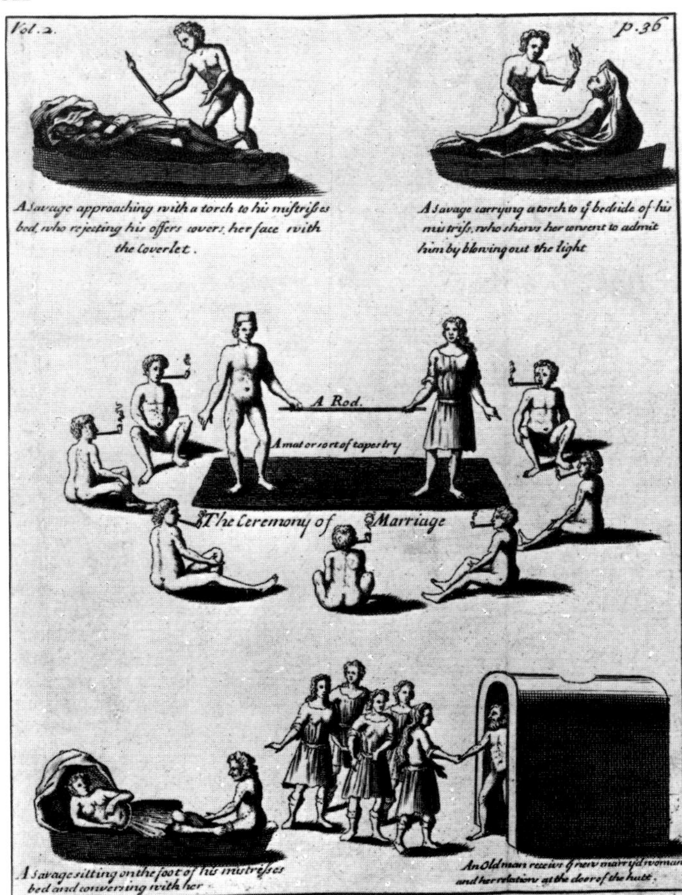

323

322 Indians hunting, from the English edition of Lahontan's *New voyages*, 1703.
In this edition, Lahontan wrote, he had 'corrected almost all the Cuts of the Holland Impression, for the Dutch Gravers had murder'd 'em, by not understanding their Explications, which were all in Franch. They have grav'd Women for Men, and Men for Women; naked Persons for those that are cloath'd, and è Contra.'

323 Indian courtship and marriage, from the English edition of Lahontan's *New voyages*, 1703.
'. . . the two Parties stand upright upon a fine Mat, holding a Rod between them, while the old Men pronounce some short Harangues. In this Posture do the two married Persons Harangue one after another, and Dance together, singing all the while, and holding the Rod in their Hands, which they afterwards break into as many pieces as there are Witnesses to the Ceremony, in order to be distributed among them . . . 'Tis allowable both for the Man and the Woman to part when they please. Commonly they give one another eight Days Warning . . . Then the little pieces of the Rod that were distributed among the Relations of the married Persons, are brought into that Hut in which the Marriage was Solemniz'd, and burnt in their Presence.'

Another is an outgrown Bear wch is good meat
His skin to gett I have used all ye ways I can
He is mans food & he makes food of man
His hide they would not me it preserve
But said it was a god & they should starve
This plain affords nothing but Beast & grass
And over it in three days time we past
Getting unto ye woods on the other side
It being about forty sixe miles wide
This wood is poplo ridges with small ponds of water
There is beavour in abundance but no Otter
With plains & ridges in the Country throughout
Their Enemies many whom they cannot rout
But now of late they hunt their Enemies
And with our English guns do make ym flie
At deerings point after the forst
I set up their a Certain Cross
In token of my being there
Cut out on it ye date of year
And Likewise for to veryfie the same
Added to it my master sir Edward deerings name
So having not more to trouble you wth all I am
Sir your most obedient & faithful Servt at Command

Henry Kelsey

Text used: A. G. Doughty and Chester Martin (Eds.), The Kelsey Papers, *Ottawa, 1929, pp. 1-4.*

4
James Knight, gold and the Northwest Passage

From Knight's York Factory journal, 1715-16

James Knight received the surrender of York Factory from the French in 1714 on behalf of the Hudson's Bay Company, and the next year sent William Stuart and some Cree Indians inland among the Northern (Chipewyan) Indians to discover the potentialities of the region to the northwest. The party returned in 1716 with a group of Chipewyans, and one of their women slaves, a chief's wife from a tribe farther west still, who between them gave the credulous Knight all the information he wanted about gold and a sea-route to the west.

[10 May 1716]. I have had abundance of discourse with them the Northern Indians about there Country and did gett them to lay down there Rivers along Shore to the Norward they chalked 17 Rivers some of them very Large. But I could not hear by them that thare is any Straights that parts Asia from America but they told me there is a very Great River that comes out of the West Sea and is in the bottom of a very Great Bay where there lyes 3 Islands in the Mouth of the Bay, allmost out of sight of Land where them Indians Inhabit thare brings a Yellow Mettle from thence and warres it as they and the Copper Indians doth Copper. . . .
[12 May 1716]. I have had a great deal of further discourse with those Northern Indians about there country they still persist in it there is 17 Rivers from Churchill River to ye Norwards but from there Discourse I begin to think there may be a Passage or Straits that parts America from Asia and it is for this Reason after you are past the third River from Churchill they tell me thare is no wood grows till they come to ye 13th River and then there begins to grow wood again and all the other 4 Rivers the woods begins to grow bigger and thicker and the 17th River is bigger than any of the rest so that I believe they go round the Land wch if they did not it is Impossible that there should be more Wood to ye Norward than to ye Southward it being the last River that has the biggest wood. . . .
[12 July 1716]. She [the slave-woman] has both seen it taken and took it up out of the River her self as it has washt out of the Bank it is very Yellow soft and heavy and that they find lumps so bigg sometimes that they hammer it betwixt stones and make dishes of it. There is likewise a white mettle they make the same use of but in the hammering they say it is a ringing Noise to what Yellow Mettle has. She further tells me that they every Summer see Sevll Ships in the Western Seas wch I cannot think to be Spaniards because they use so farr to ye Norward as 62. I rather take them to be Tartars or Jappanness Vessells and they see 'em go to some great Islands that lyes within sight of the Land and that there is very little Ice in them seas in the Winter and these Northern Indians that was with me this Spring does assure me that great Wood does grow all along the Westland Country and that shows there is an Open Sea that it is not so cold as the East part of America . . .

Text used: James Knight, York Fort Journal 1715-16, *Hudson's Bay Company Archives B.239/a/2, fos. 29d.-30, 31d., 44d.-45.*

324 Title-page of James Knight's York Fort journal for 1715-16. *Hudson's Bay Company Archives, B.239/a/2.*
It was the regular duty of a Hudson's Bay Company factor to keep a daily journal of events at his trading post and to send it to England by the yearly ship.

325 John Wigate. 'Chart of the Seas, Straits &c. thro' which his Majesty's Sloop 'Furnace' pass'd for discovering a Passage from Hudson's Bay to the South Sea', London, 1746. *British Museum, London.*
Wigate's map was produced as evidence of the continued likelihood of a Northwest Passage through Hudson Bay. It shows several openings along a largely unsurveyed coastline north of Churchill, a strait opening out through the Wager, but none to the north where Middleton had put his Frozen Strait (plate 296). See also plate 326.

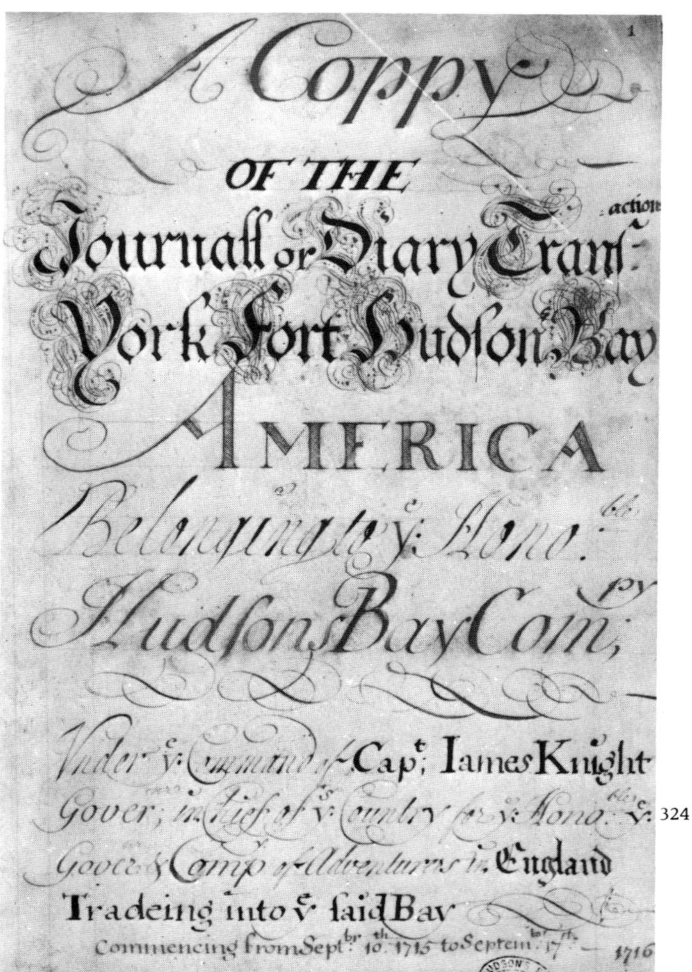
A Coppy
OF THE
Journall or Diary Transactions
York Fort Hudsons Bay
AMERICA
Belonging to ye Honoble
Hudsons Bay Compy
Under ye Command of Capt James Knight
Gover in Chief of ye Country for ye Honoble ye
Gover & Comp of Adventurers in England
Tradeing into ye said Bay
Commencing from Septbr 10th 1715 to Septembr 17th 1716

324

PARTS UNKNOWN
Lieut. Rankin was up this Strait as far as the three last Islands & notwithstanding he had a fresh of Wind & strong Tide of Flood from the W.S.W. brought him to a Grapnel so that there is the highest Probability that this whole Coast (which we did not search) consists of broken Lands & Islands & cannot be far from the Great Western Ocean especially as Whales came from the Westward into Wager Strait with every Tide of Flood as far as Deer Sound
Repulse Bay discover'd 1742
Var. 50
C. Hope
Wager Strait
Deer Sound
Savage Sound
The New Strait
Low Beach Pt.
C. Dobbs
Whalebone Pt.
C. Fullerton
This Coast unknown
Sir THO: ROE'S Welcome
Var. 35
Brook Cobham
Whale Cove
Lovegrove, a fair open S. to the Westward of Whale Cove.
Seal River
C. Churchill
Var. 18
Churchill R.
York Fort
C. Tatnam
Nelson River
R. de Terre Rouge
New Severn River
W. Pens
E. Pens
Var. 21
Mill Isles
Queen Marys Cape
Queen Anne's Foreland
White Bear Bay
Nottingham Isle
Salisbury
C. Diggs
Diggs Isle
Var. 43
C. Pembroke
Cape Southampton
Mansela I.
Var. 37
Var. 33
North Sleepers
West Sleepers
C. Smith
C. of Hope's Advance
NORT MAIN
HUDSON'S BAY
A NEW DISCOVERED SEA
Bakers Dozen
Belchers Isles
Var. 21
Marvel Head
C. Henrietta Maria
JAMES'S BAY
Bear Islands
The Cubbs
Var. 19
Twins
C. Jones
Gull I.
C. Hope
Slude River
Albany River
Albany
Cakechichouan River
Charlton I.
P. Comfort
Ruperts R.
Moose R.
Onahanna R.
LABA
NEW
NEW FRANCE
GULF OF S
R. Canada
Quebec
THE Smaller Figures in this Chart are the Depths in Fathoms. The Literal or Roman Figures shew the Hour of High Water or rather the End of the Stream The Direction of the Darts shew upon what Point of the Compass the Tide of Flood setts and the Numbers to which Var. is prefix'd shew the Degrees of the Magnetical Variation Westerly.

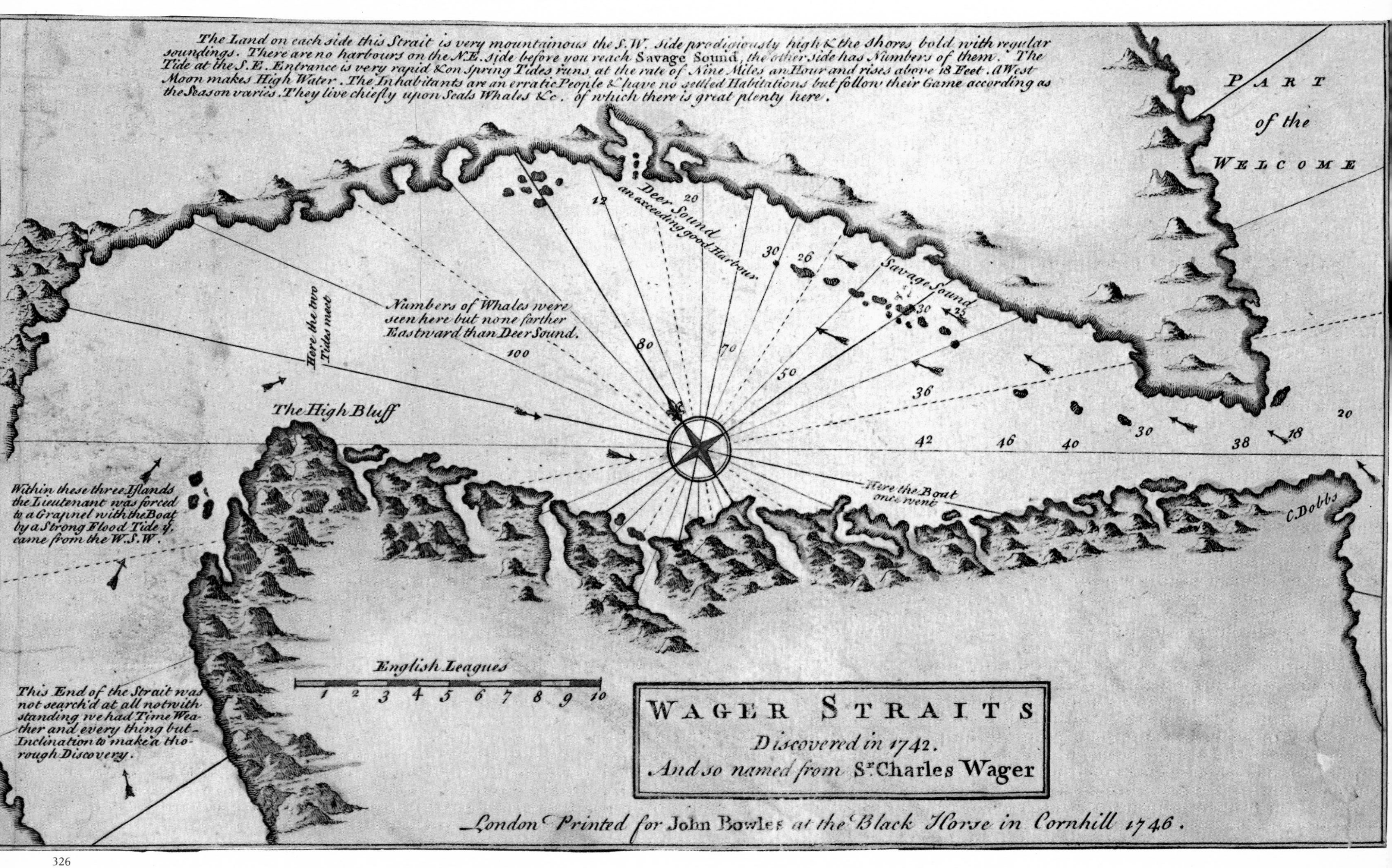
The Land on each side this Strait is very mountainous the S.W. side prodigiously high & the Shores bold with regular soundings. There are no harbours on the N.E. side before you reach Savage Sound, the other side has Numbers of them. The Tide at the S.E. Entrance is very rapid & on Spring Tides runs at the rate of Nine Miles an Hour and rises above 18 Feet. A West Moon makes High Water. The Inhabitants are an erratic People & have no settled Habitations but follow their Game according as the Season varies. They live chiefly upon Seals Whales &c. of which there is great plenty here.
PART of the WELCOME
Deer Sound an exceeding good Harbour.
Savage Sound
Numbers of Whales were seen here but none farther Eastward than Deer Sound.
Here the two Tides meet
The High Bluff
Here the Boat once went
C. Dobbs
Within these three Islands the Lieutenant was forced to a Grapnel with the Boat by a Strong Flood Tide y. came from the W.S.W.
This End of the Strait was not search'd at all notwithstanding we had Time Weather and every thing but Inclination to make a thorough Discovery.
English Leagues
1 2 3 4 5 6 7 8 9 10
WAGER STRAITS
Discovered in 1742.
And so named from Sr. Charles Wager
London Printed for John Bowles at the Black Horse in Cornhill 1746.

5
Lahontan and the 'noble savage'

From Baron Lahontan, *New Voyages*, London, 1703

The Baron Lahontan (Louis-Armand de Lom d'Arce) spent the years 1683 to 1692 in New France. His *Voyages*, published when its author was on the verge of bankruptcy, achieved immediate popularity and a wide circulation, and passed through dozens of editions and abridgements in French, English, German and Dutch. Despite Lahontan's disrespect in places for factual accuracy, his vivid style brought North America and its inhabitants before a wider reading public than any previous writer.

A short View of the Humors and Customs of the SAVAGES

The Savages are utter Strangers to distinctions of Property, for what belongs to one is equally anothers. If any one of them be in danger at the Beaver Hunting the rest fly to his Assistance without being so much as ask'd. If his Fusee bursts they are ready to offer him their own. If any of his Children be kill'd or taken by the Enemy, he is presently furnish'd with as many Slaves as he hath occasion for. Money is in use with none of them but those that are Christians, who live in the Suburbs of our Towns. The others will not touch or so much as look upon Silver, but give it the odious Name of the *French Serpent*. They'l tell you that amongst us the People Murther, Plunder, Defame, and betray one another, for Money, that the Husbands make Merchandize of their Wives, and the Mothers of their Daughters, for the Lucre of that Metal. They think it unaccountable that one Man should have more than another, and that the Rich should have more Respect than the Poor. In short, they say, the name of Savages which we bestow upon them would fit our selves better, since there is nothing in our Actions that bears an appearance of Wisdom. Such as have been in France were continually teazing us with the Faults and Disorders they observ'd in our Towns, as being occasion'd by Money. 'Tis in vain to remonstrate to them how useful the Distinction of Property is for

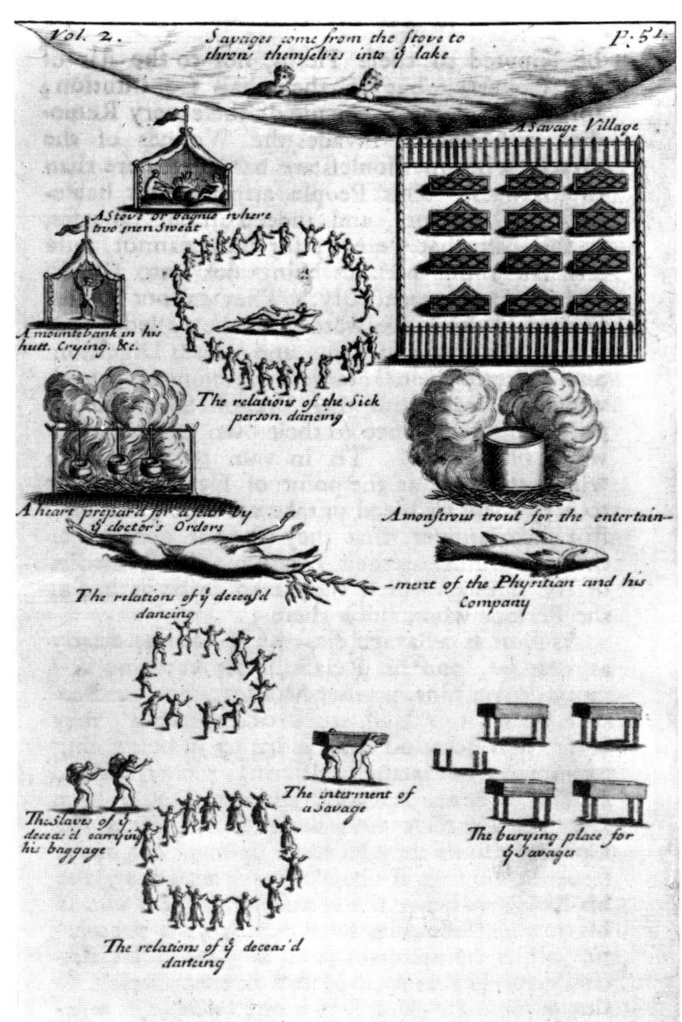

327

328

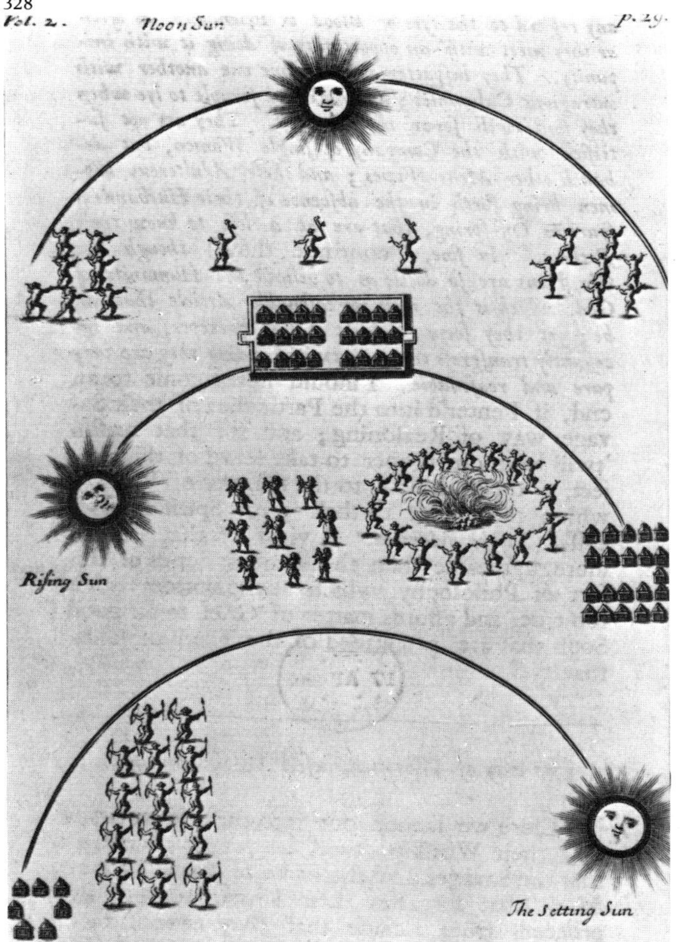

326 John Wigate. 'Wager Straits', London, 1746. *British Museum, London.* Another map drawn by Middleton's former clerk to demonstrate the possibility of a Northwest Passage. Middleton, on his expedition to Hudson Bay in search of the Passage in 1741-2, had not sailed near enough the coast between Marble Island and the Wager to have made a thorough examination, and so he missed Chesterfield Inlet. (See plates 296 and 325.)

327 Illness and death among the Indians, from the English edition of Lahontan's *New voyages*, 1703.
'The Savages are not at all alarm'd by Sickness, for they fear Death much less than the Pain and Duration of their Illness. . . . When they are ill, they are always visited by a sort of Quacks, (*Jongleurs*) . . . who being once cur'd of some dangerous Distemper, has the Presumption and Folly to fancy that he is immortal, and possessed of the Power of curing all Diseases, by speaking to the Good and Evil Spirits. . . . When the Quack comes to visit the Patient, he examines him very carefully; *If the Evil Spirit be here*, says he, *we shall quickly dislodge him*. This said, he withdraws by himself to a little Tent made on purpose, where he dances and sings houling like an Owl. . . .'

328 Sacrificial dance of the Indians, from the English edition of Lahontan's *New voyages*, 1703.
'The Savages never Offer Sacrifices of Living Creatures to the *Kitchi Manitou*; for their common Sacrifices upon that occasion are the Goods that they take from the *French* in exchange for *Beavers*. Several persons of good Credit have inform'd me, that in one day they Burnt at *Missilimackinac*, Fifty Thousand Crowns worth of such Goods. I never saw so Expensive a Ceremony, my self. . . .'

329

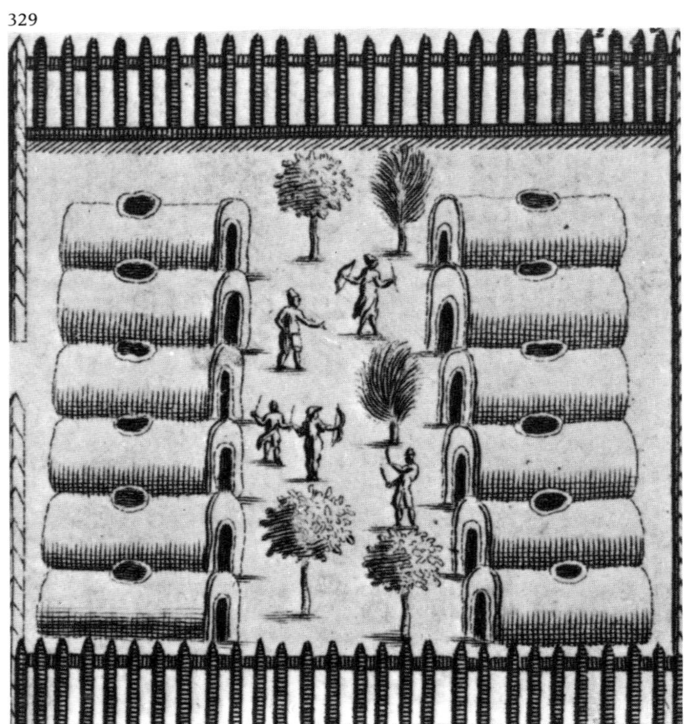

329 The village shown is probably a representation of one of the Huron villages in the Mackinac region which Lahontan knew so well; from the English edition of Lahontan's *New voyages*, 1703.

the support of a Society: They make a Jest of what's to be said on that Head. In fine, they neither Quarrel nor Fight, nor Slander one another. They scoff at Arts and Sciences, and laugh at the difference of Degrees which is observ'd with us. They brand us for Slaves, and call us miserable Souls, whose Life is not worth having, alledging, That we degrade our selves in subjecting our selves to one Man who possesses the whole Power, and is bound by no Law but his own Will; That we have continual Jars among our selves; that our Children rebel against their Parents; that we Imprison one another, and publickly promote our own Destruction. Besides, they value themselves above anything that you can imagine, and this is the reason they always give for't, *That one's as much Master as another, and since Men are all made of the same Clay there should be no Distinction or Superiority among them.* They pretend that their contented way of Living far surpasses our Riches; that all our Silences are not so valuable as the Art of leading a peaceful calm Life; that a Man is not a Man with us any farther than Riches will make him; but among them the true Qualifications of a Man are, to run well, to hunt, to bend the Bow and manage the Fuzee, to work a Cannoo, to understand War, to know Forrests, to subsist upon a little, to build Cottages, to fell Trees, and to be able to travel an hundred Leagues in a Wood without any Guide, or other Provision than his Bow and Arrows.

Text used: Baron Lahontan, New Voyages to North-America, *London, 1703, vol. II, pp. 7-9.*

6
La Vérendrye reaches the Mandans, 1738

From La Vérendrye's correspondence of 1734 and journal of 1738-9

i) In the first extract La Vérendrye reports to the Marquis de Beauharnois, governor of New France, a conversation he had with Assiniboine Indians during the winter of 1733-4 about the mysterious Ouachipouennes or Mandans to the south.

I asked them what they thought of that tribe and whether they were savages like themselves. They replied that they took them for French; their forts and houses were much like ours, except that the roofs are flat with earth and stone over them; their forts are made of double rows of stakes with two bastions at opposite corners; their houses are large and adjoin the palisades so that you can make a tour of the forts on the tops of the houses, the latter having cellars where they keep their Indian corn in large wicker-work baskets. They never leave their fort; all alike, men and women, work in the fields, the chiefs only excepted, and these have men to serve them.

These Caserniers [barrack dwellers] are of very tall stature, well-proportioned, white, and walk with their toes turned out. Their hair is light in colour, chestnut and red; a few have black hair. They have beards which they cut or pull out, some, however, allowing them to grow. They are engaging and affable with strangers who come to see them, but nevertheless are always on their guard. They do not visit the neighbouring tribes. They are clothed in leather or in dressed skins skilfully worked and of different colours. They have a kind of jacket with breeches and stockings of the same material; the shoes seem to be of one piece with the stockings. The women are dressed in long gowns, a kind of tunic which goes down to the ankles, with a girdle that carries an apron, the whole of leather finely worked. They wear their hair in tresses coiled on the head. . . . This tribe has only one great chief, and it has a large number of forts all situated on opposite banks of a great river which flows west.

ii) The second extract is from La Vérendrye's journal of his expedition of 1738-9 to the Mandans, when he was able at last to compare the reality of Mandan life with the marvelling descriptions he had been receiving from the tribes farther north. It also records the appearance of a Mandan village near the Missouri, very different from the less permanent settlements of the Indians in the St Lawrence and Great Lakes area.

330 'Carte d'une Partie du Lac Superieur avec la Decouverte de la Riviere depuis le Grand portage A jusqu'au Lac Ounipigon . . .', 1734. Copy in *Public Archives of Canada, Ottawa.*
Although crudely drawn, this 1734 map represents a distinct advance on the slightly earlier 'Auchagach map' (see plate 287). For the first time Lake Winnipeg is shown lying north to south, and the long, straight River of the West has disappeared. Instead, a small section of a very different River of the West is shown curving away in the bottom left-hand corner of the map, and is in fact the Missouri. At the southern end of Lake Winnipeg the newly established Fort Maurepas is shown, and just beyond it a line marks the limit of French exploration. An effort has been made to depict the Red-Assiniboine-Souris River system, and although several errors have been made in the attempt to translate Indian reports into map form the outline for the first time bears some relation to reality. In the south the upper Mississippi is once more depicted, though too far west, and in the north the outlets of several rivers flowing from Lake Winnipeg towards Hudson Bay are indicated.

331 'Carte contenant Les Nouvelles De couvertes De L'Ouest En Canada', 1740. *Service Historique de la Marine, Paris, Recueil 67 carte No. 23.*
This map is best viewed along its north-south line. The most obvious error

330

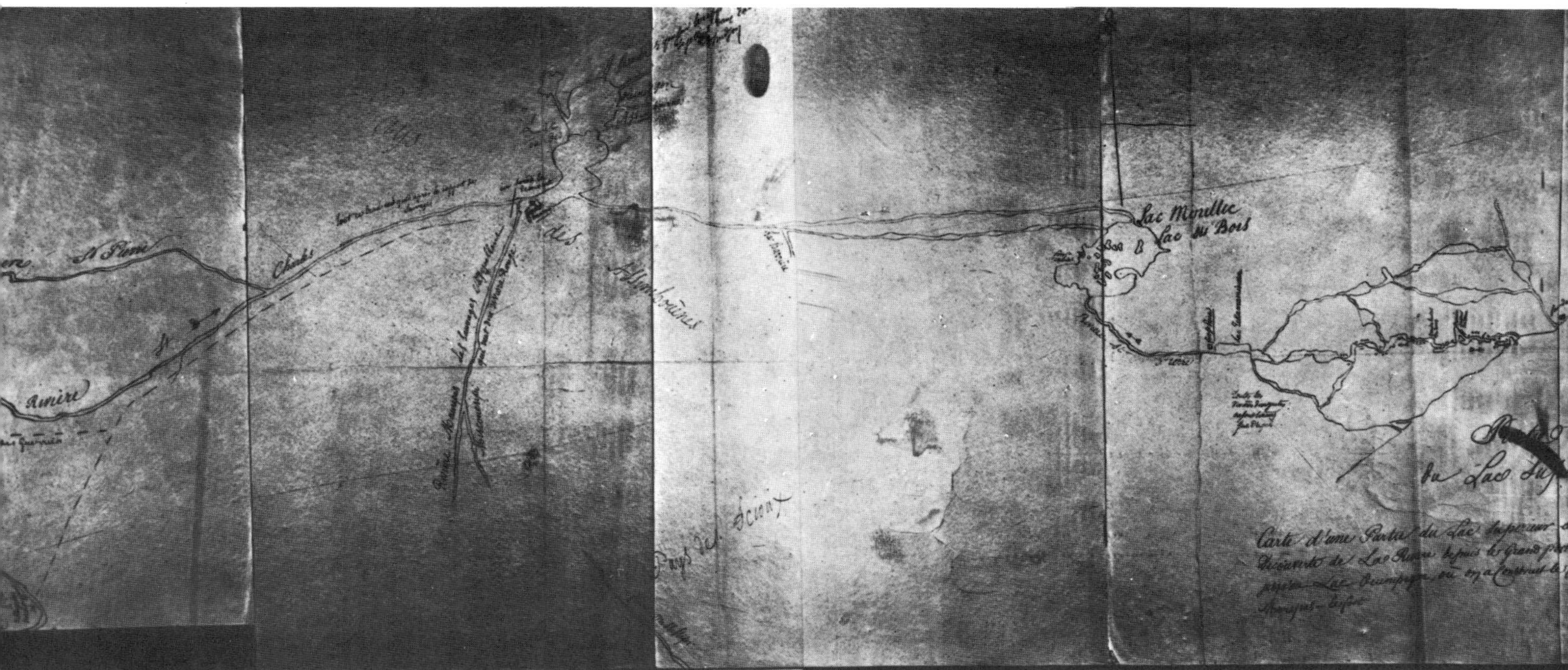

331

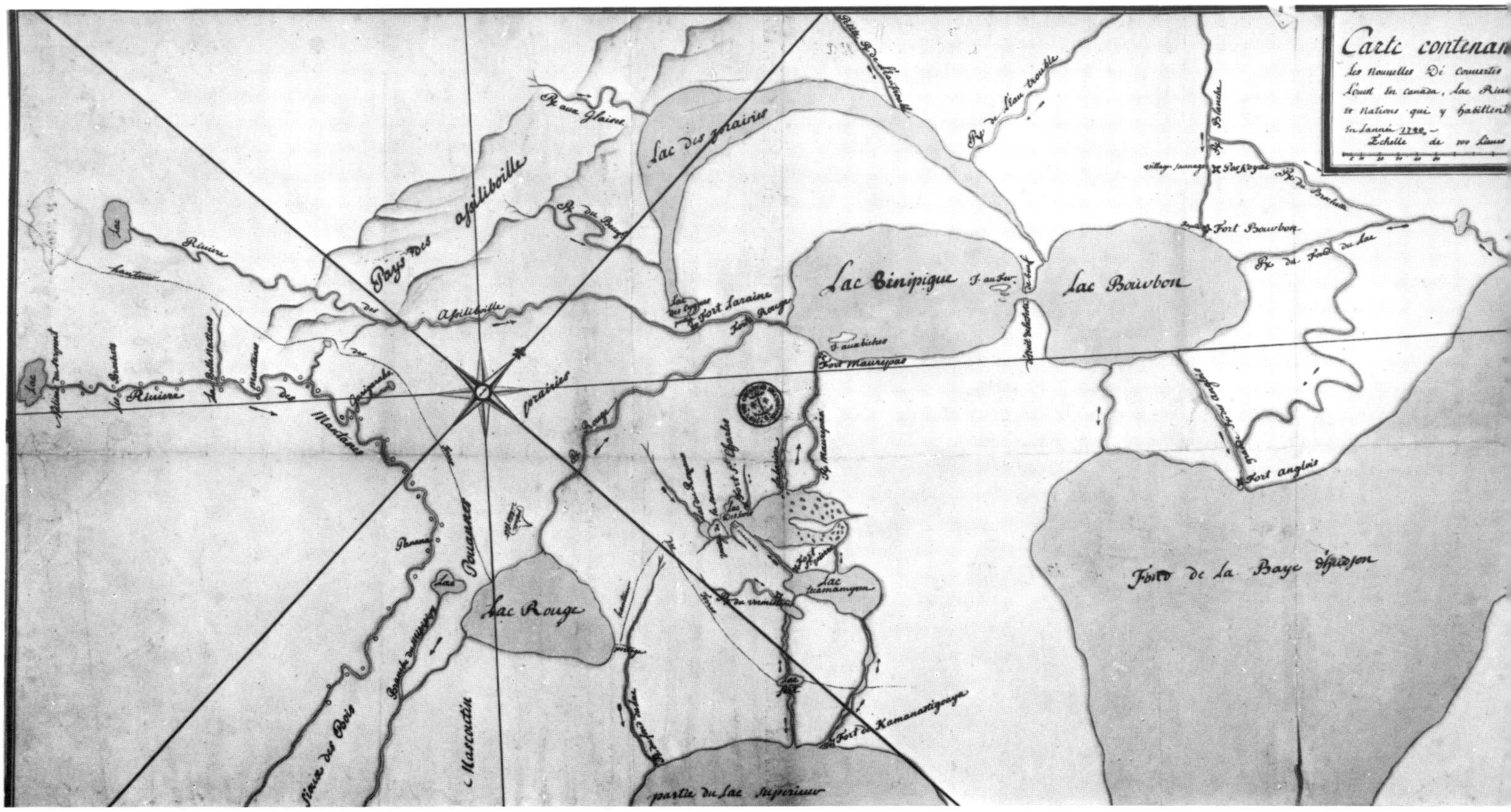

is the foreshortening between Hudson Bay and Lake Winnipeg, with only a short water-carriage indicated between the Lake and the Hudson's Bay Company posts at York and Churchill. A new feature is the presence of the Saskatchewan River (' R. Blanche') shown flowing into the northern end of Lake Winnipeg, of which the northwest part is named 'Lac Bourbon'. To the west the curious crescent-shaped 'Lac des prairies' is an attempt to represent Lakes Manitoba and Winnipegosis. Farther south the Red River is marked flowing north from a distended Red Lake ('Lac Rouge'), which is now suggested as one of the sources of the Mississippi. The Assiniboine ('Assiliboille') is correctly shown (unlike on the 1734 map, plate 330) as joining the Red River before flowing into Lake Winnipeg. Finally, the Missouri ('Riviere des Mantanes') bulks large to the south and southwest, with the Mandan villages reached by La Vérendrye in 1738 clearly indicated. By now the explorer clearly identified his River of the Mandans with the Missouri, not the River of the West, for an arrow shows its course as flowing from, not to, the west. The Mississippi is shown rising from a small lake in the 'Nations du serpent', according to La Vérendrye a warlike people (perhaps Kiowas) who blocked the way to the western ocean.

A feature of the map is the marking of the French forts, from Kaministiquia on Lake Superior to La Reine on the Assiniboine and 'Paskoyae' (Basquia or The Pas) on the Saskatchewan. The 'I. masacre', faintly marked at the southern end of Lake of the Woods, is the spot where Sioux Indians killed one of La Vérendrye's sons, Jean Baptiste, and his eight companions in June 1736. Despite its errors and crudities, the map is an impressive reminder of the accomplishments of La Vérendrye and his sons in the 1730s. French knowledge had been extended westward for 500 or 600 miles from Lake Superior in a great arc swinging from the Saskatchewan in the north to the Missouri in the south.

From the first mountain the whole route lay in a prairie country, but with a succession of hills and valleys, which it is fatiguing to climb up and down several times a day. There are some magnificent plains of three or four leagues in extent. The marching order of the Assiniboin villagers, especially when they are numerous, is in three columns, the scouts in front, the wings [extending back] to a good rearguard; the old and disabled march in the main body which is in the middle. I had all the Frenchmen kept together as much as possible. If the scouts perceive any herds of buffalo on the way, as often happens, a cry is raised which is quickly heard by the rear-guard, and all the most active men in the columns join the vanguard so as to surround the beasts, numbers of which they kill, whereupon each man takes all the meat he wants. As that arrests the march, the vanguard marks out the camping ground and no one must go any further. The women and the dogs carry all the baggage. The men carry only their arms. They often make their dogs carry firewood even, as they frequently have to camp in mid-prairie, the clumps of trees only occurring at distant intervals.

On the morning of the 28th [November] we arrived at the place indicated as a rendezvous for the Mandan, who arrived in the evening, one chief with thirty men and four Assiniboin. . . . I confess I was greatly surprised, as I expected to see people quite different from the other savages according to the stories that had been told us. They do not differ from the Assiniboin, being naked except for a garment of buffalo skin carelessly worn without any breechcloth. I knew then that there was a large discount to be taken off all that had been told me. . . . M. de Lamarque and I took a walk to examine the extent of their fortifications. I gave orders to count the cabins, and we found that there were about one hundred and thirty. All the streets, squares and cabins are uniform in appearance; often our Frenchmen would lose their way in going about. They keep the streets and open spaces very clean; the ramparts are smooth and wide; the palisade is supported on cross pieces mortised into posts fifteen feet apart with a lining. For this purpose they use green hides fastened only at the top in places where they are needed. As to the bastions, there are four of them at each curtain well flanked. The fort is built on an elevation in mid-prairie with a ditch over fifteen feet deep and from fifteen to eighteen wide. Entrance to the fort can only be obtained by steps and pieces [of wood] which they remove when threatened by the enemy. If all their forts are similar you may say that they are impregnable to savages. Their fortification, indeed, has nothing savage about it.

This tribe is of mixed blood, white and black. The women are rather handsome, particularly the light-coloured ones; they have an abundance of fair hair. The whole tribe is very industrious. Their dwellings are large and spacious, divided into several apartments by wide planks. Nothing is lying about; all their belongings are placed in large bags hung on posts; their beds are made in the form of tombs and are surrounded by skins. . . . Their fort is very well provided with cellars, where they store all they have in the way of grains, meat, fat, dressed skins and bearskins. They have a great stock of these things, which form the money of the country. The more they have the richer they consider themselves. . . . The men are big and tall, very active and, for the most part, good-looking, fine physiognomies, and affable. The women generally have not a savage cast of feature.

Text used: L. J. Burpee (Ed.), Journals and Letters of Pierre Gaultier de Varennes de la Vérendrye and his sons, *Toronto: The Champlain Society, 1927, pp. 153-5, 157, 316-20, 339-43.*

7
Middleton's explorations in Hudson Bay, 1742

From Captain Christopher Middleton's journal, 1741-2

Captain Middleton reached Hudson Bay in command of a naval expedition to search for a Northwest Passage in 1741. He wintered with his two ships, the *Furnace* and *Discovery*, at the Hudson's Bay Company post at Churchill, and in July 1742 sailed along the west coast of the Bay looking for a passage. This extract describes the failure of the expedition to find a way north through the Frozen Strait which Middleton discovered.

On the third of August, the River for the first time was a little clear of Ice, and accordingly in pursuit of our Discovery, and on the fifth by Noon got into the Latitude of 66° 14'. We had then got into a new Strait, much pester'd with Ice, and on the north Side of which we saw a Cape or Head Land bearing north; we had deep Water, and very strong Tides within four or five Leagues of it. I nam'd this Head Land *Cape Hope*, as it gave us all great Joy and Hopes of it being the extreme north Part of *America*, seeing little or no Land to the northward of it. We turned or worked round it the same Night, and got five or six Leagues to the N.b.W. before we could perceive any otherwise than a fair and wide Opening; but about Noon the sixth Day, after having got into the Latitude of 66° 40', found we were imbay'd, and by two in the Afternoon could not go above three Leagues farther, and having tried the Tides, all the Forenoon, every two Hours till two o'Clock in the Afternoon, found neither Ebb nor Flood, yet deep Waters. . . . On the seventh . . . I travelled twelve or fifteen Miles from Hill to Hill inland, till I came to a very high Mountain, from whence I plainly saw a Strait or Opening the Flood came in at, and the Mountain I stood upon being pretty near the Middle of this Strait, I could see both Ends of it; the whole being about 18 or 20 Leagues long, and 6 or 7 broad, and very high Land on both Sides of it, having many small Islands in the Middle and on the Sides of it; but it was all froze fast from Side to Side, and no Appearance of its clearing this Year, and near the 67th Degree of Latitude, and no anchoring the Ships, being very deep Water close to the Shore, and much large Ice driving with the Ebb and Flood, and but little Room if thick Weather should happen, which we continually expect in these Parts; it was agreed upon in Council to make the best of our way out of this dangerous narrow Strait . . .

Text used: Middleton's journal as printed in his A Vindication of the Conduct of Captain Christopher Middleton, *London, 1743, pp. 117-18.*

8
Indians at a fur trade post

From James Isham's 'Observations', 1743

James Isham was the Hudson's Bay Company's factor at York Factory, where he kept a volume of 'Observations' in addition to his official journal. The manuscript begins with a vocabulary of Cree words and phrases and their English equivalents (the latter only are printed here). In this Isham unconsciously reveals the relationship between the European trader and the Indians—a relationship of mutual dependence, suspicion and familiarity. The window mentioned is

332-9 In 1743 James Isham, a Hudson's Bay Company factor who had commanded at both York and Churchill, wrote a manuscript volume of 'Observations on Hudsons Bay', the text of which was illustrated with some simple but well-observed sketches of the Cree Indians. The textual comments quoted here are taken from E. E. Rich and A. M. Johnson (Eds.), *James Isham's Observations on Hudsons Bay, 1743 . . .*, the sketches from the manuscript in the *Hudson's Bay Company Archives, E.2/2.*

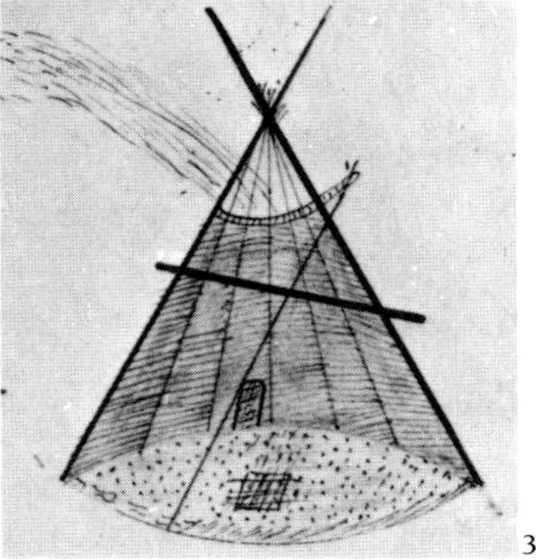

332

332 Indian skin tent. Beside the drawing is the following text: 'These tents are made of Drest Deer skins, or Drest moose skins, which is commonly ten skins, in tent, a moderate tent, will hold 12 or 14 Indians old and young, they are Very cold living on the winter, and subject Very much to smoaking w'ch the Native does not much mind, sitting on the ground, wherefore the smoak ascending does not Effect their Eyes much, tho Very troublesome to the English men, they not being us'd to such Low seats . . .'

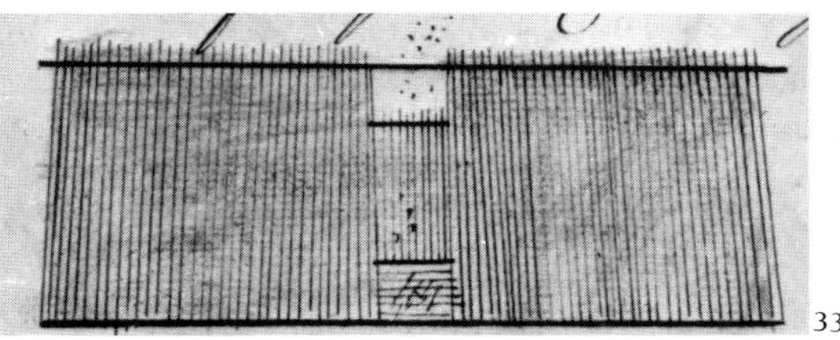

333

333 Log hut. The Company servants, when living away from the post wooding and hunting, built log huts. '. . . the Logs are round Leaning one against another with a Rig pole in the Midle, and sett close togeather taking mawse [moss] or mould to fill up the seams . . . one of these tents 14 foot Long 7 foot wide 3 [9] foot high will conveniently stove 14 men, they are not so subject to smoak as the skin tents, and Reckon'd much warmer. . . .'

334

334 Indian graves. '(1) The Graves, (2) the piles, round the Graves, (3) Hatchets, (4) a Bayonet, (5) painted sticks, (6) an Ice Chissel, (7) the Sculp, or the skin of the head, with the hair of an Ehuskemaw [Eskimo]'.

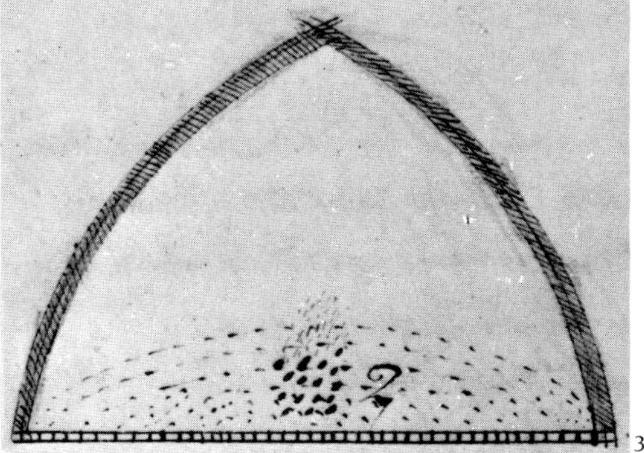

335

the hatch in the wall of the trading room through which all trade was conducted; it was a strict Company rule that the trading Indians should not be allowed inside the walls of the post itself.

DISCOURSES UPON DIFFERENT SUBJECTS OF ENGLISH & INDIAN

It's to be observed. (E) stands for the Englishman or trader, and (A) for the first Indian, (B) the second Indian, (C) the third, (D) the fourth &c. . . .

A freind come I want to trade
E presently i am Eating
A make haste it's flood I want to be gone
E presently presently
A you are always Eating give me some
B when shall we trade
E come and trade
C ope'n the window
E the window is ope'n or I have op'n'd the window
E ope'n yr. Bundles of beavr.
B I have gott no Beaver
E ho' what they are all smal fur's I suppose what was you a doing in the wntr.
B I was starv'd in the winter was the Reason I killd. no Beaver
E so make haste & trade
E Where is my debt
C how many Beaver was I in Debt
E five Beaver in martins & ten parchment Beaver
C their and what must I trade my beaver is all gone
E that is Laughing talk
B I will trade a Long gun small and handy with a Red gun case

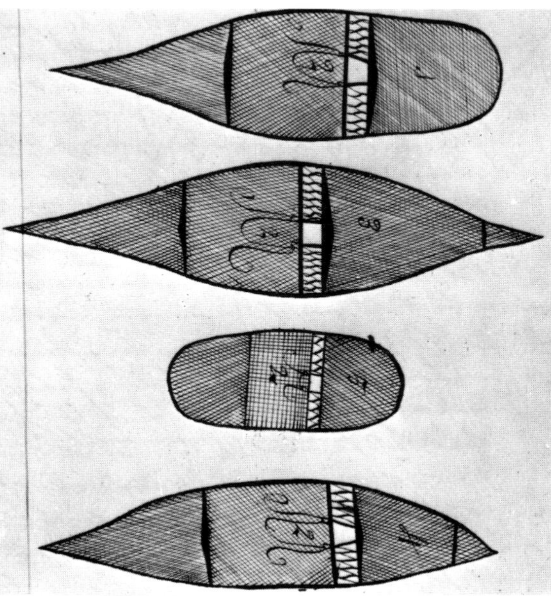

336

335 Indian sweat-house. Instructions read as follows: 'They make a little hutt or tent, about four foot high and about 6 foot over,—which Done, they take as many Coats or skin's, as they can procure, and Cover itt up close, Leaving a small Vacancy to go in att,—they then take about 20 Large stones, and heet them hott in the fire, in another tent, when hott, they put them into their hutt or swetting house. . . . they then go in Naked as they were born, their they sitt Like monkey's upon their Brich, tell they are in a perdigious sweet,—and when they think they have swetted Suffitiently, they then come out, and Run as they are in Such a heat into the River if Summer, if Winter they wash themselves with Snow . . . Such methods with Some Europians wou'd be prest. Death. . . .'

336 Indian snow shoes. The caption underneath reads: '(1) An Indian snow shoe (2) the strings which is tied to the foot (3) a Galley shoe (4) a Northern [Chipewyan] Indian shoe (5) a hoop nett, which Childn. wears made of willow, when they can not gett Birch or Juniper'.

337 Trapping foxes. '(3) the springs (4) the plates for the baite (5) the trigger (6) the notch (7) a trap up (8) 2 foxes catcht (9) a gun (10) posts its tied to (11) a post where the trigger stick is tied to (12) the sides of the trench (13) the Line (14) a Cross stick where the Baite is with a hole in't (15) a round Chawd trapp &c.' From James Isham's 'Observations', 1743.

338 Trapping foxes. '(1) Is 3 Guns Sett in a triangle form (2) false bait's (3) the Lines cov'd. with snow . . . (6) 3 casks's with pistols sett in them (7) the Lines under the snow (8) the baite.' In his accompanying text to the sketches of these rather elaborate and expensive traps Isham noted that this last method was used only for 'Very shy' foxes, 'the muzzel not to come out of the cask only a hole Something bigger then the muzzel, with the Lines also Cover'd with snow . . .' From James Isham's 'Observations', 1743.

339 Indian canoes, from James Isham's 'Observations', 1743.

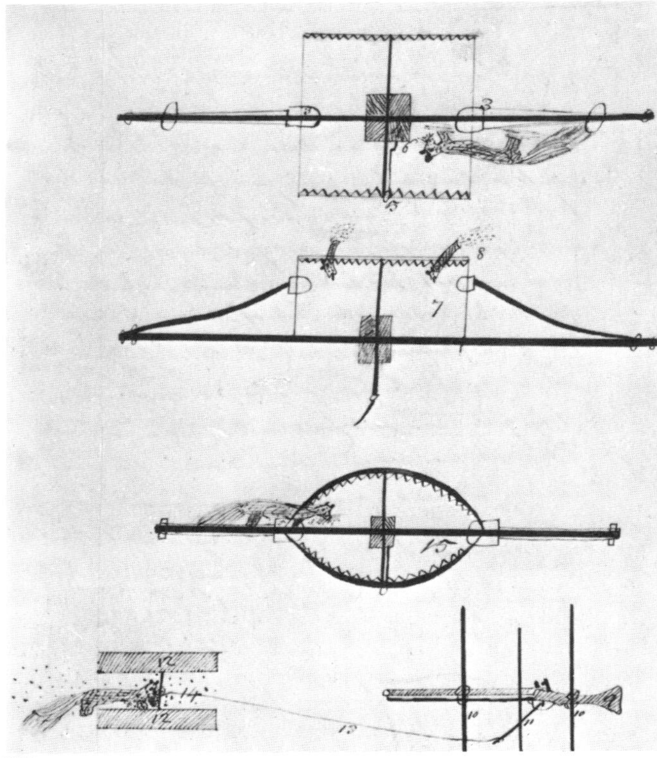

337

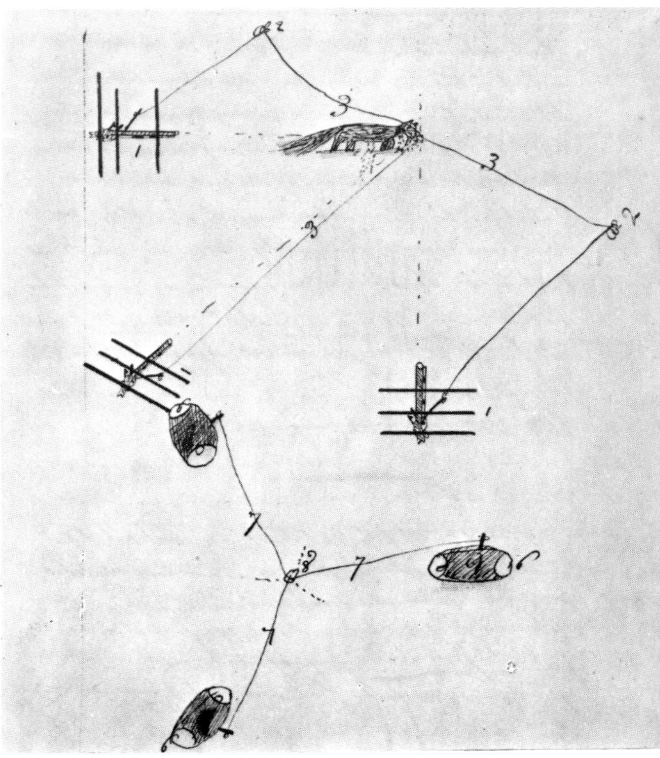

338

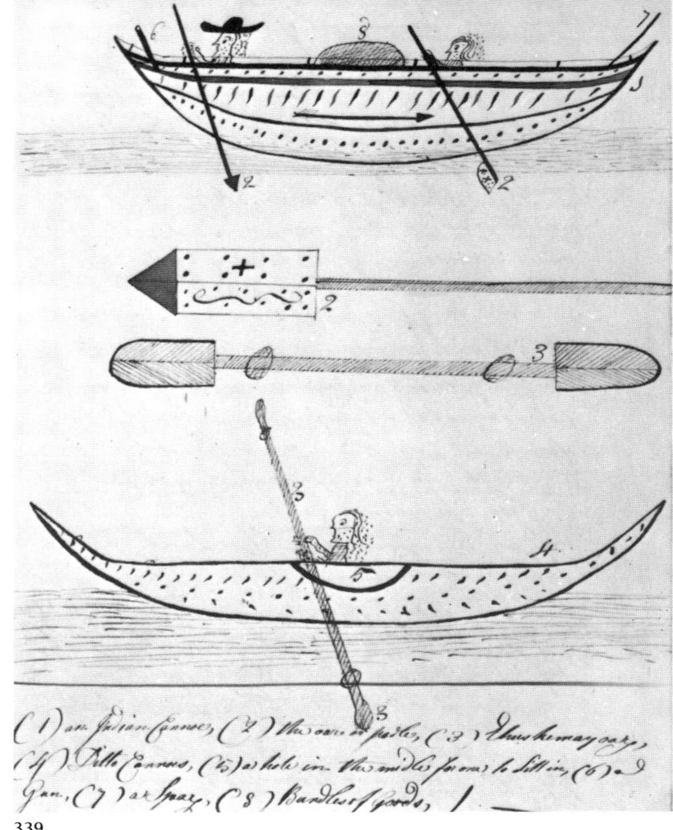

339

340

340 The Hudson's Bay Company post at Flamborough House, *c.* 1750. *Hudson's Bay Company Archives, G.1/100.*
Flamborough House was a small, temporary defensive outpost about 20 miles inland from the important trading factory at York. This sketch by James Isham shows the post as a simple building set in a stockade in a clearing on the banks of the Nelson River. The little post has a watch-tower, and nearer the river a gun platform on which cannon were mounted.

E here is a very good gunn itt will not freese in the winter
D five Beaver in powder above measure . . .
G your powder measure is sm'l
E they are the same as us'd to be
B give me a Bayonet
E put your Beaver in
B Let me Look at more
E they are all a like
B Do you think I'll steel
E who say's you'l steel
E Did you see any Ind's as you came down
A ten Canoes I see nigh hand & will be a great many more quickly
E have you done trading
B we have done all but Brandy
A a gallon cag of Brandy . . .
E have you done
A Yes you may shutt the windw.
A Give me some tobacco for Indian's to smoak as I shall see some in going up
B your tobacco is bad itt's very dry
E you have not brought many Martins do not be Lassy, Keep close to trapping in the winter
A Very well
E farewell good Luck to you

Text used: E. E. Rich and A. M. Johnson (Eds.), James Isham's Observations on Hudson's Bay, 1743. . . . *London, Hudson's Bay Record Society, 1949, pp. 47, 50, 52-4.*

9 Henday among the equestrian Indians of the plains, 1754

From Anthony Henday's journal, 1754-5

Henday's great individual journey of 1754-5 from Hudson Bay in quest of the plains Indians brought him by October 1754 to the mounted 'Archithinue' Indians of the prairies, somewhere south of Red Deer River. These were Atsina, often referred to as Waterfall or Gros Ventres Indians, members of the Blackfoot group. Some at least of Henday's colleagues back at York Factory found his descriptions hard to believe; 'The accts. of Horsemen being Inland were not credited . . .' one of them wrote later.

13 October 1754 . . . In the evening we were joined by 7 Archithinue Natives on Horse-back, who informed us we should see the Great Leader, & numbers of Archithinue Natives to-morrow.
14. Monday. Travelled 4 Miles S.W.b.W. Then came to us four men on Horse-back; they told us they were sent from the main body to see whether we were Friends or Enemies. We told them we were Friends. Attickasish, Canawappaw, Cokamanakisish, and the other of our Leaders walked in front about 4 Miles farther than we, and an opening in the middle; where we were conducted to the Leader's tent; which was at one end, large enough to contain fifty persons; where he received us seated on a clear (white) Buffalo skin, attended by 20 elderly men. He made signs for me to sit down on his right hand; which I did. Our Leader set on several grand-pipes, and smoked all round, according to their usual custom: not a word was yet spoke on either side. Smoking being over, Buffalo flesh boiled was served round in baskets of a species of bent, and I was presented with 10 Buffalo tongues. Attickasish my Guide, informed him I was sent by the Great Leader who lives down at the great waters, to invite his young men down to see him and to bring with them Beaver skins, and Wolves skins: and they would get in return Powder, Shot, Guns, Cloth, Beads, &c. He made little answer: only said that it was far off, & they could not paddle. Then they entered upon indifferent subjects until we were ordered to depart to our tents, which were pitched about a full quarter of a Mile without their lines.
15. Tuesday. Froze a little last night. Our women employed dressing Beaver skins for cloathing. About 10 o'clock A.M. I was invited to the Archithinue Leader's tent: when by an interpreter I told him what I was sent for, and desired of him to allow some of his young men to go down to the Fort with me, where they would be kindly received, and get Guns &c. But he answered, it was far off, and they could not live without Buffalo flesh; and that they could not leave their horses &c: and many other obstacles, though all might be got over if they were acquainted with a Canoe, and could eat Fish, which they never do. The Chief further said they never wanted food, as they followed the Buffalo and killed them with the Bows and Arrows; and he was informed the Natives that frequented the Settlements, were oftentimes starved on their journey. Such remarks I thought exceeding true. He made me a present of a handsome Bow and Arrows, and in return I gave him a part of each kinds of goods I had, as ordered by Mr. Isham's written instructions. I departed and took a view of their camp. Their tents were pitched close to one another in two regular lines, which formed a broad street open at both ends. Their horses are turned out to grass, their legs being fettered: and when mounted, are fastened to lines cut of Buffalo skin, that stretches along and is fastened to stakes drove in the ground. They have hair halters, Buffalo skin pads, and stirrups of the same. The horses are fine tractible animals, about 14 hands high; lively and clean made. The Natives are good Horsemen, and kill the Buffalo on them. These Natives are drest much the same as others; but more clean and sprightly. They think nothing of my tobacco; & I set as little value on theirs; which is dryed Horse-dung. They appear to be under proper discipline, & obedient to their Leader: who orders a party of Horsemen Evening and Morning to reconitre; and proper parties to bring in provisions. They have other Natives Horsemen as well as Foot, who are their Enemies: they are also called the Archithinue Indians: & by what I can learn talk the same language, & hath the same customs. They are, like the other Natives murthering one another slyly. Saw many fine Girls who were Captives; & a great many dried Scalps with fine long black hair, displayed on poles, & before the Leader's tent. They follow the Buffalo from place to place: & that they should not be surprised by the Enemy, encamp in open plains. Their fuel is turf, & Horse-dung dryed; their cloathing is finely painted with red paint; like unto English Ochre: but they do not mark nor paint their bodies.

Text used: L. J. Burpee (Ed.), 'York Factory to the Blackfeet Country', The Journal of Anthony Hendry [sic], 1754-55, *Proceedings and Transactions of the Royal Society of Canada, 3rd Series, vol. I, 1907, pp. 337-9.*

10
The Eskimos of Hudson Bay

From Andrew Graham's 'Observations on Hudson's Bay', 1767-91

Whereas the fur traders had well-established contacts with many of the Indian peoples of North America, meetings between Europeans and the Eskimos in their alien and icy environment to the north were brief and sporadic. The earliest regular contact with the Canadian (as distinct from the Greenland) Eskimos came in the mid-eighteenth century when the Hudson's Bay Company sent sloops to trade with the Eskimos who lived in the northwestern parts of the Bay. In his manuscript 'Observations' one of the Company factors of the 1760s and 1770s, Andrew Graham, wrote down his impression of the Eskimos.

These people are found in many parts of the Hudson's Bay Company's territories. Thus: they are seen annually by the ships in Hudson's Straits upon the Savage Islands in latitude 62° North; again upon the Isles of Nottingham and Salisbury at the head of the Straits in latitude 63° North. They frequent likewise the eastern coast at the back of Terra Labradore; and also the northern shore and islands as far as has been discovered; and Mr Hearne, when in search of a large river and copper mine, found them as far north as latitude 71° 54′: so that we may suppose they live even nigh the pole. Those in Hudson's Straits and Bay seem to be the same kind of people; only the latter appear to live more in tribes than the others. This race of people are not numerous; we seldom see above 150, including women and children, in passing yearly through the Straits. These are clothed mostly in seal-skins, but the Bay natives, having plenty of deer, make their garments chiefly of those skins. The amount of the Esquimaux seen annually to the northwards, does not exceed five hundred. We are of the opinion that those we see in the Straits transport themselves to the eastern shore of the Bay, and to the coast of Labrador, on the approach of winter; and they have been seen going across with their families in their luggage boats. They are certainly a very hardy race of people, to abide in places so barren that neither stick or even shrub is to be found; and oftentimes only the bare rocks, without any herbage. Many of them formerly resided upon Churchill River, but on the Company's building a Fort there, in the beginning of this present century, and the Indians resorting thither to trade, the Esquimaux retired farther to the north. They are fond of an insular situation, to be more secure from the attacks of the Indians, who are inveterate enemies to them, and glory in their destruction.

In the years 1750, 1751 and 1752 I was to the northward in the [*Churchill*] sloop, but I had no opportunity of taking a few remarks of their manners etc., only shall say I saw them eat salmon and seals' flesh raw; at the same time they were boiling meat. Upon their first discovering the vessel they

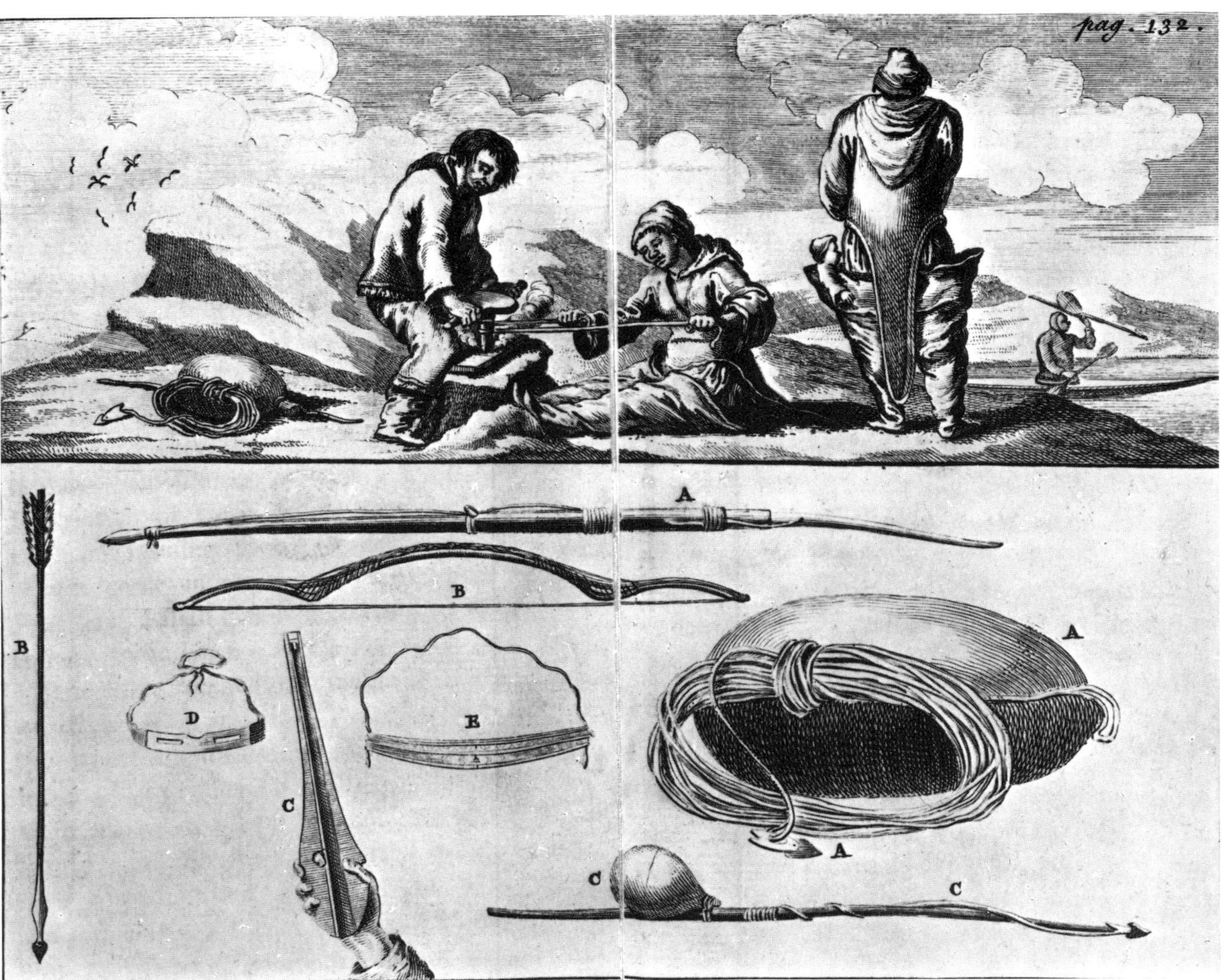

341 Eskimo implements and activities, from Henry Ellis, *Voyage to Hudson's Bay*, 1748.

341

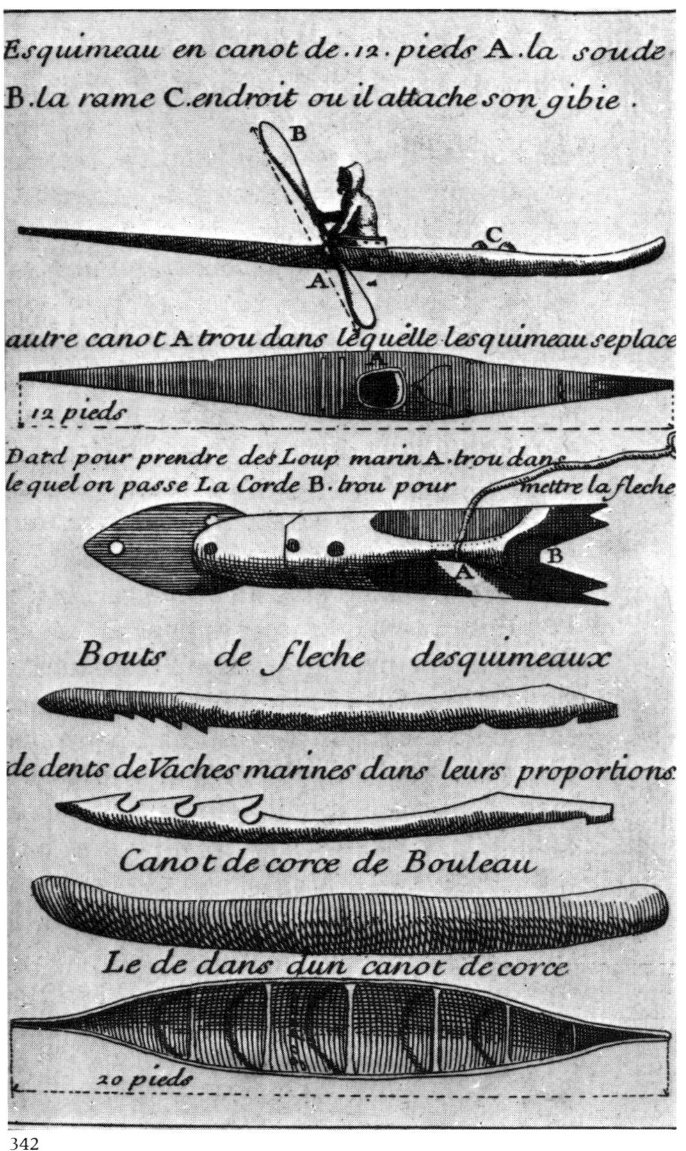

342

342 Eskimos and their kayaks. '. . . their frames are made of Wood or Whalebone, very slender, and covered with Sealskin-Parchment all over, a Hole in the middle excepted, which has a Rim of Whalebone or Wood round about to prevent the Water coming down off the Deck, and affords only room for one Man to sit in, his Feet stretched forward, and sometimes a Skin laced about his Waist from the Rim before-mentioned, which effectively shuts out all Water.' Henry Ellis, *Voyage to Hudson's Bay*, 1748.

343

343 Mammals and fish of the northern waters, from Henry Ellis, *Voyage to Hudson's Bay*, 1748.
The 'Sea Unicorn' is the narwhal; the whale is the Bowhead whale found in the northern part of Hudson Bay; the 'Sea Horse' is a walrus.

came off in their canoes, making a hideous noise, calling out, Chimo! Chimo! By clapping their breasts and other signs are seemingly overjoyed to see the sloop. We take from them train oil, and blubber, whale-bone, and two or three foxes' skins, giving them in return, knives, lances, fish-gigs and beads etc., but no fire-arms as before mentioned; the want of which gives their enemies great advantage over them.

Nothing was known of their manners and customs till the year 1765 the master of the Churchill sloop was allowed to prevail on them to let some of their young people to come to the Fort, which was accordingly granted that two young men should go with him on a promise they should be kindly used, and brought back next summer. After wintering at Churchill he delivered them safe to their friends next summer, who were overjoyed to see them again, and after finding that they had been kindly used the old people embraced the sloop master in a most friendly manner. In the year 1767 two young men came again in the sloop to winter at Churchill, and brought one canoe along with them. . . .

The men are short in stature, few exceeding five feet five inches, but exceedingly well proportioned; their face broad and flat, occasioned by the prominency of the cheek bones, and the rotundity and largeness of the cheeks; the eyes black and diminutive; the mouth small; teeth white, and the lips black; the countenance brown olive, or what we generally call the Gipsy colour; the beard eradicated; the hair of the head coarse, black, straight, and perfectly wire-like. The women in general are taller than the men. They have high full breasts, and broad shoulders. They wear their hair very long; but will sometimes part with it to Europeans in exchange for beads.

Both sexes are very light of foot; and use their hands too with dexterity and skill. They have but few maimed and infirm persons amongst them, and still fewer mis-shapen births. Their body is fleshy, and capable of enduring the cold very well with little clothing; and their heads and necks bare. They want not for strength or activity of body; but they are awkward and unapt in doing anything to which they are not accustomed; yet nothing can equal their perfection in their own business. Whether we consider the shape, workmanship, or materials of their dress, we must acknowledge nothing could be better adopted to their situation and necessities; or executed with greater ingenuity and neatness. Observe even those who never had any knowledge or intercourse with Europeans, and we will be surprised at the fineness of their sewing. . . .

They have a strong attachment to their native country and friends; and however despicable and poor their food and way of life may appear on the other side the Atlantic, yet the contented Esquimaux prefers his own. This we have experienced in such of that nation who have wintered amongst us at Prince of Wales's Fort. It was a considerable time before they could be brought to relish the European diet; and at last we were obliged to debar them access to the train oil, which stood in an out-house for the use of the watch-lamp. In the winter they would get upon the north flanker of the Fort and sit near each other, the tears in the meantime copiously distilling down their cheeks; and when the cause of their grief was enquired after, the mournful guests replied, 'they were looking towards their native country and thinking upon their absent friends.'

Text used: Glyndwr Williams (Ed.), Andrew Graham's Observations on Hudson's Bay 1767-1791, *London, Hudson's Bay Record Society, 1969, pp. 213-16, 224.*

11
The discovery of America's northern coastline, 1771

From Samuel Hearne's *Journey to the Northern Ocean,* 1795

Throughout the first half of the eighteenth century reports reached the Hudson's Bay Company posts of a great river, a copper mine and a strait somewhere far to the northwest. After several attempts to reach this region by sea had failed, Samuel Hearne was instructed to travel overland from Churchill across the Barrens. His first two attempts failed, but in 1771 he reached his objective with the aid of a remarkable Chipewyan ('Northern') Indian, Mattonabee, his followers, and not least his wives.

344

344 Samuel Hearne, 1745-92. This engraving, published shortly after his death, shows Hearne as a youngish man (he was in his mid twenties when he made his celebrated journey to the Coppermine River), but whether it was drawn from life is doubtful. *Hudson's Bay Company Archives.*

345

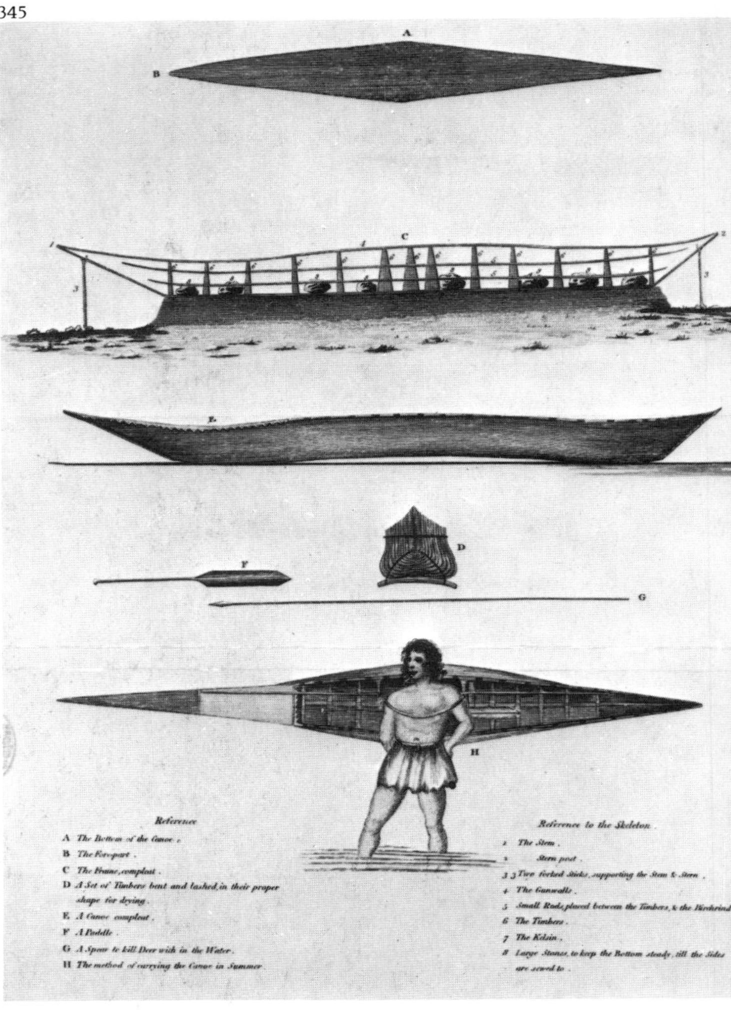

345 Method of building Chipewyan canoes, from Samuel Hearne, *A journey . . . to the Northern Ocean,* 1795.
In his text Hearne wrote: 'Those vessels, though made of the same materials with the canoes of the Southern Indians, differ from them both in shape and construction; they are also much smaller and lighter; and though very slight and simple in their construction, are nevertheless the best that could possibly be contrived for the use of those poor people, who are frequently obliged to carry them a hundred, and sometimes a hundred and fifty miles at a time, without having occasion to put them into the water. Indeed, the chief use of these canoes is to ferry over unfordable rivers . . . All the tools used by an Indian in building his canoe, as well as in making his snow-shoes, and every other kind of wood-work, consist of a hatchet, a knife, a file, and an awl.'

346 Bloody Fall, by John Hood, 1821, from J. Franklin, *Narrative of a journey to the shores of the polar sea . . .* 1823.
This spot, so named by Hearne in 1771, was reached by Franklin in July 1821 when he found relics of the Eskimos massacred by Hearne's Chipewyan Indians a half-century before. Referring to that event, Franklin wrote: 'Several human skulls were strewed about the ground near to the encampment, and as the spot exactly answers the description given by Mr. Hearne . . . we had no doubt of this being the place. . . .'

Having a good stock of dried provisions, and most of the necessary work for canoes all ready, on the eighteenth [April] we moved about nine or ten miles to the North North West, and then came to a tent of Northern Indians who were tenting on the North side of Thelewy-aza River. From these Indians Matonabbee purchased another wife; so that he had now no less than seven, most of whom would for size have made good grenadiers. He prided himself much in the height and strength of his wives, and would frequently say, few women would carry or haul heavier loads; and though they had, in general, a very masculine appearance, yet he preferred them to those of a more delicate form and moderate stature. In a country

346

347

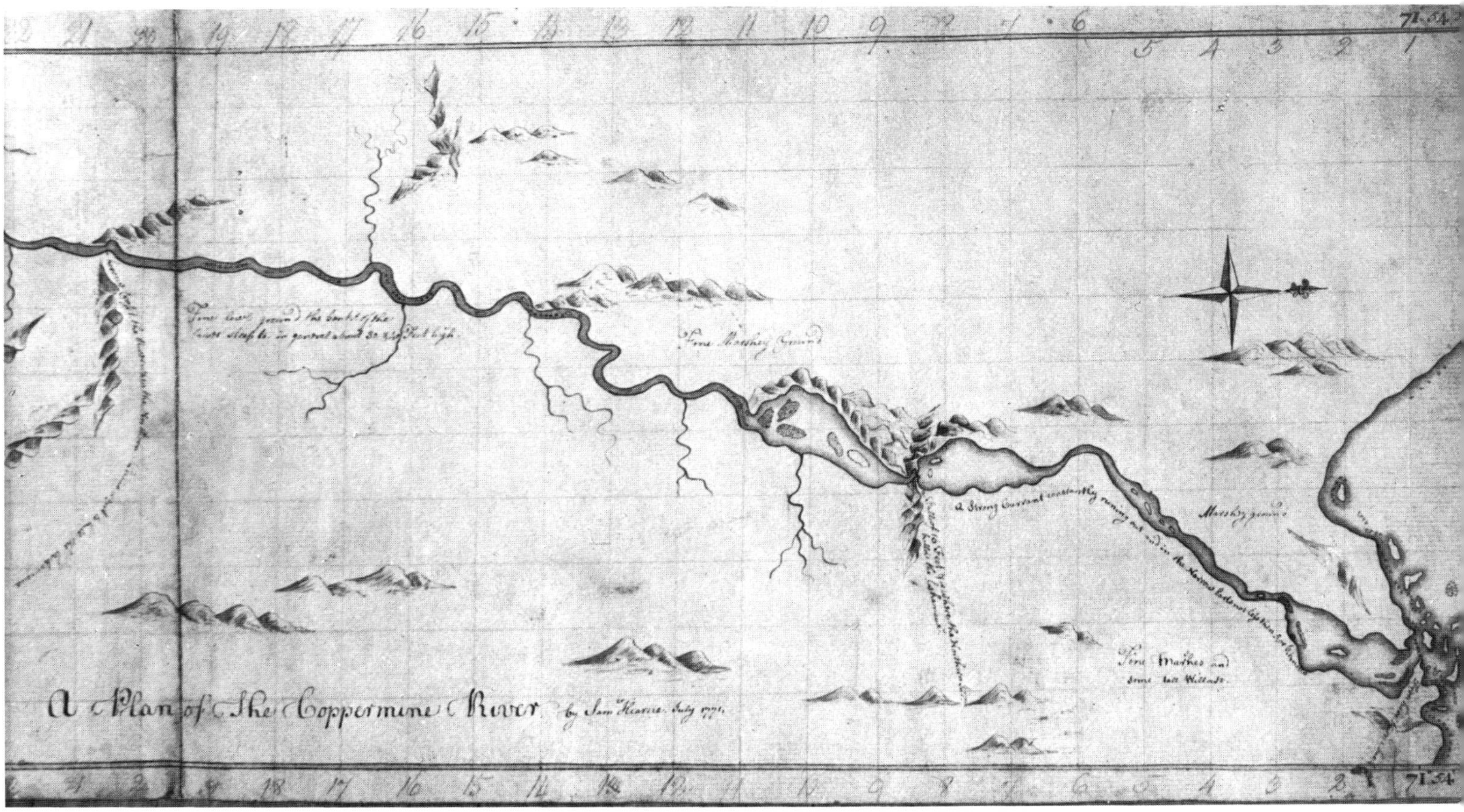

347 Samuel Hearne. Section from 'A Plan of the Coppermine River', 1771. *James Ford Bell Library, University of Minnesota.*
This map shows the last twenty-five miles or so of Hearne's epic journey to the shores of the Arctic Ocean in July 1771. It includes the 'Bloody Falls' where Hearne witnessed the massacre of a party of Eskimos by his Chipewyan Indian companions. On this map, as on his general map (plate 348) Hearne placed the mouth of the Coppermine River in latitude 71°54'N., about 200 miles too far north. Though dated July 1771 it would seem improbable that this was the actual map which Hearne drew at the time, but a note in his published *Journey . . . to the Northern Ocean* makes it clear that he took with him ample material for map-making: 'I drew a Map on a large skin of parchment, that contained twelve degrees of latitude North, and thirty degrees of longitude West, of Churchill Factory, and sketched all the West coast of the Bay on it, but left the interior parts blank, to be filled up during my Journey. I also prepared detached pieces on a much larger scale for every degree of latitude and longitude contained in the large Map. On those detached pieces I pricked off my daily courses and distance, and entered all lakes and rivers, &c., that I met with.'

like this, where a partner in excessive hard labour is the chief motive for the union, and the softer endearments of a conjugal life are only considered as a secondary object, there seems to be great propriety in such a choice; but if all the men were of this way of thinking, what would become of the greater part of the women, who in general are but of low stature, and many of them of a most delicate make, though not of the exactest proportion, or most beautiful mould? Take them in a body, the women are as destitute of real beauty as any nation I ever saw, though there are some few of them, when young, who are tolerable; but the care of a family, added to their constant hard labour, soon make the most beautiful among them look old and wrinkled, even before they are thirty; and several of the more ordinary ones at that age are perfect antidotes to love and gallantry. This, however, does not render them less dear and valuable to their owners, which is a lucky circumstance for those women, and a certain proof that there is no such thing as any rule or standard for beauty. Ask a Northern Indian, what is beauty? he will answer, a broad flat face, small eyes, high cheek-bones, three or four broad black lines a-cross each cheek, a low forehead, a large broad chin, a clumsy hook-nose, a tawny hide, and breasts hanging down to the belt. Those beauties are greatly heightened, or at least rendered more valuable, when the possessor is capable of dressing all kinds of skins, converting them into the different parts of their clothing, and able to carry eight or ten stone in Summer, or haul a much greater weight in Winter. These, and other similar accomplishments, are all that are sought after, or expected, of a Northern Indian woman.

On 14 July Hearne and the Chipewyan Indians reached the long-sought Coppermine River.

On my arrival here I was not a little surprised to find the river differ so much from the description which the Indians had given of it at the Factory; for, instead of being so large as to be navigable for shipping, as it had been represented by them, it was at that part scarcely navigable for an Indian canoe, being no more than one hundred and eighty yards wide, every where full of shoals, and no less than three falls were in sight at first view.

Near here the Indians surprised and massacred a party of Eskimos, after which, Hearne, appalled and nervous, continued his explorations.

It was then about five o'clock in the morning of the seventeenth [July], the sea being in sight from the North West by West to the North East, about eight miles distant. I therefore set instantly about commencing my survey, and pursued it to the mouth of the river, which I found all the way so full of shoals and falls that it was not navigable even for a boat, and that it emptied itself into the sea over a ridge or bar. The tide was then out; but I judged from the marks which I saw on the edge of the ice, that it flowed about twelve or fourteen feet, which will only reach a little way within the river's mouth. The tide being out, the water in the river was perfectly fresh; but I am certain of its being the sea, or some branch of it, by the quantity of whalebone and seal-skins which the Esquimaux had at their tents, and also by the number of seals which I saw on the ice. At the mouth of the river, the sea is full of islands and shoals, as far as I could see with the assistance of a good pocket telescope. The ice was not then broke up, but was melted away for about three quarters of a mile from the main shore, and to a little distance round the islands and shoals.

By the time I had completed this survey, it was about one in the morning of the eighteenth; but in those high latitudes, and at this season of the year, the Sun is always at a good height above the horizon, so that we had not only day light, but sunshine the whole night: a thick fog and drizzling rain then came on, and finding that neither the river nor sea were likely to be of any use, I did not think it worth while to wait for fair weather to determine the latitude exactly by an observation; but by the extraordinary care I took in observing the courses and distances when I walked from Congecathawachaga, where I had two good observations, the latitude may be depended upon within twenty miles at the utmost. For the sake of form, however, after having had some consultation with the Indians, I erected a mark, and took possession of the coast, on behalf of the Hudson's Bay Company.

On his return journey Hearne visited one of the copper 'mines', about thirty miles south from the mouth of the Coppermine River.

This mine, if it deserve that appellation, is no more than an entire jumble of rocks and gravel, which has been rent many ways by an earthquake. Through these ruins there runs a small river; but no part of it, at the time I was there, was more than knee-deep.

The Indians who were the occasion of my undertaking this journey, represented this mine to be so rich and valuable, that if a factory were built at the river, a ship might be ballasted with the oar, instead of stone; and that with the same ease and dispatch as is done with stones at Churchill River. By their account the hills were entirely composed of that metal, all in handy lumps, like a heap of metal. But their account differed so much from the truth, that I and almost all my companions expended near four hours in search of some of this metal, with such poor success, that among us all, only one piece of any size could be found.

Text used: Samuel Hearne, A Journey from Prince of Wales's Fort in Hudson's Bay to the Northern Ocean . . ., *London, 1795, pp. 88-90, 146, 162-4, 173-4.*

12 Alexander Henry on the prairies, 1776

From Alexander Henry's *Travels and Adventures*, 1809

Born in the American colonies of English parents, the elder Henry was among the first British traders into Canada after the conquest of 1759-60, and by 1761 he was already as far west as Michilimackinac (Mackinac). In 1776 Henry was on the eastern edge of the prairies between the north and south branches of the Saskatchewan, where he spent some time among the Assiniboine. He portrays them in the last years of their dominance and freedom of the eastern prairies, before the real impact of the white man had been felt.

In the course of the day, the great chief informed us, that he proposed hunting the wild ox [buffalo] on the following morning, and invited us to be of the party.

In the morning, we went to the hunt accordingly. The chief was followed by about forty men, and a great number of women. We proceeded to a small *island* on the plain, at the distance of five miles from the village. On our way, we saw large herds of oxen at feed; but the hunters forebore to molest them lest they should take the alarm.

Arrived at the island, the women pitched a few tents, while the chief led his hunters to its southern end, where there was a pound, or enclosure. The fence was about four feet high,

348

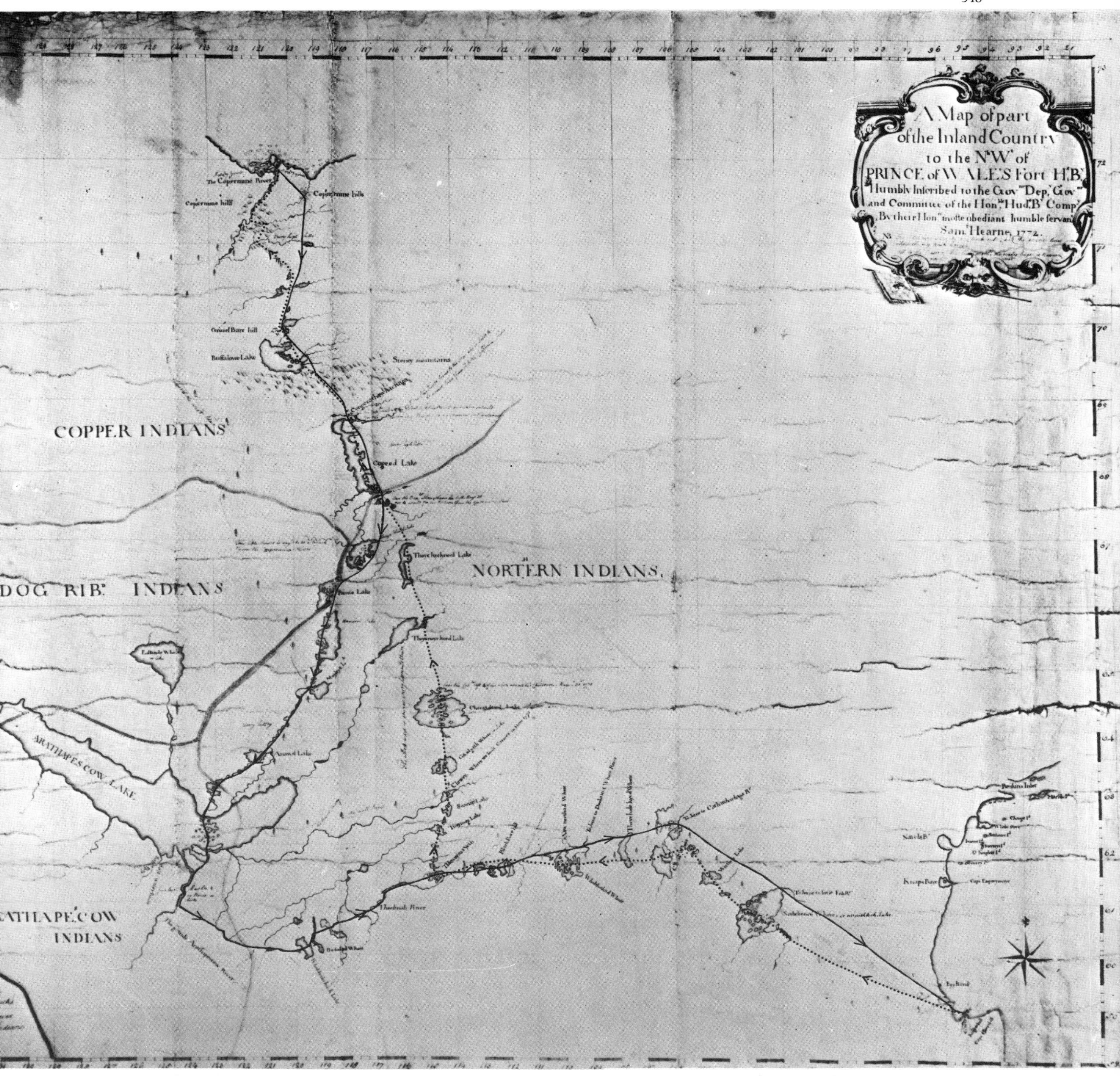

348 Samuel Hearne. 'A Map of part of the Inland Country to the NhWt of Prince of Wale's Fort HS BY', 1772. *Hudson's Bay Company Archives, G.2/10.* This map, on which the handwriting (though not the lettering) appears to be the same as on Hearne's map of the Coppermine River, shows the vast extent of country traversed by Hearne and his Chipewyan companions in 1770-2 on their overland sweep from Hudson Bay to the Arctic Ocean. It differs from, and is in some respects superior to, the printed map which accompanied Hearne's *Journey . . . to the Northern Ocean* published in 1795. A dotted line traces Hearne's outward route; a solid one his track back to Churchill. Recent investigations have suggested that the crucial landmark of 'Thleweyaza Yeth', where Hearne left his east-west path and turned north, is Delight Lake, just south of the Thoa River. Hearne's 'Arathapes Cow Lake', sometimes spelt by him 'Athapuscow Lake', was to be a fruitful source of confusion to other map-makers and explorers; it is Great Slave Lake, which here appears on a map for the first time, but for some years it was assumed to be Lake Athapaska, 200 miles to the southeast. Although no map under Hearne's name was published until 1795, the Hudson's Bay Company made his account and maps available for consultation by the Admiralty and cartographers, with the result that well before the posthumous publication of his narrative Hearne's discoveries appeared on the maps of Roberts (plate 400), Dalrymple and Arrowsmith.

349

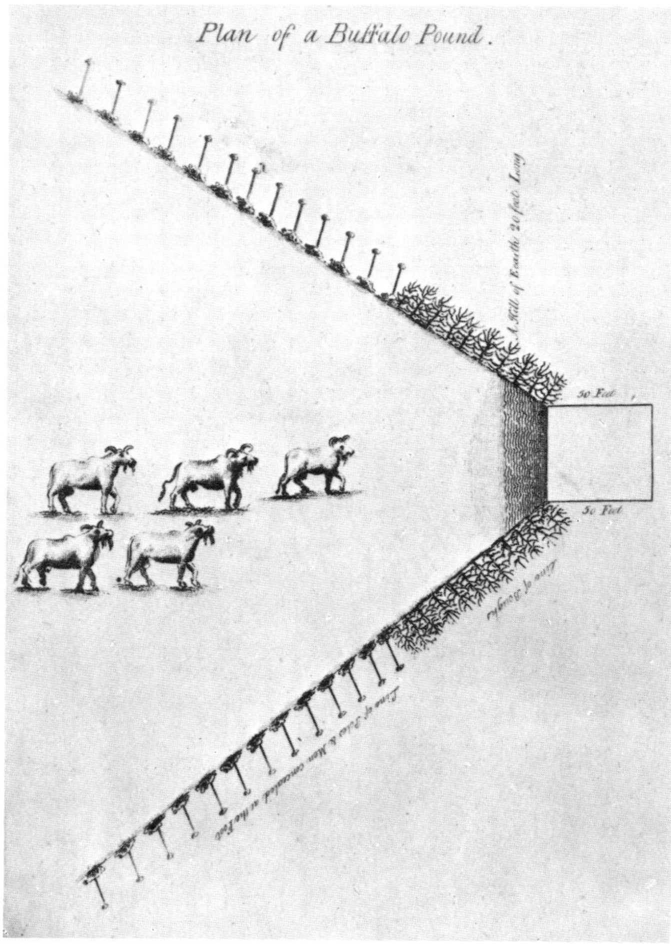

350

and formed of strong stakes of birch-wood, wattled with smaller branches of the same. The day was spent in making repairs; and by the evening all was ready for the hunt.

At day-light, several of the more expert hunters were sent to decoy the animals into the pound. They were dressed in ox-skins, with the hair and horns. Their faces were covered, and their gestures so closely resembled those of the animals themselves, that had I not been in the secret, I should have been as much deceived as the oxen.

At ten o'clock, one of the hunters returned, bringing information of the herd. Immediately, all the dogs were muzzled; and this done, the whole crowd of men and women surrounded the outside of the pound. The herd, of which the extent was so great that I cannot pretend to estimate the numbers, was distant half a mile, advancing slowly, and frequently stopping to feed. The part, played by the decoyers, was that of approaching them within hearing, and then bellowing like themselves. On hearing the noise, the oxen did not fail to give it attention; and, whether from curiosity or sympathy, advanced to meet those from whom it proceeded. These, in the meantime, fell back deliberately toward the pound, always repeating the call, whenever the oxen stopped. This was reiterated till the leaders of the herd had followed the decoyers into the jaws of the pound, which, though wide asunder toward the plain, terminated, like a funnel, in a small aperture, or gate-way; and, within this, was the pound itself. The Indians remark, that in all herds of animals there are chiefs, or leaders, by whom the motions of the rest are determined.

The decoyers now retired within the pound, and were followed by the oxen. But, the former retired still further, withdrawing themselves at certain movable parts of the fence, while the latter were fallen upon by all the hunters, and presently wounded, and killed, by showers of arrows. Amid the uproar which ensued, the oxen made several attempts to force the fence; but, the Indians stopped them, and drove them back, by shaking skins before their eyes. Skins were also made use of to stop the entrance, being let down by strings, as soon as the oxen were inside. The slaughter was prolonged till the evening, when the hunters returned to their tents. Next morning, all the tongues were presented to the chief, to the number of seventy-two. . . .

It had been my wish to go further to the Plains, till I should have reached the mountains, at the feet of which, as I have already observed, they lie; but, the chief informed me, that the latter were still at the distance of many days' journey, and that the intervening country was a tract destitute of the least appearance of wood. In the winter, as he asserted, this tract cannot be crossed at all; and in the summer, the traveller is in great danger of perishing for want of water; and the only fuel to be met with is the dung of the wild ox. It is intersected by a large river, which runs to the sun's rising, and which has its sources in the mountains.

With regard to the country of the Osinipoilles [Assiniboine], he said, that it lay between the head of the Pasquayah, or Sascatchiwaine, and the country of the Sioux, or Nadowessies, who inhabit the heads of the Mississippi. On the west, near the mountains, were the Snake Indians and Black-feet, troublesome neighbours, by whose hands numbers of his warriors fell.

The Osinipoilles have many villages, composed of from one to two hundred tents each. Few exceed the latter number. They often go to the mountains, on war-parties, and always on horse-back. When the great chief intends to go to war, he sends messengers to the several villages, directing the warriors to meet him at an appointed place and time. With regard to the latter, it is described by the moon, at the beginning, full, or end. In obedience to the summons, they assemble in greater numbers than can be counted, armed with the bow, sling and spear, and with quivers full of arrows. . . . The horse of the Osinipoilles were originally procured from white people, with beards, who live to the southward; that is, the Spanish colonists, in New Mexico.

Text used: James Bain (Ed.), Travels and Adventures in Canada and the Indian Territories between the Years 1760 and 1776 by Alexander Henry, Fur Trader, *Toronto, 1901 (reprint of original New York edition of 1809), pp. 298-301, 303-4.*

351

349-50 Two views of a buffalo pound: *top left*: by Lieutenant George Back, in J. Franklin, *Narrative of a journey to the shores of the polar sea . . .*, 1823; *bottom*: by Edward Umfreville, *The present state of Hudson's Bay*, 1790.

351 'A view near Point Levy opposite Quebec, 1788'; watercolor by Thomas Davies. *National Gallery of Canada, Ottawa.*
Of particular interest because of its carefully-observed detail of the tents, canoes and dress of the Indians.

7 THE PACIFIC COAST

1 The mystery of the North Pacific

At the beginning of the eighteenth century the waters and lands of the North Pacific were among the least-known areas of the inhabited globe. This remote region presented baffling problems to the geographers of Europe, and central to the mystery was the relationship of Asia and America. Were the two continents connected by a land-bridge, or separated by water—and, if the latter, by a narrow strait or a sea? Explorers of North America coming from the east could throw no light on the puzzle, for the course of overland exploration had not yet proceeded far beyond the line of the Mississippi and Lake Superior. On the Pacific coast the Spaniards from their Mexican ports had by the early seventeenth century carried out sketchy surveys of the shoreline as far north as Cape Blanco near latitude 43°N., but beyond that stretched the longest unexplored coastline in the world. The next known point of land was Asiatic Kamchatka, and what lay between was a matter of speculation and rumor. Dean Swift could place Brobdingnag there without fear of contradiction, and professional geographers sketched in the strait of Anian, De Fuca's inlet, Aguilar's river, and the hazy stretches of Yedso, Company Land and Gama Land on evidence little stronger than that for Gulliver's land of giants. On the opposite brinks of this great void in Europe's knowledge stood two peninsulas, California and Kamchatka, 5,000 miles apart, the one hot and arid, the other snow-covered and fogbound for much of the year. The physical contrast was indication enough of the immensity of the task attempted in the eighteenth century, which can be best visualized as a giant, if hesitant, pincer movement. The Russians in the far north, and the Spaniards from their bases in New Spain, slowly groped their way towards each other, although the final leap across the gap which still lay between them in the 1770s was made by an Englishman, James Cook.

Throughout the seventeenth century Lower or *Baja* California lay on the most northerly frontier of Spain's immense American empire. What was known of it from earlier coasting voyages, the most important of which was that of Sebastián Vizcaíno in 1602-3, held out few attractions for settlement. There was no sign either of precious metals or of populous Indian nations. Mountains and deserts on one side and a forbidding shoreline with few harbors on the other provided deterrents stronger than reports that farther north in Upper or *Alta* California Vizcaíno had found at Monterey a harbor which might serve as a port of call for the Manila galleon on its long annual voyage from the Philippines to Acapulco. Although during the course of the century missionaries slowly moved north up the Mexican mainland into the Sonora Valley, and efforts were made to cross the gusty waters of the Gulf of California to establish settlements on the western shore, not until the beginning of the eighteenth century was it discovered that California was not an island but a peninsula (see selection 1). This was the individual achievement of yet another in the long line of Jesuit missionary explorers, Father Eusebio Francisco Kino, who from his mission post at Dolores on the San Miguel River pushed north to the Colorado and Gila Rivers, and during the course of more than fifty journeys on horseback and foot carried out the first interior exploration of Pimería Alta (northern Sonora and southern Arizona). By the late 1690s Kino was absorbed in the quest for a land route to California, and by 1702 he had shown that one existed, although he himself never made the journey from Sonora across the head of the Gulf and on to the Pacific coast. Not until 1746 did Father Consag sail right round the Gulf of California, and so enable Ferdinand VII of Spain to issue a decree the next year proclaiming that

352

352 N. Witsen. Section of 'Carte Nouvelle de la Grande Tartarie', late seventeenth century.
This map is characteristic of the speculative cartography of the North Pacific before Bering's explorations in the eighteenth century. Asia ends just north of Japan in a land called Jedso or Jeso, which Jesuit reports had described; opposite Jedso is Staten Land or Island, and farther east still Company Land. These were inflated and misplaced versions of two of the Kurile Islands sighted by the Dutch explorer Marten Gerritsen Vries. There is as yet no sign of Kamchatka.

353

355

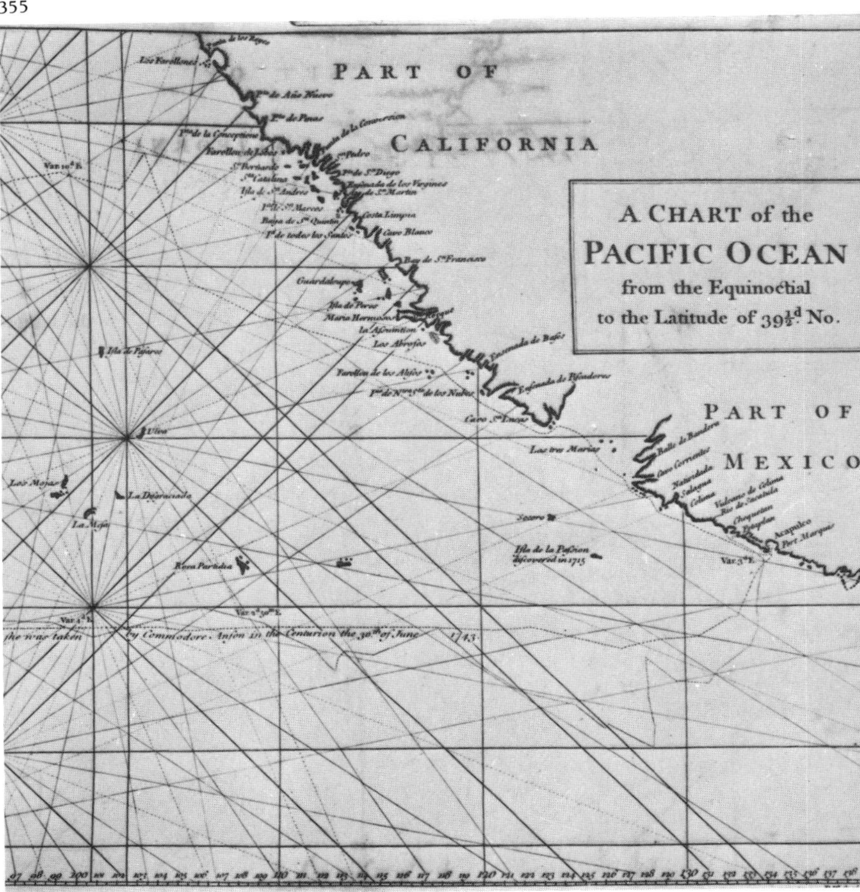

354

355 'A Chart of the Pacific Ocean', from Richard Walter, *A voyage round the world by George Anson*, London, 1748.
This pilot's chart of the Pacific, which included part of the Californian coast, was seized by the British commodore, George Anson, when he captured a Spanish galleon, the *Covadonga*, on its route from Acapulco to Manila in 1743. When it appeared in the official account of Anson's voyage in 1748 the map became one of the very few Spanish ones of the period to be printed; ironically, when *Noticia de la California* by Venegas was published at Madrid in 1757, it included a Hispanicized version of the map which was taken from the Anson narrative of 1748.

353 Indian fisherman of southern California, from George Shelvocke, *A voyage round the world*, London, 1726.
In his accompanying text, Shelvocke noted: '. . . the men being expert harpooners, they go out to sea on their bark-logs, which are only composed of five logs of a light wood, made fast to one another by wooden pegs; on these they venture out rowing with a double paddle, and with their harpoons (which are made of a sort of hard wood) strike the largest Albacores, and bring them in; this was altogether surprising to us, who had so often experienced the strength of that fish. . . .'

354 Two Californian women, from George Shelvocke, *A voyage round the world*, London, 1726.
This illustration is typical of many in the published 'voyages' of the period in that it seems to have been drawn by an artist in Europe to fit the description in the text rather than from first-hand observation; the unconvincing background is supposed to depict Lower California near Cape San Lucas.

'California is not an Island'.[1] Kino's pioneering journeys were followed by other Jesuits, who by the middle of the century had established a dozen or so mission posts on the peninsula. Even so, Lower California remained isolated, thinly-held and always vulnerable to revolt by the Indians whose characteristics were sketched in such unflattering colors in the Jesuit *Noticia de la California* of 1757 (see selection 2).

The expulsion of the Jesuits from Spanish America in 1767-8 might have marked the end of the Californian mission, but they were eagerly replaced by the Franciscans who arrived as the region was about to become a springboard for a new expansion to the north, brought about by external factors, and above all by the menace posed to Spain's pre-emptive rights over the coast to the north by the Russians. Since the days of Drake Spain had been sensitive about English seaborne forays along the Pacific shores of its American empire; and Anson's depredations along the coasts of Chile, Peru and Mexico in 1741-2 revived Spanish fears, more particularly since Anson was no buccaneer but the commander of an official British naval expedition. French thrusts from the Mississippi Valley towards Texas and New Mexico were another source of concern (see chapter 5), though calmed by the Bourbon Family Compact of 1761. Now this third threat directed Spanish attention to the far north and to the Russians.

2 Bering and the Russian explorations, 1728-71

Just as California was at the farthest extremity of a vast Spanish land empire, so Kamchatka was in the early eighteenth century the most distant area of a Russian empire which stretched from the Baltic to Siberia. From their base at Okhotsk the Russians had reached the southern tip of Kamchatka in 1706, and ten years later made the first sea crossing from Okhotsk to Kamchatka. The next step was to determine the reality of the *bolshaya zemlya* (large country) rumored to lie farther east, a quest which was bound to arouse speculation about the relation of Asia to America. A Siberian Cossack, Semen Dezhnev, had claimed that in 1648 he rounded East Cape, the eastern extremity of Asia (since renamed Mys Dezhneva by the Russians); but his report on this lay unheeded at Yakutsk, and despite the importance of his achievement it was unknown to Peter the Great. In 1716 and 1717 the Tsar was questioned about Siberia, and what lay beyond, during his visits to western European capitals; and in 1724 shortly before his death he set in train an expedition led by the Danish seaman Vitus Bering. As Bering later recorded, his orders from the Tsar were to sail from Kamchatka along the shore to the north, and 'Determine where it joins with America, go to some settlement under European jurisdiction. . . .'[2] After crossing northern Asia Bering's party built a vessel at Okhotsk, sailed to the west shore of Kamchatka, crossed overland to the peninsula's east coast, and there built another boat. In this vessel, the *St Gabriel*, Bering in 1728 reached and sailed through the strait now known by his name, but haze hid the American shore, and he failed to bring back definite information as to whether the continents were separated. Four years later Gwosdev sighted the American shore while on a voyage in Bering's old ship, but thought the land was probably part of a large island. Gwosdev seems to have made no map of his discoveries, but one drawn in the 1740s firmly states that the eastern shore of the strait seen from the *St Gabriel* in 1732 was *bolshaya zemlya*. News of Bering's momentous yet inconclusive voyage first reached western Europe through du Halde's history of China, published in Paris in 1735, which included a narrative of the voyage and a map obtained (indirectly) from Bering. This outlined the eastern tip of Asia, but showed nothing of America.

In 1731 Bering was entrusted with a second, more ambitious expedition—in effect a whole series of expeditions involving overland explorations in Siberia and voyages south through the Kurile Islands towards Japan, in addition to the main thrust led by Bering which was aimed east from Kamchatka at the American mainland. For ten years the Danish fleet-captain and a small army of associates, scientists and officials labored at St Petersburg, Okhotsk and Kamchatka, struggling against difficulties of distance and climate, financial stringency and local apathy. Finally, in the spring of 1741 Bering sailed in the *St Peter*, with the *St Paul* as consort, southeast from Kamchatka to latitude 45°N., where Company Land and Gama Land were alleged to lie. In turning northeast to search for these imaginary lands the two vessels became separated,

356

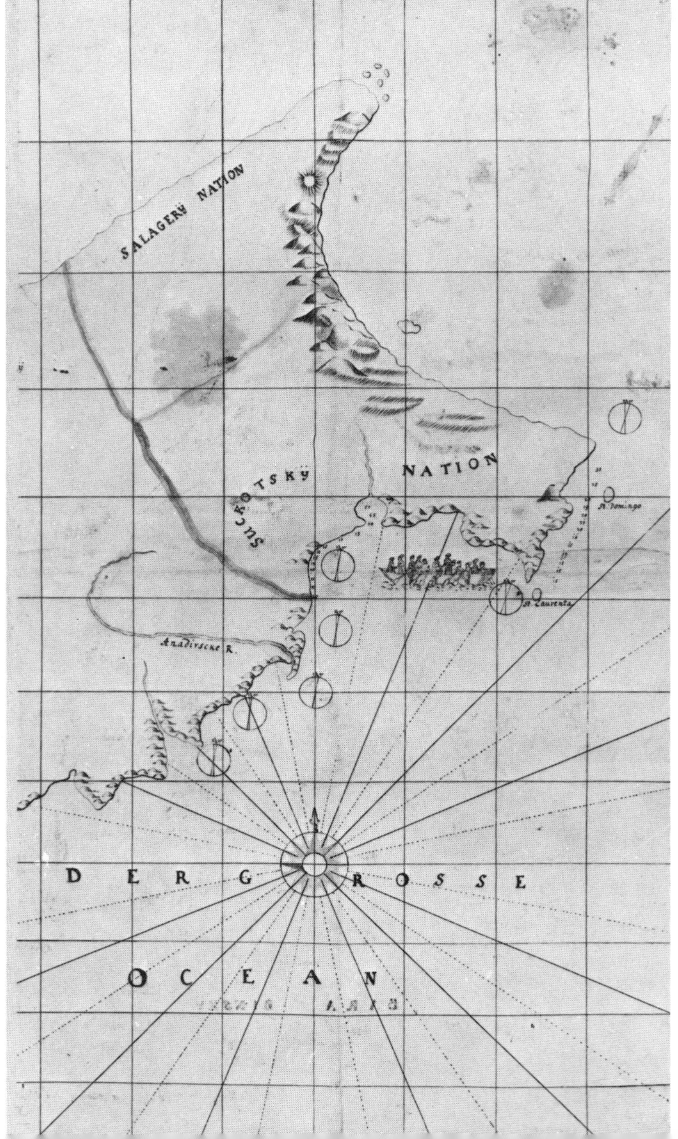

356 Two sections of a map showing Bering's explorations of 1725-8.
British Museum, London, K.Top.114 43(1).
This map, drawn in 1729, is a version with German legends of a map which exists in several variant forms in the Russian and Swedish archives.
The cartouche on the left-hand side of the map (*left*) has illustrations of the inhabitants of eastern Asia, the Tschutski and Kamchadales; the righthand side of the map shows Bering's crucial voyage of July/August 1728 to the eastern extremity of Asia. Although this is clearly delineated there is no hint of land across the water to the east.

357

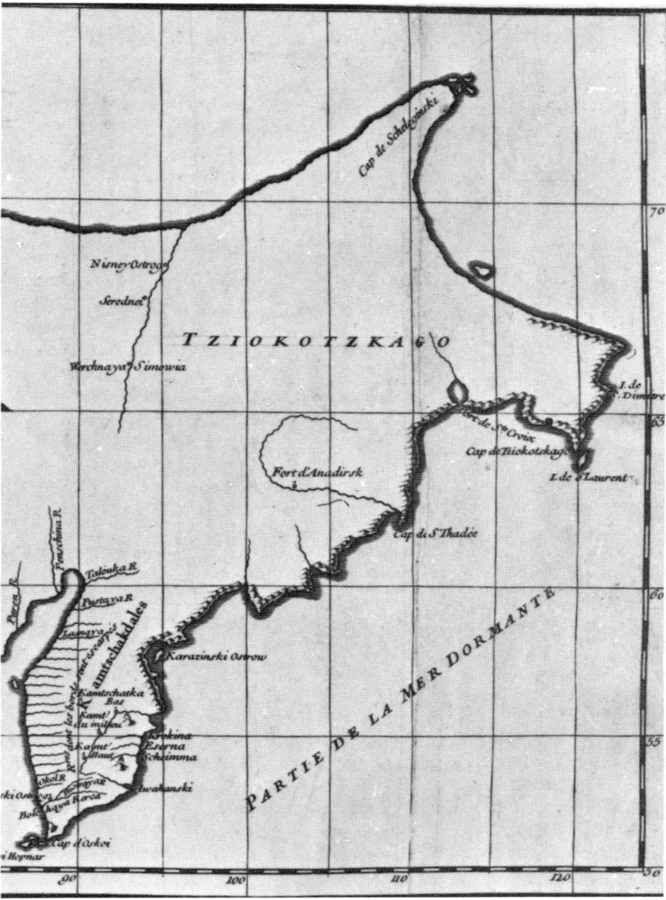

358

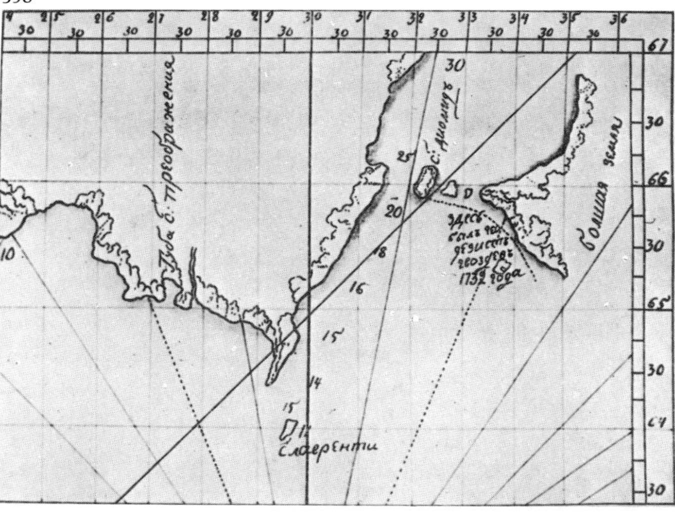

357 The first published version of the map (details of which are shown in plate 356) in Western Europe was contained in Vol IV of J. B. du Halde, *Description géographique de la Chine*, Paris, 1735, which also contained an account of the voyage and was translated into English the next year.

358 Detail from a Russian manuscript map of the voyage of Mikhail Gwosdev, 1732. *Central State Archives of Military History, Moscow.* Drawn under the direction of Martin Spanberg who had sailed with Bering in 1728, the map distinctly shows Cape Prince of Wales on the American side of Bering Strait, and Gwosdev's track in Bering's old vessel the *St Gabriel* passing along the coast towards Cape Rodney. The legend to the northeast of this landfall is significant—'bolshaya zemlya', or 'great land'. No better representation of Bering Strait was to appear until Cook's voyage almost a half-century later; but like so many Russian maps of the period this one was never published.

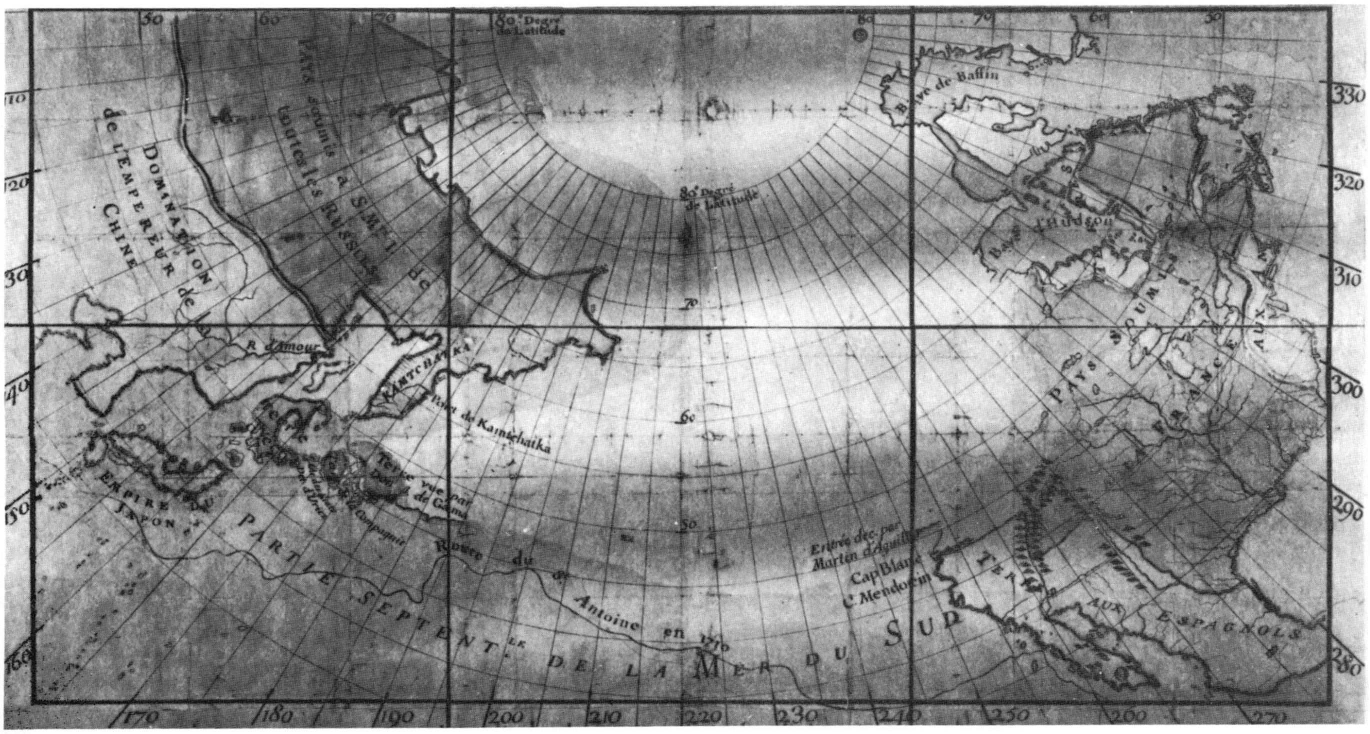

359

359 J. N. de l'Isle. 'Carte dressée en 1731 Pour Servir a la recherche des Terres et des Mers situées au Nord de la Mer du Sud'.
Younger brother of the famous Guillaume, Joseph Nicolas de l'Isle prepared this manuscript map at the request of the St Petersburg Academy of Sciences as a guide for the second Bering expedition. Although de l'Isle made no attempt to indicate the American coastline north of California, he inserted a whole chain of imaginary lands south of Kamchatka: Yedso or Yeso, Staten Island, Company Land and, stretching far to the east towards California De Gama Land. When Bering eventually sailed from Kamchatka in 1741 he headed towards this area, but in seeking these fictitious regions his two ships went far out of their way, and became separated with disastrous results. One of Bering's officers, the Swede Sven Waxell, wrote later:
'I think it would be only reasonable were such unknown lands first to be explored before they are trumpeted abroad as being the coasts of Yezo or de Gama . . . I know that I am writing all too much about this matter, but I can hardly tear myself away from it, for my blood still boils whenever I think of the scandalous deception of which we were the victims.'
Waxell (1952), p. 103.

360

361

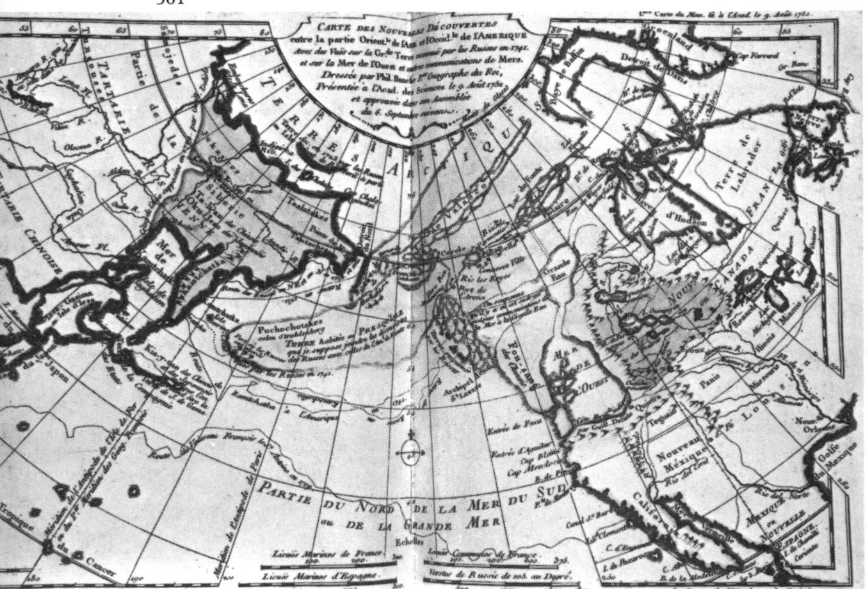

360-1 Philippe Buache. 'Carte des Nouvelles Découvertes au Nord de la Mer du Sud . . .'; 'Cartes des Nouvelles Découvertes entre la partie Orient.le de l'Asie et l'Occid.le de l'Amerique' (both Paris, 1752).
Two examples of the speculative geography produced by Buache in the 1750s, the first to support J. N. de l'Isle's Memoir of 1750, the second, one of thirteen maps presented by Buache in his *Considerations géographiques et physiques sur les nouvelles découvertes au nord de la grande mer* of 1752. The first map shows a vast Mer de l'Ouest similar to that supposedly drawn by Guillaume de l'Isle *c.* 1700, and to the north—and quite separate—the alleged discoveries of de Fonte in 1640. On the second and later map the Mer de l'Ouest is smaller, and has a suggested water connection with the De Fonte waterways to the north. These in turn point rather more openly to Hudson Bay and Baffin Bay than on the first map. A feature of both is that of the explorations carried out by the *St Paul* and *St Peter* on Bering's expedition of 1741, only the track of Chirikov's vessel (on which De l'Isle's brother Louis de la Croyère had sailed) is shown.

with disastrous results. Bering's second-in-command, Chirikov, went on to sight the American coast in latitude 55° 21'N., but there lost both his ship's boats with their crews, was unable to land, and on his return voyage to Kamchatka touched only at one of the Aleutian islands. Bering meanwhile had turned northeast until he sighted Mount St Elias in Alaska, and landed at nearby Kayak Island. He stopped there only long enough to take on water, a decision which brought from Steller, his German naturalist (see selection 3i), the biting comment that ten years of preparation had resulted in ten hours of exploration. The *St Peter*, with its crew stricken with scurvy, sailed back through the Shumagin and Aleutian islands, only to be wrecked on an island near Kamchatka where Bering and many of his crew died. The survivors, led by Sven Waxell who later wrote an account of the voyage (see selection 3ii), reached Petropavlovsk the following summer.

The journals kept on the expedition show that Bering and his officers were convinced that they had landed in America. Nevertheless, the close examination of the coastline which was necessary before it could be accepted that the land sighted was the continental coastline, perhaps part of the same land mass sighted by Gwosdev across Bering's strait in 1732, had still not been carried out. Bering's two voyages provoked more controversy than agreement. On the first he had neither proved that Asia and America were separated, nor discovered (if they were) by what extent of water. On the second there was little unanimity about the significance of the landfalls made by the two ships. Between the map published by the St Petersburg Academy of Science in 1758, with its suggestion of an immense southwestern extension of the tip of the North American continent towards Kamchatka, and the conviction of many geographers in Europe that the Russians had sighted only islands, lay many possible interpretations. This confusion, and the degree of public interest in the subject, were now heightened by the intervention of the French geographers Joseph Nicolas de l'Isle and Philippe Buache.

De l'Isle, younger brother of the famous Guillaume, had helped in the planning of the second Bering expedition, and when in 1747 he returned to France after twenty-one years in St Petersburg he brought with him a considerable collection of maps and manuscripts which he sold to Louis XV. He shared his information on the Russian discoveries with Buache, Guillaume's son-in-law, and a geographer of considerable repute himself; and when in 1750 De l'Isle read a memoir on Bering's discoveries before the Académie Royale des Sciences in Paris, it was accompanied by a map drawn by Buache. The publication two years later of the memoir and map marked the beginning of a controversy which exercised a bizarre influence on the course of exploration along the Pacific coast of North America. In his Memoir De l'Isle linked the fragmentary Russian discoveries on the northwest coast with the alleged explorations of a Spanish admiral, De Fonte, in 1640 (see selection 4); and on Buache's map northwest America was shown penetrated by the inland seas, straits and rivers described in Fonte's wondrous account. This had been rescued from a deserved obscurity by Arthur Dobbs in his *Account of the countries adjoining to Hudson's Bay* published in 1744, where it was used to buttress his theories about a navigable Northwest Passage; but in the hands of De l'Isle and Buache it became the foundation stone of an elaborate system of theoretical geography. In 1753 De l'Isle issued an entire atlas devoted to *Nouvelles cartes des découvertes de l'Amiral de Fonte*, while Buache produced a full-length work illustrated with thirteen maps, *Considerations géographiques et physiques sur les nouvelles découvertes au nord de la grande mer* (see plates 360 and 361). Accounts of voyages, some genuine, some apocryphal; reports and rumors—French, English, Spanish, Russian, Chinese (Fou-Sang was alleged to have reached northwest America from China in the fifth century)—all were accepted by Buache and welded together to support his fanciful system. Some French geographers followed De l'Isle and Buache, but two of the best-known, Bellin and De Vaugondy, as well as John Green in England, refused to accept maps based on such flimsy evidence (see plate 385).

From Russia initial criticism of De l'Isle and Buache sprang from anger at their 'evil representations' about Bering's second voyage, on which (De l'Isle asserted) the Dane played no significant part since he was shipwrecked soon after setting out from Kamchatka. Professor Müller of the St

362 G. Müller. 'Nouvelle Carte des Découvertes faites par des Vaisseaux Russiens . . .' St Petersburg, 1758.
First constructed in 1754, Müller's map of the Russian explorations was published by the St Petersburg Academy of Sciences four years later. Now the tracks of both Bering's and Chirikov's vessels in 1741 were shown; the Shumagin, Aleutian and Kurile islands were indicated, and a whole range of imaginary lands such as Yedso eliminated. The map illustrates the official Russian viewpoint that not only was the land sighted by the Russians at their farthest east part of the American mainland, but most of the coastline glimpsed on the return voyage, as well as the land seen by Gwosdev in 1732 opposite the eastern tip of Asia. This conviction led to the bloated Alaskan peninsula of the map. Although Müller warned against placing too much trust in the accuracy of the map—'My work herein has been no more than to connect together, according to probability, by points, the coasts that had been separated in various places'—it remained for many years a standard representation of the region.

362

Petersburg Academy of Sciences, who had been closely associated with the expedition, corrected De l'Isle's more elementary errors in a pseudonymous pamphlet of 1753, *Lettre d'un officier de la marine russien*. More important, the third volume of his *Sammlung Russiche Geschicte* contained in 1758 the first comprehensive account of the Russian discoveries in the North Pacific. It was translated into English (1761) and French (1766) to become the standard account of the 'Bering phase' of Russian exploration. Although Müller acknowledged that Bering on his first expedition had not brought back the conclusive information expected, he insisted that the Dane's explorations, and those of Gwosdev in 1732, had shown that 'there is a real separation between the two parts of the world, Asia, and America; that it consists only in a narrow straight'.[3] His account of the second expedition described the explorations of Bering's two ships, and of the subordinate expeditions connected with the project. He pointed out that the Russian explorations had diminished the chances of finding a Northwest Passage through Hudson Bay since they seemed to show that beyond California the American coast curved away far to the northwest. The De l'Isle/Buache system of inland seas and straits Müller emphatically rejected, adding that 'it is always much better to omit whatever is uncertain, and leave a void space, till future discoveries shall ascertain the affair in dispute'.[4] Müller's own map of the Russian discoveries (see plate 362) was published by the Academy at the same time as his book, and clearly indicated that all the land glimpsed by Bering and Chirikov in 1741 was part of the American mainland, a delusion that resulted in the enormous Alaskan peninsula of Müller's map—copied by many cartographers until Cook's explorations reduced it to more modest proportions. More useful, and less fanciful, would have been publication of the many manuscript maps made by members of Bering's crews.[5]

While the geographers pondered over the significance of Bering's discoveries, the next phase of Russian exploration in the area was already under way. The survivors of Bering's expedition had remarked on the abundance of fur-bearing mammals they had sighted; fur seals, foxes, and in particular the sea otter, with the most beautiful and coveted fur of all. Already in 1743 fur hunters had visited the island where Bering had been wrecked, and this was the forerunner of dozens of ventures which sailed east from Kamchatka towards America (at least thirty of them in the next twenty years). The *promyshleniki* were daring and brutal; in crazy vessels sometimes held together only by leather thongs they moved steadily along the stark, volcanic islands of the Aleutian chain (see selection 5). They killed not only the sea otters; they almost exterminated the native Aleuts as they burnt and looted their way from island to island, and the intimidated survivors were turned into hunters for the Russian traders. Losses from storm, disease and native attack were high, but so were profits. These trading expeditions rarely kept proper written records, and although a brief period of interest by Catherine II resulted in two government expeditions, that of Lieutenant Ivan Synd who combined survey work with escort duty for Russian traders between 1764 and 1768, and the more ambitious undertaking of Captain Krenitsyn and Lieutenant Levashev in 1764-71 among the Aleutians, the important maps which these expeditions produced were again not published.

363 Detail from plate 365 of the map by Bodega y Quadra and Francisco Mourelle, 'Carta reducida delas Costas. . . . 1775'. *Archivo General de Indias, Seville, Torres Lanzas, Carpeta de Mapas, No. 21.*
This detail shows the opening sighted by Bruno de Hezeta on his 1775 expedition in latitude 46°N. which was in fact the entrance of the Columbia River, not that of Fuca's strait.

363

3 Spanish coastal and interior explorations to the north, 1769-76

Russian activity, projects by the British to renew the search for a Northwest Passage by looking for its Pacific entrance, and the general growth of interest in the North Pacific, increased the nervous apprehension of the Spanish government. In 1761 it sent to St Petersburg its first diplomatic representative for more than thirty years, and for the next fifteen years a series of dispatches arrived at Madrid giving a remarkable amount of information (and some misinformation) about Russian movements in the north.[6] For a century and a half New Spain had made no sustained advance to the north where its inland frontier provinces were threatened by Apache raids and by Indian risings among the Pimas and Seris; but the alarmist reports arriving from St Petersburg helped to precipitate a general expansion of military and naval posts into Upper California. As Father Burriel had warned in the *Noticia de la California* of 1757, foreign settlements there would endanger the silver mines of New Spain. The discovery of a navigable Northwest Passage farther north would turn the flank of the whole Spanish position, while Britain's dominant position in eastern North America after the Treaty of Paris in 1763 made more likely a strong overland thrust towards the Pacific. Moved by these disturbing possibilities, Spain for the last time pushed forward the frontiers of its American empire. Directed by José de Gálvez, the energetic *visitador-general* of New Spain who took up temporary headquarters in *Baja* California, and helped by the inspiring presence of the venerable friar, Junípero Serra, Father-President of the Franciscan missions, seamen, soldiers and missionaries moved north along the coast to bring *Alta* California under firm Spanish control.

The first objective was Monterey, and its harbor described in such glowing, if erroneous terms by Vizcaíno in 1603 as—'the best port that could be desired . . . sheltered from all the winds'.[7] In 1769 land and sea expeditions left La Paz for the north, San Diego was reached by sea in April, and by land in May, and then in a journey along hundreds of miles of shoreline never before trodden by Europeans a party led by the governor of *Alta* California, Gaspar de Portolá, headed for Monterey. When discovered, it proved so unlike Vizcaíno's description that scouts were sent farther north, where they stumbled on the great bay of San Francisco. At first the significance of the discovery was not realized; to the Spaniards San Francisco Bay meant Drake's Bay, under Point Reyes, and the vast expanse of sheltered water which Portolá's men found was assumed to be an estuary which lay across the path of land parties attempting to reach Point Reyes (see selection 6i). On this journey the Spaniards saw for the first time at close quarters the giant redwood trees of the California and Oregon coast, so huge that eight men with arms out-

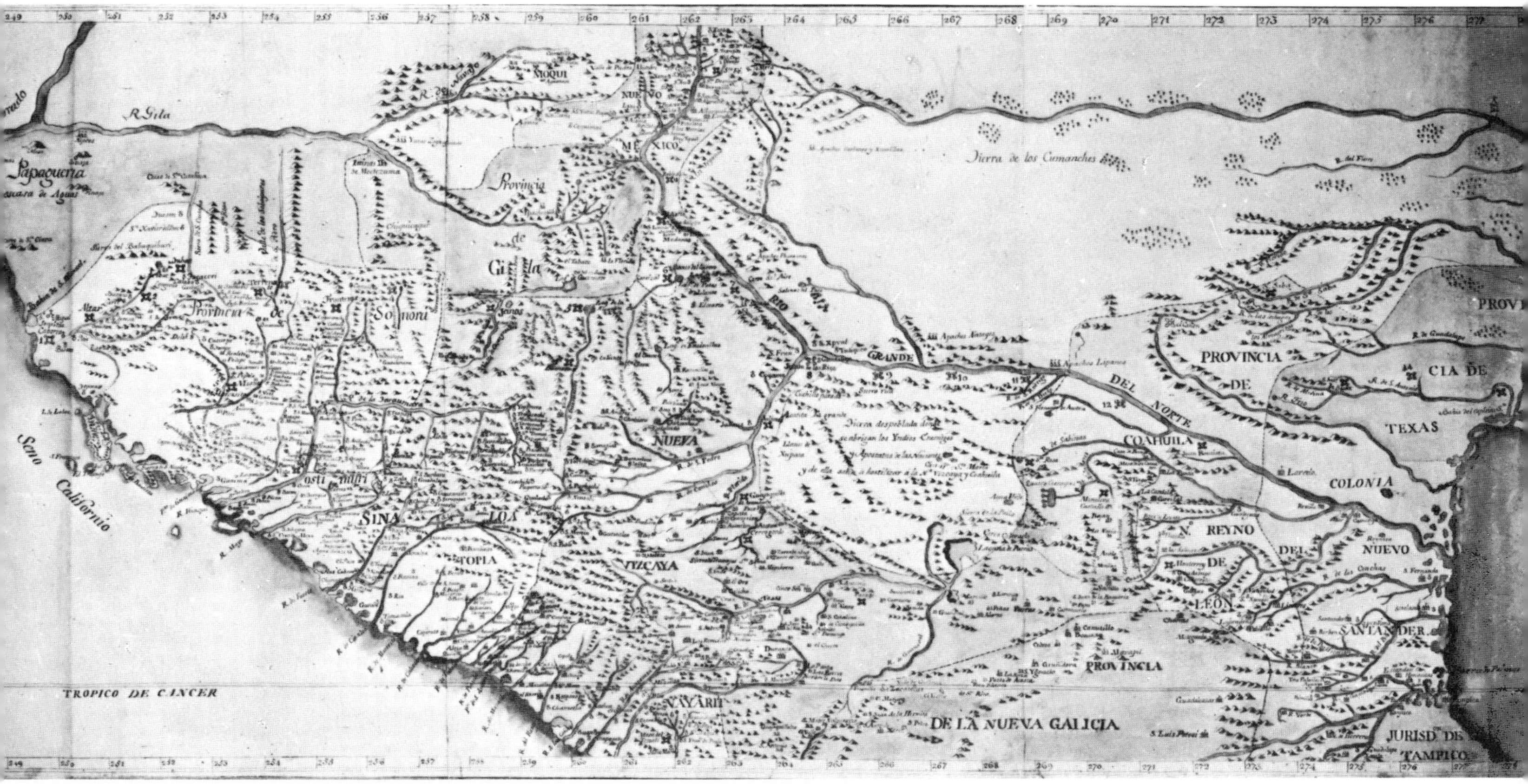

364

365

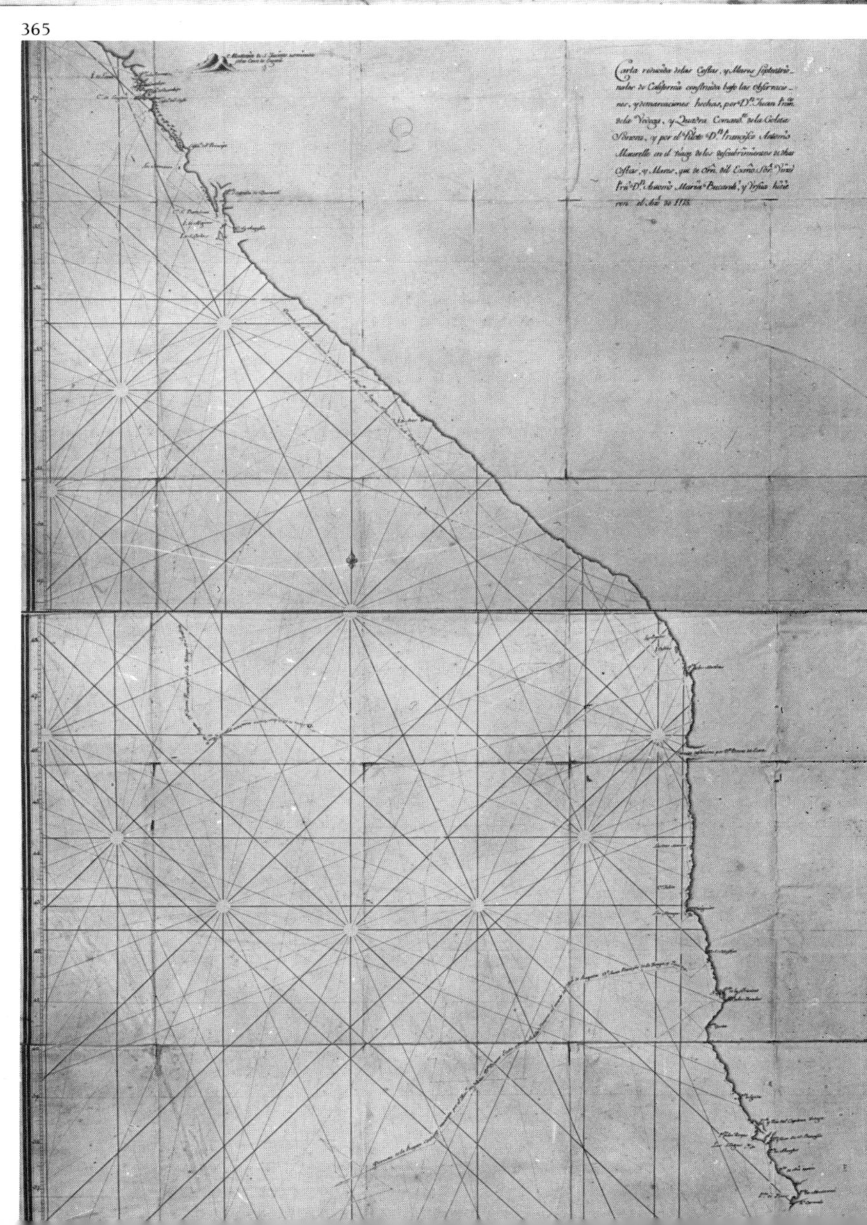

364 'Mapa de la Frontera del . . . Nueva Espana', by Nicolás de Lafora, 1771. *British Museum, London, Add. Ms. 17, 660A.*
Several manuscript versions of this map were produced by Lafora, a captain in the Spanish Royal Engineers, and his companion José de Urrútia on their return from accompanying the Marqués de Rubí on a tour of inspection of New Spain which lasted almost two years (1766-8), and extended from Texas to Sonora, and as far north as Santa Fé (see page 163). Apart from the blank stretch of Comanche territory to the northeast, and the lack of detail along the Gila, the map is an impressive production, and much superior to contemporary published maps of this vast region.

365 Juan Bodega y Quadra and Francisco Antonio Mourelle. 'Carta reducida delas Costas, y Mares Septentrionales de California. . . . 1775'. *Archivo General de Indias, Seville, Torres Lanzas, Carpeta de Mapas, No 21.*
This manuscript map of the northern expeditions of 1775 covers the long stretch of coastline from Monterey in the south fifteen hundred miles to the Alaskan coast in latitude 58°N., Bodega's farthest north (see page 230). Bucareli Sound is marked in latitude 55°40′N. The lack of detail in the middle section of the map shows that the *Sonora* was out of sight of the coastline for much of the time, and there is certainly no awareness here of the insular nature of the land to the east of the vessel's track. Even so, the map represents a bold strike north by Spain three years before the much-publicised expedition of Cook reached the coast. The map was never published, but *The London Magazine* for December 1780 constructed one from an account of the voyage by Mourelle which had reached England.

stretched could not encircle one at the base. The reality of the incomparable harbor of San Francisco Bay was not grasped for another half-dozen years, when in 1775 Juan de Ayala made the first recorded sailing through the Golden Gate, and the next year a settlement was established in the bay after an army officer, Juan Bautista de Anza, and Father Pedro Font had surveyed the area from the land side (see selection 6 ii).

Although San Diego and Monterey had been secured, and in 1771 another mission established at San Gabriel (the site of modern Los Angeles), the Spanish position in *Alta* California was still precarious. Peninsular California was too poor an area to support any permanent expansion northward, and all supplies for the new establishments had to be brought by sea from San Blas on the Mexican coast. The northward voyage,

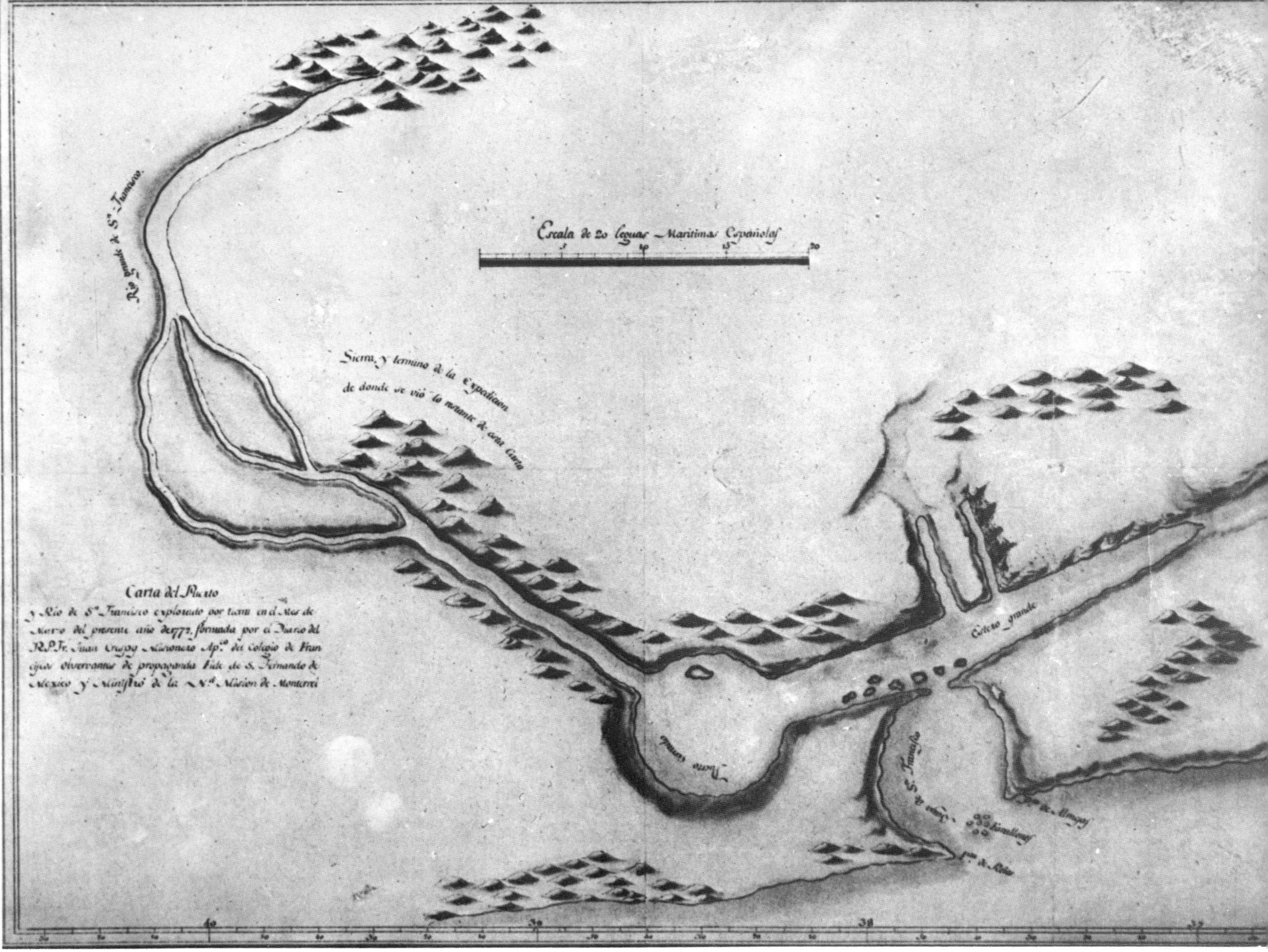

366

made difficult by headwinds, might take three or four months; and the alternative of crossing the notoriously stormy Gulf of California was even less appealing. The answer to the communications problem was a land route from Sonora across to *Alta* California, and this discovery was in the main the work of Anza and the Franciscan missionary Father Francisco Garcés. Far distant at his post at Tubac in Sonora, Anza had heard Indian reports of Portolá's expedition to Monterey in 1769. News of Spanish movements on the coast had reached the Yumas living near the junction of the Colorado and Gila Rivers, and they had passed it on to the Pimas, from whom Anza heard it. A route of sorts must exist; the question was whether it was a practicable one for settlers and supplies. In 1774 Anza made the attempt. Accompaned by Garcés, who had already carried out explorations along the Colorado and Gila Rivers three years earlier, and a party of thirty or so men, together with cattle (for food) and mules, Anza moved from Tubac across known territory to the junction of the two rivers. The Colorado desert almost defeated the expedition's efforts to reach the coast as it lay, waterless and trackless, across the Spaniards' path. A typical journal entry records Anza's frustration as he found a trail, only for it to peter out—'it led us into very dense sand dunes and we became lost entirely, because the wind moves the dunes about and carries the sand in various directions.'[8] At the second attempt the party skirted this appalling wilderness of sand-dunes, climbed the Sierra Nevadas, and reached a rocky pass, the *Puerto Real de San Carlos*. The desert lay behind; in front stretched 'most beautiful green and flower-strewn prairies, and snow-covered mountains with pines, oaks, and other trees which grow in cold countries . . . Looking toward the

366 Juan Crespí. 'Carta del Puerto y Rio de Sn Francisco . . .', 1772. *Ministerio del Ejército: 104-6-14, Madrid.*
This manuscript drawing is possibly the earliest separate map of San Francisco Bay; another version of it with different legends, but also dated 1772, is extant (and is reproduced in Harlow, 1964, opp. p. 32). Although Crespí had visited the area twice, first with Portolá in 1769-70 and then with Fagés in 1772, his map is both crude and distorted, and reflects the confusion of the first Spanish explorers. The present Golden Gate channel is identified as 'Baya de Sn Francisco', inside 'P.ta de Reies', while today's San Francisco Bay is shown in drastically flattened form as the estuary of the great river of San Francisco rising in hills to the northeast.

367 Manuel Agustín Mascaro. 'Mapa geografico de una gran parte de la America Septentrional . . .' 1782. *British Museum, London, Add. Ms. 17, 652(a).*
Drawn at Arispe, Mascaro's map sums up the substantial Spanish northward explorations of the previous fifteen years both along the Pacific coast and in the interior. Based on the maps of Costansó, Miera and others it shows the trails of Anza and Garcés in 1775, and the country covered by the Domínguez-Escalante expedition of 1776. It repeats, therefore, Miera's error about the San Buenaventura, to the west of which is shown an incomplete section of a large river which seems to be flowing down to the coast at San Francisco Bay. The map reveals that the difficult topography of the Great Basin had not yet been understood, for it clearly assumes that the rivers from the western slopes of the Rockies north of the Colorado flow into the Pacific. Although never published, the map helped to transmit the information from the manuscript surveys of Miera and others to Baron Alexander von Humboldt, who inspected Mascaro's map at Mexico City in 1803. One result of this was that Humboldt's famous map of New Spain published in 1811 owed much, though it acknowledged little, to the fine Spanish cartographers of the 1770s and 1780s whose individual efforts have remained in obscurity until illuminated and publicized by twentieth-century scholars such as Henry R. Wagner, Carl I. Wheat and Herbert E. Bolton.

Mapa
Geografic
de
gran parte de la America Septentrional comprendido entre los veinte, y quarenta grados de la
norte, y los doscientos quarenta y nueve, y doscientos ochenta y nueve de longitud oriental de Tenerife en el que
nen. las Provincias de la antigua, y nueva California, las de Sonora, Nueva Vizcaya, Nuevo Mexico, Coahuila
Texas erigidas en Capitanía General por S.M. en el año de 1769.
Arispe 29 de Julio de 1782.
Manuel Agustín Mascaró
Tropico
Provincia de Timpanogos
Provincia del Moqui
Rio Gila
Rio Colorado
Rio Grande del Norte
Rio Yaqui
Rio Mayo
Derrota del P. Garces año de 1775.
Papagos
Apaches
Pimas altos
Pimas bajos
Cabo de Corrientes

South Sea and toward our new establishments on its coasts, all the view is most beautiful.'[9]

From here the travellers descended the San Jacinto Valley through the fertile Californian coastal plain 'full of flowers, fertile pastures, and other vegetation, useful for the raising of cattle, of which species as many as one might wish could be raised',[10] and so to the mission at San Gabriel. The next year Anza proved the practicability of the trail for regular travel by leading along it a party of 240 soldiers, settlers and muleteers, and more than 1,000 animals. In a remarkable feat of careful leadership, Anza reached the Pacific with a party larger (through newborn children) than that which had left Sonora; and moreover arrived in time to defend San Diego against Indian attacks which were stretching the thin Spanish resources to the limit.

Garcés remained unconvinced that the route through the wastes of the Colorado desert was the best one, and in 1775 left Anza at the junction of the Colorado and Gila Rivers in an attempt to find a more northerly route. Travelling alone among the Indians he loved and trusted (see selection 7), he tracked along the Colorado to the Mojave River. Although he failed to find a way through to the coast he was the first European known to have entered the Great Basin, stretching from the Sierra Nevadas of California to central Utah, and unique among the major physical features of North America in not having any outlet to the sea. It was in this area that cartographers indicated the great interior sea, the Mer de l'Ouest, an illusion that the Spanish explorations were to dispel. Garcés also reaches the Grand Canyon, the first white man since Coronado's expedition of 1540 to do so, though his journal gives a disappointingly sparse description of the great chasm.[11]

Six months later another party of Spaniards entered the vast interior basin, this time from the southeast, where the two Franciscan Fathers Domínguez and Escalante left Santa Fé in quest of a route to California. Their track on the splendid maps drawn by Miero shows that they failed in the attempt, but in the great irregular circle they cut through New Mexico, Arizona, Utah and Colorado the two friars made one of the most important interior journeys of the century. In the previous dozen years several parties of soldiers, traders and prospectors had penetrated northward from Santa Fé and Taos towards the Colorado River, but from the reports they brought back of forbidding rock deserts, labyrinthic trails and bearded Indians no clear picture of the geography of the area emerged. Much of the route of the Escalante expedition lay across country never before traversed by Europeans, and Escalante's diary tells of weeks and months of struggling across a stark landscape of high plateaus trenched by awesome canyons, of featureless deserts and splintered hillsides. The quiet beauty of the Utah Valley stood in such contrast that Escalante indulged in a rare passage of hyperbolic prose (see selection 8) to describe it and its potentialities for Spanish settlement. But no Spanish force ever followed the tortuous path traced by Escalante and Miero. Their magnificent journey was one of the last notable feats of Spanish exploration, and when traders and settlers reached the Great Basin in the next century they came from the east, and they were American.

A persistent motive behind this surge of Spanish expansion remained fear of foreign activity to the north, and the early 1770s saw a fine new crop of rumors. A squadron from Russia's Black Sea fleet was to be sent around the world to Kamchatka, and from there was to descend on the northwest coast of America. An Englishman named Bings was sailing across an ice-free polar sea to California. British fur traders had reached so far west from Hudson Bay that they had made contact with the Russians in Alaska. The viceroy of New Spain, Antonio María Bucareli y Ursúa, was rightly sceptical of these reports, but they added to the general feeling of insecurity which helps to explain the decision to send exploring expeditions far along the coast to the north. In 1774 the veteran pilot Juan Pérez sailed in the frigate *Santiago* to latitude 55°N. where, off the Queen Charlotte Islands, although the Spaniards failed to land they traded with the Haida Indians who came out to the vessel in large, decorated canoes, beating drums and offering furs and superb wool blankets. On the return voyage Pérez sighted Vancouver Island and anchored off Nootka Sound, which Cook was to enter four years later, and which within two decades was to become the center of international rivalry on the coast. Back at San Blas the viceroy pronounced himself dissatisfied with Pérez's reluctance to land on the northern coast, though he appreciated the reasons for his caution:

'The darkness of the weather, the cold to which they were not accustomed, the fear of a shortage of water and of an unknown coast seem to have been the causes that the instructions with which I dispatched the expedition were not entirely complied with . . . but it will facilitate the success of later ones, and it is persuasive of the fact that in the 19° higher which we have advanced, there is no danger of foreign establishments.'[12]

The next year the schooner *Sonora* commanded by Juan Francisco de la Bodega y Quadra reached the Alaskan coast in latitude 58°N., and for the first time Spaniards landed on the northwest coast. Farther south, off the west coast of Prince of Wales Island, not far from Chirikov's American landfall of 1741, the Spaniards discovered a strait (Bucareli Sound) which led them to speculate that 'if there is a passage on these coasts to the North [Atlantic] Sea, in no place is it more likely to be than here'.[13] Meanwhile far away to the south the consort *Santiago*, which had been forced to turn back because of sickness among the crew sighted in latitude 46°N. a large bay through which 'the sea penetrates far into the land, making a horizon to the east. For this reason they thought it must be a river, but from lack of experience they could not enter and examine it.'[14] The vessel's commander, Bruno de Hezeta, reported that this was perhaps the entrance of Fuca's strait; in reality, he had seen the entrance of one of North America's major rivers, the Columbia, seventeen years before the American Robert Gray sighted it and claimed prior discovery.[15]

4 The explorations of James Cook, 1778

For the Spanish authorities the most reassuring aspect of these northern explorations was that no trace of foreign activity had been found. The reports from St Petersburg had inflated both the degree of official Russian interest in northwest America and the area of Russian activity. The fur traders were operating only in the remote Aleutians and neighboring islands; not until 1784 was the first permanent Russian establishment set up in Alaska, and then at Kodiak Island and not on the mainland. But Spanish feelings of relief were short-lived, for during 1776 a stream of intelligence reports reached New Spain from Madrid warning that a British discovery expedition was leaving for the northwest coast, commanded by the best-known explorer of the century, Captain James Cook. After two voyages to the South Pacific, Cook was now bound to the north in quest of the Pacific entrance of the Northwest Passage. Sceptical though the Admiralty was of the theoretical cartographers who concocted a northwest America broken by deep inlets and straits, the more reliable information of Hearne's journey to the Arctic Ocean (see Chapter 6) raised a new hope—that a Northwest Passage

368

368 'A Map of the New Northern Archipelago', from Von Stählin, *Account of the New Northern Archipelago*, London, 1774.
Originally published in German in 1773, Stählin's book and map purported to describe the discoveries of Russian merchants trading east of Kamchatka in the 1760s under the protection of Lieutenant Synd. Clusters of islands are scattered around the map in random fashion, but its most striking and misleading feature is the representation of Alaska as an island. Stählin's depiction of another strait through to the polar sea 15 degrees east of Bering Strait was to have a decisive effect on the instructions given to Cook in 1776. There is no indication of the Alaskan peninsula, and Unalaska, Kodiak and other major islands are wildly misplaced. A comparison with the Russian manuscript map of Synd's explorations (plate 392) shows how unfounded were Stählin's claims to have produced 'a very accurate little Map'.

might be found across the top of the North American continent, rather than through it. Coincidental with the receipt of Hearne's news came the publication in London during 1774 of a Russian map which showed another way from the Pacific to the Arctic Ocean in addition to Bering's strait. The map, constructed by von Stählin, secretary of the St Petersburg Academy of Sciences, claimed to be based on the discoveries of Lieutenant Synd and Russian traders. It marked Alaska, not as a long peninsula, but as a sizeable island. North America ended in longitude 140°W., and between it and Alaska lay a wide strait through which ships might sail into the Arctic Ocean (see plate 368).

Carrying instructions greatly influenced by the Stählin map, Cook arrived on the northwest coast in March 1778 (see selection 9). Almost 200 years after Drake, English vessels had again reached 'New Albion', and the journals of Cook's officers reflect their curiosity as they strained for a glimpse through the mist of that mysterious coastline along which (if the maps were to be trusted) Aguilar, Fuca and Fonte had discovered the entrances of great rivers and straits. But the opening now known by Juan de Fuca's name (though it leads no deeper into the continent than the Strait of Georgia), was passed unseen in the darkness; and the two ships, *Resolution* and *Discovery*, anchored in Nootka Sound off the densely-wooded oceanic shores of Vancouver Island. Here the crews met the local Nootka Indians, physically unalluring with their faces and bodies grotesquely painted and smeared with grease and filth, but a people superbly skilled on the water in handling their canoes, and on land in building wooden dwellings with intricate totemic carvings which were to fascinate generations of white visitors to the coast.

At the end of April the expedition left its haven at Nootka and headed north. Bad weather kept it well out to sea, and it did not sight land again until latitude 55° 20′N., beyond the supposed entrance of Fonte's Río los Reyes. Cook was following his emphatic instructions 'not to lose any time in exploring rivers or inlets, or upon any other account, until you get into . . . latitude 65°N.'[16] Hearne's sea far to the north was the objective, not the waterways of the apocryphal accounts. So Cook kept steadily north, along a shoreline which became bleaker and harsher, passing and naming Cape Edgecombe, Cross Sound and Cape Fairweather. On 10 May the ships' companies could see directly inland the towering peak of Bering's Mount St Elias, and the journal of one of the officers reveals the air of tense expectancy on board the ships: 'We have [Stählin's] map of the N°ern Archipelago constantly in our hands, expecting every opening to the N°ward will afford us opportunity to seperate the Continent'.[17] But the coast turned inexorably to the west, and away from the point where Hearne, more than a thousand miles distant, had sighted the shores of the polar sea. Prince William Sound was followed until its shores closed in, and then Cook Inlet farther west still. At last the long tongue of the Alaskan peninsula was rounded, and on 9 August land which Cook presumed was the western tip of the American continent came into view, and was named Cape Prince of Wales. The ships sailed west from the cape and soon sighted land again, which Cook named East Cape. They were obviously in a strait of some kind, but to identify it with any hitherto described was no easy matter. The strait of Bering's voyage of

369

370

369 Cook's ships at Nootka Sound, by John Webber, 1784. *National Maritime Museum, Greenwich.*

370 Interior of a Nootka habitation, by John Webber, 1778. *British Museum, London, Add. Ms. 23,921, fo 83.*
Cook has an interesting journal entry on this: 'At the upper end of many of the appartments, were two large images, or statues placed abreast of each other and 3 or 4 feet asunder, they bore some resemblance to the human figure, but monsterous large; the best idea will be had of them in a drawing which Mr Webber made of the inside of one of their appartments wherein two of them stood. They call them Acweeks which signifies supreme, or chief; a curtin or mat for the most part hung before them which they were not willing at all times to remove, and when they did shew us them or speak of them, it was in such a Mysterious manner that we could not comprehend their meaning.' Webber himself described in a later letter how a man armed with a knife deliberately obstructed his view of the carvings, and only moved when Webber had stripped his own coat of buttons and handed them over.

371

371 Indian houses at Nootka Sound, by John Webber, 1778. *British Museum, London, Add. Ms. 15.514, fo 7.*
Cook wrote: '. . . their houses or dwellings are situated close to the shore. They consist in a long range of buildings, some of which are one hundred and fifty feet in length, twenty four or thirty broad and seven or eight high from the floor to the roof, which in them all is flat and covered with loose boards. The Walls, or sides and ends, are also built up of boards and the framing consists of large trees or logs.'

372

373 The remarkable volcanic cone of Mount Edgecombe on the Alaskan coast in latitude 57°N. by John Webber, 1778. *British Museum, London, Add. Ms. 15,514 (1).*

1728 and Gwosdev's of 1732 was shown on Müller's map as being more than a hundred miles from shore to shore, while neither of the two northern straits marked on Stählin's map bore the least resemblance to the one the expedition was passing through. Northeast of the strait the grim reality of polar navigation was brought home to the crews as they encountered a massive wall of ice which blocked the way eastward along the northern edge of the American continent, and imperilled the ships as it heaved and crunched towards the shore. As the ships retreated through the strait it became clear that the starboard shore was indeed the eastern tip of Asia, reached by Bering fifty years earlier. But of the large island of 'Alaschka' marked on Stählin's map there was still no sign; it was, concluded an infuriated Cook, 'A Map that the most illiterate of his illiterate Sea faring men would have been ashamed to put his name to.'[18]

The whole concept of Cook's expedition had been based on two fallacies: Stählin's guess that there was a short strait east of Alaska, and the insistence of theoreticians in Europe that ice would not present a serious obstacle to navigation in the polar sea. Cook had been set an impossible task, and that under the circumstances he sometimes lacked his normal certainty of touch and professional detachment is understandable. Judged by any standards save his own, the results of his single season of exploration were extraordinary. He had charted the American coastline from Mount St Elias to Bering Strait and beyond, determined the shape of the Alaskan peninsula, and south of Mount St Elias touched (as had the Spanish explorers of 1774 and 1775) along a coast previously unvisited by Europeans. When he met Russian traders on the island of Unalaska he closed the gap between the Spanish probes from the south and the well-established Russian trade to the north. Though Cook was killed at Hawaii early in 1779, the maps brought home by his officers, and published with the three-volume official account of the voyage of 1784, showed the reality of his achievement. In outline at least the shape and position of the northwest coast of America were known at last; for the first time the region takes recognizable shape on the map. This advance in knowledge neither the Russians nor Spaniards could match; they had no seaman on the coast who approached Cook in experience and professional skill, and those surveys which were made tended to be issued in garbled form or not published at all. As the Swiss geographer Samuel Engel complained in 1777, 'Whatever happens in the Russian Empire is a secret of state'[19]; and official obscurantism, an obsessive insistence on secrecy,

374

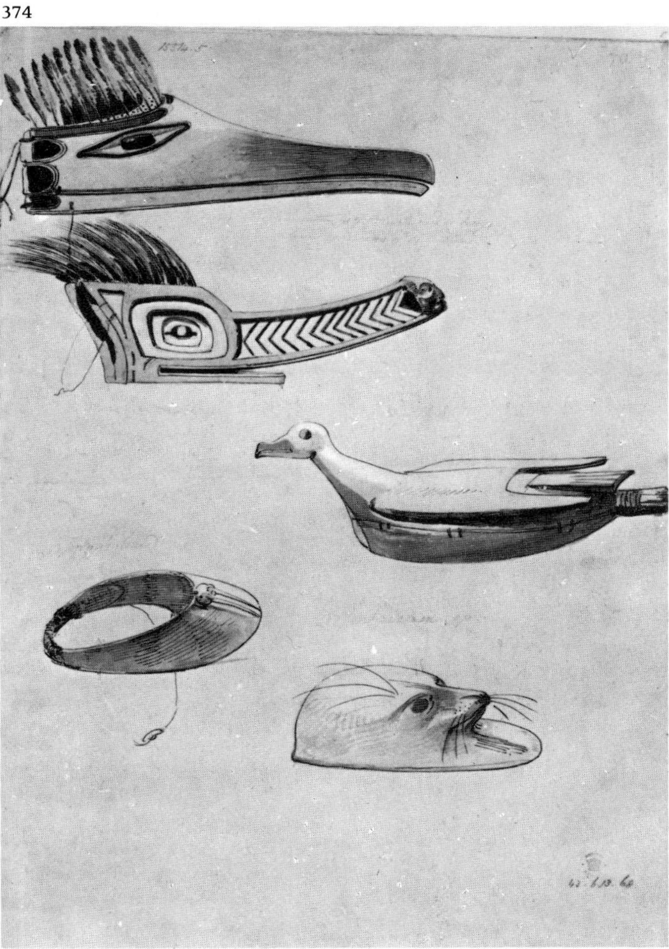

374 Artifacts from the northwest coast, by John Webber, 1778. *British Museum, London, Add. Ms. 15,514 (5).*
The top two objects are masks from Nootka used as decoys by the Indians when hunting; the bird is a 'Rattle'; at bottom left is a 'Schutzki i.e. Chukchi or Tchuktschi bonnet'; at bottom right is an 'American cap'.

375

372 Man of Nootka Sound, by John Webber, 1778. *Peabody Museum, Harvard University.*
Cook wrote: 'Both Men and Woman paint their faces, their colours are black red and white and seemed to be a kind of ochre mixed with oil, which as I have before observed they lay on with a liberal hand: in this plaster they make various scrawls on the face and particularly on the fore head. Besides this daubing they have another ornament to the Face, which is a small circular plate, or flat ring in the shape of a horse shoe, but not more in circumference than a shilling; the upper part is cut asunder, so as the two points may gently pinch the Bridle of the Nose, to which it hangs over the upper lip. These ornaments were made of either iron or copper and the rims of some of our buttons were appropriated to this use.'

375 Native canoes or kayaks at Unalaska, 1778, by John Webber. *British Museum, London, Add. Ms. 17,277 (25).*

376

377

378

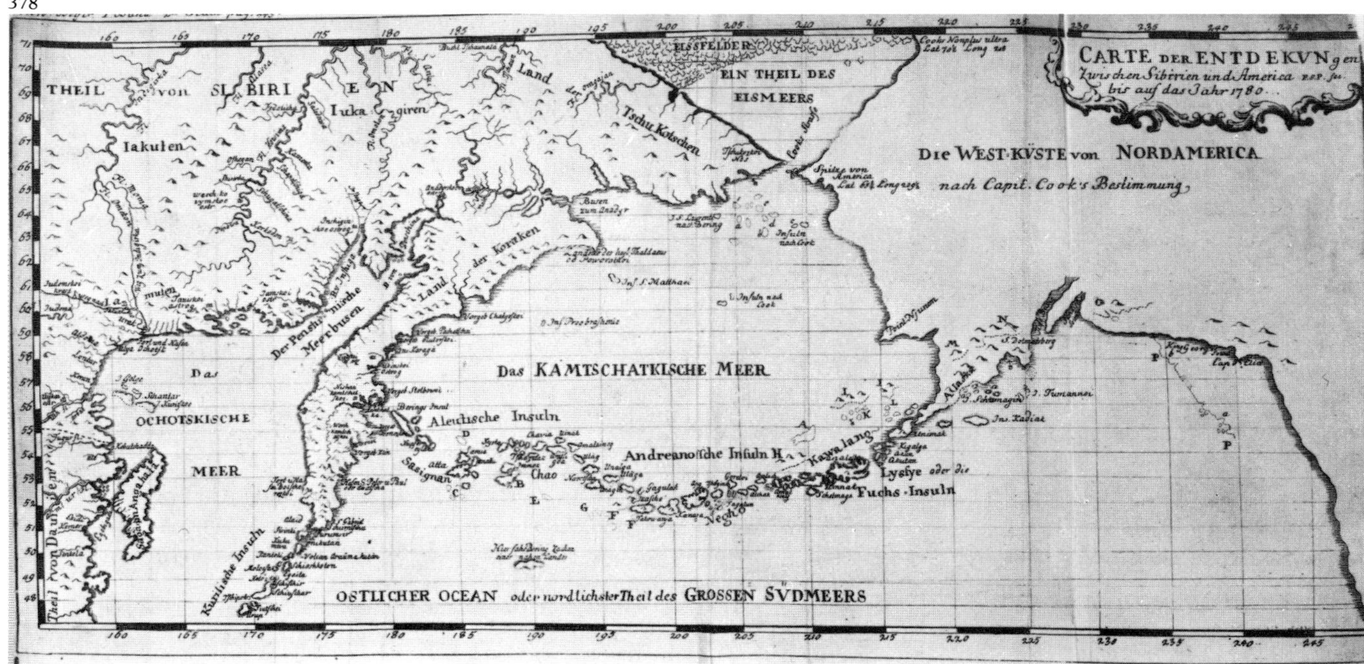

376-7 Man and woman of Prince William Sound, by John Webber, 1778. *British Museum, London, Add. Ms. 23,921, fos 89, 90.*
Cook's account suggests that the man's conical hat was made of straw, and that he was wearing a leather shirt which acted as a kind of oilskin in his kayak; and that the woman was wearing a bear skin slung over her skin dress. In a long description of their slit lips, and bored nostrils and ears, Cook concluded, 'I have nowhere seen Indians that take more pains to ornament, or rather disfigure themselves, than these people.'

378 P. S. Pallas. 'Carte der Entdekun gen Zwischen Sibirien und America', St Petersburg, 1780, from Pallas, *Neue nordische beyträge*, 1781.
This is one of the earliest printed representations of Cook's explorations on the northwest coast. Pallas, the famous German scientist resident at St Petersburg, is known to have seen in late 1779—through the good offices of Sir James Harris, British ambassador to the court of Catherine II—the letters from Cook and Clerke sent overland to Western Europe from Kamchatka. The result of this knowledge is displayed on the map. The approximate outline of northwest America appears in familiar form, though as a record of the British discoveries the map is both incomplete (there is no detail shown along the coast Cook explored between Alaska and Bering Strait) and defective (the crowded islands between Kamchatka and Alaska resemble a southern movement of the insular aberrations of Stählin's 1774 map). It is interesting that Bering Strait is named after Cook here—nomenclature which did not survive Cook's own insistence that Bering Strait should be the name adopted.

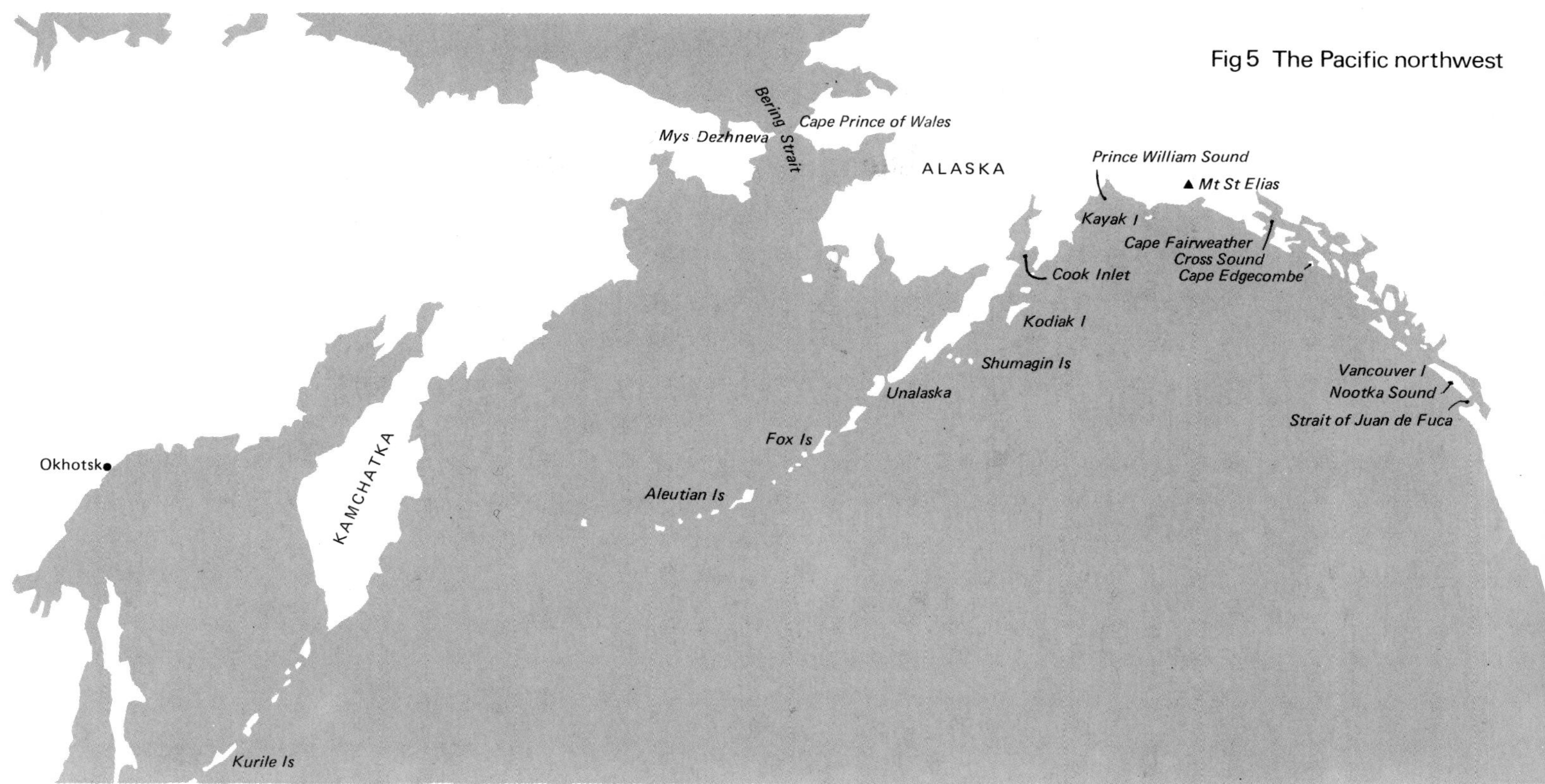

Fig 5 The Pacific northwest

were as characteristic of the government at Madrid as that at St Petersburg. One of the tragedies of the heroic explorations of missionaries, soldiers and seamen from New Spain in the last decades of the eighteenth century was that their accounts and maps remained unpublished—often until the present century. In many places he touched along the northwest coast Cook was not 'first discoverer' except in the all-important sense that he and his officers were the first to reveal fully to the world through their narratives, maps and vivid illustrations where they had been and what they had seen. In the accounts of Cook's final voyage the dramatic scenery of the northwest coast and the startling appearance of its inhabitants, from the forested shores of Nootka Sound to the bleak inlets of Alaska, became for the first time familiar sights to readers in Europe. Any publication about Cook was likely to sell well in a half-dozen European languages. The official account, lavishly illustrated, was priced formidably high at £4 14s. 6d., yet one London periodical noted of its sale: 'We remember not a circumstance like what has happened on this occasion. On the third day after publication, a copy was not to be met with in the hands of the bookseller; and to our certain knowledge, six, seven, eight, and even ten guineas, have since been offered for a sett.'[20]

In one way Cook rounded off an era in the history of the northwest coast, but his voyage was as much an introduction to a new chapter as the closing of an old. His explorations were preliminary surveys rather than the conclusive exercises they had been in the south Pacific; for neither Cook nor his Russian and Spanish predecessors had determined whether the long stretches of coastline they sailed along were islands or mainland. The interior, sometimes even a few yards from the water's edge, was still unknown. On the major problem exercising geographers as to how far north the Rocky Mountains extended, the seaborne explorations of the 1770s provided no help. The gulfs and inlets marked on the maps of the theoretical geographers might still exist almost anywhere along the coast between Nootka and Mount St Elias. The accounts, official and unofficial, of Cook's last voyage had much to say on all this, but they also drew attention to the commercial potentialities of this remote region. They described how the natives along the coast would trade a sea otter skin worth a hundred dollars for a handful of beads. The quest for beaver had drawn men from the Atlantic seaboard of the continent almost to within sight of the Rockies, and the maritime traders in their turn were quick to respond to this new lure. Expeditions were fitted out for the northwest coast, first by British merchants in China and India, and then by others in Europe and the United States (fast becoming an important maritime power in its own right). By the early 1790s so many expeditions were trading along a coast which until twenty years earlier had never seen the sails of a European vessel that, as Washington Irving put it in his novel *Astoria*, 'it was as if a new gold coast had been discovered'. Once again the close connection between exploration and exploitation had been demonstrated; the northwest coast had been opened, and the next decades were to see a struggle first for its commercial and then for its political domination.

1
Father Kino and the land passage to California, 1698-1702

From Kino's *Historical Memoirs* . . .

Father Eusebio Francisco Kino spent twenty-four years at his Jesuit mission station at Dolores in Pimería Alta. From this frontier post he pursued exploration and missionary work to the north with equal zeal, and in a series of explorations between 1698 and 1702 established the peninsular character of California.

When, ten years ago [1689], setting out from Nuestra Señora de los Dolores for the west, and passing through the lands of El Soba, I arrived after sixty leagues' journey, on three different occasions with different persons at the coast of the Sea of California, we saw plainly that the arm of the sea kept getting narrower, for in this latitude of thirty-three degrees we already saw on the other side more than twenty-five leagues of California land in a stretch so distinctly that we estimated the distance across or width of that arm of the sea to be no more than fifteen or eighteen or twenty leagues.

Therefrom arose the desire to ascertain the width higher up; and in the year 1698, at thirty-five degrees latitude, and at one hundred and five leagues by a northwest course from Nuestra Señora de los Dolores, on the very high hill, or ancient volcano, of Santa Clara, I descried most plainly both with a telescope and without a telescope the junction of these lands of New Spain with those of California, the head of this Sea of California and the land passage which was there in thirty-five degrees latitude. At that time, however, I did not recognize it as such, and I persuaded myself that farther on and more to the west the Sea of California must extend to a higher latitude and communicate with the North Sea or Strait of Anian, and must leave or make California an island. And it was with me as with the brethren of Joseph, who ate with him and made merry with him, he giving them the wheat and provisions which they required, and talked with him but knew him not, until his time.

A year afterward, at the suggestion of the father visitor, Oracio Police, I penetrated one hundred and seventy leagues to the northwest, and went beyond thirty-five degrees north latitude, with Father Adamo Gilg and Captain Juan Mateo Manje, and almost reached the confluence of the Rio Grande de Hila and the Colorado, where the natives gave us some blue shells. And still it did not occur to us that by that way there was a land-passage to California, or to the head of the sea; and not until we were on the road returning to Nuestra Señora de los Dolores did it occur to me that those blue shells must be from the opposite coast of California and the South Sea, and that by the route by which they had come thence, from there to here, we could pass from here thither, and to California.

Text used: H. E. Bolton (Ed.), *Kino's Historical Memoir of Pimería Alta . . . 1683-1711, Cleveland, The Arthur H. Clark Co., 1919, vol. I, pp. 229-30.*

379 E. F. Kino, 'Passage par terre A la Californie', from *Lettres edifiantes* . . . V, Paris, 1705.
Father Kino's celebrated map, though making no claim to knowledge beyond the extent of his actual travels, showed with great clarity the geographical significance of his explorations around the head of the Gulf of California. Although some cartographers persisted in showing California as an island almost to mid-century, most followed the lead of Guillaume de l'Isle who accepted Kino's map, which marked not only the 'land passage' from Sonora to California, but also showed the Colorado and Gila Rivers.

379

2
Lower California and its inhabitants

From Venegas, *History of California*, 1759

In 1757 a three-volume work, *Noticia de la California*, was published at Madrid. Ostensibly the work of Father Miguel Venegas, the book was largely compiled by another Jesuit, Father Andrés Marcos Burriel. Translated within a few years into English, French and Dutch, the book afforded a rare glimpse into this outlying province of Spanish America, and although the stress was naturally on the missionary endeavors of the Jesuits the writer gave detailed descriptions of peninsular (*Baja*) California and its inhabitants.

The length of California from cape San Lucas to the northern limit already conquered, is about 300 leagues: besides which, about a district of a league has been partly known and described.

Its breadth is small in proportion to its length; for at cape San Lucas it is only 10 leagues, in some places 20, in others 30, and in others 40, from one sea to the other, according to the windings of both coasts. From the extent of the country, there must naturally be a difference in the temperature of the air, and the qualities of the soil. But it may be said in general, that the air is dry and hot to a great degree; and that the earth is barren, rugged, wild, every where over-run with mountains,

380

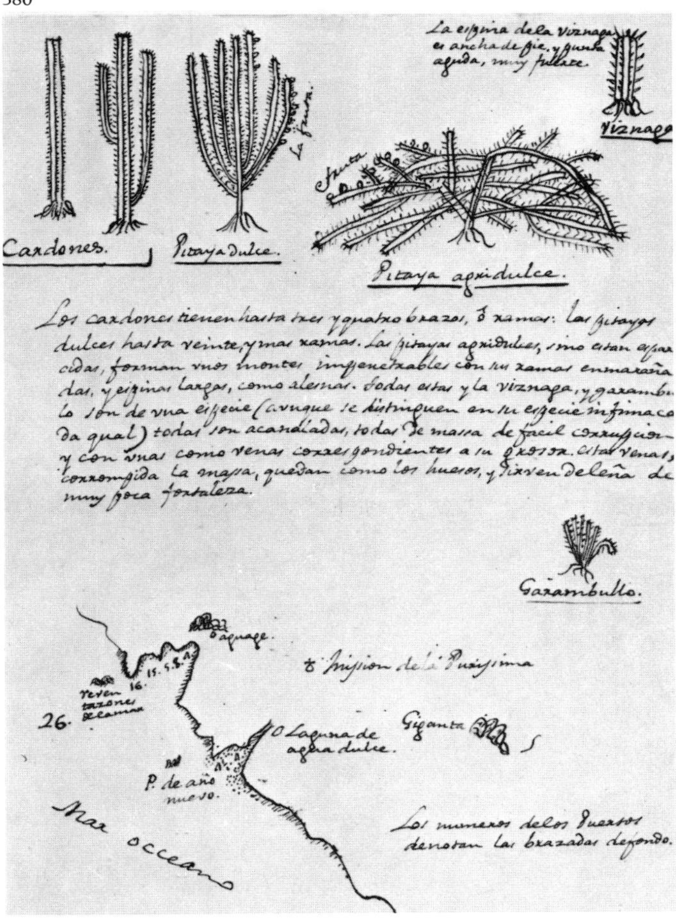

380 Line drawings of cacti in a Spanish manuscript of the mid eighteenth century, 'Descripción compendiosa de lo descuvierto y conocido de la California'. *Huntingdon Library, California, Ms. 1295.*

rocks, and sands, with little water, and consequently unfit either for agriculture, planting or graziery . . . but, notwithstanding this country in general is rugged, craggy, and barren, and the air disagreeable and unhealthy; yet near the coast there are several spots that may be greatly improved by agriculture, and would produce all the necessaries of life. The vicinity of the sea with its vapours moderates the heat of the atmosphere; the sides of the mountains send forth currents of water, without which, indeed sowing would often fail, on account of the little rain, and the uncertainty of it. Lastly, it is not without plains both for pasture and tillage. Even in the center of California there are some vallies and rising grounds of a tolerable soil, having springs for drinking and watering the grounds. In these parts it is that the poor Californians have their dwellings; and here likewise are the Cabeceras of the missions, and the villages within their jurisdiction. . . .

The characteristicks of the Californians, as well as of all the other Indians, are stupidity and insensibility; want of knowledge and reflection; inconstancy, impetuosity, and blindness of appetite; an excessive sloth and abhorrence of all labour and fatigue; and incesant love of pleasure and amusement of every kind, however trifling and brutal; pusillanimity and relaxity: and in fine, a most wretched want of every thing which constitutes the real man, and renders him rational, inventive, tractable, and useful to himself and society. It is not easy for Europeans, who were never out of their own country, to conceive an adequate idea of these people. For even in the least frequented corners of the globe, there is not a nation so stupid, of such contracted ideas, and so weak both in body and mind, as the unhappy Californians. Their understanding comprehends little more than what they see: abstract ideas, and much less a chain of reason, being far beyond their power; so that they scarce ever improve their first ideas; and these are in general false, or at least inadequate.

Text used: Miguel Venegas, A Natural and Civil History of California, *London, 1759, vol. I, pp. 26, 28-9, 64-5.*

3
Bering reaches northwest America, 1741

i) From Steller's manuscript journal, 1741-2

Among the crew of Bering's ship the *St Peter* on the momentous voyage of 1741-2 from Kamchatka to the northwest coast of America was the German naturalist Georg Wilhelm Steller. In his journal he describes the vessel's American landfall at Kayak Island, three or four miles off the mainland where the great peak of Mt St Elias towered into the clouds.

381

381 Kaye's or Kayak Island, by John Webber, 1778. *British Museum, London, Add. Ms. 15,514 (3).*
This is Bering's St Elias Island, where he landed for a few hours in 1741.

On the 17th [July], the wind being light, we gradually drew nearer the land. On Saturday, the 18th, we were so close to it towards evening, that we were enabled to view with the greatest pleasure the beautiful forests close down to the sea, as well as the great level ground in from the shore at the foot of the mountains. The beach itself was flat, level, and, as far as we could observe, sandy. We kept the mainland to the right and sailed northwesterly in order to get behind a high island which consisted of a single mountain covered with spruce trees only.

The next day Steller landed on the island for a hurried survey.

When I was once more on the top of the mountain and turned my eyes towards the mainland to take a good look at least at that country on which I was not vouchsafed to employ my endeavors more fruitfully, I noticed smoke some versts away ascending from a charming hill covered with spruce forest, so that I could now entertain the certain hope of meeting with people and learning from them the data I needed for a complete report. For that reason I returned in great haste and went back, loaded with my collections, to the place where I had landed. Through the men who were just ready to hurry back to the ship in the boat I informed the Captain Commander and asked him for the small yawl and a few men for a couple of hours. Dead tired, I made in the meantime descriptions on the beach of the rarer plants which I

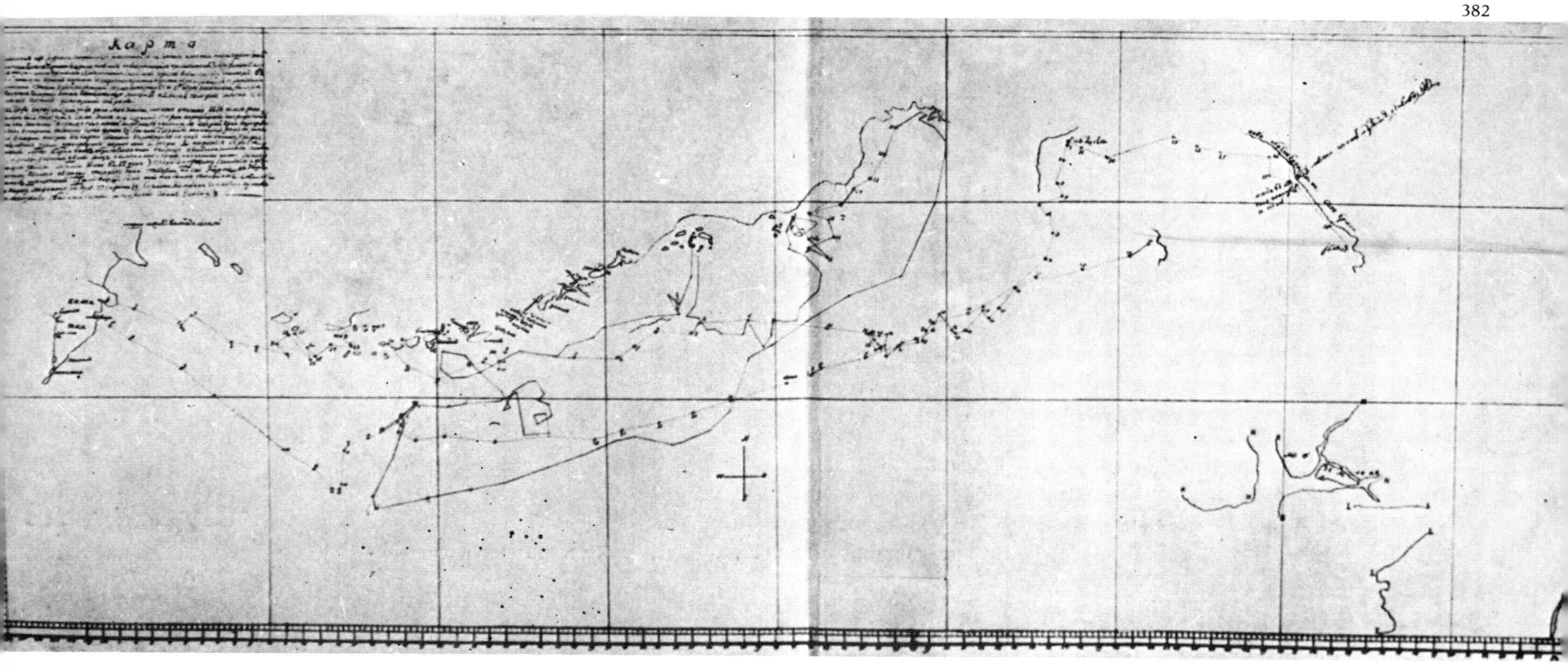

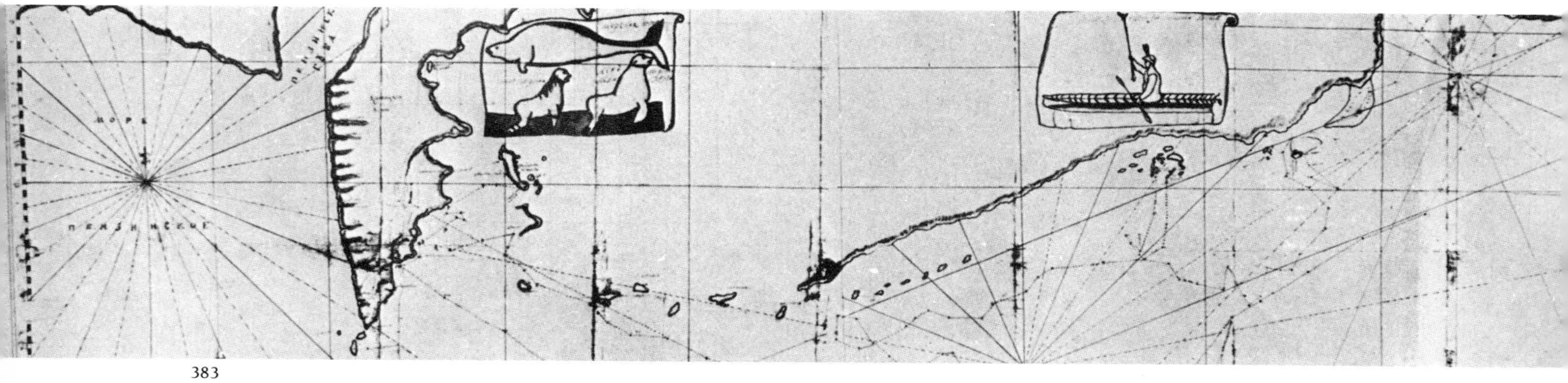

383

384

was afraid might wither and was delighted to be able to test out the excellent water for tea.

In an hour or so I received the patriotic and courteous reply that I should betake myself on board quickly or they would leave me ashore without waiting for me. . . .

I had been on the ship scarcely an hour when Khitrov with his party of about fifteen men also returned in the great boat and made the following report: He had discovered among the islands lying close to the mainland a harbor where one could anchor without danger. Although he had seen no human beings on land, he had nevertheless come across a small dwelling built of wood, the walls of which were so smooth that it seemed as if they had been planed and in fact as if it had been done with cutting tools. Out of this building he brought with him various tangible tokens, for instance, a wooden vessel, such as is made in Russia of linden bark and used as a box; a stone which perhaps, for lack of something better, served as a whetstone, on which were seen streaks of copper, as if the savages, like the ancient Siberian tribes, possessed cutting tools of copper; further a hollow ball of hard-burned clay, about two inches in diameter, containing a pebble which I regarded as a toy for small children; and finally a paddle and the tail of a blackish gray fox.

These, then, are all our achievements and observations, and these not even from the mainland, on which none of us set foot, but only from an island which seemed to be three miles long and a half mile wide and the nearest to the mainland (which here forms a large bay studded with many islands)

382 Russian manuscript map by Ivan Yelagin of the explorations of the *St Peter* and *St Paul*, 1741. *Archives of the Central Cartographic Establishment of the Navy, Leningrad.*
This map shows the more southerly track across the North Pacific of Alexei Chirikov in the *St Paul*, his American landfall in latitude 55°21'N. off the west coast of Prince of Wales Island, and the continuation of his voyage north along the coast to Chichagof Island. Near here, the legend slanting northeast across the map notes, Chirikov lost his helmsman (together with fourteen other men and both his boats). The *St Paul* then turned westward, and made a landfall at Cape Elizabeth before running for home, at first well to the south of the Alaskan peninsula, and then coming nearer to the long line of the Aleutian Islands. Vitus Bering's track in the *St Peter* is also shown, with his landing-place at Kayak Island, and a return voyage which took him closer to the Alaskan peninsula than Chirikov had ventured. The final leg of the *St Peter's* voyage through the westernmost Aleutians, and on to shipwreck at Bering Island, is not marked. One peculiarity of the map is that the American coastline discovered by Chirikov has been pushed too far east, with the result that his later landfall at Cape Elizabeth is shown to the *east* of Bering's at Kayak Island, whereas it should be well to the west. Uncertainty in the cartographer's own mind about this would seem to be shown by a duplication of Chirikov's first landfall about 12° farther west—apparently in mid-ocean—with a track leading to it bearing the correct dates for Chirikov's last three days before sighting land of 13, 14, 15 July. Chirikov's own report of December 1741 shows that he was aware that the estimated longitude (based on dead-reckoning) of his American landfall was wrong, for he pointed out that there was an apparent $11\frac{1}{2}$° discrepancy in the distance between Avacha Bay in Kamchatka and the American landfall on his outward and homeward tracks. This he ascribed to the lack of a known point of land anywhere on the voyage, and to strong oceanic currents. (See Golder (1922), pp. 308, n. 22, 313-14, 322.)

383 A contemporary Russian copy (made by Lieutenant Sofron Khitrov in 1744) of Lieutenant Sven Waxell's map of the voyage of the *St Peter* in 1741. *Archives of the Central Cartographical Establishment of the Navy, Leningrad.*
The outline of Alaska and the outlying islands is generally inferior to that on plate 382; of more interest perhaps are the representations of an Aleut in his baidarka or skin-boat, and of three mammals, including the *morskaya koro[va]* or sea cow.

384 Sections of Sven Waxell's map of Bering's second expedition reproduced in Eugen Büchner, 'Die abildungen der Nordischen Seekuh', in *Memoires de l'Académie Imperiale des Sciences de St. Petersburg,* VII Series, vol 38, 1891.
The drawings of the long-extinct sea cow are the only ones known to have been drawn by (or at least under the direction of) someone who had actually seen the mammal. It settled for example, the question of whether or not the creature had a forked tail. Although similar to the manati of warmer waters, the sea cow (*Hydrodamalis gigas*) was a separate species. Steller left a description of it in his treatise 'De bestiis marinis', but his drawings of it have disappeared, and by 1768 the creature had been exterminated by the Russian fur-traders. The other two mammals are fur seals. The second point of interest is that the fragment of Waxell's map reproduced in Büchner shows Bering Island, just off the Kamchatkan mainland, where the *St Peter* was forced to winter in 1741-2, and where Vitus Bering died.

and separated from it by a channel less than half a mile wide. The only reason why we did not land on the mainland is a sluggish obstinacy and a dull fear of being attacked by a handful of unarmed and still more timid savages, from whom there was no reason to expect either friendship or hostility, and a cowardly homesickness which they probably thought might be excused, especially if those high in authority would pay no more attention to the testimony of the malcontents than did the commanding officers themselves. The time spent here in investigation bears an arithmetical ratio to the time used in fitting out: ten years the preparations for this great undertaking lasted, and ten hours were devoted to the work itself. Of the mainland we have a sketch on paper; of the country itself an imperfect idea, based upon what could be discovered on the island and upon conjectures.

ii) From Waxell's manuscript account, *c.* 1750.

As the *St Peter* passed through the Aleutian Islands on its return voyage 'Americans' were at last encountered. This account of the meeting is given by Lieutenant Sven Waxell, a Swedish officer with Bering who wrote a narrative of the expedition some time after his return to Russia.

. . . I decided to send three men ashore, two Russians and an interpreter from the Chuckchi peninsula. They pulled off their clothes and waded ashore with the water right up under their arms. As soon as they had reached the shore, one of the Americans seated himself in his kayak and came out to me. He was evidently the eldest and I am sure also the most eminent of them all. I handed him a beaker of gin which he put to his lips, but spat the gin out again at once and turning to his fellows screeched most horribly. I had also wished to make him presents of various trifles, such as needles, glass beads, a little iron kettle, tobacco-pipes and such like, but he would accept nothing from me and turned back again. For almost an hour I remained there, the whole time making signs to them to come out to me, but I could not get them to do so. I talked to them using an English book, de la Hontan's description of North America, which I had with me. In it there is a whole number of American words in alphabetical order, with an English translation added. . . .

. . . These Americans' outer clothes or coats were made of whale guts cut up and sown together again. Their trousers were of sealskin, while their caps were of sea-lion skin set around with various feathers, most of them, naturally, hawk's feathers. Their noses were plugged with tough grass of an unknown kind and when they took this out, it gave off a quantity of fluid which they licked up with their tongues. Their faces were red, but certain of them had painted theirs blue. Their individual features were like those of Europeans, in contrast to the Kalmuks who are all flat-nosed. They were long-limbed and well formed. Their food seemed to consist of all kinds of sea animals and of the blubber, a piece of which they had wished to give me. They also eat herbs of all sorts, and wild roots. While I was watching, they pulled up some roots, shook off the sand and gobbled them up. . . .

On the following morning, 6th September, seven kayaks came out to us and lay off quite close to the ship. There was one man in each kayak, as I have already described. Two of them then came right in to the ship and took hold of our gangway. They made us a present of two of their caps and of a stick five feet long, to the thin end of which were fastened feathers of every conceivable kind. They also gave us a little human image carved out of bone, which we imagined must have been one of the idols they worshipped. They accepted presents from us as well and would have come aboard had not the wind got up and begun to blow hard, so that they had to betake themselves off in a hurry. As soon as they had got back on land, they all arranged themselves in a cluster and began screeching dreadfully. This they kept up for almost a quarter of an hour; yet I have no idea why they did so.

Text used: i) F. A. Golder (Ed.), Bering's Voyages, *New York, The American Geographical Society, 1925, vol. II, pp. 35, 50-1, 52-4; ii) M. A. Michael (Ed.),* The American Expedition by Sven Waxell, *London, William Hodge and Co., 1952, pp. 114-15, 117-19.*

4
The apocryphal voyage of Admiral de Fonte, 1640

From *The Monthly Miscellany,* London, 1708

The 'Fonte letter' first appeared, without explanation, in the April and June 1708 issues of a short-lived London periodical, *The Monthly Miscellany or Memoirs for the Curious.* At the time of publication it caused little stir, and not until British interest in the Northwest Passage revived thirty years later was it given serious attention. It was then reprinted in various forms, and in several different languages, at least ten times before the end of the century. To many the apparent refusal of the Spaniards to comment on the letter was proof of its authenticity; yet a Jesuit working in Spain produced definite evidence that the Fonte account was false, and it was the act, not of Spanish officialdom, but of an English publisher which withheld this evidence from non-Spanish readers. The third volume of the Venegas/Burriel *Noticia de la California* published in Madrid in 1757 (see Selection 2) contained a long and critical examination of the Fonte account. Burriel did more than list the narrative's inconsistencies; he gave the results of his search in Spanish archives and libraries. He had examined in vain the records at Madrid, Seville and Cadiz, contemporary accounts and maps; and nowhere had he found any reference to the voyage of 1640 or indeed to an admiral by the name of De Fonte. When the *Noticia* was translated into English in 1759 this whole section was omitted—despite the interest in England in the subject—and the omission was repeated in the French and Dutch editions since they were both translated from the English.

385

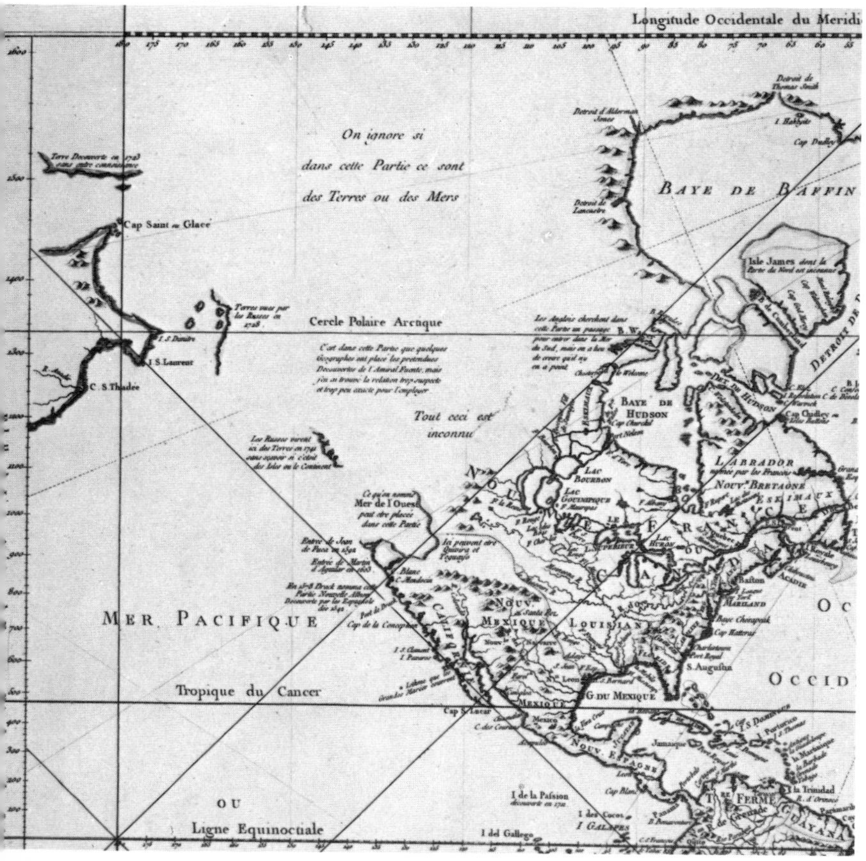

385 J. N. Bellin. 'Carte de l'Amerique Septentrionale'. Paris, 1754 (detail). A much more austere map than the bizarre Buache productions, Bellin's showed the Russian discoveries of 1728 and 1741 (but again omitted Bering's own landfall near Mount St Elias), and made a slight gesture in the direction of the Mer de l'Ouest of the de l'Isle family.

A Letter from Admiral Bartholomew de Fonte, then Admiral of New Spain and Peru, and now Prince of Chili; giving an Account of the most material Transactions in a Journal of his from the Calo of Lima in Peru, on his Discoveries to find out if there was any North West Passage from the Atlantick Ocean into the South and Tartarian Sea. . . . from the 26th of May [1640] to the 14th of June, he had sail'd to the River los Reyes in 53 Degrees of N.Latitude, not having occasion to lower a Topsail, in sailing 866 Leagues N.N.W. 410 Leagues from Port Abel to Cape Blanco, 456 Leagues to Riolos Reyes, all the time most pleasant weather, and sailed about 260 Leagues in crooked Channels, amongst Islands named the Archipelagus de St. Lazarus; where his Ships Boats always sail'd a mile a head, sounding to see what Water, Rocks and Sands there was.

The 22d of June, Admiral Fonte dispatch'd one of his Captains to Pedro de Barnarda to sail up a fair River, a gentle Stream and deep Water, went first N. and N.E.N. and N.W. into a large Lake full of Islands, and one very large Peninsula full of Inhabitants, a Friendly honest People in this Lake;

386 Manuel Agustín Mascaro. 'Plano General de la Mission y Pueblo de Arispe', 1782. *British Museum, London, Add. Ms. 17,661B.*
This beautifully colored and detailed map by Mascaro of the settlement of Arispe in northern Sonora shows the precise layout of the buildings and cultivated areas of this Spanish mission station and pueblo on the banks of the Sonora River.

387-8 Bernardo Miera y Pacheco. 'Plano geografico de la tierra descubierta, y demarcada, por Dn Bernardo de Miera y Pacheco al rumbo del Noroeste, y oeste del nuevo Mexico . . .', 1777. *British Museum, London, Add. Ms. 17,661C.*
'Plano Géographico, de la tierra descubiérta, nuevamente, à los Rumbos Norte Noroeste y Oeste, del Nuevo Mexico . . .' *British Museum, London, Add. Ms. 17,661D* (overleaf).
These splendidly illustrated maps by Miera reveal the prodigious extent of unknown country north of New Mexico traversed by the Domínguez-Escalante expedition of 1776. The maps, with their indication of relief, illustrative symbols and lengthy legends, are a treasure-house of information. They were based on Indian information, on the discoveries of earlier Spanish expeditions, but above all on first-hand knowledge gained during the journey of 1776. Miera had a quadrant, but had to estimate his longitudes. At least six manuscript copies of Miera's map are known to exist, differing in title, illustrations and legends rather than in their basic cartographic form. Both show the region north to about the 42nd parallel which included the basin of the upper Colorado and the complex river network of the central and eastern part of the Great Basin. In the extent of new country revealed, and in their accuracy, Miera's maps are among the great surveys of European discovery in the Americas, and it was a tragedy that they were not published at the time.
The maps show two major errors. The river marked as the 'San Buenaventura' is in fact Green River, but instead of joining the upper Colorado ('Zaguaganas') it is shown flowing into Sevier Lake ('Laguna de Miera') at the western edge of the map. This was to cause considerable confusion among later cartographers, many of whom were to show an apocryphal Buenaventura River flowing from the Rockies westward into the Pacific. Secondly, Miera shows in the north Utah Lake and Great Salt Lake as one body of water (given by him the Indian name, 'Laguna de los Timpanogos'), with the Tizon River flowing westward from Great Salt Lake, a concept based on the inferior map of New Spain published under the name of Joseph Antonio Alzate y Ramirez in 1768.

387 B.M. Add. Ms. 17,661C. This represents what Wheat in his *Mapping the TransMississippi West*, has called the 'undecorated' type of Miera's various maps. The legends are of particular interest: below the title the first legend points out that the Spanish explorations refuted the idea of the Sea of the West, alleged to exist in the very regions shown by Miera in such detail. The second refers to the Comanche territory, and describes how the warlike, horsed Comanche now dominated the buffalo plains as far as the Texan border, and after continual warfare had finally displaced the Apache.
In the bottom left-hand corner of the map is a reference to the Grand Canyon, where the Colorado 'flows between walls of red rock, very deep and rugged'. Most of the illustrative symbols shown in the key are self-explanatory, but it might be noted that the last of them—a cross on top of a circle—shows the daily camp sites of the Escalante expedition.

388 B.M. Add. Ms. 17,661D. Probably the original of the 'bearded Indian' type of Miera's maps (to use Wheat's classification once more), this map shows four Indians, two of them bearded, near the upper Colorado (where the expedition met them in late September 1776), and in the top righthand corner a spectacular if irrelevant depiction of the Pope. The legend on this map about the Comanches differs from that on plate 387; this gives more information about the Comanche breakthrough southward, their transition from using dogs as carriers to horses, and the effect of the turmoil caused by the Comanche-Apache rivalry on the Spanish border areas. The note on the Rocky Mountains is a perceptive one: 'This mountain range is the backbone of North America, since the many rivers that are born of it empty into the two seas, the South Sea and the Gulf of Mexico'.

386

387

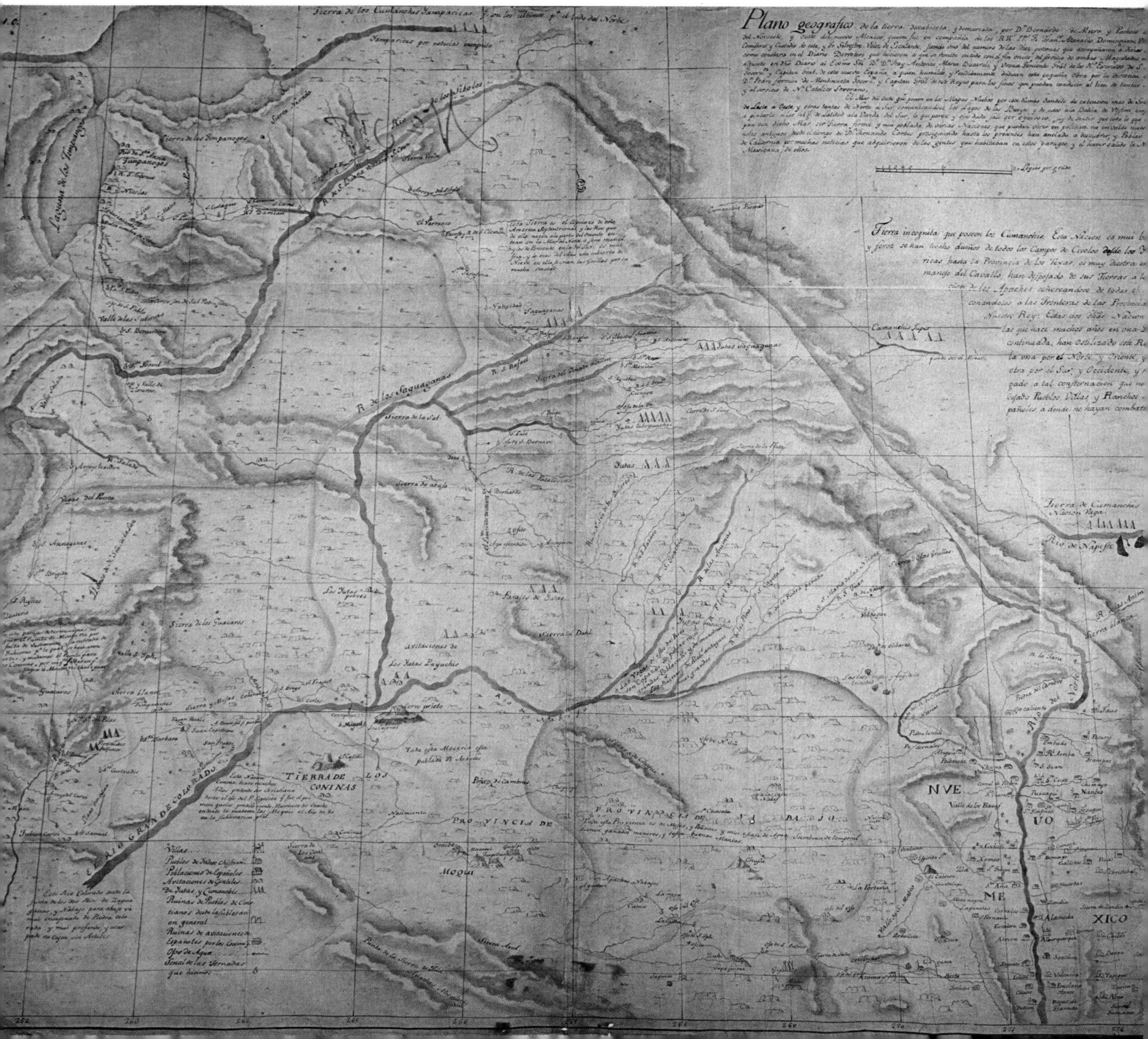

Plano geografico de la tierra descubierta, y demarcada

Tierra de los Cumanches Yamparicas

Tierra de los Timpanogos

Laguna de los Timpanogos

R. de los Saguaganas

Tierra incognita que poseen los Cumanches

Tierra de Cumanches Nacion Yaga

Rio de Napeste

Los Yutas Payuchis

Sierra de los Guacaros

TIERRA DE CONINAS

RIO GRAN DE COLORADO

PROVINCIA DE

Moqui

Rio del Norte

NUEVO MEXICO

Villas
Pueblos de Indios Christianos
Poblaciones de Españoles
Avitaciones de Gentiles
De Yutas y Cumanches
Ruinas de Pueblos de Christianos
en general
Ruinas de avitaciones
Españoles por los Comanches
Ojos de Agua
Señal de las Jornadas
que hicimos

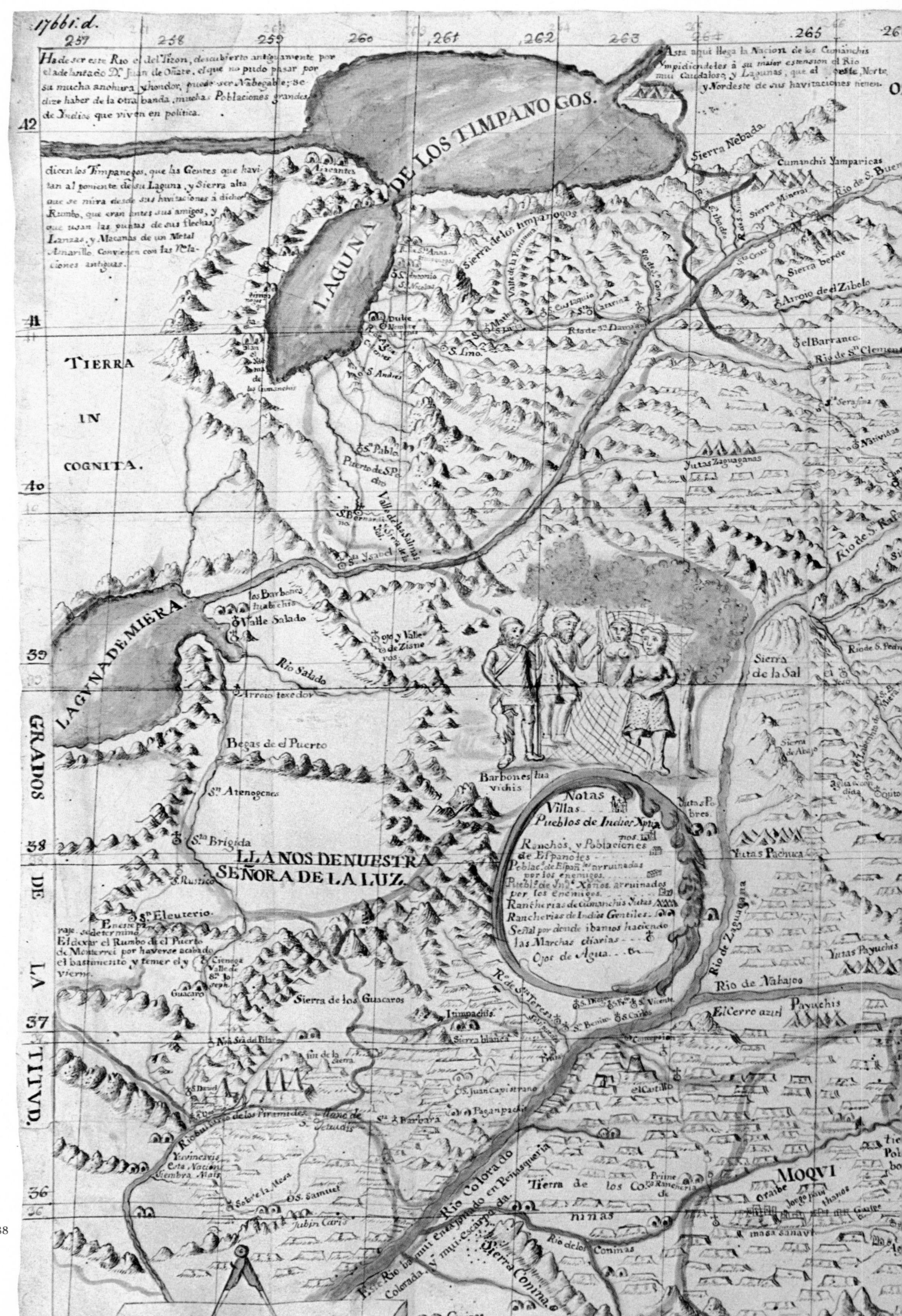

17661.d.
257
258
259
260
261
262
263
264
265
Ha de ser este Rio el del Tizon, descubierto antiguamente por el adelantado Dn. Juan de Oñate, el que no pudo pasar por su mucha anchura y hondor, puede ser Navegable; se dize haber de la otra banda, muchas Poblaciones grandes de Yndios que viven en politica.
Asta aqui llega la Nacion de los Cumanchis ympidiendoles à su maior estension el Rio mui Caudaloso, y Lagunas, que al Oeste, Norte y Nordeste de sus havitaciones tienen.
LAGUNA DE LOS TIMPANOGOS.
42
Sierra Nebada
Cumanchis Yamparicas
dicen los Timpanogos, que las Gentes que havitan al poniente de su Laguna, y Sierra alta que se mira desde sus havitaciones à dicho Rumbo, que eran antes sus amigos, y que usan las puntas de sus flechas Lanzas, y Macanas de un Metal Amarillo. Convienen con las Relaciones antiguas.
Sierra de los timpanogos
Sierra berde
Arroio de el Zibolo
41
S. Lino.
Rio de Sn. Damian
el Barranco
TIERRA IN COGNITA.
Sn. Pablo
Puerto de Sn. Pedro
Sn. Serafina
Yutas Zaguaganas
40
Valle de las Salinas
LAGUNA DE MIERA
los Barbones tiuabichis
Valle Salado
Rio Salado
Arroio texedor
39
Sierra de la Sal
Begas de el Puerto
Barbones tiua vichis
Sn. Atenogenes
Sta. Brigida
38
LLANOS DE NUESTRA SEÑORA DE LA LUZ
S. Rustico
Sn. Eleuterio
Notas
Villas
Pueblos de Indios Xptianos
Ranchos, y Poblaciones de Españoles
Poblac.s de Españ.les arruinadas por los enemigos
Pueblos de Ind.s Xptnos. arruinados por los enemigos
Rancherias de Cumanchis Yutas
Rancherias de Indios Gentiles
Señal por donde ibamos haciendo las Marchas diarias
Ojos de Agua
Yutas Pobres.
Yutas Pachuca
Yutas Payuchis
El determinar el Rumbo de el Puerto de Monterrei por haverse acabado el bastimento y temer el ynvierno.
Sierra de los Guacaros
Guacaro
Rio de Sta. Teresa
Rio de Zaguaganas
Rio de Nabajoo
37
El Cerro azul
Payuchis
Sierra blanca
S. Juan Capistrano
el Castillo
Pasanpachi
Sta. Barbara
Yuvincavis Esta Nacion Siembra Maiz
S. Samuel
Tierra de los Co
Rio Colorado
MOQUI
Oraibe
36
Jubin Caris
Rio de los Coninas
Sierra Conina
Este Rio baxa mui encajonado en Peñasqueria Colorada, y mui escarpada.
Coninas
GRADOS DE LATITUD.

267
268
269
270
271
272
273
274
275
276
LESTE.
Yamparicas
Esta Nacion Cumanchi, hace pocos años se aparecio primero a los Yutas, dicen salió por la banda de el Norte Rompiendo por entre barias Naciones, y ellos Yutas los trujeron à hacer Cambios con los Españoles. traian multitud de Perros, Cargados con sus Pieles y tiendas; se hicieron de Caballos y Armas de fierro, y se han ajilitado tanto, à el manejo de el Caballo, y à ellas que abentajaban à todas las Naciones en su agilidad y Animo, se han echo S.res y dueños de todos Campos de los Zibolos, quitandoselos à la Nacion Apache, la que era la mas dilatada que se ha conocido en la America, han destruido muchas Naciones della. y los que han quedado, los han arrinconado à las fronteras de las Provincias de Nro Rey. Causa porque se experimentã tantos daños, pues les falta su primer mantenimiento les Obliga la necesidad a mantenerse con Caballos y Mulas.
Plano Geographico, de la tierra descubierta, nuevamente, à los Rumbos Norte Noroeste y Oeste, del Nuevo Mexico. demarcada por mi Don Bernardo de Miera y Pacheco què entrò ahacer su descubrimiento, en compañia de los RR.s PP.s fr. Francisco Atanacio Doming.s y Fr. Silbestre Veles, segun consta en el Diario y Derrotero que se hizo y se remitio à S.M. por mano de su Virrei con Plano à la letra: El que dedica Al S.r D. Teodoro de la Crois, del Insigne Orden Teutonica Comandante General en Gefe de Linea y Provincias de esta America Setemptrional, por S.M. hecho en S. Ph. el Real de Chiguagua. Año de 1778.
42
41
40
39
38
37
36
Esta Sierra es el espinazo de esta America Setemptrional, pues sus Aguas que en muchos Rios que de ella Nacen Vierten, en los dos Mares El Sur y Seno Mexicano en ella se crian las grullas.
Cumanchis Jupes
Sierra del Almagre
Rio de Napeste.
Sierra de la Plata
Sierra mojada.
Sierra de las Grullas
Rio de Animas
Cumanchis Gechur Atarica
Rio de S. Joachin
Rio de las Animas
Rio florido
Rio de los Pinos
Rio de Nabajoo
Rio del Norte.
Empieza la tierra de los Yutas
El Belitrique
Las tres Mesas y tres Lagunas de la Trinidad.
Rio de la Yara
Sierra blanca
Cerro y Valle de S.n Ant.
Cerro de la Xi
Origen de el Rio Roxo
Sierra de Taos
Piedra de el Carnero
Rio de Mora
Sierra de chegui
PROVIN CIA
DE NA BA JOO
NUE BO ME- XICO
Valle de los Bacas.
Sierra de Xemes
Chusca
Chaca
El Cabezon
Sierra de Zuñi
Rio de Pecos

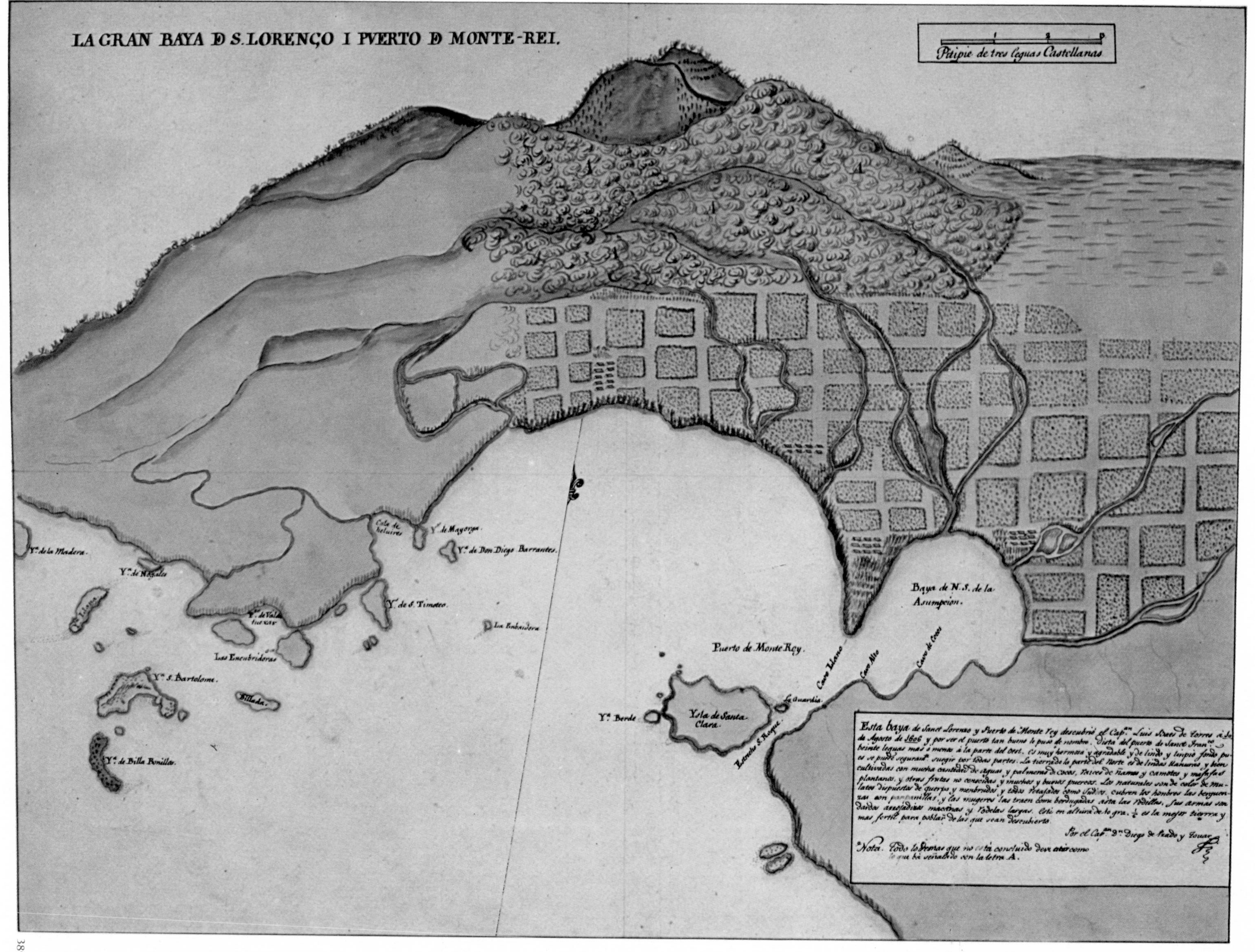
LA GRAN BAYA D S. LORENÇO I PVERTO D MONTE-REI.
Ptipie de tres leguas Castellanas
Y.ª de la Madera
Y.ª de Nogales
Cala de heluires
Y.ª de Mayorga
Y.ª de Don Diego Barrantes
Y.ª de S. Timoteo
La Enbaidera
Las Encubrideras
Y.ª S. Bartolome
Billada
Y.ª de Billa Bonillas
Puerto de Monte Rey
Baya de N. S. de la Asumpcion
Cavo Llano
Cavo Alto
Cavo de Cocos
La Guardia
Estrecho S. Roque
Yesla de Santa Clara
Y.ª Berde
Esta baya de Sanct Lorenso y Puerto de Monte rey descubrió el Cap.ⁿ Luis Baes de Torres à 30 de Agosto de 1606 y por ser el puerto tan bueno le puso de nombre. Dista del puerto de Sanct Fran.ᶜᵒ beinte leguas mas ò menos à la parte del Oest. Es muy hermosa y agradable y de lindo y limpio fondo pues se puede seguram.ᵗᵉ surgir por todas partes. La tierra de la parte del Norte es de lindas llanuras y bien cultivadas con mucha cantidad de aguas y palmeras de cocos, raices de ñames y camotes y mas fas plantanos, y otras frutas no conocidas, y muchos y buenos puercos. Los naturales son de color de mulatos dispuestos de querpo y menbrudos, y todos retasados como Judios, cubren los hombres las berguenzas con pampanillas, y las mugeres las traen como berdugadas asta las rodillas. Sus armas son dardos arrojadizos macanas y rodelas largas. Esta en altura de 10 gra. ½ es la mejor tierra y mas fertil para poblar de las que sean descubierto.
Por el Cap.ⁿ D.ⁿ Diego de Prado y Tovar
Nota. Todo lo demas que no està concluido deve estar como lo que bà señalado con la letra A.

he named Lake Valasco, where Capt. Barnarda left his Ship; nor all up the River was less than 4, 5, 6, 7 and 8 fathom Water, both the Rivers and Lakes abounding with Salmon Trouts, and very large white Pearch, some of them two foot long; and with 3 large Indian Boats, by them called Periagos, made of two large Trees 50 and 60 foot long. Capt. Barnarda first sailed from his Ships in the Lake Velasco, one hundred and forty Leagues West, and then 436 E.N.E. to 77 Degrees of Latitude.

Admiral de Fonte, after he had dispatch'd Captain Barnarda on the Discovery of the North and East part of the Tartarian Sea, the Admiral sail'd up a very Navigable River, which he named Riolos Reyes, that run nearest North East . . .

From here Fonte with two ships sailed through Lake Belle, Lake Fonte and the Strait of Ronquillo. Note that the narrative has changed to the first person.

The 17th [July] we came to an Indian Town, and the Indians told our Interpreter Mr Parmentiers, that a little way from us lay a great Ship where there had never been one before; we sailed to them, and found only one Man advanced in years, and a Youth; the Man was the greatest Man in the Mechanical Parts of the Mathematicks I had ever met with; my second Mate was an English Man, an excellent Seaman, as was my Gunner, who had been taken Prisoners at Campechy, as well as the Master's Son; they told me the Ship was of New England, from a Town called Boston. The Owner and the whole Ships Company came on board the 30th, and the Navigator of the Ship, Capt. Shapley, told me, his Owner was a fine Gentleman, and Major General of the largest Colony in New England, called the Mastechusets; so I received him like a Gentleman, and told him, my Commission was to make Prize of any People seeking a North West or West Passage into the South Sea, but I would look upon them as Merchants trading with the Natives for Bevers, Otters, and other Furs and Skins, and so for a small Present of Provisions I had no need on, I gave him my Diamond Ring, which cost me 1200 Pieces of Eight, (which the modest Gentleman received with difficulty) and having given the brave Navigator, Capt. Shapley for his fine Charts and Journals, 1000 Pieces of Eight, and the Owner of the Ship, Scimor Gibbons a quarter Cask of good Peruan Wine, and the 10 Seamen each 20 Pieces of Eight, the 6th of August, with as much Wind as we could fly before, and a Currant, we arrived at the first Fall of the River Parmentiers, the 11th of August, 86 Leagues, and was on the South Side of the Lake Belle on board our Ships the 16th of August . . .

Text used: Glyndwr Williams, The British Search for the Northwest Passage in the Eighteenth Century, *London, Longmans, Green and Co Ltd, 1962, pp. 277-9.*

5
The Russian fur trade

From Pallas, *Neue nordische Beyträge*, 1781

The most detailed accounts of the Russian voyages between Kamchatka and northwest America to reach Europe were published in German, notably the works of Gerhard Friedrich Müller (1758), Jakob Stählin von Storckburg (1774), 'J.L.S.' (1776), and lastly Peter Simon Pallas, Professor of Natural History at the Academy of Sciences, St Petersburg. Between 1781 and 1796 Pallas published seven volumes of his *Neue nordische Beyträge*; this extract describing the activities of the Russian fur traders among the islands stretching west of the Alaskan peninsula comes from the earliest of those volumes.

The remarkable chain of the new islands between Kamchatka and America (farther south than those alleged to lie nearer the Chukchi country) is already much better known through the numerous voyages made thither for furs, though darkness and uncertainty reign even here with regard to the easternmost islands and the true position and nature of that part of America where this chain ends; and furthermore the true position of each island, particularly those farthest south in the middle of the chain and least often visited, is not sufficiently determined, and their astronomical longitude is as good as entirely unknown.

This chain of islands is clearly recognizable as a continuation into the ocean of the branch of the Kamchatkan range that forms the easternmost extremities of Kamchatka in the promontories of Stolbovskoi and Kronotskoi and proceeds in the same direction, first in the so-called Bering Island and the adjacent Copper Island, then in the so-called Aleutian Islands, and finally (in a changed direction, through the islands chiefly known as the Andreanof Islands) joins the Fox Islands, which connect with the American mainland. This chain likewise encloses a part of the eastern ocean that may be conveniently named the Kamchatkan Sea. It is, indeed, to the last-mentioned, or Fox, Islands, that the now almost annual voyages from Okhotsk and Kamchatka are directed, because most of the sea otters or so-called beavers (*Lutrae*), as well as a multitude of black and gray-black foxes, are found there, which are not found at all on the nearer islands. The coasts of the latter are said to have been abandoned by the enormous herds of sea otters that formerly ranged as far as Bering Island but by this time have been frightened away by the great number of careless hunters. . . .

The pelts which are the motive and profits of these voyages cannot be carried away from here as if from a market, but the crews themselves must go hunting; and the islanders, when the Russians are satisfied that they have been made amicable by presents and by the collecting of hostages, must also be

389 'La Gran Baya de S. Lorenco I Puerto de Monte-Rei'. *British Museum, London, Add. Ms. 17651 fo r.*
Late eighteenth-century Spanish plan of the Bay of Monterey, showing the scattered settlements situated among plots of cultivated ground. In 1770 the Spaniards had established at Monterey their second Californian mission and their first presidio. The first mission was founded at San Diego in 1769.

390 A sea otter by John Webber, 1778. *British Museum, London.*

390

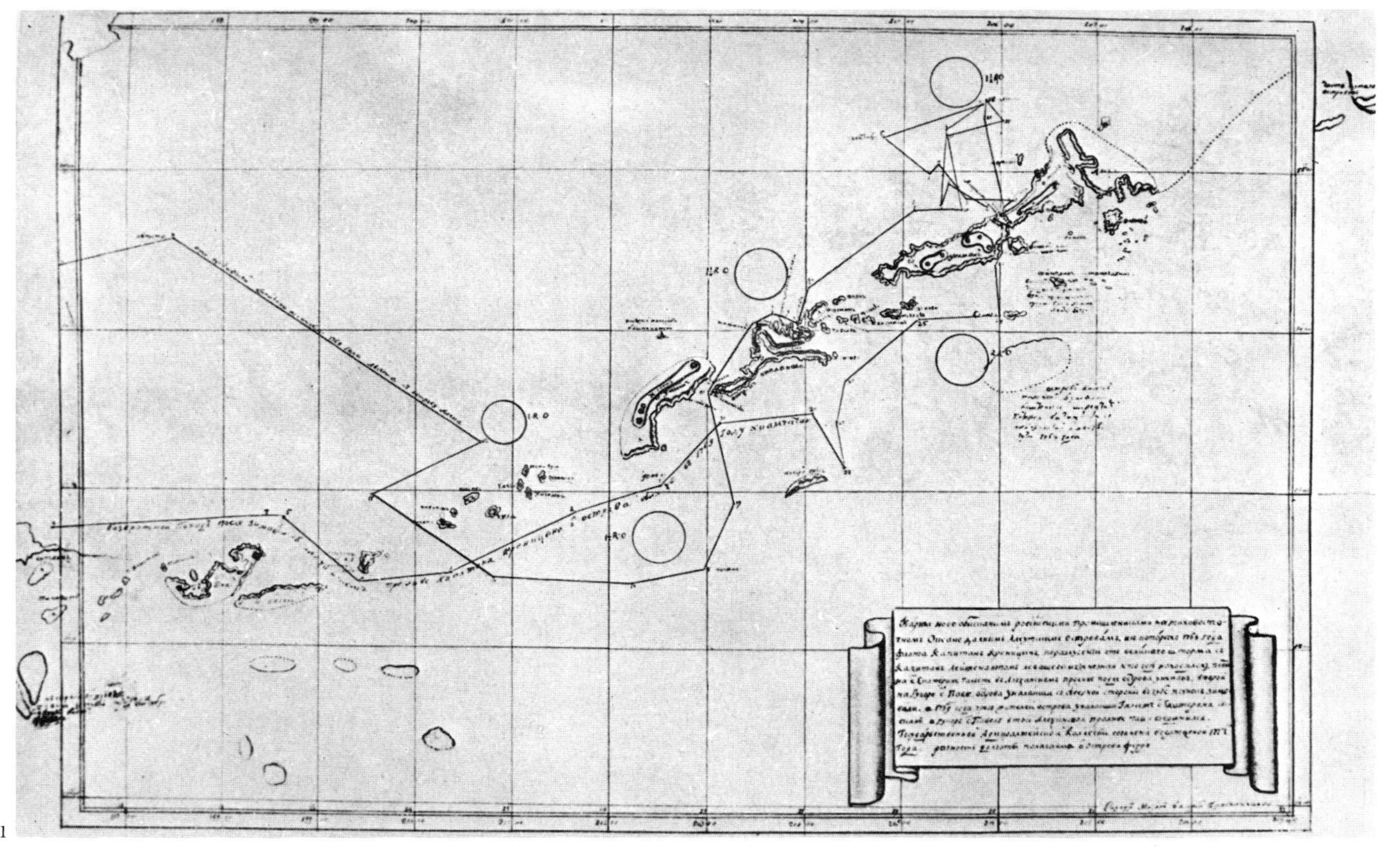

391

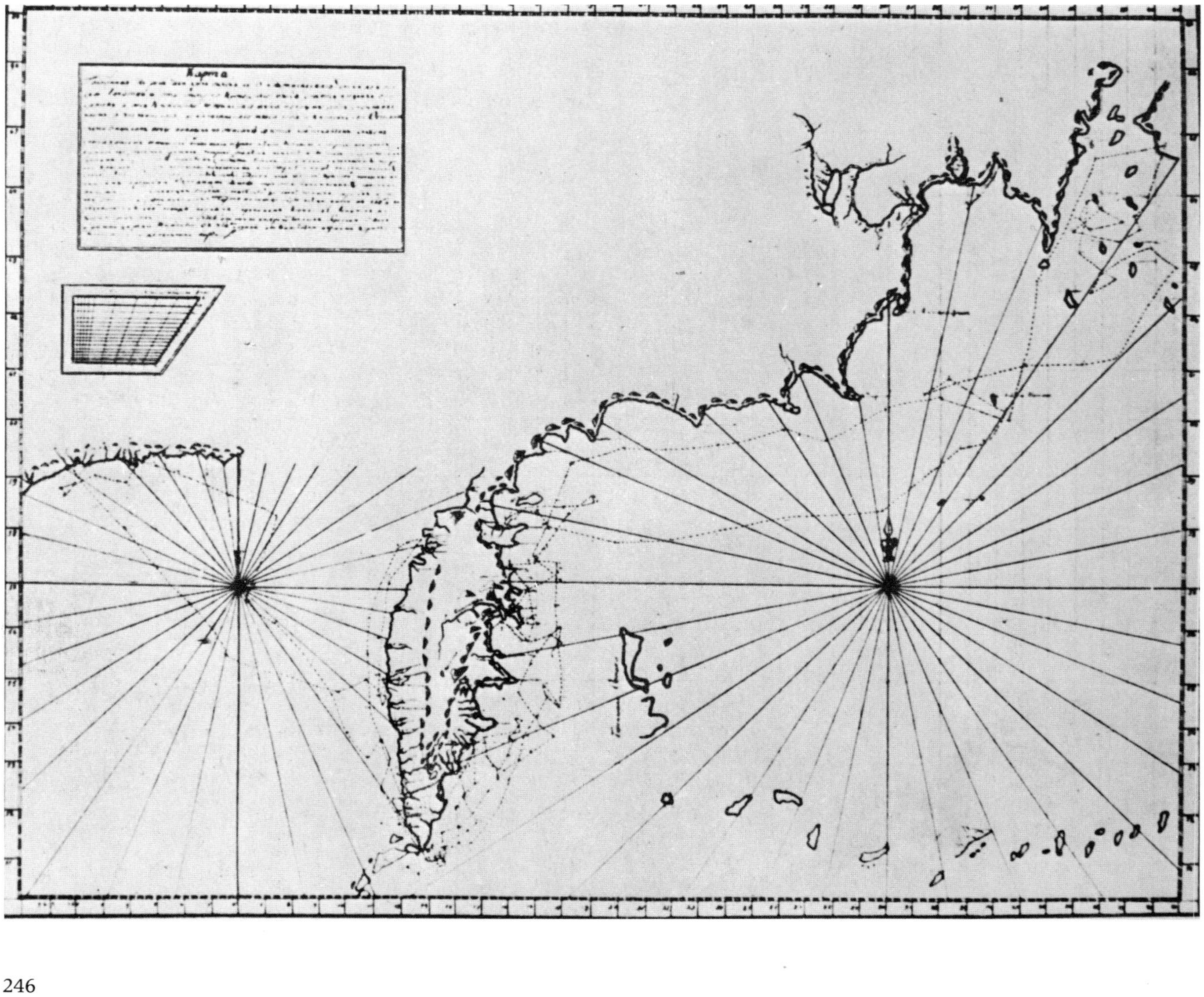

392

used in hunting, though they can be thus employed only during the stay of the voyages on those islands and after distribution of the necessary otter nets and fox traps. Consequently a crew of from fifty to seventy men must scatter in small parties on different islands and for safety's sake must avoid places that are too populous.

For this reason a voyage usually lasts four or five years, until enough pelts are collected to fill the ship and to pay at least twice the cost of fitting it out, which is from twenty to thirty thousand rubles. And yet so little is spent in constructing these vessels (which are built as two-masted galiots, of pine and birch timber, very light and almost without iron) that we must almost marvel how such badly built but usually lucky ships can make as many as a couple of voyages in that stormy ocean. And to lighten the voyage still further, they take from Okhotsk (where at present, because of the greater availability of ammunition and materials, the ships are usually fitted out) only as much meal and other provender as they consider absolutely necessary to supply the requirements and maintain the health of part of the crew (of which more than half, at the least, must be Russians), because Kamchatka furnishes nothing of the kind as yet, and everything has to be brought from Yakutsk on packhorse at very high prices.

With this small supply the ship sails in late summer round the point of Kamchatka, either first to the harbors on the east coast (Kamchatka or Avacha, in the vicinity of which the crew is to be completed with Kamchadals, who are very much needed because of their skill in hunting and their persistent healthiness in spite of the poorest nourishment) or directly to Bering and Copper Islands. There the ship is set up on supports, and the winter is passed in collecting a supply of dried sea-cow meat and hides of sea lions and the largest seals (lakhtak), which in part are used by the crew for hunting-boats and in part can be profitably bartered to the islanders for use in making their leather boats. Only in the following summer does the ship sail to the islands where the best hunting can be expected and where this previously collected supply, with what is currently obtained by hunting and fishing, must feed these bold hunters three or four years. Besides enduring this miserable way of life, they must be on guard every moment against attack from the hostile islanders, must attend to hunting, and when necessary must defend, with Russian courage and without help, the more spiritless Kamchadals.

Text used: James R. Masterton and Helen Brower, Bering's Successors 1745-1780: Contributions of Peter Simon Pallas to the History of Russian Exploration toward Alaska, *Seattle, The University of Washington Press, 1948, pp. 29-30, 31.*

391 A Russian map of the explorations of Peter Krenitsyn and Mikhail Levashev in 1767 and 1768, which shows the progress made by Russian explorers since Bering's day. The tip of the Alaskan peninsula, the Shumagin Islands, and the larger islands of Unimak and Unalaska are now clearly marked. *Archives of the Central Cartographic Establishment of the Navy, Leningrad.*

392 Russian manuscript map of the explorations of Lieutenant Ivan Synd, 1764-8. *Library of the Academy of Sciences of the USSR, Leningrad.*
A series of separate voyages by Synd is represented here, one of which had taken him to the vicinity of Bering Strait, and to a landing on the American side in the Cape Douglas or Cape Rodney area. Although the islands of the Bering Sea are poorly represented, the map is an austere production which bears no resemblance to the map of Synd's alleged discoveries published by Stählin in 1773/1774 (plate 368).

6 The discovery of San Francisco Bay

i) From the diary of Miguel Costansó, 1769-70

The engineer and diarist Costansó accompanied Gaspar de Portolá, newly-appointed governor of *Alta* California, on the arduous march north from San Diego in search of Monterey. This extract shows that the initial reaction of the party to their sighting of San Francisco Bay was disappointment that it was clearly not Monterey. They had in fact reached the Bay of Monterey at the end of September 1769 but, unable to reconcile it with Vizcaíno's description, the party continued northward along the coast.

[Tuesday, 31 October]. From the summit we saw to the northwest a large bay formed by a point of land which extended a long distance into the sea, and about which many had disputed on the preceding day, as to whether or not it was an island; it was not possible at that time to see it as clearly as now on account of the mist that covered it. Farther out, about west-northwest from us, seven rocky, white islands could be seen; and, casting the eye back upon the bay, one could see farther to the north some perpendicular white cliffs. Looking to the northeast, one could see the mouth of an estuary which appeared to extend inland. In consideration of these indications we consulted the sailing directions of the pilot Cabrera Bueno, and it seemed to us beyond all question that what we were looking upon was the port of San Francisco; and that we were convinced that the port of Monterey had been left behind.

Some members of the expedition refused to accept this, and the quest for Monterey continued.

[Thursday, 2 November]. Several of the soldiers requested permission to go hunting, as many deer had been seen. Some of them went quite a long way from the camp and reached the top of the hills so that they did not return until after nightfall. They said that to the north of the bay they had seen an immense arm of the sea or estuary, which extended inland as far as they could see, to the southeast. . . .
[Friday, 10 November]. The scouts arrived at night, very downcast, convinced now that the port of Monterey could not be farther on. . . . They stated that they had not seen any evidences whatever that might indicate the proximity of the port, and that there was another immense estuary to the northeast, which extended far inland; that it was connected with that of the southeast; [and that if they were to continue] it would be necessary to search for a way around it.

ii) From the description by Father Pedro Font, 1776

The significance of the superb harbor was not fully appreciated until the mid 70s. In 1775 Ayala became the first European for certain to sail through the Golden Gate, difficult to discern against the hills even in clear weather; and in 1776 the indefatigable Anza, hardly recovered from his second crossing from Tubac to California, journeyed there from Monterey to carry out a survey from the land side. Anza was accompanied by the Franciscan Father Pedro Font, whose account leaves no doubt about the harbor's potentialities.

We again ascended the sand hills, descended to the arroyo [stream or gulley], and crossed high hills until we reached the edge of the white cliff which forms the end of the mouth of the port, and where begins the great estuary containing islands. The cliff is very high and perpendicular, so that from

393

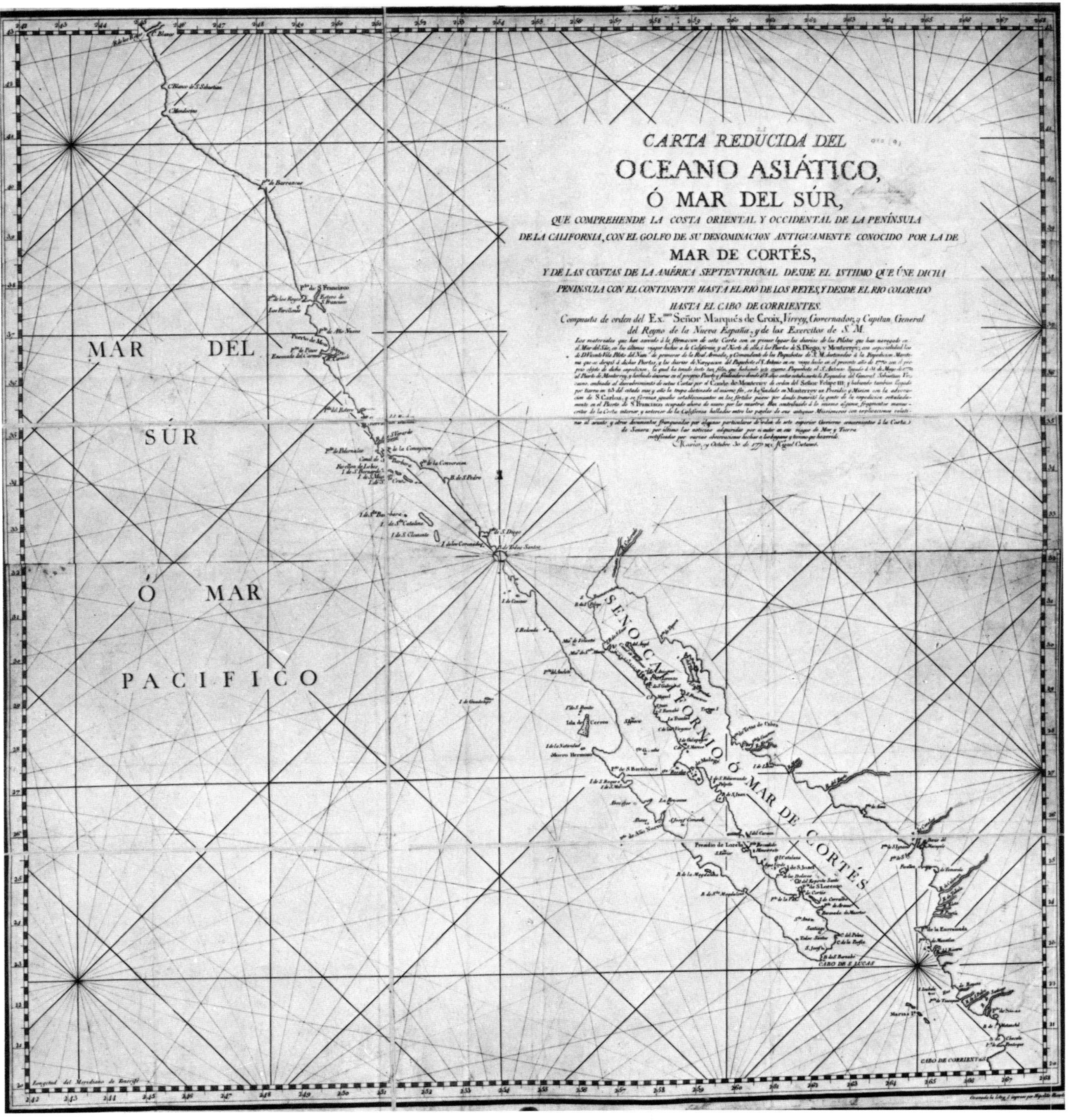

393 Miguel Costansó. 'Carta Reducida del Oceano Asiático, ó Mar del Súr, Madrid, 1771. *British Museum, London.*
When Costansó returned from the expedition of 1769-70 to San Diego, Monterey and San Francisco, he constructed a manuscript map of the Spanish discoveries. This was printed at Madrid in 1771, with some additions, notably the precise delineation of San Francisco Bay. Despite the small scale, the outline of the bay is shown more accurately here than in several later surveys.

it one can spit into the sea. From here we saw the pushing and resistance which the out-going waste of the estuary makes against that of the sea, forming there a sort of ridge like a wave in the middle, and it seems as if a current is visible. We saw the spouting of whales, a shoal of dolphins or tunny fish, sea otter, and sea lions. . . .

The port of San Francisco . . . is a marvel of nature, and might well be called the harbor of harbors, because of its great capacity, and of several small bays which it enfolds in its margin or beach and in its islands. The mouth of the port, which appears to have a very easy and safe entrance, must be about a league long and somewhat less than a league wide on the outside, facing the sea, and about a quarter of a league on the inside, facing the harbor. The inner end of the passage is formed by two very high and perpendicular cliffs almost due north and south of each other, on this side a white one and on the other side a red one. The outer end of the passage is formed on the other side by some large rocks, and on this side by a high and sandy hill which ends almost in a round point, and has on its skirts within the water some white rocks, like small farallones [headlands]. . . .

From the inner terminus of the passage extends the remarkable port of San Francisco. This harbor consists of a great gulf or estuary, as they call it, which must be some twenty-

394

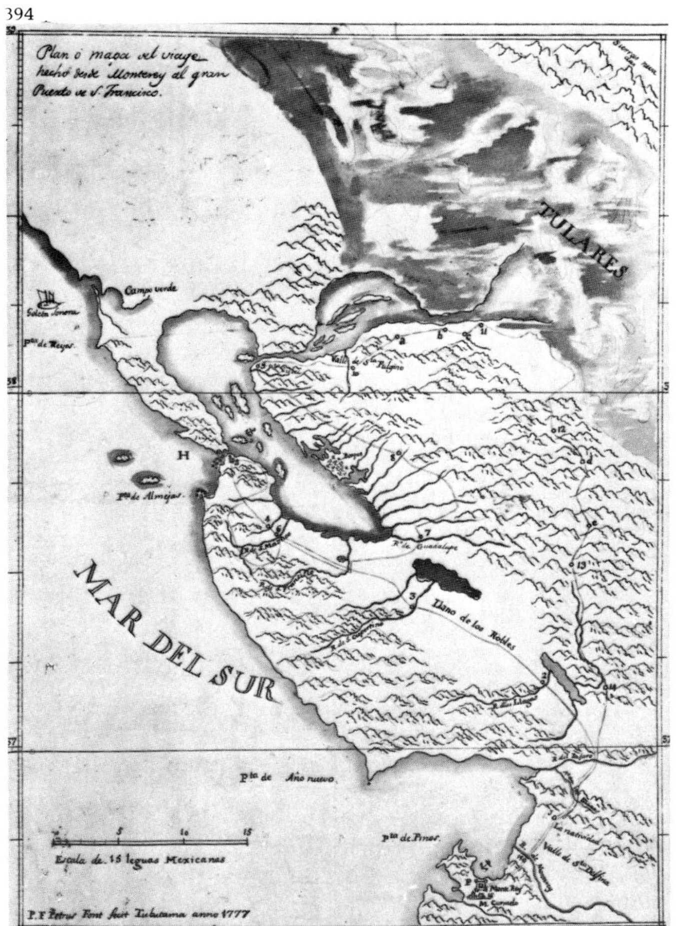

395

394 Pedro Font. 'Plan o mapa del viage hecho desde Monterey al gran Puerto de S. Francisco', 1777. *British Museum, London, Add. Ms. 17,651, fo 9.*
This neat little map shows the route of Anza's expedition of 1776, with the camp sites indicated by numbers. The shape of San Francisco Bay is much better than on Cañizares' map of the previous year, and there are a number of points of interest besides. In a reference to Bodega's northern voyage of 1775 his schooner the *Sonora* is shown outside Bodega Bay, while behind San Francisco the inland valley is indicated, and beyond it the ranges of the Sierra Nevada.

395 José de Cañizares. 'Plano del Puerto de San Francisco . . . 1775'. *Archivo General de Indias, Seville, Mapas y Planos Mexico, 305.*
This map represents part of the work of Ayala's expedition to San Francisco Bay in the late summer of 1775, where it went to prepare the way for Anza's settlers coming overland from the south. Cañizares carried out the first detailed survey of San Francisco Bay, and the soundings marked on this contemporary copy of his map reveal the thoroughness with which this great inland expanse of water was covered. Even so, as Neal Harlow has pointed out in his *Maps of San Francisco Bay* (Book Club of California, 1950), the shape of the bay is considerably distorted. Most of the Spanish names marked on the map have long since disappeared (though Isla de los Angeles remains as Angel Island), and it is worth noticing that the map's Isla de Alcatres is *not* the modern Alcatraz Island but Yerba Buena Island. Today's Alcatraz Island is shown in its correct position (though exaggerated in size) opposite the Golden Gate, but is unnamed.

five leagues long. Viewed from the mouth it runs about southeast and northwest, the estuary or mouth being in the middle. Most of the beach of the harbor, according to what I saw when we went around it, is not clean, but muddy, miry and full of sloughs, and for this reason bad. The width of the port is not uniform, for at the southern end it must be a league wide and in the middle some four leagues. At the extreme northwest it ends in a great bay more than eight leagues in extent. . . .

Indeed, although in my travels I saw very good sites and beautiful country, I saw none which pleased me as much as this. And I think that if it could be well settled like Europe there would not be anything more beautiful in all the world, for it has the best advantages for founding in it a most beautiful city, with all the conveniences desired, by land as well as by sea, with that harbor so remarkable and so spacious, in which may be established shipyards, docks, and anything that might be wished.

Text used: i) Frederick J. Teggart (Ed.), 'The Portolá Expedition of 1769-1770: Diary of Miguel Costansó', *Publications of the Academy of Pacific Coast History, University of California, Berkeley, vol. II, 1911, pp. 103-4, 107, 111-12; ii) H. E. Bolton (Ed.),* Anza's California Expeditions, *University of California Press, Berkeley, 1930, vol. IV, pp. 332, 333-4, 336, 341.*

7

Father Garcés among the Yuma Indians

From Father Pedro Font's diary, 1775

One of the most impressive of the Spanish missionary explorers of this period was Father Francisco Garcés. An untiring traveller of the region between the Colorado and Gila Rivers and the coast, Garcés was also renowned for his easy relations with the Indians of the area—the Yumas, Pimas, Opas and the rest. At the beginning of December 1775 the overland party led by Anza, which was following the route from Tubac to San Diego prospected by Anza and Garcés the previous year, had reached Yuma at the junction of the Colorado and Gila Rivers. Here Font's diary contains a vivid pen-picture of Garcés's missionary approach to the local Indians.

A great mob of Indians came to camp with their watermelons, etc., and although it was impossible to see the whole body of the people together, I estimated from what I saw that the Yumas must comprise about three thousand souls and the Cajuenches somewhat more. In the afternoon Father Garcés assembled the people and distributed among them a few beads and a little tobacco. Then he showed them the large painting of the Most Holy Virgin with the Child Jesus in her arms. They manifested great and noisy delight on seeing the image, saying, according to the interpreters, that it was good, and that they wished to be Christians in order to be white and beautiful like the Virgin, and that they would gladly be baptized. To this it was replied that for the present it could not be, but that it would be done at another time. The painting, on the reverse of which was pictured a condemned soul, was now turned around, whereupon they raised a great outcry, saying that they did not like that. The same was done with the Gileños, the Opas, and the Yumas, and all replied in the same way, without manifesting any repugnance to Christianity. On the contrary, they greatly desire it, and have asked to be baptized; but no one has been baptized because they have not been catechized. . . .

Father Garcés is so well fitted to get along with the Indians and to go among them that he appears to be but an Indian himself. Like the Indians he is phlegmatic in everything. He sits with them in the circle, or at night around the fire, with his legs crossed, and there he will sit musing two or three hours or more, oblivious to everything else, talking with them with much serenity and deliberation. And although the foods of the Indians are as nasty and dirty as those outlandish people themselves, the father eats them with great gusto and says that they are good for the stomach and very fine. In short God had created him, as I see it, solely for the purpose of seeking out these unhappy, ignorant, and rustic people.

Text used: H. E. Bolton (Ed.), Anza's California Expeditions, *University of California Press, Berkeley, 1930, vol. IV, pp. 118, 121.*

8
The Utah Valley and Great Salt Lake, 1776

From Father Escalante's manuscript diary

Two more of the characteristic missionary explorers of the period, tough physically and zealous spiritually, were the Franciscans Father Francisco Atanasio Domínguez and Father Silvestre de Vélez de Escalante, whose northern journey from Santa Fé in 1776 opened up enormous tracts of unknown country. Escalante kept an excellent diary of the journey, and in September 1776 wrote enthusiastically of the Utah Valley ('the valley of Nuestra Señora de la Merced de los Timpanocutzis'), and mentioned another 'extremely salty' lake farther on which is clearly Great Salt Lake. Escalante's 'Río de San Buenaventura' is Green River, the most important tributary of the Colorado, although the Spaniards did not know this as yet.

To the north of the Río de San Buenventura as we have said above, there is a sierra which in the parts we saw runs from northeast to southwest more than seventy leagues, and its width or breadth must be at most forty leagues, and where we crossed it, thirty. In the western part of this sierra in latitude 40° 49′ and about northwest by north of the town of Santa Fé, is the valley of Nuestra Señora de la Merced de los Timpanocutzis, surrounded by the peaks of the sierra, from which flow four fair-sized rivers which water it, flowing through the valley to the middle of it where they enter the lake. The plain of the valley must be from southeast to northwest, sixteen Spanish leagues long (which are the leagues we use in this diary), and from northeast to southwest, ten or twelve leagues. It is all clear and, with the exception of the marshes on the shores of the lake, the land is good quality, and suitable for all kinds of crops. . . .

What we have said regarding settlements is to be understood as giving to each one more lands than are absolutely necessary, for if each pueblo should take only one league of agricultural land, the valley would provide for as many pueblos of Indians as there are in New Mexico. Because, although in the directions indicated above we give the size mentioned, it is an understatement, and on the south and in other directions there are very spacious areas of good land. In all of it there are good and very abundant pastures, and in some places it produces flax and hemp in such quantities that it looks as though they had planted it on purpose. The climate here is good, for after having suffered greatly from the cold since we left the Río de San Buenaventura, in all this valley we felt great heat both night and day.

Besides these most splendid advantages, in the nearby sierras which surround the valley there are plentiful firewood and timber, sheltered places, water and pasturage for raising cattle and horses. This applies to the north, northeast, east and southeast. Toward the south and southwest close by there are two other extensive valleys, also having abundant pasturage and sufficient water. The lake, which must be six leagues wide and fifteen leagues long, extends as far as one of these valleys. It runs northwest through a narrow passage, and according to what they told us, it communicates with others much larger.

This lake of Timpanocutzis abounds in several kinds of good fish, geese, beaver, and other amphibious animals which we did not have an opportunity to see. Round about it are these Indians, who live on the abundant fish of the lake, for which reason the Yutas Sabuaganas call them Come Pescados [Fish-Eaters]. Besides this, they gather in the plain grass seeds from which they make atole [porridge], which they supplement by hunting hares, rabbits and fowl of which there is great abundance here. There are also buffalo not very far to the north-northwest, but fear of the Comanches prevents them [the Come Pescados] from hunting them. Their habitations are chozas or little huts of willow, of which they also make nice baskets and other necessary utensils. In the matter of dress they are very poor. The most decent clothing they wear is a buckskin jacket and long leggings made of the same material. For cold weather they have blankets made of the skins of hares and rabbits. They speak the Yuta language but with notable differences in the accent and in some of the words. They have good features and most of them have heavy beards. In all parts of this sierra to the southeast, southwest and west live a large number of people of the same tribe, language and docility as these Lagunas, with whom a very populous and extensive province could be formed. . . .

The other lake with which this one communicates, according to what they told us, covers many leagues, and its waters are noxious and extremely salty, for the Timpanois assure us that a person who moistens any part of his body with the water of the lake immediately feels much itching on the part that is wet. . . .

Text used: H. E. Bolton (Ed.), Pageant of the Wilderness: the Story of the Escalante Expedition to the Interior Basin, 1776, *Salt Lake City, The Utah State Historical Society, 1950, pp. 184-6.*

9
Cook on the northwest coast, 1778

From Captain Cook's holograph journal, 1776-9

Cook's two vessels, the *Resolution* and *Discovery*, first sighted the northwest coast in latitude 44° 33'N. on 7 March 1778, and by the end of the month had found a safe harbor in King George's Sound, later known by its native name of Nootka, on Vancouver Island. The ships spent most of April here, and the crews established friendly relations with the Nootka Indians.

WEDNESDAY 22nd [April]. The next Morning we were Visited by a number of Strangers in twelve or fourteen Canoes; they lay drawn up in a body a full half hour about two or three hundred yards from the ships. At first we thought they were afraid to advance nearer, in this we were misstaken, it was rather to entertain us with a Song or dance which was perform'd in concert, while two of the Canoes kept parading between the others and us. After they had finished their Songs which we heard with admiration, they came along side the Ships, and then we found that several of our old friends were among them, who took upon them the intire management of the trade between us and them very much to the advantage of the others. Having a few Goats and two or three sheep left I went in a boat accompanied by Captain Clerke in a nother, to the Village at the west point of the Sound to get some grass for them, having seen some at that place. The Inhabitants of this village received us in the same friendly manner they had d[o]ne before, and the Moment we landed I sent some to cut grass not thinking that the Natives could or would have the least objection, but it proved otherways for the Moment our people began to cut they stopped them and told them they must *Makook* for it, that is first buy it. As soon as I heard of this I went to the place and found about a dozen men who all laid claim to some part of the grass which I purchased of them and as I thought liberty to cut where ever I pleased, but here again I was misstaken, for the liberal manner I had paid the first pretended pr[o]prietors brought more upon me and there was not a blade of grass that had not a seperated owner, so that I very soon emptied my pockets with purchasing, and when they found I had nothing more to give they let us cut where ever we pleased.

Here I must observe that I have no were met with Indians who had such high notions of every thing the Country produced being their exclusive property as these; the very wood and water we took on board they at first wanted us to pay for, and we had certainly done it, had I been upon the spot when the demands were made; but as I never happened to be there the workmen took but little notice of their importunities and at last they ceased applying. But made a Merit on necessity and frequently afterwards told us they had given us Wood and Water out of friendship.

396 Cook's ships, the *Resolution* and *Discovery*, in Sandwich (Prince William) Sound, 1778, by John Webber. *British Museum, London, Add. Ms. 15,514, fo 8.*

396

From Nootka the expedition sailed north, and at Prince William Sound (named Sandwich Sound by Cook) met a different type of native from the Nootka Indians, although it is not now possible to determine whether they were of Eskimo or Athapaskan stock.

THURSDAY 14th [May] . . . Some ventured on board the Ship, but not before some of our people went into their boats. Amongst those that came on board was a good looking middle aged man who we afterward found to be the Chief; he was cloathed in a dress made of the Sea beaver skin and on his head such a Cap as is worn by the people of King Georges Sound, Ornamented with sky blue glass beads about the size of a large pea; these he seemed to set ten times more Value upon than our white glass beads which they probably thought was only crystal which they have among them. They however essteemed beads of all sorts and gave whatever they had in exchange for them, even their fine Sea beaver skins. But here I must observe that they set no more value upon these skins than others, neither here nor at King Georges Sound, till our people put a Value upon them, and even then at the last place they would sooner part with a dress made of these than one made of the skins of wild Cats or Martins. These peoples were also desirous of iron, but it must be peices eight or ten inches long at least, and three of four fingers broad for small peices they absolutly rejected; consequently they got but little from us, as it was now become rather a scarce article. The points of some of their spears or lances, were of Iron

397 Indian implements of the northwest coast, from Thomas Pennant, *Arctic zoology*, I, 1784.
These were brought back by Cook's men in 1780, and were described by Pennant as '. . . a small bow made of bone . . . on which was engraven, very intelligibly, every object of the chace . . . I could distinguish the Elk, the Rein, the *Virginia* Deer, and the Dog; birds, probably of the Goose kind; the Whale fishery, the Walrus, and the Seal.' Of the tomahawk Pennant wrote: 'the offensive part is a stone projecting out of the mouth of a sculpture in wood, resembling a human face, in which are stuck human and other teeth: long locks of scalped hair are placed on several parts of the head, waving when brandished in a most dreadful manner.'

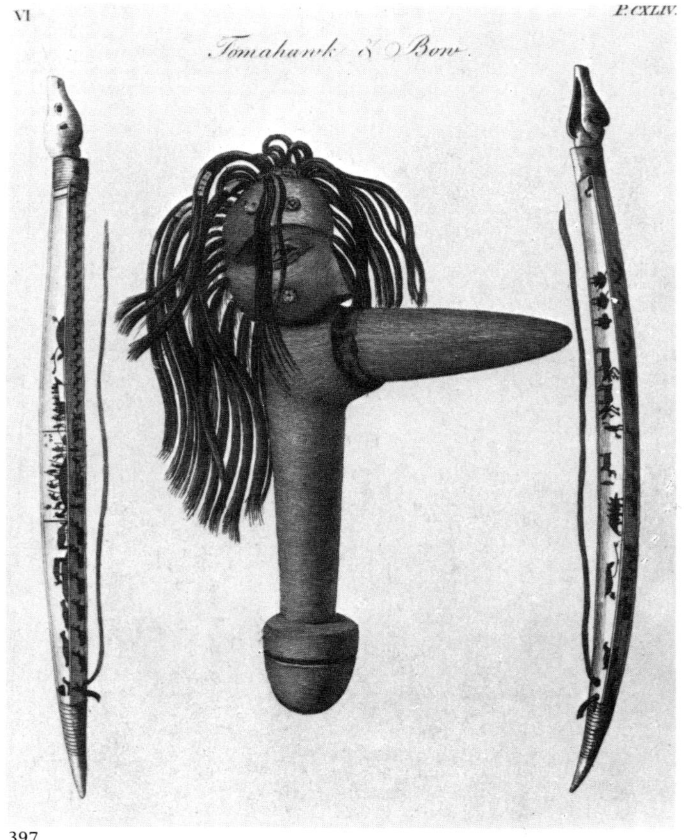

397

398

398 Indian family at Norton Sound, by John Webber, 1778. *British Museum, London, Add. Ms. 15,514, fo 18.*

shaped into the form of a Bear spear, others were of Copper and a few of bone which the points of their darts, arrows &c[a] were made of. I could not prevail on the cheif to trust himself below the upper deck, nor did he and his companions remain long on board, but while they were it was necessary to look after them as they soon betrayed a thevesh dispossission.

Throughout these weeks Cook was searching in vain for the short passage to the north marked on Stählin's map, but the only strait he found was far to the northwest, that discovered by Bering in 1728; and as the ships sailed through it and turned eastwards along the Arctic coastline of North America they found themselves confronted with an impassable barrier of ice.

[17 August]. Some time bfore Noon we percieved a brigh[t]ness in the Northern horizon like that reflected from ice, commonly called the blink; it was little noticed from a supposition that it was improbable we should meet with ice so soon, and yet the sharpness of the air and Gloomyness of the Weather for two or three days past seemed to indicate some sudden change. At 1 PM the sight of a large field of ice left us in no longer doubt about the cause of the brightness of the Horizon we had observed. At ½ past 2 we tacked close to the edge of it in 22 fathoms Water being then in the latitude of 70° 41′, not being able to stand any fa[r]ther, for the ice was quite impenetrable and extend[ed] from WBS to EBN as far as the eye could reach. Here were abundance of Sea Horses, some in the Water but far more upon the Ice; I had thoughts of hoisting the boats out to kill some, but the Wind freshning I gave up the design and continued to ply to the southward, or rather to the Westward for the Wind was from that quarter; but we gained nothing, For on the 18th at Noon our latitude was 70° 44′ and the Timekeeper shewed that we were near five leagues farther to the Eastward. We were at this time in 20 fathoms Water, close to the edge of the ice which was as compact as a Wall and seemed to be ten or twelve feet high at least, but farther North it appeared much higher, its surface was extremely rugged and here and there were pools of Water. . . .

Our situation was now more and more critical, we were in shoald water upon a lee shore and the main body of the ice in sight to windward driving down upon us. It was evident, if we remained much longer between it and the land it would force us ashore unless it should happen to take the ground before us; it seemed nearly if not quite to join to the land to leeward and the only direction that was open was to the SW. After making a short board to the Northward I made the Signal for the Discovery to tack and tacked my self at the same time.

The ships now bore away for the Sandwich Islands for the winter, but first put in at the island of Unalaska, where Russian traders and seamen were encountered for the first time.

THURSDAY 8th [October]. On the 8th I received by the hand of an Indian named *Derramoushk* a very singular present considering the place, it was a rye loaf or rather a pie made in the form of a loaf, for some salmon highly seasoned with peper &c[a] was in it. He had the like present for Captain Clerke and a Note to each of us written in a language none of us could read. We however had no doubt but this present was from some Russians in our Neighbourhood and sent to these our unknown friends by the same ha[n]d a few bottles of Rum, Wine and Porter which we thought would be as acceptable as any thing we had besides, and the event prove[d] we were not misstaken. I also sent along with Derramoushk and his party Corp[l] Ledyard of the Marines, an inteligent man in order to gain some further information, with orders, if he met with any Russians, or others, to endeavour to make them understand that we were English, Friends and Allies.

The 10th he returned with three Russian Seamen or Furriers, who with some others resided in *Egoochsac* where they had a dweling house some store houses and a Sloop of about thirty Tons burden. One of these Men was either Master or Mate of this Vessel, a nother wrote a very good hand and understood figures; they were all three well behaved intelligent men, and very ready to give me all the information I could disire, but for want of an interpretor we had some difficulty to understand each other. They seemed to have a thorough knowlidge of the attempts that had been made by their Country men to Navigate the Frozen Sea, and the discoveries which had been made in this by *Behring Tchirekoff* and *Spanburg*, but seemed to know no more of Lieutenant *Sindo* or *Sind* than his name: Nor had they the least idea of what part of the World M[r] *Staehlins* Map refered to when leaid before them; and when I pointed out *Kamtschatka* and some other known places, they asked me if I had seen the islands laid down [on] the Chart and on my answering in the negative, one of them laid his finger upon the Chart where a number of islands are laid down and said he had been cruzing there for land and could never find any. I laid before them my Chart, and found they were strangers to every part of the America Coast except what lies opposite to them. One of these Men said he was on the America Voyage with *Behring*, he must however been very young for he had not now the appearance of an old man. The Memory of few men is held in greater esteem than these Men do *Behrings*, probably from his being

399 Cook's men shooting walrus, by John Webber.
Cook entered a description of this in his journal for 19 August 1778, while near Icy Cape north of Bering Strait. 'On the ice lay a prodigious number of Sea horses and as we were in want of fresh provisions the boats from each ship were sent to get some. By 7 o clock in the evening we had got on board the Resolution Nine of these Animals . . . we lived upon them so long as they lasted and there were few on board who did not prefer it to salt meat. The fat at first is as sweet as Marrow but in a few days it grows ransid onless it is salted, then it will keep good much longer, the lean is coarse, black and rather a strong taste, the meat is nearly as well tasted as that of a bullock . . . They lay in herds of many hundred upon the ice, huddling one over the other like swine, and roar or bray very loud, so that in the night or foggy weather they gave us notice of the ice long before we could see it.'

399

the occation of thier fur trade being extended to the Eastward, which was the consequence of that able Navigators missfortunes, for had not chance and his distresses carried him to the island which bears his name, and where he died, its probable the Russians would never have thought of making further discover[ie]s on the America Coast, as indeed Government did not for what has been sence done, has been by traders.

Text used: J. C. Beaglehole (Ed.), The Journals of Captain James Cook on his Voyages of Discovery: The Voyage of the Resolution and Discovery 1776-1780, *Cambridge, The Hakluyt Society, 1967, Part One, pp. 305-6, 346-7, 416-18, 448-50.*

400

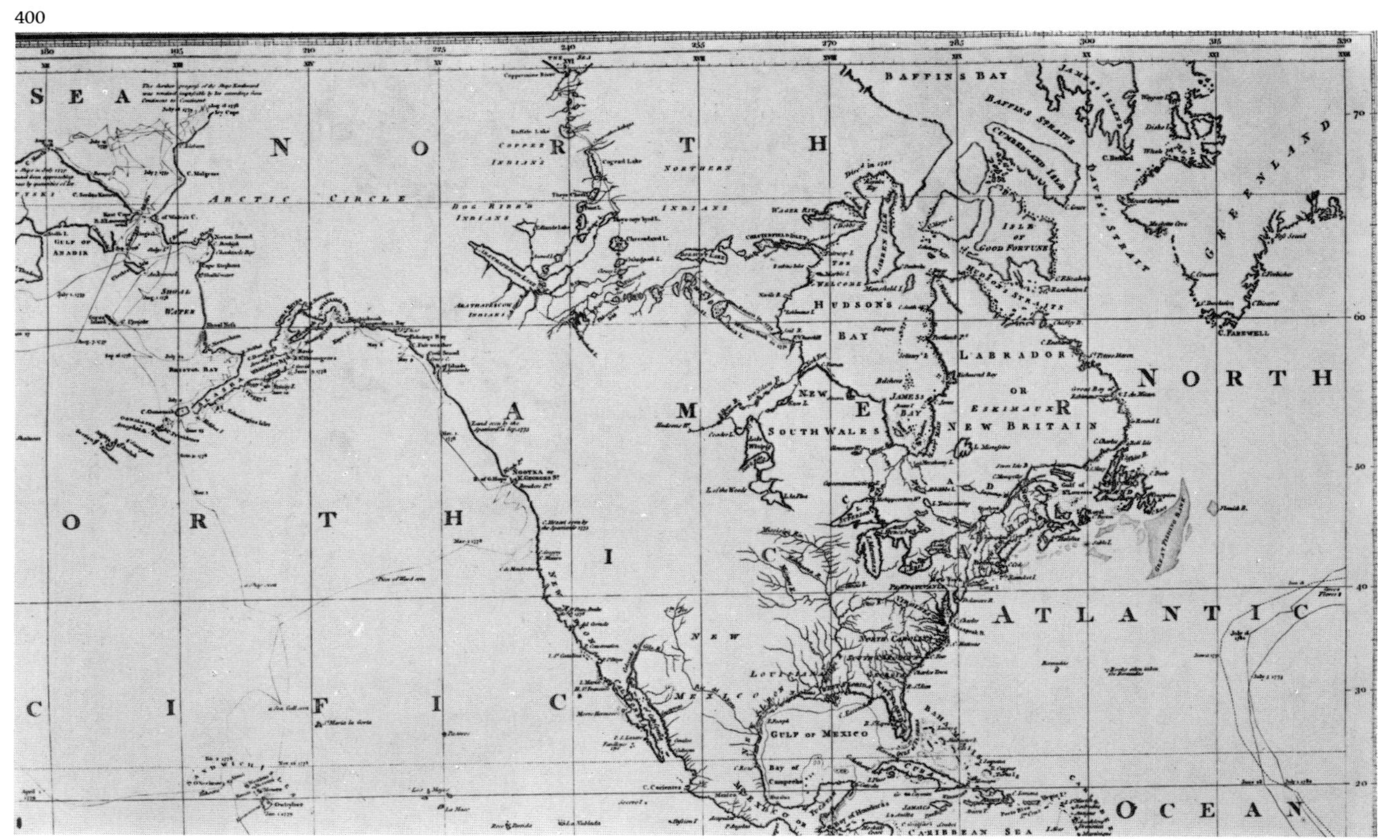

400 Henry Roberts. 'A General Chart exhibiting the Discoveries made by Capt. James Cook. . . .', London, 1784 (detail).
This map, constructed by one of Cook's lieutenants for the official account of Cook's last voyage, provided the most accurate survey to date of the northwest coast of America. The tracks of Cook (in 1778) and Clerke (in 1779) reveal the repeated attempts the ships made to force their way through the ice north of Bering Strait. The shape of northwest America shows that Cook thought he was skirting the mainland on his long haul north along the coast from Nootka; in fact, for most of the time he was off the outer coasts of the island chain which runs from Vancouver Island to Alaska. The map also demonstrates the relation between the discoveries of Cook and Hearne—erroneously so, because Hearne's discoveries are placed at once too far north and west. Farther south, little is shown of earlier French explorations in the interior, and because of the reluctance of Spain to publish the fine surveys made by its explorers in the 1770s Spanish knowledge of the vast area north of New Spain appears distinctly thin.

EPILOGUE

The impetus of exploration in the seventeenth and eighteenth centuries was uneven. There was no dramatic unrolling of the North American continent from ocean to ocean. Instead, very many men explored and re-explored territories beyond the limits of current settlement for a wide variety of reasons, most for individual personal aims, many for corporate objectives, a few for institutional ones. They went, for the most part unsystematically, westward or northward, for reasons of economic necessity or ambition, for greed for gain from furs or hoped-for precious minerals, for faith, for curiosity, careless or scientific, for the release of some kind of individual or collective tension. French and English trappers and traders crossed and recrossed each other's routes; settlers converged on western Pennsylvania alike from Connecticut, from Ulster and from Germany. Jesuits began all over again to revive missions abandoned a generation before by their predecessors; official expeditions re-traced, as if they were new, routes already well known to frontiersmen. There were few great surprises and turning points, though there were some. The final probings of the Great Lakes which brought men at last to the western end of Lake Superior; the finding, after so long, of the shores of the Northern Sea; the discovery of the long, long course of the Mississippi; and the protracted sequence of discoveries which revealed the full extent of the Missouri and Ohio basins which extended the central plain laterally over such an impressive area; all those and a few others we can see as turning points, the end of one line in the exploring process, the beginning of another. But at the time the realization of the significance of such events was not acutely felt; it emerged rather by a slow process of assimilation of converging narratives and accumulating novelties on maps. Cumulatively, the record is immensely impressive, even if it was very much less than final. This phase of exploration ended with something of a breathing space at its end, a pause in which the realities of power politics were to prepare men for a new and decisive period in American exploration.

The English wars with Spain and France between 1739 and 1763, in which the colonists of all three powers were involved, tended not so much to stop as hold up and divert both the exploration of western North America and its exploitation. Not much that was really dramatic occurred in these years in the way of opening up new areas apart from the first signs of a spread of Spanish activity from Mexico into California. Nor could much be achieved farther north until there had been some re-thinking by both the British government and the colonial assemblies. The reservation of the western areas, taken from France, to fur traders operating mainly from bases in British Canada after 1763, placed the initiative for exploration in hands other than those of the colonists. The most they could do was to move out into the nearer wilderness to begin the exploitation of the fringe areas. Spain was left, for the time being, unchallenged in a wide and ill-defined area in far western America. The preliminaries of the Revolution (1764-75) allowed little opportunity for major exploration. But the Revolution of 1776 was almost as much concerned with the desire of the new Americans to explore, conquer and exploit the western territories as it was to secure independence from British government control. The peace of 1782-3 opened the west to them, though it failed to give them Canada, which they coveted also.

The new Republic devoted much of its energies to expansion outwards from its existing boundaries, but, especially after it acquired residual French and Spanish claims, it launched out on a program of systematic exploration which at last revealed in detail the farthest west. The names of Pike, Lewis and Clark, of Fremont and others are famous in the history of exploration in the era which followed the Revolution. They are the real outriders of the American empire which was to flow over the remainder of the continent and to make the sixty years after 1783 the apotheosis of exploration, the transformation of much of North America from a wild Amerindian homeland into a field open for European farmers, businessmen, the whole subsequent apparatus of democratic institutions, bureaucracy and capitalist enterprise and exploitation. America thus became a new Europe: Canada was to follow her in another century.

CHRONOLOGY

(The numbers in brackets at the end of each entry refer to the chapters in which further information about the explorer or expedition mentioned can be found.)

1628–30	Spanish missionaries from Santa Fé reach the Jumanos in Texas (5)
1633	Oldham makes the first overland journey from New England to the Connecticut Valley (2)
c. 1634	Nicollet reaches the Indians of Green Bay, Lake Michigan (1)
	Dutch expedition travels along the Mohawk River to the Iroquois country south of Lake Ontario (2)
1641	Jogues and Raymbault journey to Sault Ste Marie (1)
1642	Field becomes the first European to reach the White Mountains of New Hampshire (2)
1647	De Quen explores the Saguenay River to Lake St John (6)
1654	Le Moyne travels south from Canada into the Iroquois country (1)
1654–60	Radisson and Groseilliers trade and explore west of the St Lawrence as far as Lake Superior, and possibly as far as the Upper Mississippi and Hudson Bay (1, 6)
1668–9	*Nonsuch* winters at Rupert River, Hudson Bay (6)
1669	Casson-Galinée expedition enters the Niagara River from Lake Ontario (1)
1669–70	Allouez journeys from Sault Ste Marie to Green Bay and the Fox River (1)
1670	Lederer reaches the Virginia Blue Ridge and crosses the Carolina Piedmont (3)
1671–2	The French make the first overland journey from the St Lawrence to Hudson Bay (6)
1673	The Jolliet-Marquette expedition reaches the Upper Mississippi, and on its course downstream sights the Missouri and Ohio (1)
1674–82	Woodward leaves Charles Town to visit the Westo on the Savannah and the Creeks in Alabama (3)
1679–80	Dulhut explores west of Lake Superior (1)
1680	Hennepin discovers the Falls of St Anthony on the Colbert River (1)
1682	La Salle reaches the mouth of the Mississippi (1)
1685	La Salle establishes settlement at Matagorda Bay on the Gulf of Mexico (5)
1690	Tonty reaches Texas south of the Red River (5)
	First Spanish mission established in Texas from the Rio Grande
1690–2	Kelsey travels inland from York Fort, Hudson Bay, to the western plains of Canada (6)
c. 1692	Couture crosses the Alleghenies from the Mississippi to Carolina (3)
1692–4	Viele journeys west from Albany to the Susquehanna, down the Ohio, and explores as far west as the Wabash (2)
1698–1702	Kino discovers the 'land passage' to California (7)
1699	Iberville enters the Mississippi delta (5)
1700	Le Sueur ascends the Mississippi to Minnesota (5)
1701	Lawson explores the North Carolina Piedmont (3)
1714, 1716	St Denys makes two journeys from the Red River to the Rio Grande (5)
1715–16	Stuart explores the Barrens northwest of Hudson Bay, possibly as far as Great Slave Lake (6)
1717–19	The French re-establish posts at the western end of Lake Superior (6)
1718	The Alarcón expedition founds San Antonio (5)
	Bienville establishes New Orleans (5)
	De Bourgmont explores the Missouri River (5)
1727	Le Tort moves along the Susquehanna to the Ohio (2)
1728	Bering sails from Kamchatka to the eastern tip of Asia (7)
1732	Gwosdev sights the American shore of Bering Strait (7)
1738	La Vérendrye discovers the Mandans on the Missouri (6)
1739	The Mallet brothers reach Santa Fé from the Missouri (5)
	La Vérendrye (The Chevalier) explores as far west as the Forks of the Saskatchewan (6)
1741	Bering and Chirikov sight the northwest coast of America; return by way of the Shumagin and Aleutian Islands (7)
1742	Middleton explores the west coast of Hudson Bay; discovers Wager Inlet and Repulse Bay (6)
	Salley crosses the Alleghenies from Virginia and descends the Ohio to the Mississippi (4)
1742–3	La Vérendrye's sons journey from the Missouri into Dakota (6)
1747	The Moor expedition explores the west coast of Hudson Bay; discovers Chesterfield Inlet (6)
1749	Coats explores the east coast of Hudson Bay (6)
1750	Walker crosses the Cumberland Gap and explores Kentucky (4)
1751–2	Gist surveys the Ohio Valley (4)
1753	Washington and Gist reach Fort Le Boeuf near Lake Erie (4)
1754–5	Henday journeys far inland from York Fort; probably sights the Rockies (6)
1758–9	Post travels to the Wyoming Valley, Pa (2)
1764–71	Synd explores the Bering Strait region, Krenitsyn and Levashev the Aleutian Islands (7)
1765	Croghan journeys down the Ohio to the Wabash and Illinois Rivers (2)
1766–7	Carver travels between Lake Superior and the Upper Mississippi; is the first English-speaking trader west of the Mississippi (2)
1766–8	Rubí-Lafora expedition surveys the northern frontier of New Spain (5, 7)
1769–71	Boone explores the Kentucky country (4)
1769	The Portalá expedition reaches San Diego, Monterey and San Francisco Bay (7)
1771	Hearne sights the Arctic coastline of North America at the mouth of the Coppermine River; on his return journey passes Great Slave Lake (6)
1772–3	Cocking explores across the Saskatchewan River as far as the Eagle Hills (6)
1773–7	Bartram journeys through the southeast (4)
1774	Pérez sails to latitude 55°N. on the northwest coast (7)
	The Anza-Garcés expedition reaches the Californian coast overland from Tubac (7)
1775	Boone clears the Wilderness Road (4)
	Quadra sails to latitude 58°N. on the Alaskan coast (7)
	Hezeta sights the entrance of the Columbia River (7)
	Garcés enters the Great Basin and rediscovers the Grand Canyon (7)
1776	The Domínguez-Escalante expedition explores from Santa Fé into Arizona, Utah and Colorado (7)
1778	Cook explores the northwest coast from Vancouver Island to Bering Strait (7)

NOTES

Chapter 1
1 Thwaites, *Jesuit Relations*, vol. XIV, p. 125.
2 *Ibid.*, vol. XVIII, p. 237
3 *Ibid.*, vol. XXXIII, p. 65.
4 For differing versions of their itineraries see Nute (1943) and Adams (1961).
5 Scull (1885), p. 136.
6 See e.g. Thwaites, *Jesuit Relations*, vol. XLI, pp. 91-129, with the report of Le Moyne's expedition, and the detailed information given in *ibid.*, vol. XLIX, pp. 257-67.
7 *Ibid.*, vol. LIV, p. 149.
8 *Ibid.*, vol. LIV, p. 231.
9 O'Callaghan (1855), p. 64.
10 See Thwaites, *Jesuit Relations*, vol. LV, pp. 105-15.
11 Lahontan (1703), vol. I, p. 54.
12 O'Callaghan (1855), p. 72.
13 Thwaites, *Jesuit Relations*, vol. LIX, p. 89.
14 Quoted in Donnelly (1968), p. 112.
15 This and the other quotations in this section are from Marquette's account in Thwaites, *Jesuit Relations*. LIX, pp. 87-163.
16 Text of Jolliet's letter to Frontenac transcribed on his map 'Nouvelle decouverte . . .' (see plate 15).
17 O'Callaghan (1855), p. 121.
18 Quoted in Eccles (1969), pp. 105-6.
19 See the various editions and translations of his three main works listed in the bibliography for 1683, 1697 and 1698.
20 See Dulhut's memoir of 1685 in Kellogg, *Early narratives*, pp. 325-34.
21 *Ibid.*, p. 297.
22 Cox (1905).

Chapter 2
1 Leach (1966), p. 3.
2 Trelease (1960), p. 3.
3 The population of New England was estimated to be 25,000 in 1600. At least one third died as a result of the epidemic, which left around 15,000 to 18,000. Mooney (1928), p. 2.
4 Hosmer (1906), vol. I, p. 61.
5 Moloney (1931), p. 48.
6 Clark (1968), pp. 388-9.
7 Baxter (1884), pp. 27-9.
8 Hosmer (1906), vol. II, p. 62, n.
9 Only the Merrimac River rises in the White Mountains. The source of the Connecticut is north of Colebrooke, New Hampshire. The Androscoggin rises in northern New Hampshire and the Saco to the east of the foothills of the White Mountains.
10 Shurtleff (1854), vol. III, p. 288. See also pp. 278, 361-2.
11 Halsby (1913), p. 32.
12 O'Callaghan (1856-83), vol. IV, pp. 96-7, 99. For his early career see vols. III and IX.
13 Trelease (1960), pp. 268-9.
14 O'Callaghan (1856-83), vol. III, p. 395.
15 No account of this expedition has remained. There are occasional references in O'Callaghan (1856-83), vol. III, pp. 436-7, 442-3, 476, vol. XI, pp. 300, 302, 308-9, 318-19, 348; and in Leder (1956), pp. 106-8. For an account of French activities in the area see Chapter 1.
16 O'Callaghan (1856-83), vol. IV, p. 749.
17 Governor Bellomont to the Lords of Trade, October 24, 1700, in O'Callaghan (1856-83), vol. IV, p. 768. See also pp. 715, 748-50, 805-6.
18 For a description of the journey see Biggar (1929), vol. III, pp. 213-26.
19 Hanna (1911), vol. I, p. 180.
20 O'Callaghan (1856-83), vol. III, p. 798.
21 Hanna (1911), vol. I, pp. 167-8. For an account of exploration carried out from the southern colonies into this area see Chapters 3 and 4.
22 Thwaites (1904), p. 230.
23 Some of these specimens have been preserved in the Natural History Museum, London. Sloane Collection, nos. 332 and 334.
24 David Brainerd's Journal in Edwards (1765), p. 356.
25 Williamson (1757), p. 24.
26 See Gist's account of this expedition in Chapter 4.
27 Croghan to Captain William Murray. Gage Papers.
28 Bourne (1905-6), vol. XI, p. 300.
29 Keating (1824), vol. I, pp. 323-5.

Chapter 3
1 Andrews (1934), vol. I, pp. 152-3.
2 Berkeley (1663), p. 6.
3 Strachey (1612 [1953]), p. 33.
4 Alvord and Bidgood (1912), pp. 49, 124, state that they reached Occaneechi Island at Clarksville, Virginia; but see Lederer (Ed.), Cumming (1958), p. 118, and Tisdale (1953), pp. 41-2.
5 *Ibid.*, pp. 123-4.
6 *Ibid.*, pp. 111, 120.
7 Morrison (1921), pp. 217-36.
8 Reprinted in Force (1844), vol. III, no. 11, p. 42.
9 Alvord and Bidgood (1912), pp. 109, 126.
10 An anonymous letter, 'A Narrative of the Country, within a few dayes of Virginia', in *A perfect description of Virginia*, London, 1649, reprinted in Force (1836), vol. II, no. 8, pp. 8-9, 13-14.
11 Lederer (Ed.), Cumming (1958), p. 20.
12 Lederer (Ed.), Cumming (1958), pp. 85-90; Cumming (1938), pp. 476-92.
13 Alvord and Bidgood (1912), pp. 183-205.
14 *Ibid.*, p. 191.
15 Parkman (1880), pp. 42-5.
16 Alvord and Bidgood (1912), pp. 17-19.
17 *Ibid.*, pp. 192-3, 194-5.
18 Swanton (1946), pp. 115, 213.
19 Alvord and Bidgood (1912), p. 217.
20 Harrison (1922), vol. XXX, p. 327.
21 *Ibid.*, p. 330.
22 Spotswood (1882), vol. I, 331.
23 Maury (1853), pp. 288-9.
24 Francis Yeardley's letter of 8 May 1754, in Salley (1911), pp. 25-6.
25 McPherson (1966), pp. 72-3; Cumming (1938), p. 83.
26 *Ibid.*, p. 87.
27 Hall (1970), pp. 89, 104.
28 Hall (1970), p. 107.
29 Salley (1911), p. 53; Cumming (1962), pp. 27, 146-7; Hall (1970), p. 98, 53.
30 *Collections of the South Carolina Historical Society* (1897), vol. V, p. 1, 13; Salley (1911), p. 77; Cumming (1962), pp. 27, 147.
31 Salley (1911), pp. 104-5.
32 *Collections of the South Carolina Historical Society* (1897), vol. 5, p. 186.
33 *Ibid.*, vol. V, p. 186, 201; location is on Gascoyne's Second Lords Proprietors' Map of Carolina (1682).
34 *Collections of the South Carolina Historical Society* (1897), vol. 5 p. 186.
35 Crane (1929), pp. 19-21.
36 *Ibid.*, p. 30; London, P.R.O. C.O.5: 287, pp. 198-202.
37 Bolton (1925), p. 50.
38 Crane (1929), p. 6.
39 *Ibid.*, p. 45.
40 Welch's route is marked on Barnwell's map: *ibid.*, p. 46; Cumming (1962), pp. 46, 190.
41 Crane (1929), p. 46; French (1851), vol. III, pp. 15-16.
42 *Collections of the South Carolina Historical Society* (1897), vol. V, p. 463, no. 1; Williams (1937), p. 26.
43 Crane (1916), vol. III, pp. 3-18; Delanglez (1944), p. 281; Adams (1962), pp. 62-3.
44 Thwaites, *Jesuit Relations*, vol. LXV, p. 117.
45 Surrey (1916), p. 339.
46 Crane (1929), p. 63-4.
47 Lanning (1935), pp. 164-90.
48 Leonard (1939), pp. 13-14.
49 *Ibid.*, p. 221.
50 *Ibid.*, pp. 54-65, 218-21; Lowery (1901), p. 359.
51 Dickenson (1699); the spelling 'Dickenson' is apparently a typographical error: see Dickinson, Ed. Andrews (1945), p. 18.
52 London, Public Record Office, C.O. 5/382/4397, fo. 24-5.
53 Crane (1929), pp. 17-18; the activities of the South Carolina expansionists are given in detail in Crane's authoritative work.
54 London, Public Record Office, C.O. 5/382/4397, fo. 25.
55 Crane (1929), p. 100; Crane has the best account of Hughes's career. The Hughes's letters were exhibited in the Library of Congress in 1929: see Maggs Bros of London, *A catalogue of rare Americana*, pp. 62-4. The present ownership of Hughes's letters is unknown.
56 Crane (1929), p. 99.
57 Spotswood (1885), vol. II, p. 331; Hughes's map is P.R.O., C.O. 700, Virginia 2.
58 Cadillac's letter of July 1714: Crane (1929), p. 104.
59 *Ibid.*, p. 168.
60 *Ibid.*
61 Mereness (1916), pp. 97-172 (Chicken's journal); pp. 176-212 (Fitch's journal).
62 Crane (1929), pp. 276-80 has the best general account; Williams (1927), pp. 115-42 reprints Cuming's journal in full; the deposition of the trader Ludowick Grant, who accompanied Cuming to the Cherokees, is found in the *South Carolina Historical and Geneological Magazine*, vol. X, 54 ff.; Williams (1937), pp. 88-94 gives additional references and comments.
63 Lawson, ed. Lefler (1967), p. 207.
64 *Ibid.*, p. xl-xliii.
65 Catesby (1743), vol. II, p. v.
66 Catesby (1743), vol. II, p. xxxiv.
67 Frick and Stearns (1961), p. 33.
68 *Ibid.*, p. 50.
69 Byrd, *Westover Manuscripts* (1841); Byrd, ed. Boyd (1929), pp. 188, 192, 216, 298.

70 *Ibid.*, p. 92.
71 *Ibid.*, p. 169-83.

Chapter 4
1 Myer (1928), pp. 779-88.
2 Mereness (1916), pp. 341, 350, 354.
3 Kegley (1938), p. 185; Fry and Jefferson's 'A Map of the Most Inhabited Part of Virginia' (1755); Brown (1937), pp. 501-13.
4 Harrison (1922), pp. 203-22.
5 Withers (1895), p. 42; Waddell (1902), p. 23; Williams (1937), p. 87; Faust (1927), vol. I, p. 367.
6 Harrison (1922), p. 206; Williams (1937), p. 117; Kegley (1938), pp. 142, 152, 158.
7 Alvord (1917), vol. I, p. 86.
8 P.R.O., C.O. 5, 1330, pp. 323-30: Alvord (1917), vol. I, p. 89.
9 Johnston (1898), pp. 8-75.
10 Bailey (1939), p. 170.
11 *Ibid.*, p. 85.
12 Gist, ed. Darlington (1893), pp. 67-8; Bailey (1939), pp. 30-1.
13 Bailey (1939), pp. 132-5.
14 Gist, ed. Darlington (1893), p. 88. Darlington is apparently wrong in stating that Gist went to Carolina to enlist Cherokees in 1756; it was his son Nathaniel: see Williams (1937), p. 149, no. 10.
15 Timberlake, Ed. Williams (1927), pp. 47-8.
16 *Ibid.*, p. 59.
17 *Ibid.*, p. 131, no. 74.
18 *Ibid.*, pp. 133-52.
19 Smith (1766) and Hutchins (1778); see also Brown (1959) for reproductions of chief maps.
20 Gordon's 'Journal' in Mereness (1916), pp. 464-89; Pittman (1770).
21 Bakeless (1939), pp. 42, 47; Williams (1937), p. 322.
22 Williams (1937), p. 323.
23 Williams (1928), p. 203-7.
24 Williams (1937), ch. 27, 'The Long-Hunters' Decade', pp. 319-33.
25 Bakeless (1939), p. 63.
26 *Ibid.*, pp. 44-8.
27 *Ibid.*, p. 64.
28 *Ibid.*, pp. 68-73.
29 Henderson (1920), pp. 216-50.
30 Jones (1883), p. 143.
31 Mereness (1916), pp. 241-55; see selection on p. 142.
32 Williams (1937), pp. 101-13.
33 *Gentleman's Magazine* 27 (1758), opp. p. 478.
34 Bartram, Ed. Harper (1942), p. 51.
35 *Ibid.*, pp. 42, 73.
36 William Bartram, ed. Evan (1968) reproduces the Fothergill drawings.
37 Bartram, ed. Harper (1958), pp. 64, 77, 79, 120, 129-31.
38 Bartram (1791), pp. 104-5; Lowes (1927), p. 366.
39 Spiller, Thorp, Johnson, Canby (1953), p. 206.
40 Published in London in 1775; edited with notes by Judge S. C. Williams as *Adair's History of the American Indians*, Nashville, Tenn., 1953.
41 De Brahm, ed. De Vorsey (1971); De Vorsey (1970), pp. 21-9.
42 Romans (1775); Phillips (1924).
43 De Vorsey (1966), pp. 20-32.

Chapter 5
1 Ogilby (1671), p. 238.
2 Benavides, ed. Hodge, Hammond, Rey (1945), pp. 37, 38.
3 Bannon (1964), p. 45.
4 Benavides, ed. Hodge, Hammond, Rey (1945), pp. 71, 72.
5 *Ibid.*, pp. 47, 48, 72, 73.
6 *Ibid.*, pp. 91, 92.
7 *Ibid.*, pp. 92-5.
8 *Ibid.*, Appendix xi, p. 135.
9 Bolton (1916), pp. 313, 314.
10 Céliz, ed. Hoffmann (1935), p. 29, note 5.
11 *Ibid.*, pp. 283-9; Bosque, ed. Bolton (1916), p. 300.
12 Espinosa (1940), pp. 13-17.
13 Bolton (1916), pp. 314-16.
14 Mendoza, ed. Bolton (1916), pp. 326, 327.
15 *Ibid.*, pp. 327-40.
16 Sigüenza, ed. Leonard (1932), pp. 59-67; in his *Mercurio Volante*, the tale is excellently told by the noted Mexican scholar.
17 Dunn (1917), pp. 14, 15.
18 Freytas, ed. Shea (1882). This bogus account of Peñalosa's journey has been discredited by Wagner and Duro; Wagner (1967), vol. II, pp. 282-3; Duro (1882).
19 La Salle's own map is lost; J.B.L. Franquelin's 'Carte de la Louisiane ou des Voyages du Sr. de la Salle . . . 1684', based on La Salle's observations before his voyage to the gulf, shows this great westward curve of the Mississippi (reprod. Winsor (1884), vol. IV, p. 228), as does the map of Minet (1685), who identifies the mouth with that of the Rio Grande (reprod. Winsor (1884), vol. IV, p. 237).
20 Margry, ed. (1879), vol. II, p. 383.
21 Joutel, ed. French (1846), vol. I, p. 86.
22 Margry, ed. (1879), vol. III, pp. 647-9; French, ed. (1846), vol. I, p. 85, note.
23 Joutel, ed. French (1846), vol. I, pp. 86, 90, 95.
24 Parkman (1869), p. 408, note 1.
25 Joutel, ed. French (1846), vol. I, p. 96.
26 Parkman (1869), pp. 351, 352, 354.
27 Joutel, ed. French (1846), vol. I, pp. 97, 99-103.
28 Margry (1879), vol. II, pp. 521-52.
29 Bolton (1915), pp. 165-82.
30 Joutel, ed. French (1846), vol. I, pp. 112-15.
31 Tonty, ed. French (1846), vol. I, p. 67.
32 *Ibid.*, p. 68.
33 Joutel, ed. French (1846), pp. 118-20, 124, 125.
34 Swanton (1952), p. 315.
35 Douay, ed. Shea, ed. French (1852), vol. IV, pp. 202-6.
36 Douay, ed. Shea, ed. French (1852), vol. IV, pp. 212-14; Joutel, ed. French (1846), vol. I, pp. 142-3.
37 Joutel, Ed. French (1846), vol. I, pp. 146, 153-5.
38 *Ibid.*, pp. 155-63; Tonty, ed. French (1846), vol. I, pp. 76-7.
39 Joutel, ed. French (1846), vol. I, pp. 166, 171, 174.
40 *Ibid.*, pp. 178, 183.
41 Tonty, ed. French (1846), vol. I, p. 70, 71.
42 *Ibid.*, pp. 72, 74.
43 *Ibid.*, pp. 77, 78.
44 Consulta of April 8, 1686; México, 61-6-20, Archivas de Indias, quoted in Dunn (1917), p. 42.
45 Dunn (1917), p. 58.
46 *Ibid.*, pp. 59-77.
47 *Ibid.*, pp. 86-9, 96-9.
48 Bolton (1915), pp. 165-82.
49 Massanet, ed. Bolton (1916), pp. 359-62.
50 Dunn (1917), p. 107, note; Massanet, ed. Bolton (1916), p. 387.
51 Massanet, ed. Bolton (1916), pp. 376-83.
52 Dunn (1917), pp. 132-43.
53 Leonard, trans. and ed. (1939).
54 Kellogg (1931-2), p. 3.
55 Winsor, (1887), vol. V, pp. 13, 15.
56 *Ibid.*, p. 18.
57 *Historical Journal* (Iberville Expedition), ed. French (1875), vol. VI, pp. 53, 54.
58 *Ibid.*, p. 52.
59 *Historical Journal* (Iberville Expedition), ed. French (1875), vol. VI, pp. 67, 71, 76.
60 Winsor (1887), vol. V, p. 19.
61 *Historical Journal* (Iberville Expedition), ed. French (1875), vol. VI, pp. 109-12.
62 La Harpe, ed. French (1851), vol. III, pp. 16, 17.
63 Sauvole, ed. French (1851), vol. III, pp. 223-7.
64 La Harpe, ed. French (1851), vol. III, pp. 17, 18.
65 Gravier, ed. Shea (1861), pp. 136-42.
66 La Harpe, ed. French (1851), vol. III, pp. 18, 19.
67 Le Sueur, in La Harpe, ed. French (1851), vol. III, pp. 23-7; and in Shea, ed. (1861), pp. 89-111.
68 La Harpe, ed. French (1851), vol. III, pp. 20, 28, 30, 35.
69 Le Page du Pratz (1763), vol. II, pp. 9, 10, 11.
70 Pénicaut, ed. McWilliams (1953); his journal is inaccurate, but good reading for customs and territory.
71 Le Page du Pratz (1763), vol. II, p. 11.
72 Céliz, ed. Hoffmann (1935). Introduction, p. 12.
73 Le Page du Pratz (1763), vol. II, pp. 12, 13.
74 Bancroft (1884), vol. I, pp. 610, 611.
75 Céliz, ed. Hoffmann (1935). Introduction, p. 14.
76 Shelby (1924), pp. 198-217.
77 Céliz, ed. Hoffmann (1935), p. 43.
78 *Ibid.*, p. 42, note 82.
79 *Ibid.*, p. 52.
80 *Ibid.*, pp. 23, 64, 65, 81-85.
81 Le Page du Pratz (1763), vol. II, pp. 20, 28, 75, 76, 91-3.
82 La Harpe, ed. French (1851), vol. III, pp. 68-72; Folmer (1941), pp. 257-8.
83 Le Page du Pratz (1763), vol. II, p. 94.
84 Le Page du Pratz, ed. Williams (1928), pp. 108-11.
85 Buckley (1911), pp. 38-66.
86 La Harpe, ed. French (1851), vol. III, pp. 73-5.
87 McRill (1963), pp. 126-59.
88 Du Tisné, quoted in La Harpe, ed. French (1851), vol. III, pp. 66, 67.
89 Nasatir, ed. (1952), vol. I, pp. 1, 2.
90 Folmer (1942), pp. 283, 284.
91 Bandelier (1893), pp. 289 ff.
92 Valverde, in Pichardo, Hackett, ed. (1931), vol. I, pp. 188, 194-7.
93 Le Page du Pratz (1763), vol. I, p. 158.
94 Le Page du Pratz (1763), vol. II, pp. 107-27.
95 Surrey (1916), pp. 42, 43.
96 D'Artaguiette, ed. Mereness (1916), p. 54.
97 Charlevoix, ed. French (1851), pp. 121, 123, 140-1, 175, 154.
98 Hachard, in Gravier, ed. (1872), pp. 73-8.
99 Le Page du Pratz (1763), vol. I, Introduction, p. ii.
100 Le Page du Pratz (1763), vol. II, pp. 162, 163, 72-6.
101 Mallet, ed. Folmer (1939), pp. 4-8.
102 Folmer (1941), pp. 264-72.
103 Nasatir, ed. (1952), pp. 43, 44, 55.
104 Folmer (1941), p. 272.
105 Bolton, ed. (1970), p. 26.
106 Dunn (1914), pp. 392-414.
107 Bolton, ed. (1970), pp. 80-7, 91, 92, 96, 97.
108 La Fora, ed. Kinnaird (1967), pp. 1-4.
109 *Ibid.*, pp. 82-7.
110 *Ibid.*, pp. 29-33.
111 *Ibid.*, pp. 79-80.
112 *Ibid.*, p. 42.
113 Bonilla, ed. West (1904), p. 9.

Chapter 6
1 Scull (1885), p. 241.
2 Public Record Office: S.P. 29/251B, fos. 271-2.
3 Delanglez (1948), p. 171.
4 *Report from the Committee* (1749), Appendix, XXVII.
5 Burpee (1935), vol. I, pp. 197-202.
6 For the most recent work on La Vérendrye see Champagne (1968), (1971).
7 Burpee (1927), pp. 44, 46.

8 *Ibid.*, p. 491.
9 See 'Memoir of the expedition of Jacques Repentigny Legardeur de Saint Pierre', in *Report on Canadian Archives 1886* (Ottawa, 1887), pp. clxi-clxv.
10 HBC Archives, A.1/33, fo. 97d.
11 See entry on Stuart in *Dictionary of Canadian Biography* (University of Toronto Press, 1969), vol. II, pp. 614-16.
12 Hearne (1795), p. xxx.
13 Robson (1752), p. 6.
14 Middleton (1743), p. 134.
15 Barrow (1852), p. 2.
16 Dobbs (1744), p. 65.
17 Rich and Johnson (1949), p. 69.
18 See Burpee (1907) for a printed version of Henday's journal. Three other variant manuscript journals are in the HBC Archives.
19 Douglas and Wallace (1926), pp. 39-40.
20 See Public Record Office: C.O. 324/17, p. 476; /18, p. 411.
21 Carver (1778), p. 122.
22 Williams (1969), section IX.
23 HBC Archives, B.198/a/9, fo. 26d.
24 Hearne (1795), p. 327.

Chapter 7
1 Tooley (1964), p. 4.
2 Golder (1922), vol. I, p. 11.
3 Müller (1764), p. 28.
4 *Ibid.*, p. 116.
5 For a whole series of manuscript maps made on this and other Russian expeditions of the period see Yefimov (1964).
6 These dispatches are printed in Tompkins and Moorhead (1949), pp. 231-55.
7 See Bolton (1959), p. 91.
8 Bolton (1930), vol. II, p. 60.
9 *Ibid.*, pp. 89, 199.
10 *Ibid.*, p. 93.
11 See Calvin (1968), p. 68.
12 Quoted in Cook (1973), p. 69.
13 Bolton (1926), vol. IV, pp. 45-6.
14 *Ibid.*, p. 32.
15 A translation of Hezeta's report is contained in Greenhow (1844), pp. 430-3.
16 Cook's original instructions, dated 6 July 1776, are in British Museum, Egerton MS.2177B.
17 Log of Captain James King, 12 May 1778. Public Record Office: Adm 55/122, fo. 31d.
18 Beaglehole (1967), vol. I, p. 456.
19 Quoted in Masterton and Brower (1948), p. 16.
20 *The Monthly Review*, LXX (London, June 1784), p. 474.

BIBLIOGRAPHY

Books and articles referred to in the notes and selections

Adair, James. *The history of the American Indians*. London, 1775. *See* Williams (ed.), 1953.
Adams, Arthur T. (ed.) *The explorations of Pierre Esprit Radisson*. Minneapolis, 1961.
Adams, Percy G. *Travelers and travel liars, 1660-1800*. Berkeley and Los Angeles, 1962.
Alvord, Clarence W. *The Mississippi Valley in British politics*. Cleveland, 1917. 2 vols.
Alvord, Clarence W., and Bidgood, Lee. *The first explorations of the Trans-Allegheny region by the Virginians, 1650-1674*. Cleveland, 1912.
Andrews, Charles M. *The colonial period of American history*. New Haven, 1934-8. 4 vols.
Bailey, Kenneth P. *The Ohio Company of Virginia*. Glendalea, 1939.
Bain, James (ed.) *Travels and adventures in Canada and the Indian territories between the years 1760 and 1776 by Alexander Henry, fur trader*. Toronto, 1901 (reprint).
Bakeless, John. *Daniel Boone*. New York, 1939.
Bancroft, Hubert H. *History of the north Mexican states and Texas*. 2 vols. In *Works*, XV. San Francisco, 1884.
Bandelier, A.F. *The gilded man*. New York, 1893.
Bannon, John F. (ed). *Bolton and the Spanish borderlands*. Norman, Okla, 1964.
Bannon, John F. *The Spanish borderlands frontier, 1513-1821*. New York, 1970.
Barrow, John (ed). *The geography of Hudson's Bay. Being the remarks of Captain W. Coats* . . . London, The Hakluyt Society, 1852.
Bartram, John. *Diary of a journey through the Carolinas, Georgia and Florida from July 1, 1765 to April 10, 1766*. Ed. by Francis Harper. Philadelphia, Transactions of the American Philosophical Society, N.S. XXXIII, part 1, 1942.
Bartram, John. *Observations on the inhabitants . . . and other matters . . . made by Mr John Bartram, in his travels from Pensilvania to Onondago, Oswego and the Lake Ontario, in Canada*. London, 1751.
Bartram, William. *Botanical and zoological drawings, 1756-1788*. Ed. by Joseph Evan. Philadelphia, 1968.
Bartram, William. 'Observations on the Creek and Cherokee Indians 1789,. Ed. by E. G. Squier. *Transactions of the American Ethnological Society*, III, New York, pl I, 1-81.
Bartram, William. *Travels*. Ed. by Francis Harper. New Haven, 1958.
Bartram, William. *Travels through North and South Carolina*. Philadelphia, 1791.
Batts, Thomas and Fallam, Robert. 'A journal from Virginia, 1671'. *See* Alvord and Bidgood, 1912, 183-95.
Baxter, James B. (ed.) *Documentary history of the state of Maine*, vol. III. Portland, Maine, 1884.
Beau, Claude le. *Adventures parmie les sauvages*. 1738.
Beaglehole, J. C. (ed.) *The journals of Captain James Cook on his voyages of discovery: the voyage of the Resolution and Discovery 1776-1780*. Cambridge, The Hakluyt Society, 1967.
Beaglehole, J. C. *The Life of Captain James Cook*. London, 1974.
Benavides, Fray Alonso de. *Revised Memorial of 1634*. Ed. by F. W. Hodge, G. P. Hammond, Agapito Rey. Albuquerque, Coronado Cuarto Centennial Publications, 1540-1940, IV, 1945.
Berkeley, Sir William. *A discourse and view of Virginia*. London, 1663.
Biggar, H. P. *See* Champlain.
Bland, Edward, and others. *Discovery of New Britaine*. London, 1651. *See* Salley (ed.), 1911, 5-19.
Bolton, Herbert E. (ed.) *Anza's California expeditions*. Berkeley, 1930.
Bolton, Herbert E. (ed.) *Arredondo's historical proof of Spain's title to Georgia*. Berkeley, Ca, 1925.
Bolton, Herbert E. (ed.) *Athanase de Mezières and the Louisiana-Texas frontier, 1768-1780*. Cleveland, 1914; reprint, New York, 1970.
Bland, Edward. *The discovery of New Britaine*. London, 1651.
Bolton, Herbert E. (ed.) *Kino's historical memoir of Pimería Alta 1683-1711*. Cleveland, 1919.
Bolton, Herbert E. 'The location of La Salle's colony on the Gulf of Mexico'. *Mississippi Valley Historical Review*, II, 1915, 165-82.
Bolton, Herbert E. (ed.) *Pageant of the wilderness: the story of the Escalante expedition to the Interior Basin, 1776*. Salt Lake City, The Utah State Historical Society, 1950.
Bolton, Herbert E. *The Spanish borderlands: a chronicle of old Florida and the Southwest*. New Haven, 1921.
Bolton, Herbert E. (ed.) *Spanish exploration in the southwest, 1542-1706*. New York, 1916; reprints 1946, 1959.
Bolton, Herbert E. and Marshall, T. M. *The colonization of North America, 1492-1783*. New York, 1920.
Bolton, *see also* Pálou.
Bonilla, Antonio. 'Brief compendium of the history of Texas, 1772'. Ed. and trans. by Elizabeth H. West. *Quarterly of the Texas State Historical Association*, VIII, 1904, 4-78.
Bonnefoy, Antoine. 'Journal of captivity among the Cherokee Indians, 1741-1742'. Trans. by J. F. Jameson. *See* Mereness (ed.), 1916, 241-55.
Boone, Daniel. 'Adventures of Col. Daniel Boon'. *See* Filson, 1784, 49-82.
Bosque, Fernando del. Diary, 1675. In 'Autos de la conquista de la Prov[a] de Coahuila . . . Expedicion de Fernando del Bosque'. MS in Archivo de la Secretaría de Gobierno del Estado de Coahuila, legajo no. 1, 1688-1736. *See* Bolton (ed. and trans.), 1916, 291-309.
Bossu, Captain M. *Travels through that part of North America formerly called Louisiana*. Trans. by J. R. Forster. London, 1771. 2 vols.
'Boston prints and printmakers'. *Colonial Society of Massachusetts Collections*, XLVI, 1973.
Boucher, Pierre. *Histoire véritable et naturelle . . . du pays de la Nouvelle-France*. Boucherville, Que., Société Historique de Boucherville, 1964.
Bourne, E. G. 'The travels of Jonathan Carver'. *American Historical Review*, XI, 1905-6, 287-302.
Brébeuf, (Saint) Jean de. *Les relations de ce qui s'est passé au pays des Hurons, 1635-48*. Ed. by T. Besterman. Geneva, 1957.
Brebner, J. B. *The explorers of North America, 1492-1806*. London, 1933, reprint New York, 1955.
Brown, Lloyd A. *Early maps of the Ohio Valley*. Pittsburgh, 1959.
Brown, Ralph M. 'A sketch of the early history of Southwestern Virginia'. *William and Mary Quarterly*, 2nd series, XVII, 1937, 501-13.
Buckley, Eleanor C. 'The Aguayo expedition into Texas and Louisiana, 1719-1722'. *The Quarterly of the Texas State Historical Association*, XV, 1911, 1-66.
Burpee, L. J. (ed.) *Journals and letters of Pierre Gaultier de Varennes de la Vérendrye and his sons*. Toronto, The Champlain Society, 1927.
Burpee, L. J. *The search for the Western Sea*. Toronto, 1935. 2 vols.
Burpee, L. J. (ed.) 'York Factory to the Blackfeet country', The journal of Anthony Hendry [sic] 1754-55, *Proceedings and Transactions of the Royal Society of Canada*. 3rd series, vol I, 1907.
Byrd, William. *William Byrd's histories of the dividing line betwixt Virginia and North Carolina*. Ed. by William K. Boyd. Raleigh, N.C., 1929.
Byrd, William. *The Westover manuscripts*. Publ. by Edmund Ruffin. Petersburg, Va, 1841.
Calvin, John (ed.) *Diario de exploraciones en Arizona y California en los años de 1775 y 1776. Fray Francisco Garcés*. Mexico City, 1968.
Campbell, Tony. 'The Drapers' Company and its school of 17th century chart-makers'. *See* Wallis and Tyacke (eds), 1973.
Caruso, John A. *The Mississippi Valley frontier: the age of French exploration and settlement*. Indianapolis, New York, Kansas City, 1966.
Carver, Jonathan. *Travels through the interior parts of North-America, in the years 1766, 1767, and 1768*. London, 1778.
Catesby, Mark. *Hortus Britanno-Americanus: or, a curious collection of trees and shrubs, the produce of the British Colonies in North America*. London, 1763.
Catesby, Mark. *Hortus Europae Americanus; or a collection of 85 curious trees and shrubs, the produce of North America*. London, 1767.
Catesby, Mark. *The natural history of Carolina, Florida, and the Bahama Islands; containing the figures of birds, beasts, fishes, serpents, insects, and plants: particularly, the forest–trees, shrubs, and other plants* . . . London, 1731–43 (1729–47). 2 vols.
Cavelier, Abbé Jean. *Relation* . . . *See* Shea (ed.), 1861, 15-74.
Céliz, Fray Francisco. *Diary of the Alarcón expedition into Texas, 1718–1719*. Ed. and trans. by F. L. Hoffmann. Los Angeles, Quivira Society Publications, V, 1935.
Champagne, Antoine. *Les La Vérendrye et le poste de l'ouest*. Quebec, 1968.
Champagne, Antoine. *Nouvelles études sur les La Vérendrye et le poste de l'ouest*. Quebec, 1971.
Champlain, Samuel de. *Voyages*. Paris, 1632.
Champlain, Samuel de. *Works*, vol. 3 (ed.) H. B. Biggar. Toronto, The Champlain Society, 1929, reprint Toronto, 1971.
Charlevoix, Father Pierre de. S.J. *Histoire et description de la Nouvelle France avec le journal historique d'un voyage fait par ordre du roi dans l'Amérique Septentrionale*. Paris, 1744. 3 vols.
Charlevoix, Father Pierre de, S.J. *Historical journal, in letters addressed to the Duchess of Lesdiguières, 1721–1722*. *See* French (ed. and trans.), III, 1851, 119-96.
Charlevoix, Father Pierre de, S.J. *Journal of a voyage to North America*. Ed. and trans. by Louise P. Kellogg. Chicago, 1923.
Chicken, Col George. 'Journal of a mission . . . to the Cherokees, 1726'. *See* Mereness (ed.), 1916, 97-172.
Clark, Andrew H. *Acadia. The geography of early Nova Scotia*. Madison, 1968.
'Codex Canadensis' MS in Thomas Gilcrease Institute, Tulsa, *c*. 1700.
Cook, Warren L. *Flood tide of empire. Spain and the Pacific Northwest 1543–1819*. New Haven and London, 1973.
Cornuti, Iac. *Canadensium plantarum*. Paris, 1635.
Cox, I. J. *The journeys of La Salle*. New York, 1905.
Coyne, James H. (ed.) 'Exploration of the Great Lakes 1669–1670 . . . Galinée's narrative and map'. Toronto, Ontario Historical Society, Papers and Records IV, 1903.
Crane, Verner W. *The southern frontier, 1670–1732*. Ann Arbor, 1929 (1956).
Crane, Verner W. 'The Tennessee River as the road to Carolina: the beginnings of exploration and trade'. *Mississippi Valley Historical Review*, III, 1916, 3-18.
Creux, François du. *Historia Canadensis*. Paris, 1664.
Crouse, Nellis M. *Contributions of the Canadian Jesuits to the geographical knowledge of New France 1632–1675*. Ithaca, 1924.
Crouse, Nellis M. *In quest of the western ocean*. New York and London, 1928.
Cuming, Sir Alexander. 'Journal, 1730'. *See* Williams (ed.), 1928, 122-43.
Cumming, William P. 'The earliest permanent settlement in Carolina: Nathaniel Batts and the Comberford Map'. *American Historical Review*, XLV, 1938, 82-9.
Cumming, William P. 'Geographical misconceptions of the Southeast in the cartography of the seventeenth and eighteenth centuries'. *Journal of Southern History*, IV, 1938, 476-92.
Cumming, William P. (ed.) *See* John Lederer.

Cumming, William P. 'Naming Carolina'. *North Carolina Historical Review*, XXII, 1945, 34-42.
Cumming, William P. *North Carolina in maps*. Raleigh, N.C., 1966.
Cumming, William P. *The Southeast in early maps*. 2nd edn, Chapel Hill, N.C., 1962.
D'Artaguiette, Diron. *Journal. See* Mereness (ed.), 1916, 17-92.
De Brahm, William G. *De Brahm's report of the general survey in the Southern District of North America*. Ed. by Louis De Vorsey, Jr. Columbia, S.C., 1971.
Delanglez, Jean. *The French Jesuits in Lower Louisiana (1700–1763)*. Washington, 1935.
Delanglez, Jean. *The life and voyages of Louis Jolliet 1645–1700*. Chicago, 1948.
Delanglez, Jean. 'The voyages of Tonti'. *Mid-America*, XXVI, 1944, 281.
De Villiers, Baron Marc. *La découverte du Missouri et l'histoire du Fort d'Orléans, 1673–1728*. Paris, 1925.
De Vorsey, Louis, Jr. 'The Colonial Southeast on "An Accurate General Map".' *Southeastern Geographer*, VI 1966, 20-32.
De Vorsey, Louis, Jr. 'William Gerard De Brahm: eccentric genius'. *Southeastern Geographer*, X, 1970, 21-9.
Dickenson, Jonathan. *Gods protecting providence*. Philadelphia, 1699.
Dickinson, Jonathan. *Jonathan Dickinson's journal: or, God's protecting providence*. Ed. by Evangeline W. and Charles M. Andrews. New Haven and London, 1945.
Dictionary of Canadian Biography. I, 1000-1700. Toronto, 1966. II, 1701-1740. Toronto, 1969.
Dobbs, Arthur. *An account of the countries adjoining to Hudson's Bay* . . . London, 1744.
Donnelly, Joseph P. *Jacques Marquette, S.J. 1637–1675*. Chicago, 1968.
Douay, Father Anastasius. *Narrative of La Salle's attempt to ascend the Mississippi*. Ed. and trans. by John G. Shea. *See* French (ed.), IV, 1852, 197-229.
Doughty, A. G. and Martin, Chester (eds) *The Kelsey papers*. Ottawa, 1929.
Douglas, R. and Wallace, J. N. (eds) *Twenty years of York Factory 1694–1714. Jérémie's account of Hudson Strait and Bay*. Ottawa, 1926.
Drake, E. C. *New universal collection of voyages*. London, 1770.
Dumont de Montigny, J. F. B. *History of Louisiana* . . . *See* French (ed. and trans.), V, 1853, 1-125.
Dumont de Montigny, J.F.B. *Mémoires historiques sur la Louisiane* . . . Paris, 1753. 2 vols.
Dunn, William E. 'The Apache mission on the San Saba River'. *The Southwestern Historical Quarterly*, XVII, 1914, 379-415.
Dunn, William E. *Spanish and French rivalry in the Gulf region of the United States, 1678–1702*. Austin, University of Texas Bulletin, no. 1705. Studies in History, no. 1, 1917.
Du Pratz, Le Page. *See* Le Page du Pratz.
Dupré, Céline. 'Cavelier de la Salle, René–Robert'. *Dictionary of Canadian Biography*, I, 172-84. Toronto, 1966.
Duro, C. F. *Don Diego de Peñalosa y su descubrimiento del reino de Quivira*. Madrid, 1882.
Eccles, W. J. *Canada under Louis XIV 1663–1701*. Toronto, 1964.
Eccles, W. J. *The Canadian frontier 1534–1760*. New York, 1969.
Edwards, George. *A natural history of birds*, pt III. London, 1750.
Edwards, Jonathan. *An account of the life of the late Reverend Mr David Brainerd*. Edinburgh, 1765.
Ellis, Henry. *Voyage to Hudson's Bay* . . . London, 1748.
Espinosa, S. M. (ed. and trans.) *First expedition of Vargas into New Mexico, 1692*. Albuquerque, Coronado Cuarto Centennial Publications, 1540–1940, X. 1940.
Faillon, M. *Histoire de la Colonie Française en Canada*, vol. III. Paris, 1685.
Falconer, Thomas. *On the discovery of the Mississippi*. London, 1844.
Faust, Albert B. *The German element in the United States*. New York, 1927. 2 vols.
Fernández-Duro, C. *Don Diego de Peñalosa y su descubrimiento del reino de Quivira*. Madrid, 1882.
Filson, James. *The discovery* . . . *of Kentucke*. Wilmington, Del., 1784.
Fisher, J. and Wieser, F. R. von. *The oldest map with the name America of the year 1509*. Innsbruck, 1903.
Fitch, Capt. Tobias. 'Journal . . . to the Creeks, 1726'. *See* Mereness (ed.), 1916, 176-212.
Folmer, Henri. 'Contraband trade between Louisiana and New Mexico in the 18th Century'. *The New Mexico Historical Review*, XVI, 1941, 249-74.
Folmer, Henri, 'Étienne Veniard de Bourgmond in the Missouri country'. *Missouri Historical Review*, XXXVI, 1942, 279-98.
Folmer, Henri. *Franco–Spanish rivalry in North America, 1524–1763*. Glendale, Cal., 1953.
Folmer, Henri. 'The Mallet expedition of 1739 through Nebraska, Kansas and Colorado to Santa Fé'. *The Colorado Magazine*, XVI, 1939, 161-73.
Force, Peter. *Tracts and other papers relating principally to the origin, settlement, and progress of the Colonies in North America*. Washington, 1836-46. 4 vols; reprint; New York, 1947.
Fothergill, Dr John. Fothergill Album of William Bartram drawings in the British Museum (Natural History). *See* William Bartram.
Franklin, J. *Narrative of a journey to the shores of the Polar Sea* . . . London, 1832.
French, Benjamin F. (ed. and trans.) *Historical collections of Louisiana and Florida* . . . New York, 1846-53. 5 vols; new series, New York, 1869; second series, New York, 1875
Freytas, Father Nicholas de. *The expedition of Don Diego Dionisio de Peñalosa . . . from Santa Fé to the River Mischipi and Quivira in 1662*. Ed. by John G. Shea. New York, 1882
Frick, George Frederick and Stearns, Raymond Phineas. *Mark Catesby. The colonial Audubon*. Urbana, Ill., 1961.
Furstenbach, Joseph. *Architectura navalis*. Ulm, 1624.
Gayarré, Charles. *Histoire de la Louisiane*. New Orleans, 1846-7. 2 vols.
Gentleman's Magazine, I (1730–).
Gist, Christopher. *Christopher Gist's journals*. Ed. by William M. Darlington. Pittsburgh, 1893.
Golder, F. A. (ed.) *Bering's voyages*. New York, American Geographical Society, 1922. 2 vols.
Gordon, Captain Harry. 'Journal'. *See* Mereness, 1916, 464-89.
Gottschalk, Louis, MacKinney, L. C. and Pritchard, E. H. *The foundations of the modern world, 1300–1775*. London. History of mankind: cultural and scientific development. Published under the auspices of UNESCO, vol. IV, pts i and ii, 1969.
Gravier, Gabriel (ed.) *Relation du voyage des dames religieuses Ursulines de Rouen á la Nouvelle–Orléans*. Paris, 1872.
Gravier, Jacques, S.J. *Relation ou journal du voyage . . . en 1700 depuis le pays des Illinois jusqu'à l'embouchure du Mississippi*. *See* Shea (ed.), 1861, 113-64.
Greenhow, Robert. *The history of Oregon and California and the other territories on the Northwest Coast of North America*. London, 1844.
Hachard, Marie-Madelaine. 'Letters', 1727. *See* Gravier (ed.), 1872, 20-85.
Hackett, Charles W. (ed.) *Historical documents relating to New Mexico, Nueva Viscaya, and approaches thereto, to 1773*. Washington, 1926. 3 vols.
Hadlock, Wendell S. and Dodge, Ernest S. *A canoe from the Penobscot River*. Salem, Mass., 1948.
Hall, Louise. 'New Englanders at sea: Cape Fear before the Royal Charter of 24 March 1662/3'. *New England Historical and Geneological Register*, CXXIV, 1970, 88-108.
Halsy, Francis W. *The old New York frontier*. New York, 1913.
Hanna, Charles A. *The wilderness trail*. New York, 1911. 2 vols.
Harper, J. Russell. *Painting in Canada*. Toronto, 1966.
Harrison, Fairfax. 'The Virginians on the Ohio and the Mississippi in 1742'. *Virginia Magazine of History and Biography*, XXX, 1922, 203-22.
Harrison, Fairfax. 'Western explorations in Virginia between Lederer and Spotswood'. *Virginia Magazine of History and Biography*, XXX, 1922, 323-40.
Hearne, Samuel. *A journey from Prince of Wales's Fort in Hudson's Bay to the Northern Ocean* . . . London, 1795.
Henderson, Archibald. *The conquest of the old southwest*. New York, 1920.
Hennepin, Louis. *Description de la Louisiane*. Paris, 1683.
Hennepin, Louis. *A new discovery of a vast country in America* . . . London, 1698.
Hennepin, Louis. *Nouvelle découverte d'un très grand pays*. Utrecht, 1697.
Hennepin, Louis. *Nouveau voyage d'un pais plus grand que l'Europe*. Utrecht, 1698.
Hennepin, Louis. *Voyage ou nouvelle découverte*. Amsterdam, 1704.
Henry, Alexander. *Travels and adventures in Canada and the Indian territories between the years 1760 and 1776*. Ed. by James Bain. New York, 1809; reprint, Toronto, 1901.
Herbst, Josephine. *New green world*. London, 1947.
Hilton, William. *Relation of a discovery . . . on the coast of Florida*. London, 1664. *See* Salley (ed.), 1911, 37-61.
Historical journal; or narrative of the expeditions made . . . to colonize Louisiana, under the command of M. Pierre Le Moyne d'Iberville, Governor General. *See* French (ed. and trans.), VI, 1875, 28-116.
Hoffman, F. L. (ed. and trans.) *Diary of the Alarcón expedition into Texas, 1718–1719*. Los Angeles. Quivira Society Publications, V, 1935.
Hosmer, James K. (ed.) *Winthrop's journal*. New York, 1906. 2 vols.
Hutchins, Thomas. *A topographical description of Virginia, Pennsylvania, Maryland, and North Carolina*. London, 1778.
Jameson, James F. (ed. and trans.) *Narratives of New Netherland*. New York, 1909; reprint, 1959.
Johnston, J. Stoddard (ed.) *First explorations of Kentucky*. Louisville, Filson Club Publications, no. 13, 1898.
Jones, Cadwallader. 'An essay Lovissinia and Virginia improved . . . 1699'. *See* Harrison, 1922, 329-34.
Jones, Charles C. *The history of Georgia*. Boston, 1883. 2 vols.
Joutel, Henri. *Journal historique du dernier voyage que feu M. de la Sale fit dans le golfe de Mexique* . . . Ed. by M. de Michel. Paris, 1713.
Joutel, Henri. *Journal historique of M. de la Salle's last voyage to discover the River Mississippi*. *See* French (ed. and trans.), I, 1846, 85-193.
Joutel, Henri. *A journal of the last voyage perform'd by Monsr de la Sale, to the Gulph of Mexico* . . . London, 1714.
Joutel, Henri. 'Relation'. MS in Dépôt des Cartes, Plans et Journaux de la Marine, Paris. *See* Margry, III, 1876, 89-534, 646-9.
Keating, William H. *Long's expedition*. Philadelphia, 1824. 2 vols.
Kegley, F. B. *Kegley's Virginia frontier*. Roanoke, Va, 1938.
Kellogg, Louise P. (ed.) *Early narratives of the Northwest, 1634–1699*. New York, 1917; reprint 1959.
Kellogg, Louise P. 'France and the Mississippi Valley: a résumé'. *Mississippi Valley Historical Review*, XVIII, 1931, 3-22.
Kenton, Edna (ed.) *Black gown and redskins. Adventures and travels of the early Jesuit missionaries in North America (1610–1791)*. With an introduction by R. G. Thwaites and a new preface by D. B. Quinn. London, 1956.
Knight, James. 'York Fort journal 1715-16'. MS in Hudson's Bay Company Archives.
Lafitau, P. *Moeurs des sauvages Ameriquains*. Paris, 1724.
Lafora, Nicolás de. *The frontiers of New Spain* . . . , *1766–1768*. Ed. and trans. by Lawrence Kinnaird. Berkeley, Quivira Society Publications, XIII, 1958; reprint New York, 1967.
La Harpe, Bénard de. *Historical journal of the establishment of the French in Louisiana*. *See* French (ed. and trans.), III, 1851, 9-118.
Lahontan, Lom d'Arce de (3rd Baron). *New voyages to North-America*. London, 1703.
Lanning, John T. *The Spanish missions of Georgia*. Chapel Hill, N.C., 1935.
La Salle, Robert Cavelier de. Mémoirs addressed to M. de Seignelay. 'Procés verbal of the taking possession of Louisiana, at the mouth of the Mississippi, 1682'. Letters, to Captain Beaujeu and others. *See* French (ed. and trans.), I, 1846, 25-49. *See also* Margry, I, II, 1879.
Lawson, John. *Allerneuste Beschreibung . . . Carolina*. Hamburg, 1712.
Lawson, John. *A new voyage to Carolina*. Ed. by Hugh Lefler. Chapel Hill, N.C., 1967.
Leach, Douglas E. *The northern colonial frontier, 1607–1763*. New York, 1966.
Le Clercq, Father Christian. *First establishment of the faith in New France*. Ed. and trans. by John G. Shea. New York, 1881. 2 vols.
Leder, Lawrence H. *The Livingstone Indian records, 1666–1723*. Albany, 1956.
Lederer, John. *The discoveries of John Lederer in three several marches from Virginia . . . translated out of Latine . . . by Sir William Talbot*. London, 1672.
Lederer, John. *The discoveries of John Lederer (1672)*. Ed. by William P. Cumming. Charlottesville, Va, 1958.
Leonard, Irving A. (ed. and trans.) *The Spanish approach to Pensacola, 1689–1693*. Albuquerque, Quivira Society Publications, IX. 1939.
Le Page du Pratz. *Histoire de la Louisiane* . . . Paris, 1758. 3 vols.
Le Page du Pratz. *The History of Louisiana* . . . London, 1763. 2 vols.
Le Page du Pratz. 'Journey into Tennessee'. *See* Williams (ed.), 1928, 108-11.
Le Sueur, Pierre. Extract from Journal, quoted in La Harpe, *Historical journal* . . . *See* French (ed. and trans.), III, 1851, 23-7.
Lincoln, Charles H. (ed.) *Narratives of the Indian Wars, 1675–99*. New York, 1913.

Lowery, Woodbury. *The Spanish settlements within the present limits of the United States, 1513–1561*. New York, 1901.
Lowes, John L. *The road to Xanadu*. Boston, 1927.
Mallet, Pierre and Paul. Abridgment of Journal sent to France by Bienville. *See* Margry (ed.), VI, 1867, 455 ff. *See also* Folmer, 1939, 4-8.
Margry, Pierre. *Découvertes et établissements des Français dans l'ouest et dans le sud de l'Amérique Septentrionale, 1614–1698*. Paris, 1879. 6 vols.
Margry, Pierre. *Relations et mémoires inédits pour servir à l'histoire de la France dans les pays d'outre-mer*. Paris, 1867.
Massanet, Fray Damian. 'Carta . . . sobre el descubrimiento de la Bahía del Espiritu Santo, 1690'. Trans. by L. M. Casis (1899). *See* Bolton (ed.), 1916, 353-87.
Masterton, James R. and Brower, Helen. *Bering's successors 1745–1780: contributions of Peter Simon Pallas to the history of Russian exploration towards Alaska*. Seattle, 1948.
Maury, Ann. *Memories of a Huguenot family. Translated and compiled from the original autobiography of the Rev. James Fontaine and other family manuscripts*. New York, 1853.
Maxwell, Hu. 'The use and abuse of forests by the Virginia Indians'. *William and Mary Quarterly*, XIX, 1910, 74-103.
McDermott, John F. *The French in the Mississippi Valley*. Urbana, 1965.
McPherson, Elizabeth G. 'Nathaniell Batts, landowner on Pasquotank River, 1660'. *North Carolina Historical Review*, XLIII, 1966, 72-80.
McRill, Leslie A. 'Fernandina: first white settlement in Oklahoma, 1719'. *Chronicles of Oklahoma*, XLI, 1963, 126-59.
Mendoza, Juan Dominguez de. 'Itinerary, 1684'. *See* Bolton (ed.), 1916, 320-43.
Mereness, Newton D. (ed.) *Travels in the American colonies*. New York, 1916.
Michael, M. A. (ed.) *The American expedition by Sven Waxell*. London, 1952.
Middleton, Christopher. *A vindication of the conduct of Captain Christopher Middleton*. London, 1743.
Moll, Herman. *Atlas Minor*. London, 1729.
Moloney, Francis X. *The fur trade of New England, 1620–1676*. Cambridge, Mass., 1931.
Mooney, James. 'The Aboriginal population of America, north of Mexico', Washington, *Smithsonian Miscellaneous Collection* LXXX no. 7, 1928.
Moravian brethren. 'Diary of a journey from Bethlehem, Pennsylvania, to Bethabara, North Carolina', *See* Mereness (ed.), 1916, 327-56.
Morfi, Fray Juan Agustin. *History of Texas, 1673–1779*. Ed. and trans by C. E. Castañeda. Albuquerque, Quivira Society Publications, VI. 1935; reprint, New York, 1967.
Morrison, A. J. 'The Virginia Indian trade to 1673'. *William and Mary Quarterly*, I n.s., 1921, 217-36.
Müller, G. F. *Voyages from Asia to America, for completing the discoveries of the north west coast of America*. 2nd edn, London, 1764.
Myer, William E. 'Indian trails of the Southeast'. *42nd annual report of the Bureau of American Anthropology, 1924–1925*. Washington, 1928, 727-88.
Myers Albert C. (ed.) *Narratives of early Pennsylvania, west New Jersey and Delaware, 1630–1707*. New York, 1912; reprint, 1959.
Nasatir, A. P. (ed.) *Before Lewis and Clark: documents illustrating the history of Missouri, 1785–1804*. St. Louis, 1952. 2 vols.
Nute, Grace Lee. *Caesars of the wilderness*. New York, 1943.
O'Callaghan, E. B. and Fernow, B. (eds) *Documents relative to the colonial history of the state of New York*. Albany, 1856-87. 12 vols.
Ogilby, John. *America*. London, 1671.
Oldmixon, John. *The British Empire in America*. 2nd ed., 1741.
Palóu, Francisco. *Historical memoirs of New California*. Ed. by Herbert E. Bolton. Berkeley, 1926.
Parkman, Francis. *La Salle and the discovery of the Great West*. 12th ed., Boston, 1880.
Pénicaut, André. *Fleur de lys and calumet*. Ed. and trans. by R. G. McWilliams. Baton Rouge, 1953.
Pennant, Thomas. *Arctic zoology*, vol. I. London, 1784.
Perfect description of Virginia. London, 1649. *See* Force, II, 1836, no. 8.
Phillips, Philip L. *Notes on the life and works of Bernard Romans*. Deland, Fla, Publications of the Florida State Historical Society, no. 2., 1924.
Pichardo, Father José Antonio. *Treatise on the limits of Louisiana and Texas*. Ed. and trans by C. W. Hackett. Austin, 1931, 4 vols.
Pinart, A. L. *Recueil de cartes, plans et vues relatifs aux États-Unis et au Canada . . .* Paris, 1893.
Pittman, Captain Philip. *The present state of the European settlements on the Mississippi*. London, 1770.
Potherie, Bacqueville de la. *Histoire de l'Amérique Septentrionale*. Paris, 1722.
Pownall, Thomas. *A topographical description . . . of North America*. London, 1776. New edition ed. by Lois Mulkearn, Pittsburg, 1949.
Relation de ce qui s'est passé de plus remarquable en la Nouvelle France 1670 et 1671. Paris, 1672.
Rich, E. E. and Johnson, A. M. (eds) *James Isham's observations on Hudson's Bay, 1743* . . . London, The Hudson's Bay Record Society, 1949.
Robson, Joseph. *An account of six years residence in Hudson's-Bay* . . . London, 1752.
Romans, Bernard. *A concise natural history of East and West Florida*, vol. I. New York, 1775.
Sagard, Gabriel. *Le grand voyage du pays des Hurons*. Paris, 1632. *See also* Wrong, 1939.
Sainsbury, W. N., Headlam, Cecil, and others (eds) *Calendar of state papers, colonial series, America and the West Indies*. London, 1893–
Salley, Alexander S. (ed.) *Narratives of early Carolina, 1650–1708*. New York, 1911.
Salley (Salling, Sally), John Peter. 'Brief account of the travels'. *See* Harrison, 1922, 211-22.
Sandford, Robert. 'A relation . . . of Carolina'. *See* Salley (ed.), 1911, 82-108.
Sauvole, M. de la Villantray de. 'Journal historique de l'établissement des français a la Louisiane, 1699–1701'. *See* French (ed.), III, 1851, 220-40. *See also* Margry, IV, 1879, 447-62.
Scull, Gideon D. (ed.) *Voyages of Peter Esprit Radisson*. Boston, 1885.
Severin, Timothy. *Explorers of the Mississippi*. London, 1967.
Shea, John G. (ed. and trans.) *Discovery and exploration of the Mississippi Valley*. New York, 1852. *See* French, (ed.), IV, 1852.
Shea, John G. (ed.) *Early voyages up and down the Mississippi*. Albany, 1861.
Shelby, Charmian C. 'St. Denis' second expedition to the Rio Grande, 1716–1719'. *The Southwestern Historical Quarterly*, XXVII, 1924, 190-217.
Shurtleff, Nathaniel B. (ed.) *Records of the governor and company of Massachusetts Bay*, vol. III. Boston, 1854.
Sigüenza y Gongora, Don Carlos de. *Mercurio Volante*. Ed. and trans. by I. A. Leonard. Los Angeles, Quivira Society Publications, III, 1932.
Smith, P. C. F. (ed.) 'The journals of Ashley Bowen (1728–1813)', *Colonial Society of Massachusetts Collections*, XLIV-XLV, 1973.
Smith, William. *An historical account of the expedition against the Ohio Indians*. London, 1766.
South Carolina Historical Society. *Collections*. Charleston and Richmond, 1857-97. 5 vols.
Spears, J. R. and Clark, A. H. *History of the Mississippi Valley from its discovery to the end of foreign domination*. New York, 1903.
Spiller, Robert E., Thorp, W., Johnson, T. H. and Canby, H. S. *Literary history of the United States*. New York, 1953.
Spotswood, Governor Alexander. *Official letters of Governor Spotswood*. Ed. by R. A. Brock. Richmond, Va, 1882-5. 2 vols.
Strachey, William. *The historie of travell into Virginia Britania*, (1612). Ed. by Louis B. Wright and V. Freund. London, The Hakluyt Society, 2nd series, CIII, 1953.
Strong, Roy. *A pageant of Canada. An exhibition*. Ottawa, National Gallery of Canada, 1967.
Surrey, Nancy M. *The commerce of Louisiana during the French régime, 1699–1763*. New York, Columbia University Studies in History, LXXI, no. 1, 1916.
Swanton, John R. *Early history of the Creek Indians and their neighbors*. Washington, Smithsonian Institution, Bureau of American Ethnology, *Bulletin* 73, 1922.
Swanton, John R. *The Indians of the southeastern United States*. Washington, Smithsonian Institution, Bureau of American Ethnology, *Bulletin* 137, 1946.
Swanton, John R. *The Indian tribes of North America*. Washington, Smithsonian Institution, Bureau of American Ethnology. *Bulletin* 145, 1952.
Taylor, E. G. R. and Richey, M. W. *The geometrical seaman*. 1962.
Teggart, Frederick J. (ed.) 'The Portolá Expedition of 1769–1770: Diary of Miguel Costansó'. Berkeley, Publications of the Academy of Pacific Coast History, 1911.
Thevenot, M. *Recueil de voyages de Mr Thevenot*. Paris, 1681.
Thomassy, R. *Géologie pratique de la Louisiane*. New Orleans and Paris, 1860.
Thwaites, Reuben G. (ed.) *Early western travels, 1748–1764*, vol. I. Cleveland, 1904.
Thwaites, Reuben G. (ed.) *The Jesuit relations and allied documents. Travels and explorations of the Jesuit missionaries in New France 1610–1791*. Cleveland, 1896–1901. 73 vols.
Timberlake, Lieut Henry. *Memoirs*. London, 1765.
Timberlake, Lieut Henry. *Memoirs, 1756–1765*. Ed. by Samuel C. Williams. Johnson City, Tenn., 1927.
Tisdale, John W. *The story of the Occoneechees*. Richmond, 1953.
Tompkins, Stuart R. and Moorhead, Max L. 'Russia's Approach to America, Pt. II. From Spanish Sources, 1761–1775'. *British Columbia Historical Quarterly*, XIII, 1949.
Tonty, Henri de. 'Mémoire adressé au Comte de Pontchartrain, 1693'. *See* Margry (ed.), 1867, 5-36. *See also* French (ed. and trans.), I, 1846, 52-78.
Tooley, R. V. 'California as an Island', *The map collectors' circle*, I. London, 1964, Appendix.
Trelease, Allen W. *Indian affairs in colonial New York: the seventeenth century*. Ithaca, 1960.
Trudel, Marcel. *The beginnings of New France 1524–1663*. Toronto, 1973.
Trudel, Marcel. 'New France, 1524–1713'. *Dictionary of Canadian Biography*, I, 26-39. Toronto, 1966.
Umfreville, Edward. *The present state of Hudson's Bay*. London, 1790.
Vail, R. W. G. *The voice of the old frontier*. New York, 1949.
Valois, Jacques. 'Douay, Anastase'. *Dictionary of Canadian Biography*, II, Toronto, 1969.
Venegas, Miguel. *A natural and civil history of California*. London, 1759.
Waddell, Joseph A. *Annals of Augusta County, Virginia*. Richmond, 1886. 2nd edition, Staunton, Va, 1902.
Wagner, Henry R. *The Spanish southwest, 1542–1794: an annotated bibliography*. Quivira Society Publications, VII, 1937; reprint New York, 1967.
Walker, Dr Thomas 'Journal'. *See* Johnston (ed.), 1898, 8-75.
Wallis, Helen and Tyacke, Sarah (eds) *My heart is a map: essays to commemorate the 75th birthday of R. V. Tooley*. London, 1973.
West, Elizabeth H. 'De Léon's expedition of 1689'. *Quarterly of the Texas State Historical Association*, VIII, 1905, 199-224.
Williams, Glyndwr (ed.) *Andrew Graham's observations on Hudson's Bay 1767–1791*. London, The Hudson's Bay Record Society, 1969.
Williams, Glyndwr. *The British search for the Northwest Passage in the eighteenth century*. London, 1962.
Williams, Samuel C. (ed.) *Adair's history of the American Indians*. Nashville, 1953.
Williams, Samuel C. *Dawn of the Tennessee Valley and Tennessee history*. Johnson City, Tenn., 1937.
Williams, Samuel C. (ed.) *Early travels in the Tennessee country, 1540–1800*. Johnson City, Tenn., 1928.
Williamson, Peter. *French and Indian cruelty exemplified in the life and vicissitudes of fortune, of Peter Williamson*. York, 1757.
Winsor, Justin. *Narrative and critical history of America*. Boston and New York, 1884-9. 8 vols.
Withers, Alexander S. *Chronicles of border warfare*. Ed. by R. G. Thwaites. Cincinnati, 1895.
Wood, Abraham. 'Letter to John Richards (on Needham and Arthur's journeys), 1674'. *See* Alvord and Bidgood, 1912, 210-26.
Woodward, Henry. 'A faithfull relation of my Westoe Voiage'. *See* Salley (ed.), 1911, 130-34.
Wrong, George M. (ed.) *The long journey to the country of the Hurons by Father Gabriel Sagard*. Trans. by H. H. Langton. Toronto, The Champlain Society, 1939.
Yeardley, Francis. 'Narrative of excursions into Carolina, 1654'. *See* Salley (ed.), 1911, 25-9.
Yefimov, A. V. *Atlas geograficheskikh otkrytiy v Sibiri i v severo-zapaduoy Ameriki XVII-XVIII vv*. Moscow, 1964.

LIST OF ILLUSTRATIONS

95 James Hunter. Ticonderoga, 1777
96 'The Country between Crown Point and Albany', 1758
97 Southack. 'The Harbour and Islands of Canso', 1720
98 Canso Harbor from Des Barres, *Atlantic Neptune*
99 Boston by Bonner, 1722
100 Indians talking to Colonel Bouquet from Smith, *An historical account*
101 Popple. Map of the Northern Colonies, 1733
102 Bartram. Iris (*color*)
103 Bartram. Bird, swamp cornus and *Galega* (*color*)
104 Bartram. Great mud tortoise (*color*)
105A Catesby. The Mock-Bird from *Hortus Europae Americanus (color)*
105B Catesby. The Wampum Snake and red lilly from *Hortus Europae Americanus (color)*
106 Huron women from Du Creux, *Historia Canadensis*
107 Sr Robert de Vaugondy. 'Partie de l'Amerique Septentrionale', 1755
108 Falls of St Anthony from Carver, *Travels*
109 'A plan of Captain Carvers Travels' . . . from Carver, *Travels*
110 Man and woman of the Naudouessie from Carver, *Travels*
111 Catesby. Pennsylvania magnolia from *Hortus Europae Americanus*
112 Hollar. Virginia Indian
113 Sasquehanok Indian village from Montanus, *America*
114 Farrer. 'A Mapp of Virginia', 1651
115 Blaeu. A new description of the southern part of Virginia . . ., 1640
116 Lederer. '. . . his three marches' from *The discoveries of John Lederer*
117 Cadwallader Jones. 'Louissiana Pars', 1699
118 Hennepin. 'America Septentrionalis', 1698
119 Catesby. Red-winged starling, *c.* 1724
120 Catesby. Goat-sucker of Carolina, *c.* 1724
121 Shapley. Hilton's discoveries along the Carolina coast, 1662
122 Locke. Map of Carolina, 1671
123 Catesby. Summer red bird, *c.* 1724
124 Catesby. Painted finch, *c.* 1724
125 Gascoigne. 'A New Map of the Country of Carolina', [1682]
126 King with attendants from Ogilby, *America*
127 Fort Carolina from Ogilby, *America*
128 Vander Aa. Shipwreck of Dickinson in 1696 from Gottfried *De Aamerkenswaadigste . . . Landreisen*
129 Moll. 'A New Map of the North Parts of America claimed by France', 1720
130 Nairne. A Map of South Carolina, 1711
131 Hughes. 'A Map of the Country adjacent to the River Misisipi', [1713]
132 Seven Cherokee chiefs in London, 1730
133 Michel. Tuscarora Indian tribunal, *c.* 1711
134 Michel. Three Americans, post-1704
135 Catesby. Angel fish from *Natural history*
136 Catesby. Largest Carolina moth
137 Catesby. Humming bird (*color*)
138 Catesby. Bison (*color*)
139 Catesby. White-bill woodpecker
140 Catesby. Red-headed woodpecker
141 Catesby. Pol-cat
142 Herrman. Virginia and Maryland, 1673
143 Vander Aa. Indians strip Dickinson's party of clothes from Gottfried, *De Aamerkenswaadigste . . . Landreisen*
144 Vander Aa. Dickinson's journey, 1696, from Gottfried, *De Aamerkenswaadigste . . . Landreisen*
145 Vander Aa. Dickinson's party reaches St Augustine from Gottfried *De Aamerkenswaadigste . . . Landreisen*
146 Frontispiece showing animals from Lawson, *Allerneuste Beschreiben*
147 Catesby. Pied-bill dopchick (*color*)
148 Catesby. Bald eagle with fish (*color*)
149 Blaeu. 'Americae nova Tabula', 1635 [1640] (*color*)
150 Catesby. Flying squirrel
151 Catesby. 'A Map of Carolina . . .' from *Natural history*
152 Catesby. Orchids growing from a branch, with a butterfly from *Natural history*
153 Catesby. Head of a Hooping crane from *Natural history*
154 Catesby. Turkey buzzard
155 Catesby. Carolina paroquet
156 Byrd. The dividing line between Virginia and Carolina, *c.* 1738
157 Byrd. 'My Plat of 20,000 Acres in N° Carolina', 1733
158 Eden in Virginia, 1736
159 Reuter. Wachovia, Dobbs Parish, NC, 1766
160 American stage wagon from Weld, *Travels*
161 Reuter. Bethabara, 1766
162 Von Redeker. 'A View of SALEM', 1787
163 Beaufort, South Carolina, *c.* 1798 (*color*)
164 Comberford. 'The south part of Virginia now the north part of Carolina', 1657 (*color*)
165 Catesby. Rock rose of Pennsylvania from *Hortus Europae Americanus* (*color*)
166 Catesby. Yellow jessamin from *Hortus Europae Americanus* (*color*)
167 Catesby. Laurel tree of Carolina from *Hortus Europae Americanus* (*color*)
168 Catesby. Water tupelo or black gum from *Hortus Europae Americanus* (*color*)
169 Virginia farmhouse, *c.* 1800
170 Walker-Washington Map, *c.* 1770
171 Mitchell. Map of the British Colonies in North America, 1755
172 Gist. 'The Draught of Genl. Braddock's Route towards Fort Duquesne', 1755
173 Washington. Sketch of journey to Fort Le Boeuf [?1754]
174 Stuart. 'A Map of the Cherokee Country', *c.* 1761
175 Kitchin. 'A New Map of the Cherokee Nation', 1760
176 Timberlake. 'A Draught of the Cherokee Country', 1765
177 Ostenaco, after Reynolds, 1762
178 Cunne Shote, after Parsons, 1762
179 Three Cherokee chiefs in London, 1762
180 Hutchins. 'A Map of the Country on the Ohio & Muskingum Rivers', 1766 from Smith, *An historical account*
181 Conference between Bouquet and the Indians, 1764, . from Smith *An historical account*
182 Tomo Chachi Mico and Tooanahomi, *c.* 1734
183 Catesby. Trumpet flower from *Hortus Europae Americanus*
184 Catesby. Tulip tree from *Hortus Europae Americanus*
185 Catesby. Dogwood from *Hortus Europae Americanus*
186 Catesby. Pellitory or 'tooth-ache tree' from *Hortus Europae Americanus*
187 Bartram. Warmouth
188 Bartram. Scarlet crowned finch
189 Bartram. Green heron
190 Lotter. 'A Map of the County of Savannah' from Urlsperger, *Der Ausführliche Nachrichten*, 1740
191 A view of Savannah by Peter Gordon, 1734
192 Charles Town, South Carolina, 1739
193 Bonar. 'A Draught of the Creek Nation', 1757
194 The governor's house in St Augustine, 1764

Maps

ACKNOWLEDGEMENTS

The authors and publishers would like to express their gratitude to the Archivist of the Hudson's Bay Company, Rev. Fr Adrien Pouliot of the Résidence des Pères Jésuites, Quebec and Mrs Benson of the Royal Library, Windsor Castle for their assistance in obtaining illustrations. They are also indebted to the following individuals, libraries, museums, archives and organizations for permission to reproduce maps, engravings, paintings and drawings:

W. P. Cumming: jacket (photograph by Earl Lawrimore); Thomas Gilcrease Institute of American History and Art, Tulsa: title page, 22, 36, 38-41, 71-6, 80, 246, 253, 255-7; courtesy of the Trustees of the British Museum and the British Library: 2-8, 12-13, 19, 21, 28, 32, 37, 43-4, 47, 49-52, 54-69, 79, 81-2, 84-8, 92-6, 98-101, 105A, 105B, 106, 108-13, 115-16, 118, 121, 125-9, 132, 135, 142-6, 149-50, 152-3, 157, 160, 171, 174-85, 190-2, 194, 196-201, 204-7, 210-11, 218, 220, 222-3, 229-34, 236-7, 241, 243, 247, 254, 259-64, 266, 268-71, 274-80, 282-6, 288-94, 296, 298-302, 312-19, 321-3, 325-9, 341-3, 345-6, 349-50, 352-7, 360-2, 364, 367-8, 370-1, 373-9, 381, 384-9, 393-4, 396-400; courtesy of The Historical Society of Pennsylvania, Philadelphia: 9, 195; Bibliothèque Nationale, Paris: 10-11, 272; Marblehead Historical Society, Mass: 14 (photograph by Mark Sexton); The John Carter Brown Library, Brown University, Providence: 15 (photograph by Stephen Karl Scher), 158, 172; La Musée, L'Hôtel-Dieu, Quebec: 16, 18; The Jesuit Collection, La Vielle Maison des Jésuites, Sillery: 17; The National Maritime Museum, Greenwich: 20, 24, 27, 369; Peabody Museum, Salem: 23; The Science Museum, London: 25-6; Photograph property of D. B. Quinn: 29; courtesy of the Trustees of the British Museum (Natural History): 31, 187-9, 202, 212-16, 390; Church of the Urseline Convent, Quebec: 33 (photograph by National Gallery of Canada, Ottawa); Crown Copyright, Public Record Office, London: 34-5, 89, 97, 107, 117, 122, 131, 173, 193; McGill University Library, Montreal: 42, Archives de la Compagnie de Jésus, Cté Terrebonne: 46; Minnesota Historical Society, St Paul: 48; Service Historique de la Marine, Paris: 53 (photograph by Sirco), 287, 295, 331, 359 (photographs by National Map Collection, Public Archives of Canada); The Bodleian Library, Oxford: 70, 156; Dépôt des Cartes et Plans de la Marine, Service Hydrographique, Paris: 77-8; Museum of Art, Rhode Island School of Design, Providence: 83; Map Division, The New York Public Library, Astor, Lenox and Tilden Foundations: 90; courtesy of The New York Historical Society, New York City: 91; The Rt Hon. the Earl of Derby: 102-4 (photographs by Elsam, Mann & Cooper); Library of Congress, Washington: 170, 267; The Huntington Library, San Marino: 114, 380; reproduced by gracious permission of Her Majesty Queen Elizabeth II: 119-20, 123-4, 136-41, 147-8, 151, 154-5; Burgerbibliothek, Berne: 133-4; Moravian Archives, Winston-Salem: 159, 161-2; National Gallery of Art, Washington: 169; The Colonial Williamsburg Collection, Va: 203; State Historical Society of Wisconsin, Madison: 208; West Virginian State Museum, Charleston: 209 (photograph by Steve Ladish); The University of Texas Library, Latin American Collection, Austin: 217; Bibliothèque Municipale, Rouen: 219 (photograph by Photo Ellebé); courtesy of The Oakland Museum, Cal: 221; Archivo General de Indias, Seville: 224-5, 227-8, 244-5, 363, 365, 395; The Newberry Library, Chicago: 226, 239; Peabody Museum of Archaeology and Ethnology, Harvard University, Cambridge, Mass: 235, 242, 248, 250, 258, 265, 372; Bancroft Library, University of California, Berkeley: 238, 251; Archives Nationales de France, section outre-mer, Paris: 240, 273 (photographs by Sirco); courtesy of the Louisiana State Museum, New Orleans: 249; Biblioteca Nacional, Madrid: 252; Hudson's Bay Company Archives: 281, 297, 303-11, 324, 332-40, 344, 348; Crown Copyright, Public Record Office of Northern Ireland, Belfast: 320; National Map Collection, Public Archives of Canada: 330; courtesy of the James Ford Bell Library, University of Minnesota, Minneapolis: 347; The National Gallery of Canada, Ottawa: 351; Novosti Press Agency (A.P.I.): 358, 382-3, 391-2; Ministerio del Ejército, Madrid: 366. Many of the photographs of originals at the British Museum were taken by John R. Freeman Ltd and those at the Royal Library, Windsor Castle were taken by A. C. Cooper Ltd. The reference maps have been drawn by Harold Bartram.

INDEX

All references are to page numbers. Roman numerals refer to the text, *italic* numerals to the captions for maps and illustrations.

Longford Library

3 0015 00056803 2

351, 848 | 9731

LEABHARLANN CHONTAE LONGFOIRT-IARMHI

Borrowers detaining books beyond the time allowed for reading—fourteen days—will be fined One Penny for each week or portion of a week afterwards.

The latest date entered is the date by which the book should be returned.